W9-BXS-039

THE AMERICAN BAR ASSOCIATION

# THE AMERICAN BAR ASSOCIATION

# FAMILY LEGAL GUIDE

## COMPLETELY REVISED AND UPDATED VERSION OF *YOU AND THE LAW*

TIMES BOOKS

RANDOM HOUSE

Copyright © 1990, 1994 by American Bar Association

All rights reserved under International Pan-American Copyright Conventions. Published in the United States by Times Books, a division of Random House, Inc., New York, and simultaneously in Canada by Random House of Canada Limited, Toronto.

Library of Congress Cataloging-in-Publication Data

The American Bar Association family legal guide / American Bar Association.—
2nd ed.
    p.    cm.
  Includes index.
  ISBN 0-8129-2361-8
  1. Law—United States—Miscellanea.  2. Law—United States—
Popular works.  I. American Bar Association.
KF387.Y655    1994
349.73—dc20
[347.3]                              93-45902

Design by ROBERT BULL DESIGN

Manufactured in the United States of America on acid-free paper

98765432

Revised Edition

This is a revised and updated edition of *You and the Law*, 1st edition, published in 1990 by Publications International, Ltd., Lincolnwood, Illinois.

# FOREWORD

George E. Bushnell, Jr., President, American Bar Association

DEFINING THE LEGAL profession seems to be increasingly more difficult. While engineers build bridges and doctors help the sick, lawyers do a wide range of tasks, depending on the client or the situation. Although it is usually clear when to consult a physician, it is not always readily apparent when to seek counsel from a lawyer. This book was written to help make clear what lawyers do and when one should consult a lawyer.

We are acutely aware of the depth and breadth of the obstacles facing those who need to use the justice system. Recently, the ABA released the "Comprehensive Legal Needs Study," the result of more than three thousand interviews with lower and moderate income families across the nation. The survey reveals that most lower and moderate income families' legal needs are related to basic, everyday issues of life: housing, personal finance, family and domestic concerns (such as divorce and child support), employment-related issues, personal injury and community problems. This book separates the many areas of law into chapters that specifically deal with these types of issues.

The chapters are further classified by specific points to make the book as readable and handy as possible. The authors use plain, direct language rather than difficult to understand and intimidating "lawyerese."

The American Bar Association is dedicated to ensuring that all Americans have a full range of options when confronted with a problem that might require a "legal" solution. I hope this book is worthwhile in helping its readers feel more comfortable with the legal system and that it will help eliminate much of the mystery and fear surrounding the legal process.

Hundreds of members of the association have contributed to the book. The Standing Committee on Public Education was the primary force behind this massive undertaking. The research was conducted by the ABA's Consortium on Legal Service and the Public and released in the Comprehensive Legal Needs Study.

This book is a big step forward in our continuing efforts to bring the law to the people, and I congratulate all those who participated.

---

*George E. Bushnell, Jr., is in private practice in Detroit, Michigan. He is a former chair of the ABA's House of Delegates and a former member of its Board of Governors. He has served as president of both the State Bar of Michigan and the Detroit Bar Association.*

# CONTENTS IN BRIEF

# CONTENTS

# INTRODUCTION

■

by Hilarie Bass, Chair, ABA Standing Committee on Public Education

AMERICANS HAVE LONG BEEN fascinated—and mystified—by the law. For years we have been delighted by the courtroom theatrics depicted in television programs and movies, but at the same time we have often feared the prospect of being personally involved in a legal case. Sometimes the very prospect of consulting with a lawyer causes us alarm. The purpose of this book is to remove some of that fear and mystery from the law. The American Bar Association has written *The American Bar Association Family Legal Guide* to help explain law, legal processes, and legal situations. It is our hope that this book will make you, the reader, better informed about the law, and better able to make decisions about legal matters.

Today we are bombarded with news stories about the law, ranging from sensational criminal trials to class action lawsuits involving defective products. The law has leapt into the public consciousness.

However, the law does not affect only the famous. It affects each of us in our daily lives—when we make a purchase, start a family, or go to work. To function effectively in our complex society, we must understand how law governs our rights and responsibilities.

That is the purpose of *The American Bar Association Family Legal Guide*—to explain the law to you in simple, easy-to-understand language. This book uses a straightforward question-and-answer format. It avoids legal jargon and technicalities; rather, it explains in everyday words how the law affects you at home, at work, and at play.

For example, you will learn many of the important legal issues about marriage, separation, and divorce. You will explore the legal aspects of buying or selling a home, the law that affects you in owning a home, and the many legal considerations of renting an apartment for yourself or to others. This book helps you understand contracts, big and little. It also gives you tips on avoiding hassles in buying consumer products. You will learn how the law affects older Americans, and get answers to frequently asked questions about major legal topics, such as personal injury and wills and estates. There is even a glossary that explains the meaning of commonly used legal terms.

*The American Bar Association Family Legal Guide* is organized so you can easily find information about those areas of law that you need to know. The question-and-answer format gives you details about the most common issues raised by each legal topic.

Other features enhance this basic approach. In every chapter, you will find brief articles on topics of great interest, which appear alongside the questions and answers. These explanations and examples give you further insight into the legal topics covered. You will also find charts and graphs that provide information about the laws in each state, as well as about federal laws that apply across the United States.

Even a book such as this cannot answer all the questions you might have on the law. To help you find additional answers, sections at the end of each chapter tell you where to get more information. These sections refer you to many free or inexpensive publications, and suggest services that government agencies, bar associations, and other groups can provide at either no or minimal cost.

When reading *The American Bar Association Family Legal Guide,* please keep several important points in mind. First, this book cannot and does not pretend to provide legal advice—only a lawyer who understands the facts of your particular case can do that. Although every effort has been made to present material that is as up-to-date as possible, laws can and do change. Decisions by state and federal courts, as well as regulations from government agencies at all levels, change how laws are interpreted and applied.

Thus, the information included in this book should be considered an introduction to the law in each area. It is not the final word. If you are thinking about pursuing any legal action, consult first with a lawyer, bar association or lawyer referral system to assure yourself of knowledgeable assistance. Armed with the knowledge and insights provided in *The American Bar Association Family Legal Guide,* you may be confident that the legal decisions you make will be in your best interests.

*Hilarie Bass is in private practice in Miami, Florida. She is president of the Florida Bar Foundation and a past member of the Board of Governors of the American Bar Association.*

# When and How to Use a Lawyer

## CONTENTS

# INTRODUCTION

ALMOST EVERYTHING WE DO—from making a purchase, to driving a car, to interacting with others—is affected by the law in some way. While it often seems hard to live with the law, it would surely be harder to live without it.

In our country, the law is, in a real sense, the people's law. It is part of the democratic heritage of Americans.

The availability of the law does, however, reveal a bewildering variety of choices. When do you need a lawyer? When can (or should) you handle a matter on your own? The purpose of this chapter is to help you make the best choices.

There are many legal situations that you can and should handle on your own, without the assistance of a lawyer. However, when circumstances and laws are unique, complicated, or confusing, you may need a lawyer's guidance. You also may need a lawyer's services when you are so close to a problem that you are unable to see your way through to a proper solution. While this chapter does not examine specific situations, it can help you determine when you should hire a lawyer, what a lawyer can and cannot do for you, and what you can do to help yourself.

## WHEN YOU NEED ASSISTANCE

**Q. Does needing a lawyer's help always mean that I have a legal problem?**

**A.** No. In fact, lawyers very often help clients in matters that have nothing to do with disputes or legal cases. For example, with their lawyer's help, people are advised about the legal aspects of starting a business or engaging in a partnership, assisted in buying or selling a home, and counseled on tax matters or estate planning, to name just a few possibilities. Often, clients receive a regular legal check-up which, like a medical check-up, is designed to prevent problems or nip them in the bud.

**Q. Do I need a lawyer every time I have a legal grievance?**

**A.** Although the law enters into many aspects of daily living, you certainly do not need a lawyer every time you become "involved" with the law. Some Americans have become too inclined to hire lawyers and proceed to court to resolve problems. For example, sports fans have sued to have a referee's controversial decision reversed, and a jilted suitor has tried to recover the cost of an evening's entertainment. Of course, lawsuits like these are not common (that is why they make news), but they illustrate that many problems are not really the business of the law or our courts.

**Q. What should I do if I have an argument with a neighbor over the boundary line between our properties?**

**A.** First attempt to talk to your neighbor. After all, you probably will have to go on living next to each other. If that fails, you may wish to seek mediation or some other form of informal dispute resolution to help the two of you resolve the problem. Perhaps you can get some guidance from public records, already existing surveys, or title searches that have been done. Maybe prior owners can cast light on the subject. If these options fail, the two of you might want to jointly pay for a survey, or jointly ask a court to decide the matter (see discussion of "quiet title" on pages 187–88 in the chapter on owning a home). As a last resort, you might want to seek legal advice on other options you can pursue.

### Q. If I buy a new stove and it stops working just as the warranty expires, should I contact a lawyer?

**A.** No. First read the warranty and see what rights you may have, notify the merchant and see if you can negotiate a satisfactory solution. If that does not work, contact the manufacturer. Though the Better Business Bureau does not resolve disputes, perhaps a complaint to them will stir the merchant or manufacturer to action. As a last resort, you can file suit in a small claims court. (See page 27 of the next chapter.) You can do all this without a lawyer.

### Q. Should I always wait until a problem becomes serious before I contact a lawyer?

**A.** No. In certain matters, if you call a lawyer as a last resort, it may already be too late. For example, it is difficult for a lawyer to protect you after you have signed away your rights or if you have waited too long to assert your rights. And some legal matters are so important or so complex that you will need a lawyer from the beginning. In such cases, having legal help early will probably save expense—and anxiety.

### Q. Why can't legal documents be in a language that I understand?

**A.** Lawyers and others trained in the law often use legal terms as shorthand to express complicated ideas or principles. The words and phrases, many rooted in Latin, are often jokingly referred to as a foreign language—"legalese." Although some legalese may be necessary in order to communicate certain ideas precisely, a document that is understood by very few of its readers is just plain poor communication.

In 1978, President Carter directed that federal regulations be "written in plain English and understandable to those who must comply" with them. Many states also have laws requiring that insurance policies, leases, and consumer contracts be written in plain English. Of particular importance here is the trend among law schools to discourage the use of legalese while encouraging writing in plain, comprehensible English.

## HELP FROM PEOPLE OTHER THAN LAWYERS

### Q. If I do not use a lawyer, who else can help me?

**A.** Unless your problem is so serious that only a lawyer can resolve it, you should first consider another source of help. If you believe a business has cheated you, help can be obtained from a consumer protection agency run by your city, county, state or federal government. Many businesses, stores, and utility companies have their own departments to help resolve consumer complaints. Some communities have an ombudsman to mediate and resolve minor landlord/tenant, consumer or employment issues. Local television and radio stations may have programs to resolve consumer-related disputes.

### Q. Are there other professionals who can be of assistance?

**A.** Yes. Do not overlook the obvious. If you have a problem with insurance, for example, discuss it with your insurance agent. Bankers, accountants, real estate agents, and stock brokers are others who may be able to help with problems in their specific fields. Of course, if your dispute is with *them* they may not be a source of unbiased information. Even so, it costs nothing to ask and they may provide free advice that can help you evaluate whether your problem needs the attention of a lawyer.

### Q. Can counseling solve some problems?

**A.** Yes. Sometimes problems that seem to be "legal" may be helped or prevented by other means. Many groups offer guidance and counseling for personal problems arising in marriage, child rearing, and managing finances. Private counselors or members of the clergy also may provide such help.

### Q. What is a small claims court?

**A.** Disputes over money are common, but often the amount of money at issue does not justify hiring an attorney or using scarce judicial resources. Small claims court is a streamlined forum where people can air their dispute and have it decided promptly and fairly. Most states have procedures that allow people to represent themselves in court if the total amount of their claim is under a certain dollar amount. The cost is minimal, procedures are simple, and there is usually little delay. Keep small claims courts in mind if your problem is not very complicated and your losses are relatively small—in the hundreds or low thousands. The next chapter provides guidance on how to file and pursue a small claims lawsuit.

### Q. A friend recommended that I try a local dispute resolution center. What does this offer?

**A.** For the right kind of case, these centers can be a quick, low-cost (or free) alternative to formal legal proceedings. These will also be discussed in the next chapter.

---

## HELP FROM LAWYERS

### Q. I understand that, under certain circumstances, going to a lawyer may be unnecessary. Are there specific cases when I should see a lawyer?

**A.** Yes, there are matters best handled by a lawyer. While these matters are sometimes hard to recognize, nearly everyone agrees that you should talk with a lawyer about major life events or changes, which might include:

- being arrested for a crime or served with legal papers in a civil lawsuit;
- being involved in a serious accident causing personal injury or property damage;
- a change in family status such as divorce, adoption, or death;
- a change in financial status such as getting or losing valuable personal property or real estate, or filing for bankruptcy.

### Q. Is there another way to determine whether I need to hire a lawyer?

**A.** Yes. Studies about how Americans actually use lawyers found that lawyers are consulted most frequently about financial/consumer matters, work-related matters, personal injury, real estate, estate planning, and marital issues. See charts on p. 5.

### Q. Is the use of lawyers growing?

**A.** Apparently. A 1993 survey of 815 adults nationwide showed that use of a lawyer for both personal and business matters had increased significantly from 1986. Researchers found that more middle and low income people were reporting that they used lawyers' services. See the chart on p. 6 indicating the percentages of Americans using lawyers for specific purposes over a three-year period.

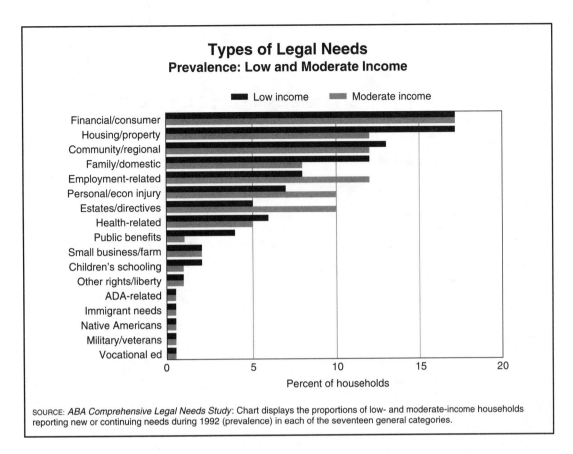

**Types of Legal Needs**
**Prevalence: Low and Moderate Income**

Low income    Moderate income

Financial/consumer
Housing/property
Community/regional
Family/domestic
Employment-related
Personal/econ injury
Estates/directives
Health-related
Public benefits
Small business/farm
Children's schooling
Other rights/liberty
ADA-related
Immigrant needs
Native Americans
Military/veterans
Vocational ed

0    5    10    15    20

Percent of households

SOURCE: *ABA Comprehensive Legal Needs Study*: Chart displays the proportions of low- and moderate-income households reporting new or continuing needs during 1992 (prevalence) in each of the seventeen general categories.

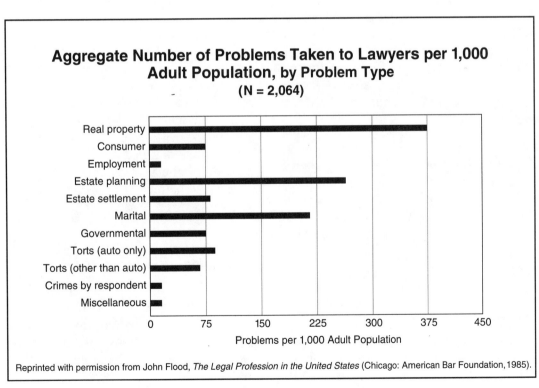

**Aggregate Number of Problems Taken to Lawyers per 1,000 Adult Population, by Problem Type**
**(N = 2,064)**

Real property
Consumer
Employment
Estate planning
Estate settlement
Marital
Governmental
Torts (auto only)
Torts (other than auto)
Crimes by respondent
Miscellaneous

0    75    150    225    300    375    450

Problems per 1,000 Adult Population

Reprinted with permission from John Flood, *The Legal Profession in the United States* (Chicago: American Bar Foundation, 1985).

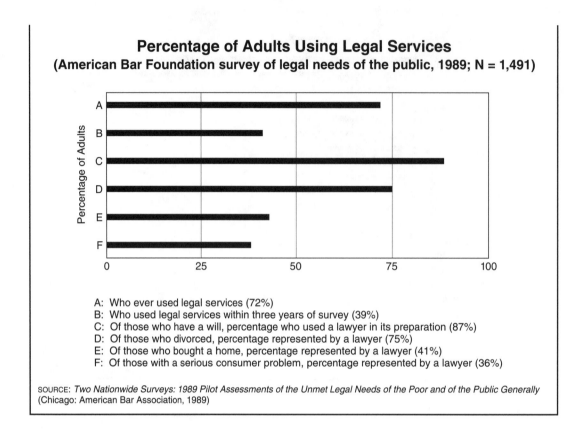

**Percentage of Adults Using Legal Services**
(American Bar Foundation survey of legal needs of the public, 1989; N = 1,491)

A: Who ever used legal services (72%)
B: Who used legal services within three years of survey (39%)
C: Of those who have a will, percentage who used a lawyer in its preparation (87%)
D: Of those who divorced, percentage represented by a lawyer (75%)
E: Of those who bought a home, percentage represented by a lawyer (41%)
F: Of those with a serious consumer problem, percentage represented by a lawyer (36%)

SOURCE: *Two Nationwide Surveys: 1989 Pilot Assessments of the Unmet Legal Needs of the Poor and of the Public Generally* (Chicago: American Bar Association, 1989)

**Q. If it is obvious that I will need a lawyer for a certain circumstance, should I save money and wait until I absolutely need the lawyer's services?**

**A.** No. Lawyers should be thought of as preventers of legal problems, not just solvers. When dealing with legal issues, an ounce of prevention is worth many dollars and anxious hours of cure. Once you have determined that you need professional legal help, get it promptly. You can get the most help if you are in touch with a lawyer as soon as possible.

**Q. What exactly is a lawyer?**

**A.** A lawyer (also called attorney, counsel, counselor, barrister, or solicitor) is a licensed professional who advises and represents others in legal matters. When you picture a lawyer, you probably think of an elderly gentleman in a three-piece suit. That picture is no longer accurate. Today's lawyer can be young or old, male or female. Nearly one-third of all lawyers are under thirty-five; the number of women lawyers has doubled since 1980 to at least 16 percent of the profession in 1992 (and many observers believe the percentage is much higher).

**Q. Is most of a lawyer's time usually spent arguing cases in court?**

**A.** No. A lawyer normally spends more time in an office than in a courtroom. The practice of law most often involves researching legal developments, investigating facts, writing and preparing legal documents, giving advice, and settling disputes. Laws change constantly. New law is enacted and prior law is amended and repealed. In addition, judicial decisions in court cases regularly alter what the law currently means, whether the source of law is the United States Constitution or a state constitution; federal or state statutes; or federal, state, and local codes and regulations. For these reasons, a lawyer must put much time into knowing how the laws and the changes will affect each circumstance.

### Q. What are a lawyer's main duties?

**A.** A lawyer has two main duties: to uphold the law and to protect a client's rights. To carry out these duties, a lawyer must know the law and be a good communicator.

### Q. What are the professional requirements for becoming a lawyer?

**A.** To understand how laws and the legal system work together, lawyers must go through special schooling. Each state has enacted standards that must be met before a person is licensed to practice law there. Before being allowed to practice law in most states, a person must:

- have a bachelor's degree or its equivalent;
- complete three years at an accredited law school;
- pass a state bar examination, which usually lasts for two or three days; it tests knowledge in selected areas of law and in professional ethics and responsibility;
- pass a character and fitness review; each applicant for a law license must be approved by a committee that investigates his or her character and background;
- take an oath swearing to uphold the laws and the state and federal constitutions;
- receive a license from the state supreme court; some states have additional requirements, such as internship in a law office, before a license will be granted.

### Q. Once licensed in one state, is a lawyer automatically allowed to practice law in all states?

**A.** No. To become licensed in more than one state, a lawyer must usually comply with each state's bar admission requirements. Some states, however, permit licensed out-of-state attorneys to practice law if they have done so in another state for several years and the new state's supreme court approves them.

### Q. If I have a legal problem, may I hire someone other than a lawyer?

**A.** In some specialized situations, such as bringing a complaint before a government agency, nonlawyers or paralegals may be qualified to represent you—and their services may cost less than a lawyer's. Ask the government agency what types of legal representatives are available.

### Q. I come from another country, and I need to hire a lawyer. Aren't notary publics actually lawyers?

**A.** A "notary public," "accountant," or "certified public accountant" is not necessarily a lawyer. Do not assume that titles such as notary public mean the same thing as similar words in your own language.

## TYPES OF LAWYERS

### Q. Do lawyers normally work alone or do most of them work for companies or the government?

**A.** About two thirds of all lawyers are in private practice; many others work for corporations or the government. Firms of various sizes employ lawyers in private practice. Almost half of the lawyers in private practice are sole practitioners who work alone. Others join with one or more lawyers in partnerships. As the table shows, about a quarter of lawyers are in partnerships that have ten lawyers or fewer.

Distribution of Private Practitioners by Practice Setting (1993)

| | | |
|---|---|---|
| In solo practice | 269,280 | 46% |
| In firms of 2–5 attorneys | 97,920 | 17% |
| In firms of 6–10 attorneys | 49,440 | 8% |
| In firms of 11–19 attorneys | 40,800 | 7% |
| In firms of 20–99 attorneys | 73,440 | 12% |
| In firms of 100 or more attorneys | 57,120 | 10% |
| Total | 588,000 | 100% |

Source: American Bar Association Membership and Marketing Research Department, Chicago, 1993.

**Q. How are lawyers split between rural and metropolitan areas?**

**A.** 88 percent of American lawyers work in metropolitan areas, and about one third of all lawyers work in large cities. Especially in rural areas and small cities, there are many general practitioners who, by themselves or with the help of other lawyers, handle most types of cases. However, the family lawyer/general practice lawyer is becoming harder to find.

**Q. On what areas of practice do lawyers normally concentrate?**

**A.** Most lawyers concentrate on one or a few specific areas, such as: domestic relations, criminal law, personal injury, estate planning and administration, real estate, taxation, immigration, and intellectual property law (see chart below).

## AREAS OF LEGAL PRACTICE

| | |
|---|---|
| Business Law | Advising about starting a new business (corporation, partnership, etc.), general corporate matters, business taxation, and mergers and acquisitions |
| Criminal Law | Defending or prosecuting those accused of committing crimes |
| Domestic Relations | Representing individuals in separation, annulment, divorce, and child custody matters |
| Estate Planning | Advising clients in property management, drawing wills, probate, and estate planning |
| Immigration | Representing parties in proceedings involving naturalization and citizenship |
| Intellectual Property Law | Dealing with issues concerning trademarks, copyright regulations, and patents |
| Labor Law | Advising and representing employers, unions and employees on questions of union organizing, workplace safety, and compliance with government regulations |
| Personal Injury | Representing clients injured intentionally or negligently, and those with workers' compensation claims |
| Real Estate | Assisting clients in developing property, rezoning, and buying, selling, or renting homes or other property |
| Taxation | Counseling businesses and individuals in local, state, and federal tax matters |

## LOOKING FOR A LAWYER

### Q. How do I go about choosing a lawyer?

**A.** The lawyer will be helping you solve your problems, so you must feel comfortable enough to tell him or her, honestly and completely, all the facts necessary to resolve your problem. No one you listen to and nothing you read will tell you which particular lawyer will be the best for you; you must judge that for yourself. Most lawyers will meet with you briefly to "get acquainted," allowing you to talk with your prospective lawyer before making a final hiring decision. In many cases, there is no fee charged for an initial consultation. However, don't assume that an initial consultation is free. To be on the safe side, ask about fees before setting up your consultation appointment.

### Q. Are there any practical considerations to keep in mind when choosing a lawyer?

**A.** Yes. The lawyer's area of expertise and prior experience are important. Seventeen states have specialization programs that certify lawyers as specialists in certain stated types of law. These states are: Alabama, Arizona, California, Connecticut, Florida, Georgia, Idaho, Louisiana, Minnesota, New Jersey, New Mexico, North Carolina, Ohio, Pennsylvania, South Carolina, Tennessee, and Texas. In states without certification programs, you may want to ask about your lawyer's areas of concentration. You may also wish to ask about the types of cases your lawyer generally handles.

Other considerations are the convenience of the lawyer's office location, the amount of fees charged, and the length of time a case may take. Although they are not always wise guidelines, consider your personal preferences about the lawyer's age, gender, and personality. These preferences may guide you in locating someone with whom you feel most comfortable.

### Q. Where should I start to look for a lawyer?

**A.** There are many sources for finding a reliable lawyer. Some of the best are recommendations from a trusted friend, relatives, or business associates. Be aware that each legal case is different and that a lawyer who is right for someone else may not suit you or your legal problem.

### Q. Are advertisements a good place to look for a lawyer?

**A.** In some ways, yes, ads are useful. Until recently, the law did not permit lawyers to advertise their services. Today, specific guidelines allow lawyers to advertise. Always be careful about believing everything you read and hear—and nowhere is this more true than with advertisements. Still, newspaper, telephone directory, radio, and television ads, along with direct mail, can make you familiar with the names of lawyers who may be appropriate for your legal needs. Some ads will also help you determine a lawyer's area of expertise. Other ads will quote a fee or price range for handling a specific type of "simple" case. Keep in mind that the lawyer may not be a "specialist" in the advertised field, and that your case may not have a simple solution. If a lawyer quotes a fee, be certain you know exactly what services the charge does and does not include.

### Q. What about a local referral service?

**A.** Most communities have referral services to help the public find lawyers. These services usually recommend a lawyer in the area to evaluate a situation—sometimes at a reduced cost. Several services offer help to groups with unique characteristics, such as the elderly, immigrants, victims of domestic violence, or persons with a disability. Bar associations in most communities make referrals according to specific areas of law, helping you find a lawyer with the right concentration. Many referral services also have competency requirements for lawyers who wish to have referrals in a particular area of law.

Still, these services are not always a surefire way to find the "right" or even a "good" lawyer for you, since some services make referrals without concern for the lawyer's type or level of experience. In the end, you must make your own decision in order to feel confident about your selection. To contact a referral service, look in the telephone book's yellow pages under "Lawyer Referral Service," or look under any local or state bar association listing.

### Q. My new job offers a prepaid legal services plan. What can I expect?

**A.** Legal services, like many other things, are often less expensive when bought in bulk. Employers, labor and credit unions, and other groups have formed "legal insurance" plans. Many plans cover most, if not all, the costs of legal consultation, document preparation, and court representation in routine legal matters. Other programs cover only advice and consultation with a lawyer. Before joining a legal plan, make sure you are familiar with its coverage and know whether you will be required to make out-of-pocket contributions. These group plans follow the same pattern as group or cooperative medical insurance plans. Employers or unions set up a fund to pay the employees' legal fees, just as they contribute to group insurance plans to cover medical costs. Legal group plans have become much more widespread in recent years. Some retail department stores and credit card companies even offer such plans to their customers.

### Q. I have heard about legal clinics, but I am not sure if I can use their services. What kind of help do they offer?

**A.** Legal clinics primarily process routine, uncomplicated legal business. These firms often advertise heavily and rely especially on TV ads. They generally use standard forms and paralegal assistants. Paralegals are those who have received special basic legal training and have learned skills through their jobs.

These clinics often charge less than traditional law firms for their services. They mainly work on wills, personal bankruptcy, divorces, and traffic offenses. Each clinic office may be small, but clinics often associate with many other offices in a multistate area.

### Q. I may want to hire a lawyer, but I do not have much money. Where can I find low-cost legal help?

**A.** People do not have a right to a free lawyer in civil legal matters (they do in most criminal cases). However, several legal assistance programs offer inexpensive or free legal services to those in need. Most legal aid programs have special guidelines for eligibility, often based on where you live, the size of your family, and your income. Some legal aid offices have their own staff lawyers, and others operate with volunteer lawyers. To find free or reduced-cost legal services in your area, call your bar association or county courthouse. You may also look in the telephone book's yellow pages under "Legal Aid," "Legal Assistance," or "Legal Services." Sometimes the telephone book will list a legal aid office under "Lawyers" or "Attorneys."

### Q. I have been accused of a crime, and I cannot afford a lawyer. What can I do?

**A.** If the government accuses you of committing a crime, the United States Constitution guarantees you the right to be represented by a lawyer in any case in which you could be incarcerated for six months or more. If you cannot afford a lawyer, the judge handling the case will either appoint a private lawyer to represent you free of charge or the government's public defender will handle your case, also at no charge.

**Q. Besides court-appointed defenders, is there any other form of government assistance available?**

**A.** Departments and agencies of both the state and federal governments often have staff lawyers who can help the general public in limited situations, without charge. The United States Attorney's Office might be able to provide guidance about federal laws. It might also guide you to federal agencies that deal with specific concerns, such as environmental protection problems and discrimination in employment or housing.

The state attorney general may also provide guidance to the public on state laws, without charge. Some states, for example, maintain consumer protection departments as a function of the attorney general's office.

Similarly, counties, cities, and townships often have staff lawyers who may provide the public with guidance about local laws. Some of these local offices also offer consumer protection assistance through their law departments. However, government lawyers may not, at the government's expense, advise or represent anyone in private legal matters.

## QUESTIONS TO ASK A LAWYER

**Q. How will I determine whether I want to hire a specific lawyer?**

**A.** Many lawyers are willing to meet with you briefly without charge so the two of you can get acquainted. During (or soon after) this first meeting, you can decide whether you want to hire that lawyer. Many people feel nervous or intimidated when meeting lawyers, but remember that you are the one doing the hiring, and what's most important is that you are satisfied with what you're getting for your money. Before you make any hiring decisions, you might want to ask certain questions to aid in your evaluation.

**HAVE FAITH**
*It is important that you trust the lawyer you hire, believing that he or she will do the best job possible in protecting your legal rights. However, remember that lawyers cannot work magic. No lawyer can be expected to win every case, and the best legal advice may turn out to be not exactly what you wanted to hear.*

**Q. What sort of questions should I ask?**

**A.** Ask about the lawyer's experience and areas of practice. How long has the lawyer and the firm been practicing law? What kinds of legal problems does the lawyer handle most often? Are most clients individuals or businesses?

**Q. Is it proper to ask the lawyer if anyone else will be working on my case?**

**A.** Since you are the one paying the bill, it is well within your rights. Ask if nonlawyers, such as paralegals or law clerks, will be used in researching or preparing the case. If so, will there be separate charges for their services? Who will be consulted if the lawyer is unsure about some aspects of your case? Will the lawyer recommend another attorney or firm if this one is unable to handle your case?

**Q. I met with a lawyer who referred me to another lawyer. Should I be angry?**

**A.** Probably not. Occasionally, a lawyer will suggest that someone else in the same firm or an outside lawyer handle your specific problem. Perhaps the original lawyer is too busy to give your case the full attention it deserves. Maybe your problem requires another's expertise. No one likes to feel that a lawyer is shifting him or her to another attorney. However, most reassignments within firms occur for a good reason. Do not hesitate to request a meeting with the new attorney to make sure you are comfortable with him or her.

### Q. What, in particular, should I ask about fees and costs?

A. How are fees charged—by the hour, by the case, or by the amount won? About how much money will be required to handle the case from start to finish? When must you pay the bill? Can you pay it in installments? Ask for a written statement showing specific services rendered and the charge for each.

### Q. When I first meet with my prospective lawyer, should I ask about the possible outcome of the case?

A. Certainly, but beware of any lawyer who guarantees a big settlement or assures a victory in court. Remember that there are at least two sides to every legal issue and many factors can affect its resolution. Ask for the lawyer's opinion of your case's strengths and weaknesses. Will the lawyer most likely settle your case out of court or is it likely that the case will go to trial? What are the advantages and disadvantages of settlement? Of going to trial? What kind of experience does the lawyer have in trial work? If you lose at the trial, will the lawyer be willing to appeal the decision?

### Q. Should I ask if and how I can help with my case?

A. Yes. It is often in your interest to participate actively in your case. When you hire a lawyer, you are paying for legal advice. Your lawyer should make no major decisions about whether and how to go on with the case without your permission. Pay special attention to whether the lawyer seems willing and able to explain the case to you and answers your questions clearly and completely. Also ask what information will be supplied to you. How, and how often, will the lawyer keep you informed about the progress of your case? Will the lawyer send you copies of any of the documents that have to do with your case? Can you help keep fees down by gathering documents or otherwise assisting the effort?

### Q. During our first meeting, should I ask what will happen if the lawyer and I disagree?

A. Yes, your first meeting is the best time to ask about resolving potential problems. Find out if the lawyer will agree to binding arbitration if a serious dispute arises between the two of you. Most state bar associations have arbitration committees that, for a fee, will settle disputes that you and your lawyer may have, say over expenses. By agreeing to binding arbitration, both you and the lawyer consent to present your cases to an outside panel and abide by its decision.

## LEGAL FEES AND EXPENSES

### Q. How can I be sure that my lawyer will not overcharge me?

A. The fee charged by a attorney should be reasonable from an objective point of view. The fee should be tied to specific services rendered, time invested, and level of expertise provided.

There are some broad guidelines to help in evaluating whether a particular fee is reasonable:

- the time and work required by the lawyer and any assistants, and the difficulty of the legal issues presented;
- how much other lawyers in the area charge for similar work;
- the total value of the claim or settlement and the results of the case;

## TALK ABOUT FEES

*Although money is often a touchy subject in our society, fees and other charges should be discussed with your lawyer early. You can avoid future problems by having a clear understanding of the fees to be charged and getting that understanding in writing before any legal work has started. If the fee is to be charged on an hourly basis, insist on a complete itemized list and an explanation of charges each time the lawyer bills you.*

*Legal advice is not cheap. A bill from a lawyer for preparing a one-page legal document or providing basic advice may surprise some clients. Remember that when you hire a lawyer, you are paying for his or her expertise and time.*

- whether the lawyer has worked for that client before;
- the lawyer's experience, reputation, and ability; and
- the amount of other work the lawyer had to turn down to take on a particular case.

**Q. Someone said that I should ask my lawyer to use the billing method that is based on contingent fees. What does this mean?**

**A.** A client pays a contingent fee to a lawyer only if the lawyer handles a case successfully. Lawyers and clients use this arrangement only in cases where money is being claimed—most often in cases involving personal injury or workers' compensation. Many states strictly forbid this billing method in criminal cases and in most cases involving domestic (i.e., family) relations.

In a contingent fee arrangement, the lawyer agrees to accept a fixed percentage (often one third) of the recovery, which is the amount finally paid to the client. If you win the case, the lawyer's fee comes out of the money awarded to you. If you lose, neither you nor the lawyer will get any money, but you will not be required to pay your attorney for the work done on the case.

On the other hand, win or lose, you probably will have to pay court filing fees, the costs related to deposing witnesses, and similar charges.

## TYPES OF FEES AND EXPENSES

*The method used to charge fees is one of the things to consider in deciding if a fee is reasonable. You should understand the different charging methods before you make any hiring decision. At your first meeting, the lawyer should estimate how much the total case will cost and inform you of the method he or she will use to charge for the work. As with any bill, you should not pay without first getting an explanation for any charges you do not understand. Remember, not all costs can be estimated exactly because of unforeseen developments during the course of your case.*

By entering into a contingent fee agreement, both you and your lawyer expect to collect some unknown amount of money. Because many personal injury actions involve considerable and often complicated investigation and work by a lawyer, this may be less expensive than paying an hourly rate. You should clearly understand your options before entering into a contingent fee agreement, which is a contract in itself.

### Q. Are all contingent fee arrangements the same?

**A.** No. An important consideration is whether or not the lawyer deducts the costs and expenses from the amount won before or after you pay the lawyer's percentage.

---

**EXAMPLE:** Joe hires Ernie Attorney to represent him, agreeing that Ernie will receive one third of the final amount–in this case, $12,000. If Joe pays Ernie his fee before expenses, the fee will be calculated as follows:

| | |
|---|---|
| $12,000 | Total amount recovered in case |
| −4,000 | One third for Ernie Attorney |
| $ 8,000 | Balance |
| −2,100 | Payment for expenses and costs |
| $ 5,900 | Amount that Joe recovers |

If Joe pays Ernie after other legal expenses and costs, the fee will be calculated as follows:

| | |
|---|---|
| $12,000 | Total amount recovered in case |
| −2,100 | Payment for expenses and costs |
| $ 9,900 | Balance |
| −3,300 | (One-third for Ernie Attorney) |
| $ 6,600 | Amount that Joe recovers |

---

The above figures show that Joe will collect an additional seven-hundred dollars if the agreement provides that Ernie Attorney collects his share after Joe pays the other legal expenses.

Many lawyers prefer to be paid before they subtract the expenses, but the point is often negotiable. Of course, these matters should be settled before you hire a lawyer. If you agree to pay a contingent fee, your lawyer should provide a written explanation of this agreement that clearly states how he or she will deduct costs.

### Q. If my lawyer and I agree to a contingent fee arrangement, shouldn't the method of settling my case affect the amount of my lawyer's fee?

**A.** Yes, but only if both of you agree beforehand. Lawyers settle most personal injury cases through negotiations with insurance companies; such cases rarely require a trial in court. If the lawyer settles the case before going to trial, this requires less legal work. You can try to negotiate an agreement in which the lawyer accepts a lower percentage if he or she settles the case easily and quickly or before a lawsuit is filed in court, though many good lawyers might not agree to those terms.

### Q. What billing method do most lawyers use?

**A.** The most common billing method is to charge a set amount for each hour of time the lawyer works on your case. The method for determining what is a "reasonable" hourly fee depends on several things. More experienced lawyers tend to charge more per hour than those with less experience—but they also may take less time to do the same legal work. In addition, the same lawyer will usually charge more for time spent in the courtroom than for hours spent in the office or library.

### Q. A friend suggested that I might want to have a lawyer "on retainer." What does this mean?

**A.** A retainer fee is a set amount of money paid regularly to make sure that a lawyer will be available for any necessary legal service you might require. Businesses and people who routinely have a lot of legal work use retainers. By paying a retainer, a client receives routine consultations and general legal advice whenever needed. If a legal matter requires courtroom time or many hours of work, the client may need to pay more than the retainer amount. Retainer agreements should always be in writing.

Most people do not see a lawyer regularly and do not need to pay a retainer fee. Sometimes, however, a lawyer will ask the client to pay some money in advance before any legal work will be done. Although often called a "retainer," this money is really a down payment that will be applied toward the total fee billed.

### Q. I saw an advertisement from a law firm that charges fixed fees for specific types of work. What does this involve?

**A.** A fixed fee is the amount that will be charged for routine legal work. In a few situations, this amount may be set by law or by the judge handling the case. Since advertising by lawyers is becoming more popular, you are likely to see ads offering: "Simple Divorce— $150" or "Bankruptcy—from $50." Do not assume that these prices will be the amount of your final bill. The advertised price often does not include court costs and other expenses.

### Q. Does the lawyer's billing method influence the other costs and expenses that I might have to pay?

**A.** No. Some costs and expenses will be charged regardless of the billing method. The court clerk's office charges a fee for filing the complaint or petition that begins a legal action. The sheriff's office charges a fee for serving a legal summons. Your lawyer must pay for postage, copying documents, telephone calls,

and the advice or testimony of some types of expert witnesses such as doctors. These expenses, often called "costs," may not be part of a legal fee, and you may have to pay them regardless of the fee arrangement you use. Your lawyer will usually pay these costs as needed, billing you at regular intervals or at the close of your case.

### Q. What are referral fees?

**A.** If you go to "Lawyer A," he or she may be unable to help but refers you instead to "Lawyer B," at another law firm, who has more experience in handling your kind of case. In return for the referral, Lawyer A will sometimes ask to be paid part of the total fee arrangement you pay to Lawyer B. The law may prohibit this type of fee, especially if it increases the final amount to be paid by a client. The ethical rules for lawyers in most states specify that two lawyers may not divide a client's fee unless:

1. the client knows about the arrangement;
2. both lawyers do some actual "work" on the case;
3. they divide the fee to show how much work each lawyer did; and
4. the total bill is reasonable.

If one lawyer refers you to another, ask whether there will be a referral fee and, if so, ask about the specifics of the agreement between the lawyers.

### Q. Should I "shop around" for the cheapest lawyer I can find?

**A.** With legal advice, as with other products and services, you often get what you pay for. Although you should not expect to get good legal advice without paying for it, you should not pay for anything that you don't actually receive. After you and your lawyer have discussed fees, make sure to follow through by examining each bill carefully. If you feel that any charge is too high or if you do not understand a billed item, ask your lawyer to explain it before you pay.

## Q. Is there anything I can do to reduce my legal costs?

A. Yes, there are several cost-cutting methods available to you. First, answer all your lawyer's questions fully and honestly. Not only will you feel better but you also will save on legal fees. If you tell your lawyer all the facts as you know them, it will save time that might be spent on the particular case and will help your lawyer do a better job.

Remember that the ethics of the profession bind your lawyer to maintain in the strictest confidence almost anything you reveal during your private discussions. You should feel free to tell your lawyer the complete details in your case, even those that embarrass you. It is particularly important to tell your lawyer facts about your case that reflect poorly on you. These will almost certainly come out if your case goes to trial.

## Q. Can I reduce my legal costs if I get more involved in my case?

A. Sometimes. Stay informed and ask for copies of important documents related to your case. Let your lawyer know if you are willing to help out, such as by picking up or delivering documents or by making a few telephone calls. You should not interfere with your lawyer's work. However, you might be able to move your case quicker, reduce your legal costs, and keep yourself better informed by doing some of the work yourself. Discuss this with your lawyer.

## Q. Should I wait for my lawyer to say what he or she needs from me?

A. No, some things should be obvious to you. Before the first meeting with your lawyer,

think about your legal problem and how you would like it resolved. If your case involves other people, write down their names, addresses, and telephone numbers. Also jot down any specific facts or dates you think might be important and any questions you want answered. Bring the information with you to the first meeting, along with any relevant documents such as contracts or leases. By being organized, you will save time and money.

## Q. If something related to my case has occurred, should I wait until my next scheduled meeting to tell my lawyer about it?

A. No, situations can vary from one day to the next. Tell your lawyer immediately of changes that might be important to your case. It might mean that the lawyer will have to take a totally different action—or no action at all—in your case. This could greatly affect your lawyer's fee.

# WHAT TO DO IF YOUR LAWYER DOES NOT SATISFY YOU

## Q. I lost my case, and I still had to pay my lawyer's bill along with costs and expenses. I am not very happy with my lawyer. What can I do?

A. First, talk with your lawyer. A lack of communication causes many problems. If your lawyer appears to have acted improperly, or did not do something that you think he or she should have done, talk with your lawyer about it. You may be satisfied once you understand the circumstances better.

## Q. I have tried to talk with my lawyer. However, my lawyer will not discuss it. Do I have any alternatives?

A. Yes. If your lawyer is unwilling to discuss your complaints, consider taking your

## EXPECTATIONS ABOUT YOUR LAWYER

*When you agree to hire a lawyer and that lawyer agrees to be your legal representative, a two-way relationship begins in which you both have the same goal—to reach a satisfactory resolution to a legal matter. To reach this end, each of you must act responsibly toward the other. In a lawyer/client relationship, acting responsibly involves duties on both sides—and often involves some hard work.*

*You have a right to expect competent representation from your lawyer. However, every lawsuit has at least two sides. You cannot always blame your lawyer if your case does not turn out the way you thought it would. If you are unhappy with your lawyer, it is important to determine the reasons. If, after a realistic look, you still believe that you have a genuine complaint about your legal representation, there are several things you can do. The accompanying questions and answers discuss your alternatives.*

legal affairs to another lawyer. You decide whom to hire (and fire) as your lawyer. When you fire a lawyer, you may be charged a reasonable amount for the work already done. Most documents relating to the case are yours—ask

for them. In some states, however, a lawyer may have some rights to a file until the client pays a reasonable amount for work done on the case.

**Q. What if I feel that my lawyer has acted unethically?**

**A.** How a lawyer should act, in both professional and private life, is controlled by codes of professional conduct in the state or states where he or she is licensed to practice. These codes are usually administered by the state supreme court through its disciplinary board.

The codes consist of rules that describe generally how lawyers should strive to improve the legal profession and uphold the laws. They also give more detailed rules of conduct for specific situations (see below). If a lawyer's conduct falls below the standards set out in the codes, he or she can be disciplined by being "censured" or "reprimanded" (publicly or privately criticized), "suspended" (having the license to practice law taken away for a certain time), or "disbarred" (having the law license taken away indefinitely).

The law sets out punishments for anyone who breaks civil and criminal laws, and that includes lawyers. But because of the special position of trust and confidence involved in a lawyer/client relationship, lawyers may also be punished for things which are not unlawful—such as telling others confidential information about a client or representing clients whose interests are in conflict.

**Q. What are some specific examples of the ethical duties of lawyers?**

**A.** Among the highest responsibilities a lawyer has is his or her obligation to a client. A number of strict rules and common sense guidelines define these responsibilities:

- *Competence.* This requires the lawyer's ability to analyze legal issues; research and study changing laws and legal trends; and otherwise represent the client effectively and professionally.

- *Following the client's decisions.* A lawyer should advise a client of possible actions to be taken in a case and then act according to the client's choice of action—even if the lawyer might have picked a different route. One of the few exceptions is a client asking for a lawyer's help in doing something illegal such as lying in court or in a legal document. In these cases, the lawyer is required to inform the client of the legal effect of any planned wrongdoing and refuse to assist with it.

- *Diligence.* Every lawyer must act carefully and in a timely manner in handling a client's legal problem. Unnecessary delays can often damage a case. If, because of overwork or any other reason, a lawyer is unable to spend the required time and energy on a case, the lawyer should refuse from the beginning to take the case.

- *Communication.* A lawyer must be able to communicate effectively with a client. When a client asks for an explanation, the lawyer must provide it within a reasonable time. A lawyer must inform a client about changes in a case caused by time and circumstances.

- *Fees.* The amount the lawyer charges for legal work must be reasonable, and the client should be told the specifics of all charges.

- *Confidentiality.* With few exceptions, a lawyer may generally not tell anyone else what a client reveals about a case. The reason for this strict rule is to enable a client to discuss case details openly and honestly with a lawyer, even if those details reveal embarrassing or damaging information about the client. A rule

called the "attorney/client privilege" helps protect confidential information from being disclosed. Ask your lawyer to explain the privilege to you.

- *Conflicts of interest.* A lawyer must be loyal to his or her client. This means that a lawyer cannot represent two clients who are on opposite sides in the same or related lawsuits unless both clients give permission. And ordinarily, there can be no representation of a client whose interests would conflict with the lawyer's interests. For example, a lawyer may not be involved in writing a will for a client who leaves the lawyer money or property in that will.

- *Keeping clients' property.* If a lawyer is holding a client's money or property, it must be kept safely and separately from the lawyer's own funds and belongings. When a client asks for the property, the lawyer must return it immediately and in good condition. The lawyer must also keep careful records of money received for a client and, if asked, report that amount promptly and accurately.

### Q. I am upset with the way my lawyer handled my case. Can I file a complaint?

**A.** Yes. In recent years, it has become easier to get action on a complaint against a lawyer. As noted above, lawyers can be disciplined for violating ethical guidelines.

### Q. Where can I file a complaint against my lawyer?

**A.** If you believe you have a valid complaint about how your lawyer has handled your case, inform the organization that grants or withholds licenses to practice law in your state. Usually this is the disciplinary board of the state supreme court. You'll find it under the government listings for your state. You can also

## A CLIENT'S RESPONSIBILITIES

*As in any successful relationship, a good lawyer/client relationship involves cooperation on both sides. As a client, you should do all you can to make sure you get the best possible legal help. This includes:*

- *Being honest. Be honest in telling all the facts to your lawyer. Remind yourself of important points or questions by writing them down before talking with your lawyer.*

- *Notifying the lawyer of changes. Tell the lawyer promptly about any changes or new information you learn that may affect your case. This responsibility is a broad one and covers things from a change of your address or telephone number to letting your lawyer know if and why you are unhappy with his or her work.*

- *Asking for clarification. If you have any questions or are confused about something in your case, ask the lawyer for an explanation. This may go a long way toward putting your mind at ease—and will also help your lawyer do a better job of handling your case.*

- *Being realistic. A lawyer can only handle your legal affairs. You may need the help of another professional—banker, family counselor, accountant, or psychologist, for example—for problems which have no "legal" solution. After you have hired a lawyer you trust, do not forget about that trust. The lawyer's judgments are based on experience and training. Also, keep in mind that most legal matters cannot be resolved overnight. Give the system time to work.*

- *Paying. A client has the duty to promptly pay a fair and reasonable price for legal services. In fact, when a client fails to pay, in some situations the lawyer may have the right to stop working on the case. Still, the lawyer must then do whatever is reasonably possible to prevent the client's case from being harmed.*

obtain its location from the local bar association. In some states, the state bar association handles lawyer discipline. The board or the bar will either investigate the complaint or refer you to someone who can help. If your complaint concerns the amount your lawyer charged, you may be referred to a state or local bar association's fee arbitration service.

Making a complaint of this sort may punish the lawyer for misconduct, but it will probably not help you recover any money. Filing a disciplinary complaint accusing your lawyer of unethical conduct is a serious matter to the lawyer. Try to resolve any differences or disputes directly with the lawyer before filing a complaint.

If you have a case pending that your lawyer has mishandled, be sure to also protect your rights by taking steps to see that your case is now properly handled.

#### Q. Then how can I get money to compensate me for my lawyer's misconduct?

**A.** You will have to file a malpractice suit against your lawyer. The discussion on medical malpractice on page 526 in the "Personal Injury" chapter will provide useful information on malpractice in general.

You may also have the right to receive compensation from a client security fund (see below).

#### Q. My lawyer settled my case out of court and refuses to pay me my share of the settlement. What can I do about it?

**A.** If you believe that your lawyer has taken or improperly kept money or property that belongs to you, contact the state (or sometimes, local) "client security fund," "client indemnity fund" or "client assistance fund." The state or local bar association or the state supreme court disciplinary board can tell you how to contact the fund that serves you. Under any name, these funds may reimburse clients if a court has found that their lawyer has defrauded them. Lawyers pay fees to maintain such funds.

#### Q. If I am having a problem with my lawyer, is there any reason that I would want to call the police?

**A.** Yes. If you believe that your lawyer has committed a crime such as stealing your money or property, you should report that crime to the police. This is a last resort that should be taken only when you feel certain of your position. However, if you are certain, do not feel intimidated because your complaint is against a lawyer.

## ALTERNATIVES TO LAWSUITS

#### Q. I am considering filing a lawsuit against someone. Is there anything I can do to avoid this?

**A.** Yes, you can try to negotiate. Before you even think of going to court, try to talk with the other person in the dispute. Most potential suits are settled long before they go to court.

### LISTEN TO THE OTHER PERSON

*Keep an open mind to possible solutions and listen to the other person's side of the story. Remember that, with or without the help of lawyers, most people settle their legal disputes out of court.*

### AFTER YOU SETTLE

*It is important to get your settlement in writing, and it is best if you and the other person involved sign the final agreement. Suppose that, after filing a lawsuit, you are able to work out the main problem with the other person, such as who owes how much to whom. It still may be necessary to appear before a judge to determine a method or schedule of payment. It is usually best to get the advice of a lawyer about any settlement before you put it into writing and sign it.*

The next chapter discusses steps to take in settling your case.

You can also explore other low-cost, informal alternatives that probably exist in your community—mediation, arbitration, and small claims court. The next chapter also provides practical information about each of these options.

**Q. I have already hired a lawyer and filed a lawsuit. Is it too late to negotiate a settlement?**

**A.** No. It's almost never too late to settle. Judges and lawyers encourage those involved in a lawsuit to reach an agreement between themselves. If you reach an agreement after filing your case, let the court know you have settled the matter, and the case will be removed from the court's calendar. If you have hired a lawyer, he or she should do this.

**Q. Can my case be thrown out of court because it is too old?**

**A.** Yes. Every state has a time limit within which a case must be filed. The logic behind such limits, called statutes of limitations, is that most lawsuits are more easily and more fairly resolved within a short time. This is another reason that it is important to act as soon as you and your lawyer feel that you may have a valid legal claim. The time limits vary for different types of cases.

## WHERE TO GET MORE INFORMATION

Many organizations and agencies act as resources for specialized areas of law. These include national groups, such as the Federal Trade Commission, and local organizations, such as the Better Business Bureau and the consumer protection department of the state attorney general's office.

State and local bar associations are also excellent sources of information. They can help by providing information about lawyer referral, dispute resolution alternatives, lawyer discipline, and other topics. They also can usually refer you to other legal and nonlegal groups that might help you.

Space prevents us from listing the many helpful organizations or the hundreds of local bar associations across the country. A listing of state bar associations appears near the back of this publication. Check the blue pages of your telephone book for governmental listings; the white pages and the yellow pages can provide additional listings of private and public organizations.

# How the Legal System Works

## CONTENTS

# INTRODUCTION

ALTHOUGH NO ONE EXCEPT A CRIMINAL expects to be charged with a crime, and few of us ever contemplate the possibility of a lawsuit, it seems that the more we know about how our legal system works, the more likely we are to respect the rights of others while demanding that our own rights are respected. Hence this chapter on how the legal system works.

Subsequent chapters will explain your legal rights in a nation dedicated to the rule of law; this chapter will give you an overview of how our legal system can give those rights meaning.

### Q. Why do we have an "adversarial" legal system?

**A.** American courtroom procedures are based on historical precedent, modified by the needs and experience of lawyers and judges. When two parties cannot agree on their respective rights and obligations, or even on what gave rise to the dispute, the system assumes each side has an equal opportunity to present its case (and to point out the weaknesses in its opponent's case) to a neutral judge or jury. The system is an adversarial proceeding, with each side championed by a lawyer following the same statutes, case law, and rules of procedure. The system is designed to permit the truth to emerge whether the case is criminal or civil in nature.

### Q. How does a civil suit differ from a criminal prosecution?

**A.** A criminal prosecution is brought by the government to punish an individual for committing a crime against society and to deter others from committing similar crimes. As appropriate, it may create an opportunity for state-supervised rehabilitation or separation of the offender from the aggrieved community. Although a criminal defendant may have directly injured only one victim, it is thought that any violation of the criminal laws harms society as well. Accordingly, the victim is not permitted to prosecute the criminal case against the defendant who harmed him or her— that is the government's job in its role as the society's representative. The crime victim, of course, is the principal witness against the criminal defendant, but it is the government alone that has the authority to file an "information" or seek a grand jury "indictment" charging someone with a crime.

On the other hand, a crime victim may file a civil lawsuit against a wrongdoer. If the victim sues, he or she is called the plaintiff; the perpetrator of the crime is called the defendant, just as in the criminal case. The civil case provides a legal forum for persons seeking compensation for their injuries or vindication of their rights. Courts may provide redress to plaintiffs who can demonstrate that a defendant has injured them while committing some legal wrong against them. Unlike a criminal case, the defendant in a civil case who is found liable for harming the plaintiff cannot be sentenced to prison but, instead, will be compelled to pay compensation or ordered to take or desist from some action.

### Q. Are there different standards for determining liability in a civil suit and guilt in a criminal case?

**A.** Yes. Because the Bill of Rights treats a criminal conviction (and the possibility of a death sentence or a prison term) as a more serious consequence than a finding of civil liability, it is more difficult to convict someone of a crime than it is to obtain a civil judgment against him or her.

In most instances, the test for whether a trial court properly found that a plaintiff met his or her "burden of proof" in a civil suit is measured by whether a reasonable person could have concluded that it was "more likely than not" that the defendant was liable for, i.e., caused, the plaintiff's injury or loss. This "preponderance of the evidence" standard means that if the evidence favors the plaintiff by even the slightest bit, he or she is entitled to a verdict. In a criminal case, however, the standard is much higher: the prosecution must demonstrate the defendant's guilt "beyond a reasonable doubt." Thus, even if it is more likely than not that a criminal defendant is guilty of the crime charged, the proper verdict is "not guilty" if there remains a reasonable doubt about his or her guilt.

As will be discussed in more detail in the chapter on criminal justice, the United States Constitution guarantees criminal defendants many other rights, including the right to a jury trial when there is the possibility of a conviction resulting in a prison term of six months or more, and the right to have an attorney appointed if the defendant cannot afford to hire one.

## SETTLING YOUR DISPUTE

### Q. Are formal, adversarial trials always necessary?

**A.** No. The majority of criminal and civil cases (non-criminal cases involving disputes between individuals or organizations) are resolved without a trial. As will be explained in the chapter on criminal justice, a criminal case can be resolved without a trial in one of three

ways. The defendant can enter a plea of guilty or a plea of *nolo contendere* (no contest) to the charges, thereby forgoing the need for a trial. Or he or she may be able to negotiate a plea bargain with the prosecution in which the two sides agree that the defendant will plead guilty to a lesser charge than the one he or she currently faces. In each of these three cases, a judge must make sure the decision is fair and voluntary.

Similarly, by some estimates upwards of 90 percent of all civil cases are "settled" before trial. The courts actively work to encourage settlements and will often require the parties to a suit to engage in pretrial settlement conferences to see if some mutually satisfactory compromise might permit them to avoid the need for a full-blown trial.

### Q. How can I settle my case?

**A.** Talk to the person with whom you have a dispute. Stay calm and reasonable. You may find that, if approached politely, your "opponent" will be willing to settle on a mutually acceptable basis. Make certain that person understands why you are unhappy and what you would consider a reasonable solution to the problem. Keep an open mind and listen to the other person's side of the story. Making an effort to settle a dispute without a lawsuit is never a waste of time. In addition, many states require that an aggrieved party first make a demand for payment or action before filing some types of lawsuits.

If you do reach a satisfactory compromise, ask your lawyer to get it in writing for both parties to sign—you'll both want to make certain what you are and are not agreeing to and what, if any, issues may still need to be resolved. Even if you and the other person involved are able to work out the main problem, such as who owes how much money to whom, it still may be necessary to appear before a judge to determine, for example, a payment schedule. Your court appearance will be made easier if the agreement is in writing and can be submitted to the judge.

### Q. *What do I do if the other party won't agree to a reasonable settlement?*

**A.** The next step is to have your lawyer write a carefully thought-out letter to the person with whom you have a disagreement. This letter should include an accurate summary of the history of the problem and a date by which you would like a response or settlement. This type of "settle or else" letter has many advantages. It helps you organize the facts and your thoughts logically. Your lawyer may be able to express your thoughts in a way that the other person might not have "heard" when you were talking to each other directly. It may be just the push needed to get the other person to settle. If the letter sets reasonable time limits, it will often help to encourage settlement. Finally, if you end up in court, your letter will give the judge important background information and will go a long way toward satisfying any state-law requirement that a demand for payment or other action be made prior to filing suit.

## ALTERNATIVE DISPUTE RESOLUTION

### Q. *If the demand letter doesn't work, do I have any other alternatives before filing a lawsuit?*

**A.** Yes. In some circumstances you might prefer to try to resolve your dispute through arbitration or some other form of alternative dispute resolution outside the formal court system.

### Q. *What is alternative dispute resolution?*

**A.** Nearly all states have established "dispute resolution centers." These centers, which, depending on the state, may be known as neigh-borhood justice centers or citizens' dispute settlement programs, specialize in helping people who have common problems. For example, there are centers that specialize in resolving disputes commonly encountered by consumers, employers and employees, landlords and tenants, neighbors, and family members.

A complete listing of the many kinds of dispute resolution programs can be found in the 1993 Dispute Resolution Directory. (For more information about this directory, write: ABA Dispute Resolution, 1800 M Street, NW, Washington, DC 20036.)

### Q. *What is the difference between mediation and arbitration as forms of dispute resolution?*

**A.** In mediation, a trained mediator will help you and your opponent resolve your disagreement by identifying, defining, and discussing the things about which you disagree. This is an informal, cooperative problem-solving process, and does not require you to know the law or to hire a lawyer. Arbitration, on the other hand, is a more formal proceeding in which you and your opponent will be asked to present evidence and witnesses to the presiding arbitrator, who usually will issue a written decision to resolve the dispute. In many cases, the decision of the arbitrator is binding on the parties and final. Most nonprofit dispute resolution centers offer mediation or arbitration services for free or at only a modest cost.

### Q. *When does it make sense to seek some form of alternative dispute resolution?*

**A.** These alternatives are generally faster, less expensive, and less stressful than a traditional lawsuit. On the other hand, some cases, either because of the high stakes involved or the complexity of the issues and facts, are simply better handled by courts operating with the full panoply of formal procedures and safeguards.

## Advantages/Disadvantages of Dispute Resolution Mechanisms

| | *Advantages* | *Disadvantages* |
|---|---|---|
| Decision Through Court Procedures | • Announces and applies public norms<br>• Follows precedent<br>• Uniformity<br>• Independence<br>• Well-established rules and procedures<br>• Partially funded by state<br>• Decisions act as a deterrence<br>• Decisions are binding<br>• Decisions are enforceable | • Lack of special expertise<br>• Can be confusing<br>• Time consuming<br>• Delays are frequent<br>• Expensive<br>• Requires lawyers<br>• Limited range of remedies<br>• Tends to divide parties<br>• Compromises are not always possible |
| Arbitration | • Privacy<br>• Parties control forum<br>• Speedy resolution<br>• Tailors remedy to individual problem<br>• Decisions are enforceable | • Lacks precedent<br>• Lacks uniformity<br>• Quality varies<br>• Becoming more structured<br>• Requiring more money and time |
| Mediation | • Privacy<br>• Reflects concerns of parties<br>• Finds harmonious solutions<br>• Addresses underlying problem<br>• Process educates<br>• Parties control process<br>• Can cost less than decision through court procedures<br>• High rate of compliance<br>• Speedy resolution | • Not binding<br>• Cannot compel participation<br>• No power to induce settlements<br>• No due process safeguards<br>• Lacks enforceability<br>• Reflects imbalance in negotiating skills<br>• Little application/development of public standards<br>• Decision may be unclear |

SOURCE: *Paths to Justice: Major Public Policy Issues of Dispute Resolution.* Reproduced by permission of the National Institute for Dispute Resolution. Call (202) 466-4764 for further information.

Arbitration also may not be possible unless both parties agree in advance to accept the arbitrator's decision as final. If either you or your opponent do not want to forgo the right to appeal an adverse decision, arbitration will not be helpful.

See the chart above for a more detailed look at the pros and cons of alternative dispute resolution.

## SMALL CLAIMS COURT

**Q. If I decide to proceed with a formal lawsuit, how should I begin?**

**A.** It depends on the type of claim you wish to make. Here a lawyer can provide you with crucial advice on not only what claims you may have, but on when, where, and how you must make them. Once your lawyer has helped you identify whether you have a valid legal claim and whether it is likely to be worth your time and money to pursue it (there are various court costs involved as well as attorney fees), you will need to determine which court has jurisdiction to hear your case. You may, for example, be able to bring your case to small claims court.

### Q. What is small claims court?

**A.** All states have these special courts, although they may have different names, such as magistrate court, justice of the peace court, or *pro se* court. As a general rule, small claims courts are available only to resolve disputes involving small claims for money. Every state limits how much money you may seek in a small claims court lawsuit. The limits may range from a few hundred dollars in some states to thousands of dollars in others.

### Q. May I represent myself?

**A.** Yes. You generally do not need a lawyer to accompany you to small claims court. Sometimes a lawyer is not permitted to represent a party in small claims court.

### Q. What are the advantages of filing a lawsuit in a small claims court?

**A.** First, since you will be acting as your own lawyer, you will save on attorney's fees. Second, small claims court procedures are simple and there is little paperwork involved. When your day in small claims court arrives, you and your witnesses can talk freely with the judge about what happened. In many states, the court will even arrange to have the trial or hearing after normal work hours. Third, there are fewer delays than in regular courts—it usually

### NO SMALL CONSIDERATIONS

*Before you decide whether you should take advantage of small claims court, answer some simple questions. Is your claim one that has only to do with money? If so, is the amount you are suing for within the limit in your state? Is the time and effort you will have to put in to learning your state's law and presenting your case worth what you are likely to collect?*

*Like other courts, small claims courts operate according to laws and rules. Even the most careful preparation and the best presentation in court will not help if you cannot prove legally that the other person owes you the money. You must be able to prove "legal liability" in your case—that you have suffered a loss because of someone else's unlawful acts.*

will take only two or three months to file, argue, and receive a decision in your case.

### Q. Can I have a jury trial in small claims court?

**A.** No, there is no jury; a judge will decide your case.

### Q. Where can I get more information about small claims courts?

**A.** There are many good "how-to" books that explain what steps to take to bring a case to small claims court. Look at a few of them if you think you might have such a case, but do not depend on books alone. The laws and rules for small claims are different in each state. For more information, check with the small claims clerk or local consumer bureaus and legal aid groups in your area.

**Q. It sounds like it won't take much work to bring my case in small claims court. Is that true?**

**A.** Not necessarily. Use a small claims procedure only if you are willing to put some time into your case. You will be acting as your own lawyer, so you will be doing research, gathering documents, and investigating factual matters to prepare and present your case.

## STATE OR FEDERAL COURT?

**Q. If small claims court is not an option, how will my lawyer determine which court is the one for me?**

**A.** After identifying the nature of the claims you may have and the remedies you are seeking, your lawyer will guide you to the court with the proper jurisdiction and venue.

**Q. What is jurisdiction?**

**A.** When we say a court has jurisdiction to hear a case, we mean it has the authority to decide the kinds of issues raised in the case. Not every court has jurisdiction to hear every kind of case. One of the first questions to answer before filing a lawsuit is whether to bring the suit in state or federal court.

**Q. What kinds of cases can federal courts decide?**

**A.** The jurisdiction of most federal courts is determined by Article III of the United States Constitution, which limits the kinds of cases federal courts can hear. These include, foremost, cases involving issues of federal law. This so-called federal question jurisdiction authorizes federal district courts to decide both civil

---

### WHY ISN'T THERE JUST ONE COURT SYSTEM?

*The United States Constitution provides for a dual system of government, with both state and federal sovereigns. While Article III of the U.S. Constitution contemplates a federal judiciary operating as a coequal branch of our national government, each state is expected to establish and operate its own court system as part of its own government. (The District of Columbia courts have a mixed state/federal quality in administering justice in our nation's capital.)*

*If there were no state or local courts, many cases could not be heard at all, for the Constitution limits the cases that can be brought in federal courts. A dual court system makes sense philosophically because it respects a state's right to establish and enforce the law with respect to its unique problems and concerns. It also makes sense practically because, as a general rule, a state's own courts are more familiar with state and local law.*

## OTHER FEDERAL COURTS

*There are several specialized courts—Tax Court, the Court of Federal Claims, the Court of Veterans Appeals, Courts of Military Review, and the Court of International Trade. Each United States District Court also has a United States Bankruptcy Court unit as well as one or more magistrate.*

*In addition, Congress has created other courts under its Article I powers to serve the people in the United States territories of Guam, the United States Virgin Islands, and the Northern Mariana Islands. These "legislative courts" operate much like the Article III courts, but the presiding officers of these courts do not have the constitutional protections accorded to Article III judges such as life tenure and the prohibition against reducing judicial salaries.*

*In every instance, a party to a federal lawsuit will have an opportunity to proceed through two levels of decision: the United States District Court or other specialized trial court and a court of appeals. In some cases, a party may receive a third level of decision from the United States Supreme Court if, for example, the Court believes that the case presents an important question of federal law.*

and criminal cases in which federal law must be interpreted or applied. The federal law at issue may have arisen out of a federal statute or regulation, treaty, or a provision of the Constitution itself.

Another category of cases that Article III has placed within the federal courts' jurisdiction can be thought of as cases in which the Constitution's framers feared that an out-of-state party might not trust the local courts to provide him or her with a neutral forum. Thus, Article III gives federal courts "diversity jurisdiction" over controversies:

- between citizens of different states;
- between two or more states;
- between citizens of the same state claiming lands under grants of different states.

Similarly, federal district courts have jurisdiction over any suit to which the United States or one of its officers is a party.

Cases involving ambassadors, consuls, and other public ministers (in other words, cases that might affect America's relations with other countries) are also entrusted to the federal courts, as are cases involving the laws relating to navigable waters (the oceans, Great Lakes, and most rivers) and commerce on those waters. In addition, Congress has created specialized federal courts such as bankruptcy courts and tax courts.

**Q. What sorts of cases are decided by state courts?**

**A.** Most states have two levels of trial courts—special jurisdiction courts with juris-

## State Court Structure Prototype

**COURT OF LAST RESORT**
or
**State Supreme Court**

Generally the court has broad discretionary jurisdiction in accepting for review either criminal or civil appeals via the intermediate court of appeals. If a petition is denied, the intermediate appellate court's ruling stands. In states with a death penalty, petitions bypass the intermediate appellate court and go directly to the court of last resort.

↑

**INTERMEDIATE APPELLATE COURTS**
or
**State Courts of Appeals**

Generally they must accept virtually all criminal appeals but have discretion in which civil appeals they will hear. Parties dissatisfied with the appellate court's decision may appeal to the court of last resort.

↑

**COURTS OF GENERAL JURISDICTION**

Courts at this level have titles such as Chancery Court, Circuit Court, District Court, Probate Court, or Superior Court. Case types may include: torts, contracts, domestic relations, estates, real property, felonies, juvenile hearings and misdemeanors.

↑

**COURTS OF LIMITED JURISDICTION**

Courts at this level have titles such as County Court, Court of Common Pleas, District Court, Family Court, Juvenile Court, Magistrate Court, Municipal Court, or Probate Court. They may hear tort and contract cases involving lower dollar amounts, misdemeanors and a limited class of felonies, drunk driving and traffic cases, and emergency juvenile hearings.

There are as many state court structures as there are states. The above information is adapted from Brian J. Ostrom, et al., *State Court Caseload Statistics: Annual Report 1991* (National Center for State Courts, 1993), which has charts showing the state court structures of all 50 states plus the District of Columbia and Puerto Rico.

diction limited to specific types of cases, and general jurisdiction courts with jurisdiction over all other cases. Special jurisdiction courts are dominated by traffic cases but also hear relatively minor civil and criminal disputes. Special jurisdiction courts often have exclusive jurisdiction over juvenile cases. These courts are variously called district, justice, justice of the peace, magistrate, county, municipal, or police courts.

Courts of general jurisdiction hear most of the serious criminal and civil cases and are sometimes divided into subject areas such as domestic relations, probate, and state and local tax. These courts are variously called circuit courts, courts of common pleas, and, in New York State, the supreme court.

Unlike the federal courts, state courts are not limited to hearing only the kinds of cases listed in Article III of the United States Constitution.

### Q. Do I ever have a choice of whether to sue in state or federal court?

**A.** Yes. Although some cases are exclusively within the jurisdiction of one or the other court systems (juvenile cases, for example, are adjudicated in state juvenile courts, while all bankruptcies are filed in federal bankruptcy court), the state and federal courts have "concurrent jurisdiction" over many cases. A typical example would be a case involving a state law that is being litigated by a plaintiff from one state and a defendant from another state. The state courts would have jurisdiction because of the state law issues. But if the case involves an "amount in controversy" of more than $50,000, the federal courts would have jurisdiction as well because the parties are citizens of different states. This is known as diversity-of-citizenship jurisdiction or, more commonly, diversity jurisdiction. Article III of the Constitution gives federal courts concurrent jurisdiction over these cases.

### Q. How is the federal court system structured?

**A.** Rather than prescribing any one rigid structure for the federal courts, Article III merely requires that the judicial power of the

# The United States Court System

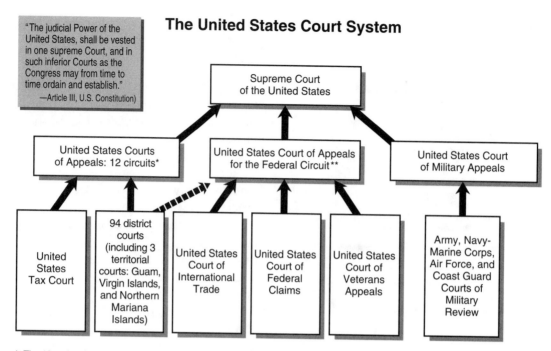

"The judicial Power of the United States, shall be vested in one supreme Court, and in such inferior Courts as the Congress may from time to time ordain and establish."
—Article III, U.S. Constitution)

Supreme Court of the United States

United States Courts of Appeals: 12 circuits*

United States Court of Appeals for the Federal Circuit**

United States Court of Military Appeals

United States Tax Court

94 district courts (including 3 territorial courts: Guam, Virgin Islands, and Northern Mariana Islands)

United States Court of International Trade

United States Court of Federal Claims

United States Court of Veterans Appeals

Army, Navy-Marine Corps, Air Force, and Coast Guard Courts of Military Review

\* The 12 regional courts of appeals also review cases from a number of federal agencies.
\*\* The Court of Appeals for the Federal Circuit also receives cases from the International Trade Commission, the Merit Systems Protection Board, the Patent and Trademark Office, and the Board of Contract Appeals.

Reprinted with permission from *Understanding the Federal Courts,* available from the Administrative Office of the United States Courts at the address given at the end of this chapter.

## NO ONE LEGAL SYSTEM

*Our American "legal system" is really composed of a number of different court systems and procedures. Although all American courts share certain attributes, how a given court will work in a particular case depends on the type of court it is and the type of dispute it is being asked to resolve.*

*The fifty state-court systems differ from one another and from the federal courts. Civil cases are adjudicated according to different rules than criminal cases. Appellate courts play a different role than the trial courts and specialized courts, such as bankruptcy and tax courts, and, accordingly, have their own customized procedures. Native American tribal courts, which generally have jurisdiction to hear cases originating on reservations, determine disputes based on Indian law, customs and codes, as well as federal law.*

*On the other hand, all American courts bear some resemblance to the federal courts established by Article III of the United States Constitution. Therefore, this chapter will primarily focus on the workings of the federal courts in general and on civil cases in particular. The criminal justice system is discussed in a separate, later chapter beginning on page 540.*

## MOST CASES DECIDED IN STATE COURT

*The fifty state-court systems together handle the overwhelming majority of all legal disputes. According to the most recent annual report of the Conference of State Court Administrators, the State Justice Institute, and the National Center for State Courts, more than ninety-three million new cases were filed in state trial courts in 1991. This enormous volume of cases included more than thirty-one million civil and criminal cases, nearly two million juvenile cases, and more than sixty million traffic cases.*

*By contrast, the Administrative Office of the United States Courts reports that in the year ending June 30, 1992, the United States District Courts received 275,237 cases, 226,895 of which were civil cases and 48,342 of which were criminal. Among the types of civil suits that entered the federal courts during this latest reporting period were: civil rights actions (23,419), cases concerning personal injury and damage to property (36,469), and prisoner petitions (46,452). Of the newly filed federal criminal cases, 70 percent were felonies. They included: homicide (195), tax fraud (849), robbery (1,804), forgery and counterfeiting (1,238), and drug offenses, the largest and fastest growing category of cases (12,512).*

federal government "be vested in one Supreme Court, and in such inferior courts as Congress may from time to time ordain and establish." Pursuant to this authority, Congress has created ninety-four United States District Courts (the trial courts in the federal system) as well as other specialized trial courts. Sandwiched between these trial courts and the Supreme Court are the intermediate appellate courts— twelve regional United States Courts of Appeals plus the Court of Appeals for the Federal Circuit, and the Court of Military Appeals.

### Q. How are the state court systems structured?

**A.** State courts are the product of the individual state's constitution and legislation. The resulting court systems vary in particulars. In addition to the two-tiered trial courts mentioned earlier, most states have an intermediate appellate court in addition to a state supreme court analogous to the United States Supreme Court.

### Q. How are judges selected?

**A.** This is another important difference between the state and federal systems. All 649 federal district court judges are appointed for life by the president with the advice and consent of the United States Senate. The nine seats on the United States Supreme Court and the 179 seats on the thirteen United States Courts of Appeals are filled in the same way.

The states, on the other hand, have a variety of procedures for filling judgeships. While many state judges are appointed by the governor for a term of years, many others are required to run for election.

Sample Complaint Form Used to Initiate a Lawsuit

## IN THE CIRCUIT COURT OF COOK COUNTY, ILLINOIS, . . . . . . . . . DISTRICT

v.

Plaintiff. . .

No. . . . . . . . . . . . . . . . . . . . . . . . . . . . . . . . . . . .

Contract . . . . . . . . . . . . . . . . . . . . . . . . . . . . . . . .

Amount Claimed $ . . . . . . . . . . . . . . . . . . . . . . . . .

Defendant. . .

Return Date . . . . . . . . . . . . . . . . . . . . . . . . . . . . . .

### COMPLAINT

The plaintiff. . . claim. . . as follows:

1.

I, . . . . . . . . . . . . . . . . . . . . . . . . . . . . . . . . . . . . . . . . . . . . . . . . . . . . . . . . . . on oath state that I am the. . . . . . . . . . . .
plaintiff in the above entitled action. The allegations in this complaint are true.

. . . . . . . . . . . . . . . . . . . . . . . . . . . . . . . . . . . . . . . . .

Signed and sworn to before me . . . . . . . . . . . . . . . . . . . . . . . . . . . . . . . . . . . . . . . . . . . . . . . . . , 19. . . .

. . . . . . . . . . . . . . . . . . . .  . . . . . . . . . . . . . . . . .Notary public

Name
Attorney for
Address
City
Telephone
Atty No.

## Q. Which method is better?

**A.** As the variety of different state procedures would indicate, there is no consensus answer to this question. Generally, supporters of the electoral method believe that elected judges are more likely to be responsive to the needs of the everyday citizen, while critics argue that the appointment method is better able to identify good judges rather than good politicians. In some states, judges are initially appointed, but then must win periodic retention elections in which voters simply vote yes or no to retain that particular judge.

## Q. How much time do I have to decide whether to file a civil law suit?

**A.** It varies depending on the kind of suit it is. An important element of all federal and state lawsuits is the "statute of limitations" that governs the amount of time you have in which to sue after the incident takes place. The concern is that it is unfair to summon a defendant into court long after the incident occurred, when memories may no longer be fresh and evidence no longer available. Thus, after the time limit has run out on the applicable statute of limitations, the plaintiff is forever barred from bringing suit—no matter how meritorious the case might be.

## Q. What begins a lawsuit?

**A.** A lawsuit begins when the plaintiff files a document with the court called a "complaint." The complaint recounts what happened to the plaintiff, what the plaintiff wants the court to do about it, and the legal reasons why the court ought to do what the plaintiff asks. The various wrongs the plaintiff claims to have suffered are listed in separate "counts" of the complaint. The complaint also sets forth the remedy the plaintiff is seeking from the court. The remedy requested is called a "prayer for relief."

### THE JUDICIARY AS A COEQUAL BRANCH OF GOVERNMENT

*First, it is important to note that a federal court's power to declare what the law means and to strike down congressional enactments as unconstitutional is in itself a powerful check against any attempt to diminish the role of the federal judiciary. In addition, federal judges enjoy two specific constitutional protections designed to maintain their independence from the executive and legislative branches. First, although Congress does have the power to determine the structure of and funding for federal courts, judges, once confirmed by the United States Senate, have life tenure—they cannot be fired except by "Impeachment for, and Conviction of, Treason, Bribery, or other high Crimes and Misdemeanors." Second, Congress cannot reduce the pay of federal judges.*

## Q. How does a defendant find out that he or she is being sued?

**A.** The clerk of the court in which the complaint is filed will issue a "summons" to the defendant. The summons tells the defendant that a suit has been filed against him or her, who filed it, and the time and place to appear in court. This summons, along with the complaint, must then be "served" into the defendant's hands. A sheriff or marshal may deliver it, or a private process server may be hired. In some instances, it may be sufficient to mail the summons and complaint by certified or registered mail.

## PRETRIAL PROCEDURES

### Q. What are the defendant's options after being served?

**A.** At this point, most defendants will hire an attorney to prepare their defense to the suit. The attorney will need to hear the defendant's version of events and scrutinize the complaint and summons. If the complaint appears deficient, legally or factually, the defendant may be advised to file one of several motions attacking it.

### Trial Progression of Civil Actions

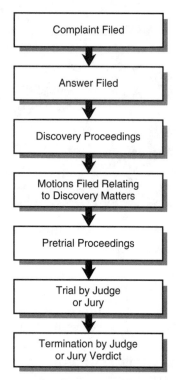

Complaint Filed

↓

Answer Filed

↓

Discovery Proceedings

↓

Motions Filed Relating to Discovery Matters

↓

Pretrial Proceedings

↓

Trial by Judge or Jury

↓

Termination by Judge or Jury Verdict

Reprinted with permission from *Understanding the Federal Courts,* available from the Administrative Office of the United States Courts at the address given at the end of this chapter.

### Q. What is a "motion"?

**A.** A motion is a formal written or oral request that the court take some specific action. Typical pretrial motions might include a defense motion to strike some allegation from the complaint or to dismiss all or part of the complaint because, for example, the issue raised has already been decided in another case or because the plaintiff has no legal right to bring this particular suit. If the service of the summons and complaint was improper (because, for example, the server delivered the documents to the wrong address or to a person 12 years old or younger), the defendant may file a motion to "quash service." In any of these cases, the parties then would be required to attend a preliminary hearing to resolve these issues.

Then the defendant will have a statutorily fixed amount of time in which to file an answer to the allegations in the complaint.

### Q. How much information should the defendant include in the answer?

**A.** Essentially, the defendant's answer must alert the plaintiff and the court to which allegations and counts in the complaint he or she is contesting, admitting, or is unable to contest or admit because of insufficient information. The defendant must respond to each and every alleged fact and count in the complaint; failure to respond can be interpreted as an admission. In addition, the answer may raise any "affirmative defenses" he or she may have beyond simple denial. If a defendant raises an "affirmative defense," he or she will be required to prove it if the case goes to trial.

In addition, although an objection that the court lacks jurisdiction to hear a case can be raised at any time, if the defendant has reason to believe that the court lacks legal authority to hear the case, he or she should raise that issue before filing an answer. Finally, if the defendant believes that the court does not have jurisdic-

# Pleadings

Pleadings are certain formal documents filed with the court that state the parties' basic positions. Pleadings are not the arguments made in court by the lawyers. Common pretrial pleadings are:

| Pleading | Function |
| --- | --- |
| Complaint | Probably the most important document in a case. It states the plaintiff's version of the facts and specifies the damages. By doing so, it records the issues of the case. |
| Answer | A statement by the defendant that responds to the charges in the plaintiff's complaint. It explains why the plaintiff should not win the case. It also may offer other facts or plead an excuse. |
| Reply | A response to new charges raised by the other party or parties in prior pleadings. Any party in the case may have to file a reply. |
| Counterclaim | Allows the defendant to sue the plaintiff, and perhaps others, for relief or damages. ("You're suing me? Well then, I'm suing you.") The defendant may file it separately or as part of the answer. If the defendant files a counterclaim, the plaintiff in turn may file a motion to answer the counterclaim. |

tion over him or her, that issue should be raised in a special appearance and determined by the court before any answer is filed.

### Q. How does a court determine whether it has jurisdiction to hear the case?

**A.** In federal court, the plaintiff bears the burden of proving, through citation of relevant statutes and case law, that the court has jurisdiction to hear his or her case under Article III of the U.S. Constitution. In most state courts, by contrast, it is up to the defendant to prove that the court does *not* have jurisdiction under applicable state jurisdictional laws.

### Q. What is a motion for change of venue?

**A.** In addition to ascertaining whether it has jurisdiction to hear the case, a trial court also may be asked to determine whether the case should be heard where it was filed or in a court in some other city, county or state. If the court determines that it would be more appropriate and convenient for the parties if the trial were held somewhere else, the court will permit a "change of venue" to that location. Congress (or, in the case of state courts, the state legislature) determines the rules regarding venue, all of which are designed to ensure that neither party is forced to travel to an unnecessarily inconvenient location to try or defend a lawsuit. In high-profile criminal cases, it is not uncommon for a defendant to seek a change of venue in an effort to find a jury that has not already formed an opinion on the case as the result of heavy local media coverage.

### Q. What if the defendant concludes that it is actually the plaintiff who is liable?

**A.** At this point, the defendant in a civil case, in addition to answering the plaintiff's claim, may file suit against the plaintiff. This action is known as a "counterclaim." If a counterclaim is filed, the plaintiff becomes a defendant and will be called on to file an answer to the allegations and counts contained in the counterclaim.

### Q. What if there are other claims or parties that should be involved in the litigation?

**A.** If the defendant believes that others not named as defendants in the plaintiff's suit are responsible, in whole or in part, for the plaintiff's injury or loss, he or she may seek to "implead" those persons, i.e., bring them into the case as additional defendants. If a person who was not named in the original suit believes he or she should be involved in order to defend his or her interests, that person may seek to "intervene," i.e., join, the suit as either plaintiff or defendant. Finally, in multiparty suits, "cross claims" may be filed. For example, one defendant could file a claim against another defendant. All of these pretrial procedures are designed to encourage plaintiffs and defendants to resolve as many of their disputes as possible in a single suit rather than in piecemeal litigation.

## DISCOVERY

### Q. Can a party force his or her opponent to disclose information and witnesses even before the trial begins?

**A.** Yes. This process, called "discovery," is a vital step in any litigation and a reminder that the goal of our legal system is to do justice rather than to reward the clever attorney or secretive litigant. "Surprise witnesses" and "secret evidence" are the province of TV and Hollywood, not the real courtroom. Among the discovery tools available to litigants are:

- *Depositions*. The attorneys for each side in a lawsuit may compel potential witnesses to answer written or oral questions under oath.

- *Interrogatories*. Each party can submit a list of written questions to the other party which again must be answered under oath.

- *Motion to produce documents*. Each party can compel the other to produce relevant documents in the other party's possession, custody, or control for the purpose of inspecting, copying or photographing them.

- *Request to admit*. Each party can ask the other to acknowledge that an allegation is true and thus spare both parties the trouble, expense and delay of having to prove it at trial.

### Q. What is summary judgment?

**A.** Even after discovery has begun, a full-blown trial still may be forestalled by a successful motion for "summary judgment." Summary judgment may be appropriate if the facts in the case are clear and the only question is how the law should be applied to those facts. In such cases, there is no need for a jury or judge to hear witnesses or view evidence regarding what happened. All that is left for the court to do is to apply the law to the known facts, and this it can do without a trial.

In considering whether to grant a party's motion for summary judgment, the trial court will review the parties' affidavits (written statements made under oath) and discovery materials to determine whether, viewed in the light most favorable to the opponent to the motion, there is no genuine dispute regarding an important fact.

If the court is uncertain whether the case contains a genuine issue of material fact, it will deny the summary judgment motion and the case will proceed to trial. If, on the other hand, the court is convinced that there is no such factual dispute, it will consider the parties' written arguments on the legal issues and then grant the motion for summary judgment, disposing of the case.

### Q. What if my opponent and I agree on some but not all of the facts in my case?

**A.** Parties can "stipulate" to the existence of certain facts and thereby forgo the need to introduce evidence at trial to prove those facts.

---

## JURIES

### Q. But doesn't the United States Constitution guarantee me a right to a jury trial in every case?

**A.** No. In criminal cases, the right only extends to defendants facing a possibility of being sentenced to a prison term of six months or more. In civil cases, the Seventh Amendment guarantees the right to a jury trial in "suits at common law." As a general rule, suits at common law encompass only those civil suits seeking money as compensation for an asserted injury or loss, for example breach of contract or personal injury actions. Thus, the Seventh Amendment's right to a jury trial does not apply if the plaintiff is seeking an "equitable" remedy for his or her injury or loss, for example an order to the defendant to cease certain conduct.

### Q. What is the difference between a legal and equitable claim?

**A.** Whether a claim is legal or equitable can generally be determined by the remedy the plaintiff is seeking. As noted above, a request for money damages is, historically, a "legal" claim, while a request that the court order a party to take or cease some action is an "equitable" claim. The question can be more complicated in cases where there are a number of different claims, some legal, some equitable, and some with both legal and equitable characteristics.

### Q. Will I automatically get a jury trial if I'm constitutionally entitled to one?

**A.** No. Trials in federal court will not be held before a jury unless a party makes a written demand for a jury trial. For tactical reasons, some parties may prefer to have their case decided by a judge alone. On the other hand, Congress can (and has) provided for the jury trial option in some instances where the Constitution does not require one.

### Q. How does a bench trial differ from a jury trial?

**A.** In a bench trial, the judge must determine the facts (what really happened, as distinguished from what the plaintiff alleged happened) and then apply the law to the facts. In a jury trial, the fact-finding function belongs to the jury. For example, in a negligence action for damages tried before a jury, the judge would decide whether state law imposes a legal duty on a host to warn guests of hidden dangers on his or her property. It would be for the jury to decide whether a loose step on the host's back porch was such a danger, whether the guest had in fact been warned not to go onto the back porch, whether that warning was sufficient under the law, whether the guest's alleged injuries were real, and whether they were actually caused by a fall off the step.

### Q. How are potential jurors identified?

**A.** The clerk of the court maintains a list of potential jurors using, for example, lists of registered voters or licensed drivers, or a combination of the two. When a case is set for trial by jury, the clerk uses this list to provide the court with a *"venire"* of potential jurors representing a fair cross-section of the community. The jurors who will actually hear the case are then chosen by the attorneys for each side in a process known as *"voir dire."*

### Q. *How do the attorneys select the jury for my case?*

**A.** Each attorney and/or the judge asks the potential juror questions designed to discover any potential bias or prejudice for or against the parties or issues in the case. If the juror concedes such a bias or if evidence suggests he or she may have one, the attorney may ask the court to strike the juror "for cause" and remove him or her from the pool of potential jurors in that case. If the judge refuses to remove the potential juror "for cause," the attorney will consider whether to use one of his or her "peremptory strikes" to remove the juror. In federal civil trials, each party can make up to

three peremptory strikes to remove a juror without providing a reason.

### Q. *May an attorney use peremptory strikes to remove jurors on the basis of their race?*

**A.** No. In the landmark case of *Batson v. Kentucky*, the Court in 1986 prohibited prosecutors from exercising peremptory strikes for racially discriminatory reasons in criminal trials. This principle has since been extended in other cases so that it is now generally agreed that neither side in either criminal or civil trials may exercise any peremptory strikes for racially discriminatory reasons. (In 1994, the U.S. Supreme Court ruled that this principle should be applied to bar gender-based peremptory strikes as well.)

### Q. *Must every jury have twelve jurors?*

**A.** No. Although most jurisdictions require either twelve or six, it is not clear what the constitutional limits might be on a jury's size.

## Roles of the Main Participants in Deciding Cases

| At Trial Level | | At Appellate Level | |
| --- | --- | --- | --- |
| Judge | Jury | Judge | Jury |
| *Before trial begins*<br>• Issues search and arrest warrants<br>• Sets and revokes bail<br>• Manages speed at which cases move through system | | • Main function is to consider how the trial court applied the laws that governed the verdict, which involves interpreting the law<br>• Also reviews procedures followed by trial court, primarily to insure that legal rights of the parties were protected | No jury involvement at appellate level |
| *During trial*<br>• Declares the law—judges' primary responsibility<br>• Determines which evidence the jury may consider<br>• Supervises procedures in court (such as ruling on motions by opposing counsel) | Within guidelines set by the judge, the jury:<br>• Decides questions of fact<br>• Evaluates credibility of witnesses<br>• Renders final verdict | • The facts are usually not reviewed by the appellate court | |

## Q. What if I am called for jury duty?

**A.** Inform your employer and appear at the time and place indicated on your jury-duty summons. Although you may be excused from jury service on the basis of hardship, the law requires your employer to permit you to take time off from work to perform your jury duty.

An obligation of citizenship, jury service is becoming less burdensome than ever before. Although jurors are paid a small stipend for each day's service, many employers will pay regular salaries to their employees for at least a portion of their jury duty. To further ease the burden on jurors, some jurisdictions have adopted a one-day, one-trial rule whereby jurors are only "on call" for one day. If they are picked for a jury on that day they will serve on that jury, but if they are not picked on that day they will not be called again for at least a year or two.

## Q. What if I am selected as an alternate juror?

**A.** Alternate jurors are selected to guard against the possibility that one of the jurors will take ill or otherwise be unable to serve. As an alternate, you would attend the trial along with the regular jurors, but would not be called to participate in reaching a verdict unless one of the regular jurors was unable to continue.

## TRIALS

## Q. My case will be tried before a jury. What does this entail?

**A.** Jury trials begin with "opening statements" presented to the jury by the lawyer for each party. The opening statement serves to introduce the jurors to each side's theory of the case and outlines what each side plans to establish during the trial. For example, in a personal injury case, the plaintiff will argue that the defendant owed the plaintiff a legal duty of some sort, that he or she breached that duty, and that, as a result, the plaintiff suffered a financial loss or other injury. The defense, meanwhile, will explain why there is reason to doubt one or more of those elements of the plaintiff's case.

## Q. How will the sides present their cases?

**A.** Through the testimony of witnesses and the introduction of relevant documentary or physical evidence. The plaintiff will present the testimony of his or her witnesses first. After each witness for the plaintiff is questioned on "direct examination" by the plaintiff's lawyer, the defendant's lawyer usually "cross examines" the witness. Cross examination may be followed by "redirect" examination by the plaintiff's counsel and "re-cross" examination by the defendant's counsel. When all of the plaintiff's witnesses have testified, the plaintiff rests. If the defendant has raised any affirmative defenses, he or she will call witnesses for direct examination in an attempt to establish these defenses. Again, each witness is usually subject to cross-examination and may be subject to redirect and re-cross examination.

Unless the jury is instructed otherwise, all of the witnesses' testimony will be evidence in the case, as will any documents or other physical evidence that the attorneys were successful in admitting.

## Q. How does a direct examination differ from a cross-examination?

**A.** Direct examination is conducted by the party calling the witness while cross-examination is conducted by the opposing party. Direct examination is intended to establish the plaintiff's case or the defendant's defense; cross-examination is intended to undermine or discredit the testimony given under direct examination.

## Q. What does it mean for a judge to "sustain" an objection?

**A.** One of your attorney's duties is to raise an appropriate "objection" to any violation of the rules governing the kinds of evidence the jury can and cannot weigh in deciding a case. When a court "sustains" your attorney's objection, it is telling your opponent's attorney that he or she is proceeding in violation of applicable procedural law and must correct his or her error. In addition, if an objection is sustained, the answer given is not in evidence and the jury will be instructed by the judge to disregard the answer.

Objections to questions may be "overruled," in which case the answer is in evidence and may be considered by the jury. However, even if the court overrules your attorney's objection, the objection will now be "preserved" in the written record of your trial and, thus, can be reviewed by an appellate court if you should lose at trial. In many instances, a failure to object at trial can be deemed to "waive" your right to complain about the matter later.

## Q. What are the rules of evidence?

**A.** Taken together, these voluminous and complex rules require fact-finding judges or juries to base their decisions solely on relevant evidence that has some minimum likelihood of being reliable. As explained in the criminal justice chapter's discussion of the exclusionary rule on page 547, some evidentiary rules are fashioned to further other important policies, such as protecting civil liberties.

## Q. What is the rule against hearsay?

**A.** Although it is one of the most familiar evidentiary rules, the rule that hearsay is generally inadmissible at trial is also one of the most complex because it is has so many nuances and exceptions. The Federal Rules of Evidence define hearsay as "a statement, other than one made by the declarant while testifying at the trial or hearing, offered in evidence to prove the truth of the matter asserted." Two major problems often arise when an attorney raises this rule at trial and asks that the jury not be allowed to hear or consider some statement that the other side wants to introduce.

First, the judge must determine why the party is seeking to introduce the out-of-court statement. For example, assume that the plaintiff's attorney objects when a defense witness named John testifies that he heard a friend named Bill yell, "Look out! Mark has a gun!" Is John seeking to relate Bill's statement in order to help persuade the jury that Mark did have a gun? If so, the statement may well be inadmissible hearsay. If the defense wants the jury to consider Bill's statement, it will have to put Bill on the stand so that he can be cross-examined about it.

On the other hand, the defense could argue that John is not introducing Bill's statement in order to prove that Mark really did have a gun, but only to show why the defendant reasonably *thought* that Mark was armed. In that case, the statement might not be hearsay because it is not being offered to prove the truth of the matter in the statement, but only to show that the statement was made or to indicate the defendant's state of mind.

## Q. Even if the statement is hearsay, could it be admitted anyway?

**A.** Actually, it could. For example, one of the many exceptions to the rule against hearsay provides that "excited utterances" may be admissible despite their hearsay nature. The rationale is that a statement is more likely to be truthful if it was made before the speaker would have had any time to think up a falsehood in the immediate aftermath of some exciting event.

## VERDICTS

### Q. Is there anything to prevent the case from reaching the jury after each side has finished presenting its case?

**A.** Yes. Before turning the case over to the jury, the judge will consider either side's motion to "direct a verdict" in its favor. A directed verdict removes the need for the jury to determine whether the defendant is liable, but such a ruling is only appropriate when the court is persuaded that no reasonable juror could reach any verdict other than the one it is being directed to reach. The court may grant, deny, or, more likely, "reserve" (postpone) ruling on such a motion until after the jury has rendered a verdict. If the jury rules against the party who requested the directed verdict, the judge can still overrule the jury's decision by granting a motion for "judgment notwithstanding the verdict." That way, if the losing party appeals, there seldom would be any need to order a new trial because the appellate court would have the option of upholding the judge's ruling or reinstating the jury's original verdict.

### Q. What happens if the court declines to direct a verdict?

**A.** Each side will be given the opportunity to address the jury directly and to summarize what he or she believes was established during the trial. At the conclusion of these talks, called "closing statements," the judge will consider each side's suggestions on how to instruct the jury regarding the proper way it should go about reaching a verdict. The judge's instructions will specify the issues the jury must decide and the law it must apply to the facts that were developed in the case. In the usual case the jury will be asked to render a "general" verdict and conclude which side won on an all-or-nothing basis. Less commonly, the judge may ask for a "special" verdict, which requires the jury to enter separate written findings on each of several issues.

### Q. What else must the verdict contain?

**A.** If the jury concludes that one of the parties is liable to the other, it must go on to decide what remedy is owed the party who was wronged. In the ordinary personal injury suit, this remedy will take the form of money "damages" which the jury will direct the defendant to pay the prevailing plaintiff. The judge may decide to separate this portion of the trial from the liability portion. In appropriate cases, such a "bifurcated" trial can simplify the issues by saving the jury from having to listen to instructions and arguments about the proper damages until after it has determined whether the plaintiff is entitled to any damages at all.

The various formulae juries may use in calculating damages seek to give effect to the overriding goal of putting prevailing plaintiffs back in the financial position they would have been in if they hadn't been wronged in the first place. It is, of course, more difficult to calculate the proper award when the defendant's wrongful act caused more than out-of-pocket expenses: How much money does it take to compensate one for pain, suffering, or loss of life's enjoyment?

In unusual circumstances, where the defendant's behavior is thought to be especially outrageous, the plaintiff may also ask the jury to direct the defendant to pay "punitive damages" in addition to compensatory damages. Punitive damages are designed to punish the defendant and to deter others from engaging in like conduct.

## POST-TRIAL PROCEDURES

### Q. Is there anything left for a victorious plaintiff to do?

**A.** Winning a civil verdict is only the first crucial step in a plaintiff's efforts to secure compensation for his or her injury or loss. After the judge enters judgment in favor of the plaintiff, he or she still must acquire a judicial order commanding the defendant to pay the compensation awarded.

If a defendant against whom you have won a judgment does not pay it, collection proceedings can be initiated. If the defendant owns property, for example, you may be able to foreclose on it. Another option would be to garnish the defendant's wages. Your lawyer—or any lawyer you contact—would be able to help you in this regard.

### Q. What options does the losing party have?

**A.** In addition to seeking a judgment notwithstanding the verdict as discussed above, the losing party may also ask the court to throw out the verdict and order a new trial on grounds that the verdict was against the weight of the evidence; that serious errors or other misconduct were committed by the judge; that there was serious misconduct on the part of a juror, lawyer, witness or party; that the damages were too large; or that vitally important evidence that could not have been discovered before the end of the trial has only now been discovered. If these "new trial" motions do not succeed, the party may choose to appeal the verdict to an appellate court.

### Q. How can a party appeal an adverse judgment?

**A.** The losing party (or a prevailing party contending that it was awarded insufficient damages) may seek review of the trial court's judgment in a higher court. In the federal system, the party will appeal to the court of appeals in the appropriate circuit.

In those states that have an intermediate appellate court, parties challenging trial court decisions generally must bring their appeal to the intermediate court first. For virtually all

criminal appeals, the intermediate appellate court must accept the case because the court's jurisdiction is mandatory. However, because intermediate appellate courts often have some limited discretion to determine which civil cases they will hear, not all civil appeals will necessarily be accepted, in which case the lower court's verdict will stand.

The most common exception to this pattern of review occurs in death penalty cases. In all instances, death-penalty appeals bypass the state's intermediate appellate court and go directly to the state's court of last resort. In the twelve states without intermediate appellate courts, civil and criminal litigants bring their appeals directly to the court of last resort.

### Q. How do appellate courts work?

**A.** An appellate court typically concerns itself solely with issues of law. An appeal is not the time to retry the case or to reargue the facts. Instead, in an appeal, the "appellant" must persuade the court to "reverse" the trial court's judgment because of some significant legal errors that occurred during the trial which could have skewed the result, such as evidence improperly admitted or excluded, or the judge instructing the jury to apply an incorrect interpretation of the law. The "appellee," on the other hand, will seek to persuade the court that no such errors were made in the lower court or that, if there was an error, it was "harmless" because it did not affect the outcome. A transcript of the district court proceedings, together with all of the original papers and exhibits, will be forwarded to the court for consideration in deciding the appeal.

### Q. What is oral argument?

**A.** Prior to oral argument, the judges who will hear the case read the briefs. The judges also examine the record compiled in the trial court. At oral argument the judges will listen to the

# TEXAS COURT STRUCTURE, 1992

**SUPREME COURT**

9 justices sit en banc

CSP case types:
- Mandatory jurisdiction in civil cases.
- Discretionary jurisdiction in civil, administrative agency, juvenile, certified questions from federal courts, original proceeding cases.

**COURT OF CRIMINAL APPEALS**

9 judges sit en banc

CSP case types:
- Mandatory jurisdiction in criminal, original proceeding cases.
- Discretionary jurisdiction in noncapital criminal, original proceeding cases and certified questions from federal court.

Courts of last resort

**COURTS OF APPEALS** (14 courts)

80 justices sit in panels

CSP case types:
- Mandatory jurisdiction in civil, noncapital criminal, administrative agency, juvenile, original proceeding, interlocutory decision cases.
- No discretionary jurisdiction.

Intermediate appellate court

**DISTRICT COURTS** (386 courts) 386 judges

**DISTRICT COURT** (376 courts)  A

376 judges

CSP case types:
- Tort, contract, real property rights ($200/no maximum), domestic relations, estate, miscellaneous civil. Exclusive administrative agency appeals jurisdiction.
- Felony, misdemeanor, DWI/DUI, miscellaneous criminal.
- Juvenile.

Jury trials.

**CRIMINAL DISTRICT COURT** (10 courts)

10 judges

CSP case types:
- Felony, misdemeanor, DWI/DUI, miscellaneous criminal cases.

Jury trials.

Court of general jurisdiction

**COUNTY-LEVEL COURTS** (434 courts) 434 judges

**CONSTITUTIONAL COUNTY COURT** (254 courts)

254 judges

CSP case types:
- Tort, contract, real property rights ($200/5,000), domestic relations, estate, mental health, civil trial court appeals, miscellaneous civil.
- Misdemeanor, DWI/DUI, criminal appeals.
- Moving traffic, miscellaneous traffic.
- Juvenile.

Jury trials.

**PROBATE COURT** (18 courts)

18 judges

CSP case types:
- Estate.
- Mental health.

Jury trials.

**COUNTY COURT AT LAW** (162 courts)

162 judges

CSP case types:
- Tort, contract, real property rights ($200/varies), estate, mental health, civil trial court appeals, miscellaneous civil.
- Misdemeanor, DWI/DUI, criminal appeals.
- Moving traffic, miscellaneous traffic.
- Juvenile.

Jury trials.

**MUNICIPAL COURT*** (853 courts)

1,214 judges

CSP case types:
- Misdemeanor.
- Moving traffic, parking, miscellaneous traffic. Exclusive ordinance violation jurisdiction.
- Preliminary hearings.

Jury trials.

**JUSTICE OF THE PEACE COURT*** (884 courts)

884 judges

CSP case types:
- Tort, contract, real property rights ($0/5,000), small claims ($0/5,000), mental health.
- Misdemeanor.
- Moving traffic, parking, miscellaneous traffic.
- Preliminary hearings.

Jury trials.

Courts of limited jurisdiction

\* Some municipal and justice of the peace courts may appeal to the district court.

SOURCE: *State Court Caseload Statistics: Annual Report, 1992* (National Center for State Courts, 1994)

# NEW YORK COURT STRUCTURE, 1992*

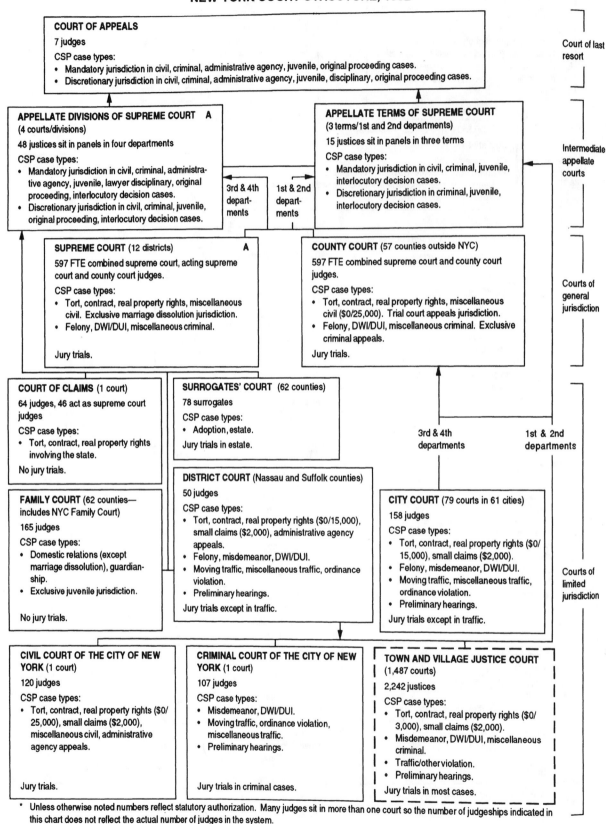

**COURT OF APPEALS**

7 judges

CSP case types:
- Mandatory jurisdiction in civil, criminal, administrative agency, juvenile, original proceeding cases.
- Discretionary jurisdiction in civil, criminal, administrative agency, juvenile, disciplinary, original proceeding cases.

*Court of last resort*

**APPELLATE DIVISIONS OF SUPREME COURT  A**

(4 courts/divisions)

48 justices sit in panels in four departments

CSP case types:
- Mandatory jurisdiction in civil, criminal, administrative agency, juvenile, lawyer disciplinary, original proceeding, interlocutory decision cases.
- Discretionary jurisdiction in civil, criminal, juvenile, original proceeding, interlocutory decision cases.

3rd & 4th departments      1st & 2nd departments

**APPELLATE TERMS OF SUPREME COURT**

(3 terms/1st and 2nd departments)

15 justices sit in panels in three terms

CSP case types:
- Mandatory jurisdiction in civil, criminal, juvenile, interlocutory decision cases.
- Discretionary jurisdiction in criminal, juvenile, interlocutory decision cases.

*Intermediate appellate courts*

**SUPREME COURT** (12 districts)      A

597 FTE combined supreme court, acting supreme court and county court judges.

CSP case types:
- Tort, contract, real property rights, miscellaneous civil. Exclusive marriage dissolution jurisdiction.
- Felony, DWI/DUI, miscellaneous criminal.

Jury trials.

**COUNTY COURT** (57 counties outside NYC)

597 FTE combined supreme court and county court judges.

CSP case types:
- Tort, contract, real property rights, miscellaneous civil ($0/25,000). Trial court appeals jurisdiction.
- Felony, DWI/DUI, miscellaneous criminal. Exclusive criminal appeals.

Jury trials.

*Courts of general jurisdiction*

**COURT OF CLAIMS** (1 court)

64 judges, 46 act as supreme court judges

CSP case types:
- Tort, contract, real property rights involving the state.

No jury trials.

**SURROGATES' COURT**  (62 counties)

78 surrogates

CSP case types:
- Adoption, estate.

Jury trials in estate.

3rd & 4th departments          1st & 2nd departments

**FAMILY COURT** (62 counties—includes NYC Family Court)

165 judges

CSP case types:
- Domestic relations (except marriage dissolution), guardianship.
- Exclusive juvenile jurisdiction.

No jury trials.

**DISTRICT COURT** (Nassau and Suffolk counties)

50 judges

CSP case types:
- Tort, contract, real property rights ($0/15,000), small claims ($2,000), administrative agency appeals.
- Felony, misdemeanor, DWI/DUI.
- Moving traffic, miscellaneous traffic, ordinance violation.
- Preliminary hearings.

Jury trials except in traffic.

**CITY COURT** (79 courts in 61 cities)

158 judges

CSP case types:
- Tort, contract, real property rights ($0/15,000), small claims ($2,000).
- Felony, misdemeanor, DWI/DUI.
- Moving traffic, miscellaneous traffic, ordinance violation.
- Preliminary hearings.

Jury trials except in traffic.

*Courts of limited jurisdiction*

**CIVIL COURT OF THE CITY OF NEW YORK** (1 court)

120 judges

CSP case types:
- Tort, contract, real property rights ($0/25,000), small claims ($2,000), miscellaneous civil, administrative agency appeals.

Jury trials.

**CRIMINAL COURT OF THE CITY OF NEW YORK** (1 court)

107 judges

CSP case types:
- Misdemeanor, DWI/DUI.
- Moving traffic, ordinance violation, miscellaneous traffic.
- Preliminary hearings.

Jury trials in criminal cases.

**TOWN AND VILLAGE JUSTICE COURT** (1,487 courts)

2,242 justices

CSP case types:
- Tort, contract, real property rights ($0/3,000), small claims ($2,000).
- Misdemeanor, DWI/DUI, miscellaneous criminal.
- Traffic/other violation.
- Preliminary hearings.

Jury trials in most cases.

\* Unless otherwise noted numbers reflect statutory authorization. Many judges sit in more than one court so the number of judgeships indicated in this chart does not reflect the actual number of judges in the system.

SOURCE: *State Court Caseload Statistics: Annual Report, 1992* (National Center for State Courts, 1994)

arguments of the attorneys for the parties and may question the attorneys about the case and how the law should be applied to the case. Typically each side is allotted one half hour in which to orally present its case. However, an appellate court is free to grant more or less time, based on the significance or complexity of the case. After oral argument, each judge votes on whether to affirm or reverse the trial court's judgment, in whole or in part. The court then issues a written opinion explaining its decision. As a general rule, the parties will not know the outcome of the case until the written opinion is released.

An appellate court is not required to hear oral argument in any case. Thus, the court may issue a decision or summary order based solely on its review of the record and the written briefs that present the arguments of the parties in detail. As a general rule, however, appeals cases are scheduled for oral argument. If the case is before an intermediate appellate court, the argument will be heard by a panel of three judges. However, in certain important cases before an intermediate court, the oral argument will be heard *"en banc,"* that is heard by all of the judges of the court. (Oral arguments before the United States Supreme Court and state supreme courts are *en banc.*)

### Q. Must an appellate court reach a unanimous decision?

**A.** No. The judge or judges who disagree with the majority's result may write a dissent to explain the disagreement. If a judge agrees with the result reached by the majority but disagrees with its explanation of why the law compelled that result, he or she may write a separate opinion "concurring" in the judgment.

### Q. What recourse is there for the party who loses at the intermediate appellate level?

**A.** He or she now can seek review in the highest court in the system. In the federal sys-

tem, of course, that court is the Supreme Court of the United States. In addition to the decisions of the United States Courts of Appeal, the United States Supreme Court has the jurisdiction, but not the obligation, to review the final decisions of state supreme courts (or even of lower state courts if the party was unable to secure additional review within the state courts) so long as the case is the sort of case described in Article III of the U.S. Constitution and was not decided on "adequate and independent state grounds." When the U.S. Supreme Court declines to hear a case, which it does in the vast majority of cases that are presented to it, the decision of the lower federal or state court remains the last word on the matter.

### Q. How does the U.S. Supreme Court decide whether to hear a case?

**A.** In the usual course, a party seeking review in the U.S. Supreme Court will file a petition asking the Court to issue a "writ of *certiorari.*" This petition will include a copy of the lower court's opinion in the case and a brief stating why the Court should agree to review it. The "respondent," who typically does not wish the Court to hear the case because he or she is satisfied with the opinion by the court of appeals, may file a brief in opposition to the petition. The Court will then either deny the petition (its action in most cases) or grant it, and command the federal or state court to transmit the record of the case to the U.S. Supreme Court for its review. In his book *The Supreme Court: How It Was, How It Is* (New York: Morrow, 1987), Chief Justice Rehnquist describes the process of selecting which petitions to grant as being influenced by the justices' views on three major factors: whether the lower court's opinion is in conflict with the opinions of other courts; the general importance of the case; and whether the lower court's decision may be wrong in light of the U.S. Supreme Court's previous opinions.

## Q. *What is the effect of granting* certiorari?

**A.** If a writ of *certiorari* is granted, the case will be set for briefing and oral argument in much the same way it was in the intermediate court of appeals. If the Court reaches the "merits" of the case (that is, the ultimate issues), its decision will be binding, final and the law of the land. Frequently, however, the Court will "remand" the case back to the lower court with instructions that the court reconsider its earlier opinion in light of the Supreme Court's clarification of how the relevant constitutional or statutory provisions should be applied and interpreted.

## Q. *What is the effect of denying* certiorari?

**A.** In a civil case, the opinion of the trial court or, if there was an intermediate appeal, the opinion of the appellate court stands as the final judgment and the case will be over. If *certiorari* was sought from a decision in a criminal case, however, the unsuccessful petitioner may have one more avenue to pursue.

Federal courts have the power to issue writs of *habeas corpus* to permit prisoners to challenge their convictions as having been wrongfully obtained in violation of the U.S. Constitution. Thus, if a state criminal defendant has "exhausted" his state remedies by seeking review in both the state intermediate court of appeals and state supreme court (and perhaps even through the state version of *habeas corpus*), the U.S. Supreme Court's denial of *certiorari* does not foreclose the prisoner from obtaining another round of review in the federal court system through the writ of *habeas corpus*. This is so because the U.S. Supreme Court's denial of *certiorari* is in no way a ruling on the merits of the case, but merely a "decision not to decide" the case.

## WHERE TO GET MORE INFORMATION

### The Federal Court System

For details about the U.S. Supreme Court, write to the Public Information Officer, the Supreme Court of the United States, Washington, DC 20543, telephone (202) 479-3211. For facts about other federal courts, contact the Public Information Officer, Administrative Office of United States Courts, One Columbus Circle, NE, Suite 7110, Washington, DC 20002-8003, telephone (202) 273-1120. The Information Service of the Federal Judicial Center is also a very useful source of data about federal courts. Write to the Center at the Thurgood Marshall Federal Judiciary Building, One Columbus Circle, NE, Washington, DC 20002-8003, telephone (202) 273-4153.

The Administrative Office of the U.S. Courts offers several useful, brief handbooks on the federal court system. Write to the address listed above. One example is *The United States Courts: Their Jurisdiction and Work*. In only 27 pages, it quickly compares state and federal jurisdictions. It also examines the work of the various courts. Another useful handbook is *Glossary of Terms Used in the Federal Courts*. It provides a very readable introduction to some of the most common terms and procedures.

*Preview of United States Supreme Court Cases* is a unique resource. It supplies journalists, lawyers, and other interested parties with up-to-date information on cases the Supreme Court is considering but has not yet decided. This resource analyzes each case's issues, facts, background, and significance. It helps readers understand decisions when the Court makes them. Yearly subscriptions are available from the American Bar Association's Public Education Division, 541 N. Fairbanks Ct., Chicago, IL 60611-3314.

Another interesting publication is *Equal Justice Under Law: The Supreme Court in American Life* (Washington: Supreme Court Historical Society, 1982), by Mary Ann Harrell and Burnett Anderson. This lively history of the Court is available from The Supreme Court Historical Society, 111 Second Street, NE, Washington, DC 20002.

*The Supreme Court and Its Justices* (Chicago: American Bar Association, 1987) includes various articles from the *ABA Journal*. It discusses the Court's internal operation, the appointment of justices, and lawyering before the Court. You can obtain it from Order Fulfillment, product code number 299-0013, American Bar Association, 750 N. Lake Shore Drive, Chicago, IL 60611.

## State and Local Courts

The public information office of the National Center for State Courts provides data on state courts. You can contact it by writing to 300 Newport Avenue, Williamsburg, VA 23187-8798, telephone (804) 253-2000. Courts in your locality are a natural, useful source of information. Many courts have handbooks that explain their procedures to the general public. They also often publish materials for jurors, witnesses, and other interested persons. To find out more about your local courts, contact your state court administrator or the state supreme court. Both have offices in the state capital.

Your local or state bar association also can be a good source of information. Bar associations often provide guides to the courts and handbooks for jurors and witnesses. In addition, they offer materials that explain the court system to the general public.

Many bar associations also sponsor bar-bench-media conferences. These meetings improve communication between the press and the courts. Some local and state bar associations offer informative materials that are specially designed for reporters covering the courts in their area.

*Explaining the Courts: Materials and Sources* (Chicago: American Bar Association, 1983) lists a wide range of publications. It includes various materials explaining state and local courts. You can obtain it from Order Fulfillment, product code number 410-0001, American Bar Association, 750 N. Lake Shore Drive, Chicago, IL 60611.

Finally, many public libraries have books of state laws and other useful references.

## The ABA Standards

The American Bar Association (ABA) has set up standards and guidelines in many areas of court procedure. They guide the work of state and federal courts. However, not every area has adopted them.

Many different ABA standards deal directly with the courts. See *Standards for Traffic Justice, Standards of Judicial Administration*, and *Standards Relating to Court Delay Reduction*. Also see *Standards Relating to Court Organization, Standards Relating to Juror Use and Management*, and *Standards Relating to Trial Courts*. All are available from Order Fulfillment, American Bar Association, 750 N. Lake Shore Drive, Chicago, IL 60611.

### Other Aspects of Law and the Courts

Booklets from many state and local courts explain the role of jurors. For general questions about juries contact the Center for Jury Studies, 1110 Glebe Road, Suite 1090, Arlington, VA 22201, telephone (703) 841-0200.

The National Criminal Justice Reference Service offers information on various matters about criminal procedures. For details, call (800) 851-3420; Maryland residents call (301) 251-5500.

Several publications explore alternative dispute resolution. *Alternative Dispute Resolution: An ADR Primer* (Washington: American Bar Association, 1987) is a useful look at several options. It is available from the ABA's Standing Committee on Dispute Resolution, American Bar Association, 1800 M Street, NW, Washington, DC 20036. Another related publication is *Dispute Resolution in America: Processes in Evolution* (1984), by S.B. Goldberg, E.D. Green, and F.E.A. Sander. You can obtain it from the National Institute for Dispute Resolution, 1726 M Street, NW, Suite 500, Washington, DC 20036.

# CHAPTER THREE

# Family Law

# INTRODUCTION

THE GOVERNMENT HAS ALWAYS HAD AN INTEREST IN MARRIAGE AND FAMILIES. State legislatures have passed many laws regulating the requirements for getting married and for obtaining a divorce. In addition, today's laws also affect couples who live together outside of marriage.

It is hard to give simple answers to many of the legal questions that a person may have about marriage, parenthood, separation, or divorce, because the laws change often and vary from one state to another. In addition, judges in different states with identical laws may decide cases with similar facts in different ways.

This chapter describes the laws and court rulings common to most states. If you have other questions, contact a lawyer in your state. You may wish to contact a specialist. Many lawyers (particularly in urban areas) work only on family law or make it a large part of their general practice. Lawyers specializing in family law also may refer to themselves as specialists in "domestic relations" or "matrimonial law."

## MARRIAGE

### Requirements of Getting Married

#### Q. Legally, what is marriage?

**A.** Most states define marriage as a civil contract between a man and woman to become husband and wife.

The moment a man and woman marry, their relationship acquires a legal status. Married couples have financial and personal duties during marriage and after separation or divorce. State laws determine the extent of these duties. As the United States Supreme Court said about marriage in 1888: "The relation once formed, the law steps in and holds the parties to various obligations and liabilities."

Of course, marriage is a private bond between two people, but it is also an important social institution.

Today, society also recognizes marriage as:

- a way to express commitment, strengthen intimate bonds, and provide mutual emotional support;
- a stable structure within which to raise children;
- a financial partnership in which spouses may choose from a variety of roles. Both spouses may work to support the family, the husband may support the wife, or the wife may support the husband.

As our society becomes more complex, there is no longer a short answer to the question "What is marriage?" Definitions and opinions of the proper functions of marriage continue to change. The women's rights movement and gay rights movement have changed some people's ideas of marriage. Marriage will remain, but it will also continue to evolve.

#### Q. What are the legal requirements for getting married?

**A.** The requirements are simple, although they vary from state to state. In general, a man and woman wishing to marry must obtain a license in the state in which they wish to be married, usually from a county clerk or a clerk of court. The fee usually is low.

Many states require the man and woman to have blood tests for venereal disease—but not for AIDS—before the license is issued. Some states do not require this test if the two have already been living as husband and wife. If the test shows that a would-be spouse has a venereal disease, certain states may not issue a license. Other states will allow the marriage if the couple knows the disease is present.

In some states a couple must show proof of immunity or vaccination for certain diseases. A few states demand a general physical examination.

If one or both of the parties have been married before, the earlier marriage must have been ended by death, divorce, or annulment.

Parties who wish to marry must have the "capacity" to do so. That means the man and woman must understand that they are being married and what it means to be married. If because of drunkenness, mental illness, or some other problem, one of the parties lacks "capacity," the marriage will not be valid.

Close blood relatives cannot marry, although in some states, first cousins can marry. Of those states that allow first cousins to marry, a few states also require that one of the cousins no longer be able to conceive children.

Most, but not all, states require a waiting period, generally one to five days, between the time the license is issued and the time of the marriage ceremony.

## Q. At what age may people marry?

**A.** In most states, a man or woman may marry at age eighteen without parental consent. Most states also allow persons age sixteen and seventeen to marry with consent of their parents or a judge.

## Q. When does a couple truly become married?

**A.** Most states consider a couple to be married when the ceremony ends. In a few states, lack of sexual relations may allow a spouse to

have the marriage annulled (see below). In most states, however, nonconsummation does not affect the validity of the marriage. In all states the proper official must record the marriage license. Recording the marriage license acts as proof that the marriage happened.

## Q. Is a particular type of marriage ceremony required?

**A.** A marriage ceremony may be religious or civil. The person or persons conducting the ceremony should indicate that the man and woman agree to be married. A religious ceremony should be conducted under the customs of the religion, or, in the case of a Native American group, of the tribe. Most states require one or two witnesses to sign the marriage certificate.

## Q. Who may conduct a marriage ceremony?

**A.** Civil ceremonies usually are conducted by judges. In some states, county clerks or other government officials may conduct civil ceremonies. Religious ceremonies normally are conducted by religious officials, such as ministers, priests, or rabbis. Native American ceremonies may be presided over by a tribal chief or other designated official. Contrary to some popular legends, no state authorizes ship captains to perform marriages.

## Q. Are common-law marriages allowed?

**A.** In most states, no. In times past, particularly the frontier days, it was common for states to consider a woman and man to be married if they lived together for a certain length of time, had sexual intercourse, and held themselves out as husband and wife, even though they never went through a marriage ceremony. Today, only about one-fourth of the states recognize common-law marriages. In order for there to be a legal common-law marriage, the couple must clearly represent themselves to

# Age Requirements for Marriage

| State | Age with parental consent | | Age without parental consent | | State | Age with parental consent | | Age without parental consent | |
|---|---|---|---|---|---|---|---|---|---|
| | Male | Female | Male | Female | | Male | Female | Male | Female |
| Alabama* | 14(a) | 14(a) | 18 | 18 | Montana*(k) | 16 | 16 | 18 | 18 |
| Alaska | 16(l) | 16(l) | 18 | 18 | Nebraska(k) | 17 | 17 | 18 | 18 |
| Arizona | 16(l) | 16(l) | 18 | 18 | Nevada | 16(l) | 16(l) | 18 | 18 |
| Arkansas | 17(c) | 16(c) | 18 | 18 | New Hampshire | 14(g) | 13(g) | 18 | 18 |
| California | (b) | (b) | 18 | 18 | New Jersey | 16(c)(l) | 16(c)(l) | 18 | 18 |
| Colorado* | 16(l) | 16(l) | 18 | 18 | New Mexico(j) | 16(d) | 16(d) | 18 | 18 |
| Connecticut | 16(l) | 16(l) | 18 | 18 | New York | 14(g) | 14(g) | 18 | 18 |
| Delaware | 18(c) | 16(c) | 18 | 18 | North Carolina | 16(c)(f) | 16(c)(f) | 18 | 18 |
| District of Columbia* | 16(a) | 16(a) | 18 | 18 | North Dakota | 16 | 16 | 18 | 18 |
| Florida | 16(a)(c) | 16(a)(c) | 18 | 18 | Ohio* | 18(c)(l) | 16(c)(l) | 18 | 18 |
| Georgia* | (b) | (b) | 16 | 16 | Oklahoma* | 16(c) | 16(c) | 18 | 18 |
| Hawaii | 16(d) | 16(d) | 18 | 18 | Oregon | 17 | 17 | 18 | 18 |
| Idaho* | 16(l) | 16(l) | 18 | 18 | Pennsylvania* | 16(d) | 16(d) | 18 | 18 |
| Illinois | 16 | 16 | 18 | 18 | Puerto Rico | 18(c)(d) | 16(c)(d) | 21 | 21 |
| Indiana | 17(c) | 17(c) | 18 | 18 | | (l) | (l) | | |
| Iowa* | 18(l) | 18(l) | 18 | 18 | Rhode Island* | 18(d) | 16(d) | 18 | 18 |
| Kansas*(j) | 18(l) | 18(l) | 18 | 18 | South Carolina* | 16(c) | 14(c) | 18 | 18 |
| Kentucky | 18(c)(l) | 18(c)(l) | 18 | 18 | South Dakota | 16(c) | 16(c) | 18 | 18 |
| Louisiana | 18(l) | 18(l) | 18 | 18 | Tennessee | 16(d) | 16(d) | 18 | 18 |
| Maine | 16(l) | 16(l) | 18 | 18 | Texas*(j) | 14(g)(h) | 14(g)(h) | 18 | 18 |
| Maryland | 16(c)(e) | 16(c)(e) | 18 | 18 | Utah | 14 | 14 | 18(i) | 18(i) |
| Massachusetts | 18(d) | 18(d) | 18 | 18 | Vermont | 16(l) | 16(l) | 18 | 18 |
| Michigan | 16(c)(d) | 16(c) | 18 | 18 | Virginia | 16(a)(c) | 16(a)(c) | 18 | 18 |
| Minnesota | 16(l) | 16(l) | 18 | 18 | Washington | 17(d) | 17(d) | 18 | 18 |
| Mississippi | 17 | 15 | 21 | 21 | West Virginia | 18(c) | 18(c) | 18 | 18 |
| Missouri | 15(d) | 15(d) | 18 | 18 | Wisconsin | 16 | 16 | 18 | 18 |
| | 18(l) | 18(l) | | | Wyoming | 16(d) | 16(d) | 18 | 18 |

*Indicates that in 1987 common-law marriage recognized. For example, some states not marked with an asterisk once recognized common-law marriage but have changed their laws and no longer do so. In these states, common-law marriages that preceded the change in law would still be valid.

(a) Parental consent not required if minor was previously married.

(b) No age limits.

(c) Younger parties may obtain license in case of pregnancy or birth of child.

(d) Younger parties may obtain license in special circumstances.

(e) If parties are under 16 years of age, proof of age and the consent of parents in person is required. If a parent is ill, an affidavit by the incapacitated parent and a physician's affidavit to that effect required.

(f) Unless parties are 18 years of age or more, or female is pregnant, or applicants are the parents of a living child born out of wedlock.

(g) Parental consent and/or permission of judge required.

(h) Below age of consent parties need parental consent and permission of judge.

(i) Authorizes counties to provide for premarital counseling as a requisite to issuance of license to persons under 19 and persons previously divorced.

(j) Marriages by proxy are valid.

(k) Proxy marriages are valid under certain conditions.

(l) Younger parties may marry with parental consent and/or permission of judge. In Connecticut, judicial approval.

SOURCE: Gary L. Skoloff, Skoloff & Wolfe, Livingston, New Jersey.

others as being husband and wife; merely living together is not enough to create a marriage.

In states that recognize a common-law marriage, the partners have the same rights and duties as if there had been a ceremonial marriage. Most other states will accept as valid a common-law marriage that began in a state that recognizes common-law marriage.

A legal common-law marriage may end only with a formal divorce.

### Q. Does the law recognize same-sex marriages?

**A.** No. As of 1993, no state has passed a law recognizing homosexual marriages. If two members of the same sex were to go through a marriage ceremony, the courts would not consider the marriage to be valid, and, in the event the parties split up, they could not seek a legal divorce. Periodically, there are proposals before state legislatures to allow homosexual marriages, but so far none has become law. However, in May 1993 the Hawaii Supreme Court ruled that denying same-sex couples the right to marry might violate the equal protection provisions of Hawaii's state constitution.

### Q. What is a domestic partnership?

**A.** Some cities have passed laws providing for "domestic partnerships" which can be used by homosexual couples and by heterosexual couples who are living together without being married. To become domestic partners, the couple usually must register their relationship at a government office and declare that they are in a "committed" relationship. Domestic partnerships provide some—but not all—of the legal benefits of marriage. Some of the common benefits are the right to coverage on a family health insurance policy, the right to family leave to take care of a sick partner (to the same extent a person would be able to use family leave to care for a sick spouse), bereavement leave, visiting rights to hospitals and jails, and rent control benefits (to the same extent a spouse would retain reduced rent if his or her partner died).

### Q. Does a woman's last name change when she gets married?

**A.** Only if she wants to change it. In the past, some people assumed that a woman would change her last name to her husband's name when she married. Now society recognizes a woman's right to take her husband's name, keep her original name, or use both names. The general rule is that if a woman uses a certain name consistently and honestly, then that is her true name. See page 76 for a detailed discussion of how names may be changed.

## Invalid Marriages

### Q. What if someone thinks he or she has a genuine marriage but it turns out to be invalid?

**A.** Sometimes people who live as a married couple learn that their marriage is not legal. For example, one supposed spouse may have kept a prior marriage secret, or both may have thought incorrectly that an earlier marriage had ended in divorce or the death of a spouse. Or a marriage may be invalid because it is between close relatives, underage persons, or people incapable of entering into the marriage contract because of mental incompetence.

In a few states the putative (supposed) spouse doctrine offers some protection if the parties went through a ceremonial marriage. A putative spouse may be entitled to the benefits and rights of a legal spouse for as long as she or he reasonably believes the marriage to be valid. In states that do not accept the putative-spouse doctrine, people who mistakenly believe they are married usually have the same status as unmarried couples who live together.

Sometimes people discover that their marriage is invalid only when filing for divorce. After a long union that a couple believed was a valid marriage, a court may refuse to declare the marriage invalid and require a divorce to end the marriage.

### Q. What other legal rules affect invalid marriages?

**A.** Sometimes the law treats an invalid marriage as valid if one person tricked the other into thinking they are married. If so, a court might not allow the deceiver to declare the marriage invalid. In legal terms, the court "estops" the deceiver from denying that the marriage exists. A court may find that the doctrine of laches (long delay) prevents even the innocent party who originally did not know about the invalid marriage from declaring it invalid, if he or she did nothing for a long time after learning that the marriage was not valid.

### Premarital Agreements

### Q. What is a premarital agreement?

**A.** A premarital or antenuptial agreement is a contract entered into by a man and woman before they marry. The agreement usually describes what each party's rights will be if they divorce or when one of them dies. Premarital agreements most commonly deal with issues of property and support—who is entitled to what property and how much support, if any, will be paid in the event of divorce.

### Q. Why do people enter into premarital agreements?

**A.** Sometimes persons intending to marry use premarital agreements as a way of clarifying their expectations and rights for the future.

Another reason for making such agreements is to try to avoid uncertainties about how a divorce court might divide property and decide spousal support if the marriage fails. A man or woman who wants a future spouse to enter into a premarital agreement often has something he or she wants to protect, usually money. One or both partners may want to avoid the risk of a major loss of assets, income, or a family business in the event of a divorce. For people marrying for a second or third time, there might be a desire to make sure that a majority of assets or personal belongings are passed on to the children or grandchildren of prior marriages rather than a current spouse.

### Q. What does the less wealthy spouse give up by signing a premarital agreement?

**A.** The less wealthy spouse is agreeing to have his or her property rights determined by the agreement rather than by the usual rules of law that a court would apply on divorce or the death of the wealthier spouse. As will be discussed later, courts have certain rules for dividing property when a couple divorce. In some states (such as California), courts automatically divide equally the property acquired by the husband and wife during the marriage. In more states, courts divide property as they consider fair, and the result is less predictable; the split could be fifty-fifty or something else. If one spouse dies, courts normally follow the instructions of that person's will, but the surviving spouse usually is entitled to one-third to one-half of the estate regardless of what the deceased spouse's will says. If the husband and wife have signed a valid premarital agreement, that agreement will supersede the usual laws for dividing property and income upon divorce or death. In many cases, the less wealthy spouse will receive less under the premarital agreement than he or she would receive under the usual laws of divorce or wills.

**Q. Why would the less wealthy spouse sign a premarital agreement if he or she would receive less under the agreement than under other laws?**

**A.** The answer to that question depends on the individual. Some people prefer to control their fiscal relationship rather than to leave it to state regulation. They may want to avoid uncertainty about what a court might decide if the marriage ends in divorce. For some, the answer may be "love conquers all"—the less wealthy person may just want to marry the other one and not care much about the financial details. For others, the agreement may provide ample security, even if it is not as generous as a judge might be. Still others may not like the agreement, but they are willing to take their chances and hope the relationship and the financial arrangements work out for the best.

**Q. What is necessary to make a valid premarital agreement?**

**A.** Laws vary from state to state. In general, the agreements must be in writing and signed by the parties. In most states, the parties (particularly the wealthier one) must disclose their income and assets to each other. This way the parties will know more about what they might be giving up. In some states, it may be possible to waive a full disclosure of income and assets, but the waiver should be done knowingly and it is best if each party has a general idea of the other's worth.

The agreements also must not be the result of fraud or duress. An agreement is likely to be invalid on the basis of fraud if one person (particularly the wealthier one) deliberately misstates his or her financial condition. For example, if a man hides assets from his future wife so that she will agree to a low level of support in case of divorce, a court probably would declare the agreement invalid. Similarly, if one person exerts excessive emotional pressure on

the other to sign the agreement, a court also might declare the agreement to be invalid because of duress.

**Q. When should the agreement be signed?**

**A.** Most states do not set a specific time at which premarital agreements must be signed. Generally, it is better to negotiate and sign the agreement well before the wedding, to show that each person has considered it thoroughly and signed it voluntarily. If the wealthier person shows the agreement to the prospective spouse only one day before the wedding, a court may later find that agreement invalid because of duress. While a last-minute premarital agreement is not automatically invalid, timing may be a significant factor in determining whether the agreement is valid.

**Q. Must the parties to a premarital agreement be represented by lawyers?**

**A.** No, but lawyers can help make sure that the agreement is drafted properly and that both parties are making informed decisions. The lawyer for the wealthier party usually prepares the initial draft of the agreement. The less wealthy party does not need to have a lawyer in order to have a valid agreement, but the agreement is more likely to be enforceable if that person's interests are represented and some back-and-forth negotiations take place.

**Q. Do premarital agreements need to provide for a certain amount of support?**

**A.** No, the law does not set a specific amount. In some cases, a court may decide that an agreement is enforceable even if it leaves one spouse with no property and no support from the other one. If, when the marriage ends, the less wealthy party does not have marketable job skills or is not able to work, a court would be likely to refuse to enforce an agreement denying support. Some states will enforce an agreement to provide no spousal support, so long as waiver of support does not leave the less wealthy party so poor that she or he is eligible for welfare.

Many courts will apply broader notions of fairness and require support at a level higher than subsistence. Some states provides that the support cannot be "unconscionably" low. That is a vague term that means different things to different courts.

Many lawyers think it is a good idea for premarital agreements to contain an "escalator clause" or a "phase-in provision" that will increase the amount of assets or support given to the less wealthy spouse based on the length of the marriage or an increase in the wealthier party's assets or income after the agreement is made.

### Q. May premarital agreements decide future issues of custody and child support?

**A.** No. A court will consider a premarital agreement the parties have reached regarding child custody or support, but the court is not bound by it. Broadly speaking, courts do not want parties to bargain away rights of children, particularly before children are even born. (A later section on child support beginning on page 87 will discuss child support guidelines.)

### Duties of Marriage

### Q. Are one or both spouses required to work outside the home?

**A.** No. While the husband and wife are married and living together, a court is not going to get involved in private family decisions of who works and who does not. That's left to the husband and wife to sort out. Today, more than half of married women—including women with preschool-age children—work outside the home. A

husband or wife cannot, as a matter of law, force his or her partner to work.

### Q. If the wife and husband separate or divorce, can a court require them to work outside the home?

**A.** No, not directly. If a wife and husband separate or divorce, a court still cannot directly order one or both of them to work. The court can, however, declare that one or both parties owe a duty of financial support to the other party or to the children. A duty of financial support means that person who is supposed to pay support must come up with the money somehow—usually from work or from savings. If the person who is supposed to pay support does not pay the money and does not have a good excuse why the money has not been paid, that person could be held in contempt of court. The possible penalties for being held in contempt of court include payment of fines and incarceration. Payments of child support and alimony will be discussed later.

### Q. Are there legal remedies if a husband or wife refuses to have sexual relations with his or her spouse?

**A.** In some states, the refusal to have sexual relations with a spouse is a specific ground for divorce or annulment of the marriage. In other states, refusal to have sexual relations could be considered a ground for divorce because it is an "irreconcilable difference" or "mental cruelty." A court, of course, would not order a person to have sexual relations with his or her spouse. In fact, in many states a spouse who forces sexual relations with a partner can be charged with rape under the state's criminal laws.

### Q. What is loss of consortium?

**A.** Loss of consortium refers to the loss of companionship and sexual relationship with one's spouse. (The concept also can apply more broadly to the loss of companionship and affection from other family members such as a child or parent.) In personal injury actions, plaintiffs may seek monetary damages for loss of consortium in addition to payment for other losses such as medical expenses, lost wages, and physical pain and suffering. For example, if a man is injured in an auto accident caused by a negligent driver and the man is unable to have sexual relations with his wife for two years because of the accident, both the husband and wife may seek damages for that loss.

### Q. *May wives and husbands sue each other?*

**A.** Yes. They can sue each other, of course, in connection with a divorce. They also usually can sue each other in connection with financial deals in which one may have cheated the other. A growing number of states also will allow one spouse to sue the other for deliberate personal injuries, such as those suffered in a beating. Some husbands and wives may try to sue each other in connection with an auto accident in which one of them, as the driver, accidentally causes injury to the other, who was a passenger. In effect, the person suing may be trying to collect money from an insurance company rather than from the person's spouse. Many states do not allow such lawsuits.

### Q. *Can a husband or wife testify against each other in court?*

**A.** Yes. Husbands and wives routinely testify against each other in divorce cases. There is an old rule of law in many states that husbands and wives cannot testify about communications between themselves made during the marriage. Although the rule may be applied in some circumstances, it generally does not apply if the husband and wife are involved in a lawsuit against each other.

## Living Together Outside of Marriage

### Q. *Can two people live together without being married?*

**A.** Of course. The Census Bureau reports that such arrangements are quite common. Some zoning laws do prohibit more than three unrelated persons from living together in one house or apartment, but two unrelated people generally can live together anywhere they want. A few states still have laws on the books prohibiting "fornication"—sexual relations between a man and woman who are not married—but such laws are virtually never enforced. Some states also have laws against "sodomy" which, among other things, prohibit sexual relations between people of the same sex. Those laws are rarely enforced if the conduct is private, consensual, and between adults (although in the 1980s, the United States Supreme Court in a divided decision did uphold a Georgia law criminalizing private sexual relations between two men).

### Q. *May two people who are living together enter into agreements about sharing expenses or acquiring property?*

**A.** Yes. The law allows people to enter into many types of contracts. If two people want to agree about who will pay what and how they will share in property that they might acquire, such an agreement can be valid and enforceable by courts in most states. From a legal standpoint, it is best to make the agreements specific and in writing. An oral agreement might be enforceable, but it is a lot harder to prove. Each party to the agreement should give some benefit to the other party, such as agreeing to pay a certain portion of expenses. If an agreement looks as though it is only creating a gift from one party to the other with the recipient giving nothing in return, the agreement might not be enforceable.

**Q. Will a court enforce an agreement by which one unmarried partner agrees to keep house and the other promises financial support?**

**A.** Probably not. To begin with, such agreements rarely are in writing, so they are hard to prove in court. Second, to the extent that one person is promising financial support to the other, that promise usually is contingent on a continuation of the relationship. If, for example, one partner says, "I'll take care of you," the statement may be too vague to be enforceable; if it means anything, it probably means something along the lines of "I'll support you financially as long as we are living together." So, if the couple breaks up, a court probably would not find an enforceable promise for continued support.

There is a potential third problem: if a court thinks an agreement amounts to providing financial support in exchange for sexual relations, the court will not enforce it. Such an agreement is uncomfortably close to a contract for prostitution.

Courts are more inclined to enforce agreements for tangible items such as payments of expenses or rights to property. A promise of housekeeping services or emotional support for a partner may be sincere, but it is much more amorphous than a promise to pay half the phone bill or share the proceeds of a condominium sale.

## MONEY MATTERS DURING MARRIAGE

### Ownership of Property

**Q. Which spouse owns what property in a marriage?**

**A.** Most property that is acquired during the marriage is considered marital or community property. For example, the wages earned by both husband and wife during the marriage are considered marital property. If one or both spouses buy a house or establish a business during the marriage, that usually will be marital property, particularly if the house or business is purchased with the husband's and wife's earnings.

Separate property is property that each spouse owned before the marriage. It also includes inheritances and gifts (except perhaps gifts between spouses) acquired during marriage. During the marriage (and afterward), each spouse usually keeps control of his or her separate property. Each spouse may buy, sell, and borrow money on his or her separate property. Income earned from separate property, such as interest, dividends, or rent are generally separate property. However, in some states that recognize community property, these profits may become marital property.

Separate property can become marital property if it is mixed with marital property. If, for example, a wife owned an apartment building before the marriage and she deposited rent checks into a joint checking account, the rent money probably would become marital property, although the building is likely to remain the wife's separate property as long as she kept it in her name. If the wife changed the title on the building from her name alone to the names of both herself and her husband, that probably would convert the building into marital property. In addition, if one spouse put a great deal of work into the other spouse's separate property, that could convert the separate property into marital property, or it could give the spouse who contributed the work a right to some form of payback. A later section in this chapter will discuss how courts divide marital property in a divorce.

**Q. May a couple own property together?**

**A.** Yes. In community property states, this occurs automatically. Nine states—Arizona, California, Idaho, Louisiana, Nevada, New

Mexico, Texas, Washington, and Wisconsin, as well as Puerto Rico—use the community property system. These jurisdictions hold that each spouse shares equally the income earned and property acquired during a marriage. This is true even if one spouse supplied all the income. In the other states, spouses probably share property under one of the following three forms of co-ownership:

- Joint Tenancy. A form of ownership that exists when two or more people own property that includes a right of survivorship. Each person has the right to possess the property. If one partner dies, the survivor becomes the sole owner. Any two people—not just spouses—may own property as joint tenants. A creditor may claim the debtor's interest in joint tenancy property.

- Tenancy by the Entirety. Allowed only in some states, this is a type of co-ownership of property by a husband and wife. Like joint tenancy, it includes a right of survivorship. But a creditor of one spouse may not "attach" (seize) the property. Each party usually must consent to the sale of the property. Divorce may result in a division of the property.

- Tenancy in Common. This form of co-ownership gives each person control over his or her share of the property, and the shares need not be equal. The law does not limit tenancy in common to spouses. A tenancy in common has no right of survivorship; when one spouse dies, his or her share passes to the heirs, either by will or state laws.

Tenancy rules vary from one state to another. Some tenancies are complex and must be created in a precise manner, otherwise the courts may not enforce them.

For more information on the various forms of ownership, see pages 150–156 of the chapter on home ownership.

## Debts and Taxes

**Q. Is a husband or wife responsible for debts incurred by the other?**

**A.** That depends on the nature of the debt as well as where the couple are domiciled. If both husband and wife have co-signed for the debt, both will be responsible for paying it. For instance, assume the husband and wife apply together for a charge card. If both sign the application form and promise to pay the charge bills, both will be responsible for paying off the balance to the credit card company or store, even if only one of them made the purchases and the other disapproved. Similarly, if a husband and wife co-sign on a mortgage for a home, both of them are potentially liable to the mortgage company, even if one of them no longer lives in the home. In community property states, a husband and wife may likewise be responsible for debts incurred by the other.

**Q. Is a husband or wife liable for the debts of the other without co-signing for the debt?**

**A.** That again depends on the nature of the debt and the domicile of the marriage. Some states have "family expense statutes" that make a husband or wife liable for expenses incurred for the benefit of the family, even if the other spouse did not sign for or approve of the expense in advance. Still other states impose this family expense obligation by common law without a statute. Thus, if the wife charged groceries at a local store or took the couple's child to a doctor for care, the husband could be liable because these are expenses for the benefit of the family. On the other hand, if the wife runs up bills for a personal holiday or the husband buys expensive coins for his coin collection, the other spouse normally would not be liable unless he or she co-signed for the debt. Again, in community property states, a husband or wife is generally obligated for the debts of the other.

**Q. Do a spouse's credit rights depend on marital status or the other spouse's financial status?**

**A.** The law forbids denying credit on the basis of marital status. See page 252 of the chapter on consumer credit.

**Q. Is one spouse responsible for debts the other spouse brought into the marriage?**

**A.** Not in most states. In states that do not recognize community property, such debts belong to the spouse who incurred them. But in community property states, a spouse may, under special circumstances, become liable for the other spouse's premarital debts.

**Q. Which spouse is responsible for paying taxes?**

**A.** If each spouse's name appears on a state or federal personal income tax return, both parties signing the return are liable for the taxes. If a couple files jointly, the Internal Revenue Service holds each one responsible for the entire debt.

## Child and Dependent Care Tax Credit

A tax credit for actual expenses incurred for child or dependent care is available to an employed person if the expenditures enable that person to be gainfully employed. The credit is computed at 30 percent for taxpayers with incomes of $10,000 or less, with the rate of the credit reduced one percentage point for each additional $2,000 of income above $10,000.

When incomes are over $28,000, the credit is computed at 20 percent. The limits on expenses for which the credit may be taken are $2,400 for one dependent and $4,800 for two or more dependents. The chart below shows the amount of credit that may be taken at various income levels.

| Family Income Before Taxes | Percentage Tax Credit | Maximum Dollar Amount of Credit | |
| --- | --- | --- | --- |
| | | One Dependent | Two or More Dependents |
| Up to $10,000 | 30% | $720 | $1,440 |
| $10,001 to $12,000 | 29% | $696 | $1,392 |
| $12,001 to $14,000 | 28% | $672 | $1,344 |
| $14,001 to $16,000 | 27% | $648 | $1,296 |
| $16,001 to $18,000 | 26% | $624 | $1,248 |
| $18,001 to $20,000 | 25% | $600 | $1,200 |
| $20,001 to $22,000 | 24% | $576 | $1,152 |
| $22,001 to $24,000 | 23% | $552 | $1,104 |
| $24,001 to $26,000 | 22% | $528 | $1,056 |
| $26,001 to $28,000 | 21% | $504 | $1,008 |
| $28,001 and over | 20% | $480 | $ 960 |

SOURCE: U.S. Department of Labor

## Q. Do the tax laws penalize married couples?

**A.** That depends on the tax bracket of each person. If one has a high taxable income and the other a relatively low taxable income, they will generally pay less income tax if they are married and filing a joint return than they would pay if single and filing as single persons. They also will pay less by filing a joint return than by filing separate returns (as married persons). For couples in which both wife and husband have a high income, the total tax will be higher for those who file jointly.

Years ago, there were stories about financially well-off married couples who would go to the Caribbean each December, obtain a divorce, file tax returns as single persons for that year to save money, and then remarry in the new year. Such a practice could be regarded as tax fraud. In any case, the savings are not as great as they were in years past.

## Q. May one spouse make a tax-free gift to the other spouse?

**A.** A person may give his or her spouse any amount of money without paying federal gift taxes if the spouse is a U.S. resident. However, it must be an outright gift or set up as a proper trust. Most, but not all, state laws do away with taxes on gifts between spouses. But the same is not true with respect to gifts to other family members. Gifts to children or other relatives may be taxable if they exceed a certain amount per year.

## Doing Business Together

## Q. May husbands and wives go into business together?

**A.** Certainly. Wives and husbands can be business partners, just as any other two people, whether related or not. They could set up a corporation and both be owners and employees of the corporation; they could form a partnership; or one could own the business and employ the other. Wages and benefits can be paid, just as they would for any other employee. If wages and benefits are being paid to a spouse or child, the amount usually should not be more than what is reasonable or a fair market value. If artificially high payments are made, the business could get into trouble with the Internal Revenue Service.

## Q. Is a wife or husband liable for the other's business debts?

**A.** Usually, no—unless the husband or wife had co-signed on the debt or they reside in a community property state. It is common, however, for institutions that lend money to small businesses to want personal guarantees of payment from the owner of the business, and not just from the business itself. In the event the debt is not paid, lenders would like as many pockets to reach into as a possible. If the owner of the business owns a home, the lender may want to use the home as collateral for the business loan. That means that the spouse of the business owner may be asked to sign a paper allowing use of the home as collateral. Thus, the home could be lost if the business cannot pay off its debts. As long as a spouse does not co-sign for the business debts, the spouse normally will not be liable for business debts incurred by his or her mate. An exception may exist in community property states.

## Q. May a couple file jointly for bankruptcy?

**A.** Yes. Bankruptcy provides relief for people who have more debts than they can pay. See the chapter on bankruptcy, beginning on page 277.

**Q. Must a working spouse provide a pension for a dependent spouse?**

A. The law does not specifically require this, but most pension plans provide for it. Also, depending upon the type of pension plan, a dependent spouse is given certain rights under federal law regarding the working spouse's pension benefits. See the chapter on "The Rights of Older Americans," beginning on page 571.

## Domestic Violence

**Q. What are legal remedies for domestic violence?**

A. In recent years, state legislatures and courts have been paying increasing attention to domestic violence. Many states have elaborate laws designed to protect spouses from domestic violence by their spouses or other family members. In many states, protection also is available for people in dating relationships that have become abusive. A common remedy is for a court to issue a "protective order" ordering the alleged abuser to stop abusing or harassing someone else. In addition, the orders often will order the abuser to stay away from the spouse, the spouse's home, or place of work. If the person continues to abuse his or her spouse (or another person protected by the order), the abuser can be charged with a criminal violation of the order in addition to being charged with other offenses, such as battery.

**Q. What kind of actions are considered domestic violence.**

A. Domestic violence statutes in most states apply not only to physical attacks, but also to other types of conduct. Some examples of conduct that could be considered domestic violence: creating disturbance at a spouse's place of work, harassing telephone calls, surveillance and threats against a spouse or family member (even though the threat may not have been carried out).

**Q. Do protective orders actually protect the victim of domestic violence?**

A. In many cases, yes. Studies have shown that issuing a protective order or arresting a person who commits an act of domestic violence does reduce future incidents of domestic violence. When perpetrators of domestic violence see that the police and court system will treat domestic violence seriously, many persons who commit domestic violence may be deterred from future violence. But orders of protection are not guarantees of protection or safety. For some individuals with intense anger or rage, no court order will stop their violence, and a court order might even add to the rage. Newspapers periodically carry stories of women murdered by their husband or boyfriend despite numerous arrests and orders of protection. The legal system cannot offer perfect protection, although it can reduce violence.

**Q. Where does one turn for help in cases of domestic violence?**

A. In a crisis situation, a call to the police is a good place to start. Many people complain that police do not take accusations of domestic violence seriously. That can be true in some circumstances, but on the whole, police are treating domestic violence situations more seriously, and police officers are receiving increased training on the subject. The local state's attorney or district attorney also may be able to offer some help. An increasing number of hospitals, crisis intervention programs, and social service agencies have programs to help victims of domestic violence. Agencies offering help in cases of domestic violence might be found in the yellow pages under "Domestic Violence Help," "Human Services Organizations," or "Crisis Intervention."

# CHILDREN

## Decision to Have Children

**Q. Who makes the decision to become a parent?**

**A.** The Supreme Court in *Roe v. Wade* and other cases has declared that the decision of whether or not to have a child is a very personal one and that the decision is protected by the right of privacy under the United States Constitution. This means that individuals who wish to have a child cannot be barred from doing so (unless perhaps they are incarcerated). Individuals who do not wish to have a child have a legal right to obtain and use contraceptives.

**Q. What if one spouse wants children and the other does not?**

**A.** Obviously, this is a significant emotional issue that can be very difficult. If one member of the married couple wants a child and the other does not, that could be a basis for a divorce. A disagreement on such a fundamental issue could be an "irreconcilable difference" under the no-fault divorce laws of most states. In states that have grounds for divorce based on someone being at fault, a disagreement on the question of whether to have children could be viewed as "mental cruelty," and thus a basis for ending the marriage.

Beyond divorce, remedies are limited. The courts cannot force a pregnant woman to stop the pregnancy, nor does the law require a wife to have her husband's permission for an abortion.

## Abortion

**Q. What is the current status of abortion law?**

**A.** As of 1994, women still have a right to an abortion. In 1992, the U.S. Supreme Court in the case of *Planned Parenthood v. Casey* reaffirmed its 1973 decision in *Roe v. Wade* that women have a constitutional right to seek an abortion during the early stages of pregnancy. States, however, do have a right to regulate how abortions are performed and states may ban abortions after the fetus is viable (able to live outside the womb) unless the mother's life or health is endangered. The scope of regulation and funding of abortions by the government varies from state to state. In *Casey*, the Supreme Court held it was permissible for states to impose a 24-hour waiting period on obtaining abortions and to require a minor to have consent of one parent or a judge for an abortion.

## Childbirth

**Q. Are there any rules prohibiting parents from having their children born at home?**

**A.** No, at-home births generally are an option for parents. The mother should have good prenatal care, and she should make sure the health care provider believes the delivery will not pose significant risks to the mother or child. If the delivery is risky for the mother or child, it is much better to use a hospital. Some states allow nurse-midwives to deliver children at the parents' home or at a birthing center. Other states allow nurse-midwives to practice only at hospitals or under the direct supervision of a physician.

**Q. If the delivery is at a hospital, may the father or a sibling be present?**

**A.** At most hospitals, the father may be present at birth. Hospitals often prefer that the father and mother have gone through some training before the delivery. Parents should check with their hospitals about other rules and about whether siblings would be allowed in the delivery room.

## Rights and Responsibilities of Parents

### Q. What are the rights of parents?

**A.** Parents have a right to direct the care, control, and upbringing of their children. This gives them the power to make various decisions, including where to live, what school to attend, what religion to follow, and what medical treatment to obtain.

Normally the state may not interfere in these decisions. Only in life-threatening or extreme situations will the courts step in to overrule parents. For example, when a child might die without the medical care that the parents refuse to provide, a judge may make the child a ward of the court and order that the care be provided. Parents have even been prosecuted for withholding medical treatment from seriously ill children. This is true even in situations where parents act out of religious belief.

There may be certain medical procedures, however, that the law allows "mature minors" to decide upon for themselves, even if their parents disagree. For example, parents have no absolute veto power over a minor's decision to use contraceptives or to get an abortion.

Parents also have the legal authority to control their children's behavior and social lives. Children have a duty to obey their parents' reasonable rules and commands. Parents may discipline or punish their children appropriately. They may not, however, use cruel methods or excessive force; that constitutes child abuse.

### Q. What are the legal rights of children?

**A.** Children have a unique status under the law. This chapter cannot explain this special status fully. However, it can point out a few of the major differences between the rights of adults and children.

Most important, children have a right to be supported by their parents. At minimum, this

**WHO CONTROLS THE MONEY CHILDREN EARN OR INHERIT?**
*Generally, parents do not have unlimited, direct control over their children's money. If children earn or inherit money, that money must be used for their benefit. Some states require the appointment of a guardian under court supervision if a child has money. Unless a court appoints someone else, parents are the guardians of their children's money. The parents are legally responsible for managing the money properly and using it for their children's needs.*

means food, shelter, clothing, medical care and education.

The law defines children as unmarried persons under the age of majority—usually eighteen—who have not left home to support themselves. The law protects children from abuse and neglect. It also entitles them to the protection of the state. They may be removed from their home if it is necessary to ensure them a safe, supportive environment. This removal may be temporary or permanent.

The law allows children to sue. However, in most instances an adult legal representative must begin the suit. Children accused of committing crimes are subject to the juvenile courts of their state, not the regular criminal justice system. (In some states, children accused of serious crimes who are above a certain age—usually sixteen—may be tried in court as adults.) Juvenile courts entitle children to only some of the due process safeguards that adults receive. In return, these courts have more freedom to deal with juveniles in an effort to rehabilitate them.

### Q. How long do parents' legal obligations to their children continue?

**A.** Parents are legally responsible for their children until they reach the age of majority (usually eighteen), marry, or leave home to support themselves. In some states, divorced parents may be obliged to pay for a child's college education or trade school. In addition, a parent's duty to support a disabled child might continue for the child's entire life.

### Q. Are parents financially responsible for the acts of their children?

**A.** The law on this varies from state to state. Some states do make parents financially responsible for damage caused by their children, but the states may place limits on the amount of liability. In Illinois, for example, parents or guardians may be required to pay no more than $1,000 for the "willful or malicious acts" of minor children who harm another person or property.

Generally, if a child has an auto accident while driving a parent's car, the parent's auto insurance policy will cover the loss to the same extent it would if the parent had been driving the car (although parents usually have to pay higher insurance premiums to cover young drivers).

## Adoption

### Q. How does one adopt a child?

**A.** Adoption laws vary from state to state. For adopting a child who is not related to the adoptive parent or parents, there generally are two types of adoptions: agency adoptions and private adoptions.

### Q. What is an agency adoption?

**A.** As the name implies, the parents work though a licensed agency. The agency often supervises the care of biological mothers who are willing to give up their children, and it assists in the placement of children after birth. Agencies screen adoptive parents—often extensively—before the adoption proceeds. Some agencies have long waiting lists of parents. Some agencies also specialize in placing children born in foreign countries.

### Q. What is a private adoption?

**A.** Private adoptions bypass the use of agencies and they may help bypass the long waiting lists as well. The process may begin when people who seek to adopt a child contact an attorney who specializes in adoptions. The attorney may work with physicians who are aware of women willing to give up children for adoption. Sometimes would-be parents will place ads in newspapers seeking women who are willing to place their babies for adoption.

In most states, adoptive parents are allowed to pay a biological mother's medical expenses and certain other costs during the pregnancy. But adoptive parents are not allowed to pay the biological mother specifically to give up the child. The law treats this as a "black market adoption," the buying and selling of children, and it's a crime in every state.

### Q. Is court approval necessary for an adoption?

**A.** Yes. Court approval is needed for both agency and private adoptions. Many states also require that the adoptive parents be approved by a social service agency.

### Q. Can a biological mother revoke her consent to adoption?

**A.** Yes, but there are limits on her right to revoke consent. In most states, a biological mother who initially consents to a child's adoption before birth, may revoke that consent after birth. In other words, the mother's consent usually is not final or binding until a certain period of time after birth. In most states that time period is relatively short, such as 48 to 72 hours, although some states may allow a longer period in which a mother may revoke her consent. If a biological mother consented to adoption during the proper period of time after birth, it is much harder for her to revoke her consent. Following an after-birth consent, a biological mother generally may revoke her consent only if she can show that there was fraud or duress. Fraud could be found if the adoption agency or

attorney lied to her about the consequences of what she was doing. Duress might exist if a person at the adoption agency threatened the biological mother with humiliation if she did not sign. A biological mother's change of heart normally is not enough by itself to revoke an after-birth adoption consent. Although a mother may feel emotionally drained and under stress after birth of a child that she plans to give up for adoption, that type of stress usually is not enough to revoke an adoption unless the person or agency that obtained the mother's consent used harsh tactics to obtain her consent.

### Q. Is the biological father's consent necessary?

**A.** Generally, yes—at least if he is known. He should be notified of the birth and pending adoption so that he may consent or object. If the father is not known, the adoption may proceed without his consent (although adoptive parents can feel safer about the validity of their adoption if the biological father has been notified and agreed to it). If a biological father is not notified, he may later contest the adoption if he acts within a certain period of time after the child's birth or adoption. (Six months is a typical time period, although the period varies between states.)

### Q. What is a "related adoption"?

**A.** A "related adoption" is one in which a child's relatives, such as grandparents or an aunt and uncle, formally adopt a child as their own. This might occur if the child's biological parents are deceased or are otherwise unable to care for the child.

### Q. What is a stepparent adoption?

**A.** A stepparent adoption is one in which a child's biological parent marries someone who wishes to adopt the biological parent's child and is able to do so.

**Q. What happens if the child's other biological parent does not agree to the adoption by the stepparent?**

A. If a biological parent does not consent to the adoption of a child, the child cannot be adopted by another person unless a court first finds that the biological parent is unfit.

**Q. What is the definition of an unfit parent?**

A. Parental unfitness is determined by state law. Normally, an unfit parent is one who has failed to have regular contact with a child or to contribute to his or her support. A parent is also unfit if he or she has been abusive or has otherwise failed to provide adequate care for the child.

**Q. What happens if a stepparent adopts his spouse's child and the parents later divorce?**

A. A divorce does not affect the legality of the adoption. The stepparent continues to have all the rights and responsibilities of a biological parent, including a right to seek custody or visitation and a duty to support the child.

**Q. Can a single person adopt a child?**

A. Yes, although some agencies strongly prefer to place a child with a married couple. Other agencies—particularly those dealing with children who might be hard to place—are willing to place a child with a single person. Single-parent adoptions usually are possible in private adoptions.

**Q. Can lesbian or gay couples adopt a child?**

A. Yes, in some states, such as New York and California, gay and lesbian couples are able to adopt a child.

**Q. What is an "open adoption"?**

A. An "open adoption" is one in which the adoptive parents agree to let the biological mother (or biological father) have some continued contact with the child after the adoption. This contact might be periodic visits or an exchange of pictures and other information between the adoptive family and the biological parent or parents. The nature of the contact often is specified in the adoption agreement. Open adoptions have become more common as more birth mothers have become involved with choosing which adoptive family will receive their child. But open adoptions are a relatively new phenomenon, and in many states it is not certain whether an open adoption agreement is enforceable by the birth mother.

**Q. Who has access to adoption records?**

A. In most states, court adoption records are sealed and can only be opened by court order. Procedures and standards for opening records vary by state. Increasingly, states require that certain nonidentifying information, such as the medical history of the biological family, be made available to the adoptive parents at the time of adoption. Some states also have registries where parties to the adoption can agree to a later exchange of information, including names and addresses.

**Q. What is the legal status of an adopted child?**

A. An adopted child has exactly the same rights as one born to his or her parents. Similarly, adoptive parents have the same obligations to the child as they would to one born to them.

**Q. What about medically assisted pregnancies?**

A. As medical science advances, there are a variety of ways in which individuals who wish to become parents can be helped to do so by medically assisted means, including artificial insemination and in vitro fertilization. These medical procedures have legal implications which vary by state. Generally, however, if both husband and wife consent to artificial insemination or in vitro fertilization, the rights and duties of the husband, wife, and child will be the same as if the child had been naturally conceived.

### Q. What is surrogate parenthood?

**A.** In this arrangement, a woman agrees, with or without payment, to bear a child for another couple. This usually occurs when the wife cannot conceive or carry a child to term. In nearly all cases, through artificial insemination, the husband's sperm fertilizes an egg belonging to either the wife or the surrogate mother. This makes the husband the biological father of the child. The surrogate mother agrees to give up all parental rights at birth. Then the wife of the biological father legally adopts the child. A few states outlaw this arrangement when the surrogate mother receives payment. Other states are considering laws that would restrict it. Persons contemplating such an arrangement should seek legal advice before entering into such an arrangement.

### Paternity

### Q. May an unmarried mother legally force the father of her baby to support the child?

**A.** Yes. Both parents, married or not, have a duty to support the child. If the father admits paternity, the mother should have him sign a statement to that effect. Then, if necessary, it will be easier to force the father to help support the child. If he does not admit to being the father, the mother may file a paternity suit against him. If this civil action succeeds, the court will require the father to provide support. Sometimes the court also will require the father to pay for the mother's pregnancy and childbirth expenses.

### Q. If a court decides that a man is a child's father, how much will he have to pay in support?

**A.** The law requires unwed parents to support their children the same as married parents. Child support guidelines in every state will determine the amount of support. As with children born to married parents, the obligation of support usually lasts until the child is an adult. If a father refuses to support his child, a court may garnish his wages, seize his property or bank accounts, perhaps even send him to jail.

### Q. What may a husband legally do if his wife bears a child that is not his?

**A.** The law presumes that a married woman's child is her husband's. He must support the child unless he can prove in court that

---

**PATERNITY AND MODERN SCIENCE**

*Paternity cases increasingly use scientific evidence. The blood tests used during much of this century were useful only up to a certain point. They might prove that a man was not the father of a certain child, but could not prove that he was the father. New tests that sample the DNA (genetic material) of the child and the supposed father are nearly 100 percent certain in proving or disproving paternity.*

he is not the father. Some states assume the husband is the father no matter what proof he presents. These states do not allow a husband to disprove paternity of a child born during the marriage.

## Abuse and Neglect Laws

**Q. What is child neglect?**

**A.** State laws make it a criminal offense for parents and legal guardians to fail to meet children's basic needs, including food, shelter, clothes, medical treatment, and supervision. Such failure constitutes child neglect.

**Q. What persons and what types of actions are covered by child abuse laws?**

**A.** It is a crime for adults to abuse children in their care. Such adults include parents, legal guardians, other adults in the home, family members, and baby-sitters. Supervising adults may not go beyond reasonable physical punish-

ment. For example, adults who beat children so severely that they require medical treatment have violated these laws. Child abuse laws involve not only physical abuse (such as beatings or starvation), but other types of cruelty, such as sexual molestation, that endanger children's moral and mental health. The laws also cover emotional abuse, such as subjecting a child to extreme public humiliation.

A person may be guilty of child abuse that he or she did not personally commit if that person had legal responsibility for the child and failed to protect the child from the abuser.

**Q. Who has a duty to report suspected child neglect and abuse?**

**A.** The law compels a wide range of people who have contact with children to report suspected child abuse or neglect. Such people include doctors, nurses, teachers, and social workers. A person who is required to report suspected neglect or abuse may face civil or criminal penalties for failure to do so. In addition, states often encourage the reporting of suspected abuse by others such as neighbors and family members through special hot lines. The laws of most states encourage persons to make reports of abuse by granting them immunity from defamation suits by the accused parents if they make the report in good faith. Some states keep central lists of suspected child abuse cases. This helps identify parents, for example, who take their children to different hospitals in order to conceal the evidence that they have repeatedly abused their children.

**Q. If the law takes children away from their parents, is the removal temporary or permanent?**

**A.** The goal usually is to reunite the family after correcting the problems that led to the removal. This, however, is not always possible. For example, the parents may make little or no

> ## TAKING CHILDREN AWAY FROM THEIR PARENTS
>
> *Whether or not a criminal case is brought, the state may remove children from the custody of their parents if there is reason to believe the parents are physically, sexually, or emotionally abusing one or more of them. The state also may remove the children if the parents are unable or unwilling to provide adequate care, supervision, and support.*

effort to improve the children's care. Then the state may ask a court to end all parental rights. If this happens, the legal bonds between parents and children are completely and permanently cut. Then another family may adopt the children.

---

# SEPARATION, ANNULMENT, AND DIVORCE

Sometimes marriages do not succeed. Despite the efforts of husband and wife, despite the help of counselors and clergy, there is nothing to do but end the relationship. And, as the state was involved in creating the marriage, so it becomes involved in dissolving it.

## Separation and Separate Maintenance

### Q. What is a legal separation?

**A.** A formal legal separation is a judicial determination of separation whereby all the issues have been adjudicated (decided or approved by a court), except that the parties do not become divorced, whether for religious reasons or otherwise. Most people use "legal separation" in a more general sense, meaning that the husband and wife are living separately, and they have formalized the arrangement by a court order or a written agreement between themselves. The order or agreement usually will state that the parties are living separately, and it will specify what support, if any, one spouse will pay the other. If the husband and wife have children, the agreement or court order might specify arrangements regarding custody or visitation with the children.

A legal separation is not the same as a divorce. For one thing, it recognizes the possibility that the couple might reunite. In any case, its terms can be modified by the parties or the court when the couple divorce. Most impor-

tantly, persons who are legally separated may not remarry. They must wait until a divorce is final before being able to remarry.

### Q. Does a person have to be legally separated before obtaining a divorce?

**A.** No. In most states a couple can proceed straight to a divorce without first seeking a legal separation. While waiting for the divorce, the couple might live separately (without a formal agreement) or, in some states, they could even live together pending the final divorce.

### Q. Is there an advantage to a legal separation?

**A.** That depends on the needs of the parties. A legal separation offers a structure for the parties while they are waiting for a divorce (or while they are considering a divorce). If one spouse is paying support for the other spouse or for the children, the spouse receiving the support may want the terms put in writing. Similarly, one or both parties may want a fixed schedule of who will be with the children at what times. If these terms are part of a written agreement or court order, the parties know what to count on, and one can go to court to seek enforcement if the other does not abide by the agreement or order.

### Q. Are there any tax advantages to a legal separation?

**A.** Yes, potentially. If one spouse is paying support for the other, the payer can deduct that money from his or her income for tax purposes. The payment will then be considered taxable income to the recipient. If the payer is in a higher tax bracket than the recipient, this will reduce the couple's combined tax liability. In any case, it will reduce the payer's taxes and raise the recipient's. To obtain such a deduction the parties must be legally separated by written agreement or court order. The deduction is not available for those in an informal separation.

**Q. Why would a spouse who is receiving support agree to this arrangement if it results in more taxes for her or him and a tax advantage to the other spouse?**

A. The tax advantage to the payer may encourage paying support in the first place and it may result in a greater amount of support. Some couples and their lawyers may figure out a tentative amount of support that would be paid without any tax benefit to the payer. Then they calculate the tax benefit of creating a deduction for the payer and income for the recipient. They split the tax savings by increasing the level of support. The increased support usually exceeds the added taxes the recipient will pay, and the payer will have less money out-of-pocket for the year because of the tax savings. (This scenario is much less common now that tax brackets are compressed, putting most middle class people into the same bracket.)

**Q. Are there psychological advantages of a legal separation?**

A. For some people, yes. Some men and women may want to separate but are not sure they want to go through a divorce. The separation might be a "trial separation"—relieving some immediate pressures while the husband and wife sort out what they want to do with their lives. And a formal legal separation may provide some structure, security, and financial advantages during the period of separation.

## Annulment

**Q. What is an annulment?**

A. An annulment is a court ruling that a supposed marriage was never valid. The most common ground for annulment is fraud. For example, one person may have not disclosed to the other a prior divorce, a criminal record, an infectious disease, an inability to engage in sex or have children. Annulment may also be granted for duress, bigamy, incest, or marriage to an underage person.

**Q. How common are annulments?**

A. They are uncommon because divorces are easy to obtain and the bases for an annulment are narrower than the bases for a divorce. One party may prefer an annulment, however, in order to avoid some obligations that a court might impose in a divorce. Also, in a few states, spousal support that terminated because of the recipient's second marriage may be reinstated if the second marriage is annulled.

## Divorce

**Q. What is a divorce?**

A. A divorce—referred to in some states as a "dissolution of marriage"—is a decree by a court that a valid marriage no longer exists. It leaves both parties free to remarry. It usually provides for division of property and makes arrangements for child custody and support.

**Q. May a couple get a divorce without lawyers?**

A. Most states permit such divorces. But the complexities of property division and taxes may make it advisable for both parties to have expert legal and financial advice.

**Q. Are most divorces contested?**

A. No. Although divorces may be emotionally contentious, most divorces (probably more than 95 percent) do not end up in a contested trial. Usually the parties negotiate and settle such things as property division, spousal support, and child custody between themselves, probably with attorneys' help. Sometimes par-

# Grounds for Divorce and Residency Requirements

| | No Fault Sole Ground | No Fault Added to Traditional | Incompatibility | Living Separate and Apart | Judicial Separation or Maintenance | Durational Requirements |
|---|---|---|---|---|---|---|
| Alabama | | X | X | 2 years | X | 6 months |
| Alaska | | X | X | | X | None |
| Arizona | X | | | | X | 90 days |
| Arkansas | | X | | 18 months | X | 60 days |
| California | X | | | | X | 6 months |
| Colorado | X | | | | X | 90 days |
| Connecticut | | X | | 18 months | X | 1 year |
| Delaware | X | | | | | 6 months |
| D.C. | X | | | 1 year | X | 6 months |
| Florida | X | | | | | 6 months |
| Georgia | | X | | 1 year | | 6 months |
| Hawaii | X | | | 2 years | X | 6 months |
| Idaho | | X | | | X | 6 weeks |
| Illinois | | X | | 2 years | X | 90 days |
| Indiana | | X | | | X | 6 months |
| Iowa | X | | | | X | None |
| Kansas | | | X | | X | 60 days |
| Kentucky | X | | | | X | 180 days |
| Louisiana | | X | | 6 months | X | None |
| Maine | | X | | | X | 6 months |
| Maryland | | X | | 2 years | X | 1 year |
| Massachusetts | | X | | | X | None |
| Michigan | X | | | | X | 6 months |
| Minnesota | X | | | | X | 180 days |
| Mississippi | | X | | | | 6 months |
| Missouri | X | | | | X | 90 days |
| Montana | X | | X | 180 days | X | 90 days |
| Nebraska | X | | | | X | 1 year |
| Nevada | | | X | 1 year | X | 6 weeks |
| New Hampshire | | X | | 2 years | | 1 year |
| New Jersey | | X | | 18 months | X | 1 year |
| New Mexico | | X | X | | | 6 months |
| New York | | X | X | 1 year | X | 1 year |
| North Carolina | | | | 1 year | X | 6 months |
| North Dakota | | X | | | X | 6 months |
| Ohio | | X | X | 1 year | | 6 months |
| Oklahoma | | X | | | X | 6 months |
| Oregon | X | | | | X | 6 months |
| Pennsylvania | | X | | 1 year | | 6 months |
| Rhode Island | | X | | 3 years | X | 1 year |
| South Carolina | | X | | 1 year | X | 1 year |
| South Dakota | | X | | | X | None |
| Tennessee | | X | | 2 years | X | 6 months |
| Texas | | X | | 3 years | | 6 months |
| Utah | | X | | | X | 90 days |
| Vermont | | X | | 6 months | | 6 months |
| Virginia | | X | | 1 year | X | 6 months |
| Washington | X | | | | X | 1 year |
| West Virginia | | X | | 1 year | X | 1 year |
| Wisconsin | X | | | 1 year | X | 6 months |
| Wyoming | X | | | | X | 60 days |

SOURCE: *Family Law Quarterly*, Vol. 27, No. 4, Winter, 1994, published by the ABA Family Law Section.

ties reach an agreement by mediation, with a trained mediator who tries to help husband and wife identify and accommodate common interests. The parties then present their negotiated or mediated agreement to a judge. Approval is virtually automatic if the agreement is fair.

If parties are unable to agree about property, support, and child custody, they may ask the court to decide one or more of those matters. One spouse may sue the other for divorce, alleging certain faults or offenses by the defendant. But this has become far less common than it once was. Most divorces now are no-fault divorces.

### Q. What is a no-fault divorce?

**A.** It is a divorce in which neither person blames the other for breakdown of the marriage. There are no accusations, no need to prove "guilt." A common basis for a no-fault divorce is "irreconcilable differences" or "irretrievable breakdown." As those terms imply, the marriage is considered to be over, but the court and the legal documents do not try to assign blame. Another common reason is that the parties have lived separate and apart for a given period of time, such as for six months or a year, with the intent that the separation be permanent.

### Q. Why does the law provide for no-fault divorces?

**A.** No-fault divorces are considered a more humane and realistic way to end a marriage. Husbands and wives who are divorcing usually are suffering enough without adding more fuel to the emotional fires by trying to prove who did what to whom. The laws of no-fault divorce recognize that human relationships are complex and that it is difficult to prove that a marriage broke down solely because of what one person did. However, some critics of no-fault divorces are concerned that an economically

dependent spouse may not be adequately protected when it is so easy for the other spouse to obtain a divorce.

All states have some form of no-fault divorce, but most also retain fault-based grounds as an alternative way of obtaining a divorce. Some spouses want the emotional release of proving fault by their mates. Courts are not a very good forum for such personal issues, and the accuser is usually less satisfied than he or she expected to be.

### Q. What are grounds for obtaining a divorce based on fault?

**A.** States that allow fault-based divorce vary somewhat on the allowable grounds. Many permit divorce for adultery, physical cruelty, mental cruelty, attempted murder, desertion, habitual drunkenness, use of addictive drugs, insanity, impotency, and infection of one's spouse with venereal disease. Spouses in the mood for revenge could probably come up with a multicount complaint.

### Q. Will use of fault grounds affect other aspects of the divorce?

**A.** That depends on the state. In some states, fault may be taken into consideration in deciding property and spousal support, even if the divorce is granted on no-fault grounds. For example, in some states fault will be considered if it directly causes waste or dissipation of marital assets. In many states, the fault of a party in causing a breakdown of the marriage is not supposed to be a factor in dividing property or deciding spousal support. In a few states, however, a spouse who commits adultery may not be able to receive spousal support. In custody cases, the marital fault of a party usually is not supposed to be considered unless that fault caused a harmful impact on the child. For example, a discreet extramarital affair normally would not be a major factor in deciding custody.

But an affair or series of affairs which placed the child in stressful situations could be a factor in deciding custody.

**Q. May a woman resume her unmarried name when she divorces?**

A. Yes, that is her option. She may resume her unmarried name or keep her married name. If she is changing her name, she should notify government agencies and private companies that have records of her name. Examples of places to notify: Internal Revenue Service, Social Security Administration, Passport Agency (within U.S. State Department), Post Office, state tax agencies, driver's license bureau, voter registration bureau, professional licensing agencies, professional societies, unions, mortgage company, landlord, banks, charge card companies, telephone company, other utilities, magazines, newspapers, dentists, and schools and colleges that the woman attended or that her children attend. It can be useful to have the divorce decree state that the wife will resume her unmarried name, but generally it is not necessary to do so in order for a woman to make a valid name change.

## Property

**Q. In divorce cases, how often do judges decide who gets what?**

A. Judges rule on major contested issues in only a relatively small number of cases. As noted earlier, probably more than 95 percent of divorce cases are not decided by the court. Instead, the parties—usually with help from attorneys—have reached an agreement between themselves which they present to a judge for approval. If the agreement is fair, approval usually is granted after a short hearing.

Nonetheless, the rules of law that a judge would use to decide a contested case influence the settlements that the parties reach. If it is predictable that a matter would be decided in a certain way, it is seldom worth taking the issue to trial. In many cases, the cost of pursuing a disputed property issue at trial will exceed the possible monetary gain of a victory in court.

**Q. How do judges decide disputed property issues?**

A. Laws vary from state to state. As a starting point, many states allow parties to keep their "nonmarital" or "separate" property. Nonmarital property includes property that a spouse brought into the marriage and kept separate during the marriage. It also includes inheritances received and kept separate during the marriage. It also may include gifts received by just one spouse during the marriage. Some states permit division of separate as well as marital property when parties divorce, but the origin of the property is considered when deciding who receives the property. After allocating separate property, the court divides marital or community property.

**Q. What is marital or community property?**

A. Marital or community property is defined somewhat differently by different states, but it generally includes property and income acquired during the marriage. Wages earned during the marriage would be marital property. A home and furniture purchased during the marriage usually would be marital property.

**Q. What if the property obtained during the marriage is in the name of one party only?**

A. That too usually will be marital property if it was paid for with marital funds such as wages. For example, if a wife buys a car during the marriage and pays for it with her wages, the car is marital property, even though it is in her name only. A pension also is usually marital property, even though it may have been earned by the labor of only one spouse during the marriage. A pension can be a very significant piece of property; it and the family home often are the most valuable assets acquired by a couple during the marriage. (If a pension was completely earned before the marriage, it probably would be nonmarital property.) Marital or community property can be divided by the court between the parties.

### Q. How does a husband or wife keep nonmarital property separate and thus less likely to be lost in a divorce?

**A.** The main way to keep nonmarital property separate is to keep it in one's own name and not mix it with marital property. For example, if a wife came into a marriage with a $20,000 money market account and wanted to keep it as nonmarital property, she should keep the account in her own name and not deposit any marital funds in the account. She should not, for instance, deposit her paychecks into the money market account, because the paychecks are marital funds and could turn the whole account into marital property.

Another example: If a husband inherits some stock from his mother during the marriage and he wants to keep it as nonmarital property, he should open his own investment account and should not use the account for any investments that he and his wife own together.

If a husband or wife decides to use some nonmarital funds for a common purpose, such as purchasing a home in joint tenancy, that money normally will become marital property. The nonmarital property will be viewed by the courts of most states as a gift to the marriage. The property distribution laws have many intricacies and variations between states; understanding them usually requires a lawyer's help.

### Q. How do courts divide marital or community property?

**A.** Again, the answer varies from state to state. A few states, such as California, take a rather simple approach. They believe property should be divided equally because they view marriage as a joint undertaking in which both spouses are presumed to contribute equally, though often in different ways, to the acquisition and preservation of property. All marital property will be divided fifty-fifty, unless the husband and wife had a premarital agreement stating otherwise. (Premarital agreements were discussed on pages 56–58.) Most states, however, apply a concept called "equitable distribution."

### Q. What is "equitable distribution"?

**A.** That means a court divides marital property as it thinks is fair. States applying principles of equitable distribution view marriage as a shared enterprise in which both spouses usually contribute significantly to the acquisition and preservation of property. The division of property could be fifty-fifty, sixty-forty, seventy-thirty, or even all for one spouse and nothing for the other (although that would be very unusual). Under equitable distribution, courts consider a variety of factors and need not weigh the factors equally. That permits more flexibility and more attention to the financial situation of both spouses after the divorce. However, it also makes the resolution of property issues less predictable. Here are some examples of factors that are considered by states applying principles of equitable distribution.

- *Nonmarital property.* If one spouse has a lot more nonmarital property than the other, that could be a basis for giving more marital property to the less wealthy spouse.

- *Earning power.* If one spouse has more earning power than the other, that could

# Property Division

| | Community Property | Only Marital Property Divided | Statutory List of Factors | Nonmonetary Contributions | Economic Misconduct Considered | Special Contribution to Education |
|---|---|---|---|---|---|---|
| Alabama | | X | | | | |
| Alaska | | | X | X | X | X |
| Arizona | X | | X | | | X |
| Arkansas | | X | X | X | | |
| California | X | | X | X | X | X |
| Colorado | | X | X | X | X | |
| Connecticut | | X | X | X | X | X |
| Delaware | | | X | X | X | |
| D.C. | | X | X | X | X | |
| Florida | | X | X | X | X | X |
| Georgia | | X | | | | |
| Hawaii | | | X | X | X | |
| Idaho | X | | X | | | |
| Illinois | | X | X | X | X | |
| Indiana | | X | X | X | X | |
| Iowa | | X | X | X | | X |
| Kansas | | | X | | X | |
| Kentucky | | X | X | X | X | X |
| Louisiana | X | | | | | |
| Maine | | X | X | X | | |
| Maryland | | X | X | X | | |
| Massachusetts | | | X | X | | |
| Michigan | | | | | | |
| Minnesota | | X | X | X | X | |
| Mississippi | | | | | | |
| Missouri | | X | X | X | | |
| Montana | | | X | X | X | |
| Nebraska | | X | | X | | |
| Nevada | X | | | | | |
| New Hampshire | | | X | X | X | X |
| New Jersey | | X | X | X | | X |
| New Mexico | X | | | | | |
| New York | | X | X | X | X | X |
| North Carolina | | X | X | X | X | X |
| North Dakota | | | | X | | |
| Ohio | | X | X | X | X | X |
| Oklahoma | | X | | | | |
| Oregon | | | | X | | |
| Pennsylvania | | X | X | X | X | X |
| Rhode Island | | X | X | X | X | X |
| South Carolina | | X | X | | X | X |
| South Dakota | | | | X | X | |
| Tennessee | | X | X | X | X | X |
| Texas | X | | | | X | |
| Utah | | | | | X | |
| Vermont | | | X | X | X | X |
| Virginia | | X | X | X | | X |
| Washington | X | | X | | | |
| West Virginia | | X | X | X | X | X |
| Wisconsin | X | | X | X | | X |
| Wyoming | | | X | | | |

SOURCE: *Family Law Quarterly*, Vol. 27, No. 4, Winter, 1994, published by the ABA Family Law Section.

be a basis for giving more marital property to the spouse with less earning power.

- *Who earned the property.* That can be a factor favoring the party who worked hard to acquire or maintain the property.

- *Services as a homemaker.* Courts recognize that keeping a home and raising children are work. In addition, those services often enable the spouse who is working outside the home to earn more money. Thus, services as a homemaker are a factor in favor of the homemaker. Some courts also apply a related concept of considering whether one spouse had impaired her or his earning capacity because of working as a homemaker. That factor also would favor the homemaker-spouse.

- *Waste and dissipation.* If a spouse wasted money during the marriage, that could count against him or her when it comes time to divide property. This factor is sometimes labeled "economic fault," and may be considered even by courts that do not consider other kinds of fault.

- *Fault.* Non-economic fault, such as spousal abuse or marital infidelity, is considered in some states, but most states do not consider it relevant to property division.

- *Duration of marriage.* A longer marriage may be a factor in favor of a larger property award to the spouse with less wealth or earning power.

- *Age and health of parties.* If one spouse has ill health or is significantly older than the other, that factor could favor a larger award to the sicker or older spouse.

### Q. Who is likely to get the house?

**A.** That depends on the facts of each case. If the parties have children and can afford to keep the house, even though they will be living separately, the law usually favors giving the house to the spouse who will have custody of the children most of the time. If the parties cannot afford to keep the house, it may be sold and the proceeds divided (or perhaps given to one party).

In some cases, there is a middle-ground approach: The spouse who has primary custody of the children will have a right to live in the house for a certain number of years. At the end of that time, that spouse will buy out the other spouse's interest or sell the house and divide the proceeds.

### Q. What if the parties have a negative net worth—owing more money than they have?

**A.** In that uncomfortable but common situation, the court (or the parties by agreement) will divide whatever property they have and then allocate the responsibility of each party to pay off particular debts.

### Alimony/Maintenance

### Q. What is alimony or maintenance?

**A.** Alimony or maintenance—sometimes also referred to as "spousal support"—is money paid from one spouse to another for day-to-day support of the spouse with fewer financial resources. Sometimes alimony also can be used to pay back a debt. For example, if one spouse paid to put the other spouse through college or graduate school, alimony might be used to pay back the spouse who provided financial support for the education.

### Q. When do courts award alimony?

**A.** At one time, courts commonly ordered husbands to pay alimony to their former wives until the ex-wives married again or died. Today,

# Alimony/Spousal Support Factors

| | Statutory List | Marital Fault Not Considered | Marital Fault Relevant | Standard of Living | Status as Custodial Parent |
|---|---|---|---|---|---|
| Alabama | | | X | | |
| Alaska | X | X | | X | X |
| Arizona | X | X | | X | X |
| Arkansas | | X | | | |
| California | | X | | | |
| Colorado | X | X | | X | X |
| Connecticut | X | | X | X | X |
| Delaware | X | X | | X | X |
| D.C. | | | X | | |
| Florida | X | | X | X | |
| Georgia | X | | X | X | |
| Hawaii | X | X | | X | X |
| Idaho | X | | X | | |
| Illinois | X | X | | X | X |
| Indiana | | X | | | X |
| Iowa | X | X | | X | X |
| Kansas | | X | | | |
| Kentucky | X | X | | X | |
| Louisiana | X | | X | | X |
| Maine | | | X | | |
| Maryland | X | | X | X | |
| Massachusetts | X | | X | X | X |
| Michigan | | | | | |
| Minnesota | X | X | | X | X |
| Mississippi | | | X | | |
| Missouri | X | | X | X | X |
| Montana | X | X | | X | X |
| Nebraska | | X | | | |
| Nevada | X | X | | | |
| New Hampshire | X | | X | X | X |
| New Jersey | | X | | | |
| New Mexico | | X | | | |
| New York | X | X | | | X |
| North Carolina | | X | X | | |
| North Dakota | | | X | | |
| Ohio | X | X | | X | X |
| Oklahoma | | X | | | |
| Oregon | X | X | | X | X |
| Pennsylvania | X | | X | X | X |
| Rhode Island | X | | X | X | |
| South Carolina | | | X | | |
| South Dakota | | | X | | |
| Tennessee | X | | X | X | X |
| Texas | | X | | | |
| Utah | | | X | | |
| Vermont | X | X | | X | X |
| Virginia | X | | X | X | |
| Washington | X | X | | X | |
| West Virginia | | | X | | |
| Wisconsin | X | X | | | |
| Wyoming | | | X | | |

SOURCE: *Family Law Quarterly*, Vol. 27, No. 4, Winter, 1994, published by the ABA Family Law Section.

alimony is ordered by a court on the basis of one spouse's need or entitlement and the other spouse's ability to pay. Although most alimony payments are made from men to women, it is possible that a well-off woman could be required to pay support to her economically dependent husband. Maintenance is awarded less often now because there are more two-income couples and fewer marriages in which one person is financially dependent on the other. A person who pays support may deduct it from his or her income for tax purposes; the one who receives it must pay taxes on it (unless the parties agree otherwise).

## Q. What is rehabilitative support?

**A.** The most common spousal support today is rehabilitative support. It is intended to provide a chance for education or job training so that a spouse who was financially dependent or disadvantaged during marriage can become self-supporting. It should help make up for opportunities lost by a spouse who left a job to help the other spouse's career or to assume family duties. It may be awarded to a spouse who worked outside the home during the marriage, but sacrificed his or her career development because of family priorities. Rehabilitative support is usually awarded for only a limited time, such as one to five years.

## Q. What is permanent support?

**A.** Courts award permanent spousal support to provide money for a spouse who cannot become economically independent. The most common reason for ordering permanent maintenance is that the recipient, because of advanced age or chronic illness, will never be able to maintain a reasonable standard of living without the support. When deciding the amount of permanent support, courts often use the same criteria as for dividing property.

Although it is called permanent support, it can change or cease if the ability of the payer or the needs of the recipient change greatly. It ends if the recipient remarries, and it may end if the recipient decides to live with someone else.

## Q. If one spouse supports the other through graduate or professional school, does the supporting spouse have a right to be compensated for increasing the earning capacity of the other spouse?

**A.** Some courts offer a new kind of compensation when neither property distribution nor traditional spousal support is appropriate. For example, one spouse may have supported the other through graduate or professional school. The supporting spouse may have expected that both would benefit from the educated spouse's enhanced earning capacity, but the marriage ends before any material benefits were earned.

The supporting spouse does not need rehabilitation because that spouse has worked during the entire marriage, and there is no significant property to be distributed because marital resources went to the educational effort. In cases such as this, the courts may award this new compensation, usually as periodic payments, to the supporting spouse. The amount paid may be based upon the contributions of the supporting spouse to the educational expenses and general support of the spouse who leaves the marriage with an advanced degree, or it may be for a portion of the increased earnings of the educated spouse. The courts may change or end such payments if the expected increased earnings do not occur, but the payments are not ended by remarriage of the recipient. These types of payments sometimes are called "reimbursement alimony" or "alimony in gross."

## Q. Does the law help newly divorced spouses who must now get their own health insurance?

**A.** Yes. A federal law passed in the 1980s requires most employer-sponsored group health plans to offer divorced spouses of covered workers continued coverage at group rates for as long as three years. The divorced spouse of a worker must pay for the coverage, but the coverage is available. Health care reforms under consideration by Congress in 1993 and 1994 also may make health insurance easier to obtain.

## Custody

### Q. What is child custody?

**A.** Child custody is the right and duty to care for a child on a day-to-day basis and to make major decisions about the child. In sole custody arrangements, one parent takes care of the child most of the time and makes major decisions about the child. In joint custody arrangements, both parents share in making major decisions, and both parents also might spend substantial amounts of time with the child. Joint custody will be described in more detail later in this section.

### Q. How do courts decide custody?

**A.** If the parents cannot agree on custody of their child, the court decides custody according to "the best interest of the child." Determining the best interest of the child involves consideration of many factors.

### Q. Do mothers automatically receive custody?

**A.** No. Under the laws of almost all states, mothers and fathers have an equal right to custody. Courts are not supposed to assume that a child is automatically better off with the mother or the father. In a contested custody case, both the father and mother have an equal burden of proving to the court that it is in the best interest of the child that the child be in his or her custody. There are a few states (mostly in the South) that have laws providing that if

everything else is equal, the mother may be preferred; but in those states, many fathers have been successful in obtaining custody, even if the mother is a fit parent.

### Q. How have the laws changed in deciding custody disputes between mothers and fathers?

**A.** The law has swung like a pendulum. From the early history of our country until the mid-1800s, fathers were favored for custody in the event of a divorce. Children were viewed as similar to property. If a husband and wife divorced, the man usually received the property—such as the farm or the family business. He also received custody of the children. Some courts viewed custody to the father as a natural extension of the father's duty to support and educate his children.

By the mid-1800s, most states switched to a strong preference for the mother—sometimes referred to as the "Tender Years Doctrine." Under the Tender Years Doctrine, the mother received custody as long as she was minimally fit. In other words, in a contested custody case, a mother would receive custody unless there was something very wrong with her, such as she abused the child or suffered from mental illness or alcoholism. The parenting skills of the father were not relevant. This automatic preference for mothers continued until the 1960s or 1980s, depending on the state. Then principles of equality took over, at least in the law books of almost all states.

### Q. Are judges prejudiced in favor of mothers or fathers in deciding custody cases?

**A.** Although judges are supposed to be neutral in custody disputes between mothers and fathers, many observers believe some judges are biased. Some judges, based on their background or personal experience, may have a deep-seated belief that mothers can take care of children

# Custody Criteria

| | Statutory Guidelines | Children's Wishes | Joint Custody Laws | Cooperative Parent | Domestic Violence | Health | Attorney or GAL for Child |
|---|---|---|---|---|---|---|---|
| Alabama | X | | X | | | | |
| Alaska | X | X | X | X | X | X | X |
| Arizona | X | X | X | X | X | X | X |
| Arkansas | | | | | | | |
| California | X | X | X | | X | | X |
| Colorado | X | X | X | X | X | X | X |
| Connecticut | | X | X | | | | X |
| Delaware | X | X | | | | X | X |
| D.C. | X | X | | | X | X | X |
| Florida | X | X | X | | X | | X |
| Georgia | X | X | X | | | | X |
| Hawaii | X | X | | | X | | X |
| Idaho | X | X | X | | X | X | |
| Illinois | X | X | X | X | X | X | X |
| Indiana | X | X | X | | | | X |
| Iowa | X | X | X | X | X | X | X |
| Kansas | X | X | X | X | X | X | |
| Kentucky | X | X | X | | X | | X |
| Louisiana | X | X | X | | X | | |
| Maine | X | X | | | X | | X |
| Maryland | | | X | | X | | X |
| Massachusetts | | | X | | X | | X |
| Michigan | X | X | X | X | X | | X |
| Minnesota | X | X | X | | X | | X |
| Mississippi | X | | X | | | | |
| Missouri | X | X | X | | X | | X |
| Montana | X | X | X | | X | | X |
| Nebraska | X | X | X | | | X | X |
| Nevada | X | X | X | | X | | X |
| New Hampshire | X | X | X | | X | | X |
| New Jersey | X | X | X | X | X | X | X |
| New Mexico | X | X | X | X | X | X | X |
| New York | | X | X | | | | X |
| North Carolina | | X | X | | | | |
| North Dakota | X | X | | | X | X | X |
| Ohio | X | X | X | | X | X | X |
| Oklahoma | X | X | X | | X | | |
| Oregon | X | | X | | X | | |
| Pennsylvania | | | X | X | X | | X |
| Rhode Island | | | X | | X | | X |
| South Carolina | | X | X | | | | |
| South Dakota | | X | X | | | | X |
| Tennessee | | X | X | | | | |
| Texas | | X | X | | X | X | X |
| Utah | X | X | X | | | | X |
| Vermont | X | | X | | | | X |
| Virginia | X | | X | | | X | X |
| Washington | X | X | | | X | X | X |
| West Virginia | | X | X | | X | | |
| Wisconsin | X | X | X | X | X | X | |
| Wyoming | | X | | | X | X | |

SOURCE: *Family Law Quarterly*, Vol. 27, No. 4, Winter, 1994, published by the ABA Family Law Section.

better than fathers and that fathers have little experience in parenting. Conversely, some judges may believe that fathers automatically are better at raising boys—particularly older boys. Judges with such biases may apply these views when they decide custody cases, although they are supposed to base decisions on the facts of each case and not on automatic presumptions. As a group, judges are less biased in deciding custody cases today than in times past, although bias probably still exists.

### Q. What is the most important factor in deciding custody?

**A.** That will vary with the facts of each case. If one parent in a custody dispute has a major problem with alcoholism or mental illness or has abused the child, that could be the deciding factor. If neither parent has engaged in unusually bad conduct, the most important factor often is which parent has been primarily responsible for taking care of the child on a day-to-day basis. Some states refer to this as "the primary caretaker factor." If one parent can show that he or she took care of the child most of the time, that parent usually will be favored for custody, particularly if the child is young (under approximately eight years old). Use of this factor promotes continuity in the child's life and gives custody of the child to the more experienced parent who has shown the dedication to take care of the child's day-to-day needs. If both parents have actively cared for the child or if the child is older, the factor is less crucial, although it is still considered.

### Q. May a child decide where he or she wants to live?

**A.** The wishes of a child can be an important factor in deciding custody. The weight a court gives the child's wishes will depend on the child's age, maturity, and quality of reasons. Some judges do not even listen to the preferences of a child under the age of seven and instead assume the child is too young to express an informed preference. A court is more likely to follow the preferences of an older child, although the court will want to assess the quality of the child's reasons. If a child wants to be with the parent who offers more freedom and less discipline, a judge is not likely to honor the preference. A child whose reasons are vague or whose answers seem coached also may not have his or her preferences followed.

On the other hand, if a child expresses a good reason related to the child's best interest—such as genuinely feeling closer to one parent than the other—the court probably will follow the preference. Although most states treat a child's wishes as only one factor to be considered, two states (Georgia and West Virginia) declare that a child of fourteen has an "absolute right" to choose the parent with whom the child will live, as long as the parent is fit.

### Q. How does a judge find out about the child's preferences?

**A.** Often judges will talk to the child in private—in the judge's chambers rather than in open court. In some cases, the judge may appoint a mental health professional, such as a psychiatrist, psychologist, or social worker, to talk to the child and report to the court.

### Q. If a parent has a sexual relationship outside of marriage, how does that impact on a court's decision on custody?

**A.** That depends on the law of the state and the facts of the case. In most states, affairs or nonmarital sexual relations are not supposed to be a factor in deciding custody unless it can be shown that the relationship has harmed the child. If, for example, one parent has had a discreet affair during the marriage, that normally would not be a significant factor in deciding custody. Similarly, if after the marriage is over, a parent lives with a person to whom he or she is not married, the live-in relationship by itself normally is not a major factor in deciding custody. In the case of live-in relationships, the quality of the relationship between the child and the live-in partner can be an important factor in a custody dispute.

If the parent's nonmarital sexual relationship or relationships have placed the child in embarrassing situations or caused significant stress to the child, then the relationship would be a negative factor against the parent involved in the relationship. In a few states, courts are more inclined to automatically assume that a parent's nonmarital sexual relationship is harmful to the child. As with the issue of a preference for mothers in custody cases, the issue of a parent's sexual conduct can be one in which individual judges may have personal biases that influence their decisions.

### Q. If a parent is homosexual, what impact does that have on custody?

**A.** The impact varies dramatically from state to state. Courts in many states seem more willing to assume harmful impact to a child from a parent's homosexual relationship than from a heterosexual relationship. On the other hand, some states treat homosexual and heterosexual relationships equally and will not consider the relationship to be a significant factor unless specific harm to the child is shown. A homosexual parent (or a heterosexual parent) seeking custody will have a stronger case if he or she presents evidence that the child does not witness sexual contact between the partners and that the child likes the parent's partner.

### Q. If one parent is trying to undermine the child's relationship with the other parent, how does that affect custody?

**A.** Most states declare a specific policy favoring an ongoing, healthy relationship between the child and both parents. If one parent is trying to undermine the child's relationship with the other parent, that is a negative factor against the parent who is trying to hurt the relationship. If other factors are close to equal, a court may grant custody to the parent who is more likely to encourage an open and good relationship with the other parent.

### Q. If one parent is religious and the other is not, may the court favor the more religious parent?

**A.** Normally, no. Under the First Amendment to the United States Constitution, both parents have a right to practice religion or not practice religion as they see fit. A judge is not supposed to make value judgments about whether a child is better off with or without religious training or about which religion is better. If a child has been brought up with particular religious beliefs and religious activities are important to the child, a court might favor promoting continuity in the child's life, but the court should not favor religion *per se*. In some cases, a parent's unusual or nonmainstream religious activities may become an issue. Normally, a court should not consider a parent's unusual religious practices in deciding custody or visitation unless specific harm to the child is shown.

### Q. Can custody decisions be changed?

**A.** Yes. A court may always change child custody arrangements to meet the changing needs of the growing child and to respond to changes in the parents' lives. A parent seeking to change custody through the court usually must show that the conditions have changed substantially since the last custody order. The parent also must show that changing the custody arrangement would be better for the child. Sometimes the parent must show that not changing custody would be detrimental to the child.

## Visitation

#### Q. If a parent does not receive custody, how much visitation is he or she likely to receive?

**A.** That will vary with the desires of the parents and the inclinations of a judge. A common amount of visitation, however, is: every other weekend (Friday evening through Sunday); a weeknight (for dinner); half of the child's spring breaks; alternate major holidays; and several weeks in the summer. If parents live far apart and regular weekend visitation is not feasible, it is common to allocate more summer vacation and school holidays to the noncustodial parent. For parents who do not like the term "visitation" or "custody," it is possible to draft a custody and visitation order that leaves out those terms and just describes the times at which the child will be with each parent.

#### Q. Under what circumstances may the custodial parent deny the other parent visitation?

**A.** The parent with custody must have a good reason to deny the other parent visitation. For example, if the noncustodial parent has molested the child, is likely to kipnap the child, or is likely to use illegal drugs or excessive amounts of alcohol while caring for the child, a court probably will deny visitation or restrict visitation. If visitation is restricted, visitation might be allowed only under supervision, such as at a social service agency or in the company of a responsible relative.

## Joint Custody

#### Q. What is joint custody?

**A.** Joint custody—sometimes referred to as "shared custody" or "shared parenting"—has two parts: joint legal custody and joint physical

custody. A joint custody order can have one or both parts.

#### Q. What is joint legal custody?

**A.** Joint legal custody refers to both parents sharing in major decisions affecting the child. The custody order may describe the issues on which the parents must share decisions. The most common issues are school, health care, and religious training (although each parent has a right to expose the child to his or her religious beliefs). Other issues on which the parents may make joint decisions include: extracurricular activities, summer camp, age for dating or driving, and methods of discipline. Many joint custody orders specify procedures parents should follow in the event they cannot agree on an issue. The most common procedure is for the parents to consult a mediator. Mediation will be discussed later in this chapter on page 92.

#### Q. What is joint physical custody?

**A.** Joint physical custody refers to the time the child spends with each parent. The amount of time is flexible. The length of time could be relatively moderate, such as every other weekend with one parent; or the amount of time could be equally divided between the parents. Parents who opt for equal time-sharing have come up with many alternatives such as: alternate two-day periods; equal division of the week; alternate weeks; alternate months; and alternate six-month periods. If the child is attending school and spends a substantial amount of time with both parents, it usually is best for the child if the parents live relatively close to each other. Some parents, on an interim basis, have kept the child in a single home and the parents rotate staying in the home with the child.

#### Q. Are courts required to order joint custody if a parent asks for it?

**A.** No. In most states, joint custody is an option—just as sole custody is an option. Courts may order joint custody or sole custody according to what the judge thinks is in the best interest of the child. In some states (eleven in 1993), legislatures have declared a preference for joint custody. That usually means the courts are supposed to order joint custody if a parent asks for it, unless there is a good reason for not ordering joint custody. The most common reason for not ordering joint custody is the parents' inability to cooperate. Courts are concerned that a child will be caught in the middle of a tug of war if joint custody is ordered for parents who do not cooperate with each other. Parents who do not cooperate also will have trouble with sole custody and visitation, but the frequency of conflicts may be somewhat less since they will need to confer less often on major decisions and the logistics of a joint physical custody arrangement.

### Q. What are the pros and cons of joint physical custody?

**A.** Supporters of joint physical custody stress that it is in the best interest of children to protect and improve their relationship with both parents. They believe shared custody is the only way to make sure that the children do not "lose" a parent because of the divorce. Critics fear that shared-time parenting is unworkable and worry about instability and potential conflict for the child. The success of joint physical custody may depend on the child. Some researchers have said that children who are relatively relaxed and laid back will do better with joint physical custody than children who are tense and become easily upset by changes in routine. Because joint physical custody usually requires keeping two homes for the child, joint physical custody often costs more than sole custody.

As with joint legal custody, the best forecast of success usually is whether the parents

shared most of the child care when their marriage was working. It is usually easiest on the children to make the custodial arrangement after the divorce similar to the parental pattern before the separation. However, children's needs for each parent change as they grow. Parents probably should avoid locking in any parenting plan forever. Rather, they should plan to review the custody arrangement as the children grow and the children's needs change.

## Child Support

### Q. How do courts set child support?

**A.** Under federal law, all states must have guidelines by which courts determine child support. The guidelines were established because variations in the amounts of support set in similar circumstances were too wide and because levels of child support were considered too low. The guidelines are formulas that consider the income of the parties, the number of children, and perhaps some other factors. The formulas are based on studies of how much families ordinarily spend for child-rearing. They try to approximate the proportion of parental income that would have been spent for child support if the family had not been divided by divorce. Courts plug numbers into the formula and come up with an amount of support that should be paid for the child or children. The parties can argue that because of special circumstances, a court should order greater or less support than the guideline amount.

### Q. When working with guideline formulas, how are the parents' incomes determined?

**A.** Many states use a parent's net income. That means the gross income (total income from wages, investments, and other sources) minus federal and state income taxes, Social Security tax, Medicare tax, health insurance,

# Child Support Guidelines

| | Income Share | Percent of Income | Extraordinary Medical Formula | Child-Care Formula | Post-Majority Support |
|---|---|---|---|---|---|
| Alabama | X | | | | X |
| Alaska | | X | | | |
| Arizona | X | | | | |
| Arkansas | | X | | | |
| California | X | | X | X | |
| Colorado | X | | X | X | X |
| Connecticut | X | | | | |
| Delaware | | | X | X | |
| D.C. | | | | | |
| Florida | X | | | | |
| Georgia | | X | | | X |
| Hawaii | | | X | X | |
| Idaho | X | | | | X |
| Illinois | | X | | | X |
| Indiana | X | | X | X | |
| Iowa | X | | X | X | |
| Kansas | X | | X | X | |
| Kentucky | X | | | | |
| Louisiana | X | | X | X | |
| Maine | X | | X | X | |
| Maryland | X | | X | X | |
| Massachusetts | | | | | |
| Michigan | X | | X | X | |
| Minnesota | | X | | | |
| Mississippi | | X | | | X |
| Missouri | X | | | | |
| Montana | | | X | X | |
| Nebraska | X | | | | |
| Nevada | | X | X | X | |
| New Hampshire | | X | | | |
| New Jersey | X | | X | X | |
| New Mexico | X | | X | X | |
| New York | | X | X | X | |
| North Carolina | X | | X | X | |
| North Dakota | | X | | | |
| Ohio | X | | | | |
| Oklahoma | X | | | | |
| Oregon | X | | X | X | |
| Pennsylvania | X | | | | |
| Rhode Island | X | | | | X |
| South Carolina | X | | | | |
| South Dakota | X | | | | X |
| Tennessee | | X | | | |
| Texas | | X | | | |
| Utah | X | | X | X | |
| Vermont | X | | X | X | |
| Virginia | X | | X | X | X |
| Washington | X | | X | X | |
| West Virginia | | | X | X | |
| Wisconsin | | X | | | |
| Wyoming | X | | | | |

SOURCE: *Family Law Quarterly*, Vol. 27, No. 4, Winter, 1994, published by the ABA Family Law Section.

and perhaps union dues. Some states base their guidelines on gross income rather than net income.

For self-employed persons, the determination of income may be complex. Courts will allow deductions of reasonable business expenses before determining net income. But courts may disallow unusually high business expenses and depreciation that reduce income artificially without hurting the parent's cash flow. Thus, certain expenses that are deductible for tax purposes may not be deductible from income for the purpose of setting child support.

### Q. How much child support should a noncustodial parent expect to pay?

**A.** That question is difficult to answer precisely because guidelines vary between states and because courts may depart from the guidelines. But some examples can be given.

### Q. What is an example of a guideline for child support based on the income of only the noncustodial parent?

**A.** Here is the "percentage of obligor's income" guideline that was in effect in Illinois in June 1993:

| Number of children | Percent of supporting party's net income |
| --- | --- |
| 1 | 20% |
| 2 | 25% |
| 3 | 32% |
| 4 | 40% |
| 5 | 45% |
| 6 or more | 50% |

Under this guideline, if a noncustodial parent ("supporting party") had a net income of $40,000, the annual level of child support would be $8,000 for one child; $10,000 for two children; $12,800 for three children, etc.

### Q. What's an example of a support formula based on the incomes of both parents?

**A.** Support guidelines based on the incomes of both parents often are referred to as "income shares models." Under these guidelines, the court first adds the net income (or in some states, the gross income) of both parents. Then the court consults a long table—or computer program—that assesses the total obligation of support as a percentage of the combined incomes and the number of children. Generally, the percentage drops as the combined incomes rise, on the assumption that financially well-off parents need to spend a smaller portion of their incomes on their children than parents who are less well-off. The court multiplies the combined incomes by the percent figure and obtains a dollar amount that the child or children are considered to need for support. Then the responsibility to pay that support is divided between the parents in proportion to each parent's incomes.

Here is an example using Colorado's child support schedules. Assume a father and mother have two children and a combined annual gross income of $60,000—$40,000 earned by the father and $20,000 earned by the mother. The schedules put the guideline amount for support at $11,508 per year ($959 per month). Since the father earns two-thirds of the parties' combined income, he would pay two-thirds of the children's support ($7,672 a year) and the mother would pay one-third ($3,836). If one parent had primary custody of the children, the other probably would make a cash payment to that parent. The parent with primary custody probably would not make a cash payment as such, but would be assumed to be spending that amount on the children. Alternatively, the parents might set up a checking account for the children's expenses and both would deposit their respective shares into the account.

**Q. What are reasons for ordering more support than the guideline amount?**

**A.** This will vary from state to state and will depend, in part, on what expenses the guidelines include and do not include. But some common reasons for giving support above the base guideline amount include: child-care expenses, high medical or dental expenses of the child that are not covered by insurance, and voluntary unemployment or underemployment of the parent who is supposed to pay support. Expenses for summer camps and private schools also might be a basis for setting higher support levels, particularly if private schools or summer camps were part of the family's lifestyle during the marriage.

**Q. What are reasons for setting support below the guideline amount?**

**A.** Again, this can vary from state to state, but common reasons for setting support below the guideline amounts include support obligations from earlier marriages and large debts to pay off (particularly if the debts are related to family expenses). If the support guidelines are based on the income of only the noncustodial parent and if the custodial parent has an unusually high income, then the noncustodial parent can argue that the custodial parent's income is a reason for setting support below the guidelines.

Also, if the guidelines do not have a cap or maximum level of income to which they apply, the very high income of the noncustodial parent is a basis for setting support below the guidelines. For example, using the Illinois guidelines described earlier, if a noncustodial parent has three children and an annual net income of $200,000, that parent can argue that the children do not need the $64,000 per year that the guidelines call for.

**Q. What is the effect on child support if the parents have joint custody of the children?**

**A.** That depends on the nature of the joint custody arrangement. If the parents have joint *legal* custody (by which they share in making major decisions regarding the child), that will have little effect on child support. If the parents have only joint legal custody, one parent still has primary custody of the child and handles payments of most of the child's day-to-day expenses. The custodial parent's expenses for the child have not been reduced by the joint custody arrangement. If the parents have joint *physical* custody and the child spends a substantial amount of time with each parent, support might be set at less than the guideline amount since both parents are likely to handle day-to-day expenses for the child. (Parents, however, will need to coordinate payments on major expenses such as camp, school, clothing, and insurance.)

**Q. Is child support paid while the child is with the noncustodial parent for summer vacation or long breaks?**

**A.** In most cases, yes. Courts figure that many major expenses for the benefit of the child—such as rent, mortgage, utilities, clothes, and insurance—have to be paid whether the child is with the custodial parent or not. So, usually, a full support payment is due, even if the child is with the noncustodial parent. On the other hand, the parties themselves (or the court) are free to agree on payments in different amounts during vacation periods when the child is with the noncustodial parent. The lower amount for vacation periods with the noncustodial parent might reflect savings to the custodial parent for food expenses or child care.

**Q. Do divorced parents have to pay for their child's college expenses?**

**A.** That depends on the state and the parties' agreement. Courts in some states will require parents to pay for a child's college expenses (assuming the parents can afford it and the child is a good enough student to benefit from college). Courts in other states note that married parents are not required to pay for their child's college expenses, and, therefore, divorced parents are not required to do so either. Regardless of the state's law on compulsory payment of college expenses, the mother and father can agree as part of their divorce settlement to pay for these costs. Courts usually will enforce those agreements.

### Q. How is child support enforced if a parent does not pay?

**A.** The state and federal governments have a variety of techniques for enforcing payments of child support. The most common is a wage deduction, by which the employer sends a portion of the parent's wages to a state agency which then sends the money to the parent who has custody of the child. Beginning in 1994, all child support orders require an automatic wage deduction unless the parties have agreed otherwise or unless a court waives the automatic order. The state also can intercept the federal and state tax refunds of persons who have not paid support. Liens can be placed on property, such as real estate and automobiles. A parent who has not paid support can be held in contempt of court, which may result in a fine or a jail term. State's attorneys or district attorneys may help with collection of child support, though their efficiency varies from district to district.

Child support enforcement is a matter of increasing federal concern. Under the Child Support Recovery Act of 1992, it now is a federal crime to willfully fail to pay child support to a child who resides in another state if the past-due amount has been unpaid for over one year or exceeds $5,000. Punishments under the federal law can include fine and imprisonment.

A parent may not reduce child support payments without a court order: the unpaid amounts will accumulate as a debt, even if a court later decides that there was a good reason for the reduction.

### Q. To what extent is child support not paid?

**A.** In 1989 (the last year the federal government comprehensively surveyed the issue), there were about 10 million mothers living with a minor child or children whose father was not living with them. Only 58 percent of those mothers received an order of child support. (Many women who did not receive orders of support had their children out of wedlock.) Of the mothers who had a court order of support, approximately 50 percent received payment in full, 25 percent received partial payment, and 25 percent received no payments.

### Q. What legal remedies are available if a child is abducted by a parent?

**A.** Abduction of a child by a parent is a crime under federal law and the laws of most states. Local police, state police, and in some cases the FBI can help in locating missing children. Parents who abduct their children also can be forced to pay the expenses incurred by the other parent in trying to find and return the child. To recover such expenses, a parent usually would need the help of a private attorney.

## Grandparents and Stepparents

### Q. What are grandparents' rights to visitation?

**A.** Though their son or daughter is divorced, grandparents probably still have the right to a continuing relationship with their grandchildren. If their son or daughter does not have custody and the custodial parent denies

## A STEPPARENT'S DUTIES AND RIGHTS

*The responsibilities of a stepparent depend on state law. A stepparent usually is not liable for a spouse's children from another marriage, unless the stepparent has adopted the children. Until then, the children's biological parents are liable for their support. Some states, however, make stepparents liable for the stepchildren's support as long as the stepparent and stepchildren are living together.*

*A stepparent who does not adopt a spouse's children normally may not claim custody of them if the marriage ends in divorce, although some states allow a stepparent to seek visitation. Stepchildren usually do not share in the estate of a stepparent, unless the stepparent has provided for the stepchildren in a will. However, unmarried stepchildren under eighteen may receive supplemental retirement benefits or survivor's benefits under Social Security.*

grandparents for a significant period of time, such as one year.

A few courts and legislatures have extended the right to grandparent visitation in cases in which the parents are not divorced and are still living together. One state supreme court, however, has held that such visitation is an unconstitutional intrusion into the parents' family privacy.

Before ordering visitation for grandparents, a court must find that the visitation is in the best interest of the child. If the child is placed in a particularly stressful situation because of the visitation, the visitation might not be ordered, or if visitation already is underway, it may be stopped.

### Q. May courts award grandparents custody of their grandchildren?

**A.** Yes, but usually only if neither parent wants the children or if the parents are unfit. Courts examine such factors as the grandparents' age, general health, and ability to care for the children. Courts will not deny grandparents custody because of their age, as long as they are healthy.

Some custody disputes between grandparents and parents arise when the grandparents have been raising their grandchildren for a considerable length of time under an informal arrangement. The grandparents may have become the "psychological parents" of the grandchildren by the time the parent or parents seek to regain custody. In this circumstance, courts in many states will allow the grandparents to retain custody, even if the parents are fit.

## Mediation

### Q. What is mediation?

**A.** Mediation is a process in which the parties to a divorce (or some other dispute) try to

the grandparents access to the grandchildren, the grandparents may ask the court to grant them visitation. Grandparents may also have a right to visit with the children of their deceased child, even though the surviving parent prefers that they not. Some states also will give grandparents visitation if the child had lived with the

resolve their disagreements outside of court with the help of a mediator. The mediator cannot force a settlement, but tries to assist the parties to clarify their interests and work out their own solution. In divorce actions, mediators often are involved in custody and visitation disputes. They also can handle property disputes, support disputes, and other issues. If the parties resolve their disagreements through mediation, the attorneys for one or both of the parties still may be involved in finalizing and approving the agreement.

### Q. Is mediation mandatory in divorce actions?

**A.** That depends on the rules of the local court. Many courts do require mediation of custody and visitation disputes—the mother and father must talk with a court-appointed mediator to try to resolve the problem before putting their case before a judge. The mediator cannot force a resolution, but the parties can be told to try mediation before coming to court.

### Q. What is the professional background of divorce mediators?

**A.** Most mediators are either mental health professionals or attorneys. Many mediators, particularly those associated with court mediation services, have degrees in social work or psychology. Private mediators (which the parties may choose to hire) often are attorneys, although many are mental health professionals. Mediators who are mental health professionals are not serving as therapists, and mediators who are attorneys are not serving as attorneys. Instead, they are professionals who are trying to help two (or more) people work out their differences.

### Q. What are the advantages of mediation?

**A.** Mediation often is cheaper and quicker than taking a case before a judge. A good medi-

ator also can help the parties build their problem-solving skills, and that can help them to avoid later disputes. Most people who settle their cases through mediation leave the process feeling better than they would have if they had gone through a bitter court fight.

### Q. What are the disadvantages of mediation?

**A.** Mediation can be a problem if one or both parties are withholding information. For example, if the purpose of mediation is to settle

---

**WHAT HAPPENS WHEN ONE SPOUSE DIES?**

If the spouse left a will—which is always a good idea—his or her property should be distributed according to his wishes. But if the will or a premarital agreement makes no provision for the surviving spouse, a court may invalidate it and assign at least some of the deceased person's assets to the survivor.

If there is no will, the property will be distributed according to the laws of the state, with a certain percentage to the surviving spouse, a certain percentage to surviving children, and perhaps some for surviving parents, brothers, and sisters.

See the chapter "Estate Planning," beginning on page 653.

financial issues and one party is hiding assets or income, the other party might be better off with an attorney who can vigorously investigate the matter. Mediators usually are good at exploring the parties' needs, goals, and possible solutions, but they do not have the legal resources of an attorney to look for hidden information.

Another problem with mediation can arise if one party is very passive and likely to be bulldozed by the other. In that situation, the mediated agreement might be lopsided in favor of the stronger party. A good mediator, however, will see to it that a weaker party's needs are expressed and protected. Some mediators may refuse to proceed with mediation if it looks as though one side will take improper advantage of the other.

Some professionals think that mediation is not appropriate if the case involves domestic violence. One concern is that mediation will just give a forum in which the abuser can harm the victim again. Another concern is that victims of physical abuse are not able to adequately express and protect their own interests. However, other professionals believe that disputes in families with a history of domestic violence still can be mediated.

Finally, if mediation does not succeed, the parties may have wasted time and money on mediation and still face the expenses of a trial.

## WHERE TO GET MORE INFORMATION

### Adoption

Every state has a state adoption officer. These officials usually have offices in the state capital. The state government information operator can help you locate the officer for your state. For information about agency adoptions, contact the Child Welfare League of America, 440 First Street, NW, Suite 310, Washington, DC 20001-2085. Its telephone number is (202) 638-2952. You also may wish to contact the National Committee for Adoption, 1930 17th Street, NW, Washington, DC 20009-6027. Its telephone number is (202) 328-1200. For information on independent adoption, check with your state or city bar association. Ask if independent adoptions are legal in your state. Also ask if the bar association will refer you to lawyers who handle independent adoptions.

### Battered Spouses

Many communities offer shelters for battered spouses and their children. Details on these shelters are available from the police, crisis intervention services, hospitals, churches, family or conciliation courts, local newspapers, or women's organizations. A resource is the National Coalition Against Domestic Violence, P.O. Box 18749, Denver, CO 80218-0749. The telephone number of this national information and referral center is (303) 839-1852. The local or state chapter of the National Organization for Women (N.O.W.) also should be able to provide information to help battered spouses.

## Child Support

Every state has Regional Child Support Enforcement Units that help custodial parents establish and enforce child support orders and locate absent parents. (These offices are sometimes called IV-D Offices because they are required by Chapter IV-D of the Social Security Act.) You can locate the offices by looking under county or state government listings in the telephone book or by asking the state government switchboard. Another resource is the Office of Child Support Enforcement Reference Center, Office of Child Support Enforcement, 6110 Executive Boulevard, Rockville, MD 20852. This office can help parents find their state's enforcement officers.

## Credit and Bankruptcy

Two chapters in this publication discuss these topics: "Consumer Credit," beginning on page 239, and "Consumer Bankruptcy," beginning on page 277. The "Consumer Credit" chapter also lists many free publications.

## Divorce

Most local public libraries offer books written about divorce. Ask the librarians for help.

## Mediation

A source for information on mediation is the Academy of Family Mediators, 1500 S. Highway 100, Suite 355, Golden Valley, MN 55416. Its telephone number is (612) 525-8670. The academy lists family mediators in every state by training and experience. Local courts also may have information regarding mediation services.

## Missing Children

Various agencies can offer help in finding children who are missing. They include:

> Missing Children Help Center, 410 Ware Boulevard, Suite 400, Tampa, FL 33619; Telephone: (813) 623-KIDS or (800) USA-KIDS (toll-free).

or

> National Center for Missing and Exploited Children, 2101 Wilson Boulevard, Suite 550, Arlington, VA 22201. Telephone: (800) 843-5678 (toll-free).

## Pensions

One resource on pensions is the U.S. Department of Labor. The address is: Pension and Welfare Benefits Administration, U.S. Department of Labor, Division of Technical Assistance and Inquiries, Room N5658, 200 Constitution Avenue, NW, Washington, DC 20210.

The Pension Rights Center informs employees of their rights involving pensions. This private organization also offers booklets that explain related topics. Write to: Pension Rights Center, 918 16th Street, NW, Suite 704, Washington, DC 20006. Or call (202) 296-3776.

## Social Security

Your local Social Security Administration office can provide information and literature on benefits. You can find its address and telephone number in your local telephone directory—usually under "U.S. Government."

## Taxes

The basic resource on federal income taxes is the Internal Revenue Service (IRS). You can find your regional office in the phone book under "U.S. Government." You may also wish to contact an accountant or a tax lawyer.

Free publications on family taxes available from the IRS include *Community Property and the Federal Income Tax* (Publication 555), *Tax Information for Divorced or Separated Individuals* (Publication 504), and *Tax Rules for Children and Dependents* (Publication 929).

## Wills and Estate Planning

The "Estate Planning" chapter beginning on page 653 discusses these topics and lists related resources.

## Women's Issues

The Legal Defense and Education Fund of the National Organization for Women (N.O.W.), 99 Hudson Street, New York, NY 10013 will send you a free list of publications from N.O.W.

# CHAPTER FOUR

■

# Buying and Selling a Home

# INTRODUCTION

A HOME IS THE LARGEST PURCHASE most Americans will ever make. It's surprising, then, that people sometimes plunge into buying or selling a home with less care than they give to buying or selling a car.

If you are one of the millions of Americans about to buy or sell a home, it's important to understand the ramifications of the decisions you will make. For example, state and federal law, the economy, your personal preferences, your financial situation, the prevailing real estate market, current mortgage rates, and tax considerations, are among the many factors that affect you as either a buyer or seller. You will also need to work with a variety of people—attorneys, lenders, home inspectors, appraisers, and insurance agents, to name a few. In short, buying and selling a home is not the simple matter it might appear.

Whether you are buying your first home or selling your tenth, you will want to make sure that you understand how the law affects your decisions. This chapter begins with questions related to buying and selling a home. It's a good idea to become familiar with the legal aspects of both the buying and selling side of the process. This is particularly true if it has been a while since you bought or sold a home.

Practices and laws change. You will want to be aware of how these changes affect your responsibilities as buyer or seller, as the case may be.

Remember, someone must be willing to buy a home before you can sell it, and vice versa. The sale will involve negotiation and will have legal consequences. Like any other contract negotiation, it's a good idea to understand the goals of both parties in the transaction.

## GETTING STARTED

**Q. Why is the purchase or sale of a home more complicated than buying or selling some other object, such as an expensive car?**

**A.** Taxes, financing considerations, and other factors affect the transactions involving such items as cars and boats. Under the law, however, these items are considered personal property as distinguished from real estate, also known as real property. Personal property and real estate have different characteristics and, as a general rule, the law treats each type of property differently.

Personal property is usually easily moved and, in many cases, is owned for a relatively short period of time. Possession of personal property also is a strong indicator of ownership. With real estate, on the other hand, the property cannot be moved and possession does not necessarily mean ownership. To illustrate, unless property is fenced in, it may be difficult to distinguish a neighbor's property from your own. And, while you may own real estate, you may not have possession of it, if, for example, you are renting the property to someone else.

Other factors that distinguish real estate from personal property are: many different people can have an interest in the same real property; foreclosing on real property is much more difficult than repossessing a car; and real estate is taxed differently than personal property.

## ELEMENTS OF REAL ESTATE

*An ownership interest in real estate is illustrated by the following examples:*

- *the land and everything under it, including minerals and water;*
- *anything of value on the land such as crops or timber;*
- *the airspace over the land;*
- *improvements on the land such as buildings, for example a garage, barn, or fence.*

*Ownership of these elements may be separate or shared and may also be subject to legal claims or liens. (A lien is a claim against property representing an unpaid debt of the owner or an unpaid judgment entered against the owner by a court of law.)*

*Here's an example of how several different persons can have a legally recognized interest in the same real estate. A farmer might lease land owned by a school district. While the district owns the land, the farmer owns the crops he or she plants on the land. The district also might have sold mineral rights to the land to yet another person.*

## WHAT IS A HOME?

*A home is more than a single-family dwelling built on an individual parcel of land. Townhouses, condominiums, and cooperatives are also homes. Each one of these types of homes has unique features which are discussed later in this chapter.*

costs as they get older. Other benefits include favorable tax considerations and more control over one's personal living environment than might be possible in the context of renting.

A common view of prospective home buyers is to think of a home solely or, at least, primarily as an investment. This view, however, may be mistaken. There is no reason to assume that home prices will always rise. As many owners have discovered in the last five years or so, home prices can fall, sometimes dramatically. And, depending on the home prices in your area of the country, renting may be far more economical than buying, particularly if the renter invests the difference between a mortgage payment and rental payment. Nonetheless, while the decision to buy a home is not just an investment decision, it may be wise to give it the same care.

**Q. What is a "buyer's market"?**

**A.** A buyer's market occurs when home sales are slow. Here are some of the ways to determine if the home market in your area is a buyer's market:

- Is it taking longer and longer to sell homes?
- Are foreclosures increasing?
- Are there large reductions in home prices?

**Q. Why should I buy a home?**

**A.** Most people buy a home because they want to own it and, thus, reduce their living

- Has there been a decline in the number of building permits issued?
- Is unemployment increasing?

These factors indicate a "soft" market for home sales. A soft market tends to make sellers anxious and puts buyers in a stronger position than sellers. In a soft market, buyers have many homes to choose from and can demand special considerations from sellers.

### Q. What is a "seller's market"?

**A.** The best time to sell your home is when homes are selling fast, there are few homes on the market, and the local economy is good. These are all characteristic of a seller's market and operate to move home prices upward. Sellers can and do demand high prices for their homes and often dictate the terms of the contract. In a seller's market, sellers often receive several competing offers and are in a position to sell quickly, perhaps in a matter of days or weeks.

If you are a potential seller in a seller's market, you're well situated to sell quickly and at your price. On the other hand, if you're a potential buyer in a seller's market, you'll want to be particularly careful that you don't rush into a decision that you may later regret. The best way to avoid this situation is to do your homework to ensure that you know what you want and what you can afford.

---

## MEETING THE PLAYERS

### Q. Who is involved in a real estate transaction?

**A.** Although it's possible for a home to be bought and sold strictly between principals—the buyer and seller—this rarely happens today. Usually, a home buyer will want to use the services of a real estate agent, an attorney, and a home inspector to check out the property. To obtain financing, home buyers will consult the staff of one or more lending institutions. They also may consult with a financial planner or accountant about financing and an insurance agent to obtain home-owner's insurance.

While some sellers choose to sell their home without the services of a real estate agent, few would forgo the services of an attorney once a purchase offer has been made. The seller also may turn to a financial planner or accountant for assistance in sorting out the tax consequences of selling.

### Q. What is the real estate agent's role in a home sale?

**A.** Typically, two real estate agents are involved in the sale of the home—the listing agent, with whom the seller lists the property, and the agent who shows the property to prospective buyers. For the buyer, it is important to keep in mind that both the listing agent and the agent showing properties are agents for the seller. This means that both of these individuals work for and on behalf of the seller, not for the buyer. For a prospective buyer, this is an absolutely crucial point. It means, for example, that neither the listing agent nor the showing agent is permitted to disclose negative information to a buyer about the property, that is, information that is adverse to the seller's interest in selling the property.

As a buyer, you can avoid this information gap by hiring a buyer's agent. Because this individual represents you as the buyer, he or she will be required to disclose to you all relevant information—the bad as well as the good—about the property you are considering. In addition, a buyer's agent is there to negotiate the best possible purchase terms for you. Under recent changes made by the National Association of Realtors, a buyer's agent can be compensated from the total commission generated by a sale. This change is expected to increase the number of buyer's agents and, thus, to expand the level of information available to buyers. Because this is an area of law that is rapidly changing, it is important for the buyer to have a knowledgeable attorney.

### Q. What is the role of the seller's agents?

**A.** The seller's listing agent helps determine the price of the home, suggests how to market the home, schedules advertising and open houses, shows the home to prospective buyers, and otherwise facilitates the sale. The showing agent works with buyers to show homes, contacts the listing agents, monitors the transaction, and, perhaps, helps to obtain financing. In most cases, the seller pays the sales commission which is shared by the two agents.

### Q. When should I see an attorney about buying or selling a home?

**A.** It probably isn't necessary to consult a lawyer when you begin your search for a home. If you are a buyer, you probably will want your attorney to enter the process when you are ready to make an offer and, certainly, before you sign an offer to purchase. If you are a seller, you probably will want to consult an attorney early in the process and before signing a listing agreement with a real estate agent.

Buying and selling real estate almost always entails a contract. So, keep in mind that a typed or handwritten "letter of agreement" or "letter of understanding" signed by the parties will be binding if it meets the legal requirements of a contract. Don't sign something assuming it's not a contract and, therefore, not important. If something goes wrong, you don't want to discover too late that you've signed away important rights, failed to include important protections, or failed to receive what you expected. And beware of making oral promises. Many kinds of contracts don't have to be in writing to be valid.

For example, if a seller verbally promised to update the electrical system, the buyer might be able to insist that the system be updated even if the matter doesn't arise in later negotiations. Legal advice will be much more helpful— and less expensive—before rather than after signing a purchase contract.

## Selecting a Real Estate Agent to Sell Your Home

### Q. Why should I list my home with a real estate agent?

**A.** Experienced, reputable agents can be an invaluable asset to a seller. Real estate agents can offer advice on the suggested listing price, can give you an educated guess as to how long it may take to sell, and can offer valuable suggestions about how to best show your home. The major advantage, however, is that by listing with an agent, information about your home is immediately available to hundreds of other agents and buyers in your area through a Multiple Listing Service (MLS).

The agent with whom you sign a listing agreement is known as the listing agent—most are members of the local MLS. Usually, within twenty-four hours of signing an agreement with an MLS agent, all MLS offices in your area will get a notice that your home is for sale. Because most home buyers work with agents, this makes information about your home available immediately to a wide range of potential buyers.

### Q. How do I choose an agent to sell my home?

**A.** Choosing an agent requires that you do your homework both on the qualifications of the real estate firm and the individual agent who will handle your sale. You may want to interview several agents from various local firms with the following in mind:

- Is the firm a member of the National Association of Realtors, a national voluntary professional organization whose members exchange information and hold seminars in order to enhance their skills and improve the services provided to buyers and sellers of real estate?

- Ask about sales for the last six months or one year. How do these figures compare to the sales figures of other real estate agencies?

- How long do homes stay on the market?

- How much and where does the agency advertise?

- How close is the actual sale price to the listing price for homes sold over the past six months or year?

You also may want to know how familiar various firms and agents are with your area. How well do they know its schools, facilities, and public transportation? The answers to these and similar questions can help you select someone who is knowledgeable and interested in working for you.

Ask to see the Multiple Listing Book and compare the listings of various firms and agents. A large firm may also have a large number of listings. In this case, you will want assurance that the firm's agents have the time and energy to devote to an additional listing. On the other hand, a small office with fewer listings may be preferable, particularly if that means better, more personal service, and, therefore, a quicker sale at or near the desired price.

Once you've settled on an agency, interview potential agents. Ask them about their plans to market the home. Who do they think are the best potential buyers and how do they intend to target them? For example, retirees and young families are usually interested in different amenities. If your home is a natural fit with a particular age group, ask each prospective agent how he or she intends to show your home's advantages to its target market.

It's a good idea to avoid agents who want to list your home at a much higher price than other agents suggest. This may be just a device to get the listing. Within a few weeks, you may find yourself being pressured to reduce the price drastically.

Finally, make sure you are comfortable with the agent you choose. You should have confidence in your agent's ability. Your agent should be responsive to you by telling you who has expressed interest in the home and following up on the visits of potential buyers. For example, if many buyers have seen your home but no offers have been made, your agent should be trying to discover why. Is the price too high? Is the decor too detracting? Should some minor repairs be made?

### Q. What is the listing agreement?

**A.** Once signed, the listing agreement is a binding contract between the seller and the listing real estate firm. Its provisions include length of the listing period, commission rate and payment date, responsibilities of the firm and its agents, and who is responsible for the cost of advertising and the other costs associated with the home sale.

Read the listing agreement carefully. Do not hesitate to discuss any provisions you would like to change. To further protect your interests, resist signing an agreement until your attorney has reviewed and approved it, especially if you have requested changes that have been resisted.

One final suggestion could save you a lot of money. Before signing a listing agreement, let your friends and neighbors know you're selling. If any of them express an interest in buying, exclude them from the listing agreement. Then, if one of them ultimately buys the property, you will not be required to pay any commission at all.

## DIFFERENT TYPES OF LISTING AGREEMENTS

*Most real estate firms prefer "exclusive right to sell" listings. These listings guarantee that a commission will be paid no matter who sells the property as long as it is sold during the time period covered by the listing.*

*Other types of listings include open listings and exclusive agency listings. Exclusive listings require that the listing agency work the property and actively promote its sale. In some states, an exclusive agency listing may be offered under which the seller can avoid paying commission if he or she sells the house personally and not through an agent.*

*Most real estate agencies avoid open listings for residential sales because these listings allow sellers to list with other agencies or to sell the homes themselves. Under an open listing, the commission is paid only to the agency who finds the buyer.*

*Real estate firms that are members of a Multiple Listing Service combine their exclusive right to sell listings. This makes the home available to a wide variety of prospective buyers. The multiple listing agreement defines how the firms share the sales commission when the property is sold.*

**Q.  *What fee will I pay on the sale of my home?***

**A.** Typically, real estate firms charge 5 to 7 percent of the sale price. On some higher-priced homes, a firm may charge the full commission on the first $100,000 or $200,000 and a lower percentage of any amount above that price. If the agency that lists the home is also the agency that sells it, the commission is shared by the agency and the individual agent who actually handled the sale. If the listing firm and the selling firm are different, the commission is shared by the two firms.

Other less common forms of fee payments include the flat-fee method, in which a set fee is charged regardless of the home's price, and the net method. The latter, which is not favored and is illegal in some states, allows the broker to retain any amount of the selling price higher than an agreed sale price.

It is important to keep in mind that all commission agreements are negotiable, particularly in a seller's market.

**Q.  *What other terms in the listing agreement are negotiable?***

**A.** In theory, they all are. At the very least, the real estate agency should be willing to negotiate provisions on:

- The length of the contract. Many of the standard forms provide that the contract renews automatically. Many firms want a six-month listing. If you're in a hurry to sell your home, try to get a 60-day or 90-day listing.

- When the commission is earned. For example, this might occur only when the seller and buyer actually complete the sale, not when they sign the purchase agreement.
- Who will be responsible for the advertising expenses—the seller or the agency.

### Q. What legal protection do I have after signing a listing agreement?

**A.** The listing agreement between a seller and a real estate firm carries a fiduciary responsibility. The firm and all of its agents act for the seller. They owe the seller the duties of care, obedience, accounting, loyalty, and notice.

### Q. Is the real estate agent liable if a potential buyer steals something from my home?

**A.** Unless the agent showing your home was negligent, such as giving your house keys to a buyer, it's unlikely that he or she is responsible for thefts. Sellers should take the precaution of securing small, valuable items. If your agent wants to use a lock box, which allows agents access to keys to your home, make sure the agent uses an electronic lock box. Unlike a manual lock box, an electronic lock box gives a printed record of all the agents who have shown the home. This deters any agent who might be unscrupulous.

### Q. What can I do if my real estate firm doesn't seem to be working very hard to sell my home?

**A.** The housing market and the salability of your home are usually the chief problems when a home isn't selling. But, sometimes a firm or a particular agent is at fault for one reason or another. The best way to prevent this problem is to limit the term of the listing agreement to 90 days or less. If your home doesn't sell in that

period of time, you're legally in a position to try another firm

You also may want to change firms if its agents don't return your telephone calls, don't keep you informed about the progress of your home sale, fail to schedule open houses, or, generally, appear uninterested in the sale. On the other hand, do not be unduly upset if you are presented with offers that seem unreasonably low. Your firm and its agents have an obligation to present you with all offers, even those that may seem insulting. Of course, you are not required to accept any offer presented. But, if you feel that undue pressure is being applied, it may be time for a change—another reason to limit the length of a listing agreement.

## Selecting a Real Estate Agent to Help You Buy a Home

### Q. How does a buyer choose a real estate agent?

**A.** Buyers have two options in selecting a real estate agent—they can work within the traditional system of listing and showing agents, both of whom represent and are paid by the seller, or they can hire a buyer's agent. If the second option is selected, the buyer may pay a fee to the agent for his or her services but the agent is responsible only to the buyer. In either case, you will want to look for an experienced agent familiar with the neighborhood that interests you. Interview several agents. Ask about the agent's sales for the last six months or a year; what was the average time needed to find homes for buyers; how many people have bought homes through them; and what kind of homes were sold. Ask the agent for the names of recent buyers who used his or her services and talk to them. You should be interested in how much time the agent spent with the buyers, how helpful he or she was during negotiations, and whether they were satisfied with the services provided.

Most people prefer to work with experienced real estate agents. Two years of experience is a good rule of thumb. Experience in handling closings is important as well. Obviously, if an agent has had two years' experience but has closed only two transactions during that time, the agent may be less experienced than one might like.

Also make sure that your agent has a good record of locating the types of homes specified by prospective buyers. For example, an agent who customarily has clients seeking $500,000 homes may not spend much time working for a client seeking a $100,000 home. Remember, unless a buyer is working with a buyer's agent, the agent's commission depends on the selling price of the home. Thus, an agent may spend more time with a client looking for a more expensive home.

Most importantly, before you start working with an agent, try to make decisions about the type of home you want, the amount you are willing to pay, and all the other important aspects of home buying. Shop open houses to get a feel for various neighborhoods and the style of home you are seeking.

Couples should be in agreement on how much they are going to spend and what type of home they want. Agents quickly become frustrated when a couple, or any two people buying a home together, seem to have different things in mind.

### Q. What is the fee relationship with a buyer's agent?

**A.** Most buyers prefer to have their agent's fee paid by the seller to avoid additional costs. But, remember, this preference may commit the buyer to the traditional arrangement in which the listing and showing agents both work for the seller. Any buyer who is uncomfortable with this situation may enlist the help of a buyer's agent who will represent only the buyer.

A buyer's agent may require a nonrefundable fee, which will vary with the length of the home search and the extent of the services provided. If you choose this option, you will want to have a specific contract which, as with all written contracts, should be reviewed and approved by your lawyer. The contract should specify the services to be provided and the fees you will pay. If possible, avoid having the fee connected to the purchase price of the home. You do not want to provide an incentive for your agent to encourage a more expensive sale than you want. It may be possible, however, to specify in your purchase offer to the seller that your agent's fee will be paid by the seller at closing.

To find a buyer's broker, check the yellow pages of your telephone book or call the local real estate association for referrals.

### Q. What should I tell a real estate agent about my personal situation?

**A.** If you have a buyer's agent, you may feel free to discuss all aspects of the sale. If you are working with a traditional agent, you may want to withhold certain information that could be useful to the seller. Remember, unless you have hired a buyer's agent, the showing agents you are working with actually represent the seller and are required to disclose all relevant information you might give to the seller.

Some people suggest that you disclose only home styles, prices, and amenities you want when working with a traditional agent. Personal information, such as the fact that your lease expires in two months or that you are willing to bid a higher price on a home, could be conveyed to the seller and ultimately hurt you in the negotiation process. You should also avoid discussing financial information that could be shared with a prospective seller by prequalifying for a loan.

### Buying and Selling Without an Agent

#### Q. Are there advantages to selling my home without an agent?

**A.** Yes. If you sell your home on your own, you will not have to pay a sales commission. While this may seem like a large savings, you must prepare yourself to assume all the responsibilities and costs associated with selling your home. These include advertising your home, spending time with potential buyers, and negotiating the sale.

Sellers familiar with local sales procedures and the real estate market may choose to sell their homes themselves, and there are various books that can help guide you through the process. Experts generally recommend that the seller hire both a lawyer and appraiser at the beginning of the process. An appraiser can help you establish a price for your home, and the attorney can help you with the legal issues, legal filings, and other necessary documentation.

#### Q. Are there disadvantages to selling my home myself?

**A.** There are three distinct disadvantages:

- First, you will lack the many resources that real estate agents have to attract buyers. For example, your home will not be listed in your local Multiple Listing Service, so it is unlikely that many buyers will be shown your home.

- Second, you will have to find time to show your home and talk to potential buyers and you will need to pay for all advertising.

- Third, you will be directly involved in negotiating the sales price and other contract provisions.

At first glance, this last task may seem easy enough. However, many sales fall through without the mediating influence of a third person who has the experience to bring the buyer and seller together on a variety of issues. A professional real estate agent is on the alert for "deal-breakers," the kind of petty disagreements over small items that break up negotiations. If you've decided to sell on your own and also don't hire an attorney to negotiate for you, remember that settling on the terms and conditions of sale, including the price, is a give-and-take process. The fact that you love your renovated kitchen won't influence a potential buyer who intends to remodel anyway. If, after some reflection, you conclude that you lack the necessary experience, it may be wise to turn to a real estate agent or your attorney.

---

## SOME ADVANCE WORK BEFORE YOU BUY

*If you are a prospective buyer, postpone offers and negotiations until you get a feel for various neighborhoods and the style of home you are seeking. Shopping open houses is an excellent way to do this. You also may want to be prequalified by a lender for a mortgage before you have a specific home in mind, which will require filling out financial statements, making the necessary financial disclosures, and having your credit record checked. This will give you a rough idea of how much money the lender will loan you and, thus, make it easier for you to pinpoint your price range.*

## Q. Are there advantages to buying a home directly from the owner?

**A.** The major advantage of buying a For-Sale-by-Owner, or FSBO, home should be a lower purchase price because the seller will not be paying a commission on the sale. The truth is, however, that many FSBOs are priced as high as they would be if they were listed with a real estate firm. If you are interested in a FSBO, make sure you check the prices of comparable homes on the market as well as recent sales in the area.

## Q. How can I buy a foreclosed property?

**A.** Foreclosed properties, called REOs (for Real Estate Owned by the lender), are owned by the lending institution or government agency that backed the mortgage. For one reason or another, the owner has failed to make payments on the loan and the lender has "foreclosed" on the property. This means that the lender has taken title to the property and has become an owner seeking to sell.

Foreclosed properties include both single-family homes and condominiums. They are sold individually or through auctions. Some institutions advertise their lists of foreclosed properties; others deal strictly through real estate agents. Local real estate agents usually have a current list of the foreclosed homes in their area and can provide information on these properties.

Fannie Mae, the Federal National Mortgage Association, is a large government holder of mortgages. It offers a toll-free telephone number that buyers can call to get a list of foreclosed properties in their area. The number is (800) 553-4636; (800) 221-4636 in Maryland.

The Federal Housing Administration (FHA) usually sells its foreclosed properties through an auction announced in the classified sections of local newspapers. Potential buyers submit bids on the day of the auction, accompanied by a certified check for a percentage of the bid price. The highest bid usually gets the home.

---

## DISCLOSURES

## Q. What is the seller obligated to disclose to the buyer?

**A.** Disclosure is covered—or not covered—by state law. In other words, disclosure is treated differently among the states.

Some states require sellers to fill out a long form that explicitly asks about the seller's knowledge of various material defects that might be present in the home. For example, the form might ask the seller if he or she is aware of any material defects in the basement, leaks in the roof, unsafe concentrations of radon gas, etc. Another form might specifically question the condition of various parts of the home, such as the age of the roof, whether the home contained insulation, etc. In other states, sellers are not required to fill out disclosure forms but are required to disclose any defects in equipment that should be functioning at the time of sale such as the furnace, central air conditioning, the hot-water heater, etc.

Most states, however, do not require disclosure. Thus, in most states, the phrase *caveat emptor*—or buyer beware—prevails. Unless the buyer asks specific questions about defects, the seller is not required to disclose them even if he or she has specific knowledge that one or more substantial defects exist. As a result, any problems discovered by the new owner after the sale is closed are his or her problems. The moral? As a buyer, when in doubt, ask.

As a seller, you may want to disclose known material defects that seriously affect the home's value even if your state does not mandate such disclosure. This will help you avoid any future legal problems involved with the sale of your home. Many of the lawsuits filed about real-estate transactions involve the seller's misrepresentation or failure to disclose. Responding honestly to the buyer's questions and either repairing material defects or disclosing them is an effective way to avoid future litigation.

**Q. What are the real estate agent's obligations with respect to disclosure?**

**A.** The Code of Ethics of the National Association of Realtors governs real estate firms and agents who are members. This Code calls for disclosure of all known pertinent facts about the property. Members also will try to get all the buyer's questions answered. For example, if the buyer has spotted water damage in the basement, a member agent should ask the seller about it and tell the buyer about the cause of the problem.

## WORKING WITH AN ATTORNEY

**Q. How do I choose an attorney?**

**A.** To choose an attorney, you will want to consider the following factors:

- Area of specialty: While it is not necessary to engage an attorney who specializes in real estate transactions, you will want an attorney who is familiar with the laws and practices regarding real estate in your area. It's a good idea to select an attorney who has had some recent experience in handling real estate matters.

- Office location: Your attorney will need to review agreements and papers and appear at the closing. Costs can be minimized with a local attorney.

- References: Friends and colleagues can be a good source for references. Ask them what they liked and didn't like about the attorneys with whom they worked.

- Comfort level: Real estate transactions can be very trying. You will want to hire an attorney who can smooth the way, not one who will create obstacles to your purchase or sale of a home.

State and local bar associations, the yellow pages, and even your real estate agent can provide you with names of attorneys in your area. You'll want to interview the attorney, ask about his or her approach to a real estate transaction, discuss fees, and, generally, get an idea of whether or not this attorney is right for you. Along with advice and help in negotiations, your attorney will ensure that your interests are protected.

**Q. What will I have to pay for the lawyer's services?**

**A.** Lawyers' fees vary from city to city and state to state. Fees for services normally are competitive, but the major factors in determining the fee will be the complexity of the transaction and the time required to complete it.

### DISCUSS ATTORNEY'S FEES IN ADVANCE

*Most people feel uncomfortable discussing fees with professionals, but the only way to avoid surprises is to ask about fees during your first visit. Most professionals, including attorneys, expect to discuss fees. In fact, you might be wise to avoid working with an attorney who wants to postpone this discussion. Most attorneys charge by the hour, but some have an established fee for a real estate transaction.*

The estimated fee the lawyer discusses on your first visit usually is just that—an estimate. The actual fee will depend on the type and amount of work involved. For example, if your attorney reviews a purchase offer only once or twice and the transaction moves forward without problems, the estimated fee should be close to the actual fee. If your attorney reviews several purchase offers or problems arise that require your attorney's intervention, the fee will be higher than the estimate. Attorneys who are familiar with real estate work should be able to give you a fairly accurate estimate of what their work will entail. If you run into problems, be sure to ask your attorney how much the extra time is affecting your final bill.

It may be helpful to remember that spending a bit more in attorney's fees so that potential problems are resolved before closing on your purchase may save you time and money later when you decide to sell the property. As the seller, it is likely that you will have to bear the cost of resolving these deferred problems before you're able to sell.

## SETTING THE PRICE

### The Seller's View

**Q. How do I establish the price of my home?**

**A.** First of all, there is no "right" price. The value of your home is almost entirely dependent on what someone is willing to pay for it and how long you are willing to wait to find that person. Most sellers are not in the position to wait for the "ideal" buyer who will pay their "ideal" price. They want to find the optimum price at which their home will sell in a limited amount of time. To do this, they typically rely on comparisons with recently sold homes in the area. A real estate agent can help you by giving you a list of homes sold through the local Multiple Listing Service during the past year or so. For

example, if your home is a three-bedroom, two-bath ranch on a typical lot, your agent can point out sales prices of similar homes to determine a listing price. Try to limit your study to homes that are very similar to yours. If Victorian homes are prized in your area, even a Victorian needing work will be priced higher than other styles of homes of similar size.

To narrow the price further, you'll want to look at amenities sought by buyers. An attached garage, wood-burning fireplace, updated kitchen and baths, large lot, and spacious rooms are among the factors that generally increase a home's price. Conversely, expect the selling price to be lower if your home does not have these or similar amenities.

Location is also a factor. Most buyers want good schools, good transportation, quiet neighborhoods, and little if any commercial activity. The presence or absence of these factors all affect the selling price of your home.

Perhaps equally important are your reasons for selling and how long you can wait. Typically, the most interest is generated in the first few weeks a home is listed. If you want to sell your home fast, you'll want to price it so that it stands out among comparable homes on the market. If you're willing to wait (and remember that you'll be responsible for keeping the house in tip-top shape during the time it remains on the market), you can afford to price it above the competition. Sellers who try to hold out for the highest price, however, may find themselves reducing the price down the line. A house that has been on the market beyond the average marketing time generates little interest from buyers, even when the price is reduced dramatically. Most buyers will assume that the home has problems which they, understandably, want to avoid.

**Q. Should I consult a professional appraiser?**

**A.** Those few people who cannot find comparable homes may want to consult a professional appraiser before settling on a selling price. An appraisal is the fair market value of the home, so it should be close to the probable selling price. (Lenders usually order their own appraisals, often paid for by the buyer, before approving a loan in order to ensure that the home is worth at least as much as the money being lent plus the buyer's down payment.) If you intend to sell your home on your own, without a real estate agent, an appraisal can provide valuable market information. Remember, however, that determining market value is not an exact science. A home is worth what someone will pay for it.

### The Buyer's View

**Q. How much home can I afford?**

**A.** This is one of the first things to consider when buying a home. First of all, knowing what you can afford will narrow your range so you will not waste time by looking at homes that cost too much. First-time buyers often become disappointed when they find the home of their dreams only to discover they cannot afford it.

Unless you are paying cash for a home, how much home you can afford depends on your income, your assets, your expenses and debts (including automobile or education loans and outstanding credit card balances), prevailing interest rates on mortgages, the cash needed for a down payment (10 to 20 percent of the purchase price), and closing costs (four to six percent of the purchase price).

**Q. Is there a formula for determining what I can afford?**

**A.** The prevailing rule says that a home should cost no more than 2.5 times your annual income. Thus, if your income is $50,000, your price limit would be $50,000

## CAN YOU AFFORD A HOME?

*Consider the following factors to determine whether or not you can afford to purchase a home:*

- *How much money have you saved for a down payment?*
- *What is the status of your current income and expenses, such as car payments?*
- *Do you have a good credit history?*
- *What are the current interest rates on mortgages?*
- *What are your priorities and lifestyle?*

multiplied by 2.5, or $125,000. Typically, a lender expects you to pay no more than about 28 to 30 percent of your gross income for housing, which includes the loan payment, property tax, home owner's insurance, and estimated utility costs. A lender will look at your debts. As a general rule, your total indebtedness, including monthly housing expenses, should not exceed 36 percent of your gross income.

Along with these guidelines, consider your lifestyle and priorities. If costly vacations, dining out, and entertainment are important to you, you may want to buy a less expensive home than the lender says you can afford. Many people, however, find that they are willing to give up some luxuries or even stretch their budget for the home they want.

Use the worksheet on page 111 to help calculate how much of a mortgage a lender would be willing to grant you. Remember that your total debts plus potential housing costs cannot exceed 36 percent of your gross income.

## GROSS MONTHLY INCOME

|  | Borrower | Co-Borrower | Total |
|---|---|---|---|
| Base income | $_____ | $_____ | $_____ |
| Overtime | $_____ | $_____ | $_____ |
| Commissions | $_____ | $_____ | $_____ |
| Dividends/interest | $_____ | $_____ | $_____ |
| Other | $_____ | $_____ | $_____ |
| Total | $_____ | $_____ | $_____ |

**LIABILITIES:**

|  | Monthly Payments | Unpaid Balance | Months left to pay |
|---|---|---|---|
| Automobile loan | $_____ | $_____ | _____ |
| Student loans | $_____ | $_____ | _____ |
| Personal loans | $_____ | $_____ | _____ |
| Credit cards | $_____ | $_____ | _____ |
| Other | $_____ | $_____ | _____ |
| **Total Monthly Payments** | $_____ | $_____ | _____ |

## Q. How much money will a lender provide for my home purchase?

**A.** The total loan amount a lender will agree to provide is directly tied to your income and expenses. As a homeowner, you will be paying a monthly loan payment, along with the cost of insurance, property taxes, utilities, and maintenance. A lender looks for a solid history of income, employment, and credit. The lender also will review your expenses, including automobile payments, credit-card debt, education loans, child support, alimony, etc. If you are borrowing money for your down payment, the lender will treat the interest payments on that loan as expenses.

## Q. What do I need for a down payment?

**A.** Some people may qualify for special government-insured loans offered through the Federal Housing Administration (FHA) or Veterans Administration (VA). The down payment needed for these loans is minimal. But, unless you can qualify, you will need a down payment equal to 20 percent of the purchase price to avoid paying the extra cost of Private

## How Much Home Can You Afford?

| Annual Gross Income | Monthly Gross Income | 29% of Gross Income* |
|---|---|---|
| $15,000 | $1,250 | $ 363 |
| 20,000 | 1,667 | 483 |
| 25,000 | 2,083 | 604 |
| 30,000 | 2,500 | 725 |
| 35,000 | 2,917 | 846 |
| 40,000 | 3,333 | 967 |
| 45,000 | 3,750 | 1,088 |
| 50,000 | 4,167 | 1,208 |

*Average housing expense as a percent of gross income.

SOURCE: Department of Housing & Urban Development

Mortgage Insurance (PMI). With less than a 20-percent down payment, banking regulations require the buyer to carry PMI. This insures the lender against nonpayment of the difference between the customary down payment and the down payment actually paid. The charge for PMI may be as much as $50 or $60 per month, although the amount declines as the loan ages and you begin to pay off more of the principal.

## Q. Do I have to pay PMI for the life of the loan?

**A.** If you cannot put down 20 percent, the only way to end the PMI payments is to demonstrate in the future that your equity in the home has increased to 20 percent. This can sometimes be done if you refinance and your home has increased in value to the point where the balance of your loan is less than 80 percent of the home's value. Or, if you have owned your home long enough to build up equity through principal payments, you may be able to eliminate PMI. Be aware, however, that the insurer will need written support from a certified appraiser as to the value of your home. The value assessed by a municipality for real estate tax purposes is seldom considered in evaluating home equity.

## Q. What will I need for closing costs?

**A.** Along with the down payment, you will need between 4 and 6 percent of your loan amount to pay for closing costs, unless you are obtaining an FHA or VA loan. These costs include fees for your attorney, the lender's appraisal, lender's title insurance, title search, escrow deposits for property taxes and/or homeowner's insurance, as well as other expenses such as recording fees. If you are obtaining a loan, the law requires the lender to provide an estimate of these costs at the time you apply.

### Q. Is the seller responsible for any costs?

**A.** Yes. The seller is responsible for paying the commission on the sale and must pay any taxes owed on the property, any money due his or her lender, and any liens that may be outstanding on the property. Usually, the seller is required to pay the cost of a title insurance policy for the buyer that insures the buyer against any defects in the title to the property.

The seller is sometimes required to pay "points." Points are the difference between prevailing interest rates and the rate the buyer is actually paying for his or her loan. For example, if the prevailing rate is eight percent and the actual rate being paid by the buyer is seven percent, the seller would pay one point, or one percent, of the amount of the buyer's loan.

### Q. How do interest rates affect my choice of a home?

**A.** The interest you pay on your loan is part of the cost of owning a home. For example, a one percent increase in the interest rate on a $100,000 loan adds approximately $75 to your monthly loan payment over the life of a 30-year loan. Obviously, the lower the interest rate, the more you can afford to borrow. Be aware that home interest rates can change quickly. They usually are the last rates to decline when other interest rates are falling and are among the first to rise when other rates are climbing.

### Q. Should I prequalify for a loan?

**A.** If you are unsure about your price range and, especially, if you are a first-time buyer, prequalifying for a loan can help smooth the purchase process. You will know exactly what you can afford and avoid the disappointment of being unable to buy the home you thought you could afford.

To prequalify for a loan, you will need to go through most of the steps entailed in applying for the actual loan. If you decide to prequalify, be sure to do so through a loan originator, that is, an actual lender. A mortgage broker, who brings together borrowers and lenders, cannot prequalify you for a loan.

### Q. I want to buy a home but my credit history is poor. Is there anything I can do?

**A.** Yes, there are several options. First, before you attempt to buy, you will want to improve your credit record by paying your bills on time and by curtailing your borrowing.

Second, credit-reporting agencies can and do make mistakes. Major credit-reporting companies such as Equifax, Trans Union, and TRW maintain computer files on your financial history. Credit-reporting agencies are authorized by law to disclose credit information to any person or organization with a legitimate business need for the information. On the other hand, the law also gives you the right to examine your own file. A summary of the report must be made available to you free of charge; however, there is a fee if you request a full credit report.

If you believe your credit report is in error, you may challenge the report by explaining the error in writing. The information must be verified by the agency if it is kept in the report. If you discover inaccuracies and you can prove them, you can demand that the agency correct them within a reasonable period of time. If there are no errors, you have the right to include a letter of explanation of up to 100 words in your report. The agency must include your statement, or a clear and accurate summary of it, in all future reports. For example, if you were unable to pay a loan because you were out of work or suffered a severe illness, you could add this information to the report. You may want to consult your lawyer if you are unable to have your report changed as required by law. (See the "Consumer Credit" chapter for more details.)

## Payment Tables*
## 15-Year Mortgage

| Amount Financed | 6% | 7% | 8% | 9% | 10% | 11% | 12% | 13% | 14% | 15% |
|---|---|---|---|---|---|---|---|---|---|---|
| $ 50,000 | $421.93 | $449.41 | $477.83 | $ 507.13 | $ 537.30 | $ 568.30 | $ 600.09 | $ 632.63 | $ 665.88 | $ 699.80 |
| $ 80,000 | $675.09 | $719.06 | $764.52 | $ 811.41 | $ 859.68 | $ 909.28 | $ 960.14 | $1,012.20 | $1,065.40 | $1,119.67 |
| $100,000 | $843.86 | $898.83 | $955.65 | $1,014.27 | $1,074.61 | $1,136.60 | $1,200.17 | $1,265.25 | $1,331.75 | $1,399.59 |

*Table gives the amount of monthly payments (principal and interest) to repay loans that fully pay off the debt over the term of the loans.

## Payment Tables*
## 30-Year Mortgage

| Amount Financed | 6% | 7% | 8% | 9% | 10% | 11% | 12% | 13% | 14% | 15% |
|---|---|---|---|---|---|---|---|---|---|---|
| $ 50,000 | $299.78 | $332.65 | $366.88 | $402.31 | $438.79 | $476.16 | $ 514.31 | $ 553.10 | $ 592.44 | $ 632.23 |
| $ 80,000 | $479.65 | $532.24 | $587.01 | $643.70 | $702.06 | $761.86 | $ 822.90 | $ 884.96 | $ 947.90 | $1,011.56 |
| $100,000 | $599.58 | $665.30 | $733.76 | $804.62 | $877.57 | $952.32 | $1,028.62 | $1,106.20 | $1,184.88 | $1,264.45 |

*Table gives the amount of monthly payments (principal and interest) to repay loans that fully pay off the debt over the term of the loans.

Credit-reporting agencies are allowed to retain negative information in your report for seven years and bankruptcy information for ten years.

## MAKING AN OFFER: THE PURCHASE CONTRACT

### Q. How do I begin negotiations to buy a home?

**A.** Negotiations are handled in various ways in different parts of the country. Typically, most transactions begin with negotiation over price, although other items such as date of possession may also be negotiated. The real estate agent will provide a form, usually called a contract to purchase or, simply, a real estate contract. In any case, this is a formal, written offer that conveys your terms to the seller. If you intend to have the home inspected, it should include an inspection rider; if you intend to apply for a mortgage, it should include a mortgage-contingency clause; if your attorney has not reviewed the contract, it should include an attorney-approval rider. In other words, it should cover the basics. Remember, once this document is signed by both parties, it is legally binding.

The offer should specify a date after which it is no longer valid. This may be as little as 24 hours from the time the seller or the seller's agent receives it. The offer to purchase also is usually valid only if both the buyer and seller sign it within a certain time period. As a general rule, an earnest money deposit of perhaps $500 or $1,000 accompanies the offer to purchase.

Often this is the start of negotiations. The offer to purchase may be passed back and forth

## WHAT IS EARNEST MONEY?

*When the buyer signs the offer to purchase, the buyer usually deposits a sum of money with the seller, the seller's real estate agent, or the seller's attorney. Your offer should specify that the earnest money deposit will be placed in an interest-bearing account with the interest credited to the buyer.*

*Earnest money is not the same thing as the buyer's down payment although, if the sale goes through, it will be applied to the down payment. Earnest money symbolizes the buyer's commitment to take the necessary steps to complete the purchase, for example obtaining a loan. Thus, if a prospective buyer does little or nothing to complete the sale, he or she risks losing the earnest money deposit.*

between the buyer and seller before being accepted by both. Remember, however, that any changes agreed to during negotiations must be initialed by both parties. Once you have agreed on terms, you will want to arrange for a home inspection and review the document with your attorney if, as noted above, you included these riders in your offer. In most cases, you will not want to apply for financing until the home inspection is completed and satisfactory.

In some areas, the purchase contract will include all provisions of the transaction; in other areas, another document will be drawn up by the buyer or the seller that covers such items as conveyance of title, provision for insurance, etc. In either case, you will want your attorney to make sure that the final document covers all aspects of the sale.

**Q. What is the purchase contract?**

**A.** The purchase contract may be called a sales contract, real estate contract, purchase agreement, sales agreement, or purchase and sale agreement. Whatever it is called, it is a legal document that, when signed by both parties, is a legal contract that will govern the entire transaction. Before signing such a contract, you will want to review it carefully and have your attorney review it. Remember, once it is signed, you are obligated to fulfill your part of the contract.

**Q. What are the key provisions of the purchase contract?**

**A.** A purchase contract, in most cases, is a standard form contract with any necessary riders attached. The contract can include many provisions but should include the following items:

- the date of the contract;
- the purchase price of the home;
- amount of the down payment;
- all items to be included in the sale such as wall-to-wall carpeting, window treatments, appliances, or lighting fixtures;
- any items to be excluded from the sale such as an heirloom chandelier;
- the date when the deed will be transferred (or the closing date);
- a mortgage contingency clause if the buyer intends to apply for a loan. This states that the buyer intends to obtain a loan in a specified amount at a specified

interest rate within a specified period of time. If the buyer is unable to obtain financing, the buyer may be released from his obligation. The seller usually allows the buyer 30 to 60 days to obtain a loan commitment.

- an inspection rider. This allows the buyer to have the home inspected, usually within 10 days of the date of the contract. If the inspection is unsatisfactory, the buyer ordinarily is released from the contract. However, the buyer may not be released if the contract allows the seller to make repairs and the repairs, when made, meet applicable standards of workmanship.

- an attorney-approval rider for both the buyer and the seller if either or both parties are signing the contract before it is reviewed by their respective attorneys;

- a legal description of the property;

- provision that the seller will provide good title to the home or what is sometimes called marketable title. Generally, the seller fulfills this obligation by providing an abstract of title, certificate of title, or a title insurance policy. This indicates that the seller has the authority to sell the home. In some states, for example Connecticut, the seller is required to deliver good title which the buyer is expected to verify, at his or her own expense, by securing an abstract of title, certificate of title, or a title insurance policy. If the buyer encounters problems in establishing title, he or she can reject the title at closing.

- any restriction or limitations that could affect title;

- provision for paying utility bills, property taxes, and similar expenses through the closing date;

- provision for return of the buyer's earnest money deposit if the sale is not com-

pleted as, for example, when the buyer has been unable to obtain financing after reasonable or good faith efforts to do so;

- provision for taking possession. Along with a firm date for transferring possession from the seller to the buyer, the buyer should include a provision that requires the seller to pay a specific amount of rent per day if the seller does not leave the home by the agreed date. If the buyer and seller already know that possession will be delayed, the buyer may ask for a certain amount of money to be held in escrow at the closing to cover the rent for the expected time period.

- provision for a walk-through inspection within a specified period before the date of closing to allow the buyer to make sure conditions are as they should be according to the contract;

- terms of any escrow agreement;

- provision for who is responsible for maintaining insurance until the closing. The Uniform Vendor-Purchaser Risk of Loss Act applies in some states, which means that the seller assumes the risk of loss until either the transfer of title or possession. In some states, the common law requires the seller to assume this risk.

- signatures of the parties.

## Q. *What does an inspection rider provide?*

**A.** The inspection rider is a very important safeguard for the buyer. Two types are commonly used. The first gives the buyer the right to have the property inspected by a professional home inspector of the buyer's choice and at the buyer's expense. If the inspector finds defects, the buyer has the right to cancel the contract within a specified time. This type of rider raises some of the same issues as an unrestricted attorney-approval rider, since inspectors often find problems in homes. Thus, it can give buyers a few extra days to decide whether they want to follow through with the purchase.

The second type of inspection rider gives the seller time to either repair any problems uncovered by the inspection or agree to reduce the selling price contained in the contract by the cost of repairs. If a seller opts to do nothing, he or she must inform the buyer. Unless the buyer and seller can come to terms based on the buyer's inspection report, the buyer can cancel the contract and seek return of any earnest money previously paid.

Some people prefer the first inspection rider described above. Although it is open to occasional abuse by fickle buyers, its simplicity generates fewer back-and-forth discussions between the buyer and seller. If there is a serious problem and the seller really wants to sell, the parties usually can make a new deal.

Still, the choice is yours. Just remember that a real estate purchase contract is no different in principle than any other contract—its terms are negotiable. By using properly drafted riders, you may quickly turn a form contract into one that deals with your personal concerns.

## Q. What is an attorney-approval rider?

**A.** One common rider makes the purchase contract subject to approval by the buyer's and seller's respective attorneys within a short period of time, usually five to ten days after acceptance of the offer. In such cases, the standard contract form should include the phrase, **"Subject to the Approval of the Attorneys for the Parties Within ___ Days,"** with the number of days written in. Without such a condition in the contract, both the seller and the buyer are bound by the terms of the contract, which may be unclear or may differ from the parties' intent.

## Q. Does an attorney-approval rider give a buyer an "out" from the contract?

**A.** Yes, like the inspection rider and the mortgage-contingency rider, it does allow a buyer to get out of a purchase contract. In fact, this is the reason some sellers will not accept such clauses.

An attorney-approval rider could avoid this pitfall by limiting the attorney's approval to legal matters as, for example, the state of the title. In addition, the rider could specify that a lawyer must state such disapproval in writing, with the seller having the option to correct the problem causing disapproval. This type of rider ensures that the contract need not bind the parties if their lawyers find an unsatisfactory provision in the small print. Meanwhile, the buyer and seller can sign the

**THE WALK-THROUGH**
*Many buyers like to inspect the property 24 hours or so before the closing to be sure it is in the same condition as it was when they signed the offer to purchase and to make sure that all property to be included in the sale remains in place. If something has been removed that was included in the sale under the terms of the purchase contract (such as a chandelier or appliance), the buyer should quickly notify his or her attorney or the seller's agent to see if the item will be returned before closing. Or, if agreeable to both parties, the buyer and seller may decide to reach a financial compromise instead.*

contract knowing that the other party may not easily back out of the contract because of a minor defect or objection.

### Q. What is a mortgage-contingency rider?

**A.** This common provision allows the buyer a certain period of time to obtain a commitment for financing at a specified interest rate for a certain amount of money. It usually lasts for 30 to 60 days, depending on the average time needed to obtain a loan commitment.

The clause might read, for example, that the contract is contingent on the buyer obtaining approval for a 30-year mortgage for $100,000 at no more than eight percent interest within 45 days. For additional protection, the buyer might specify the type of loan he or she prefers, for example fixed or variable.

> **BEWARE OF CONTINGENCIES**
>
> *If an offer to purchase your home contains any contingency, you should include a time period for compliance, after which the offer expires. Otherwise, your home could be off the market for months, with no assurance that the sale will go through.*
>
> *If a buyer extends an offer that is contingent on Veterans Administration financing, note that your acceptance of the offer could obligate you to pay points (percentages of the loan amount). In this case, you would want to place a limit on the points to be paid.*

A mortgage-contingency rider provides critical protection to the buyer. For example, it allows the buyer to void the purchase contract without penalty in those cases in which the buyer is unable to obtain financing on the terms specified in the contract after making a reasonable or good faith effort to do so within the time provided. Because this type of clause favors the buyer, some real estate agents suggest that the buyer obtain "prequalification" from a lender, which gives the seller a degree of confidence that the buyer will not use the clause to void the contract unless some extraordinary circumstance arises.

The seller may refuse to agree to a mortgage-contingency rider. This can and does happen in a very hot seller's market—in which case, there is not much the buyer can do. But the absence of a mortgage-contingency rider might mean that the buyer will be forced to finance his or her home purchase at an unfavorable interest rate. Because of this risk, buyers should be cautious about signing a purchase contract that does not contain this clause.

### Q. May the seller refuse a mortgage-contingency rider or an inspection-contingency rider?

**A.** Yes. Sellers are not required to accept any of the buyer-protection riders we've discussed. However, as a general rule, most sellers will accept these and similar riders unless they are selling in a very hot market.

Sellers should ensure that the proposed interest rate is reasonable, based on current rates, and also allow a limited but reasonable time for the mortgage commitment. Similarly, most sellers accept an inspection rider but should make sure that this rider expires relatively quickly—say, ten days from signing. Unlike a mortgage commitment, there's no reason that an inspection can't be done within a week or so.

### Q. Should I allow the seller to remain in the home after closing?

**A.** Most buyers want possession upon closing, because they will be paying the mortgage as of that date and will not want to pay for two residences. Sometimes, however, a buyer may allow the seller to remain for a specified period of time. For example, the seller may be moving to another state one month after the closing or, perhaps, the seller is waiting for a builder to finish a new home. If you find yourself in this situation, do not rely on oral promises or a statement about the date on which the seller promises to vacate the premises. Make sure your purchase contract states how long the seller may occupy the home after closing and specifies the rent owed to you for that period.

The contract also should specify any penalties in the event the seller does not move, does not pay rent after closing, or does any damage prior to vacating the premises. Sometimes your attorney will prepare a separate lease, or use an occupancy agreement, to cover these and similar contingencies.

### Q. What happens to my earnest money deposit if we do not complete the sale?

**A.** Generally, the purchase contract allows the buyer to get back his or her earnest money and any interest earned on it, unless the buyer has in some way violated the contract. If the seller refuses to return the deposit, the buyer may have to sue the seller for return of the deposit.

### Q. Can a buyer sue a seller for backing out of the contract?

**A.** Yes, if the seller violates the terms of the contract or refuses to close the sale, the buyer can sue to force the seller to complete the trans-

action. It also is possible for the buyer to sue for damages. For example, a buyer who had incurred costs for obtaining a mortgage or costs for renting temporary housing caused by the seller breaking the contract would have a case for damages.

## Home Inspections

### Q. What is involved in a home inspection?

**A.** A professional home inspection can vary among localities, but, generally, the aim is to discover any problems with the home that might not be readily apparent. Most inspectors check to make sure there are no material defects or problems with such items as the electrical, plumbing, heating, and air-conditioning systems. The inspector also may check for termites, the age of the roof and when it might need replacement, condition of the basic structure including the foundation, evidence of basement seepage, and other problems. Some inspectors check for radon concentrations, lead paint, or other environmental hazards.

A professional inspection should not be alarmist. The idea is to point out problems without exaggerating defects. It's a good idea for the buyer to accompany the inspector during the inspection. In this way, the buyer is able to ask questions and to get an idea of the cost of any repairs that are necessary or advisable. Further, the inspector also may suggest ways to better insulate the home or offer maintenance suggestions that can prolong the life of operating systems such as heating and air conditioning.

Most buyers do not want to pay for an inspection until they have settled on other terms with the seller. To do this, the buyer often uses an inspection rider to provide that the offer to buy is contingent on a favorable inspection of the home.

## WHAT TO EXPECT FROM THE HOME INSPECTION

*The buyer normally hires a contractor or home inspector to check out the home. The inspector does not care about cosmetic problems that the buyer could easily see such as peeling wallpaper, torn carpet, or flaking paint. The inspector shows an interest only in the structural and mechanical aspects of the home, looking for problems that a buyer is unlikely to notice. These include termite damage, foundation and structural problems, and the age and condition of the roof. The inspector also will examine the condition of the chimney, storm windows, gutters, electrical wiring, and plumbing.*

*If possible, you will want to accompany the inspector and take notes. Some inspectors charge a smaller fee if the potential buyer does not require a written report. However, be aware that a written report may be required if the buyer intends to cancel the purchase contract because of defects revealed by the inspection.*

*Inspection fees vary based on such factors as the size and type of building inspected. As a general rule, anticipate a fee somewhere between $250 and $500.*

**Q. What should the buyer do if the inspection uncovers material and costly defects?**

**A.** There are several choices. Although the inspection rider may simply allow you to walk away from the purchase, this may not be desirable, especially if the home has other qualities you are seeking. One alternative is to negotiate with the seller to lower the previously agreed-upon price. For example, if the seller was unaware that the furnace was corroded and in need of replacement or that there was rotting timber that needed replacement, he or she may be amenable to reducing the purchase price by the estimated cost of repairs. Alternatively, the price could remain the same with the seller repairing the problem at his or her expense.

While some buyers use an inspection to extract further concessions from the seller, it's unlikely that a seller is going to agree to reduce the cost of a home to reflect the cost of correcting minor problems such as a repairing a porcelain chip or replacing peeling wallpaper or worn carpeting. A seller facing a long list of minor repairs the buyer wants made before closing may want to end negotiations unless he or she has no other alternative than selling the home to this particular buyer.

**Q. What can the seller do if he or she disagrees with an inspection report?**

**A.** Your response as a seller to a negative inspection report will depend on the buyer. Sometimes, such a report may scare away the buyer. If you strongly disagree with the inspection, you may want to obtain your own written inspection, copies of which you can provide to prospective buyers.

One response to a negative inspection report is negotiating a resolution to the problems discovered by the inspector. For example, if the inspector discovers that your home has inadequate or outdated electrical wiring, the seller may offer to have the wiring updated or to reduce the price by an agreed-upon sum to cover the buyer's costs of updating the wiring.

As a seller, you should be aware that some home buyers will take any problems and turn them into major roadblocks, hoping to force an anxious seller to reduce the selling price. If you find yourself dealing with such a buyer, you may be better off to simply refuse further negotiations, let the offer expire, return the buyer's deposit, and place the home back on the market. But, if you believe that the buyer's complaints are without merit, you could insist on compliance with the purchase contract; this, however, could lead to a lawsuit.

### Q. Should a seller get a home inspection?

**A.** If you are worried about possible problems in your home, it may be a good idea to pay for an inspection before you put your house up for sale. The inspection would allow you to take a look at your home from a buyer's perspective and allow you time to fix any problems or reduce your asking price.

Most buyers will probably want to pay for their own inspections. If you do share your pre-sale inspection report with a buyer, be sure to provide the entire report; otherwise, a court might construe that you intentionally withheld negative information.

## FINANCING A HOME PURCHASE

### Q. How do I finance the purchase of a home?

**A.** Few people have enough cash to buy a home outright—most need to finance their pur-

chase by borrowing money. Usually, this is done by contracting with a financial institution such as a bank or savings and loan. The buyer agrees to pay interest on the money borrowed and the lender retains a lien (mortgage) on the property. In some cases, buyers are able to obtain seller-financing in which the buyer pays interest to the seller and the seller retains a lien on the property. In other cases, a buyer is able to assume the seller's mortgage. That is, the buyer pays the difference between what is owed on the mortgage and the purchase price and takes over the seller's payments on the mortgage. (Note that this can occur only if provisions in the mortgage state specifically that it is assumable. Most mortgages written today include a due-on-sale clause that prohibits assumption of a mortgage.) In the event that a buyer can assume the seller's mortgage, the seller should remember that he or she remains liable to pay the mortgage unless the seller's lender specifically and in writing releases the seller from this obligation.

Today, a wide variety of financing mechanisms exist to finance a purchase. Some buyers may qualify for federally insured loans which permit smaller-than-normal down payments and lower interest rates than prevailing market rates.

### Q. How do lenders determine the interest rate?

**A.** Interest rates for home loans are determined by the overall market in interest rates. Short-term rates, such as those paid on a six-month certificate of deposit, are usually the lowest. The highest rates are usually paid on unsecured loans, such as credit-card debt.

Home loan rates are very interest-sensitive; that is, when rates are declining, they are usually the last to be lowered, but when rates are rising, they are among the first to go up. This is because most home loans are made at a fixed rate over a fairly long term—

## SHOPPING FOR INTEREST RATES

*You can and should shop for rates. As noted earlier, a 1 percent change in the interest rate on a one-hundred-thousand-dollar thirty-year fixed-rate loan could mean a seventy-five dollar difference in each monthly loan payment. The market is competitive. Lending institutions often will offer lower-than-market rates to attract borrowers.*

*There are several ways to shop for home loans. Many metropolitan newspapers carry a weekly listing or sampling of rates offered in their areas. Rates can change very rapidly, which might mean that these listings may not be up to the minute. However, they can give you a good general idea of the market. In addition, several reporting services offer details on the variety of loan types and interest rates available from area institutions. Prices of these services range from ten to thirty dollars. Therefore, you may want to use a reporting service only when you are ready to apply for a loan. You also can call a real estate mortgage broker for information.*

low rates by taking a go-slow approach to reducing interest rates.

Interest rates for home loans have fallen dramatically since the early 1980s. These lower rates have made home buying much more affordable. These rates can and will rise very quickly, however, if the prevailing trend changes and other interest rates begin to escalate. Anyone interested in an adjustable-rate mortgage, in which the interest rate changes during the life of the mortgage, should be aware that rates could climb rapidly and significantly increase the amount of the mortgage payments.

**Q. Does it pay to shop around for an interest rate?**

**A.** Yes. Lenders are very competitive. Interest rates and fees charged to originate a loan vary among financial institutions. Typically, lenders charge the prospective buyer a fee to obtain a loan—this may be a flat fee or a percentage of the loan (one point is 1 percent of the loan amount).

One lender might offer an 8 percent, thirty-year fixed-rate loan with a flat fee of two hundred dollars. A second lender might offer a 7 percent, thirty-year fixed-rate loan with two points. A third lender might offer the loan without points or other fees but at a higher interest rate. This could be advantageous for a buyer who wants to put as much as possible into his or her down payment. Another buyer might prefer to pay higher points in exchange for a lower interest rate because the IRS allows points to be deducted against taxable income in the year the home is purchased.

**Q. What is a land contract?**

**A.** A land contract is a common form of seller financing. The buyer pays the seller a down payment and agrees to make payments of interest and principal on the outstanding balance. In other words, the seller acts as a lending

fifteen to thirty years—during which time interest rates may increase substantially. Thus, lenders attempt to protect themselves from making too many long-term loans at

institution. Typically, the buyer takes possession of the property, but the seller retains the right to sue to recover the property if the buyer fails to fulfill his or her contractual obligations. As a general rule, legal title is not transferred to the buyer until all payments are made. Evidence of title, such as a warranty deed, usually is placed with a third person who holds the document until payment is completed, at which time he or she delivers it to the buyer, who should make sure that it is recorded in the proper local records office—for example, the recorder's office or county clerk's office. Once again, because a contract is involved, attorneys for both parties should be consulted to review its terms. Finally, since title is not transferred until full payment has been made, the contract should be recorded by the buyer with the recorder's or county clerk's office so that his or her interest in the property is protected until payment is made in full.

**Q. I want to buy another home, but I haven't sold my present home yet. Is there a way to finance until I can sell?**

**A.** Many lenders offer a bridge loan to allow a buyer to buy another home while waiting to sell his or her present home. You can obtain a bridge loan if you have a contract to sell your present home and you need the loan only for a specific, relatively short, period of time.

It is much more difficult to obtain a bridge loan if you do not have a buyer for your home and, thus, need to pay loans on two properties. Bridge loans usually carry a higher interest than a traditional home loan.

**Q. What is a fixed-rate loan?**

**A.** Most prospective buyers prefer a fixed-rate loan because the interest rate cannot be increased during the term of the loan, typically 15, 20, or 30 years. Under a fixed-rate loan, buyers can feel more comfortable knowing the

exact amount of their monthly loan payments throughout the life of the loan.

Although the interest rate does not change, the way in which the payment is divided changes over the loan period. At the beginning, most of the payment is applied to the interest owed to the lender. As the loan progresses, more money is applied to the principal—the face amount of the loan. This also means that the amount of interest deductible for federal income tax purposes will decline over the life of the loan.

The major difference between a fifteen- or twenty-year fixed-rate loan, on the one hand, and a thirty-year fixed-rate loan, on the other, is that the borrower will pay higher monthly payments on the shorter term loans than would be the case with a thirty-year loan for the same amount of money. Over the life of the loan, however, the buyer pays far less interest, because he or she is using the money for a shorter period of time.

**Q. What is an adjustable-rate loan?**

**A.** Adjustable-rate loans vary, but they all share one common factor—some aspect of the terms of the loan can be changed by the lender during the life of the loan. The specific type of adjustable mortgage is tied to whether the change is in the rate of interest, amount of payment, or length of time for repayment.

If you are considering applying for any type of adjustable-rate loan, make sure you understand exactly how the mortgage works, including the spread between the interest rate and the index to which the rate is tied; how often the loan can be adjusted; the maximum allowable increase (or decrease) each year as well as over the life of the loan.

Adjustable-rate loans include:

- Adjustable-rate mortgages (ARMs). These loans typically offer a lower-than-market interest rate in the first year. The future interest rate, usually adjusted annually, is tied to an index that may move up or down but is not under the control of the lender. The index might be the one-year Treasury bill (the T-bill rate) or some other rate that reflects the changes in interest rates.

Note that the rate is tied to the index—it is not the same as the index. The mortgage might specify, for example, that the future rate would be two points above the average T-bill rate. Typically, ARMs are adjusted once a year on the anniversary date of the loan. Additionally, ARMs usually have a provision for a cap, that is, the highest rate that could be charged. Some may include a minimum rate as well.

- Convertible ARMs. These loans usually offer a conversion factor that allows the borrower to convert to a fixed-rate loan at a specified period of time. For example, a convertible ARM could allow the borrower the option to convert to a fixed-rate loan once a year over the first five years of the loan. The interest rate to be paid would also be tied to an index.

- Renegotiable-rate mortgage (rollover). These loans typically set the interest rate and monthly payments for several years and then allow both the rate and principal payments to be changed depending on general market conditions. If the new terms are unacceptable to you, you can pay the loan in full or refinance at prevailing interest rates.

- Graduated payment mortgage (GPM). With this type of loan, typically sought by young buyers who expect their incomes to rise, the payments are low in the first couple of years and set to rise gradually for five to ten years.

- Shared-appreciation mortgage. These loans offer lower-than-market rates of interest and low payments in exchange for a lender's share in appreciation of the property. Usually, the lender will require that its share of equity will be turned over when the home is sold or at a specified date set out in the loan agreement.

### Q. What is a balloon loan?

**A.** With a balloon loan, the buyer is expected to pay off the loan completely within a short period of time, usually in three, five, or seven years. In other words, this is a short-term loan. The interest rate can be fixed or variable, but in all cases the unpaid balance on the principal is due at the time specified. The borrower must either refinance or sell the home to pay off the loan.

To attract buyers, builders often offer balloon loans during periods of high-interest rates when home sales are sluggish. In most cases, the interest rate will be lower than prevailing home loan rates. However, if interest rates are high when full payment is due, refinancing may not be possible. The balloon will burst, resulting in foreclosure and loss of the home.

### Q. How do FHA and VA loans work?

**A.** The Federal Housing Administration (FHA) offers insured low-interest loans made by the federal government and approved lending institutions. The cost for this loan insurance varies and is charged at the closing. While FHA loans are not available through all lenders, in some areas they are very popular and can make the difference in obtaining a loan for some potential buyers who do not qualify for conventional financing. The Veterans Administration (VA) offers government-insured loans to qualified veterans.

Income qualifications, required down payments, and the maximum allowable loans under these plans are changed periodically. Currently, the maximum FHA loan is about

## Highlighting the Essentials

| Type | Description |
|---|---|
| **Fixed-rate mortgage** | Fixed interest rate, usually long-term; equal monthly payments (applied unequally toward principal and interest) until debt is paid in full. |
| **15-year mortgage** | Fixed interest rate. Requires down payment or monthly payments higher than 30-year loan. Loan is fully repaid over 15-year term. |
| **Adjustable mortgage** | Interest rate changes over the life of the loan, resulting in possible changes in your monthly payments, loan term, and/or principal. Some plans have rate or payment caps. |
| **Balloon mortgage** | Monthly payments based on fixed interest rate; usually short-term; payments may cover interest only with principal due in full at term end. |
| **Graduated payment mortgage** | Lower monthly payments rise gradually (usually over five to ten years), then level off for duration of term. |
| **Assumable mortgage** | Buyer takes over seller's original, below-market mortgage. |
| **Land contract** | Seller retains original mortgage. No transfer of title until loan is fully paid. |
| **Reverse mortgage** | Lender makes monthly payments to borrower, using owner's equity in property as collateral. |

SOURCE: Federal Trade Commission.

$150,000 in certain high-priced areas of the country.

For first-time home buyers, the federal government as well as state governments offer loan assistance to prospective buyers who meet eligibility requirements. For current information about these loan programs, consult local FHA and VA offices as well as your real estate agent.

### Q. What are jumbo loans?

**A.** Jumbo loans exceed the amount of loans allowed by the Federal National Mortgage Association (Fannie Mae) and the Federal Home Loan Association (Freddie Mac), the federal agencies that oversee the secondary market in mortgage loans. The maximum mortgage amount for Fannie Mae and Freddie Mac can go up or down and presently stands at $203,150.

Fannie Mae and Freddie Mac are not loan guarantors, they are purchasers from primary lenders. Fannie Mae and Freddie Mac purchase loans from lenders and then resell the loans to other organizations such as insurance companies and banks. On the other hand, FHA and VA are loan guarantors. Many FHA and VA loans are purchased by Fannie Mae and Freddie Mac.

Interest rates on jumbo loans typically are slightly higher than on other loans, but this isn't always the case. Lenders who intend to keep the mortgage in their portfolio tend to offer competitive interest rates.

### Q. What is negative amortization?

**A.** In a typical home loan, the borrower pays off the interest and principal in installments. This is known as amortization because the debt is gradually reduced.

Negative amortization can occur when the installment payments do not cover all the interest due each month. This unpaid interest is added on to the principal that is owed, resulting in a debt that increases, rather than decreases.

The worst problem with negative amortization occurs in a market in which home values decrease. Then the size of your debt could increase to the point where it would exceed the equity in your home. Sadly, you could sell your home and not be able to repay what you owe.

Most professionals advise buyers to avoid a negatively amortized loan. The risks outweigh the benefits of the lower payments. It may be better to postpone buying a home until you can make higher payments or investigate a lower-cost loan from the FHA or VA.

### Applying for a Home Loan

### Q. How do I apply for a loan?

**A.** Obtaining a loan requires a lot of paperwork and sometimes a lot of fortitude. The savings and loan scandals and the large number of foreclosures in recent years have forced lenders to take a much more critical look at their lending practices. While you won't be asked for your blood type, it's a good bet that you will be asked about everything in your financial history. Loan applications vary, but most require the following information:

- Employment history, salary history, and proof of employment. This may require you to obtain a letter from your employer as well as recent wage stubs. You may be asked for copies of your federal tax returns for recent years or copies of your W-2 statements. While there is no law that requires you to submit this information, the lender has the right to turn down your request for a loan if you refuse to supply pertinent information. If you are using other income to qualify for the loan, such as income from property, child support, or income from investments, you will need to provide proof of these as well.

- Credit history. This includes all the account numbers of all credit cards that you currently have. You may be asked to submit year-end statements that reveal how much interest was paid on these cards during the preceding year.

- Outstanding debts. These include automobile loans, alimony, child support payments, credit-card debt, etc.

- Assets. These include the value of any items you own, such as automobiles, rental property, stocks, bonds, cash, savings accounts, IRAs, retirement accounts, mutual funds, etc.

- Source of your down payment. The lender will want to make sure that you are not borrowing money to make your down payment. (If you are borrowing money and will be making interest payments, this will be taken into consideration.) If you are receiving a gift from relatives for a down payment, the lender will expect proof that the gift will be forthcoming.

### Q. How long does it take to get a home loan application approved?

**A.** When you apply for the loan, ask the lender how long the approval process is expected to take. It can take anywhere from twenty-four hours to three months, depending on a variety of factors. If you have included a mortgage-contingency clause in your purchase contract, be sure to inform your lender when you apply for the loan of the date the clause expires. Usually, your lender will work with you to meet the deadline or alert you that approval will take more time. At that point, you may be able to get an extension from the seller on the contingency.

Once your loan is approved, the lender will provide you with a loan commitment, which agrees to lend a specific amount of money on specific terms. A copy of this commitment can be provided to the seller to assure him or her that your financing is in place.

### Q. What is the lender obligated to tell me about the loan?

**A.** Federal law requires that the lender reveal all costs of the loan, including such items as appraisal fees, escrow fees, fees for the lender's attorney, service charges, and, of course, the interest rate on the loan. The interest rate must be presented as the annual percentage rate or APR. This is calculated by including the interest to be paid along with other fees, such as any points paid to originate the loan.

Under the terms of the federal Truth in Lending Act, lenders are required to use the same methods for computing the cost of credit and disclosing credit terms. This requirement allows borrowers to fairly compare the costs and terms of home loans. It is a much more reliable method for comparing costs than the advertised rate of the loan.

The federal Equal Credit Opportunity Act prohibits discrimination in any aspect of a home loan transaction on the basis of race, religion, age, color, national origin, receipt of public assistance funds, sex, marital status, or the exercise of any right under the Consumer Credit Protection Act. If a lender rejects your

loan application, you are entitled to know the specific reasons in writing.

Lenders are also prohibited from doing anything that discourages you from obtaining credit, including taking an excessively long time to process your application, being unwilling to discuss available types of loans, or failing to provide information required to apply for a loan. If you suspect that you are being discriminated against in applying for a loan, a complaint can be filed with the Office of Fair Housing and Equal Opportunity of the Department of Housing and Urban Development, Room 5204, Washington, D.C. 20410-2000. You also may file a complaint with the Federal Reserve Board of Governors or the District Reserve Bank serving your area. Check the government pages of the telephone book for their addresses. When making a complaint, be sure to include your name and address along with the name and address of the person or financial institution you are filing the complaint against, a short description of the alleged violation, and the date of the alleged violation.

### Q. What documents must I sign to secure the loan?

**A.** The borrower will sign many documents; however, two documents are essential to completing the loan transaction. One is a promissory note agreeing to repay the lender the money borrowed plus interest. This promissory note is a legally enforceable contract. The borrower may be responsible for repaying the note even if he or she later sells the home to a buyer who assumes the mortgage. The second document is a mortgage, or deed of trust, and gives the lender a security interest in the real estate. Having a security interest in your home means the lender may enforce repayment of the loan by selling the property. If you do not pay, you could lose your home.

## Key Provisions of the Mortgage

**Q. What is an assumable mortgage?**

**A.** An assumable mortgage allows you to transfer your existing mortgage debt to the buyer of your home. The new owner would "assume" (take over) your mortgage and pay you the difference between the amount you still owe and the agreed-upon sale price. Most lenders no longer allow buyers to assume mortgages. They generally insist on a "due-on-sale" clause under which the buyer must get a new mortgage. Some assumable mortgages remain on the market, however. If the interest rate is attractive, you should explore these. Some lenders will allow a mortgage to be assumed by charging a fee or adjusting the interest rate on the assumed mortgage.

Prior to assuming a mortgage, a prospective home buyer should obtain a written statement from the original lender stating:

- the amount still owed on the loan;
- the rate of interest for the remainder of the loan;
- the length of the repayment period remaining; and
- when the lender has the right to call in the loan (order payment of the entire amount) or change any of the existing terms.

Before the loan can be assumed, the lender may require the buyer to go through the lender's normal loan-application process so that the lender is sure the buyer is creditworthy. The particular form of loan-assumption agreement will vary depending upon your location.

**Q. What is a due-on-sale clause?**

**A.** Most—but not all—home loans made today contain a due-on-sale clause which requires that the seller pay his or her loan in its entirety at the time the sale is closed. This

## INSURING YOUR HOME LOAN

*Several types of insurance contracts pay your home loan if you die or become disabled. This type of insurance establishes an annual premium cost for the life of your loan. Because your loan declines as you pay down the principal (main amount of the loan), the amount of insurance coverage decreases each year, although the cost stays the same. In most cases, a term life insurance policy that can be used to pay off the loan in the event of your death is preferable to a mortgage insurance policy. Term life insurance is less expensive and offers better protection and more flexibility. All insurance products are relatively complicated. You may want to consult a financial professional or an attorney to check these policies before you buy one.*

*Because temporary or permanent disability can threaten your ability to pay your home loan, you may also want to consider buying a disability policy or participating in any disability insurance offered by your employer. Disability insurance can add to your peace of mind and that of your lender.*

means that the buyer cannot assume the seller's mortgage. Federal law has replaced state law in this area and due-on-sale clauses are enforceable.

## Q. *What is a late-payment charge?*

**A.** Most home loans include a late-payment charge. The lender charges it to the borrower if the monthly mortgage payment is late. These charges can be very expensive. You'll want to make sure you know when your loan payment is due and allow enough time for it to arrive by the due date if you are mailing your payment.

## Q. *What is a prepayment penalty?*

**A.** Although illegal in some states, where permitted, home loans include a prepayment penalty. This is a charge imposed if the borrower pays off the loan ahead of schedule. This penalty is usually one or two percent of the loan. It is not unusual for home loans to include a prepayment penalty for the first few years; however, you should avoid mortgages that require a prepayment penalty beyond the third year.

## Buying a Home from a Builder

## Q. *Are there any special considerations when you are buying a home from a builder?*

**A.** A buyer purchasing a new home from a builder may or may not work through an agent. If you are not working with an agent, you may want to consult your lawyer to ensure that the purchase contract with the builder contains no surprises. In addition, you may want to consider having the finished structure inspected notwithstanding its newness. Remember, it's the quality of the construction, not its newness, that is important. An independent inspection can give you this assurance.

If you are contracting with a builder on a home that is not built or finished, you will want to make sure you will get what you think you are buying. For example, model homes typically include options, rather than standard features. Along with superior windows and siding, these could include better-quality kitchen cabinets, higher-grade carpeting, and more expensive lighting fixtures. Make sure that the builder provides you with a complete list of standard and optional features. If you are choosing options, make sure the purchase contract includes the specific cost of all options.

You will want to know other facts as well, such as the type and extent of any landscaping to be provided by the builder, known plans for the development of surrounding property, and the exact provisions of any warranty from the builder. If possible, you will want a warranty that is insured by an insurance company, rather than a warranty guaranteed only by the builder. Finally, the builder should provide you with evidence that his or her subcontractors and material suppliers have waived any liens they might have against the property in the event the builder does not pay them for their work.

Specified dates for completion and occupancy should be included if the home is not yet built. You can provide for a penalty or for the right to cancel the contract if the builder exceeds these dates.

## THE TITLE

## Q. *How do you obtain title to a property?*

**A.** Title to real estate consists of ownership of and the right to use the property. A title search will help the buyer find out what rights the seller has, including the authority to sell.

Unlike personal property, title to which may pass when the property changes hands, the rights to the various components of real estate may be owned, leased, or affected by claims or liens of different people. Among the many possible existing claims against real estate are: mineral rights; unpaid mortgages; liens of workers such as plumbers and liens of persons supplying construction material, both of which are known as mechanic's liens; outstanding court judgments; liens for unpaid taxes; and power-line easements, road rights-of-way and drainage easements.

Second, there may be questions about whether the seller can convey good title. A title search reveals this by discovering whether there are any breaks in the chain of title all the way back to the original owner. Gaps in the property's chain of title might make it impossible for the person who appears to be the seller to transfer good title to a prospective buyer.

An attorney, an abstract company, or a title company can conduct a title search of the public records of all deeds, mortgages, and other instruments that affect the seller's title to the real estate in question. The results of this search are usually compiled in an "abstract of title" or title insurance commitment to help the buyer determine who has actual title to the property, whether there are any restrictive covenants that could limit the use of the property, and whether any individuals or institutions have some interest or claim on it.

Government regulations, such as zoning or occupancy laws, also affect your use of the real estate. As a buyer, you will want to know how these restrictions might affect your use of the property.

There also may be subdivision covenants or common-ownership association bylaws that restrict the use you can make of your property. They could, for example, restrict you from using your property to store liquor, prevent you from renting your home, or place architectural controls on your property. Covenants written long ago may contain restrictions that are unenforceable today, such as prohibitions against selling your home to members of certain racial or ethnic groups. These can be ignored but

covenants that are enforceable should be understood. Ask for a copy of these restrictions before you make an offer to purchase. Your attorney can help you decide if a covenant is legal and binding.

Any defects in the title should be corrected before the closing. Typically, the seller is responsible for remedying title defects. For these reasons, even in areas of the country where the buyer receives a title insurance policy, buyers and sellers may want the advice of a lawyer. Buyers and sellers should check to see what types of title insurance policies are available, their costs, reliability, and so forth.

### Q. What is title insurance?

**A.** An owner's title insurance policy is an agreement that the title insurance company will defend against and pay losses involved in any claim covered by the policy's terms, as long as the buyer or the buyer's heirs own an interest in the property. The policy will cover a prior owner if, in selling the property, he or she gave a deed containing certain warranties with respect to title.

The policy provides two types of coverage. First, if someone contests the buyer's insured title in a legal action, the insurer will defend the title at no expense to the buyer. Second, if there is a defect in the title that cannot be eliminated, title insurance provides financial indemnity to protect the buyer from loss due to the defect, up to the amount of the policy.

Title insurance is available from title companies and, in some states, from lawyers' groups. Title insurance varies in price in different parts of the country. The extent of the protection is only as broad as the language of the policy itself. The buyer's attorney can help gauge whether the policy is adequate.

Lenders usually require buyers to obtain title insurance that protects only the lender. This is known as a lender's title policy. The buyer may have to pay for additional title insurance to protect his or her interests or negotiate with the seller to purchase such a policy. For more on title insurance, see page 149 of the chapter on owning a home.

An additional consideration is what legal title to hold your property in (joint tenancy, tenancy by the entirety, etc.) This topic is discussed fully on pages 150–156 of the chapter on home ownership.

## THE CLOSING

### Q. What happens at the closing?

**A.** The real estate closing is the final stage in the process of buying a home. The closing is a meeting at which the buyer and seller, usually accompanied by their respective lawyers and real estate agents, complete the sale. At this meeting, the buyer usually makes all the required payments. The seller produces all documents necessary for the transfer of good—that is, marketable—title and delivers a deed that transfers the title to the buyer.

Before the closing, the parties and their lawyers will review all documents to see that everyone is fulfilling all conditions and promises of the contract. A closing statement or settlement sheet is prepared, fully listing the financial aspects of the closing. The Real Estate Settlement Procedures Act (RESPA) will apply in any transaction in which a buyer is obtaining a federally insured mortgage from a financial institution. This requires use of a settlement sheet developed by the Department of Housing and Urban Development. In other closings in which the buyer is not obtaining a mortgage, another form of settlement sheet is usually prepared.

Both buyers and sellers should expect to sign a lot of papers at the closing. Buyers should expect to sign the following:

- A promissory note promising to pay in full the loan and interest.

- The mortgage document which secures the promissory note by giving the lender an interest in the property and the right to take and sell the property—that is, foreclose—if the mortgage payments aren't made.

- A truth in lending form that requires the lender to tell you in advance the approximate annual percentage rate of the loan over the loan's term.

- A typed loan application form.

- A payment letter telling the buyer the amount of the first payment and when it is due.

- An affidavit that the buyer's various names (if he or she has used more than one) all refer to the same person.

- A survey form stating that the buyer has seen and understands the survey of the property and that it fairly depicts the property.

- A private mortgage insurance application, usually required on loans with a down payment of less than 20 percent.

- A termite inspection or other inspection form, indicating that the buyer has seen a report of any inspections that were made.

The seller can expect to sign the following documents:

- The deed transferring title in the real estate from the seller to the buyer.

- A bill of sale transferring ownership of any personal property that may be included in the sale of the real estate.

- An affidavit of title in which the seller states that he or she has the legal right to sell the real estate and that there are no liens or encumbrances (judgments, mortgages, or taxes owed) on the property.

- An affidavit as to mechanic's liens and possession indicating that the seller has not had any work done on the property that would give rise to a mechanic's lien and that there are no parties other than the seller entitled to possess the property.

- An occupancy certificate indicating that a new home complies with the local housing code.

Both buyer and seller will also sign the following:

- An affidavit specifying the purchase price and indicating the source of the purchase price. (This affidavit assures the lender that the buyer has not received any undisclosed loans from the seller that could negatively affect the buyer's ability to repay the lender's loan.)
- A RESPA form developed by the federal Department of Housing and Urban Development and sometimes a separate closing statement, specifying all costs associated with the transaction.

### Q. What are some financial aspects of the closing?

**A.** At the time of closing, the seller and buyer will total up various credits in order to determine how much money the buyer must pay. The seller will receive credits for such items as fuel on hand (such as oil in the home heating tank), unused insurance premiums, prepaid interest, and escrow deposits for insurance, taxes, and public utility charges such as water and sewer fees. These credits also will include any other items prepaid by the seller that will benefit the buyer.

The buyer normally will receive credits for such items as the earnest money deposited and taxes or special assessments that the seller has not paid. The settlement sheet also will specify who is responsible for the payment of various expenses. These will include the sales commissions and the costs of the title search, inspections, recording fees, transaction taxes, and the like. The allocation of such expenses will depend on the terms of your contract as well as the law and customs in your area. Your real estate agent or attorney should advise you ahead of time of how much money you will need at the closing. Typically, you will be required to have a certified check in the amount required to meet these expenses.

The chart below by no means exhausts the list of fees that might be charged at closing. Other common fees include: loan origination fee to cover the lender's administrative costs in processing the loan; credit report fee; lender's appraisal fee; mortgage insurance application fee; mortgage insurance premium; and hazard insurance premium. Buyers also may have to put money into escrow to assure future payment of such recurring items as real estate taxes. Also, there often are separate document fees that cover the preparation of final legal papers such as the promissory note and mortgage or deed of trust.

### Closing Costs

Closing costs usually include all or most of the following:

| | |
|---|---|
| Appraisal fee | This is the fee paid for an appraisal of the property. It is required by the lender and often is paid for by the buyer. The Federal Housing Administration and Veterans Administration establish the appraisal fees for mortgages that they guarantee. |
| Attorney's fee | The buyer and seller pay the fees for their own lawyers. In some states, buyers are required to pay for the lender's attorney. This fee may be a certain percentage of the mortgage or a fixed fee. |

# A Sample Settlement (Closing) Worksheet

This is a sample worksheet for a family purchasing a $100,000 house and getting a new $80,000 loan. Line 103 assumes that their total settlement charges are $4,000. This figure is merely illustrative. The amount may be higher in some areas and for some types of transactions, and lower for others.

| J. Summary of Borrower's Transaction | |
|---|---|
| **100. Gross Amount Due From Borrower** | |
| 101. Contract sales price | 100,000.00 |
| 102. Personal property | |
| 103. Settlement charges to borrower | 4,000.00 |
| 104. | |
| 105. | |
| Adjustments for items paid by seller in advance | |
| 106. City/town taxes          to | |
| 107. County taxes          to | |
| 108. Assessments **6/30 to 7/31 (owners assn)** | 40.00 |
| 109. **Fuel Oil 25 gal. $1.00/gal.** | 25.00 |
| 110. | |
| 111. | |
| 112. | |
| **120. Gross Amount Due From Borrower** | **104,065.00** |
| **200. Amounts Paid By Or In Behalf Of Borrower** | |
| 201. Deposit or earnest money | 2,000.00 |
| 202. Principal amount of new loan(s) | 80,000.00 |
| 203. Existing loan(s) taken subject to | |
| 204. | |
| 205. | |
| 206. | |
| 207. | |
| 208. | |
| 209. | |

| Adjustments for items unpaid by seller | |
|---|---|
| 210. City/town taxes                to | |
| 211. County taxes **1/1 to 6/30 $1,200/year** | 600.00 |
| 212. Assessments **1/1 to 6/30 $200/year** | 100.00 |
| 213. | |
| 214. | |
| 215. | |
| 216. | |
| 217. | |
| 218. | |
| 219. | |
| **220. Total Paid By/For Borrower** | **82,700.00** |
| **300. Cash At Settlement From/To Borrower** | |
| 301. Gross Amount due from borrower (line 120) | 104,065.00 |
| 302. Less amounts paid by/for borrower (line 220) | ( 82,700.00) |
| 303. Cash  ☒ From  ☐ To Borrower | 21,365.00 |

Source: Department of Housing and Urban Development.

| | |
|---|---|
| Survey fee | If the lender requires a registered survey, the buyer probably will pay the fee. You may be able to avoid this fee if the lender agrees to accept a recent survey done for the seller. However, the seller must sign a document stating that the property lines have not changed since the completion of the survey and there have been no additional improvements to the property since the survey was taken. Even then, a title insurance company may require a new survey unless the survey is current or has been recertified recently. |
| Loan discount fee | This is the lender's charge to the buyer (points) to obtain the loan. The buyer may have paid some of this fee in advance to secure the loan. |
| Inspection fees | Charges for general inspections or inspections required by local laws. The buyer or seller may be responsible for |

these fees depending on the contract and local law and custom.

Title fees — Cost of title search.

Title insurance — The cost of title insurance, usually divided between the seller and buyer. The seller pays for the buyer's policy and the buyer pays for the lender's policy.

Recording fees — The cost for recording change of ownership such as a deed; recording the buyer's mortgage; recording the release of the seller's mortgage by the seller's lender; and recording the release of any liens found in the record of title.

## Ownership Options

**Q. What form of ownership is best for a home?**

**A.** To take title to the home, ownership must be declared in one of various ways. This may be as a single owner, joint tenancy, tenancy in common, or tenancy by the entirety. Each offers various advantages and disadvantages, depending on your personal situation. These options are discussed in the chapters on home ownership and estate planning.

**Q. How is ownership affected if I live in a community property state?**

**A.** Community property states include Arizona, California, Idaho, Louisiana, Nevada, New Mexico, Texas, Washington, and Wisconsin. If you live in a community property state, state law holds that the property you bought while married belongs to each member of the couple equally, no matter whose money actu-

ally paid for it and regardless of whose name is on the title.

This provision generally applies to property acquired during the marriage, rather than property owned before the marriage or property that is inherited during the marriage. But state laws vary and you would be wise to discover how community property laws in your state apply to any real estate purchase under consideration and what form of ownership is best for your situation.

## OPTIONS FOR OWNING PROPERTY

*Most married couples own property in joint tenancy or as tenants by the entirety. There are other options and the option that is best for you will depend on a variety of factors such as your estate tax situation and provisions you may want to make for children, stepchildren, or other relatives. For example, couples who have children from previous marriages may want their home equity transferred to their children upon their death, rather than to the spouse. Couples who are joint tenants may want to provide in their wills for the distribution of property if both die simultaneously. Be sure to consult an attorney about the various advantages and disadvantages of different types of ownership so that you can make an informed decision about the form of ownership that is best for you.*

## TAX CONSIDERATIONS

**Q. What is a transfer tax?**

**A.** Depending on your state and local laws, there may be state or local transfer taxes due on the amount paid to purchase a home. A transfer tax is a tax paid for the privilege of transferring ownership of real property.

If the home is financed, there may be a documentary tax on the note and an intangible tax on the loan. Generally, the seller pays the cost of the transfer tax but in most cases it is negotiable. The buyer generally pays the cost of the documentary tax on the note and the tax on the loan.

**Q. What is property tax?**

**A.** Most homes are assessed a property tax. This is a yearly tax based on the assessed value of your property, usually paid to the local community. As a general rule, the tax is divided among the municipality (city and town), county, school districts (including the local school district and community colleges), and other governmental units. Currently, these taxes are deductible against taxable income on your federal tax return.

Depending on your state's laws, the amount you pay in property tax also may be deductible on your state income tax return.

**Q. How can I find out the current property taxes on a home?**

**A.** The seller should be willing to reveal the property taxes paid on the home over the last few years. If not, you or your attorney can obtain this information from the local tax assessor's office.

**Q. Will my purchase of a home affect the property taxes?**

**A.** Depending on how your state assesses property, a purchase can affect the amount of property taxes to be paid. For example, in some states, property tax increases occur only when a home changes ownership. The tax assessor reassesses the home using the price paid as its new value; in some cases, the taxes may skyrocket. In addition, many states reassess property every three or four years. If you are buying the home at the end of that cycle, you may see a large increase in property taxes. While the amount of tax may not be the deciding factor in your decision to buy, you will want to take it into account in determining your total monthly housing costs.

**Q. What is the difference between "assessed value" and "appraised value"?**

**A.** The assessed value of a home, determined by the tax assessor, is the basis for property taxes. It may or may not reflect the market value, that is, the price at which the home would be expected to sell. If you know the assessed value of a home, you can then determine the taxes to be paid on it. Contact the assessor's office of the city or county in which the home is located for the total tax rate. The tax rate usually is stated in "mills" and is applied to each one thousand dollars of assessed valuation. For example, a tax rate of ten mills on a home assessed at one hundred thousand dollars would be one thousand dollars. Be aware that not all states assess homes at their full market value. Some states assess on only a portion of the home's value.

The appraised value is an estimate of the property's market value made by a trained appraiser. A lender normally will require an appraisal to determine that the selling price does not exceed the property's market value or fall below the lender's mortgage.

**Q. Is there anything I can do if my home is assessed at a higher value than I paid for it?**

**A.** You may be able to appeal the assessment, based on your purchase price. Once you have purchased the home at fair market value, you can appeal to the assessor's board or office. You must prove, however, that the sale was an "arm's-length transaction." In other words, you cannot purchase the home from a relative at a below-market cost and expect that your appeal will be successful. If the assessor grants your appeal and reduces the assessment, future taxes to be paid would be lowered. See pages 183–184 in the chapter on home ownership for more on lowering property taxes.

### Q. What items involving home ownership are deductible against federal income tax?

**A.** Both property tax and interest on loans of up to one million dollars in principal are deductible against your taxable income when you file your federal income tax form. Federal law also permits you to borrow up to one hundred thousand dollars through a home equity loan and deduct the interest, as long as the total debt on the home (including the first mortgage) does not exceed the fair market value of the home. Remember, however, that you must itemize to claim these deductions; they are not available to taxpayers who claim a standard deduction. New buyers may deduct any loan fees or points paid to obtain a mortgage in the tax year in which the points were paid, but only if the points were paid by funds other than the mortgage funds borrowed by the buyer. A point is equal to 1 percent of the amount borrowed. As noted earlier, loan fees or points paid to refinance a mortgage cannot be claimed in a single year; they must be spread out over the life of the loan.

Be aware that transfer taxes and most other local real estate taxes payable in a real estate transaction are not deductible. The same is true for other closing costs such as appraisal fees and recording fees. See pages 182 and 184 for more on possible federal tax breaks.

## Tax Considerations When Selling Your Home

### Q. Do I have to pay federal taxes on the sale of my home?

**A.** If you are selling a home, the profit realized on the sale is generally taxable as a capital gain. However, there are ways to defer or avoid this tax if your home is your primary residence.

The IRS Code 1034 "roll-over" residence replacement rule may allow you to defer paying any capital gains tax if you sell a primary residence and purchase a new primary residence of equal or higher value within twenty-four months either before or after the sale of your home. This provision also allows you to buy a home of lesser value if you use the difference in price to renovate the new home within twenty-four months. Note, however, that this provision only applies to a primary residence; it does not apply to second homes. As a general rule, this provision can be used only once in a twenty-four-month period. However, if a job change requires you to move at least thirty-five miles from your former job, the provision can be used more than once in a twenty-four-month period.

Even though you intend to defer paying taxes on any profits realized from the sale of a primary residence, you still must file a form with the IRS for the year in which the sale occurred. This form requires you to disclose the price of the home, the cost of any allowed improvements, real estate fees deducted from the sale, and any other eligible deductions against the sale price. If you have not yet purchased a new home but intend to within twenty-four months, you must still fill out this form and then submit another form when you purchase a new primary residence.

Certain people, including some military service employees and people who have lived outside the United States, may be eligible for a longer time within which to exercise the "roll-over" provision. Check with your attorney or tax adviser for details.

### Q. How do I determine my profits?

**A.** You can calculate your profits by subtracting the adjusted cost basis of your home from its adjusted sales price. You can compute the adjusted cost basis by subtracting certain items—such as the sales commission, lawyer's fees, and fix-up expenses—from the price of your home when you bought it.

To calculate the adjusted sales price, start with the selling price. Then subtract the cost of capital improvements made while you owned the home and closing costs not deducted when you bought it. Note that you may not subtract the cost of repairs. The IRS is very strict about what it considers improvements. For example, repairing a water heater is not considered an improvement but adding a dishwasher is. Also, you may deduct the labor costs paid to a tradesperson (such as a carpenter) but not any costs for your own labor. The IRS requires home sellers to complete a form in the year of the sale that includes these calculations. You also will want to keep all receipts for any costs you are deducting from the sale. Without such written proof, the IRS is not likely to allow your deductions.

### Q. Now I have figured my profits. What about figuring my taxes?

**A.** First, remember that if there is no profit, you do not have to worry about paying taxes; however, the IRS does not allow you to deduct any loss on a primary residence. If you do not buy a new primary residence within twenty-four months, if your new primary residence does not cost as much as or more than the sales price of your old home, or if you choose to pay the taxes, you owe taxes on at least some of the profits. Profits are treated as capital gains, currently taxed at 28 percent.

### Q. What about the home exemption for senior citizens I have heard about?

**A.** Taxpayers aged 55 and older are eligible for an exclusion of up to $125,000 of capital gains on the sale of their main residence. This means they do not have to pay taxes on up to $125,000 in profits on the sale of their home. This is a once-in-a-lifetime exclusion. You should use it only after careful consideration. For example, the IRS views a married couple as one person for purposes of this exclusion. If one spouse has already used the exclusion, the other spouse may not use it on the sale of another jointly owned home.

The IRS requires specific criteria to use this exclusion:

- one of the owners must be 55 or older;

- you must have lived in the home as your primary residence for a minimum of three of the last five years before the sale;

- you may not rent out your home or fail to live there for more than six months of at least three of the five years before the sale.

If you fail to meet any of these guidelines, the IRS will not allow the exclusion.

The law also allows you to combine the $125,000 exclusion with the "roll-over" residence replacement rule. This allows a homeowner to avoid any capital gains tax. For example, if you sold your home and realized $250,000 in profits, you could use the $125,000 exemption and purchase a new home that cost at least $125,000 within twenty-four months. This would avoid any tax.

The $125,000 exclusion is complicated, as is determining profits on the sale of a home. If you are considering using this exclusion, consider consulting a financial planner, accountant, or tax attorney to determine if you qualify for the exemption and whether or not you have correctly figured your profits.

### Q. Will I also owe state and local taxes on my profits?

**A.** It depends. You may live in a state or city that will require you to pay state or local taxes on the profits of a home. Some states or local communities also charge a "transfer tax" on the sale of property. This tax is usually levied as a percentage of the sales price.

### Q. What is a sale-leaseback?

**A.** A sale-leaseback occurs when you agree to sell your home to a buyer who agrees to rent the home to you for a certain period of time. Usually, this type of arrangement occurs between retired parents and their adult children. A sale-leaseback often provides the most advantages to retirees in low tax brackets who have children in high tax brackets. The family can structure it so that the children carry the burden of paying interest and take the benefit of deducting the interest from their taxes. The parents benefit by receiving income to offset expenses.

The sale-leaseback can be established in two ways. Either the buyer can obtain a loan to buy the home outright or the seller can provide some of the financing. In the first case, the seller would pay rent to the buyer. In the second case, the seller would pay rent to the buyer while the buyer would make payments to the seller on the loan given by the seller.

If you are considering this arrangement between relatives, be sure to have your agreement in writing and make sure that it conforms to IRS rules. For example, the IRS requires that the buyer pay a fair market price for the home and that the seller pay a fair market rent in order for the arrangement to avoid qualifying as a gift. In other words, the IRS will not permit you to structure a sale-leaseback to lower your estate taxes. An attorney can help you draw up the necessary papers to make sure you don't inadvertently run afoul of the IRS rules and end up with a penalty or gift tax. See the chapter in this book on older Americans for more on sales-leasebacks, reverse mortgages, gift annuities, and other options of particular interest to older persons.

## Gift Annuities

### Q. How does a gift annuity work?

**A.** A homeowner interested in converting home equity into income may want to consider a gift annuity in which the homeowner donates the home to a qualified charitable institution and is eligible for a tax deduction against taxable income in the year in which the donation is made. In return, the institution provides an annuity to the donor and grants the donor a life estate in the home. This means that the donor may remain in the home for his or her lifetime and is responsible for all taxes and maintenance on the home. At the donor's death, the property becomes the possession of the charitable institution.

This arrangement offers several tax advantages, particularly for homeowners who do not have heirs or who want to reduce the size of their taxable estate. Again, a financial professional or tax attorney should be consulted.

## BUYING IN A MULTI-UNIT DWELLING

### Q. What is the difference between a condominium and a co-op?

**A.** A condominium is a common-interest community in which individual units are separately owned but the owners share an interest in common areas, for example, hallways, roofs, and exteriors. With a cooperative, or co-op, buyers purchase shares of stock in a corporation that owns a building. A condominium owner has title to his or her unit; a co-op owner receives a proportionate amount of shares in the corporation that owns the building, based on the unit's proportion of the building.

For the purposes of income tax laws and other laws regarding real estate, a condominium is treated as a single-family home. But an association has the right to impose

## OWNERSHIP IN A COMMON-INTEREST COMMUNITY

*A common-interest community is real estate in which ownership of individual portions of the property carries an obligation to pay money to another person, usually an association, for maintenance, taxes, upkeep and insurance of property other than the individually owned portion of the property. Common-interest communities can come in many forms. There are condominiums, cooperatives, planned-unit developments and private-easement communities. In most of these common-interest communities involving residences, there is a homeowners' association charged with providing common services and maintaining the common areas. The homeowners' association may also have jurisdiction over use and occupancy within the individual units.*

*Almost all common-interest communities are described in a declaration, master deed, or declaration of covenants, conditions, and restrictions found in the land records.*

maintenance fees, demand escrow payments for large repair bills, and manage the overall operation of the entire building. Owners of co-ops must abide by the corporation rules; additionally, if they fail to pay their fees, they may be evicted because they do not hold title to their unit. (See the section on shared ownership in the chapter on home ownership—especially page 201—for more on living in this kind of property.)

**Q. Are there differences between common-interest home ownership and single-family home ownership?**

**A.** In single-family home ownership, the control, decisions, and expenses are the responsibility of the owner, subject to zoning restrictions established by local law and any restrictions contained in the declaration of the builder who originally developed the property. As a general rule, multi-unit ownership is subject to more extensive regulation than single-family ownership. For example, there are statutes, rules, and regulations governing what you may and may not do with your condominium, co-op, or other multi-unit dwelling.

Be sure to obtain all the information on the terms of sale and such regulations. Ask to see the bylaws, operating budget, management agreement, and regulating agreement. Many states require disclosures to the purchasers of units in a common-interest community. Some states have a central agency that licenses and regulates the development and sale of common-interest community units.

The cost of the unit is not the limit of your financial obligation with multi-unit real estate. There will be monthly assessments to cover maintenance and related expenses for operating the common areas. These assessments will be in proportion to the percentage you own of the total complex. If all the apartments in a ten-unit building are the same size, each owner would have a 10 percent ownership stake. This means that each owner will pay 10 percent of its assessments.

These costs may well increase over time. You should determine the amount of the monthly assessment and the potential increase before signing an offer to purchase. In addition, unit owners are subject to special assessments above and beyond the basic assessment, to pay for unforeseen improvements or repairs. Always ask about pending projects and their approximate cost. You also should be sure that there is enough liability insurance coverage for the entire development.

### Q. Can I obtain a mortgage for a co-op?

**A.** The law defines owning a condominium as owning a piece of real estate. Owning a co-op, however, means that you own shares of stock in a building. Formerly, it was not easy to get a mortgage to buy a co-op. That was why prices on co-ops usually were much lower than condominium prices. Once the federal government amended the law to allow the Federal National Mortgage Association (Fannie Mae) to buy co-op loans, it made it much easier for prospective co-op buyers to obtain mortgages. Today, it is only slightly more difficult to obtain a mortgage for a co-op than for a condominium, but prices generally remain lower because of the extra restrictions placed on co-op owners.

### Q. What criteria should be considered when buying a condominium or co-op?

**A.** One of the best ways to find out information about a condominium association, cooperative corporation, or other common-interest property is to talk to owners or shareholders. Ask them what they like best about where they live and what their complaints are. Along with all the things one would consider about a single-family home, such as neighborhood, prospective common-interest buyers should consider the following:

- Percentage of owner-occupants and renters. A high percentage of renters could indicate poor sales and/or absentee landlords who are less interested in maintaining the building. Because of these risks, it is often difficult for prospective buyers to obtain loans for units in buildings with a high percentage of renters.

- Monthly maintenance fees, special assessments, and the history of such items. You also will want to ask whether the association or corporation is involved in any lawsuits brought by builders, neighbors, or former owners.

- Financial condition of the association or corporation. You will want to get a copy of the most recent financial statement and budgets.

- Quality of construction. Hire an inspector and make certain that he or she checks the soundproofing, the condition of shared common areas, such as the roof and patios, and the electrical, heating, and plumbing systems.

- Bylaws and/or covenants. If these are too restrictive, you may have trouble in obtaining a loan or selling your unit or share in the corporation.

The chapter on home ownership beginning on page 145 contains detailed information about shared ownership.

## THE FAIR HOUSING ACT

### Q. Can a homeowner legally refuse to sell a home to a potential buyer?

**A.** The Fair Housing Act, Title VIII of the Civil Rights Act of 1968, covers housing discrimination. This law prohibits housing discrimination by real estate firms and homeowners. This means that homeowners may not refuse to lease or sell property based on race, religion, gender, color, or national origin. In some localities, special housing discrimination ordinances or laws also cover sexual orientation. This does not mean, however, that sellers must sell you their home. It means that you could take legal action if the seller refuses to sell and you believe it was due to discrimination.

A homeowner can face serious financial penalties if found in violation of this law. The potential buyer could sue for actual monetary losses as well as attorney's fees, court costs, and even punitive damages.

A homeowner may lawfully discriminate on economic grounds. Without too much fear of legal action, a seller could refuse the bid of a buyer with a poor credit rating or inability to obtain a loan. The homeowner's argument could be that he or she cannot be forced to remove the home from the market while waiting for a loan commitment that had little chance of materializing. Perhaps the safest thing for the seller to do if the economic viability of an offer is in question is to tell the buyer that offer might be accepted once the loan commitment is obtained—if no other offers were received in the interim.

**Q. What is steering?**

**A.** Real estate firms and agents also are covered by the Fair Housing Act, which prohibits them from steering, a practice of showing potential buyers homes located only in certain neighborhoods. For example, a firm or agent might be accused of steering if the homes shown to prospective black buyers were located only in black neighborhoods.

**Q. How can I tell if discrimination is occurring, and what can I do about it?**

**A.** You may suspect discrimination if:

- somebody tells you that a listed home is no longer for sale but it remains on the market;
- an agent avoids showing you homes in areas you have requested;
- a seller refuses a full-price bid on a home.

If you suspect that someone has discriminated against you, request a complaint form by calling the federal Department of Housing and Urban Development (HUD) at 1-800-424-8590. Its job is to investigate such complaints. You also may be able to contact a local civil rights organization to find out if your area has specific organizations to contact. Usually, you will have to consult a lawyer about possible legal action against the homeowner.

---

## WHERE TO GET MORE INFORMATION

Nearly every state has federal information centers where information on federal services, programs, and regulations is available to consumers. Check the government pages of your local telephone directory for the office nearest you. The local library also can be a good source of helpful, free information. Various nonprofit agencies, such as the Better Business Bureau offices, can help you get more information on your legal rights and obligations in buying and selling a home. Look in your local telephone directory for the BBB office nearest to you.

The federal government publishes a listing of many free or low-cost pamphlets on home ownership and home buying. This listing can be obtained from the Consumer Information Center–4B, P.O. Box 100, Pueblo, CO 81002; telephone (719) 948-3334.

For information on HUD programs, contact the federal Department of Housing and Urban Development (HUD), Library and Information Services, 451 Seventh Street, SW, Room 8141, Washington, DC 20410; telephone: (202) 708-1422. This information also may be available at some local HUD offices.

*Home-Made Money: A Consumers Guide to Home Equity Conversion* is available from the American Association of Retired Persons (AARP), AARP Fulfillment, Home-Made Money, Department BHG, 1909 K Street, NW, Washington DC 20049.

The Internal Revenue Service (IRS) is an excellent source of information on tax questions relating to owning a home. Its national toll free number is 1-800-829-3676. Its tele-tax service has recorded tax information on 140 topics. You can find the toll-free phone number for your state by calling the IRS office in your area. Topics include the sale of a home, reporting gains from home sales, installment plans, and exclusion of gain for people aged 55 or older.

The IRS also publishes several free pamphlets dealing with common tax questions. These include: *Real Estate Taxes* (Publication 530), *Limits on Home Mortgage Interest Deductions* (Publication 936), and *Tax Information on Selling Your Home* (Publication 523).

# C H A P T E R   F I V E

■

# Home Ownership

# INTRODUCTION

THE RIGHT TO OWN PROPERTY is so deeply embedded in the American legal system that the Bill of Rights places the right to property on an equal level with the right to life and liberty. The Fifth Amendment to the Constitution declares that no one may deprive someone of life, liberty, or property without due process of law and prohibits the government from taking private property for public use without paying just compensation for it.

Owning property carries with it responsibility on the part of the homeowner. You may be able to hire someone to change a faucet washer, fix a broken windowpane, or cope with rising water in the basement, but there are some legal matters that you should understand to make sure your ownership is not jeopardized. This section covers a basic introduction to the law of home ownership, including rights and restrictions, title questions, financial issues, ownership options, liability and insurance, remodeling, working with contractors, and issues involving shared ownership in condominiums, cooperatives, and other common-interest communities.

## PROPERTY RIGHTS AND RESTRICTIONS

### Q. What are my rights as a homeowner?

**A.** Generally, what you do with the home you own is up to you. You have a right to maintain or neglect, preserve or remodel, keep, sell or give away, and enjoy your home as you see fit. These rights, however, are limited by federal, state, and local laws and statutes. For example, under the federal Fair Housing Act, you may not discriminate when renting your property. In terms of local statutes, your home must conform to zoning and building codes in your municipality. If your garage is falling down and thus creating a potential hazard, the community may be able to force you to repair or raze it. Likewise, zoning codes may prevent you from adding a three-story addition.

Although the rights our society and the law afford to homeowners are extensive, they are not absolute. The people who live around you also have rights, so the law places certain restrictions on the use of your property. If you are not mindful of zoning, building codes, easements, water rights, and local ordinances on noise, you could find yourself in trouble.

### Zoning Limitations

### Q. How do zoning codes affect my property rights?

**A.** To avoid urban mishmash, municipalities often restrict business and industry to particular designated areas. Other areas are zoned residential, including apartment buildings, or zoned strictly for single-family homes. If your neighborhood is zoned residential, you won't have to worry about a pool hall or gas station going up next to your house, but it also means that there are certain restrictions on what you can do with your property.

Zoning laws vary among communities. While some municipalities mandate few if any zoning restrictions, others enforce very strict zoning laws, controlling such items as the maximum size of a dog house and the height of a

## RIGHTS TO NATURAL RESOURCES

*You may use, sell or restrict the use of your property's natural resources, from stands of timber on the surface to minerals lying beneath. Note, however, that because surface and underground water, oil, and gas move about without regard to property lines, you don't necessarily have the right to pump out as much as you want from a well on your property. Removing resources such as these is subject to state and federal regulation. For example, if there is a stream running through your land, in most states you cannot dam it up to the point where downstream neighbors do not get water.*

fence. If you are planning to build any sort of addition or new structure, check with your local building department about zoning restrictions on your property. If you are still unsure, consult a lawyer.

### Q. Can zoning codes prohibit me from running a business in my home?

**A.** A typical residential zoning law probably would not preclude you from operating a home-based business that would not alter the character of the neighborhood, such as telephone sales, freelance writing, or mail-order distribution. But if the home-based business will require signs and frequent traffic from customers, check with the local department of building and zoning before making any kind of

investment. Also, be sure to ask about anything you must do to license your business.

### Q. Is there a way to avoid zoning restrictions?

**A.** Most communities allow you to apply for a variance if you wish to make a minor change to your property that would violate zoning restrictions. Essentially, a variance is permission from the governing body to deviate from the zoning laws. The zoning department can provide materials explaining how to seek a variance. The steps may involve a public hearing, an appearance before the planning commission, and approval by the town governing board. It is up to you to show that the proposed change is required by a hardship caused by the shape, condition, or location of your property, and will not alter the character of the neighborhood or reduce neighboring property values.

If your plans call for a major change, you may apply for a zoning change. For example, if you live near the boundary of an area zoned commercial and you want to turn your 19th-century house into a doctor's office, you might be able to persuade the zoning authorities to extend the boundaries a bit. Again, you would have to show that the change would not hurt property values and convince your neighbors that it would not diminish their property rights.

## Restrictive Covenants

### Q. What are covenants?

**A.** Covenants, also called conditions, consist of private restrictions designed to maintain quality control over a neighborhood. A builder may draw up covenants affecting a new subdivision he or she is developing, although they also exist in older subdivisions. Covenants typically restrict such things as lot size, square footage, and architectural design; they also may prohibit satellite dishes, boats and motor homes, certain types of fences, and unsightly activities such as auto repair.

### Q. How do covenants affect my property rights?

**A.** Covenants "run with the land," which means that they bind all future owners of the property unless all property owners in the affected subdivision join in releasing them. Covenants may restrict your use of your land even if municipal zoning laws permit the proposed use. You should have received a list of the covenants from your real estate agent when you bought your home. If not, a list should be available from any existing homeowner association. As with zoning codes, you may be able to negotiate a minor variance, such as building an addition slightly higher than the covenant's limit.

Note that covenants must comply with state and federal laws. Old covenants that prohibit homeowners from selling their homes to persons of certain races and religions are not enforceable.

## Easements

### Q. What is an easement?

**A.** An easement on your property indicates that someone else may have a right to use part of it for a specific purpose. A common example is a power company's easement to run a power line over your backyard. The developer normally establishes these types of easements when the subdivision is plotted or the house is built in order to provide utilities to the development.

Neighbors also may have an easement on your property, whether to use your driveway to get to their house (a positive easement) or one that restricts you from blocking their view of the lake (a negative easement). Or they might have a profit (short for the French term *profit a prendre*, which means "profit to be taken"), allowing them to remove something from your property such as raspberries, coal, or timber.

### Q. How are easements created?

**A.** An easement or profit may be created by a deed, by a will, or by implication—such as if a previous owner divided a single lot in half and the only access to the back lot may be through the front one. Or, if a neighbor has been using your property in some way for a long time, such

### CHECKING OUT EASEMENTS

*Easements are recorded at the county courthouse, but they may be scattered among various plats, deed books, and mortgage books. The best way to find out about them is through a professional title search, which most likely transpired if you obtained title insurance or an opinion of title before buying the house. If you discover an easement, check the wording. When a document grants an easement to a particular person, the restriction may cease when he or she dies or sells the property. But if it's granted to someone and "his heirs and assigns," it's probably in effect no matter who owns the property. Unless and until the easement expires, your legal obligation is to refrain from interfering with that right.*

as by driving on your private road, he may be able to secure a prescriptive easement to continue doing so whether you want him to or not. Courts are willing to grant prescriptive easements when the neighbor has been engaging in the activity in question for a period of years that varies by state (usually between five and fifteen years) and the property owner has not physically stopped him, such as by erecting a locked gate. Oddly, one of the requirements for gaining a prescriptive easement is the property owner's objections—such as your telling him not to drive on your road over and over for years, without putting up a gate. The reasoning seems to be that if I give you permission to do something, you cannot claim it as a right.

## Other Restrictions

### Q. What other restrictions might affect my property rights?

**A.** If your home is listed on the National Register of Historic Places, other restrictions may exist. But generally, private owners are free to alter, add to, convert, or even demolish their home—even if it is on the historic places list. The only restriction if a home is listed is that no federally funded or federally licensed program may harm a home on the list without a hearing before a federal agency.

Some communities have their own historic preservation ordinances, which may affect what you can do to your property. In Marblehead, Massachusetts, for example, homes in the historic district are prohibited from exterior renovations without permission from a local committee.

### Q. What about regulations on activities in my home?

**A.** The general rule is that activities in the privacy of your home are your own business

with three exceptions: when your activities are illegal; when you are violating zoning codes, such as by running a prohibited business from your home; and when the activities make it difficult for other people to enjoy their own homes. Common sense dictates that if you mow your lawn at 4 a.m. or blast your stereo at midnight, you should not be surprised if someone calls the police. Local noise ordinances may restrict the hours in which you can conduct certain noisy activities.

Likewise, most activities that are illegal in public are also illegal in private—such as selling cocaine or serving alcohol to minors. Police generally need a search warrant to enter your home. To get a warrant they must show a judge "probable cause"—reasonable evidence that they are likely to find something illegal inside.

## SAFEGUARDING PROPERTY RIGHTS

### Title Insurance

### Q. What is meant by the term "good title"?

**A.** Good title, also called "marketable title," means you legally own your home and have the authority to sell it. Traditionally, this was determined by a study of the public record to determine the chain of ownership back to the very beginning of the property, as well as any encumbrances such as liens on the property. This study is called an abstract, and some buyers, especially in rural areas, still rely on an abstract and a lawyer's opinion as to what it shows for evidence of title. But metropolitan mortgage lenders, who rarely know much about any specific property, have made abstracts obsolete by insisting on title insurance.

The chief problem with the abstract system is its lack of accountability. What happens if the abstract company or the lawyer issuing an opinion on the property fails to uncover a flaw in the title and it costs you, the new owner, a great deal of money? You could sue, but you'd have to prove that someone was negligent. With title insurance, the insurer agrees to pay covered claims whether anyone was negligent or not. Essentially it's a thorough search of the public record, just like abstract and opinion, but backed by insurance.

### Q. How does title insurance work?

**A.** Title insurance is the opposite of your home's casualty and liability insurance, which repay you in case of injury or damage occurring after the effective date of the policy. Title insurance only covers matters that occurred before the policy's effective date, but were discovered later. Instead of having to pay premiums year after year to maintain the coverage, you only have to pay once to be covered as long as you own the property. Note, however, that many lenders insist on a new policy before refinancing, to make sure their new loans will have first priority. They want to know if you have taken out a second mortgage, obtained a home improvement loan, or been subject to a court judgment between the original mortgage and this one. (For more information about title insurance, see page 130 of the "Buying and Selling a Home" chapter.)

### Q. What's the difference between an owner's policy and a mortgagee policy?

**A.** The owner's policy covers losses or damages you suffer if the property really belongs to someone else, if there is a defect or encumbrance on the title, if the title is unmarketable, or if there is no access to the land. The latter could occur, for example, if you would have to cross a private road to get home and the owner of the road refuses permission.

The lender's mortgagee policy includes all four of these protections. But it protects only the lender (although the owner is protected indirectly if the home is lost since the loan is paid off and the owner's personal liability is limited). Particularly important policy clauses for the lender are the ones that cover losses the lender would suffer if another creditor were first in line.

Owner's policies are more expensive, and in fact, if the same insurer issues both, the concurrent mortgagee policy will probably cost far less—in part because the insurer doesn't have to search the records twice. The limit of the owner's policy is typically the market value of the house at the time of the purchase, while the mortgagee policy is for the amount of the mortgage. The premium is based on the amount of coverage, and may vary greatly by state.

If you are refinancing, your new title insurer will probably rely on the work of the individual or company who did a title search when you bought the home. If you provide the prior policy as evidence of a good title, the new insurer will simply bring it up to date by checking what you have done to affect it, such as loans or partial sales. If a big problem surfaces that the original title insurer should have caught, the second insurer may go after the first to cover the claim. Likewise, if you have an abstract, the insurer may bring it up to date and base the policy on that. Contact a lawyer if you have questions about your title policy.

## Ownership Options

### Q. How does the deed affect property ownership?

**A.** The ownership description on the deed has long-term significance—both in the duration of the title and whether you are free to transfer your interest to someone else. Today, the most common form of ownership is "fee simple." (The term "fee simple" comes from feudal England, where a noble landholder would grant an estate, called a fee, to a faithful

## WHAT ISN'T COVERED BY TITLE INSURANCE

*Title insurance policies are standard in most states, although the forms may vary somewhat from state to state. An owner's policy usually does not cover one or more of the following matters (often referred to as "standard exceptions"), unless, in most states, an additional premium is paid and the necessary evidence is furnished to the title company. (In some states all you have to do is ask to eliminate the standard exceptions, and furnish appropriate information.) When the evidence is furnished and the insurance coverage is given, this is frequently referred to as "extended coverage." The standard exceptions are:*

- *claims of people who turn out to be living in the house (such as the prior owner's tenants or someone living without your knowledge in your lake cabin) if their presence there is not a matter of public record;*

- *boundary line disputes;*

- *easements or claims of easements not shown by public records;*

- *unrecorded mechanic's liens (claims against the property by unpaid home improvement contractors); and*

- *taxes or special assessments left off the public record. (In addition, in much of the country, and particularly in the western states, mineral and/or water rights are a standard exception.)*

*Other important exclusions from coverage include zoning; environmental protection laws; matters arising after the effective date of the policy; subdivision regulations, building codes and the effect of any violation of these rules; matters known to be created, suffered, or assumed by the insured; and matters not shown in the public records and not disclosed to the insurer. Exclusions need to be removed by special endorsements and probably will result in additional premiums. As noted, title insurers will also list as a special exception anything they find that might turn into a claim, whether it be this year's property taxes or the power company's easement across the property, even in a policy "without exceptions." Check your current policy to see what's on the list, in case there's anything you should be concerned about.*

subject in exchange for service or money. If the lord intended for the tenant to be able to keep the estate in the family after he died, he would include the phrase "and his heirs" in the legal document. That's still the phrase to include on a deed if the owner is to hold the property in fee simple, able to sell it or bequeath it.)

Fee simple is the most complete form of ownership, because, in theory, title in fee simple is valid forever. People who own property in fee simple may sell it, rent it out, transfer it to their beneficiaries, and to some extent limit its use in the future. Under some of the older forms of ownership, such as an "estate for years," the title reverts to the former owner at some specified time.

While it is still possible to transfer property as a life estate, it is rarely done because it severely restricts the new owner's ability to sell the property. A life estate, for example, would allow owner A to bequeath or give the house to B, perhaps his wife, until she dies, then to C, their child. Owner B could not sell the house, but only has the right to live in it. People often used a life estate to lower estate taxes, but today most people would prefer the flexibility of a trust to gain the same end. Sometimes people use a life estate to give title to a descendant who may better qualify for financing, while retaining an assured roof over their head.

The way in which your deed lists ownership has critical long-term implications, including who can transfer interests to someone else, how much of the property is available to one owner's creditors, whether the property goes through probate when one party dies, and whether the surviving owner faces a tax on any capital gain when it is time to sell. Couples who have children from previous marriages may want their home equity transferred to their children at death rather than to their spouses. It is important to think about what you want the deed to accomplish, because depending on your state law, at least four ownership options are available—sole ownership, joint tenants, tenants in common, and tenants in partnership. In some states, married couples also may opt for tenants by the entirety. (For more on these topics, see the chapters on buying and selling a home and estate planning.)

### Q. What is the most common form of ownership?

**A.** For couples, whether or not married, joint tenancy is the most common form of own-ership. Under joint tenancy, each person owns an undivided interest in the real estate. At the death of one joint tenant, the interest of the decedent, by operation of law, is immediately transferred to the surviving owner, who becomes the sole owner of the property. When property is held in joint tenancy, the beneficiaries of a deceased joint tenant have no claim to the property, even if the deceased mistakenly tried to leave the property to them. Most couples choose this form of ownership to avoid having their home involved in probate.

Tenancy by the entirety operates similarly but requires that the tenants be spouses and the property be their homestead. This form of ownership is not recognized by some states. Consult an attorney to determine the form of ownership most advantageous to you.

### Q. What is a tenancy in common?

**A.** Tenancy in common gives each owner separate legal title to an undivided interest in the property. This allows the owners the right to sell, mortgage, or give away their own inter-ests in the property, subject to the continuing interests of the other owners. When one owner dies, the interest in the property does not go to the other owners. Instead, it transfers to the decedent's estate. This might be an appropriate form of ownership for those who want their beneficiaries, rather than the other owners, to inherit their interest in the property.

### Q. What's the difference between joint tenants and tenants in common?

**A.** Two or more people who own a home as joint tenants or as tenants in common are each considered the owner of an undivided interest in the whole property. That is, if there are two owners, each owns half, but not a specific half such as the north half. If there is a court judgment against one owner, the creditor may wind up owning that person's interest in the house. In some states, an owner may sell his or her interest to someone else whether or not the other owner approves. Such a sale ends a joint tenancy, so the new owner becomes a tenant in common with the remaining original owner(s). (The arrangement is complex if, say, A, B, and C own a house as joint tenants and A sells her interest to D. B and C are still joint tenants with respect to two-thirds of the property, but tenants in common with respect to D's third.)

The chief difference between joint tenants and tenants in common is the "right of survivorship." If one joint tenant dies, the property automatically belongs to the other owner or owners, avoiding probate. If three people own it and one dies, the other two automatically each own half. If the owners are tenants in common, the other owners have no rights of survivorship—they would inherit the deceased's interest in the property only if it was specified in his or her will.

### Q. How do you stipulate that you are joint tenants?

**A.** The deed must specify that the property is held as joint tenants. The usual language for this is "Mary Smith and Amy Smith, as joint tenants with right of survivorship and not as tenants in common." That way if there is a question, say from Mary Smith's children who think they should inherit her half-interest in the property, the intent of the owners will be clear.

It is especially important to specify joint tenancy on the deed. Otherwise the law assumes that the owners are tenants in common (except, in some states, where their ownership constitutes tenancy by the entirety if they are married to each other, as explained below).

### Q. What is tenancy by the entirety?

**A.** If the co-owners are married to each other, at least one other option may be available, depending on their state law. The other form is for married couples to share ownership as a "tenancy by the entirety." Its roots lie in

the common-law concept that a husband and wife are one legal entity. As with a joint tenancy, this form bears a right of survivorship; if one spouse dies, the other automatically owns the property.

In most states that still recognize this form, a husband and wife who purchase property together are considered tenants by the entirety unless the deed very specifically states that they are tenants in common (or joint tenants) and not tenants by the entirety. Otherwise, a deed saying "to John Smith and Mary Smith, his wife," creates a tenancy by the entirety.

What if one spouse wants to transfer a half interest to someone else during the marriage? The ability to do so depends on where the couple live. In most states that recognize tenancy

---

## DOES OWNING A HOME AFFECT YOUR ESTATE?

*Ownership in a property could very well affect your estate, depending on its terms and the type of ownership you have in the home. For example, if you are a joint tenant, your home will pass directly to your joint tenant and will not be a part of your estate. As you acquire equity in your home, your estate could be vulnerable to federal estate tax or state inheritance tax if the equity along with your other assets exceeds certain statutorily established sums. If you do not have a will, you should consider preparing one now that you own a home. (For more details, see the chapter on estate planning, beginning on page 651.)*

by the entirety, the property can be sold only if both spouses sign the deed, indicating that each is selling one-half interest. However, in some states either spouse may transfer his or her interest—including the right to survivorship. Therefore, it is important to know what law applies in your state.

### Q. In what states are these various options available?

**A.** Sole ownership, joint tenancy, and tenancy in common are available in all states, though certain specific details of ownership may vary by state. Tenancy by the entirety is available in about 40 percent of the states, most of them in the eastern half of the country. See the next answer for the community property states.

### Q. Are there any special considerations if you live in a community property state?

**A.** Nine states—Wisconsin, Louisiana, Texas, New Mexico, Arizona, Idaho, Nevada, Washington, and California—plus Puerto Rico have adopted a different concept of the relationship of husband and wife, which is rooted in Spanish law. These states consider any property acquired during a marriage, except by gift or inheritance, to be "community property." Each spouse owns half of the community property. Each may transfer his or her interest without the other's signature. But there's no right of survivorship; when one spouse dies, half of the couple's property—including half of the house—goes through probate.

If you live in a community property state, the law assumes that if you acquired your house during the marriage by the efforts of either spouse, it is community property unless you specifically say otherwise in the deed. Both husband and wife must sign to transfer the property to someone else.

### Q. Which form of ownership is best?

**A.** That depends on your circumstances. You or your spouse may want to be able to bequeath half of your house to someone else. For example, if you are in a second marriage with children from the first, you will want to avoid joint tenancy with your spouse because your children could not inherit your interest. But if you want to avoid having the house tied up in probate after one of you dies, joint tenancy might be a good idea. If you are married and have reason to expect creditors to come after your house, you may want the protection offered by a tenancy by the entirety, if available in your state, because property owned by both of you in that form generally isn't subject to a judgment against one spouse.

If you live in a community property state, be aware of two significant tax advantages of holding the house as community property rather than as a joint tenancy. The first advantage has to do with tax on capital gain, which is the difference between the selling price and the house's "basis," its cost when you took possession. If you hold the property as community property, when the surviving spouse inherits the whole, the property receives a new tax basis (called a "stepped-up" basis) which reflects its current value. The practical effect of this is to minimize capital gains taxes if the survivor sells it soon thereafter. Let's say the property was purchased initially for $50,000 and is now worth $150,000. Without the stepped-up basis you could owe capital gains taxes on $100,000, but with it you would owe nothing if it sold for $150,000. But if you hold it as joint tenants, only half an interest changes hands when one spouse dies, which means that only half the property gets a stepped-up basis. The capital gain upon sale is likely to cost you thousands of dollars.

The other tax advantage to community property involves estate taxes. Every American may bequeath up to $600,000 without paying federal estate taxes. (In some states, you still may be liable for state inheritance tax on lower amounts.) If you and your husband have more than $600,000 and hold all your property as joint tenants, it will not be part of your husband's estate when he dies. You will own all the jointly held property free of federal estate taxes. However, your estate has increased substantially, and since it exceeds the $600,000 exemption it will be subject to federal estate taxes when you die. If you live in a community property state, your husband's one-half share of the couple's community property is his estate. The portion passing to you as his spouse would not be subject to federal estate tax because of the marital deduction. The remaining portion of the estate, if it exceeds $600,000, would be subject to tax.

## Q. Should a married couple ever title their house in only one name?

**A.** One of the chief concerns when considering property ownership in a single name is liability for court judgments. For example, take the case of a house in the husband's name alone. Let's say he loses a lawsuit over a car accident and his insurance won't cover the judgment. Because the property is solely his, it could be sold to cover the judgment. (In twenty-two states some protection is offered through a homestead exemption, which allows families of two or more people to keep a small house to live in. But the maximum lot size and value are usually quite small; in Arkansas, for example, it is a quarter acre and $2,500 value.)

Some people might want to title the house in only one name precisely to avoid such judgments. For example, a doctor without malpractice insurance might want to deed the house to her husband. But consult an attorney about all the aspects of your situation, including tax and possible fraud implications, before making such a decision.

## Q. How does the form of ownership affect the property settlement in a divorce?

**A.** In about 90 percent of all divorces, the property is divided up by the parties themselves in out-of-court settlements, often with the help of lawyers and mediators. Husband and wife decide what is fair and reasonable in a process of give and take. In contested divorces, it's up to the judge to decide who gets what. Years ago, courts in most states had no authority to redistribute property in a divorce, so their job was to sort out the legal titles. Only jointly held property was subject to judicial division. But today courts are more concerned with what is fair than with whose name is on a deed. They consider a wide range of factors, from the length of the marriage to the needs of each party.

So who gets the house? If there are minor children, usually the home goes to the custodial parent. If there are other assets to divide, the noncustodial parent may get a bigger share of them to balance out loss of the home. If not, courts typically award possession of the house

### CHANGING THE FORM OF OWNERSHIP
*It's fairly simple to take care of the paperwork of changing the form of ownership. Basically you sign a new deed and file it with the local recorder of deeds. But using the wrong deed or the wrong wording can result in serious consequences. Consult an experienced property lawyer to make sure you consider all the aspects of your situation and get it done correctly. A straightforward change will probably have a minimal cost.*

to the custodial parent until the children grow up. Then the house is to be sold and the proceeds divided between the parties. If neither party can afford to maintain the home, the court may order it sold promptly and the equity split.

## Handling Property Constraints

### Q. What is a lien?

**A.** A lien, which dates back to English common law, is a claim to property for the satisfaction of a debt. If you refuse to pay the debt, whoever files the lien may ask a court to raise the money by foreclosing on your property and selling it, leaving you with the difference between the selling price and the amount of the lien. (Your mortgage lender, though, should be first in line for payment.) It is possible to lose a $200,000 house over a $5,000 lien, though any homeowner with a house of such value probably would find a way to satisfy the lien.

There are several types of liens, any of which creates a cloud on your title. For example, a "mechanic's lien" or "construction lien" can occur if contractors or subcontractors who worked on your house (or suppliers who have delivered materials) have not been paid. They may file a lien at the local recording office against your property. If the lien is not removed, it can lead to foreclosure or inhibit your ability to sell your home. Liens often are filed in connection with divorce decrees. If two homeowners divorce, the court often will grant one of them the right to remain in the house. When that owner sells it, however, the ex-spouse may be entitled to half the equity. The divorce decree would probably grant that spouse a lien on the property for that amount. If everything goes as it should, the ex-spouses will get the full payment of their respective shares at the closing.

Unfortunately, things don't always go as they should. Suppose the woman you bought your house from was subject to such a decree, but her ex-husband had given her a quit-claim deed to the property conveying ownership to her but not mentioning his lien. She might leave town with both halves of the equity—and the lien would stay with the property. The ex-spouse still has a right to extract his equity from the sale. In that case the title insurer may disclaim responsibility, because the lien was not filed in the land records; however, some courts have ruled that insurers cannot do that. When a divorce occurs, insurers are on notice that this problem could arise—they should check the divorce decree. The best protection for someone purchasing a house subject to a divorce decree is to have a lawyer examine all relevant documents to make sure this problem does not occur.

Likewise, if you bought a home with your spouse but later divorced, your own divorce decree might give your former spouse a lien on the home for half the proceeds. That lien can hinder your ability to sell the home if your former spouse refuses to release the lien. A careful divorce lawyer will build a release mechanism—such as an escrow containing the deed and release—into the divorce decree.

### Q. Can a lien be filed for unpaid child support?

**A.** Many states impose a lien on the property of divorced parents who fail to pay child support. That lien would have to be paid off before the property could be sold.

### Q. What is "adverse possession"?

**A.** Although you have a right to keep trespassers off your land, under the law it is possible for a trespasser who uses the property for many years to actually become the owner. This entitlement is called adverse possession. It is very unlikely to occur in an urban or suburban area, where lots are relatively small and home-owners know when someone else has been using their property continuously. But if you own an unvisited beach house or hunting cabin, you might not know that someone has been living there continually for years.

Adverse possession is similar to a prescriptive easement, where a court declares that, for example, your neighbor has a right to keep his hedge on a strip of your land because it has been there for forty years. The difference is that while prescriptive easements concern use of the land, adverse possession concerns actual ownership. For a claim of adverse possession to succeed, the trespasser must show that his occupation of your property was open and hostile, which means without permission. As with prescriptive easements, granting the person permission to use the property cancels his claim to ownership by adverse possession. The occupa-

---

### REMOVING A LIEN

*If you discover a lien on your property, see an attorney to determine the best course of action. If the lien is valid, and for an affordable amount, the advice might be to pay it and clear the title. However, just paying it off is not enough. Have the payee sign a release-of-lien form, and file it at the county (or "land title") recording office to clear the recorded title. You can then decide whether to pursue the person responsible. If the amount of the lien is major and you believe it is not your debt, consult with your attorney about what action to take.*

---

tion must also have continued for a certain number of years, generally ten to twenty years but sometimes fewer, depending on the state. And in many states, the trespasser must have paid local property taxes on the land.

This last requirement provides a way to avert loss of a property through adverse possession. If you suspect that someone has been living in your hunting cabin, check the property tax records for that county to see whether anyone has made tax payments on it.

A bit of vigilance will prevent problems in this area. You should post "no trespassing" signs to warn people that this is private property. Erect gates at entry points and keep them locked. Ask trespassers to leave, and call the police if they refuse. If you suspect that someone will keep on using your property (such as for a road to obtain lake access) despite your efforts, consider granting written permission to keep on doing so, especially if the use doesn't interfere with your use. This will bar adverse possession, which requires that permission not have been granted. To make the arrangement clear, ask for a written acknowledgment, and, if reasonable, a fee or payment.

**Q. What constitutes an encroachment?**

**A.** An encroachment occurs when your neighbor's house, garage, swimming pool, or other permanent fixture stands partially on your property or hangs over it.

In the case of a neighbor's roof overhanging your property or his fence being two feet on your side of the line, your rights might be tied to the prominence of the encroachment and how long it has been in place. If it was open, visible, and permanent when you bought your home, you may have taken your property subject to that encroachment. The neighbor may have an implied easement on your property to continue using it in that manner. If the encroachment is less obvious, you may only discover it when you have a survey conducted for some other purpose. In that case, you might have a better chance of removing the encroachment.

A house addition could be an encroachment if it starts twenty-three feet back from the sidewalk and the local setback ordinance requires twenty-five feet. The neighbors could band together and sue you, hoping you would be forced to raze your addition. Or you might have to live with your neighbors' disapproval, perhaps after paying a fine to the city for the violation.

It is even possible to encroach on an easement, for example, by locating the apron of your swimming pool on the telephone company's easement across your property for underground cables. In that case, the company would have a right to dig up the concrete and charge you for it.

### Q. What can you do about an encroachment?

**A.** First, demand that the neighbors remove the encroachment. If they refuse, you could file a quiet title lawsuit or ejection lawsuit and obtain a court order. Of course, this isn't the best if you wish to maintain neighborly feelings, especially if the fixture in question is merely the cornice of his house. Further, if prior owners of the neighboring property have used that bit of your land for quite a few years, your current neighbor could ask a court to declare a prescriptive easement to maintain the status quo.

Second, you can sell the strip of land to your neighbors. Perhaps you didn't know quite where the boundary line was anyway, so you might agree on a new one on your side of the encroachment and file it with the county recording office.

Third, you can grant written permission to use your land in that way. This maneuver can actually ward off a claim for prescriptive easement or adverse possession, because perfecting either of these claims requires showing that the use was open and hostile (without permission).

If you like this neighbor but may not like those who follow, you might grant permission only as long as that neighbor owns the property. Your attorney could draw up a document granting permission and file it for you.

The primary question when someone has encroached slightly onto your property is how important it is to you. Typically, disputes over encroachments arise when discord is present among neighbors. If everyone is getting along fine, chances are you can live quite happily even though your neighbors' fence does creep onto your land.

## Government Rights to Property

### Q. Can the government force me to sell my property?

**A.** Since ancient times, governments have had the right to obtain private property for governmental purposes. In the United States, this power, called eminent domain, is limited by the Constitution's Bill of Rights, which grants people the right to due process of law and just compensation if deprived of their property. The federal government and individual states may delegate their condemnation power to municipalities, highway authorities, forest preserve districts, public utilities and others. These authorities may force the purchase of private land for public purposes, such as constructing a new freeway or expanding a school playground. The scope of government's activity has expanded so much in recent years that almost anything counts as a public purpose.

If the government wants your land, you may hear about it informally at a public hearing on the matter. The best approach at this time may be to rally the neighbors in hopes of influencing the authorities' plans. For example, the town might be persuaded to narrow the proposed road that would eat up some of your yard. Your first official notice will be a letter indicating interest in acquiring your property (or a portion of it) for a certain purpose. That's when informal negotiations should kick into high gear. With or without your consent, the government then has your property appraised and makes you an offer, called the "pro tanto award," which you may accept or refuse. If you accept it, the government may ask you to sign a document waiving your right to sue for more money. Some governmental units offer a bonus to entice people into accepting the pro tanto award, because it's cheaper than going to court. In a typical project, about 75 percent of the property owners accept the government's initial offer. The rest sue for more, but three-quarters of them settle the case before trial.

If you think the offer is too low, retain a lawyer experienced in eminent domain cases to negotiate for you and prepare your case for possible trial. If the case does go to trial, it's a battle of experts who testify to the value of the property, which is ultimately set by the jury.

### Q. Can the government seize my property without paying me?

**A.** Although the federal government is scrupulous about due process of law in cases of eminent domain, it is far less diligent in a different and relatively new area. If the police suspect you of certain specific crimes, particularly drug trafficking, the law allows them to seize any of your property that might have been used in the commission of the crime or purchased with the proceeds of the crime. For example, if your tenant grows marijuana in the basement of your rental house, the police might seize the house, sell it, and keep the equity to fund further law enforcement efforts. Since 1985, law enforcement officials have seized more than $2.6 billion worth of houses, cash, cars, and other assets.

> ## FEES FOR EMINENT DOMAIN CASES
> *Some attorneys who specialize in eminent domain cases work on a contingency basis; their fee is a given percentage of the difference between the initial offer and the ultimate settlement. You might want to set up a fee arrangement where you pay a flat fee or hourly rate for initial review, negotiation, and counteroffer, then switch to a contingent fee if the matter turns into a lawsuit.*

Many critics are disturbed because civil forfeitures do not require that the owner be convicted of a crime. Government officials are free to seize property without warning or compensation if they believe it is linked to criminal activity. So it is up to the owners to prove that their property should be returned. The value of the property forfeited has no relation to the seriousness of the crime, as an Iowa man learned when he lost his $6,000 boat because he caught three fish illegally. In a California case, a couple held a second mortgage on a house occupied by a businessman convicted of running an interstate prostitution ring. Federal agents seized the house and kept it for five years while it fell into disrepair. The owners had to go to court to regain their property.

A growing number of critics are calling for legal reform in this area, but in the meantime, make sure there is not even an appearance of criminal activity in any house or vehicle you own. If your property is seized by the government, retain a knowledgeable, assertive lawyer as fast as you can.

## LIABILITY ISSUES

**Q. Am I responsible if someone has an accident in my home or on my property?**

**A.** The question of legal responsibility hinges on whether your negligence or carelessness contributed to an accident or injury. Homeowners are liable only if a court finds them in some way negligent (though many settle before this point if they or their insurer believes that a court would find them negligent). For example, a homeowner might be considered responsible if someone slips and falls on his icy sidewalk. Other common injuries and negligence suits involve power lawn mowers, swimming pools, boats, and other recreational vehicles. Most homeowners carry insurance, and the insurance company generally handles any claims against the homeowner. It is only when the insurer believes the claim is unreasonable that the matter is likely to land in court. Even then, the insurer will furnish the attorney and pay any damages awarded (up to the limit of the policy), along with court costs.

Still, facing a lawsuit and going to court is no fun. Lawsuits involve months of depositions, motions, and counter motions before the trial even gets started. Even after a verdict is rendered, a party may appeal and the battle could go on for years. As a homeowner, you are far better off both preventing injuries on your property in the first place and protecting yourself with a solid insurance policy in the event the unavoidable and unexpected does occur.

**Q. Am I responsible for anyone who enters my property?**

**A.** Historically, the law identified various categories of people who might be injured on your property, and the category of the injured party dictated the homeowner's duty of care. Although in a few jurisdictions a trespasser is still categorized separately from "lawful" visi-

tors, the courts in most states hold property owners to the same standard with respect to everyone: a duty to employ reasonable care in maintaining your property and to warn people of hazards. This means, for example, that if you permit someone to pick gooseberries on your property, you are obliged to warn the berry picker that the local gun club is holding target practice nearby.

Generally, courts hold homeowners responsible only if they are in some way negligent. The law does not expect the homeowner to guarantee that someone visiting his or her house will not get hurt. But it is the homeowner's responsibility to take reasonable care to protect people from known hazards.

**Q. What happens if someone is injured on my property and we are both at fault?**

**A.** While your best defense to any charge of negligence is that you exercised due care, there are several other defenses available. In some cases, a jury may decide that although a homeowner was partially responsible for what happened, the person injured was also partially responsible. This is called "comparative or contributory negligence." For example, if you forget to tell your houseguest that you have just dug a pit in your backyard for the new septic system, and the guest decides to get a breath of fresh air and wander around in the backyard in total darkness, a jury might find both of you partly responsible for your guest's broken leg. In that case, the jury might reduce the amount of the damage award you might otherwise have to pay.

In other cases, the jury might decide to absolve you of any responsibility because of what the law calls "assumption of risk." For example, when a Georgia homeowner and his neighbor were trying to get rid of a nest of wasps, the neighbor climbed a ladder and sprayed the nest with insecticide. The wasps swarmed out, and the frightened neighbor fell off the ladder. When he sued the homeowner for the resulting injuries, the court ruled that the neighbor knew perfectly well that wasps tend to swarm, yet he assumed the risk. Accordingly, the homeowner was not liable.

## Q. What is the difference between natural and artificial hazards?

**A.** Generally, courts do not hold homeowners liable for injuries stemming from natural hazards such as lakes and streams, even if a child is hurt, unless some other negligence is involved. Homeowners are more likely to be responsible if the hazard was created artificially. For example, a man who was pushing a child on a tree swing while attending a barbecue in New York stepped back onto a rotted plywood board covering a sewer trap, which gave way under his weight. A court found the homeowners liable because they knew about the danger and made it worse by hanging the swing where anyone pushing a child on it would have inevitably stepped on the rotted cover.

On the other hand, take the case of a Nebraska man who just finished shoveling snow off his driveway in the freezing mist. While he was inside getting some salt to finish the job, the mail carrier slipped and fell on the driveway. The mail carrier sued, but the court ruled the homeowner was blameless because he did not create the hazard and was doing his best to eliminate it.

## Q. What about liability in regard to children?

**A.** The law concerning a property owner's responsibility for children, even when they are trespassing, has changed over the years. In 1901, when a five-year-old drowned after falling into a water-filled uncovered excavation, the court ruled that because the child was a trespasser and the property owners didn't know there were children around the pit, they weren't liable. Even then, however, another legal doctrine was evolving, stemming from injuries caused to children playing on railroad turntables left unsecured in areas frequented by the public. In a series of late nineteenth-century cases involving such injuries, the courts found the railroads negligent. The courts ruled that some dangerous places look like such fun that landowners should expect children to come play.

The law calls these "attractive nuisances." Even though an uninvited child wandering into your yard to inspect the swimming pool might well be a trespasser, the law says you have a

---

### LIABILITY RISKS

*Negligence is usually the basis of a liability suit. Take steps to avoid the conditions that would prove carelessness. Some examples of cases in which a court might find you negligent:*

- *failure to maintain your property or creation of a condition that may result in injury or damage to someone else's property;*
- *knowledge of a hazard and lack of intent to eliminate the hazard, erect barriers, or warn people who enter your property;*
- *lack of care in maintaining or creating hazards that might attract children;*
- *actions or inaction that might cause damage to your neighbors' property.*

special duty to erect barriers to protect children from harm's way. That's why the Supreme Court of Georgia recently refused to dismiss a case against the owners of a swimming pool where a two-year-old drowned. The swimming pool was in the side yard of their home on a corner lot, three blocks from an elementary school. The yard and swimming pool were not fenced in, and the pool had both a diving board and playground-type slide.

Another case involved a Michigan family that stopped at a private home to buy raspberries. While the adults were talking, two preschool boys wandered into the garage, where they found a loaded gun and one boy shot the other. The court ruled that although homeowners cannot be expected to make their homes childproof, those who have reason to expect children to come around—such as the couple who sold raspberries from their home—should expect children to act on childish impulses and should take steps to protect them.

The message is clear: If there is a way in, the child may find it and may get injured and you may be liable. That is why precautions such as fences, locked gates, and swimming pool covers—and good liability insurance—are so important.

### Q. Am I responsible for damage caused by my children?

**A.** As a rule, parents are liable for injury and damage caused by their minor children (eighteen years of age and younger). Usually, such damage caused by children thirteen or under will be covered by your homeowner's policy. In many homeowner's policies, damage and injury are not covered if the children are older than thirteen and intentionally cause the damage or injury. The best way to avoid liability is to teach your children to respect other people and their property.

### Q. If I host a party in my house, am I liable for my guests' actions?

**A.** Some courts have ruled that a host is not responsible for the conduct of guests, unless your parties routinely turn into brawls. Likewise, if one of your guests is horsing around and hurts himself, you probably will not be liable. But you might be liable if you let your guest drink too much, then put him into his car and send him out on the highway. That is what happened in a landmark New Jersey case, where the homeowners had been drinking whiskey for a couple of hours with one of the husband's subcontractors. They walked him to his car, saw him off, and called shortly to see if he'd made it home. He had not. Thoroughly drunk, he was in a head-on collision in which a woman was seriously hurt. The case went to the state Supreme Court, which held the hosts liable. It is a lesson worth remembering. Host liquor liability insurance policies are available.

### Q. What about liability concerning my pets?

**A.** The law holds people responsible for the actions of their pets. Most states have so-called dog-bite statutes, holding owners legally liable for injuries inflicted by their animals. If your state has no such statute, you may still be found liable under the common-law rule that owners are legally responsible if they knew the animal was likely to cause that kind of injury. You may also be found liable if you violated a leash law or a requirement to keep your pets fenced.

Many states and municipalities also have enacted "vicious dog statutes," which enable an animal control officer or a judge to declare a particular dog or specific breed of dog vicious and require the owner to confine the dog securely or muzzle it in public. Some states make it illegal even to own a breed of dog that has been declared vicious. Some cities have

**RECREATIONAL USE OF PROPERTY**

*If you own a lot of land and allow someone to use it free of charge for hunting, fishing, skiing, or some other recreational activity, you are probably not liable if the person gets hurt. In the 1970s, virtually all states enacted "recreational use statutes," designed to encourage people to open their land for recreational use without fear of liability. The statutes do not protect you if you charge a fee or if you're malicious in your failure to warn of hazards. For more information about such statutes in your area, contact a local attorney.*

imposed an outright ban on all pit bulls, which they consider inherently vicious. Many jurisdictions ban wild animals such as wolves, bears, and dangerous snakes from being kept as pets.

If you own a dog or another animal that might injure someone, call your locality's animal control office to find out the laws in your area. Know your pet's temperament and keep it out of the path of strangers. Keep vaccinations current, and post warning signs if you think your pet might injure someone. These signs should be prominent and straightforward, such as BEWARE OF DOG, so people are clearly informed of the danger involved. However, the signs may not absolve you from liability if a child climbs into the yard or the dog gets out.

### Q. Can I be held liable if my tree falls on my neighbor's house?

**A.** Traditionally, property owners were not responsible for damage caused by falling tree limbs and other natural occurrences on their property. However, they were responsible for damage caused by artificial conditions, such as a loose board from your lumber pile being carried by the wind through your neighbor's plate glass window. The current trend suggests that the courts are applying an ordinary standard of care/negligence in both cases. This means that maintaining your property in good condition is an important protection against a negligence suit.

For example, if your trees have visible rot, you should cut them down or trim rotted limbs before they can fall on your neighbor's property. Trees should be maintained well enough that, short of a tornado or hurricane, the wind won't blow things from your place over to your neighbor's.

If you excavate near the property line and cause your neighbors' land to sink, you may be liable whether or not their house is affected. Check with a civil or geological engineer if you think you have reason to be concerned. Your builder or contractor will know of one, or you can find one yourself through the yellow pages.

Similarly, if changes you make to the contours of your land cause excess rain water to pour onto your neighbor's property and result in damage, you may be liable. If you are planning to change the contours of your land, ask an attorney or your local building inspector about your state law.

### Q. Are there other areas to be concerned about liability?

**A.** Basically, if you're acting reasonably and responsibly, maintaining your property and carrying homeowner's insurance, you shouldn't fret about liability. If you're planning any changes to your property, however, you should investigate local laws to ensure that any changes will not violate them. The following areas can hold special concern:

- **Waterfront areas.** If you live along a river or stream, state and local laws designed to protect wildlife habitats may preclude your clearing brush or changing the lay of the land. Do not act without checking with your department of conservation, natural resources, or wildlife, usually located in the state capital.

- **Pollution.** You could be liable for the cost of cleaning up pollution stemming from underground oil tanks or old dump sites on your property, whether or not you caused the problem in the first place. Look into this before you buy a piece of property, because there is not much you can do about it afterward. Ask the seller if there are any such problems, and have your attorney include a clause in your purchase agreement that covers you in the event such problems arise. If there is special concern because of the unique nature of the property, you might even consider hiring an environmental consultant.

## A CHECKLIST FOR A SAFE HOME

- *Repair steps and railings.*
- *Cover holes.*
- *Fix uneven walkways.*
- *Install adequate lighting.*
- *Clear walkways of ice and snow as soon as possible.*
- *Be sure children do not leave toys on steps and sidewalks.*
- *Replace throw rugs that slip or bunch up.*
- *Reroute extension cords that stretch across traffic lanes.*
- *Repair frayed electrical cords.*
- *Keep poisons and other hazards out of the reach of children, even if you don't have children.*
- *Warn guests about icy conditions and other hazards.*
- *Restrain your pet.*
- *Erect barriers to your swimming pool; an automatic pool cover or a tall fence with a good gate that you lock, and an alarm on doors leading to the pool.*
- *Remove all guns or keep them securely locked and out of sight, where children cannot see them or gain access to them.*
- *Remove nails from stored lumber; secure any lumber piles.*
- *Don't leave ladders standing against the side of the house or garage.*
- *Don't let children stand nearby when you mow the lawn.*
- *Don't let your guests drink and drive or drive under the influence of drugs.*

- *Wetlands.* Federal laws govern the draining and filling of wetlands. If you have places on your property that are boggy even part of the year, avoid serious legal trouble by finding out what your responsibilities are before making changes. You might start with your state's department of environmental protection, probably located in the state capital. The federal Office of Wetlands Protection in Washington, DC, also might be able to help.
- *Utility lines.* As a rule you are not liable for maintenance of utility lines crossing your property, but to be safe don't do anything to cause potential damage to them, such as planting fast-growing trees under them.

### Q. What should I do if someone is injured on my property?

**A.** First and foremost, do all you can to help—express concern, ask what injuries might have been suffered, make the victim as comfortable as possible, call for medical assistance, etc. Do not, however, say anything to suggest or admit guilt or negligence. While it is natural to empathize with the injured party and want to soothe any pain and suffering, as well as your own feelings of guilt, it is not a good idea to complicate your potential liability with such statements. Rather, leave it up to the law to decide who was responsible.

Notify your insurer in writing (and speak to your attorney) as soon as possible. Do not talk with the other party or their attorney about liability until you have taken these steps. You may well decide later to offer to defray some medical bills of the injured party, but do this after you have had the chance to review the situation with a clearer head and the appropriate parties.

There is one other situation where the law requires you to act. If someone has been hurt on your property or is in danger, you may have a legal duty to offer humanitarian aid even though you had nothing at all to do with the injury. For example, a Minnesota cattle buyer became severely ill while inspecting a farmer's cattle. A court later ruled that the farmer had a duty not to send the man, who was helpless and fainting, out on the road alone on a cold winter night.

### Liability Insurance

### Q. What is liability insurance?

**A.** The liability portion of your homeowner's policy is designed to cover unintentional injuries on the premises and unintentional damage to other people's property. In other words, injuries caused by your negligence are covered; those you inflict on purpose are not covered. Given your potential liability as a homeowner, you are asking for trouble if you do not carry adequate liability insurance. It takes only one person who is seriously injured by your negligence to generate a huge liability award and deplete your financial nest egg, not to mention your psychological well being.

### Q. What kind of liability coverage is provided by a typical homeowner's policy?

**A.** A typical homeowner's policy includes $100,000 of liability insurance, which won't go far if someone is severely injured. For a slight increase in premium you can raise that to $300,000 to $500,000, and some companies offer coverage of $1 million or more. Typically, coverage includes harm caused by your children and pets, except intentional harm if the child is over thirteen. If your pet attacks people routinely, the insurer may cancel your policy or refuse to renew it.

Most standard homeowner's policies **do not** cover:

- employees and clients of your home-based business, including the children in your home-based day care if you take in more than three children and have no special endorsement;
- claims by one member of the household against another;
- any disease you pass on to someone.

### Q. What is an "umbrella" liability policy?

**A.** An umbrella liability policy, also called a "personal excess liability" policy, is designed to protect you in case of a big judgment that would quickly eat up your regular policy coverage. These policies are relatively inexpensive because the insurers are betting you'll never need to file a claim. Their coverage takes up where your home and auto policies leave off; thus you will need to have certain levels of basic home and auto liability insurance before you can qualify for an umbrella policy. Generally, these would be $100,000 in liability coverage on your homeowner's policy and $250,000/$500,000 on your auto ($250,000 per person, $500,000 per accident; or sometimes $300,000 in single-limit coverage).

You also have to meet certain eligibility requirements, such as owning no more than four cars. If you've been convicted for driving under the influence of alcohol in the past three years, you are not likely to get approved for coverage.

Some umbrella policies pay the deductible amount that isn't covered by basic policies. Others impose a deductible, called a "retained limit," in certain circumstances. For example, if your homeowner's policy doesn't cover slander or libel (most don't without a special endorsement), an umbrella policy with a retained limit might require you to pay the first $250 of a judgment for slander. The other kind would pay

### WORKERS' COMPENSATION

*If you have a home-based business that involves people coming to your house, be sure to obtain a separate business rider. Also, if you have a swimming pool or other special hazard, check the policy provisions to make sure you're covered. If you have domestic employees, even part-time help such as nannies, you may be required to carry workers' compensation insurance, which costs a little more than $100 per year. Workers' compensation sets limits on awards; if you don't have it, you could have to pay far larger damages, and there may be civil and criminal penalties if you don't carry it. Contractors working on your house should already have workers' compensation for their employees. You should ask to see proof of such coverage, and don't hire them if they don't produce sufficient verification or don't have adequate coverage.*

from dollar one. Note that most umbrella policies don't cover injuries you cause with your motorcycle and certain water craft, such as high-powered speed boats.

Your premium for the umbrella policy will be determined based on the number of houses, rental units and vehicles you own. If you have one house and two cars, a typical premium costs $100-150 for $1 million in coverage. You will get $2 million in coverage for only about $50-$100 more in premium costs.

## PROTECTING YOUR PROPERTY

### Homeowner's Insurance

**Q. What kind of homeowner's insurance do I need?**

**A.** Broadly speaking, a homeowners' policy is a package deal designed to pay for the repair or replacement of your house and belongings, plus extra living expenses if, say, you and your family have to stay in a motel for several months while your home is being rebuilt. It also covers claims and legal judgments against you for injuries people suffer in your home or damage you cause. How much the insurer pays depends, of course, on the limits of your policy, which in turn depends on how much you've paid in premiums.

Although details of insurance policies vary among companies, the general forms of coverage are fairly standard. Many homeowners opt for an inexpensive "basic" policy, called HO-1 or HO-A, which provides actual cash value of your home and contents in case of loss due to specific causes, such as fire. This minimalist type of policy usually satisfies lenders, because they are interested only in your ability to repay the mortgage, not rebuild your house.

Many financial professionals recommend policies that provide at least 80 percent replacement value, rather than actual cash value, of your home in the event of damage from specific causes, such as fire and theft. These are called "broad" policies or HO-2 or HO-B. In most cases, you're better off with replacement value, because it usually costs more to replace it than its "market" or "cash" value. Note that "replacement cost" is estimated by the insurance agent, and for an additional small fee,

### WHO NEEDS AN UMBRELLA POLICY?
*People usually determine their need for umbrella liability coverage not so much by how many hazards they have on their property as by the assets they have to protect. After all, the wealthier you are, the more you have to lose if someone is injured on your property. Some people buy $5 million in coverage, and some even take out umbrellas over their umbrellas. Consult your insurance agent to help decide what type and amount of coverage is best for you.*

guaranteed replacement cost coverage will protect you if your agent has underestimated the cost of replacing your home. Another way to guard against under-insurance is with an "inflation guard clause," which increases the face value of the policy either according to the annual increase in local construction costs or by a given percentage every three months. This rider can reduce the chances of your being under-insured, but it doesn't guarantee replacement cost.

For the best protection, a comprehensive or "all-risk" policy covers any kind of damage except specific exclusions, such as floods and earthquakes. Even with this type of policy, however, insurance for luxury items, jewelry, art, and antiques may require separate riders. If you live in a condo or cooperative, an HO-6 policy gives you coverage similar to HO-2. A few companies do offer all-risk coverage for condo and co-op owners. As with any other type of significant purchase, it pays to shop around.

## Insurance Coverage Reported by U.S. Households

| | % of public | % have insurance | % don't have insurance | % not sure |
|---|---|---|---|---|
| Home owners: | | | | |
| 1989 | 67 | 96 | 3 | 1 |
| 1986 | 69 | 95 | 3 | 2 |
| 1984 | 67 | 93 | 4 | 3 |
| | | | | |
| Renters: | | | | |
| 1989 | 28 | 26 | 70 | 4 |
| 1986 | 27 | 23 | 69 | 8 |
| 1984 | 29 | 28 | 65 | 8 |

SOURCE: Insurance Information Institute.

## IS YOUR HOME A FIRETRAP?

*The majority of house fires are caused by improper maintenance or use of heat sources or electrical appliances, or careless use of smoking materials. Fatal fires occur most often when there is no functioning smoke alarm to wake everyone. So take a few precautions to avoid becoming another fire death statistic.*

- *Keep combustible materials away from your furnace, wood stove, or other heating device.*
- *Use the proper fuel for the appliance. For example, don't rekindle your wood stove or kerosene heater with gasoline.*
- *Check electrical cords and replace them if they're frayed.*
- *Periodically have an electrician check your wiring to make sure it is safe.*
- *Make sure matches, cigarette butts, and ashes are extinguished before you go to sleep.*
- *Install a smoke detector on each level of your home near the stairwell. Test them regularly to make sure the batteries are fresh.*
- *Teach everyone in your family how to escape safely in case of fire:*

    *drop and crawl because the good air is near the floor, test doors for heat before opening them, and don't be afraid to break windows to get out.*

- *Arrange a meeting place outside so no one goes running back into a burning house to rescue someone who's already safely outside.*

### Q. What isn't covered by a homeowner's insurance policy?

**A.** Most policies specifically exclude damage caused by floods and earthquakes, and some policies will exclude or limit theft in high crime areas. This doesn't mean that you can't necessarily purchase insurance for these threats; it simply means that if you can, you must pay for riders on your policy. Homeowner's policies also provide little if any coverage for home businesses. If you're operating a home business, check with your agent to see whether your business is adequately protected.

### Q. Does homeowner's insurance cover natural disasters?

**A.** Not necessarily, because the differing nature of these perils is treated differently by the insurance industry. Consumers are often confused about what their homeowners' policy covers and what it doesn't. The following guide shows what coverage is available for specific types of disasters and how you get it:

*Floods.* Homeowner's policies absolutely exclude damage from flooding, except for a narrow range of cases such as a pipe or water tank bursting. You can't get an endorsement to cover it at any price; however, if your community is in a flood-prone area, you can probably buy a special policy as part of the National Flood Insurance Program, administered by private insurers and backed by the federal government. Any insurance agent can sell flood policies. Cost depends on what measures your community has taken to reduce the risk of flood damage. Until your community meets the standards of the federal flood-control program, only limited coverage is available: up to $35,000 for a single-family house and $10,000 for its contents, for a cost of about $250 per year. Once the community meets the standards you can get up to $185,000 for a single-family house and $60,000 for its contents. The premiums depend on the structure of the house and how close it is to the river, but in a moderately flood-prone area, $60,000 of coverage on a house and its contents might cost about $150.

*Earthquakes.* The state of California requires insurance carriers to offer earthquake coverage to anyone in the state who carries one of their homeowner's policies. Usually it's an endorsement to the regular policy, expanding the coverage for a fee. But if a California policyholder decides not to buy or renew the endorsement, the carrier isn't obligated to give him or her a second chance. Of course, given the risk, earthquake endorsements in that part of the country don't come cheap. The annual premium on a $100,000 house could be anywhere from $150 to $1,200, depending on the location of the house and the materials used in its construction. Brick houses, for example, would be at the high end of the spectrum. Deductibles on earthquake endorsements are usually 10 percent of the coverage for the structure and its contents, figured separately. In other parts of the country you can get earthquake endorsements, often for next to nothing—but most people don't because they don't expect to need them.

*Tornadoes and hurricanes.* Although standard homeowners' policies cover windstorms, you may need extra protection if you live in an area such as Florida or Texas that is especially prone to hurricanes or tornadoes. In these areas, standard coverage may not be available; you have to buy a special policy such as the beach and windstorm insurance plans available in seven Atlantic and Gulf Coast states. As with flood insurance, any licensed agent or broker in those states can sell it.

*Volcanoes* are specifically listed as a covered peril in standard homeowners' policies, so that's one natural disaster you don't have to worry about.

## SHOPPING FOR INSURANCE

*Whether you're buying your first policy or shopping for better price and coverage, begin by listing your possessions and estimates of their value. Get your house appraised, either by an insurance representative or an independent appraiser, to figure out what it would cost to rebuild at current prices. Note valuables that might require special coverage. Then take the following steps:*

- *Talk with several different agents about your insurance needs. Ask them to quote premium costs with higher and lower deductibles. Compare costs and coverage.*
- *Check the reputation of the companies you're considering. Rating services such as A.M. Best & Co., Moody's Investor Services, Standard & Poor's Corporation, and Duff & Phelps study companies' financial stability and ability to pay claims. Your insurance agent should have the latest ratings for the companies he or she works with.*
- *Ask your agent to help you interpret the ratings scales, which vary between the services and can be confusing. You want to be reasonably sure your insurer will be able to pay your claim.*
- *Watch out for policies that limit recovery on personal possession to "four times the actual cash value." This could mean you would get less than you need to replace your old furniture and drapes.*
- *Avoid policies that limit reimbursements to what the insurance company would be able to pay for a given item, because the company could probably buy it wholesale.*
- *Keep your agent informed of additions to your house and major purchases that might affect the level of coverage you need.*
- *Periodically review your coverage to make sure you're adequately insured.*

### Q. How much does homeowner's insurance cost?

**A.** The cost of homeowner's insurance varies greatly with the policy coverage and the age, location, and replacement cost of your home. It pays to shop around and compare insurance premiums, but be sure that you are comparing similar, if not identical, coverage. Another way to reduce costs substantially is to opt for a high deductible, such as $500 or $1,000 if you can afford to pay this amount yourself in case of damage. You also may qualify for a discount if you've taken particular safety precautions such as installing deadbolt locks or cabling your mobile home to the ground. Ask your insurance agent what discounts are available and what you would need to do to qualify.

### Q. What should I do if I need to file a claim?

**A.** The claims process for theft or damage to your home or its contents is fairly basic, but it will go more smoothly if you have taken inventory of your possessions and their worth ahead of time. In case of theft, first call the

## TAKING INVENTORY

*Although you don't need a detailed inventory to buy insurance, and you can eventually get a sizable check from the insurance company without one, the claims adjusting process goes a lot more smoothly if you have clear, accurate records. The time-honored method is to fill in a "household inventory" booklet available from your agent, recording purchase dates of furniture, equipment, and valuables and estimating replacement costs. It helps to attach bills of sale, canceled checks, or appraisal records. The more detail you can include, the better.*

*Another option is to use a computer software package designed to categorize records of personal possessions and make it easy to update them. Some of these programs can print out the records room by room, in case of partial damage to your house.*

*For a visual record, consider either photographs or a videotaped tour of your house, complete with commentary. Include the insides of closets and cabinets, and take close-ups of computers, jewelry and other valuables.*

*Send a copy of your inventory to your attorney, store it in a safe-deposit box, or leave it with a friend, but be sure to have a back-up in a safe place.*

police. Then call your agent or company immediately. Ask whether you are covered for the situation, whether the claim exceeds your deductible, how long it will take to process the claim, and whether you will need estimates for repairs. Follow up your call with a written explanation of what happened. If you need to make temporary repairs to secure your home or protect it from the elements, keep track of expenses, but don't make permanent repairs until the adjuster has inspected the damage.

### Q. What can you do if you have a problem with your insurance company?

**A.** If you're dissatisfied with the way your adjuster handles your claim, first talk to your agent. If that doesn't help, call the company's consumer affairs department. Then try the National Insurance Consumer Helpline (1-800-942-4242), which might be able to suggest a course of action. Finally, you could call your state's insurance department to complain and ask for help. If these approaches do not bring a satisfactory settlement, consider hiring your own, independent adjuster for an independent appraisal of your damage. You'll have to pay a fee of 10 to 15 percent of your final settlement. Check with your state insurance department, though, to find out whether public adjusters have to be licensed in your state. Don't do business with someone who comes to your door after a loss, claiming to be an adjuster; there are scam artists out there eager to take advantage of your misfortune.

If necessary, you could insist on arbitration of the dispute with your insurance carrier. An independent arbitrator selected by the attorneys for both sides will hear the arguments and decide what compensation you're entitled to. For the name of an arbitration organization near you, contact Arbitration Forums, P.O. Box 217500, Tampa, FL 33688-1500 (1-800-967-8889) or the American Arbitration Association (1-212-484-4000). For disputes involving just a few thousand dollars, it's probably cheaper to present your own case in small claims court.

## Security Issues

### Q. What should you do if there is an intruder in the house?

**A.** Everyone's afraid of finding someone in the house at night. If it happens, avoid a confrontation—your life is more important than your possessions. If possible, run away and call the police. If you can't get yourself and your family out of the house, lock yourselves in a room. If you're face to face with an intruder, stay calm and be cooperative.

What about self defense? You do have a legal right to protect yourself and your property, but recognize that you may end up in court if you shoot an intruder or whack him over the head with an iron pipe. You would have to argue that you really did act in self defense or in defense of your property, and it would be up to the jury to decide whether or not to believe you.

Basically, the law says that you can use reasonable force to defend yourself if you're being attacked or if you have a reasonable belief that you will be attacked. That is, you don't have to wait until the intruder is actually coming at you with a knife. The key word here is "reasonable"; the jury would have to decide whether a reasonable person would have thought that a toy gun was real or that a hand going into the pocket was reaching for a weapon.

### Q. What is considered "reasonable force"?

**A.** States vary widely on what they consider "reasonable force." In general, if you use force against an intruder, use no more than appears necessary. That is, if a shout sends the burglar running, don't pull a gun and shoot him in the back. If a single blow stops a burglar in his tracks, don't beat him to a pulp. If the intruder isn't threatening bodily harm to someone in the house, you're on shaky ground if you use deadly force. Some courts have held that a homeowner who could retreat safely isn't justified in beating or killing the intruder. Likewise, courts have held that a homeowner isn't justified in attacking a burglar if it appears that a shout or warning would be enough.

What about booby-trapping your home to keep burglars out? Despite the popularity of the movie "Home Alone," people have gotten into serious legal trouble for that sort of thing. Even if you're fed up with repeated break-ins, you can't set up a gun rigged to shoot anyone who comes through the window. First, it's not up to you to impose a death sentence on someone who might try to break in, and second, the next person through the window might be a firefighter trying to save you.

### Q. Does the law prohibit me from destroying wild animals on my property?

**A.** It depends on the animal. Many states allow killing of gophers, rattlesnakes, and coyotes without a permit, but most states impose hefty fines for killing other wild animals without a permit. Your state department of fish and wildlife has jurisdiction over wild animals, and a call to the nearest office will probably get you some advice. In some cases it isn't difficult to deter an invading animal. An eight-foot-high fence will stop most deer, and dried blood, as well as commercial mixtures, appears to repel rabbits. Storing trash so that it is not accessible to raccoons quickly forces these very smart (and often rabid) animals to find new stomping grounds.

It is true, however, that some animals are difficult to deter. Farmers lose thousands of dollars of crops to deer, pronghorns, and other graceful neighbors. In the West, ranchers cope with marauding bears and coyotes. Many states assist farmers with reducing the damage, and some reimburse farmers and ranchers for wildlife damage.

Note that in most cases reimbursement programs, which are funded by hunting license fees, aren't open to farmers who bar hunters from their land.

## A CHECKLIST ON HOME SECURITY

*How easy would it be for a crook to get into your home? Experts advise homeowners to begin by looking at their home as a burglar might. Identify the easiest place to get in and make it harder.*

- *Are there exterior lights on the front and back sides?*
- *Are there shrubs around your doors and windows that a burglar could use for cover? Better trim them.*
- *Do you have a privacy fence that could provide burglars with too much privacy?*
- *Do you have deadbolt locks on your doors? Do you keep them locked, even if you're out working in the yard?*
- *Are your doors solid, at least 1 1/4 inch thick, and do they fit snugly in the frame?*
- *Have you put in a specially designed lock for your sliding glass door? Could a burglar slide a window open from the outside and climb in? If you have double-hung windows, a removable nail pinning the upper and lower halves together is quite effective.*
- *Should you consider grates for your street-level windows? (Be aware that they can trap you inside in case of fire.)*
- *Would an alarm go off if an intruder stepped inside? Burglars hate noise.*
- *A sticker on your window declaring you have an alarm system may be enough to scare off some would-be intruders (whether you actually have an alarm system or not).*
- *Do you ever leave your house keys with your car keys when you have your car parked? Do you carry house keys on a key ring with a name and address tag? Do you hide a key in a secret place outside your home? Burglars know where to look.*
- *When you go on vacation, could strangers tell you're gone? Don't let mail and newspapers pile up outside, and make sure your lawn stays mowed and your walks stay shoveled. Use automatic timers for lights and a radio, and leave your blinds open in their usual position.*

## Environmental Hazards

**Q. What kinds of environmental hazards should I be concerned about?**

**A.** A home can look and smell fine, yet have deadly lead dust in the air, cancer-causing radon in the basement, or an underground oil tank leaching oil into the water table. Although toxic waste regulations apply to homeowners in much the same way as they apply to businesses, no laws require asbestos, lead, and other contaminants to be removed from owner-occupied residences. It's a matter of health and safety for you and your family.

**Q. How do I determine if there's an environmental problem in my home?**

**A.** In some cases, you may find out about a problem accidentally, such as when a painter points out lead-based paint on your woodwork or a remodeling contractor finds asbestos around the furnace and won't proceed until it's removed. You might learn about lead the hard way when your children can't think straight, or about contaminated water when the whole family gets sick. Health problems from asbestos or radon, however, wouldn't show up for another thirty years. The only way to discover and correct the problem may be to hire an expert to conduct the right tests.

In a growing number of states, sellers are required by law to inform potential buyers of knowledge about asbestos or other toxic substances in the house. Then it's up to the buyer and seller to work out who's responsible for dealing with it. The seller might lower the price to compensate the buyer for having to cope with the problem. In other states, the general rule is "buyer beware." A seller can't set out to misrepresent or hide the condition or lie if asked, but there's no obligation to disclose the problem. These days, though, home buyers often make the offer contingent on a satisfactory result of testing. Regular home inspectors

aren't usually qualified to test for lead or radon, so getting an accurate test would require hiring a qualified specialist.

If you intend to test for radon, asbestos, lead, or other household toxins, be careful about who you hire to test and deal with it. For example, people claiming to be asbestos consultants and contractors may find asbestos and try to convince you that it must be removed right away, even though the proper treatment for asbestos in many cases is to leave it in place. Then they'll remove it unnecessarily, which is a waste of money, and do so improperly, which can increase the health risk. To avoid such scams, do some research on the nature of each home toxin, and find out what services are available and what procedures and precautions the job involves to be done correctly. For names of licensed professionals in your area, check state or local health departments or Environmental Protection Agency (EPA) regional offices. As with any home improvements contractor, ask for references from previous clients, make sure the contractor has done similar projects, and get estimates from more than one. (See the "Home Improvement and Repairs" section beginning on page 194 for information on hiring contractors.)

**Q. What is asbestos?**

**A.** Asbestos is a fibrous material found in rocks and soils worldwide. Until the early 1970s it was widely used in flooring, walls, shingles, ceiling tiles, as insulation or fire retardant for furnaces and wiring. When the material crumbles or flakes, tiny asbestos flakes escape into the air. You breathe the fibers, they persist in your lungs, and with repeated long-term exposure you're likely to develop lung or stomach cancer.

**Q. What should I do about asbestos in my home?**

**A.** If the asbestos-containing material is in good shape—not flaking or peeling—and not likely to be disturbed, the best thing to do is leave it in place. But if it's going to be scraped, hammered, sawed, or otherwise disturbed in a remodeling project, a trained professional should be contacted to find a way to minimize the dissemination of the material.

Since total removal is expensive and difficult, intermediate options include applying a sealant or covering it with a protective wrap or jacket. It's tricky business, and even the cleanup needs to be done with a special vacuum cleaner to avoid scattering asbestos fibers. Don't try any of this yourself. Make sure the contractors you hire don't track it through the house or break the old material into small pieces.

To avoid conflict of interest, anyone you hire to survey your house for asbestos shouldn't be connected to an asbestos correction firm. The federal government, as well as some state and local governments, offers training courses for asbestos consultants and contractors. Ask to see documentation proving that everyone working with asbestos in your home has completed state or federal training.

### Q. Why is lead dangerous?

A. Lead is a soft, metallic element occurring naturally in rocks and soil all over the world. Until fairly recently, it was commonly used in pipes, plumbing solder, paint, and gasoline. If you breathe particles of lead dust or drink lead-contaminated water, it accumulates in your blood, bones, or soft tissue. High concentrations of lead can cause permanent damage to the brain, central nervous system, kidneys, and red blood cells. Lead is especially dangerous for infants, children, pregnant women, and the unborn because growing bodies absorb lead more easily and their tissues are more sensitive to it. Also, a given concentration of lead is worse on a child's smaller body than an adult's. In residential buildings, lead in drinking water and lead paint pose the major dangers.

### Q. What can you do about lead in drinking water?

A. Lead-based solder has been banned since 1988, but homes built before then often have lead solder that corrodes into drinking water. You can't tell whether pipes leach lead by looking at them, but a simple chemical test can identify it. If you want to have your water tested, ask your local, county, or state health or environment department about qualified testing laboratories. If you're having plumbing work done in an older home, check for lead pipes and make sure the plumber doesn't use lead solder. Even new faucets and fixtures can put some lead into the water. One way to reduce the risk is to run the faucet for one minute before using water for drinking or cooking. Never use hot water for drinking, cooking, or especially for making baby formula. Heat increases the leaching of lead into water.

If you do have lead in your water, several devices are available to reduce corrosion, including calcite filters, distillation units, and reverse-osmosis devices. Be aware that water softeners and carbon, sand and cartridge filters are not effective for removing lead. Get qualified advice before buying or leasing a device, as their effectiveness varies.

### Q. What should be done about lead paint?

A. Lead-based paint was applied to some two-thirds of the houses built before 1940 and a third of those built between 1940 and 1960, according to the EPA. Lead paint tastes sweet, so children have been poisoned from chewing on flakes of paint. Also there is a potential danger from lead dust that is stirred up when lead-based painted woodwork is scraped, sanded, or heated with an open flame stripper. Then it settles in fibers and fabric and gets stirred up again by normal cleaning.

The only accurate way to tell whether your house has lead-based paint is to remove a sample and have it tested in a qualified laboratory. Contact a local, county, or state health or environmental department about where to find one.

If lead-based paint is in good condition and there is no possibility that it will be nibbled on by children, it's best to leave it alone. Otherwise, you can cover it with wallpaper or some other building material or completely replace the woodwork. Removing lead paint properly and safely is a time-consuming and expensive process that requires everyone else to leave the house during removal and clean-up.

If the house was painted on the outside before 1950, the surrounding soil is probably contaminated with lead. Don't leave patches of bare soil, and clean your floors and windowsills regularly with wet rags and mops. Make sure everyone in the family washes their hands frequently.

Also note that some states have strict laws regarding lead paint and rental units. In Massachusetts, for example, few landlords would rent their units to people with children under age six unless the unit had been de-leaded. That's because landlords can be held liable for any lead-induced illnesses that later develop in these children if the unit had not been de-leaded.

### Q. *What is radon?*

**A.** Radon is a colorless, odorless, tasteless gas resulting from the natural decay of uranium in the earth. It comes into your house through small cracks, floor drains, wall/floor joints, and the pores in hollow block walls, and tends to accumulate in the lowest level of the home. It can also get trapped in ground water, so homes with wells are more likely to have a radon problem. Radon particles get trapped in your lungs, where they break down and release bursts of radiation that can damage lung tissue and cause cancer.

### Q. *How do you test for radon?*

**A.** Testing for radon in well water requires sending a sample to a laboratory for analysis. Inexpensive test kits for radon in the air are available at hardware stores, but be sure they have been approved by a federal or state health, environmental or consumer protection agency. Long-term testing over a year is most accurate, but short-term testing can let you know if you have a potential problem.

Most homes contain from one to two picocuries of radon per liter of air (pCi/L). If rooms in your home have more than four picocuries of radon per liter of air, it should be reduced. This normally isn't a do-it-yourself project, but professional radon-reduction contractors can determine the source of the gas and seal leaks and install fans, pumps, or other equipment to keep it out. Special filter systems can remove radon from your water supply. Depending on the number of sources, the amount of radon and the construction of the home, installing radon-reduction equipment costs anywhere from several hundred to several thousand dollars but in most cases is less expensive than de-leading.

### Q. *What is considered toxic waste?*

**A.** Usually toxic waste is associated with chemical companies or nuclear reactors. But a residential property also can harbor toxic wastes that are potentially dangerous to the homeowner and neighbors. For example, many family farms have a ravine or back lot that's long been a handy place to dump discards, such as rusting metal objects or empty pesticide containers that haven't necessarily been rinsed out according to label instructions. Or a private home may have a leaky heating-oil tank buried under the backyard, either one still in use or an abandoned one that was never emptied when the heating system was converted to natural gas. Oil, pesticides, or other toxic substances from these sources can seep fumes into a neighbor's basement, contaminate nearby wells, or migrate through the water table until there's an oil slick on the nearest creek.

### Q. Who is responsible for cleaning up toxic wastes?

**A.** The law may hold homeowners responsible for the cost of cleaning up toxic waste sites whether or not they had anything to do with creating the problem. Responsible parties are "jointly and severally" liable, including the current homeowner, the owner of the property when the pollution was caused, and the person or company who caused it (which could be a third party altogether). "Jointly and severally" means that any one of them can be forced to pay the entire cost. That may be the current homeowner, who is probably the easiest one to find. Then it is up to the homeowner to find the others and sue to recover the cost.

When someone discovers the problem and the city or county health department is contacted, an inspector will be sent out to conduct tests and determine the source of the pollution. The cost of investigation alone can be expensive. Then the department begins the process of cleaning up the site to enforce state regulations. The clean-up process might involve ordering the homeowner to hire a consultant and a remediation crew. If it is an emergency or an immediate threat to water quality, the agency may send someone in to clean it up, then sue the homeowner for reimbursement. But that is a difficult process; usually agencies first try to get the homeowner to take care of a problem.

The clean-up process may involve judgment calls and negotiation. Oil in the soil from a leaking tank, for example, will eventually degrade. Instead of hauling all the old soil out and replacing it, it might be less expensive to drill new wells for those affected. If your property has a toxic waste problem, hire an attorney experienced with environmental matters to help you through the process. It might involve obtaining an analysis to estimate how long before the waste would degrade and how far and fast it's likely to migrate until then. In some cases, the negotiations turn into a battle of experts.

What if you don't think you should have to pay for clean-up because you didn't have anything to do with causing the pollution? Your only hope is the "innocent landowner defense," under the Superfund Amendments and Reauthorization Act of 1986, which limits the liability of a landowner who made "all appropriate inquiry" into the environmental condition of the property before buying it. That means the only way you would be off the hook is if you had the foresight to have an environmental survey done before buying the property to see whether it was contaminated by hazardous substances. That would include a visual inspection of the property and compilation of a history of past owners and their waste disposal practices, contaminant releases and violations, and other information. Chances are you didn't do that; it's the sort of thing lenders sometimes require for commercial loans because lenders also can be on the hook for toxic waste sites.

To prevent future problems, check with your local health authority to find out how to meet state regulations for disposal of motor oil, paint, antifreeze, and other toxic substances.

---

## FINANCIAL ISSUES

### Understanding Your Mortgage

### Q. Who owns the mortgage on my house?

**A.** Traditionally, banks and savings and loan institutions owned most residential mortgages. Today, it is much more common for mortgages to be securitized and sold to investors such as mutual funds and insurance companies. This means that borrowers are usually dealing with a mortgage servicer, rather than the actual person or institution that holds the mortgage.

### Q. What happens when your mortgage is transferred?

**A.** Most mortgages are sold soon after they are originated. This means that most mortgage holders will be dealing with at least two and possibly more mortgage servicing agents during the life of the mortgage. The mortgage servicer is responsible for collecting monthly payments and handling the escrow account, such as paying property taxes. The National Affordable Housing Act, passed in 1990, addresses the responsibilities of a mortgage servicer and consumer protection in this area. Under this act, lenders are required to do the following:

- Notify you at least fifteen days before the effective date of the transfer of your loan servicing. (The servicer has up to thirty days after the transfer for notification if you have defaulted on the loan, the original servicer filed for bankruptcy, or the servicer's functions are being taken over by a federal agency.)

- Notice must include the following: name and address of the new servicer; date the current service will stop accepting mortgage payments and date the new servicer will accept them; and a free or collect-call telephone number for both servicers if you have questions about the transfer.

- The new servicer may not change any terms or conditions and this must be disclosed to the borrower. For example, if your former lender did not require that property taxes or homeowner's insurance be paid from an escrow account, the new servicer cannot demand that such an account be established.

- During a sixty-day grace period, a late fee cannot be charged if you mistakenly send your mortgage payment to your former servicer, and the new servicer cannot report late payments to a credit bureau.

### Q. What can you do if you have a problem with a mortgage servicer?

**A.** Contact your servicer in writing if you believe a late penalty was improperly imposed, or for any other problem. Include your account number and explain why your account is in error. The servicer must acknowledge your inquiry in writing within twenty business days and has sixty business days to either correct your account or explain why it is accurate. During this time it is important that you not withhold any disputed amount of mortgage payment, which could allow the mortgage to be declared in default.

If you believe your servicer has not complied with the law, you may want to file a complaint. For a complaint about a HUD-certified servicer, write to the Office of Single Family Housing, HUD, Room 9282, Washington, DC 20410 (telephone 202-708-3175). You also may want to contact an attorney to advise you. Under the National Affordable Housing Act, consumers may initiate class action suits and obtain damages for a pattern or practice of non-compliance.

### Q. What is an escrow account?

**A.** This is the account established by lenders to pay for such items as property tax and homeowner's insurance. The lender establishes the monthly amount required to maintain escrow by adding up the annual costs of property tax and possibly insurance and dividing by 12. This is the amount that is stipulated in your monthly payment.

The Real Estate Settlement Procedures Act limits the amount of money that can be held in an escrow account. The calculation is rather complex. Let's say the expenses paid by your escrow account add up to $3600, or $300 a month. The law requires that at least once a year, the escrow account be no more than two times the monthly payment required, or $600. The practical effect of this is that taxes are usually collected once or twice a year. Between collections, the account may have a sizable balance, but immediately after the collection it should have no more than $600 in the account. If you notice on your monthly statement that your escrow is larger than that sum, you have the right to question the lender. This happens more frequently than one might imagine, so take the time to figure out if your lender is following escrow regulations. Otherwise, you are paying more in monthly payments than you should be.

### Q. How do I determine how much equity I have in my home?

**A.** Equity is the value of your unencumbered interest in your home. It is determined by subtracting the unpaid mortgage balance and any other home debts, such as a second mortgage or home equity loan, from the home's fair market value. For example, if your mortgage is $50,000 and your home is worth about $100,000, you would have $50,000 in equity or 50 percent equity in your home. On the other hand, if the value of your home has fallen, you may have less equity than when you purchased the home.

### Q. What can I do if falling home prices have cut my equity?

**A.** Many homeowners have found themselves in this sorry state, particularly if they bought their home in the mid to late 1980s when home prices were soaring. Now that prices have fallen drastically in some areas, homeowners are faced with the problem of having no or little equity in their property.

This is a particularly horrible situation if you are trying to sell or refinance. If you sell, you may owe the lender more money than you receive from the sale of the home, because the sale price is lower than the remaining mortgage. If you're trying to refinance, a lender will want to know that you have at least 20 percent equity in the home, but an appraisal may not bear this out. Be sure, however, to not accept the first appraisal. You may find another appraiser will value your home more highly.

Unfortunately, if your equity has fallen below what you owe on your mortgage, there is little you can do in this situation. If you must sell, you'll have to take a loss on your home and perhaps pay the bank to retain a good credit rating. If you are trying to refinance, you may be able to talk to your lender and renegotiate more favorable rates on your outstanding mortgage. The one exception is for homeowners who have FHA and VA loans, who can apply for a special refinancing without an appraisal. (See sidebar "Refinancing FHA and VA Loans" on page 182.)

### LIABILITY ON AN ASSUMPTION

*If you allow buyers to assume your mortgage, are you liable for the loan if they default? That depends on when and how your mortgage originated. For example, some assumable mortgages may dictate your responsibilities in case of an assumption. With loans insured by the FHA before Dec. 15, 1989, and on most assumable conventional loans, you remain liable for the life of the loan. On FHA mortgages originated after that date, you would share liability with the new owner for five years.*

## LENDERS DON'T WANT TO FORECLOSE

*Lenders do not like to foreclose on property because they usually will not retrieve the full amount of their loan. In most cases, the homeowner would sell and repay the mortgage if he or she could do so; so the practical consequences of foreclosure mean that the bank ends up with a property that is not worth the outstanding amount on the mortgage. A lender may recover all its money only if it is foreclosing on a home that has much more equity than the money owed on the mortgage.*

### Q. Is there anything I can do if I can't pay my mortgage?

**A.** Most people get behind on their mortgage payments because of job loss, divorce, illness, and medical bills. The first thing to do if you are having trouble making your mortgage payments is to take the matter seriously. Many people refuse to face the facts that their home is on the line and delay doing anything until it is too late.

Most financial institutions do not like to foreclose on properties (see sidebar, this page), and there may be ways to work with the lender to reduce your monthly payments or at least delay foreclosure until you can sell your house. That is why it is important to contact your lender as soon as possible. Call or write to explain your problem, and be sure to notify the lender of your account number to speed the process. Sometimes the lender will allow you to defer paying principal or may even refinance

the loan at a lower rate to help make your payments affordable. If you can prove that you are actively trying to sell your home, your lender also may cooperate with reducing monthly payments.

Next, contact the nearest housing counseling agency, which offers advice and services to help you ward off foreclosure. If your loan is HUD-insured, for example, a HUD-approved agency can help you apply for federal mortgage-relief programs that may provide temporary aid. If you have a VA-insured loan, contact a local VA office for assistance.

In some states, filing for bankruptcy also may ward off immediate foreclosure, but you are well advised to contact an attorney to begin bankruptcy proceedings.

### Q. What happens when a lender forecloses on the mortgage?

**A.** Depending on the state where you live, certain protections are afforded homeowners, but generally all your rights to your home will end if a foreclosure sale occurs or soon thereafter (usually no more than six months). This means that once a lender files a foreclosure suit, you must act immediately. In Illinois, for example, when a foreclosure suit is filed, the homeowner has ninety days to make up the back payments to reinstate the mortgage. After that date, the lender can legally require that the mortgage be paid in full within seven months of the original foreclosure notice. The important fact to remember is that you must act immediately to protect your home if your lender intends to foreclose.

## Refinancing and Home Loans

### Q. How can you figure out whether it makes sense to refinance your mortgage?

**A.** This is an easy question for some homeowners—if you have a double-digit interest rate on your mortgage when rates have dropped to below 8 percent, there is no question that you will save money by refinancing. Other homeowners may need cash out of their home equity to fund other expenses, such as college tuition. Borrowing the money on your house and deducting the interest is almost always going to be cheaper than taking out a personal loan.

For others, the question is more difficult. First you need to compare interest rates to figure out how much you would save on your monthly payments, as well as the life of the mortgage. For example, on a $100,000 mortgage, a mortgage interest rate of 7 percent versus 8½ percent results in a savings of about $100 a month, or $1,200 a year on a thirty-year loan. To more precisely calculate the difference, you will want to get an amortization chart from a banker or real estate agent. Compare what you are currently paying in principal and interest per month with what you would be paying on the new loan.

Second, add up the costs of points, closing costs, title insurance, etc. of the refinancing. Third, you may want to also calculate the difference between your current payment's after-tax cost versus your future payment's after-tax cost. Because Uncle Sam gives you a tax break (fifteen to thirty-one cents per every dollar of interest paid, depending on your tax bracket) on mortgage interest, it is important to figure this into your calculations, particularly if you are in the top tax bracket and/or expect to be in an even higher bracket. Simply multiply the annual interest you pay currently by .15 or .31, depending on your tax bracket, to figure out your current tax savings. Then multiply your annual interest paid on the new loan versus the same number. For example, if you're currently paying $7,800 in mortgage interest annually ($650 per month) and you're in a 31 percent bracket, you currently have an annual tax savings of $2,418 ($7,800 multiplied by .31).

**Q. Are there times when it doesn't make sense to refinance?**

**A.** In almost all cases, you won't recover the closing costs for a few years, so if you are planning to sell your home in the near future, it makes little sense to refinance unless you can obtain a no-points adjustable-rate mortgage at a low "teaser" rate.

**Q. What's the difference between a home equity loan and a second mortgage?**

**A.** They are similar in that the interest on both is tax deductible (on loans up to $1 million), and the home serves as collateral for both types of loans. They differ because a second mortgage usually consists of a fixed sum for a fixed period of time, while a home equity loan usually works as a line of credit on which you may draw over time. Typically, a home equity loan carries an adjustable interest rate, while a second mortgage carries a fixed rate, although this is not always the case in today's market.

**Q. Which is better?**

**A.** If you need a lump sum of cash, you are probably better off with a second mortgage because you will get a better interest rate on the loan. If you need money over a longer period of time, such as to pay college tuition or to pay for renovations planned over the next few years, it may be better to obtain a home equity loan. That way, you won't be paying interest on the money until you actually withdraw it when you need it.

**Q. Do the same rules apply to original mortgages and refinancing?**

**A.** When you refinance, you pay off the original mortgage and take on a new one. State and federal laws protect consumers in both cases, but you will want to go through the same steps as you would in obtaining a first mortgage. (See pages 121–126 of the "Buying and Selling a Home" chapter for advice on shopping for mortgage interest rates and mortgages.)

**Q. Can I deduct on my federal tax return the points I paid to refinance my mortgage?**

**A.** With one exception, points paid on a refinancing must be amortized over the life of the loan, while points paid to obtain an initial mortgage may be deducted in the year the home was purchased. For example, if you paid two points to refinance a new thirty-year mortgage, you would be allowed to deduct one-thirtieth of the points paid each year over the next thirty years. If you pay off the loan before it is due, however, you may deduct any remaining amount in the year the loan was paid in full.

The exception to this rule is if you pay the points yourself and use part of the proceeds of the refinancing to pay for home improvements. Then you are allowed to deduct a portion of the points in the year of the refinancing. For example, if you paid $2,000 or two points to refinance a $100,000, fifteen-year mortgage and you used $25,000 to renovate your kitchen, you would be able to deduct 25 percent of the

> **REFINANCING TIPS**
> - *Get a copy of your credit report before you apply and correct any errors.*
> - *Make sure you have a minimum 20 percent equity in your home; otherwise, you'll be expected to put down more money or be forced to pay Private Mortgage Insurance (PMI).*
> - *Make sure you understand the fee you will be charged when using a mortgage broker.*
> - *Consider shortening the term of the loan, perhaps from thirty to fifteen years; you will pay more each month but save a lot in interest payments over the life of the loan.*
> - *Be prepared to wait. Refinancing can take three months or more, because when mortgage interest rates decline, many homeowners jump at the chance to refinance.*

> **REFINANCING FHA AND VA LOANS**
> *Homeowners who have an FHA or VA loan may be able to qualify for a special program, called FHA Streamline Refinancing, which does not require a home appraisal, employment verification, or qualifying ratios as long as the mortgage is current. If you want to refinance an FHA or VA loan, call your local HUD office for information.*

$2,000 or $500 in the year that you refinanced; the other $1,500 would have to be divided over fifteen years, allowing a $100 annual deduction.

### Tax Considerations

**Q. What tax breaks are available to home-owners?**

**A.** On your federal tax return, both your local property tax and mortgage interest paid on your home loan (up to $1 million) are deductible against other income as long as you itemize and do not use a standard deduction. "Deductibility" simply means that you don't have to pay federal taxes on the income you spend on mortgage interest and state and local taxes. In the early years of a home loan, for example, when most of your payment goes toward interest, you might shelter as much as a quarter to a third of your income. This deduction can be spread over both a first home and a vacation home, as long as the vacation home is not being used principally as a rental property.

Federal tax law also allows you to deduct interest paid on up to $100,000 of a home equity loan as long as the total debt on the home (including the first mortgage) does not exceed the fair market value of the home.

You also may be eligible for a deduction of property tax paid on your home on your state income tax return, but this is not the case in all states. In Massachusetts, for example, local property taxes may not be deducted against income on the state tax return.

## Q. Is there any way to lower the property taxes on my house?

**A.** To lower property taxes, you need to lower the assessed value of your property, which is the basis of your taxes. By providing evidence that the assessed value of your home or business property is too high, you should succeed in lowering the assessment, as well as your property taxes.

In most states, an assessor or a board of assessors places a value on your property for tax purposes. If the property has recently been sold, its sale price will be an important factor in setting the value. If there has been no recent sale, they will estimate its market value using other evidence. This assessment may be done annually or on some other schedule, such as every four years. In most cases, then, the assessor uses a complicated schedule to get from appraised value to dollar amount of taxes owed. For example, in many states, the value is reduced by a certain percentage, then multiplied by the local

property tax or millage rate to establish the amount of taxes you will actually pay.

Your role in the process should begin when you get a notice indicating the assessed value placed on your property. If you think it is too high, you will want to file an appeal as soon as possible. To challenge the assessment, first look for obvious mistakes in the notice. Make sure the address and description of your property are correct. It may be necessary to look up the information about your home at the assessor's office. Check to make sure the number of rooms, bathrooms, square footage, etc. is accurate, and make a note of any discrepancies.

Next, check to see if you qualify for a special tax break. Some jurisdictions provide tax breaks to certain categories of property owners. For example, tax waivers of 10 percent or more may be available to owner-occupied homes, owners age sixty-five and older, disabled veterans, and persons with certain disabilities. Lastly, make sure the assessor has any information about damage to the property, such as flood or fire damage. If any of these conditions apply, ask your local assessor's office how to file an appeal and note any of these problems in your appeal.

Even if none of these special conditions apply, investigate whether the market value determined by the assessor is higher than the true market value of your property. Local real estate agents or the county registrar of deeds should be able to provide recent sales of comparable or similar properties in your area. Also, check the assessed value of similar neighboring properties; this is public information in most places. Remember, however, that the assessed value may reflect one-year-old values; in other words, the assessment usually is based on the market value of your home the previous year, not its current value. Once you have the information you need to protest your assessment, you will either be required to fill out a form or make an appointment with the assessment board. Be prepared to bring facts and figures. If your appeal fails, depending on your state you may appeal that decision to a special board of equalization, a board of appeals, a state court, or a special tax tribunal. State laws vary as to how and when property is assessed and appeal procedures. For specific information, consult your local government officials or your lawyer.

### Q. How can you qualify for a tax deduction on a home office?

**A.** In 1993, the U.S. Supreme Court upheld IRS rules regarding home office deductions, making it much more difficult to qualify for the deduction if you provide most services away from your home office. Both self-employed persons and employees who are not provided an office at work are affected by this ruling. Under the IRS rules, the home office must meet one of the following conditions:

- It is the taxpayer's principal place of business—the taxpayer must either spend most of his or her working days there or produce goods or services in the office.

- It is used by clients or customers of the taxpayer.

- It is a separate structure not attached to the dwelling unit. This means, for example, that a contractor who does most of his work in other places and who does not meet clients in his office could qualify for the deduction only if the office is a separate structure.

Additionally, financial professionals suggest that if you spend working time away from the office, to ensure that you qualify for the deduction you also should do the following:

- Set up a separate phone line for the business.

- Have clients or customers visit you in the home office and keep records of the visits.

- Have all business-related correspondence sent to the home office.

### Q. What is deductible in a home office?

**A.** All maintenance, repairs, and equipment in the home office are deductible against income associated with the business conducted in the office. These would include a new desk, office paper, and painting the room. In addition, self-employed persons are allowed to deduct a percentage of annual household expenses, including maintenance and repairs of items that affect the entire house, utilities, homeowner's insurance, and mortgage insurance. These costs are proportioned relative to the size of the house and must be calculated according to a complicated IRS formula based on the percentage of hours you work at home. Note, also, that the deduction for household expenses of an employee who is required to maintain a home office is limited to two percent of adjusted gross income.

A home office also may be depreciated using a 31.5-year straight line commercial depreciation rate, but this deduction is recaptured if you sell your home.

### FILING AN ASSESSMENT APPEAL

*Most municipalities allow a limited time for assessment appeals; don't wait until you get your tax bill, which is usually too late. In most states, the procedures for tax appeals are relatively simple and homeowners may be able to represent themselves. If the case is complex or involves a large amount of money, you may want to consult an attorney or real estate appraiser.*

# MANAGING NEIGHBORHOOD PROBLEMS

**Q. What's the best way to handle a dispute with a neighbor?**

**A.** Unless you intend to move, resolving a problem amicably is in your best interest. Neighborhood spats typically originate from minor disputes over boundary lines, fences, junk cars, noise, pets, and trees. If the problem cannot be solved between the two of you, different disputes call for different remedies.

If a neighborhood problem is addressed in your local government's zoning code, which regulates which activities are permitted in a neighborhood, you may be able to turn to municipal officials. If you live in a condominium, cooperative, or planned subdivision, private regulations and a homeowners' association to back them up may provide support. If the offending activity is classified under common law as a nuisance, it might be either a crime or a civil offense under local law. And if the appropriate agency doesn't take action, you could file a lawsuit in court to stop the activity or in small claims court for monetary damages.

In all cases, you will want to know how the law, as well as municipal and subdivision regulations, can be put to use if you are unable to resolve things quietly.

**Q. How can I tell if my neighbor is violating a zoning ordinance?**

**A.** City or county zoning regulations may limit the height of fences, the use of property for commercial purposes, or the decibels of noise allowed at night. In some cases, city officials notice a violation and issue a citation, but usually it is up to the neighbors to complain. If you suspect a zoning violation is causing the problem—such as the transformation of your vegetable garden into a shade garden thanks to your neighbor's new 12-foot fence—check with your city hall or town council to see if there's a regulation on the books. Either town hall or the local library should have copies of municipal ordinances.

**Q. What can I do if my neighbor is violating a zoning ordinance?**

**A.** Notifying the neighbor that he is violating an ordinance may take care of the problem. To file a complaint, you may have to contact the city attorney or the controlling agency, such as the local zoning board. If the city takes up the cause for you, it will require less effort and expense on your part than filing a nuisance suit. You won't receive money, however, because your neighbor will either be ordered to comply with the zoning rules, pay a fine to the city, or both.

**Q. What constitutes a nuisance?**

**A.** A nuisance is the legal term for a person's unreasonable action that interferes with your enjoyment of your property. Anything from noxious gases to annoying wind chimes may constitute a nuisance. The law of nuisance involves a balancing test, weighing the social value of the activity against the social value of your use and enjoyment of your property. Accordingly, authorities who have to deal with nuisance complaints expect them to be reasonable. For example, your distaste for your neighbor's cooking odors will not be enough to sustain a nuisance complaint.

**Q. What can you do about a nuisance problem?**

**A.** If your local ordinances make nuisance a crime (usually a misdemeanor), the offender might be given a citation to appear in court at a given date, or he or she might even be arrested, held until posting bond, and ordered to appear in court. If convicted, he or she may be fined and/or jailed. If your local ordinances make nui-

## STEP-BY-STEP GUIDE FOR RESOLVING NEIGHBOR PROBLEMS

**Step 1:** *Discuss the problem with the neighbor, who may not be aware that the late-night parties bother you or that Fifi is digging up your flower bed.*

**Step 2:** *Warn the neighbor. Obtain a copy of the applicable local ordinance (look in the "municipal code," which should be found in your local library or in City Hall or contact your local council representative). Mail it with a letter of warning alerting your neighbor of a violation of the law. Wait a reasonable time to see if the problem is resolved.*

### SAMPLE WARNING LETTER

Dear Neighbor,

Just as you enjoy playing your stereo, I enjoy a quiet environment in my home. It is impossible for me to do so when your stereo is played at such a loud volume.

Please read the enclosed municipal noise ordinance. You will see that the law requires that you comply and keep your stereo to a reasonable volume.

I trust that we can resolve this matter amicably so that I will not be forced to contact the authorities. Thank you for your anticipated cooperation.

**Step 3:** *Suggest mediation. Try to work out the problem with an impartial third-person mediator to resolve the dispute informally.*

**Step 4:** *Contact the authorities. If all else fails, call the police and/or file a civil lawsuit against the neighbor.*

sance a civil violation, he or she would face civil charges in court. The penalty for a civil violation is a fine.

Whether the alleged nuisance violates a civil or criminal city ordinance, the city carries the burden of prosecuting the case. Your role as the complaining neighbor is limited to testifying if the case goes to trial. Again, any money collected will be in the form of fines paid to the city, not to you.

The other option is to file a nuisance suit yourself. Here you would bear the expense of

bringing the case to trial, including filing fees and legal counsel, but if you won you could collect monetary damages from the neighbor. A less expensive approach that may be available in your area is to file in small claims court, which would cost less and probably be faster. Either way, to prevail against your neighbor in court you will have to show the following elements:

- The neighbor is doing something that seriously annoys you. It helps to show a copy of a letter you wrote asking the neighbor to stop or modify his behavior.

- The neighbor's actions have reduced your ability to use and enjoy your property.

- The neighbor is responsible for his actions.

- In some states (New Jersey, New Mexico, North Dakota, Oklahoma, and South Dakota), the neighbor's conduct must also be unreasonable or unlawful.

- A specific amount of money or an injunction directing the neighbor to do or to refrain from doing something would adequately deal with the annoyance.

### Q. How can I handle disputes over boundary lines?

**A.** Disputes about boundary lines are less common than other neighbor-related problems, in part because of modern surveying techniques. As a rule, boundary lines are set forth in the property description in your deed. Sometimes, though, if the property was originally recorded decades or even centuries ago, that description may be a bit murky.

If you and your neighbor are unsure where the boundaries lie, there are a number of alternatives:

- Spend a few hundred dollars to hire a surveyor.

- File a "quiet title" lawsuit asking a judge to determine the location of the boundary line. This is even more expensive because you will have court filing fees and possibly a survey if the court so requires.

  (Quiet title is a type of lawsuit that asks a court to make a final determina-

## HANDLING DISPUTES IN COMMON-INTEREST COMMUNITIES

*If you live in a common-interest community, check the bylaws and regulations of your development to see whether there is a rule against the activity in question. Your homeowners' association can be a powerful ally. After all, if a neighbor's actions are bothering you, they may be equally troublesome to other residents of the development. If your neighbor refuses to comply with your initial requests, consider asking other neighbors if the situation bothers them, too. They may be willing to sign a petition or a joint letter to the homeowners' association, which is more likely to draw the attention of the board than a complaint from an individual.*

*The association will investigate the complaint, ask for input from the offending neighbor, then take a vote as to whether official action is warranted. If the board feels your neighbor has violated its governing rules, it will likely begin by issuing a formal warning letter. In extreme cases of noncompliance, homeowners' associations have referred the matter to the city attorney or have filed their own nuisance suits against the offending resident.*

tion about the title of a piece of property. An example would be when someone needs to show that she is the rightful owner of a piece of land before she can sell it. She could ask the court to examine the records and confirm her ownership.)

- Agree with your neighbor that a certain imaginary line or a physical object, such as a fence or a large tree, will serve as the boundary. Each party should sign a "quit-claim" deed, granting to the other neighbor ownership to any land on the other side of the line. Be sure to record the deed by filing it in the county records office (often called the "registry of deeds").

### Q. What can I do about noise?

**A.** In densely populated areas, noise is one of the most common sources of neighborhood tension. Some municipal ordinances limit noise to a given number of decibels. If the police have a decibel machine, you can ask them to measure the noise your neighbor is creating. This provides useful documentation should you need to proceed against your neighbor in court.

Timing is critical, though. Accordingly, many municipalities regulate noise levels during certain "quiet times" when most people sleep. They typically begin between 10:00 p.m. and midnight and last until 7:00 or 8:00 on weekdays; on weekends they often extend to 9:00 or 10:00 a.m. But some noises may be unreasonable at any time, such as playing an electric guitar so loud that it makes a neighbor's walls shake.

As with any nuisance, start by asking the neighbor to tone down the volume and explain why. Keep a log of the noise—when it occurred, how loud it was, and how it affected your household. If the neighbor doesn't respond even to a letter, consult with your town council about local ordinances that might need enforcement. Consider a lawsuit only as a last resort.

### Q. My neighbor is letting his property fall apart. Is there anything I can do?

**A.** Blighted property decreases the value of surrounding homes and will frequently incur the wrath of surrounding neighbors; but unless they are governed by subdivision rules on exterior maintenance, homeowners are generally free to choose how their property looks. The exception occurs when a place is so neglected that it becomes a neighborhood eyesore, such as a yard overgrown with weeds or filled with trash, or a safety hazard, such as a dangerous structure.

If deterioration is a matter of the offenders' financial problems, perhaps you and other neighbors could pitch in for a "cleanup" day. If it's simply a matter of sloth, ask the offenders to clean up or repair what is broken. If they refuse your request that they clean up their property to a reasonable standard, you may be able to get the city to do it for you, provided it has an ordinance declaring blighted property to be a nuisance. If so requested by a resident—or if a city official observes the nuisance—the city may issue repeated notices to the offenders. In about 95 percent of the cases, homeowners clean up their property after the first notice. About one percent of the cases are actually prosecuted in court.

And if you are the one at fault, you may want to clean up your act. A California man was jailed twice after the city prosecuted him on misdemeanor charges over the piles of trash and junk cars on his property. While he was in jail, the city undertook the cleanup of his property—then placed a $15,000 lien on his home to recover the cleanup costs.

### Q. What can I do if my neighbor is engaging in illegal activities?

**A.** First, if the problem is with tenants, contact the property owner, who may or may not know that the tenants are doing something illegal, such as selling illegal drugs. Some cities

## WATCH THOSE BOUNDARIES

*Before you erect a fence or other structure on your land, make sure that it is indeed your land. If you innocently but mistakenly erect a fence on your neighbor's property, you may be liable for trespassing on your neighbor's land. Your neighbor could ask the court for an injunction to make you tear down the fence, as well as money for any damage you may have caused to his or her property. The same applies in reverse: if your neighbor starts building on a parcel you feel is rightfully your land, notify him or her immediately. If you allow the construction to continue and wait too long to complain, you may be giving up your right to that strip of land. After many years of uncontested use, courts sometimes grant the party that has used the land a "prescriptive easement" allowing them to continue doing so. How far over the boundary is enough to complain about? The reasonableness of the circumstances may dictate whether a court will support you. For example, a judge may not be too sympathetic to your request that a neighbor relocate a building that is an inch over your property line. However, if that building is flush with your windows and blocking your sunlight and air, the court may feel differently.*

require that such tenants be evicted or fine landlords who allow such a nuisance to continue. In some cases, state and federal laws provide for the government to seize property that is being used for illegal financial gain. The threat of forfeiting the house to the government is likely to persuade the homeowner to evict the undesirable tenants. Another approach is for you and your neighbors to pursue a private lawsuit against a neighborhood nuisance. Neighbors can be a powerful, unifying force against a common "enemy."

### Pets

**Q. What can I do if my neighbor's animals are creating a problem?**

**A.** Some neighbors get along like cats and dogs—and in some cases, the problem is real cats and dogs. Consider the situation of two southern California neighbors whose yards were separated by a thick concrete wall. On one side was a litter of normally well-behaved Chinese chow dogs; on the other, two mellow cats. No problem—until the cats learned how to climb the wall, perch atop it, and glare down at the dogs. The dogs took to barking and yapping whenever anything stirred on the other side of the wall.

The entire neighborhood was unhappy. The cat owner blamed the dogs for the noise; the dog owner blamed the cats for teasing the dogs. Even more infuriated was a third neighbor, who worked nights and was trying to sleep when the "dog alarm clock" went off every morning. The trouble escalated when the dog owner started hurling shoes, balls, and other objects at the cats to chase them off the wall. One unidentified flying object sailing over the wall smacked the cat owner's child on the head. By that point, everyone was threatening to sue everyone else.

The solution? The cat owner suggested a truce: the cats would go out in the mornings and the dogs in the afternoons. By late afternoon, all the animals could go out because the third neighbor would already be at work. The dog owner agreed to stop pitching objects at the cats; the cat owner agreed to pluck the cats off the wall whenever she found them tormenting the dogs. The animal war ended as quickly as it had begun.

If you have a problem with a neighbor's pet, knowing your local laws can add clout to your efforts to resolve it. Your town probably has one or more applicable ordinances indexed under "Dogs" or "Animal Control" that can be enforced in court. Such laws often limit the number of animals per household, the length of time a dog may bark, or the frequency of barking allowed. Leash laws require that dogs not run at large, and "pooper scooper" laws require owners to clean up after their pets. If polite requests to your neighbor don't work, call your local animal control service, which is likely to be more receptive to your problem than the police or other city officials. Unless the animal control authorities consider your complaint unreasonable, they will probably call the offending animal's owner with a warning, followed by a citation if the problem persists.

A citation resembles a ticket; it requires the offender either to pay a fine or to challenge the citation in court. After being punished in the pocketbook, many people will change their animals' behavior to conform with the law. If they continue to allow their animal to annoy you, they can be fined repeatedly if you continue to complain.

If the problem persists, you may need to bring a civil lawsuit for "nuisance" to get a court order. The offender is likely to obey, because one who disobeys a court order may find himself in contempt of court, which can mean time in jail or at the bank, withdrawing hefty sums to pay a fine.

For animal problems, call the police only as a last resort. Police are generally not very interested in problem dogs, as they have more serious matters to worry about. Bringing the police into the equation also may sever any further relations with your neighbor.

## CREATURE COURT

*When the fur flies between pet owners and their neighbors in Ventura County, California, the confrontation can end up in "animal court," a voluntary program and an alternative to formal court proceedings. There, the county's "poundmaster" presides over about one hundred cases each year, which have included a cat that bit a woman, a rooster that rudely awakened the neighborhood, and a variety of disputes over dogs that bit, barked, or intimidated children.*

## Trees

### Q. What's the law regarding trees?

**A.** Trees can cause as much contention between neighbors as yapping dogs, whether they block people's view, crack their foundation, or drop debris on their driveway. The ground rules state that a tree whose trunk stands entirely on the land of one person belongs to that person; if the trunk stands partly on the land of two or more people, it usually belongs to all the property owners. Someone who cuts down, removes, or harms a tree without permission owes the tree's owner money for compensation for that harm done.

### Q. Is there any way I can be prevented from cutting down the trees on my own property?

**A.** In most cases, the answer would be no, but trees are not strictly private property like barbecue grills. In some instances, neither the tree owner nor the neighbor has unlimited control over the fate of a tree. One subdivision overlooking scenic Farmington Valley in Simsbury, Connecticut, has a restrictive covenant in its deeds bearing homage to trees: homeowners cannot cut them down, even on their own land. They can, however, trim diseased limbs or branches that block their view of the valley below.

Subdivision rules such as this are designed to restrict the use of each lot in a tract for the benefit of all who reside there. One lot owner can enforce the restriction against another. If you are considering buying property in a subdivision, ask about any such restrictions in the general building plan.

### Q. Can I trim the overhanging limbs of my neighbor's tree?

**A.** You may trim the branches of a neighbor's tree that hang over your property, with certain restrictions:

- you may trim up to the boundary line only;

- you need permission to enter the tree-owner's property (unless the tree poses "imminent and grave harm" to you or your property);

- you may not cut down the entire tree;

- you may not destroy the tree by trimming it.

It's always best to notify the tree owner before starting any trimming, pruning, or cutting. If the owner objects to the trimming, offer reas-surance that the job will be done professionally and responsibly, within the mutual rights of both parties involved.

### Q. Am I liable for the encroachment of my trees or shrubbery on a neighbor's property?

**A.** The law varies from state to state, but generally it depends largely on the extent of damage done. It's best to avoid a confrontation—legal or otherwise. Tree roots are a more serious (and potentially costly) problem. You will save money in the long run by hiring a landscaper or "tree surgeon" to take whatever steps are necessary to prevent root damage to your neighbor's home or wall.

### Views

### Q. What are my rights regarding the view from my property?

**A.** Generally there is no absolute right to a view, air, or light, unless granted in writing by a law or subdivision rule. Such provisions are more common in coastal areas or other scenic-view locations. If view is important to you or to the value of the property you are considering buying, be sure to investigate your legal rights to protect that view before closing the deal.

### Q. Can my neighbor legally block my view?

**A.** What can you do if you wake up one morning and find a new fence on your neighbor's land blocking your view of Big Sur? That depends in part on where you live. The best way to protect a view is to purchase an easement from your neighbor, guaranteeing that no obstruction of your view will be built on the land described in the easement. (See page 148 for more on easements.) You may cringe at the thought of paying for a view that is already there, but in the long run it is likely to be less

## THE FRUITS OF YOUR NEIGHBOR'S LABOR

*Fruit-bearing trees that overhang a neighbor's property pose a tasty dilemma—when apples drop onto the neighbor's property, is the fruit considered manna from heaven? According to a long-standing common law doctrine, no. The fruit belongs to the owner of the tree—and so it has been since the 1800s, when a man named Hale scooped up twenty bushels of pears from the orchard trees of his neighbor. A court ordered Mr. Hale to return his booty to the orchard owner, even though Hale had been standing on his own land when he plucked the fruit.*

*What if your neighbor's fruit is a problem for you? If rotting fruit habitually falls from a neighbor's tree into your yard, notify him. Ask him to clean the fruit from your yard and to trim the tree to avoid such droppings in the future. If he ignores your request or refuses to comply, your neighbor may be liable for any damages the errant fruit causes to your grass or garden. (The same thing goes for the fruit of a neighboring tree that may cause physical injury to you, such as a coconut that falls from a high tree and smacks you on the head.)*

costly—and more scenic—to buy an easement now than to bring a lawsuit in the future.

For example, a Los Angeles Superior Court judge ordered the rock star Madonna to trim her driveway hedges to eight feet in height and to trim a pine tree down to her roof level—and to pay the legal fees of the neighbor who brought the lawsuit against her. The neighbor contended that the untrimmed foliage blocked his Hollywood Hills view of the city lights below and reduced the value of his property. He was able to prevail because he had a longstanding written agreement with her regarding his view, so he simply went to court to enforce that contract.

Unless you live in a community that has a view ordinance, you are unlikely to get relief in the courts without such a contract. But even given a view ordinance, the mayor won't necessarily jump in and order your neighbor to tear down the obstruction. If the city does not feel your complaint has merit, you will have to initiate a lawsuit and wait until your day in court to request an order requiring your neighbor to restore your view. Depending upon the backlog in your local courts, that wait could be months. And of course your neighbor might appeal the decision, causing another lengthy delay. In the interests of time and sanity, it may be advisable to forgo the legal wrangling and negotiate with your neighbor.

If your city does not have a view ordinance, you can still ask a court to have the offending fence or trees removed if you can show that by erecting or planting it, your neighbor was "deliberately and maliciously" trying to block your view. This would fall under the category of "spite fences" (see below).

## Fences

### Q. What constitutes a fence?

**A.** The word "fence" is not limited to a picket or stockade-type barrier. Fence ordinances generally cover anything that serves as an enclosure or partition, including trees or hedges. Many zoning regulations restrict the height of fences, whether they are made of cut timber or living trees.

### Q. Who owns a boundary fence?

**A.** A fence that sits directly on the property line of two neighbors is known as a "boundary fence." The legal rights and responsibilities depend on a number of factors, including who "uses" the fence. Generally, boundary fences are somewhat like trees that straddle a property line—they belong to both property owners, both are responsible for the upkeep of the fence, and neither may remove or alter the fence without the other's permission. Of course, the owners are free to agree otherwise. One may wish to "buy" the fence from the other and have it recorded in his deed for posterity. Or one neighbor may be willing to give up his "share" of the fence if the other agrees to pay for the maintenance.

### Q. What can you do about a "spite" fence?

**A.** A spite fence is one that is excessively high, has no reasonable use to your neighbor, and was clearly constructed to annoy you. For example, suppose you live atop a canyon view and you've been feuding with your neighbors, who live farther down the slope. The neighbors suddenly erect a 20-foot-high stockade fence near the property line. Unless your neighbors can demonstrate a reasonable need for such a high fence, such as extra privacy concerns, you can sue them under the doctrine of private nuisance. The case may be difficult to win, how-ever, because most fences or other structures have some arguable utility to the owner.

Your remedies, depending on the law of the state where you reside, may include an injunction to have the fence removed (or at least lowered to a less offensive height) or compensatory damages (a financial payment to you). Factors the court will consider in determining the appropriate amount of compensation include the diminished value of your property and any annoyance caused by the erection and maintenance of the fence; however, you cannot recover for "hurt feelings" or embarrassment due to the fence.

Most spite fences spring from a history of bad feelings in the neighborhood, which deteriorate into anger and spite. That's why it pays to be neighborly in the first place.

---

### HOG-TIED BY A FENCE LAW

*If you live in a historic part of the country, beware of obscure fence laws that may still be on the books. In Maryland, a Howard County landowner was subjected to an anachronistic county law that not only required him to share the cost of a fence on the property line with his neighbor but required the fence to be "hog-tight"—low enough so that a hog could not squeeze under it. And no, neither of the neighbors had any hogs on his property. (At last report, county officials were working to repeal the law.)*

# HOME IMPROVEMENTS AND REPAIRS

## Legal Protections

### Q. Which federal laws are applicable to remodeling projects?

**A.** Federal Trade Commission (FTC) rules address the problem of false advertising. It is illegal for a vendor to advertise any product or service for less than it really costs or to engage in the old bait-and-switch tactic. This happens when you are "baited" by an ad for a product or service, then told that one isn't available and "switched" to another, more expensive version. The law requires vendors to offer a rain check whenever demand for an advertised bargain exceeds supply, unless the limited supply is clearly stated in the ad.

The federal Truth in Lending law protects consumers who obtain outside financing for their projects. A lender must prominently state the annual percentage rate (APR) of interest you will be charged. So whether you finance your home improvement through a bank, a credit union, or the contractor himself, at least you will know what the interest rate is. Note that even if the terms appear reasonable, it is a bad idea to have the contractor secure financing for your project and in some areas it may also be illegal. Even though he may approve you as a credit risk when a bank won't, he has good reason: his guarantee that you will pay him back is ultimately your house. It is probably worth a lot more than whatever you are doing to improve it. So if you cannot pay for work right now, try to postpone it until you can.

These laws help keep most contractors honest, but they can't keep the bad apples off the streets. Even if you report violations to the Federal Trade Commission in Washington or one of its ten regional offices, the FTC is not likely to prosecute a small contractor. Federal enforcement tends to concentrate on major violations or patterns.

### Q. What protection do I have once I sign a contract?

**A.** Given the number of scam artists working the streets, your best federal protection may be the cooling-off period mandated by the Truth in Lending Act. Called a "right to rescission," the law gives you three business days to cancel any contract that was signed in your home (or any location other than the seller's place of business) that implies any kind of financial claim to your home. This occurs, for example, when the contract gives the contractor the right to file a lien against your home to enforce payment. This law also applies to any contract that involves the borrower making four or more payments, such as when the contractor finances a project by using your home as collateral for a second mortgage.

Contractors pay attention to this law because if they don't comply, you have the right to rescind for three years from the date on the contract—or until you transfer interest or sell the property.

If circumstances entitle you to a cooling-off period, the contractor must give you two copies of the Notice of Right of Rescission at the time you sign the contract. It must be separate from the contract—not buried in fine print—and a copy given to each owner, because any one owner may cancel. The notice must identify the transaction, disclose the security interest, inform you of your right to rescind, tell you how to exercise that right, and give you the date the rescission period expires.

### Q. What kind of state and local laws apply to contractors?

**A.** State laws often are modeled after federal laws, and states and local agencies are much more apt to pursue a small contractor who may have violated them. If you suspect that a contractor is breaking the law, get in touch with your state attorney general's office or local department of consumer affairs.

Some state laws specifically target dishonest contractors. For example, Illinois's Home Repair/Fraud Act, strengthened in July 1992, makes it a crime to misrepresent the terms of a home repair contract, deceive people into signing one, damage someone's property to drum up home repair business, or charge an unconscionable fee for home repair services. A contractor who preys on disabled people or those older than sixty may be committing aggravated home repair fraud, a felony punishable by three to seven years in jail and a fine of up to $10,000.

Localities also can impose tough laws against unscrupulous contractors. A local law in Putnam County, New York, provides such punishments as suspension or revocation of the contractor's license, both criminal and civil penalties, and punitive damages against the contractor.

For information about legal protections and enforcement options in your state, contact your state or local consumer protection agency, or the consumer fraud division of the local prosecutor's office.

**Q. What's the best way to guard against swindlers?**

**A.** Despite all the statutes, if you have to rely on the law to get your money back from a shoddy contractor, you will have to wait a long time. Take matters into your own hands by carefully checking the reputation of any contractor ahead of time. Be wary of contractors who:

- Claim to work for a government agency. Check it out.

- Offer free gifts. Ask the following questions: What exactly are the gifts? When will you receive them? Can you get a price reduction instead?

---

**MEDIATION**

*Mediators are trained to listen to both sides in a dispute, identify problems, and suggest compromises and equitable solutions. They provide an impartial and unbiased forum for neighbors to talk. The key to mediation, unlike a lawsuit, is that it is not an adversary process. No judge makes a decision for either party. The outcome of the dispute is in the hands of both parties. Until both agree, there is no resolution. The parties are more likely to comply with the agreement, since both have agreed to it. You may be able to find dispute resolution services through the yellow pages (look under "mediation services" or "arbitration services"). Many bar associations offer nonprofit programs, and many states' departments of consumer affairs have dispute resolution offices. Consult the "State Government" listings in your telephone directory.*

---

- Engage in door-to-door sales or try to get your business by telephone solicitations. Be especially wary if the sales pitch demands an immediate decision to take advantage of prices that won't be available tomorrow. Most reputable contractors don't engage in such tactics.

- Offer an unsolicited free inspection of your furnace or basement. Rip-off artists use this ruse to get into a home and either fake a problem or damage a sound furnace and good pipes.

- Claim your house is dangerous and needs immediate repair—unless you already know it does.

- Have a company name, address, and telephone number and other credentials that can't be verified. Fly-by-night operators often use a mail drop and an answering service while hunting for victims.

- Promise a lower price for allowing your home to be used as a model or to advertise their work. (Has the price really been lowered? What does the "use of your home" entail?)

- Engage in bait-and-switch tactics. After luring you with an ad that offers an unbeatable deal on a job, these contractors tell you the materials aren't available for that job but they can give you a bargain on another, more expensive, job.

- Leave delivery and installation costs out of their estimates.

- Offer to give you a rebate or referral fee if any of your friends use the same contractor.

- Insist on starting work before you sign a contract.

### Hiring a Contractor

#### Q. *How do I find a reputable contractor?*

**A.** After thinking through what you want and what you can afford, ask for recommendations from people who have had similar work done and talk to building inspectors, bankers, and trade association representatives—people who should know first-hand the work and reputation of contractors in your community.

For a large job, interview and solicit bids from two or three contractors from your list, but make sure they are bidding on exactly the same job to allow comparisons. The lowest bid is not necessarily the best, because a contractor with a reputation for excellent workmanship and for standing behind the work might be worth more. Even if the job is small enough to warrant only one bid, take time to check out your contractor's reputation and credentials.

Make sure a contractor's references had similar work done. For a kitchen remodeling, for example, ask for former clients who have had kitchens done by the contractor. Chances are any such references provided by the contractor will be happy clients, so try to go a step or so beyond "He's a great guy" and "No problems at all." Ask exactly what the contractor did, and how this person found out about him. Jot down any more names that are mentioned, with addresses and telephone numbers. Was the client comfortable with the way things were left at the end of a day as well as at the end of the project? What does the client wish he had done differently to make the job go even more smoothly? What did the client's spouse (or roommate, neighbors, or children) think about the work and the construction process? What is the next project this person wants to hire the contractor to do?

#### Q. *What kinds of certification should the contractor provide?*

**A.** If you are satisfied with a contractor's reputation, check his credentials before signing the contract. Ask if he is licensed and bonded. Although not all states require licensing for home contractors, those that do have at least a record of each contractor's name and address, compliance with insurance laws, and agreement to operate within the law. If the company is a corporation, the state has a record of the individual responsible. While some states only require contractors to register their names and addresses, quite a few require them to have some experience and pass an exam.

A state license doesn't ensure that the contractor will do a good job, but it is an indication that he has made an effort to comply with the law. Check with the state contractors licensing board to see if the license is current. Some states will also tell you if there have been complaints against a given contractor and whether they proved to be valid; otherwise you can get that information from the local Better Business Bureau or office of consumer affairs.

Being bonded provides important protections for you, but be aware that the word has two meanings. "Fully insured and bonded" generally means the contractor's insurance coverage protects against his employees' theft, vandalism, or negligence. If you have valuables to consider, ask to see a certificate or letter certifying such a policy.

A performance bond is an insurance company's assurance that the contractor can finish the job as stated in the contract. If he defaults, the insurance company will pay another contractor to complete the work. Contractors must take out a separate bond for each job, so bonds are usually limited to jobs of $25,000 or more, and contractors pass on the cost to the homeowner. It is an expensive proposition, up to 10 percent of the contract price for a residential swimming pool; but a contractor who has been approved by a bonding company is a very good risk. You're the one who decides whether to require (and pay for) a bond.

Make sure that the contractor carries workers' compensation insurance, to cover injuries he and his workers might sustain on the job. If he doesn't carry it, you could be responsible for some hefty bills. Ask if he belongs to a trade association. Many associations require a contractor to have been in business a certain length of time, to have passed a credit check, and to meet all legal requirements of his state. It

wouldn't hurt to call the association to make sure the contractor's membership is current and inquire about complaints.

Also ask if there is a warranty on his work and materials and the time limit on the warranty. Make sure any warranty is included in the contract. (Even if there is no specific warranty, most jurisdictions recognize an implied warranty of good workmanship that gives you some protection.) For an additional fee, some contractors offer an extended warranty such as the five-year policies available through the Home Owners Warranty Corporation.

To check whether any civil judgments or lawsuits are pending against the contractor, call the local clerk of court. If someone sued the contractor over something like poor workmanship, consider it a warning. Likewise, you might want to check with the nearest federal bankruptcy court to see whether this contractor has ever filed for bankruptcy—a strong indication of financial instability.

### Q. *What should the contract include?*

**A.** A complete home improvement contract should address the following:

*Preamble.* An introduction that states names, addresses, phone numbers, and the date the contract is executed. It should specify whether the contractor's business is a sole proprietorship, partnership, or corporation. (If it is a partnership or corporation, make sure the person who signs is an authorized representative.) The preamble should also state that the remodeler is an independent contractor, not your employee. Otherwise, you might be responsible if the builder injures someone. For another layer of financial accountability, add the contractor's social security number. The contract price should state the total dollar amount, including sales tax, to be paid by the homeowner for services agreed to in the contract.

*Starting and completion dates.* No contractor is likely to begin until after your right to rescission has safely passed. Specify an end-date, stating exceptions such as weather, strikes, etc. You may want to add a bonus-penalty clause if the date is critical. Specify a daily starting time if that matters to you. Consider interim completion dates for key phases of big jobs.

*Scope of work.* Contractors may shy away from a clause as broad as "all labor, materials, and services necessary to complete the project." But don't allow them to be so specific in the work listed that anything else becomes an "extra" or a "change order," which may be billed separately.

*Description of materials.* See that complete descriptions of agreed-to products—including brand names and order numbers—are listed. Plans, bids, estimates, and all other documents relating to the project are part of the scope of work. Make sure that copies of these are attached to all copies of the contract before you sign it.

*Permits, licenses, and zoning.* Specify that the remodeler will obtain all necessary licenses and permits and satisfy all zoning regulations and building codes, and indemnify the homeowner in case he fails to do so.

*Cleanup policy.* Will the contractor clean up daily? After each project? Only at the end? Where is refuse to be placed?

*Storage.* Specify where materials and equipment will be kept. You are probably liable for damage to materials and equipment from fire or accidents, so be sure to check your homeowner's policy and make sure these are covered.

*Parking.* If it is a problem, arrange for the contractor's vehicle as well as subcontractors'.

*Noise.* Some is inevitable and may even provide a safety valve for workers, but place limits on time and volume, according to local laws and neighborhood needs.

*Theft.* Building materials are often stolen. The contract can make either the contractor or the owner responsible.

## THE IMPORTANCE OF A WRITTEN CONTRACT

*Don't allow any work to begin until there is a signed contract—one that protects you. (Some people might take a chance on very small jobs—under $1,500—but it is a chance.) Oral agreements can be enforced in court, but it is difficult to prove who said what if you don't get it on paper. Ask to see an insurance certificate to make sure the contractor is covered in case one of his subcontractors is injured on your property. If the contractor gives you a standard contract to sign, take it home and study it carefully at your leisure. Strike out clauses you think are unreasonable and have both parties initial the change. If you are uncertain about the meaning of provisions and/or if it is a major, expensive job, make sure your attorney checks the contract.*

*Damage.* What if the retaining wall collapses when they're digging for the new swimming pool? You'll want the contract to state that the contractor is responsible for damage to your property.

*Change orders.* Very few jobs go exactly as planned, which requires that the contract have a provision that enables it to be amended simply and easily. The contract should provide that change orders can be written up, signed by both parties, and attached to the contract as plans change or delays occur. See the sample on page 200 for specific wording of this contract clause.

*Warranties.* The contract should assure that the materials are new, and that you will receive all warranties from manufacturers for appliances and other materials used on the job.

*Progress payments.* Contractors don't expect to be paid entirely in advance, but they also don't expect to wait until all work has been done. It is customary to pay one-third upon signing a contract to allow the contractor to buy supplies and get started. In smaller projects, two payments may suffice. In larger ones, plan to make payments after completion and approval of major phases of the work. In all cases, make your final payment as large as possible, usually at least 10 percent. DO NOT MAKE FINAL PAYMENT until all work is completed, inspected, and approved; subcontractors are paid and any liens canceled; and warranties are in the proper hands.

*Financing contingency.* If your ability to proceed with the project depends on securing outside financing, include a contingency clause stating that the contract is not binding if you are unable to secure the needed funds on acceptable terms.

*Suppliers and subcontractors.* Ask for a list of subcontractors and suppliers and attach it to the contract with their addresses, telephone numbers, and social security numbers. Although you are not their boss, they probably have a right to place a lien on your home if the contractor does not pay them in full. It's only fair that you know who they are, should legal action become necessary. If you prefer, arrange to pay suppliers and subcontractors directly.

## Troubleshooting the Project

### Q. *Who should obtain building permits and when should they do it?*

**A.** To find out whether you will need building permits, contact your local building department. Some municipalities require permits for just about anything; others require permits for only major remodeling projects. The person who takes out the permit is considered liable for the work, so follow the usual custom of having the architect or contractor obtain it. As a homeowner, you don't want to be responsible if the work doesn't conform to standards or codes, but you need to know which permits are required and make sure they are obtained.

### Q. *What's the point of getting a permit, besides giving the town money?*

**A.** First of all, the point is to abide by the law. Second, the inspector who checks your house can assure you that the work you are paying for is safe. Plumbing and electrical inspectors, for example, assure that the work is done according to code. Additionally, if you have followed proper procedures, your house will be free of encumbrances when you want to sell it. In New York, for example, real estate inspectors can stop property sales when they find disparities between original and remodeled plans of a property. Altered fire-escape routes, often caused by a door or doorway altered without permit and inspection, can be dangerous. Such noncompliance puts the homeowner—and buyer—in an expensive bind.

If you live in a condominium or cooperative apartment, or other common-interest property, your rights to renovate and remodel differ from those of single-family homeowners. Check your condominium declaration—or check with your board—to see if your renovation will be permitted.

### Q. *What should I watch out for when the job begins?*

**A.** Be sure to keep a handle on the documents that can help you avoid problems later. In consultation with your contractor, draw up a schedule of what will be done when, and make sure this is followed. If you don't have the wiring inspected before the drywall goes up, for example, the inspector may require you to tear out the drywall.

Contractors report that their biggest problems with homeowners arise because owners request additional work along the way, then object when they see the bill. The best way to avoid misunderstanding is with a specific change order. This document, signed by both parties and added to the original contract, specifies the additional work to be done, the materials, and any change in the schedule. For a large project, type up and duplicate blank change-order forms to fill out as you need them.

### Q. What happens if someone is hurt on the job?

**A.** If you are dealing with an independent contractor, his insurance should cover expenses; but if you hired someone down the street to paint your house, someone who doesn't maintain a separate business and who relied on you for tools and supervision, that person is your employee and any injuries are your responsibility. If someone gets hurt later because, for example, the new basement steps were not nailed down, your insurance company may pay the injured party but then go after the contractor responsible.

### Q. What can I do if the contractor violates the contract?

**A.** If you believe there has been a contract violation, first bring the matter to the attention of the contractor with a telephone call or conversation. For example, if you came home from work one day and found that the new picture window was in the wrong place, call the contractor immediately. To protect yourself, make a note of the conversation, summarizing your concerns and any agreements, and send it to him. Keep a copy yourself. Next, ask your lawyer to write a letter stating your concerns and asking for the correction.

---

### CHANGE/ORDER CLAUSE

*The following wording can be used to provide for a change/order clause:*

*Without invalidating this contract, the owner may order changes in the work, including additions, modifications, or deletions. Price and time will be adjusted accordingly. All such changes in the work shall be in writing, and signed by the contractor and owner and attached to this document.*

---

If that doesn't work, check to see if your contract specifies alternative dispute resolution (ADR)—that is, mediation or arbitration. That means you and the contractor will have agreed to call in a mutually acceptable third party to resolve the dispute without going to court. If your contract does not specify ADR, your initial letter and the lawyer's letter will provide you with a base for further action with a consumer-protection agency or a lawsuit, possibly in small claims court.

Either way, your options are to push for "specific performance" of the contract, which means forcing the remodeler to do the work as agreed, or for the remodeler to pay any extra costs you incur by having someone else do it.

### Q. What is a construction lien?

**A.** Construction liens (also called mechanic's liens) are subordinate to any prior mortgage on your house, so it is a difficult route to payment. In some states, contractors and subcontractors must notify a homeowner if they intend to take out a lien. In others, you only learn about it after it is filed at the local recording office. If you find out someone has filed a lien, call your lawyer immediately because the next word might be notice of foreclosure.

### Q. How can I prevent a construction lien from being filed?

**A.** It is possible to add a clause to the contract stating that the contractor agrees to give up his lien rights, but the contractor may not agree to it. And, even with a contractor's waiver, any subcontractor or supplier who is not paid for his work or materials by your contractor can file a lien against your home. Unless your job is covered by a performance bond, or your state has some sort of fund to protect homeowners from paying twice when the contractor doesn't pay subcontractors or laborers, your chief protection against a lien is holding back final payment until all work has been completed to your satisfaction and your contractor supplies proof in writing that he has paid everyone who worked for him on your job. A release-of-lien form is useful, because it provides places for all the subcontractors to sign. (This is one reason to have all subcontractors and suppliers named up front in your contract, so you can make sure everyone has signed off on the release-of-lien form.)

## SHARED OWNERSHIP

### Cooperative Living Arrangements

### Q. What is a common-interest community?

**A.** Thanks to creative developers, common-interest communities exist in various configurations with a confusing array of names and forms of ownership. Still, certain characteristics are shared—they are designed specifically for a certain type of community living by a single developer (or in the case of existing buildings, a single converter). They are created by a specific set of documents, usually drawn up by the developer and subject to change by the membership. And when the developer or converter departs, the community's affairs are governed by an association of all unit owners through its elected board. The board has the authority to enforce the restrictions and collect assessments to pay for maintenance and improvements.

Because these ownership forms are governed by the laws of so many different states, the terminology can be confusing. Whatever the general term, there are three distinct types of common-interest communities with three distinct types of ownership: the cooperative, the condominium, and the planned community or planned unit development (PUD). You can't tell which is which by looking at the architectural form of the buildings. For example, in some states, "site condominiums" look just like single-family detached homes but the land—not the home—is part of the condominium. However, the form of ownership has significant legal implications. Be sure you know what type yours is—the form of ownership is specified in the community's declaration, which is essentially its constitution.

### Q. What's the difference between a cooperative and a condominium?

**A.** In cooperatives, found primarily in New York and Chicago, the members are stockholders in a corporation that owns the entire building, including the residential units and all common elements such as corridors, elevators, and tennis courts. Stockholders don't actually own any real estate; the corporation owns it all. Instead, stockholders are entitled to lease their individual units from the corporation. Each stockholder pays a monthly "maintenance charge," which is a proportionate share of the corporation's cash requirements for mortgage payments, operation, maintenance, repair, taxes, and reserves. The corporation, governed by an elected board of directors, may veto a proposed transfer of stock, so it has considerable control over potential buyers.

Condominium ownership provides exclusive title to the "airspace" within your own unit, and ownership of the common elements is shared among all unit owners as tenants in common. Within limitations, you are free to mortgage your unit or sell it. As in a cooperative, all unit owners must pay their share of the assessment for operation, maintenance, repair, and reserves. The association is responsible for enforcing the rules and managing the common elements, but it doesn't actually own anything.

### Q. How does a planned community work?

**A.** A planned community, also called a "homeowner association," is a hybrid subdivision combining certain aspects of cooperatives and condominiums. In these developments, each owner holds title to a unit—in many cases, a single-family, detached house. But all common areas, such as parks and playgrounds, belong to the incorporated association, which all owners are required to join. The association is responsible for maintaining common areas and, in some cases, house exteriors. Homeowners pay a periodic assessment for common area expenses and reserves.

Some planned communities include sections organized as condominiums or cooperatives. Others include commercial or even industrial areas, designed to allow people to live within walking distance of stores and work. Some of these developments are huge—such as Reston, Virginia, a planned community of 19,000 units. Further, several adjoining community associations may belong to a master association, also known as an "umbrella association," a "master planned community," or a "mixed-use association," which charges an additional assessment to pay for certain community-wide services.

### Q. What kind of restrictions can be imposed in common-interest communities?

**A.** The extent of restrictions imposed on owners varies. In a planned community of freestanding houses, rules may be limited to preserving the quality and cohesiveness of the development by requiring approval of any architectural or other exterior changes. Condo-

---

**BY ANY OTHER NAME**
*"Common-interest community" is the term preferred by the National Conference of Commissioners on Uniform State Laws, a group devoted to drafting model laws for adoption by state legislatures. But the Community Association Institute (CAI), a national trade group for anyone connected with this type of development, prefers the term "community association." Other terms in use are "common interest realty association," "common interest development," "residential community association," "common property subdivision" and "interdependent covenanted subdivision." Depending on who is talking, the association might be a "community association," a "homeowners' association," or a "property owners' association." If you're talking about these developments with someone from another area, make sure you're talking about the same thing.*

miniums and cooperatives tend to have much more extensive rules and regulations, because generally people are living much closer together and often in the same building.

Mid-rise and high-rise condominiums rely on the concept of the "airspace block." The title to a single-family house or townhouse often includes the land underneath it and the air above it, but if you own a high-rise apartment there are other owners above and below. So you hold title, in effect, to a block of air—within four walls, a ceiling, and a floor.

Within that airspace block, you may alter or remove nonsupporting walls, replace the light fixtures, change the carpet however you wish, and make other changes that don't infringe on your neighbors' property rights. On the other hand, you are responsible for the maintenance and repair of paint, wallpaper, fixtures, and appliances, except for wires and pipes running through your walls that serve other units. Sometimes people accustomed to rental apartments are surprised to learn that their condo building manager isn't responsible for fixing their hot water heater.

## Legal Rights and Restrictions

**Q. What federal laws apply to common-interest communities?**

**A.** Few federal laws directly affect the organization and operation of common-interest communities, but two consumer-oriented federal laws apply directly. Under the Fair Housing Amendments Act, effective since March 1989, developments may no longer discriminate against families with children unless the development meets the act's strict qualifications for senior citizen developments. Otherwise, it is no longer legal to advertise a development as being for adults only or to steer would-be buyers elsewhere because their children wouldn't

be welcome. It is still legal to prohibit occupancy by, for example, people forty years old or younger, but even then a forty-five-year-old with legal custody of a child under 18 couldn't be denied access to housing.

The Fair Housing Amendments Act also prohibits discrimination against disabled persons. Developments must permit construction of facilities for disabled residents, although the disabled resident may be required to remove the construction upon leaving. Further, all new multifamily buildings must provide access for the disabled in every unit on the ground floor or accessibility by elevator. Under HUD regulations, this includes wide doors, free passage for wheelchairs through units, bathroom walls strong enough for grab bars, and access to at least a representative portion of the amenities.

**Q. How do state laws apply to common-interest communities?**

**A.** Most of the substantive law—and confusion—lies in an ever-changing patchwork of state statutes. The governance of cooperatives falls under state statutes governing corporations and nonprofit corporations, because residents of a cooperative own stock in the corporation that owns their building. The same statutes apply to the associations governing planned communities, which likewise own the common areas.

Condominiums, however, do not have a corporation responsible for liabilities, taxes, and governance. That is why each state has a special set of laws detailing how condominiums must be organized and operated. These laws require each condominium to file a declaration and bylaws, with specific requirements regarding the rights and duties of the association. Planned communities require no specific statute, but some states include them in an act governing all common-interest communities.

Condominium statutes vary considerably, from state to state, and many lack protections for consumers. While some states provide only the barest framework for creating a condominium, others are incredibly complex and detailed. For example, Florida, where nearly three million people live in condominiums, understandably has the most complex, extensive regulation of all the states.

### Q. What else governs a common-interest community?

**A.** Along with federal and state laws, each individual community is governed by its own declaration and articles, a set of bylaws, and various regulations and decisions promulgated by the association board. Finally, given the extensive litigation over the authority of particular associations, various courts have interpreted statutes, rules, and regulations, often based on common law (nonstatutory) principles.

A community association gains its authority from the legal documents that created it: the declaration, articles, and bylaws. State statutes often back up that authority, whether in the statutes governing nonprofit corporations, the specific condominium or common-interest community act, or both. Broadly speaking, a community association may hold property, sue and be sued, receive gifts and bequests, make charitable contributions, make contracts, borrow or invest money, and assess unit owners for their share of the expense of maintaining and operating the community. Some state statutes grant even more far-reaching powers.

By law, each common-interest community must file a set of master regulations, plus subsidiary documents called articles, plus a set of bylaws. For planned communities, the master regulations are called the covenants, conditions, and restrictions. The same document for a condo is called a declaration or a "master deed."

A condominium declaration describes the land, building, and other improvements; the location of each unit; the common elements; and the intended use of each unit. Basically, the declaration involves the physical arrangement, including a floor plan with tax lot numbers for the various units. But under the laws of many states, it need not contain much in the way of operational detail.

The articles of incorporation, called articles of association in nonincorporated associations, involve the legal establishment of the association, including the name, address, and purpose of the association; the aggregate number of shares permitted; whether cumulative voting is permitted; and, in general, the power of the board to make, alter, and repeal reasonable bylaws.

---

### UNIFORM CONDOMINIUM ACT

*In hopes of bringing some uniformity to the law, the National Conference of Commissioners on Uniform State Laws has proposed model laws in the area, which twenty-three states have adopted or adapted, and numerous others are considering. The Uniform Condominium Act (UCA) allows flexibility for developers while offering protection to consumers, such as requiring extensive disclosure before sale. It covers such matters as insurance and tort liability. The Uniform Common Interest Ownership Act (UCIOA) extends the same provisions to cooperatives and planned communities. So far, only a handful of states have adopted UCIOA.*

### Q. What do the bylaws regulate?

**A.** Bylaws dictate how the managing board will be elected and define their duties and powers. Bylaws cover such matters as whether the board will manage the property or engage a management firm; rules critical to settling disputes that might arise; how assessments and reserves are to be determined; what restrictions apply to the lease and sale of units; and to what extent board decisions bind unit owners.

Although bylaws in most corporations may be altered freely by the board or by a simple majority of the members, many condominium statutes require a two-thirds or even three-quarters majority to change them. States that have adopted the Uniform Condominium Act allow a bit more flexibility, to reduce the chance that a subdivision will be unable to adapt to changing conditions. Wherever you live, though, get used to your development's bylaws because they are rarely changed.

## The Board of Directors

### Q. How is the board established?

**A.** The board of directors is elected by the membership to carry out day-to-day operations and oversee enforcement of the rules. A typical board has five to seven members who are elected on a rotating basis. The board in turn elects officers, such as a chairman or president, secretary, and treasurer.

### Q. What is the role of the board of directors in managing a multi-unit dwelling?

**A.** Typically, the board has broad powers under state law. The board may raise or lower assessments and impose special assessments to cover specific repairs or improvements. It also may insist that unit owners obey the policies of the association. Major restrictions on the pur-

chaser's right to lease, finance, or resell his or her unit may exist.

Many multi-unit associations grant the board of directors a right of first refusal to buy a unit. The way this generally works in practice is that the owner must offer to sell the unit to the board before offering it for sale to any other person.

### Q. How does the board enforce the association's rules?

**A.** When a unit owner ignores the rules, the board usually levies fines against the owner. If the fines pile up and the owner refuses to pay, the board may file a lien against the property and, if necessary, foreclose on it to get the money. Another approach is for the association to sue the violator, seeking an injunctive order to stop the practice in question. A violator who refuses to follow the court order could be in contempt of court.

In theory, any unit owner may sign a complaint against a neighbor to initiate a process that could lead to fines. In practice, though, most unit owners are hesitant to sign formal complaints against people next door, even though they voice their concerns loudly to the board. If the community hires a management company—standard practice in larger communities—the company's routine maintenance inspections include checking for violations of the rules. The employee who discovers the infraction then serves as a complaining witness to the board, which more than likely will start by sending someone to talk to the violator. Most board members try to be even-handed in their enforcement, as they don't want to be criticized for punishing one violator and showing leniency toward another.

If the board decides to resort to the courts, it must do so promptly or risk losing the authority to enforce the rule. If the rules say you cannot build a tool shed and you do it anyway, board members cannot walk past it every day for a year and then sue to have you remove it.

## Q. How does the board handle assessments?

**A.** One of the most onerous tasks of an association board is raising the monthly assessment that pays for maintenance and various services, from trash collection to snow removal. Some state statutes mandate certain levels of reserves to guard the community's financial stability and prepare for inevitable capital expenditures. Even without a mandate, a board is wise to build up a substantial reserve to avoid having to require a massive special assessment when the furnace needs to be replaced.

In some states, associations may not raise the assessment higher than a set amount without membership approval. In Illinois, for example, condominium boards must hold a referendum of unit owners if the budget increase rises above 15 percent. Many condominium declarations adopted ten or fifteen years ago set similar dollar caps on assessments without owner approval.

When unit owners are doing well, they may grouse about the assessment but chances are they will pay it. But what if a unit owner is in serious financial trouble, with several thousand dollars worth of assessments unpaid? If the owner goes bankrupt, the creditors line up for their share of what is left—and the community association is normally far down the line, well behind the bank that holds the mortgage. If the association cannot obtain the bankrupt owner's assessment, all the other property owners in the community will have to cover it.

One provision of the Uniform Common Interest Ownership Act, in effect in Connecticut, Alaska, and several other states, gives community associations a "super-priority lien," putting them first in line for the bankrupt unit owner's share of the past six months' assessments. Numerous states are considering this provision, although it is opposed by the banking lobby.

## CHALLENGING ASSOCIATION RULES

*In the course of operating the association, boards periodically enact other rules and regulations regarding the details of community life, such as how parking spaces are allocated. These are subject to judicial review if a unit owner believes that the board overstepped its authority in a given regulation. In reviewing regulations, courts tend to consider four questions:*

- *Is the rule consistent with the declaration and other superior documents?*
- *Was the rule adopted in a good faith effort to serve a purpose of the subdivision?*
- *Are the means adopted to serve the purpose reasonable?*
- *Is the rule consistent with public policy?*

*If a court rules that the answer to one of these questions is no, it might throw out the rule in question.*

## Q. What can I do if the board isn't doing its job?

**A.** Most problems arise if a board neglects the enforcement of rules or misuses the funds entrusted to them. If you suspect financial problems, you are entitled to review the association's financial documents, including its budget, financial report, bank loan documents, and record of reserves. Together with other concerned unit owners, you may hire an independent accountant for an audit even if the board refuses to do so.

If you believe the board has become autocratic and tyrannical, review the minutes of the board meetings to see whether decisions were made in accordance with the association's bylaws, rules, and regulations. Was there proper notice of meetings? Were all procedures proper? If not, some of the board's actions may be void.

When the board has seriously mismanaged its responsibilities, you have two basic options. One is to file a lawsuit against the board for breaching its duties. Be aware, though, that the board has a right to assess the unit owners to pay for its own defense, so you will be paying for both sides. Arbitration or mediation may be a less costly approach, if your bylaws permit them. The other option is to run for a position on the board yourself and convince some well-qualified neighbors to do the same. In the long run, that's probably the best solution.

## Handling Problems

### Q. Can an owner obtain a variance from the association rules?

**A.** Under the rules of most community associations, you cannot make changes to the exterior of your home without the consent of the board. Normally the board delegates the review of plans to an architectural control committee, which sets standards and uses them to rule on whether you can add a skylight or put on a screen door. As a homeowner, you submit your plans to the committee and cross your fingers. Be aware, though, that courts have found that covenant committees do not have the authority to approve major violations of the restrictive covenants.

If the board denies your request, you will either have to change your plans or steel yourself for a major battle. One New Jersey homeowner sued his association in 1982 after its board denied him permission to build a deck. The case was in and out of court for years, with neither side willing to budge.

### Q. What can I do if my neighbor is a problem?

**A.** The first step is to check the bylaws and regulations governing the association to see whether the practice in question is a violation. Then talk about it, first to the neighbor posing the problem and then to one of the members of the board, which often acts as a mediator to help unit owners informally work things out. If one party is clearly violating the rules, the board may ask you to sign a formal complaint to begin a proceeding that could lead to fines against your neighbor or even a court injunction to stop the behavior. If the problem isn't addressed in the documents and a polite request doesn't help, one option is to try alternative dispute resolution. Again, it is important to act promptly if a neighbor's behavior makes life unpleasant for you. If you have put up with it without comment for ten years, you may have trouble proving your point.

### Q. What can you do if the community has too many rental tenants?

**A.** Owner-occupants often object to renters, who are perceived as not caring about the property enough to maintain it properly. Likewise, absentee owners generally want to keep up the rental value but don't want to pay for extras. And although restrictions apply to tenants as well as to owner-occupants, they are more difficult to enforce. But if the board slaps a lien on a unit owner because of the tenant's behavior, the owner may well terminate the tenant. If a majority of the unit owners believe the number

## IS YOUR ASSOCIATION ADEQUATELY INSURED?

*Condominium associations typically carry several insurance policies to cover damage to building exteriors and common elements, as well as liability for injuries on the premises. In a common-interest community containing attached dwellings or dwellings within a single building, most lenders and enabling statutes require a single policy of property insurance covering the entire building or all of the buildings in the project. This policy should not name the unit owners as insureds, but name the association or a trustee as insured for the benefit of unit owners and their mortgage lenders. In such a community you would only have to purchase property insurance covering your unit's contents, including paint, wallpaper, furniture and possibly appliances, carpeting and the customized built-in portions of the unit. Your unit owner's insurance should also include a small amount, from $1,000 to $2,500, covering uninsured losses to the overall community. This coverage would pick up your share of large deductibles in the community association insurance or it may cover losses that are not covered by the association's insurance.*

*In an attached-unit project, liability insurance should be maintained by the association to cover the entire project. Once again, this liability insurance should not name each unit owner individually as insured, but should name the association as the insured for the benefit of the unit owners. The association policy will cover the unit owner's liability for association activities on the common areas and within the community, and other association activities that occur outside of the community for which the unit owner might be liable.*

*The unit owner's individual policy should cover the unit owner's individual liability for actions such as those that would occur outside the community or negligently undertaken by the unit owner that were not the responsibility of the association.*

*In a common-interest community that consists of detached dwellings on their own lot, often the insurance only covers the common areas or those areas that are the responsibility of the association. In these kinds of communities, the insurance on the dwelling is the normal home owner's insurance that would be carried on any single-family detached dwelling. However, the association insurance should cover the liability of the homeowners for the association's activities as well as the property of the association.*

*In addition, associations usually carry liability policies on directors and officers in case the board members are sued over their decisions, and an umbrella liability policy to cover catastrophic judgments.*

*Unit owners pay the premiums on all their association insurance as part of their regular assessments.*

*You have a right to see the association's master policy, which the association generally must supply within thirty days of your request. For a quicker response, ask the insurance company directly for a copy of the building policy. With that and a copy of the association's declaration in hand, your insurance agent can help you determine how much homeowner's insurance you need.*

*While you are looking at the master insurance policy, ask your agent if the association is adequately insured. Full replacement cost is important, as the victims of Hurricane Andrew learned. And if someone is seriously injured on the property and the association's liability policy doesn't cover the judgment, each unit owner could be assessed for a portion of the cost. Your own homeowner's policy, if broad enough, should protect you against these and other emergency assessments resulting from a casualty or liability loss. Without your own coverage, however, you could be subject to a catastrophic assessment.*

of renters is a problem, they may be able to band together and convince the board to call for a vote on a change to the bylaws that would restrict leases.

### Q. What can be done if the converter of a cooperative defaults?

**A.** Although cooperative ownership is rare in most parts of the country, it is the primary form of home ownership in New York City. Over the past few years, a glut of cooperative conversions in New York and some changes in the laws governing them have put some conversion sponsors in deep financial trouble.

When the owner of an apartment building decides to convert it to a cooperative, the building's residents have a legal right to remain as rent-controlled tenants for as long as they wish, unless 50 percent of them decide to buy. The result is that a typical building being converted has a large number of rental apartments owned by the sponsor, who is responsible for paying more in monthly maintenance fees than he receives in rent. Many sponsors have defaulted, whether for not paying maintenance on unsold shares, not paying the mortgage, or both. The entire corporation then faces foreclosure or bankruptcy.

If that happens to your cooperative, there are several ways to avoid disaster. If the sponsor has financed the unsold shares, the sponsor's lender would do well to begin paying maintenance on those apartments as quickly as possible to protect the value of the collateral, then try to sell the shares to the tenants or pay them to move and resell the units. If not, the shareholders need to take control of the board of directors, terminate the sponsor's proprietary lease, and cancel the sponsor's stock. Then the rent goes to the corporation. Quick action is critical to keep the building from deteriorating in the meantime.

### Q. What can I do if I have a problem with the developer?

**A.** In an increasing number of cases, condominium associations have sued their developers over shoddy construction, breach of contract, negligence, or fraud. These lawsuits are complex, time-consuming, and expensive, often involving hundreds of people and millions of dollars. But the law expects a developer who cuts corners on construction or breaks promises to the unit owners to make up for the damage.

If only your unit is involved in the problem, it is up to you to engage an attorney and try to settle the matter out of court, if possible. But if the problem involves common areas or common funds, the association may assess all unit owners to pay its legal fees in pursuing the developer. In some cases the developer may agree to arbitration to save the time and expense of a lawsuit. The important thing, though, is to act quickly because the longer you wait, the harder it is to find witnesses or collect a judgment.

## WHERE TO GET MORE INFORMATION

Nearly every state has federal information centers where information on federal services, programs, and regulations is available to consumers. Check the government pages of your local telephone directory for the office nearest to you. The local library also can be a good source of helpful, free information. Various nonprofit agencies, such as the Better Business Bureau (BBB), can help you get more information on your legal rights and obligations in owning property. Look in your local telephone directory for the BBB office nearest to you.

The federal government publishes a listing of many free or low-cost pamphlets on home ownership and home buying. This listing can be obtained from the Consumer Information Center N, P.O. Box 100, Pueblo, CO 81002, (719) 948-3334.

In addition, the Federal Trade Commission has free publications on homes and real estate. Write to Public Reference, Federal Trade Commission, Sixth and Pennsylvania, Washington DC 20580, telephone (202) 326-2222, for a list of currently available publications.

# Renting Residential Property

# INTRODUCTION

RENTING AN APARTMENT can be a headache, whether you are the prospective tenant or the landlord, and disputes between landlords and tenants are never pleasant. This chapter offers some help over the rough spots.

Keep in mind that state and local laws on this subject vary widely and are frequently different from the established principles of common law. For specific answers you may need to get help from your local government, tenants association, or building managers association. The examples in this chapter concern rental arrangements between private parties; the rules may be different if you are renting from a government agency, such as a city or county housing authority.

---

## CHOOSING A LANDLORD/TENANT

The first decision in a rental relationship requires that both the landlord and the tenant choose each other. The wisdom of this decision will probably affect each party's satisfaction until the tenant moves out or the landlord turns over the property to someone else, and that could mean years. A "problem" tenant or a "problem" landlord usually does not improve over time. Both the landlord and the tenant should do all they can to make sure of a good match.

If you are a landlord, do not be so anxious to rent a place that you will accept a poor tenant. If you are a prospective tenant, do not accept a poor dwelling or lease just because the place is available today. Check each other out.

### Q. How can tenants choose a good landlord?

**A.** If you look at a house or apartment to rent, you will naturally check out the space and the amenities: the number of bedrooms and bathrooms, the presence of kitchen appliances and air conditioning, and so forth. You should check out the landlord as well.

The single most important question is whether the landlord will make repairs if something breaks. If possible, get the answer to this question before you move in.

You can also check out the landlord with the local building management association, apartment association, or Board of Realtors, the local office of the Institute of Real Estate Management, and whatever agency handles tenant complaints in your locality.

One quick way to judge the quality of a building is to look at the mailboxes and doorbells at the front door.

Are the tenants' names all uniform, such as generated by a plastic label gun? If so, they were probably put there by an above average landlord who cares about the appearance of the building.

Are the name labels all different, as if the tenants put them there themselves? That is a sign of a landlord who is indifferent to the appearance of the building.

> **CHECK IT OUT**
> *In choosing an apartment you will want to check the overall condition of the grounds and the building, the common areas, parking areas, the interior painting, cleanliness, and maintenance. Look at it at night as well as in daylight. Talk to present tenants.*

Are the names written on the mailboxes with a felt marker or scratched into the metal? Are the mailboxes broken or lacking locks? That looks as though the landlord and tenants don't care at all about appearances. You should look elsewhere.

**Q. Suppose the landlord says he'll fix anything that's broken. Why should I believe him?**

**A.** If you inspect the apartment and see some things that are broken or need to be repaired, ask the landlord when repairs will be made.

If the landlord is willing to write down a list of repairs to be made and sign it, that is an indication of good faith. This is an above average landlord.

If the landlord makes only an oral promise to repair things, you cannot be sure of the real intention. Some things may be repaired and some may not.

If the landlord won't even give an oral promise, it's a clear sign that repairs won't be made. This landlord is below average. Look someplace else.

But remember the difference between repairs and improvements. A tenant is entitled to have things in good working order. A tenant may not be entitled to a new refrigerator.

**Q. How can landlords go about choosing tenants?**

**A.** If you are offering a place to rent, have the prospective tenants complete a rental application. Standard application forms are usually available at stationery stores.

The two most important elements of the application are the employment history and the rental history. Get information for the past three or five years. Then contact each of the applicant's employers and landlords for that period. If the applicant has worked at the same job and lived in the same apartment for that

## LET'S LOOK AT THE RECORD

*It may be difficult and time-consuming, but one way to check the quality of a landlord is to visit the courthouse and check the public records.*

*Has the municipality sued the landlord for failure to maintain the property up to the requirements of local codes? If there is no record of such a suit, it's a probably a sign of a good landlord (though it could also indicate an inattentive municipality). If the landlord has been sued, you should be suspicious. If a suit is pending now, run away.*

*If the municipality has a local code inspection agency, its files may be matters of public record. Check them if you can. A code violation in the past does not necessarily indicate a bad landlord. Not all code violations are equally serious, and many buildings will have some violations. Municipalities will issue complaints or file suits against the landlord only in cases of serious code violations and only if repairs are not made promptly.*

time, you have as good an indication as possible of a quality tenant.

A prospective tenant who undergoes such a check might well be thankful. The landlord will have checked the building's other tenants as well, and so the neighbors will probably be reliable people.

### Q. How else can landlords evaluate prospective tenants?

**A.** Many areas have companies that specialize in tenant records. They can tell you if someone has been evicted in the past or failed to pay the rent.

General credit bureaus can supply a history of credit payments to landlords if the prospective tenant authorizes a search of the records. This credit information will include the timeliness with which car and credit card payments have been made, bankruptcies, judgments against the tenant, and adverse information from other creditors.

### Q. Are there any legal pitfalls in choosing a tenant?

**A.** Landlords need to take special care to treat all prospective tenants in the same way. The law prohibits many kinds of distinctions that landlords used to make in selecting tenants. Fair housing laws forbid discrimination on the basis of race, of course, but go far beyond that. See the section on fair housing, on page 235.

---

## LEASES

When the landlord has decided to rent to the tenant and the tenant has chosen to rent from the landlord, they will enter into a lease or rental agreement.

### Q. What is a lease or rental agreement?

**A.** They are contracts, either written or oral, in which the landlord grants to the tenant exclusive possession of the premises in exchange for rent for a period of time.

### Q. Do all tenants have the same kind of lease?

**A.** No. Most tenants fall into one of two categories.

If the tenant rents for a fixed period of time (that is, a term) and no notice is required to terminate, the tenancy is called a tenancy for years. This tenancy is usually in writing. It must be in writing if the term of the lease is longer than one year.

If the tenancy continues indefinitely, automatically renewing from one period to the next, and if a notice is required to terminate, the tenancy is called periodic. This lease or agreement may be written or oral.

### Q. What are the advantages of an oral versus a written lease?

**A.** For tenants with an oral month-to-month agreement, the major advantage is the ability to terminate the lease and move out without further rental liability with only a short notice to the landlord. The notice usually must be the same as the term of the agreement, commonly 30 days. Tenants are very mobile (20 percent move each year) and the ease of moving can be an important consideration.

For landlords, an oral lease provides an easy way to terminate the lease and make the tenant move out with only a short notice, or to raise the rent. The landlord is usually not required to state a good reason for the termination, as must be done in other cases. (See the sections on termination of leases and security of tenure beginning on page 226.)

### Q. What are the disadvantages of an oral lease?

**A.** Because nothing is written down, the major disadvantage is the possibility of misunderstandings between the landlord and the tenant about the conditions of the tenancy.

## Q. What are the advantages of a written lease?

**A.** The chief advantage of a written lease is the landlord's right to hold the tenant to pay rent for the entire duration or term of the lease.

The tenant may also have an advantage, in that the landlord cannot raise the rent beyond the amount specified in the lease during the term of that lease. There is no evidence, however, that landlords with oral leases increase rent more often than landlords with written leases. Furthermore, since most standard lease forms are written by attorneys who work for landlords or the real estate industry, the slant of the lease is usually in favor of the landlords.

## Q. What are the disadvantages of a written lease?

**A.** The major disadvantage for the tenant is that the landlord may write in express provisions that void certain protections that the law ordinarily gives to the tenant. Also, in most written leases the landlord's responsibilities are not very well spelled out.

## Q. What are the most important lease clauses from the point of view of landlords?

**A.** The most important clause to landlords is the duty of the tenant to pay the rent in full and on time. This includes the right to charge a fee for damages if payment is late. Other important clauses grant the landlord the right to enforce the rules and regulations written into the lease.

## Q. What are the most important lease clauses for tenants?

**A.** The lease states the duty of the landlord to maintain the physical condition of the premises. Other clauses should state the right of the tenant to terminate the lease if the land-

**CHANGING THE RULES**

*Leases are not written in stone, even though standard forms may seem that way.*

*Most standard leases are written by lawyers who favor landlords. Tenants should try to remove clauses they do not like. They should try to add conditions that they want, such as the right to own pets or to have the landlord paint the apartment.*

*Likewise, of the scores of standard forms available, none is likely to meet the needs of every landlord. Some fail to spell out which utility services the tenant pays for and which ones the landlord pays. Others fail to allow the landlord the right ever to enter the premises without the consent of the tenants.*

*Landlords have as much right as the tenants to alter the lease terms to cover such things.*

lord fails to make needed repairs. Where the law allows it, the tenant should have a clause specifying the right to hire workers to correct defects in the premises and to charge the landlord for the cost or deduct it from the rent. A clause giving the tenant the right to pay reduced rent is important if the landlord fails to make repairs.

# Read Before You Sign!

Leases vary widely. Below are explanations of clauses found in a typical pro-landlord lease and in a lease that is more balanced between the rights of landlord and tenant. Leases similar to these are available in many stationery stores. The pro-landlord lease has few rights for the tenant and many tenant obligations; the balanced lease has obligations for both landlord and tenant and rights for both. Whether you are a landlord or a tenant, make sure you read and understand any lease before you sign it.

| Clause | Pro-Landlord Lease | Balanced Lease |
| --- | --- | --- |
| Interest on security deposit | No interest unless required by state law. | Interest at 5% per year. |
| Return of security deposit | Will return after deducting for tenant's failure to comply with terms of lease. | Landlord required to provide a written statement of repairs done to premises, with receipts. |
| Condition of premises/repairs | By signing lease, tenant acknowledges that premises are in good repair, except as noted in lease. No specific space provided on lease to write in repairs that are needed. | Landlord expressly warrants that premises are fit and comply with all applicable codes. Space provided for repairs needed and date repairs will be completed. |
| Limitation of liability/ regulations | Restricts or eliminates landlord's liability for failure to keep premises in repair (e.g., damage caused by plumbing failures or leaks in roof). Landlord not responsible for damage caused by his or her actions or by neglect of his or her duties to keep premises in repair. | No clause waiving landlord's liability. |
| Default | If tenant fails to pay any part of rent, or breaks any other part of lease, landlord is authorized: to terminate lease without notice; to enter premises without process of law to remove tenant; to possess and sell tenant's property to recover rent owed; and to have a first lien on all personal property of tenant as security. | No comparable clause. |
| Fire and casualty | Landlord has 30 days to repair damage that makes dwelling unfit for use, or landlord can simply terminate lease. | Tenant has right to terminate lease in case fire or other casualty makes unit uninhabitable. |
| Confession of judgment | In the event that landlord sues tenant, tenant appoints landlord's attorney to represent tenant in court; tenant waives right to be served and to notice of the suit; tenant confesses judgment (admits to the complaint filed against him by the landlord); agrees to pay landlord's court costs and attorney fees; waives all errors that might be made at trial; waives all rights to appeal; consents to immediate eviction. | No comparable clause. |
| Option to renew lease | None. | Tenant has option to lease for another period of time, at a stated rent. Landlord cannot arbitrarily refuse to renew lease. |
| Duty to maintain/ warranty | None (no part of lease says that landlord will make repairs if something breaks during the tenancy). | By warranting that premises are fit and meet code requirements, landlord is promising to keep them that way. |
| Entry by landlord | Landlord has free access without notice. | Only with 24-hour advance notice, and only for specified purposes. |
| Additional landlord obligations | None. | Spelled out in detail (e.g., adequate exterminator services for unit, adequate locks, screens, secure mail boxes). |
| Tenant remedies if landlord does not maintain premises | None. | Tenant has right to hire repairpersons and buy materials, and deduct costs from rent, after giving landlord adequate notice of the need for repairs. |
| Tenant's right to terminate | None. | Tenant has right to end lease in event of job loss or transfer. |

## Q. How should the tenant or the landlord change the lease if either doesn't like certain clauses?

**A.** If either one can persuade the other to remove a particular provision, that provision should be marked out in ink on all copies. The marked-out sections should then be initialed by both the landlord and the tenant.

Many preprinted forms contain large blank spaces for the landlord and tenant to write additional agreements, which become part of the lease. These inserted paragraphs should be initialed by both landlord and tenant. If the spaces are absent or are too small, the additional terms should be written on a separate sheet of paper and signed by both the landlord and tenant.

## Q. Does the law regulate the provisions in a lease?

**A.** Yes. Both courts and legislative bodies have made laws restricting the provisions in a lease.

For example, state courts have struck down lease clauses that provide that the tenant accepts the apartment in "as is" condition and that the tenant must pay the rent regardless of whether the landlord maintains the property. So, if a landlord sues to evict for nonpayment of rent, tenants can defend themselves by arguing that the premises were not worth the full contract rent because of the deteriorated condition. This legal concept is called the implied warranty of habitability, which is discussed later. It prevents the landlord from evading the responsibility to maintain the premises even if the tenant signed a lease waiving the right to maintenance.

Many states and municipalities have enacted laws that prohibit some clauses from residential leases. An example of a commonly prohibited clause is "confession of judgment." Such a clause would permit the landlord's attorney to go into any court and to represent the tenant without any prior notice, service or process. The tenant would waive a jury trial, confess judgment to whatever the landlord sues for without any defense, waive all errors or omissions made by the landlord in making the complaint, and authorize an immediate eviction or wage deduction.

## Lease Clauses to Consider

## Q. Can the tenants own pets?

**A.** With an oral agreement or lease, tenants would probably have the right to own a pet. Without a clause in a written lease prohibiting pets, it would be hard for a landlord to prove that tenants were told that pets were forbidden.

Written leases usually have a clause prohibiting pets on the premises or requiring tenants to get written permission for them from the landlord. A tenant who violated this clause could be evicted if the pet remained after the landlord asked for its removal.

## Q. Is the lease canceled because the landlord sells the building or the tenant dies?

**A.** Most preprinted standard lease forms contain a paragraph on heirs and successors. This paragraph provides that the lease does not expire upon the sale of the building or the death of the tenant. If the tenant dies during the term of the lease, the tenant's estate will continue to owe the rent until legally released; it will also have the right to occupy the premises.

## Q. Does the tenant owe the landlord a late fee if the rent is not paid on the date specified in the lease?

**A.** Not unless a late fee is specified in the written lease. Some municipal ordinances restrict the amount of late fees that a landlord may charge. State courts have also ruled that such a fee may be charged for damages but cannot be so large as to constitute punishment.

Only the government has the right to punish or penalize someone for misconduct.

**Q. Can tenants be forced to waive their rights by signing a lease?**

**A.** Maybe. It depends upon whether the local or state law prohibits landlords from requiring such waivers. For example, the landlord's duty to maintain the property cannot usually be waived by the tenant. However, the landlord's duty to notify the tenant before suing for eviction can be waived in most places.

**Q. If the landlord loses the building to the bank by foreclosure for failure to pay the mortgage, is the tenant's lease still valid?**

**A.** No. Most leases provide that the lease is subordinate to any mortgage. This means that if the landlord fails to make payments to the mortgage holder, the landlord can lose the property through a lawsuit, called a foreclosure. Since the lease is subordinate to the mortgage, the bank can disregard it and evict the tenant.

**Q. Is the landlord liable for the damages incurred by a tenant who was injured because of inadequate maintenance of the property?**

**A.** Many leases contain clauses, called exculpatory clauses, in which the tenant automatically excuses the landlord from any liability for damages from any cause whatsoever. Only about half of the states prohibit such clauses in residential leases.

If the lease does not contain an exculpatory clause or if the state makes such a clause illegal, it will be up to a court to decide whether the injury resulted from some negligent act by the landlord.

Some courts have held that if the tenant's injury resulted from the landlord's violation of the housing code, the landlord is plainly negli-

> ### PLEASE DON'T COME IN
>
> *Normally a landlord has no right to enter a tenant's apartment unless the tenant gives consent. Under the general concept of landlord-tenant law, the landlord has surrendered possession of the premises entirely to the tenant for the term of the lease.*
>
> *But a written lease will almost always give the landlord the right to enter to show the premises to prospective buyers or prospective tenants and to make necessary or agreed repairs. A lease may require the landlord to give a 24-hour notice, but some leases do not require any prior notice or restrict the time or frequency of entry.*
>
> *State and local laws may also give landlords the right of access. Usually these ordinances require landlords to give reasonable advance notice and to enter only at reasonable times and not so often as to be harassing.*

gent and liable. Other courts have required the tenant to prove negligence. That is, there must be evidence that the landlord knew or should have known of the defective condition before the tenant's injury. Furthermore, the landlord must have failed to make repairs within a reasonable time or in a careful manner.

**Q. If the property burns down, does the tenant still owe rent under the lease?**

**A.** In most cases, no. But a few state laws still on the books call for continued payment.

**Q. If the government condemns the property and decides to tear it down, is the tenant's lease still valid?**

**A.** No. Most leases state that the landlord or the government may terminate the tenant's lease if the government condemns the property. The right of the government to condemn private property is called eminent domain. The government must compensate landlords for taking their property. The lease may provide that the tenants are not entitled to any of this money, but in some areas the law may entitle them to a portion of the settlement.

**Q. Can the tenant, with the landlord's consent, operate a business out of the rented premises?**

**A.** How residential property may be used legally is governed by local zoning ordinances. In residential areas, some ordinances permit white-collar work, such as accounting, word processing, tutoring, and counseling, but forbid any commercial, retail, industrial, or manufacturing use. Likewise, local zoning may prohibit people from living in a commercial, retail, industrial, or manufacturing building. Therefore, if the landlord rents manufacturing space to a residential tenant in violation of the zoning ordinance, the lease is unenforceable because it is for an illegal purpose.

Most leases provide that the tenant must use the premises solely for residential purposes. Thus, business uses would be illegal even if the zoning law allowed them.

**Q. If the landlord provides laundry facilities in the building at the time that the tenant signs the lease but later discontinues this service, does this violate the lease?**

**A.** Maybe. Most leases provide that the tenant's use of any facility in the building outside of the apartment is a license and not a lease. These facilities include laundry in the building, storage areas, garages and parking spaces, bike rooms, swimming pools, workout rooms, and party and recreational areas. A license conveys permission to exercise a privilege in the use of the property and can be revoked by the landlord.

But state statutes or municipal ordinances may define the term "premises," which are rented to the tenant, to include the common areas of the property. In that case, such services

---

### WHOSE CHANDELIER IS IT?

*Disputes often arise when tenants install more or less permanent fixtures, such as chandeliers or ceiling fans, in their apartments. Can they remove them when they move out?*

*Under the general concept of landlord-tenant law, tenants may do anything they wish as long as they do not damage the property. But most leases do not allow a tenant to install such fixtures without the landlord's approval. Sometimes the lease provides as well that such fixtures become the landlord's property when the lease expires. Some leases permit removal of the fixtures if the wall or ceiling is restored to its original condition.*

**CONDOS ARE SPECIAL**

*A tenant who rents a condominium has two obligations, one to the condo unit's owner and one to the condo association.*

*The condo owner is the landlord. But the association sets the rules and regulations for the building and controls the common areas. Depending on local law, the association may have the right to seek eviction of a condo tenant who violates the rules. It may also have the right to seek the tenant's eviction if the condo owner fails to pay the regular association assessments.*

*All states and many municipalities have passed special condo laws, although in some cases they do not apply to buildings with only a few units. If you rent a condo, check the local law.*

cannot be discontinued by the landlord. If the landlord discontinues services that are included in the rent, the tenant probably would be entitled to a reduction in rent.

**Q. What can the tenant do if other tenants in the building make noise and interfere with the tenant's "right of quiet enjoyment" of the premises?**

**A.** Traditionally, other tenants cannot interfere with the "right of quiet enjoyment." But that legal phrase does not refer to noise; it refers to the tenant's legal right to occupy the apartment. The landlord would violate the right by renting the same apartment to two different tenants or by removing the tenant's belongings.

As for noise, some courts have held recently that the landlord has the duty to keep tenants from annoying others where the lease contains a clause requiring tenants not to disturb their neighbors. Because they control who may rent in the building, it is appropriate to require landlords to enforce their own rules.

**Q. In a legal dispute between the landlord and the tenant, does the tenant have to pay the landlord's attorney's fees?**

**A.** Most leases make the tenant responsible for the payment of all attorney's fees incurred by the landlord in the enforcement of the provisions of the lease. But some state or local laws restrict that provision to situations where the landlord wins a lawsuit and the court awards fees; if the tenant wins, the landlord pays the fees.

## MAINTENANCE OF RENTAL PROPERTY

A major source of conflict between landlords and tenants concerns the maintenance and repair of the rental property. Regardless of how high or low the rent is, there is an inherent tension between the desire of landlords to make money and the desire of tenants to have money spent on the property.

**Q. Does the landlord have the obligation to maintain the premises and to make repairs if defects occur?**

**A.** Yes. The lease makes the landlord responsible, and so do many court rulings and state and local laws.

**Q. Does the tenant have any obligation to the landlord regarding the maintenance of the premises?**

A. Traditionally, the tenant has the duty not to "commit waste." That means the tenant may not cause unreasonable and permanent damage to the property.

The common law, leases and landlord-tenant laws have modified this concept. The tenant must comply with the sections of housing codes concerning keeping the premises clean and disposing of trash in a reasonable manner and in the facilities that the landlord supplies. The tenant must obey the rules of the lease and may not damage the property negligently or deliberately. When moving out, the tenant must return the property to the landlord in clean and repaired condition, except for reasonable wear and tear. (See the section on security deposits on page 231.)

**Q. What is the express warranty of habitability?**

A. The lease may explicitly say that the landlord shall maintain the premises and make repairs. Such promises are called express warranties of habitability.

When the lease is signed, the tenant should make sure it lists all repairs that are needed now and contains a clause by which the landlord agrees to make future repairs when needed. Then, if the landlord fails to maintain the premises up to the express standard written into the lease, that would constitute a breach of contract and the tenant could sue or seek other remedies.

**Q. What is the implied warranty of habitability?**

A. The traditional concept of landlord-tenant law was that unless the lease explicitly provided for the landlord to maintain the property and make repairs, the tenant accepted the premises "as is." The landlord had no duty to make the property fit for habitation before the tenant moved in or to repair the premises if they became defective while tenant was living there.

Beginning in the late 1960s, courts ruled that the lease of every residential tenant contained an implied (that is, unwritten but understood) warranty that the property was in good condition and the landlord would keep it that way. Lease clauses in which the tenant waived the right to maintenance were declared illegal and unenforceable. Almost all of the state courts have made such rulings. By passing laws requiring the landlord to maintain the property, state legislatures and municipalities have also created an implied warranty in leases.

Habitability is sometimes defined as the minimum standard for decent, safe, sanitary housing specified in the state or local housing code.

This implied warranty of habitability gives tenants the right to withhold rent if the landlord fails to comply with the state or local housing code. Tenants can also sue landlords and can defend themselves against eviction for nonpayment of rent by arguing that the landlord violated the implied warranty of habitability.

The court rulings generally do not require the landlord to correct all violations of the housing code but only to achieve substantial compliance.

**Q. What are housing codes?**

A. A housing code is an ordinance enacted by the state or municipality requiring property owners, including landlords, to maintain their property and to make repairs.

To qualify for funding from the federal urban renewal program, about five thousand municipalities passed these codes between 1954 and 1965. They also hired inspectors to enforce the codes.

A standard provision in the codes prohibits a landlord from renting a property that does not meet the minimum code standards.

**Q. Do the implied warranty of habitability and housing codes apply only to tenants living in slum buildings?**

**A.** They apply to everyone. It is true that the original lawsuits that led to the adoption of the implied warranty of habitability were brought on behalf of poor tenants living in slum conditions. However, the courts make no legal distinction between the rights of tenants based on income. The standard of maintenance required applies to all buildings, all landlords, and all tenants.

It cannot be stressed too much that tenants at all income levels have problems with landlords providing adequate maintenance. It is not uncommon for very expensive apartments to have dozens of severe code violations, such as corroded plumbing, defective or missing locks, and faulty furnaces.

**Q. What kind of standards do housing codes require landlords to maintain?**

**A.** Tenants should know what the local housing code requires because they have the right to demand these conditions of the landlord. Landlords should know the requirements because the municipality expects them to maintain these conditions in the property.

The following conditions are typical of the broad areas covered in detail in local housing codes:

- the building outside the apartment, such as garbage and refuse removal, and safe and structurally sound stairs, porches, railings and handrails, windows and doors, screens, storm windows, walls and siding, roofs, chimneys, foundations, basements, signs, awnings, and other decorative features;
- the interior of the apartment, such as walls, floors, and ceilings without holes, cracks or other defects, no lead-based

paint, waterproof bathroom and kitchen floors, no rodent or insect infestation;
- light, ventilation and space, such as minimum lighting for halls and stairways, window or mechanical ventilation, minimum adequate space for occupants;
- plumbing facilities and fixtures, such as running water, adequate hot water, sufficient water flow, no leaks, working fixtures;
- mechanical systems, such as hot water tanks, furnaces, air conditioning, cooking equipment, fireplaces;
- electrical systems, such as elevators, sufficient circuits and capacity, working fixtures, switches and receptacles;
- fire safety, such as smoke detectors, fire extinguishers, automatic sprinkler systems, adequate exits, control over storage of flammable materials;
- security, such as locks on the windows and doors, peepholes in the doors, shatterproof glass on windows.

**Q. Can the tenant do anything if the landlord refuses to make repairs?**

**A.** Yes. The tenant has a number of options, though not all are available in all states. The tenant might complain to the municipal code enforcement agency, take the landlord to court, repair the defect and deduct the cost from the rent, reduce the rent payment, or terminate the lease.

## Municipal Code Enforcement

**Q. Can the municipal government force the landlord to maintain the property and make repairs?**

**A.** If the municipality has adopted a housing code, it will probably have also adopted a mechanism for enforcing that code against violators. The tenant can report the landlord to the municipal department responsible for enforcing the code. The municipality hires employees to inspect properties for code violations.

### Q. How does municipal code enforcement work?

**A.** Municipalities make two basic types of inspections: upon complaint from residents and upon a preset plan.

Some landlords have contested the right of municipal inspectors to enter their property; they call it trespassing. The municipality may have to go to court to get a search warrant if the landlord refuses to let an inspector enter. The municipality does not need a warrant, however, if the inspector is invited onto the property by tenants.

Some courts have restricted the right of the municipality to enter apartments in a building unless the inspection is part of a preset plan. A municipality's plan is simply a schedule of inspections. It may call for inspection of the common areas of every rental building every year, or inspections of all buildings with more than three stories every two years, or every building in a certain neighborhood every three years, or any variation of that timetable.

If a local inspector finds any violations of the housing code, a citation can be issued against the landlord. Besides stating the violations, the citation may give the landlord a specified number of days to comply with the law.

If the landlord does not make the required repairs, the next stage of enforcement will probably be an administrative hearing. If the landlord fails to correct the code violations after a hearing, the municipality can take the landlord to court.

State laws authorize the courts to order the landlord to make repairs, to fine the landlord, to place the building in receivership until the violations are corrected, or even to condemn the building and order it demolished.

### Q. Is municipal code enforcement effective?

**A.** Where local government and courts are committed to code enforcement, this is probably the single most effective way to maintain the quality of housing in the community. But many municipalities are not making the persistent effort that is needed.

## Suing the Landlord

### Q. Can the tenant take the landlord to court for failure to maintain the premises and make repairs?

**A.** Yes. There are three legal theories that apply.

- The concept of the implied warranty of habitability, which was established by tenants attempting in court to force landlords to comply with local housing codes.

- Many local landlord-tenant ordinances permit the tenant to seek a court order if the landlord fails to maintain the premises. These ordinances may also require the landlord to pay the tenant's attorney's fees.

- A number of state statutes on consumer fraud include the landlord-tenant relationship. Under these laws it is a fraud for a landlord to rent premises in defective condition. The statutes often provide for punitive damages and for the landlord to pay the tenant's attorney's fees.

## Repair and Deduct

### Q. What is repair and deduct?

**A.** Repair and deduct is a law that permits the tenant to hire someone to make essential repairs and then to deduct the cost from the rent. In many places, state or local law covers

**SHOULD YOU GO TO COURT?**

*If the state courts are responsive to municipalities' lawsuits for code enforcement, they will be responsive to tenants' lawsuits as well. In those cases, suing will be quite effective.*

*The major problem is that the complexity of the court system really requires tenants to be represented by an attorney. Poor tenants may have access to free or low-cost legal services, but most tenants are not eligible for such assistance. Middle-income tenants will have to find an attorney willing to represent them on a contingency fee basis (that is, paid upon winning the case). Thus, suing the landlord is not easy. However, some lawsuits in California have resulted in judgments against landlords for millions of dollars, including paying the fees of the tenants' attorneys.*

*On the other hand, if the courts have not become responsive to municipal code enforcement, then the tenants will not do well in court. The ability to sue successfully, particularly under the consumer fraud law, depends upon the sensitivity of the courts.*

only repairs that are required to keep the premises habitable, such as repair of a broken furnace or leaking roof.

### Q. How does a tenant use repair and deduct?

A. The tenant would serve a written notice on the landlord. This notice would list specifically what repairs the tenant needs, provide a period of time for the landlord to comply, and state that if the landlord fails to do so, the tenant will hire someone to make the repairs and will deduct that cost from the rent.

### Q. Are there any limitations on the use of repair and deduct?

A. Local laws may place a maximum dollar amount that the tenant can spend on repairs. For example, a Chicago ordinance limits a ten-ant's repairs to five hundred dollars. Some laws limit repair costs to one month's rent.

However, in jurisdictions that have no explicit repair and deduct legislation and rely on the implied warranty of habitability, the right to use repair and deduct is limited only by the reasonableness of the repairs. A tenant may even be able to buy a new furnace and deduct the cost from the rent.

### Reduced Rent

### Q. What is reduced rent?

A. When the premises do not comply with the standards of the local housing code, the tenant can pay the landlord a rent reduced from the full contract amount, which reflects the reduced value of the premises.

**Q. How does a tenant go about paying reduced rent?**

**A.** The tenant would serve a written notice on the landlord. This notice would list specifically what repairs the tenant needs, provide a period of time for the landlord to comply, and state that the tenant will pay a reduced rent unless the landlord makes the repairs within the time specified.

**Q. May the tenant withhold all the rent?**

**A.** A tenant might do that, especially to get the landlord's attention. But the landlord could reply with a notice to pay up or get out. And if the premises remained habitable at least to some extent, some rent would be owed. It would be up to a court to decide how much of a reduction is justified.

**Q. Must the tenant put the withheld rent money in an escrow account?**

**A.** There is no legal requirement to do that. But it might be a good idea, so that the money would be readily available if needed. Some local landlord-tenant ordinances might require that the rent money be placed in escrow in the event of litigation. When a case goes to court, the judge is likely to ask if the disputed money is available.

**Q. What is a rent strike?**

**A.** Some localities allow tenants to withhold all of the rent money in a dispute about repairs. Provided they have the money to pay the landlord back for any rent which the court finds to be owed, they will not be evicted. A rent strike is usually a collective action by a number of the tenants in the same building. They may withhold all of the rent or perhaps only a portion. It is a good idea to place the rent money in escrow in a rent strike so that all tenants know that their neighbors are participat-

ing; this also protects the money and limits each individual tenant's liability.

**Q. How do the courts calculate rent reductions?**

**A.** There are several standards, but they are not consistent across the country. Some courts have permitted reductions based on the fair market rental value of the premises. This means that the rent is reduced from the contract amount to the value the court considers fair with the defects. Other courts have adopted a proportional use standard. This means the reduction is determined by how much the defects reduce the use of the premises. If the use is reduced by 40 percent, for example, the rent may be reduced by 40 percent.

**Q. If the tenant paid full rent but the premises were defective, can the tenant seek a rent reduction for past months?**

**A.** Maybe, but the tenant would have to sue the landlord to collect. This concept is called retroactive rent abatement.

Both the implied warranty of habitability and local ordinances provide that the tenant has the right to recover damages from the landlord for failure to maintain the premises.

For example, suppose that the lease called for rent of $500 a month and the tenant paid that amount for six months, $3,000 in all. And suppose that the court later determines that the value of the premises was only $300 a month, $1,800 in all. The court could order the landlord to refund the $1,200 overpayment to the tenant.

## Lease Termination for Code Violations

**Q. Can the tenant terminate the lease if the landlord fails to maintain the premises?**

**A.** Yes. Three different legal theories justify such an action. They are called illegal lease, constructive eviction, and material non-compliance.

### Q. What is an illegal lease?

**A.** If the landlord has been cited by the municipality for serious violations of the housing code, the tenant can argue that the lease is illegal because the code makes it against the law for the landlord to rent the premises in defective condition. This theory holds that the landlord should not benefit economically from the illegal act.

### Q. What is constructive eviction?

**A.** Constructive eviction means the property is in such poor condition that the tenant really cannot live there. For example, there is no water, no electricity, no heat, or there is a seriously leaking roof in danger of collapse.

The tenant has to serve notice on the landlord of the conditions but there is usually not a minimum time period before the tenant can vacate. The tenant must actually move out in order to argue constructive eviction. If constructive eviction applies, the tenant will not be responsible for paying the rent.

### Q. What is material noncompliance?

**A.** Material (that is, substantial) noncompliance means the premises don't meet the minimum standards of the local or state housing code. The concept is similar to the standard of the implied warranty of habitability invented by the Uniform Residential Landlord and Tenant Ordinance (see page 232 below).

To terminate the lease on these grounds, the tenant would have to serve written notice on the landlord, specify the conditions that represent material noncompliance, demand the correction of the conditions within a specified period of time, and inform the landlord of the date that the lease will terminate if the conditions are not corrected.

## Other Lease Terminations

### Q. Does the landlord need a reason to terminate the lease at the expiration of the term?

**A.** The landlord does not need a reason to terminate the lease unless the lease requires a written notice or provides for automatic renewal. However, the nonrenewal of the lease may be governed by a security of tenure law or a retaliatory conduct law, which are discussed below in this section.

### Q. How does the landlord terminate the lease at the expiration of the term?

**A.** It depends upon the type of lease.

If there is an oral lease with month-to-month tenancy, the landlord ends it by serving a written notice of the same length. For example, the notice must give the tenant thirty days

### FORCING A TENANT OUT

*A landlord can terminate the lease and force the tenant out for good cause. The most common causes are nonpayment of rent, damage to the premises, and violation of the rules and regulations of the lease. The most common violations are disturbing the neighboring tenants with noise, possession of pets, and occupancy by persons who are not named on the lease. Often the landlord must give the tenant a short period in which to correct the problem before eviction action begins.*

to vacate if rent is paid monthly, and seven days if it is paid weekly, although some states have different rules. Most cities or states require that this notice be delivered personally to the tenant, although some permit delivery by mail.

If there is a written lease with a specific duration or term, the lease automatically ends on the last day of the term. However, some municipal ordinances require a 30-day written notice to the tenant before the end of the term. Without such a notice the tenant does not know whether the landlord wants to renew the lease or not. It is always a good idea for the landlord and tenant to discuss the matter well before the term ends.

### Q. Can the landlord terminate the lease because the tenant is paying reduced rent?

**A.** If the tenant is paying reduced rent because of the landlord's breach of the implied warranty of habitability or violation of the housing code, the landlord may not have the right to terminate the lease. A retaliatory conduct law may prohibit such a termination.

### Q. What kinds of actions by the tenant are protected from landlord retaliation?

**A.** The landlord may not retaliate if the tenant exercises any right or remedy under the law. These rights include complaining to the government agency responsible for code enforcement, complaining to the landlord about code violations and the failure to make repairs, and organizing or joining a tenants union.

### Q. What kinds of conduct by the landlord does the law consider retaliatory?

**A.** Landlord-tenant laws define four actions as retaliatory: eviction action or the threat of it, nonrenewal of the lease, increasing the rent, and decreasing the services.

### Q. How does the tenant prove that the landlord's conduct was retaliatory?

**A.** The tenant does not have to prove it. The law assumes that the conduct was retaliatory if it followed the tenant's protected actions within a specified period of time, sometimes as long as six months. The landlord has the burden to prove some other valid motive in terminating the lease. The tenant can further assure legal protection by keeping a log of events and communications pertaining to the landlord's conduct.

### Q. How does the landlord terminate the lease for cause?

**A.** For nonpayment of rent the landlord can serve a written notice threatening to terminate the lease unless the tenant pays the past due rent within a certain number of days (depending upon the area, from three to ten days). If the rent is paid, the tenant may remain.

For violation of the rules and regulations of the lease or damage to the premises, the landlord can serve a written notice terminating the tenancy after a certain number of days (from ten to thirty days, depending upon the area). Some localities, but not all, provide that the tenant may remain if the violation ends, for example, getting rid of a forbidden pet or repairing the damage to the premises.

### Q. What does all this emphasis on written notices mean to the landlord?

**A.** In every jurisdiction the law imposes specific statutory obligations on the landlord as to the method of termination of leases. If the landlord fails to give the written notice where required or if the notice is not properly written or not properly served on the tenant, the landlord will not have the right to terminate the tenancy. When the landlord goes to court, it is already too late to correct any deficiencies in the written notice.

# SAMPLE LEASE CLAUSE ON TERMINATION

*21. LANDLORD'S REMEDIES. Landlord shall have the remedies specified in this paragraph for the following circumstances:

A. Termination for Failure To Pay Rent. If all or any portion of the rent is unpaid when due and Tenant fails to pay unpaid rent within five (5) days after written notice by Landlord of an intention to terminate Lease if rent is not so paid, Landlord may terminate Lease. Landlord may also maintain an action for rent and/or damages without terminating Lease.

B. Termination for Breach of Lease. If there is a material noncompliance by Tenant with this Lease, Landlord may deliver written notice to Tenant specifying the acts and/or omissions constituting the breach and that the Lease will terminate upon a date not less than ten (10) days after receipt of notice, unless the breach is remedied by Tenant within that period of time. If the breach is not remedied within the ten (10) day period, Lease shall terminate as provided in the notice.

C. Self-Help. If there is a material noncompliance by Tenant with Paragraph 16 (other than Subparagraph G thereof) and Tenant fails to comply as promptly as conditions permit in case of emergency or in cases other than emergencies within fourteen (14) days of receipt of written notice by Landlord specifying the breach and requesting that Tenant remedy it within that period of time, Landlord may enter the Apartment and have the necessary work done in a manner required by law. Landlord shall be entitled to reimbursement from Tenant of the costs of repairs under this subparagraph.

D. Damages and Injunctive Relief. If there is a material noncompliance by Tenant with this Lease, Landlord may recover damages and obtain injunctive relief. If Tenant's noncompliance is willful, Landlord may recover reasonable attorney's fees.

E. Disturbance of Others. If Tenant violates Paragraph 16G within sixty (60) days after receipt of a written notice as provided in Subparagraph 21B above, Landlord may obtain injunctive relief against the conduct constituting the violation, or may terminate the Lease on ten (10) days' written notice to Tenant.

F. Rights upon Termination. If this lease is terminated, Landlord shall have a claim for possession and/or for rent.

SOURCE: The Fund for Justice and The Chicago Council of Lawyers

---

Besides hiring an attorney to advise on the entire procedure, the landlord can get standardized termination forms from stationery stores, the local apartment association, or the Board of Realtors. Landlords should use these forms and fill in every blank space accurately to be sure that they follow the law.

**Q. What can the landlord do if the tenant doesn't move after the lease is terminated?**

**A.** The landlord has to take the tenant to eviction court. The landlord cannot evict the tenant; only a court can do that.

**Q. How long does the eviction process take?**

**A.** After the notice period expires, the landlord may file a lawsuit alleging forcible entry and unlawful detainer. The court will assign the case for trial as a "summary" or quick proceeding. Assuming proper service of the summons and complaint on the tenant, the court will render judgment after a default proceeding or trial. The trial may be scheduled as soon as two weeks after the suit is filed. In some states, the judge can order eviction immediately at the end of the trial.

But customarily the court gives the tenant time to move out, usually one to four weeks. If the tenant remains after that period, the landlord has to hire the sheriff or marshal to carry out a forcible eviction. That will take several weeks more. Further delays are possible if the tenant files a motion for more time or objects to the court determination.

Thus, the eviction process from the end of the notice period can take from five weeks to three months. And that assumes there are no delays.

### Q. What can delay the judgment?

**A.** Many things. First, the landlord must hire the sheriff, a licensed process server, or an attorney to serve the summons and the complaint on the tenant. If that agent is unable to serve the papers properly, the trial cannot go forward on the scheduled date and the landlord has to try again. In some jurisdictions the landlord's agent may "nail and mail" the summons and complaint (that is, post the papers on the tenant's front door and then mail copies to the tenant). In some other areas the landlord has to employ an agent to serve the papers the first time but may "nail and mail" the second time.

The trial may be delayed by procedural matters, such as problems with the landlord's termination notice or problems with the method of service of that notice or of the court summons and complaint. Or the tenant may request certain procedural rights, such as pretrial investigation of the facts or a jury trial.

Action may also be delayed if the tenant has substantive defenses against the eviction, such

> ## CHANGING THE LOCKS
> Most people have heard stories of landlords changing the locks or shutting off the water or electricity to force a tenant out. That sort of thing is illegal.
>
> In fact, some jurisdictions consider such action a criminal offense. Unless the tenant is allowed back in, the landlord could be arrested. The law might also provide a process by which the tenant could sue the landlord for monetary damages and attorney's fees for an unlawful interruption of the occupancy.

as the landlord's violation of the implied warranty of habitability, discrimination, or retaliation.

### Q. What happens if the tenant does not show up in court?

**A.** If the tenant does not respond properly to the lawsuit or show up in court, the judge will issue a default judgment in favor of the landlord. This is what happens in most eviction suits. It is obviously not in the tenant's interest to fail to appear.

### Q. What kind of judgment may the court enter in an eviction case?

**A.** If the court rules in favor of the landlord, it may require the tenant simply to vacate the premises or to vacate and pay back rent, damages, court costs, and, in a few places, the landlord's attorney's fees.

**Q. Can the landlord take the tenant's possessions or physically throw the tenant out after the court allows eviction?**

**A.** No. The landlord must have the sheriff or other proper authority carry out the physical eviction. Only the court can evict a tenant, and the purpose of the court proceedings is to prevent the landlord from "self-help" evictions. If the court issues a judgment for unpaid rent, the landlord must use the normal debt-collection procedures, which may include partial wage garnishment and attachment of bank accounts.

**Q. Is any of the tenant's property protected from seizure?**

**A.** Yes. All jurisdictions exempt some property from seizure by creditors, but they vary greatly in specifying which property is exempt. States may exempt used cars of low value, household furnishings, clothing, tools or equipment used in the tenant's business, and most of the tenant's wages.

**Q. Does the tenant owe rent after the termination of the lease and being evicted?**

**A.** The landlord and the court may terminate the right of the tenant to occupy the premises. However, in many areas the tenant can still be held liable for the payment of rent if the lease provides for it. But it is unusual for the landlord to sue the tenant a second time if the reason for the first lawsuit was nonpayment of rent.

## Lease Termination by Tenants

**Q. If the tenant moves out before the expiration of the lease, is the lease terminated?**

**A.** No. The lease does not terminate just because the tenant moves out. The lease is a contract in which the tenant promises to pay the landlord for the right to possess the premises whether the tenant actually lives there or not.

**Q. How can the tenant terminate the legal obligation of the lease?**

**A.** There are three ways for the tenant to get out of the rental obligation: termination for legal misconduct by the landlord, replacement in the premises by a new tenant, or agreement between the landlord and tenant.

Failure to maintain the premises may constitute legal misconduct. Local laws may provide for termination of the lease if the landlord violates other provisions of the law, such as by abusing access to the premises or failing to disclose code violations cited by the municipality.

If another tenant replaces the existing tenant, the first tenant can avoid the rental obligation. The landlord cannot legally collect from the original tenant if the replacement tenant pays the full rent.

Obviously, the landlord and tenant can end the tenancy by mutual agreement. This simple approach is often overlooked.

**Q. How is one tenant replaced by another?**

**A.** Under the common law, if there is no written lease, the tenant has the unrestricted right to transfer the leasehold to anyone else. A written lease will undoubtedly contain a provision giving the landlord the right of approval over prospective replacement tenants. Whether the landlord is acting reasonably in approving or disapproving of the replacement tenant can be an issue.

**Q. Does the landlord have the duty to mitigate the rental obligation of the tenant who moves out?**

**A.** In many places, the landlord is obligated to make a good-faith effort to find a new tenant promptly so that the old tenant can discontinue paying rent. The first tenant can also help find a new tenant.

### Q. What is the difference between subleasing and reletting?

A. In reletting, the landlord signs a completely new lease with the replacement tenant and releases the original tenant from the obligation to pay rent.

In subleasing, the first tenant rents to another one. Although the subtenant now has the obligation to pay rent, the original one still remains responsible for the remainder of the lease term. Therefore, if the subtenant fails to pay, the landlord may sue the original tenant for the rent even though that tenant is no longer using the premises.

The original tenant may also be liable for damages if the subtenant breaches the lease or destroys the property.

### Q. Can the tenant stay after the expiration of the lease?

A. A tenant who stays after the expiration of the lease is called a tenant at sufferance. The landlord can sue for eviction or can choose to continue accepting rent, thus renewing the lease. The renewal will be on a month-to-month basis or for another year, depending on the terms of the lease and the provisions of the law. Moreover, a provision of the lease or a statute may give the landlord the right to charge double the current rent during the withholding period.

Since the landlord has the choice of eviction or renewal, the tenant who needs to stay past the expiration of the lease should try to negotiate an agreement with the landlord and should get it in writing.

## SECURITY DEPOSITS

### Q. What is a security deposit?

A. It is money to protect the landlord in case the tenant damages the property or fails to pay rent. Usually the tenant pays the security deposit before moving in. The landlord may ask for any amount, but some local laws restrict the deposit to the equivalent of one or two months' rent.

### Q. What does the lease say about security deposits?

A. A preprinted standard lease form will probably contain a paragraph explaining that the tenant has made the deposit to assure compliance with all the terms of the lease. The lease will also set forth the conditions under which the landlord will return the deposit to the tenant. Most leases allow the landlord to keep all or part of the deposit if the tenant owes rent upon moving out or has caused property damage beyond normal wear and tear. Some of it may also be kept to pay for cleaning the premises for the next tenant.

### Q. Are deposits for cleaning, pets, parking, or garage door openers considered security deposits and, thus, refundable?

A. Yes. If the tenant performs the duties set forth in the lease, the landlord does not have a legal reason to keep the money whether the lease calls it a security deposit or not.

### Q. Must landlords hold security deposits in a separate bank account apart from other assets?

A. Not unless the law imposes such a requirement. But if there is such a requirement, a landlord who fails to keep the security deposit separate from other money may owe damages to the tenant.

### Q. Under what conditions does the landlord owe a refund of the security deposit?

A. The landlord will owe the tenant at least a partial refund if the rent was paid in full and

## INTEREST ON DEPOSITS

*Most states have statutes requiring the landlord to pay interest on the security deposit. In those states, the landlord cannot avoid paying interest simply because a lease says the deposit does not earn interest.*

*Some landlords try to get around this by calling the security deposit "prepaid rent." But some laws say prepaid rent earns interest as well.*

*After the passage of the local landlord-tenant ordinance in Chicago requiring the payment of interest on security deposits, a number of landlords converted the deposits to prepaid rent for the last month of the lease. So the City Council amended the ordinance to require the payment of interest on prepaid rent.*

the cost of repairs beyond normal wear and tear was less than the amount of the deposit.

### Q. *What should the tenant do if the landlord does not refund the deposit or refunds what the tenant believes is too little?*

**A.** The tenant should first try to negotiate with the landlord, perhaps with the help of a mediator. If that fails, the tenant should take the landlord to small claims court. Many states have a special small claims court where persons can sue to collect money owed to them without the need to hire an attorney. These courts are sometimes called *pro se* courts (Latin for "for oneself") because the tenant, who will be the plaintiff in the lawsuit, is often required to appear without a lawyer. (In most places, the landlord may still hire an attorney.) This type of court is not as intimidating as regular court because the judge does not expect legal sophistication from the tenant.

## UNIFORM RESIDENTIAL LANDLORD AND TENANT ACT

In response to the civil rights movement of the 1960s, the federal government funded a legal services project to draft a model residential landlord-tenant code. From this model code the National Conference of Commissioners on Uniform State Laws drafted the Uniform Residential Landlord and Tenant Act (URLTA) in 1972. The American Bar Association approved this act in 1974. Subsequently, most states and many municipalities passed laws based upon this act.

### Q. *Does the URLTA favor tenants over landlords?*

**A.** No. URLTA provides for both landlord and tenant obligations and remedies.

### Q. *Are there tenants' rights not covered in URLTA?*

**A.** Yes. URLTA does not provide for security of tenure; control over rent increases; payment of reduced rent for reduced services; freedom of speech in relationship with a landlord; appointment of a receiver to manage the building if the landlord fails to do so; payment of interest on the security deposit; separate handling of the deposit and the rent money; or condominium conversion protection for tenants.

## Q. What is security of tenure?

**A.** Security of tenure provides that the tenant has the legal right to continue the tenancy indefinitely unless the tenant violates certain rules or regulations or the landlord has a compelling reason to reclaim possession of the premises. This provision is a major departure from the traditional concept that the landlord had the arbitrary right to terminate the lease at the end of any term. The right of the landlord to raise rent is the major area of conflict in the enforcement of security of tenure. All municipalities with rent control have security of tenure laws. New Jersey has the only statewide security of tenure law.

---

**VOTE FOR . . .**

*A landlord may be able to force you to remove a political sign from your window.*

*The First Amendment to the Constitution provides that the government may not abridge any citizen's right to freedom of speech, and that means political expression of any kind. But the amendment does not cover private relations, such as between a landlord and tenant.*

*It is common for a lease to contain a clause that forbids the tenant to exhibit any sign, political or otherwise, in the window or elsewhere in the apartment without the approval of the landlord.*

---

## Q. What is condominium conversion protection for tenants?

**A.** During the late 1970s thousands of rental buildings were converted to condominium ownership by real estate developers. The tenants had to buy the apartments if they wanted to stay in the buildings. This was financially impossible for many tenants, and they had to move out.

Protests by tenants led to the passage of laws in many communities controlling the method of the conversion and in some cases even the right of developers to convert buildings at all. These laws' most common restriction required the developer to bring the building fully up to the standard of the local housing code. The restriction most desired by tenants was the requirement that a certain percentage of the existing tenants had to buy in order for the conversion to go forward. Sometimes the existing tenants who did not buy had the right to continue to rent in the building even if the conversion occurred.

In no area, however, has legislation stopped conversions entirely.

---

## RENT CONTROL

## Q. What is rent control?

**A.** The words "rent control" apply to laws or governmental regulations that limit the amount of rent or rental increase that the landlords can charge.

## Q. Has there ever been nationwide rent control in the United States?

**A.** Nationwide rent controls existed during World War II. President Nixon also imposed rent controls in 1971 during the initial phase of the effort to control inflation.

> ### ABILITY TO PAY
> *Rent control does not consider a tenant's ability to pay. It is not a social welfare program providing subsidies to the tenant. Even in communities with rent control, there are tenants spending too large a percentage of their incomes on rent. Rent control does not make housing affordable for everyone.*

All public housing has rent control by definition, because the government sets the rent level for each tenant. Privately owned rental housing in which the government gives some special subsidy to the developer or landlord has rent control because the landlord must secure the approval of the government before raising rents.

Most privately owned rental housing is subject to rent control only if the local or state government has passed a rent control ordinance or statute.

### Q. What areas of the country have rent control?

A. The District of Columbia and some municipalities in Massachusetts, New York, New Jersey, and California have passed rent control ordinances. Some state legislatures have outlawed local rent control ordinances. Perhaps 10 percent of the tenants in the country are covered by some form of rent control.

### Q. What kind of rent control laws are there?

A. New York City was the only municipality in the country to retain rent control after the end of World War II. The law there did not permit rent increases without specific permission from an administrative board. Rents could be raised based upon a pass-through of certain expense increases, such as the cost of fuel.

From the late 1960s through 1978 other communities adopted rent control. Most of these laws allow automatic but limited rent increases without any requirement of showing expense increases. Landlords are allowed to petition for larger increases on the basis of major repairs or extraordinarily large expenses that the normal rent increase would not cover. These so-called second generation rent control laws have prevented some of the large rent increases experienced by tenants in other cities.

### Q. How does rent control regulate the amount of rent?

A. Usually the mayor of the city with rent control appoints a board to administer the law. That board determines how much the annual rent increases will be and whether individual landlords get extra rent increases. Some communities elect the rent control board members directly. Some observers think the elected boards are more independent from landlords.

### Q. Are there state laws against rent control?

A. Yes. Legislatures in about half of the states have forbidden municipalities to enact rent control ordinances. For example, in 1987, after the voters of Detroit enacted rent control by referendum, the Michigan Legislature passed a law revoking the right of cities to adopt rent control laws.

### Q. What is vacancy decontrol?

A. Vacancy decontrol is a provision of a rent control law that allows landlords to charge whatever rent they can collect from a new tenant who moves in to fill a vacancy. This is really an anti-rent-control provision. Within a few years, new tenants in the same building can be paying twice as much as old tenants. Not only does the landlord collect more rent with vacancy decontrol, but public support for rent control is undermined by the unfairness of treatment.

## FAIR HOUSING

**Q. Is a landlord allowed to discriminate in the selection of tenants?**

**A.** Yes. The landlord can use legal criteria to select tenants, such as their past history of tenancy, the amount of income they have with which to pay the rent, their credit history, and their past criminal record. The landlord may also use personal criteria in selecting tenants, such as purple hair or nose rings. In some places, a landlord may even refuse to rent to certain people because of their occupation.

**Q. What is fair housing?**

**A.** "Fair housing" is a legal term applied to federal, state, and municipal laws that prohibit landlords from refusing to rent property because the prospective tenant falls into one or more of certain protected classes.

The Fair Housing Act (Chapter 42 of the United States Code, beginning at Section 3601) forbids landlords to discriminate in choosing tenants because of their race, religion, ethnic origin, color, sex, physical or mental handicap, or family status. Landlords cannot refuse to rent to a family with children. It is also illegal under the Fair Housing Act for landlords to harass, intimidate, threaten, interfere with, or evict a tenant because of the same factors. Furthermore, the same law prohibits the landlord from attempting to evict a tenant for filing a complaint or lawsuit charging the landlord with discrimination.

The Civil Rights Act of 1866 (Chapter 42 of the U.S. Code, Section 1982) prohibits discrimination because of the race, ethnic origin, or color of the tenants. This federal law applies to all landlords without any exceptions.

All the states and many cities have enacted fair housing laws as well. Some of these laws are not as strict as the federal law, but some are more strict because they protect additional classes of persons.

Some states and municipalities forbid rental discrimination based on marital status, age (over 40 especially), less than honorable discharge from the military, sexual orientation, or source of income (welfare, social security, alimony, or child support).

**Q. What can a prospective tenant do against a landlord who discriminates illegally?**

**A.** The fair housing laws provide for two remedies. A prospective tenant can file an administrative complaint with the agency enforcing the law or can sue the landlord in court.

The U.S. Department of Housing and Urban Development (HUD) is responsible for enforcing the federal fair housing laws. The complaint must be filed within one year of the date of the discriminatory conduct. States and many cities have human rights agencies that accept complaints. HUD has the authority to award monetary damages to the person discriminated against; the agency of the state or municipality may have similar authority.

The prospective tenant may also file a lawsuit in federal court to enforce the Fair Housing Act or the Civil Rights Act. The person may file an administrative complaint with HUD and sue in court at the same time. The prospective tenant may file a lawsuit in the state court to enforce the state or local law.

**Q. How can the prospective tenant prove that the landlord has illegally discriminated?**

**A.** The prospective tenant has the burden of proving that the landlord's conduct was discriminatory. The person can establish a case against the landlord by proving four things: that the plaintiff is a member of a protected group; that the plaintiff applied for and was qualified to rent a certain property; that the plaintiff was rejected by the landlord; and that the property remained unrented thereafter.

**Q.** *What are the possible outcomes for a prospective tenant who files a complaint or a lawsuit for discrimination?*

**A.** If the prospective tenant wins, the landlord can be ordered to rent the premises and perhaps to pay actual and punitive monetary damages as well. The landlord can also be assessed the attorney's fees incurred by the prospective tenant. The landlord may also have to submit to periodic review of documents and practices for a certain number of years.

## WHERE TO GET MORE INFORMATION

Many states and cities have departments of housing, departments of fair housing, or departments of human affairs. Employees there can usually answer questions and accept complaints of discrimination. Municipal housing departments can also receive complaints of inadequate maintenance. Check government listings in the local telephone directory.

The U.S. Department of Housing and Urban Development (HUD) has offices in many large cities and has involvement in many landlord-tenant issues. HUD has regulations governing public housing, publicly subsidized housing, and fair housing. HUD can answer questions and accept complaints of housing discrimination.

Tenants may seek the assistance of the National Housing Institute, which provides information and referral to local tenant organizations. NHI is located at 439 Main Street, Orange, NJ 07050. Telephone (201) 678-3110.

Landlords may seek the assistance of local real estate or building management organizations.

Bar associations may provide referral to local attorneys who are familiar with landlord-tenant law or fair housing law in the community.

Information on local housing codes is available from the local code enforcement department.

There are three national or regional organizations that write model housing codes. They typically provide written materials to both the public and professionals.

American Public Health Association

    1015 15th St., NW
    Washington, DC 20005
    Telephone (202) 789-5667

Building Official and Code Administrators International

    4051 West Flossmoor Road
    Country Club Hills, IL 60478
    Telephone (708) 799-2300

Southern Building Code Congress International

900 Montclair Road
Birmingham, AL 35213-1206
Telephone (205) 591-1853

Two national publications discuss landlord-tenant law in layperson's terms:

*Landlord Tenant Law Bulletin*
Quinlan Publishing Company
23 Drydock Avenue
Boston, MA 02210-2387
Telephone (617) 542-0048

*Managing Housing Letter*
CD Publications
8204 Fenton Street
Silver Spring, MD 20910
Telephone (301) 588-6380

# Consumer Credit

# INTRODUCTION

THE USE OF CREDIT is a way of life in the United States, almost as American as apple pie. At any one time, about two-thirds of American families have installment debts outstanding. They owe money for their credit purchases of cars, appliances, clothing, vacation trips and other goods and services. For these families, payments on their installment debts absorb about 14 percent of the family income. About one-third of families have home mortgage loans, which are another form of consumer debt. The "Buying and Selling a Home" and "Home Ownership" chapters in this publication cover mortgages.

This chapter can help you better understand how to use credit, how to determine if you are reaching or have reached your credit limit, and what to do if you have exceeded that limit.

This chapter also will help you better understand the rules, regulations, and laws about consumer installment credit, designed to protect you, the consumer. In addition, this chapter will help you decide when you may need a lawyer to handle your credit problems. (If you are married, see pages 61–62 of the "Family Law" chapter for topics regarding credit and marriage. "The Rights of Older Americans" chapter also contains credit-related discussions, beginning on page 572.)

## CREDIT: WHAT IS IT AND WHAT DOES IT COST?

### Q. What exactly is credit?

A. Credit allows you to buy and use goods and services now, and pay for them later. For example, credit lets you use a car or a washing machine before (and, usually, long after) you have fully paid for its services. You pay for the services as you use them. Of course, you could save now to buy the car in the future, but you may want or need the car now, not three years from now. Similarly, you may buy a pair of shoes or a dinner on your credit card now and pay for them later.

### Q. What are the basic forms of consumer credit?

A. There are three basic forms of consumer credit: *noninstallment credit* (sometimes called thirty-day or charge-account credit), *installment credit* or *closed-end credit*, which is legally defined as credit that is scheduled to be repaid on four or more installments (usually monthly) and *revolving* or *open-end credit*. In addition, some lease arrangements operate like consumer credit and may be subject to similar laws, so these are discussed briefly in this chapter. However, credit secured by real property—your home, for example—is discussed in the chapters on "Buying and Selling a Home" on pages 121–126 and "Home Ownership" on pages 177–182.

### Q. Why does credit cost money?

A. To buy now and pay later, you usually must pay a finance charge. This is because the supplier who waits for payment, or the lender who lent you the money to pay a supplier, could have invested the money instead and earned interest. Thus the finance charge you pay compensates them for that lost interest, as well as covering some of the costs involved in extending you credit. The supplier may be the car dealer, appliance dealer, shoe store, or restaurant. The

## How Credit Operates

| Type of Credit | Basic Operation |
| --- | --- |
| Charge-account or 30-day credit | Balances owed on such accounts usually require payment in full within 30 days. Such arrangements are not considered to be installment credit, since the debt is not scheduled to be repaid in two or more installments. Travel and entertainment cards, such as American Express and Diners Club, operate this way, as do most charge accounts with local businesses, especially service providers: doctors, plumbers, and so on. |
| Installment or closed-end credit | A consumer agrees to repay the amount owed in two or more equal installments over a definite period of time. Automobile loans and personal loans are examples of this type of consumer credit. |
| Revolving or open-end credit | In this more flexible method, the consumer has options of drawing on a pre-approved open-end credit line from time to time and then paying off the entire outstanding balance, only a specified minimum, or something in between. With this type of credit, the consumer may use the credit, make a payment, and use the credit again. Bank credit cards, such as Discover, MasterCard, and VISA, and those issued by major retail establishments are examples of revolving credit. |

lender may be a bank, credit union, or finance company. Only you can decide whether it is worth the cost of the finance charge to have a car or other goods and services now, rather than later.

Many states regulate by law how much finance charge you can agree to pay and provide penalties if the supplier or lender charges too much. However, some states allow your agreement and competition among credit extenders to determine what you pay. You should shop for credit much as you shop for the best deal on a car or television set. The Truth in Lending Act and similar state laws allow you to do that.

**Q. I keep seeing references to the Truth in Lending Act. What is it?**

**A.** The Truth in Lending Act (TILA) is a federal law that requires that all creditors provide

**CAREFULLY EVALUATE YOUR OPTIONS**

*The examples on these pages illustrate the importance of checking all financing options before making a decision. Fortunately, the law allows you to obtain the information that you need to comparison shop. You should use this information, and, factoring it in with your own situation and needs, determine which loan or credit arrangement is best for you.*

information that will help you decide whether to buy on credit or borrow, and if so, which credit offer is the best for you. Creditors (sometimes valued credit grantors) include banks, department stores, credit card issuers, finance companies, and so on.

Under the law, before you sign an installment contract, creditors must show you, among other information, the amount being financed, the monthly payment, the number of monthly payments and—very important— the annual percentage rate (APR). The APR is an annual rate that relates the total finance charge to (1) the amount of credit that you receive and (2) the length of time you have to repay it. Think of the APR as a price per pound, like 20 cents per pound for potatoes. You may buy five pounds for one dollar or ten pounds for two dollars. In either case the rate is 20 cents per pound. However, the total cost in dollars depends on the amount of potatoes you buy. When you buy credit instead of potatoes, you buy a certain amount of credit for a given number of months. The total dollar amount of your finance charge will depend upon how many dollars worth of credit you obtain initially and how many months you use those dollars.

The TILA also regulates credit advertising, which makes it easy to credit shop. For example, if an automobile ad emphasizes the low monthly payment (giving a dollar figure), it also must tell you other pertinent information, like the APR.

Of course, the APR can help you in shopping for a credit card and other forms of open-end credit.

## Q. *How do I select the best way to finance the purchase of, for example, a car?*

**A.** Let's see how you can use the information required by the TILA to get the best deal for you in financing a used car having a cash price of $5,000. You have $1,000 in savings to make a down payment on the car and need to borrow the remaining $4,000. Suppose that by shopping around you find the four possible credit arrangements shown below.

[Please note that the figures for total finance charge are correct, even though not precisely equal to the sum of the payments less the amount financed ($4,000). Creditors often round off monthly payments to the nearest dollar, and adjust the final payment to make up the difference.]

Let's begin with an easy decision. Notice that the four-year loan of Creditor B is a better deal than the four-year loan of Creditor C. Since their lengths are equal, we know that an 11-percent loan is cheaper than a 12-percent loan for the same amount of money. Forget about Creditor C.

However, look what happens when the lengths of the loans vary: Even though Creditors A and B charge an APR of 11 percent, the total dollar finance charge is a good deal greater on the 4-year loan from Creditor B than on the 3-year loan from Creditor A. Of course, the difference makes sense, since with Creditor B you would have another year to use the lender's money. You have to decide whether you would like to have the lower monthly payment that is available on the longer loan. Note that it doesn't help to look just at the total finance

|  | APR | Length of Loan | Monthly Payment | Total Finance Charge |
|---|---|---|---|---|
| Creditor A | 11% | 3 years | $131 | $714 |
| Creditor B | 11% | 4 years | $103 | $962 |
| Creditor C | 12% | 4 years | $105 | $1,056 |
| Creditor D | 12% | 2 years | $188 | $519 |

charge, which is lowest on the loan from Creditor D. But that creditor charges 12 percent rather than the 11 percent available from Creditors A and B. The only reason the total finance charge is the lowest of the four is that you would have the use of the creditor's money for only two years. Forget Creditor D.

Thus, your choice narrows to Creditor A vs. Creditor B, and which you choose depends on how easy it will be to meet the monthly payments. And, a big decision is whether having a car today, rather than later, is worth the monthly payments at the 11 percent financing rate.

### Q. Does this mean that I should look only at the APRs when shopping for credit?

**A.** No, when buying on credit, you will not be shopping wisely if you merely compare APRs. For example, your car dealer may be pushing "incentive financing" by offering an APR that is way below the rate being offered by, say, your credit union. Alternatively, the auto dealer may also be advertising a cash rebate if you buy the car for cash. To see which is the best deal, you need to find out which arrangement would yield the lowest monthly payment. You can do this if you do not change the down payment and the length of the loan from the dealer or credit union. In essence, you make all the terms of the two credit arrangements the same, except the monthly payment. Then take the deal that gives you the lowest monthly payment to buy the car.

For example, a major car maker once offered a choice of a $1,500 cash rebate or 5.8-percent financing for four years on certain models. Assume that the car you would like to buy costs $16,000. If you have $2,000 for a down payment, you have the following choices:

1. Finance through the dealer's finance company. A $2,000 down payment would leave $14,000 to be financed over four years at 5.8 percent. Monthly payments disclosed under the TILA would be $327.51.

2. Finance directly from a bank, credit union, or another credit grantor. With the $1,500 cash rebate from the dealer and your $2,000, you have $3,500 to apply to the purchase price of $16,000. This leaves $12,500 to borrow ($16,000 − $3,500 = $12,500). If you borrow $12,500 for four years at 11.17 percent, you will find from the TILA disclosures that your monthly payments would be $324.10. Take it.

### Q. Are there any other points to consider when using installment credit?

**A.** Yes, consider whether the interest that you pay for the credit is deductible when calculating your federal income taxes. Almost all homeowners may still deduct their entire mortgage interest for tax purposes. However, the interest that you pay on credit-card debt, student loans, auto loans, and other debts is no longer deductible.

If you itemize deductions in preparing your taxes, you might consider financing major credit purchases through a home equity loan. This type of loan is discussed on page 181 in the chapter on owning a home. However, remember that if you use a home equity loan, you are placing your home at risk. And if the items that you are permitted to deduct for tax purposes are less than your standard deduction, you will find that the interest on home equity credit will not help you cut your tax bill.

There is another factor to consider. What if you pay the loan off early? You need to check how the rebate of unearned finance charges will be calculated.

## CHOOSING A CREDIT CARD

### Q. Who provides revolving credit?

**A.** Revolving or open-end credit is becoming increasingly popular in this country, as more people have credit cards than ever before.

Discover, MasterCard, Optima and Visa are examples of the many credit cards issued by banks, savings and loans, and credit unions. In your shopping for a bank credit card, you need to recognize that credit cards with the Visa and MasterCard logos or marks are issued by thousands of different savings and loans and credit unions. Hence, if you do not like the terms on one Visa card, you can always check with other issuers to see if their terms are preferable. Major retailers issue their own credit cards, and oil companies also have their cards, although many of the oil companies do not offer revolving credit, only 30-day credit (except on purchases of tires, batteries and accessories).

### Q. How may I choose a credit card that is right for me?

**A.** Selecting a credit card is like selecting a suit or dress; you want a good "fit." Because there are many card issuers, you have a wide choice among cards. In this section, we will examine terms that are typically offered to consumers by banks and other issuers of credit cards. It is illegal for card issuers to send you a credit card unless you have asked for it or unless it replaces a card you previously asked for. Furthermore, under the TILA, every solicitation for a credit card must contain a brief disclosure statement. Disclosures more extensive in nature are due before the first time you use the credit card you have applied for, and specific disclosures about finance and other charges and transactions are required with your periodic statement (usually monthly). In this section we use examples from actual solicitations and explain how they might affect the "fit" of the card offered to your own credit needs.

### Q. How should I judge the APR shown in the solicitation?

**A.** The law requires credit grantors to quote the APR and to tell you the balance calculation method they use to figure the finance charge you pay. Since credit grantors use many different methods to compute that balance to which the APR is applied, credit grantors who quote identical APRs may charge you very different dollar finance charges each month. It depends on how you use the account and how they calculate the unpaid balance for assessing the charge.

### Q. How do credit grantors figure an account's balance?

**A.** The most common system used by card issuers is to apply the APR to the average daily balance in your account over the billing period. A typical offering of a credit card states:

**Method of Computing the Balances for Purchases**

Average Daily Balance (including new purchases)

Occasionally, retailers compute the balance by subtracting payments made or credits given during the billing period from the total amount you owe. They refer to this as the adjusted balance method. A few credit grantors do not subtract from the balance any payments made during the billing period. This previous balance method can cost you more than the other two methods; it depends on how you use your account. Other methods are also employed, but these three methods can be used to illustrate the differences.

As you can see from these examples, finance charges may vary greatly depending on how the credit grantor calculates them. In the first example, the average daily balance of $300 determines the amount of finance charge owed. The average daily balance is the average of the $500 owed for half a month and the $100 ($500 minus $400) owed for the other half. You owe the $500 and the $100 each for half a month because you paid the $400 in the middle of the month. In the adjusted balance method, which is used by rela-

| | Average Daily Balance | Adjusted Balance | Previous Balance |
|---|---|---|---|
| Monthly interest rate | 1.5% | 1.5% | 1.5% |
| Previous balance | $500 | $500 | $500 |
| Payment on 15th day | $400 | $400 | $400 |
| Finance charge | $4.50 | $1.50 | $7.50 |
| Calculation of finance charge | Average balance of $300 × 1.5% | $100 × 1.5% | $500 × 1.5% |

tively few creditors, you owe a finance charge only on the amount owed at the end of the period. Since you paid $400, and thus only owe $100, you pay a finance charge only on the $100. In the previous balance method, you owe a finance charge on the amount owed at the beginning of the pay period—the entire $500.

## Q. Can I avoid paying a finance charge?

**A.** Many credit cards offer a grace period for purchases, which is the time between the end of the billing cycle and the date that you must pay the entire bill to avoid paying a finance charge. It is usually between 20 and 25 days. The grace period is shown on the disclosure statement in the following manner:

> **Grace period for repayment of the balance for purchases**
>
> No finance charges are assessed on current purchases if the balance is paid in full each month within 25 days after billing.

Note that the full balance must be paid each month to avoid finance charges and that the grace period applies only to purchases. If you obtain a cash advance on your bank credit card, you will almost always pay finance charges from the date of the advance and probably a cash advance fee as well.

The credit grantor may adjust the grace period under another method of assessing monthly charges on your bill called the retroactive or two-cycle balance method. Under this system, if your opening balance on your bill

was zero, and then you made credit purchases, but did not pay your entire bill, your next monthly bill will include a finance charge for these purchases from the dates that they were posted to your account.

For example, assume that you used a credit card on an account with no outstanding balance to buy a $500 item that the credit grantor posted to your account on March 15. Say that the credit grantor bills you on April 1, and you must pay in full by April 20 to avoid a finance charge. However, assume further that you make a payment of only $200, which the credit grantor credits to your account on April 18. Then your next bill (say May 1) will include a finance charge composed of two parts. One portion of the finance charge will be for the use of $500 for the period from March 15 to March 31. The other charge will be for the period from April 1 through April 30. You must read the disclosure statement or cardholder agreement very carefully to determine whether the card issuer uses this retroactive method.

## Q. Does the APR on a credit card always stay the same?

**A.** Not if there is a variable-rate provision. More and more credit card issuers set APRs that vary with some interest-rate index, such as the market rates on three-year U.S. Treasury bills (T-bills) or the prime rate charged by banks on short-term business loans. These issuers must disclose in their solicitation to you that the rate may vary and how the rate is determined. This may be done by showing the index and the spread. The latter is the percentage points added to the index to determine the rate you will pay. An example of a disclosure on a variable-rate credit card offering is shown below:

**Variable Rate Information**

Your Annual Percentage Rate may vary quarterly. The rate will be the Prime Rate as published in The Wall Street Journal plus 9%. The rate will not go below 15.0% or exceed 19.9%.

## Q. *What other fees and charges should I look for on the disclosure statement?*

**A.** In your disclosure statement, you will find a statement something like the following (assuming these fees are part of the plan):

**Transaction fee for cash advances, and fees for paying late or exceeding the credit limit**

Transaction fee for Cash Advances: 2% of the amount of the advance ($1.00 minimum; $10 maximum).

Late payment fee: $15, if the amount due is $2 or more. Over-the-limit fee: $15.00.

(There may be other fees as well, such as replacement card fees, copy fees, wire transfer fees, and insufficient funds fees.)

Unless you expect to be late in your payments, your choice of a card should not be heavily influenced by the size of the late fee. An over-the-limit fee may be more troublesome. Most credit card issuers set a limit on the amount of credit that they are willing to provide you at any one time. To encourage you not to exceed this limit some banks may charge an over-the-limit fee. Unless you keep careful track of your charge slips, it is difficult for you to know how much you owe in relation to the credit limit. If you believe that you might be close to your credit limit from time to time, you might want to shop for a bank credit card

that does not have an over-the-limit fee, or a very low charge.

## Q. *Is there a charge each year for the right to use a credit card?*

**A.** Whereas few, if any, credit cards issued by retailers have annual fees, many credit cards issued by financial institutions have annual fees. These may range from $15 to $25, and perhaps $35 to $60 for "premium cards" that provide a higher line of credit. (And charge accounts, such as American Express or Diners Club, have annual fees that probably exceed annual fees charged for bank cards.) If you usually pay your credit card accounts in full each month and do not expect to pay a finance charge, you should shop for a credit card with no annual fee or one that is low. However, if you often don't pay the balance in full each month, then a low APR may be better for you than a low annual fee. A credit card solicitation must disclose any annual or other periodic fee, and certain other fees such as transaction, cash advance, and late fees if they are imposed.

## Q. *What if I can't get a credit card from a financial institution—either because of a bad credit record or because I have not established a credit record?*

**A.** You may want to consider applying for a secured credit card. This is a credit card issued by a bank or other financial institution that is secured by a savings account that you have deposited with the bank or other financial institution. Because this is a fairly new financial service, you need to shop carefully for the best terms. Generally, you should be able to avoid an application fee. In the past these have been quite high. Your line of credit will typically be limited to 90 percent to 100 percent of your savings account. In shopping for a secured card, compare the rates paid on savings accounts, the APR charged and the annual fees. The APR is

## CHOOSING A CREDIT CARD

*A credit card must fit your financial habits. If you often do not pay your account in full each month, you will pay more attention to the annual percentage rate (APR) than someone else who never pays a finance charge. That person will be more concerned with an annual fee that would be levied.*

*Just knowing the APR is not enough, since there are different ways of calculating the balances against which the APR is applied. If you don't think that your income will rise if interest rates go up, you might prefer a credit card with a fixed APR rather than one with a variable rate.*

*If you expect to use the credit card to obtain cash advances, the cash advance fee is important to consider. If you have a hard time keeping track of charges on your credit cards, a high over-the-limit fee may be worth avoiding. And, if late fees promise to be a major problem, perhaps you should not take on another credit card.*

important, since you are likely not to be repaying your account in full each month. Also important are the late fee and any over-limit fee. These are sometimes quite high on secured credit cards.

Having a secured card may be something like using training wheels on a bicycle. Once that you have shown you can handle a revolving credit account, you should ask the institution that has issued you the secured credit card to offer you the opportunity to switch to an unsecured card with more favorable terms. If the offer is not made, even after you have established a good credit record, apply for a regular credit card from another financial institution.

Evaluate carefully pitches for "guaranteed" credit cards or "gold" cards. You may see advertisements for such cards on television or in the print media, with the promise that credit is readily available by calling a 900-number. The call itself may cost $50 or more and get you nothing but a list of banks offering credit cards or a booklet on how to manage your credit. Other cards that you might be offered have limited use, since they apply only to purchases from a catalog issued by the promoter. Often, the merchandise is overpriced.

## PROTECTIONS FOR THE CONSUMER

**Q. How does the Truth in Lending Act affect me?**

**A.** The federal Truth in Lending Act (TILA) helps you to choose credit wisely by requiring credit grantors to give you plenty of information before you make a choice. However, the law alone cannot protect you fully. You have to make it work by being an informed consumer.

The TILA does not set finance charges, nor does it tell you what rates are fair or unfair—even if we knew what those terms mean. In many states, laws exist to prevent you from paying finance charges that are too high, but in most cases it is competition that serves to keep credit card rates in line, and they have been declining in recent years. But for competition to be effective in controlling rates, you must use the information provided by the TILA to select the credit card that best fits your needs.

### Q. How can I limit the amount of finance charges that I pay for credit?

**A.** Your shopping for credit plays a key role in limiting and minimizing the finance charges that you must pay. It does not matter whether you are looking for closed-end credit (installment credit) or open-end credit (revolving credit). And even though most states impose rate ceilings on various credit grantors or types of credit—for example, state law usually limits the rates that finance companies may charge—your shopping can still save you money.

In shopping for the best terms for you, check *The Wall Street Journal* and other newspapers that frequently publish shopping guides to credit cards from financial institutions that cover all of the relevant terms discussed above. You can also obtain such guides to regular and secured credit cards from RAM Research Corporation, Box 1700 (College Estates), Frederick, MD 21702. Call 1-800-344-7714 for information about consumer publications. Currently, a summary of about 500 low-priced Visas and MasterCards is available for five dollars. The Federal Reserve Board also gathers credit card rate terms for publication.

### Q. In shopping for a credit card, I found that one credit card issuer charges a higher rate than that allowed by my state law. How can that be?

**A.** Many states impose rate ceilings on retail or bank credit cards. However, these limits do not always apply across the board. For example, under federal law national banks may "export" their finance charge rates on credit cards. (State-chartered, federally insured institutions generally have the same exportation rights.) Thus, a national bank may issue cards from an office in South Dakota, a state that has no rate ceiling on bank cards, so the bank may charge cardholders in Iowa any rate the agreement specifies. While most retailers selling to Iowa consumers may not charge rates on their credit cards higher than Iowa law permits, some major retailers have established credit card banks and issue cards from those banks. In those instances, they abide by the laws of the state in which the bank is located. In real life, competition forces national banks and retailers to keep their rates in line with those charged by state-chartered banks, other financial institutions, and retailers. In this example the pressures of the marketplace—the choices made by informed consumers—set the rates. The law does not set them.

Nonetheless, if you believe that the rate being charged violates state law, you should report the case to the office of consumer protection (or similar office) or your state's attorney general. Competition and enforcement activities usually prevent such violations, but if there is a violation, you may be able to recover all of your finance charges plus a penalty, depending upon your state's law.

### Q. What if a credit grantor fails to obey the TILA?

**A.** You should inform the proper federal enforcement agency, as listed in the back of this chapter. Violations include failing to disclose timely information as required under the Truth in Lending Act or giving you inaccurate information. To enforce your rights, you may bring a lawsuit for actual damages (any money loss you suffer). You may also sue for the greater of twice the finance charge or $100. However, the most you can recover, even if the finance charge is high, is $1,000. If you win the

# Protect Your Credit Cards and Know Your Rights

(1) Sign new credit cards as soon as they arrive. Cut up and throw away expired credit cards. Destroy all unused pre-approved credit applications.

(2) In a safe place, keep a list of your credit-card numbers, expiration dates, and the toll-free phone number of each card issuer to report missing or stolen credit cards and possible billing errors (see pages 260–263).

(3) Don't lay your credit card down on a counter or table. Hand it directly to the clerk or waiter. Keep an eye on your card after you give it to a clerk. Make sure that he or she imprints only one charge slip and, if he or she makes an error and has to imprint a second charge slip, tears up the first one. Take back your card back promptly after the clerk is finished with it, and make sure that it is yours. Tear up the carbons when you take your credit-card receipt.

(4) Never leave your credit card or car rental agreement in the glove compartment of a car or the credit card in an unlocked desk drawer, grocery cart or hotel room.

(5) Never sign a blank credit-card receipt. Draw a line through any blank spaces above the total when you sign receipts.

(6) Open credit-card bills promptly, and compare them with your receipts to check for unauthorized charges and billing errors. If your monthly statement doesn't arrive on time, call the issuer immediately.

(7) Write the card issuer promptly to report any questionable charges. Written inquiries should not be included with your payment. Instead, check the billing statement for the correct address for billing questions. The inquiry must be in writing, and it must be sent within 60 days of the statement date to guarantee your rights under the federal Fair Credit Billing Act.

(8) Never give your credit-card or checking-account number over the telephone unless you make the call. Never put your credit-card number on a postcard or on the outside of an envelope.

(9) If any of your credit cards is missing or stolen, report the loss as soon as possible to the card issuer. Follow up your phone calls with a letter to each card issuer. Send each letter by certified mail and keep a copy. The letter should contain your credit-card number, the date the card was missing and the date you called in to report the loss.

(10) If you report the loss before a credit card is used, the issuer cannot hold you responsible for any subsequent unauthorized charges under federal law. If a thief uses your card before you report it missing, the most that you will owe for unauthorized charges on each card is $50, though if you lose a number of cards you could be out hundreds of dollars.

(11) Federal law requires that creditors who allow a grace period to pay your monthly bill get the bill to you so you have two weeks to pay before the grace period ends.

(12) Federal law requires a creditor to post your payment promptly; to credit overpayments or other credits to your account and refund the money to you on request or after six months; to promptly notify card issuers of returns and card issuers to promptly credit returns; and prohibits a credit card issuer from setting off your credit card debt against your checking account or savings account without your consent.

lawsuit, the law also entitles you to court costs and attorney's fees.

## PROTECTIONS FOR CONSUMERS WHO LEASE PRODUCTS

**Q. What is the Consumer Leasing Act?**

**A.** The Federal Consumer Leasing Act applies to any lease of consumer goods for more than four months. (It does not apply to leases of real estate.) This law requires the lessor (the owner of the auto you lease, for example) to disclose information before you sign the lease. Among the most important items are:

- total amount of any initial payment you are required to pay;
- number and amounts of monthly payments;
- total amount for fees, such as license fees and taxes;
- any penalty for default or late payments;
- the annual mileage allowance and the extra charges involved if you exceed that allowance;
- whether you can end the lease early, and the extra charge required;
- whether you can purchase the auto at the end of the lease and for what price;
- any liability that you may have for the difference between the estimated value of the auto and its market value at the time you end the lease;
- any extra payment that you must make at the end of the lease.

You have the same rights to sue for violation that you have under the TILA. You can report apparent violations of the Consumer Leasing Act to the same agencies that enforce the TILA (see page 272).

## HOW TO APPLY FOR CREDIT

### Equal Credit Opportunity Act

**Q. When I apply for credit, are there factors that credit grantors must consider in a fair manner?**

**A.** The federal Equal Credit Opportunity Act (ECOA) says that credit grantors may not use certain factors to discriminate against you in a credit deal. A credit grantor may not use age (providing that you are old enough to enter into a legally binding contract), race, color, national origin, sex, marital status, religion, receipt of public aid, or the exercise of rights under the Consumer Credit Protection Act, TILA, and related federal law to:

- discourage or prevent you from applying for credit;
- refuse you credit if you otherwise qualify;
- extend you credit on terms different from those granted someone with similar risk (as determined by such factors as ability to repay, credit history, stability and assets); or
- give you less credit than you asked for, if someone with similar risk would have received that amount or more. The Equal Credit Opportunity Act does not, however, guarantee that you will receive credit. You still must meet the credit grantor's standards of whether you are worthy of receiving credit.

### Age Discrimination

**Q. When I apply for credit, may a credit grantor ask my age?**

**A.** Yes, but if you are old enough to sign and be liable for a contract (usually 18 to 21, depending on state law), a credit grantor may not:

# Determining Creditworthiness

Credit grantors may use any of the following factors to decide whether to extend credit to you. However, if your credit history is bad, they usually will not give you credit or else will charge you a high finance charge for the risk they will accept.

| Factor | Explanation |
|---|---|
| Ability to repay | This depends on the stability of your current job or income source, how much you earn, and the length of time you have worked or will receive that income. Credit grantors also may consider your basic expenses, such as payments on rent, mortgage loans or other debts, utilities, college expenses, and taxes. |
| Credit history | This shows how much money you owe and whether you have large, unused lines of open-end credit. A very important consideration is whether you have paid your bills on time and whether you have filed for bankruptcy within the past ten years or had judgments issued against you. |
| Stability | Your stability is indicated by how long you have lived at your current or former address and the length of time you have been with your current or former employer. Another consideration is whether you own your home or rent. |
| Assets | Assets such as a car or home may be useful as collateral for a loan. Credit grantors also look at what else you may use for collateral, such as savings accounts or securities. |

- refuse to give you credit or decrease the amount of credit just because of your age;
- refuse to consider your retirement income in rating your credit application if the creditor considers income in evaluating creditworthiness;
- cancel your credit account or require you to reapply for credit just because you are a certain age or have retired;
- refuse you credit or cancel your account because you cannot get credit life (or related) insurance due to your age.

The law does allow a credit grantor to consider certain age-related facts. These include how long your income will continue or how long it will be until you reach retirement age. Consider, for example, a loan that will take a long time to pay back. If an older applicant does not provide adequate security, he or she may not be a good credit risk.

## Public Assistance

**Q. May a credit grantor deny credit if I receive public assistance?**

**A.** Not if you receive Social Security or public assistance payments such as Aid to Families with Dependent Children. Then a credit grantor may not deny you credit for that reason alone. However, credit grantors may ask the age of your dependents, since you may lose federal benefits when they reach a certain age. A credit grantor also may consider whether you will con-

## PROTECTING YOUR RIGHT TO CREDIT

*The Equal Credit Opportunity Act offers equal opportunity to obtain credit, but does not assure you of credit—only the opportunity to obtain it. Essentially, the law requires that credit grantors may not treat an applicant less favorably than other equally creditworthy applicants on the basis of age (as long as you're old enough to make a legally binding contract), race, color, sex, national origin, marital status, religion, receipt of income from a public assistance program, or exercise of rights under federal consumer protection laws. Some state laws may be even more protective; for example, they may preclude discrimination because a couple has children.*

you are married, single, widowed, divorced, or separated. Specific prohibitions include:

- a credit grantor usually may not ask your gender when you apply for credit (one exception would be a loan to buy or build a home, or to repair, rehabilitate, or remodel a home, when asking your gender helps the federal government look for housing discrimination by determining whether equally qualified females and males are able to obtain residential mortgage loans; however, you may refuse to answer this question);

- you normally do not have to use a gender title (Mr., Miss, Mrs., or Ms.) when applying for credit; sometimes credit grantors may ask whether you are married, unmarried, or separated if your marital status relates to their right to obtain repayment; such a request would most likely be made in a state with community property laws or if the credit will be secured;

- a credit grantor may not ask women if they use birth control or whether they plan to have children; and

- you do not have to reveal child support or alimony payments to a credit grantor unless you wish the credit grantor to consider it as income.

tinue to meet residency requirements for receiving benefits and whether the creditor can reach the benefits by legal process if you do not pay.

### Discrimination Against Women

**Q. Does my gender or marital status affect whether I am worthy of credit?**

**A.** No, the law protects both men and women from discrimination based on gender and marital status. In general, a credit grantor may not deny you credit or take any adverse action, such as lowering your credit limits or raising your APR, just because of your gender or because

### Marital Status and Separate Credit Accounts

**Q. May married people open credit accounts that are not also in their spouses' names?**

**A.** Yes, you may open credit accounts or take out loans in your own name and do not have to open joint accounts or take out loans with your spouse. Moreover, if you have a joint account with your spouse, when a creditor sends a credit bureau information about your account, it must report the information in both your names. The credit bureau will also maintain a separate file on you and may rely only on your credit history when making a credit decision.

A credit grantor may not:

- refuse to open a separate credit account just because of your gender or marital status;
- require your spouse to cosign your account, unless you live in a community property state where spouses are liable for each other's debts; or
- ask about your spouse or ex-spouse when you apply for credit based on your own income. However, a credit grantor may seek this information if a community property state is involved or if you are relying in part on your income from alimony, child support, or maintenance payments from your ex-spouse for the purpose of obtaining credit.

## Change in Marital Status

**Q. If my marital status changes, may a credit grantor force me to reapply for credit?**

**A.** No, a credit grantor may not require you to reapply for credit just because you marry or divorce, or your spouse has died.

A credit grantor also may not close your account or change its terms for these reasons alone. There must be a change in how worthy of credit you are, such as a decrease in your income. For example, if your spouse dies or you get a divorce, and you had used your spouse's income to get credit, a credit grantor may have you reapply. The credit grantor must allow you to use the account while considering your new application.

## Denial of a Credit Application

**Q. What happens if a credit grantor denies credit to me?**

**A.** Under the Equal Credit Opportunity Act, a credit grantor must notify you whether it has approved or denied your credit application within thirty days after you have completed your credit application. If the credit grantor denies credit to you, the notice must be written and list the reasons for denying credit or tell you how to request an explanation. Another law, the Fair Credit Reporting Act, affects credit denials, as well. It requires that the notice tell you if the credit grantor used a credit report to deny you credit and, if so, the name and address of the credit bureau that provided the report. These rights also apply if a credit grantor takes any adverse action, such as closing an existing credit account or reducing an open line of credit.

**Q. What may I do if a credit grantor will not say why it has taken an adverse action against me?**

**A.** First, ask the credit grantor to supply a written explanation as required by law. If you think the credit grantor has discriminated against you, tell the credit grantor why you think this, then try to resolve the issue through negotiation. If the credit grantor continues the adverse action and has not given a satisfactory explanation, you may sue (see below) or complain to the appropriate federal enforcement agency (see the end of this chapter).

**Q. Can I sue if a credit grantor has discriminated against me?**

**A.** Under the Equal Credit Opportunity Act, you may sue for actual damages (the actual losses you suffered), plus punitive damages of up to $10,000. The amount of punitive damages awarded depends on whether the credit grantor should have known it was violating the law and other factors like the number of violations. Punitive damages penalize the credit grantor because it has violated the law.

## CREDIT INSURANCE

### Q. What is credit insurance?

**A.** There are many different types of credit insurance. Credit life insurance will pay off the balance owed should you die. Credit accident and health insurance will make the monthly payments on the covered debt for the period of time that you cannot work as a result of an accident or illness. The coverage may not become available until after you have been disabled for four or more days. Occasionally, you may be offered unemployment insurance, which would provide for payments on the covered debt during the period that you become unemployed. (Again, there may be a waiting period.)

### Q. What requirements must creditors follow when they offer credit insurance?

**A.** There are certain basic requirements that creditors must observe in offering you any of these forms of credit insurance:

- whether or not you accept the insurance will normally not be a factor in the approval of your loan, and that fact should be disclosed to you in writing; however, if the credit insurance is required, the premiums for the insurance must be included in the annual percentage rate (APR) that is disclosed to you;
- the cost of any credit insurance offered must be disclosed to you in writing;
- you must give affirmative, written indication of your desire to have such insurance. Usually this means that you must check the "yes" box on the loan form and sign that you want the insurance.

### Q. Do I have to have credit insurance?

**A.** No. If possible, you should decide ahead of time whether or not you want credit insur-

ance. Once you are at the point of sale, you may be pressured to accept it, just as you may be pressured to buy a more expensive TV set or more options on a car. Buying a car can be pretty exciting, but be sure that your decision prevails when it comes to the credit insurance. Tell the salesperson whether or not you want the insurance. If you are told to "sign here, here and here," be sure to study the loan agreement to see that your wishes on credit insurance have been observed. When you are at the final closing, check again. If you have made arrangements over the phone for a loan, and specified "no credit insurance," check the loan document when you are at the lender's office to get the loan. If you had stated that you did not want credit insurance but find that it is provided on the loan agreement, don't sign it, even if the lender moans that the form will have to be completely redone.

### Q. Is credit insurance a good idea?

**A.** Whether or not you should buy any credit insurance is a personal decision. Surveys of consumers who have purchased credit insurance indicate that they have done so because they did not have much other life insurance and did not wish to leave their family with the obligation to pay off the debt. The cost per $100 of credit insurance is definitely higher than the cost per $100 of a term life insurance policy. However, if the credit life insurance covers a $5,000 auto loan, the comparison is not very meaningful, since most consumers cannot buy $5,000 term life policies. The minimum amount purchasable is usually $50,000 or $100,000, depending on the insurer. Thus, you should expect to pay more per $100 of coverage for credit life insurance than for a $50,000 term life insurance policy—just as you expect to pay more per ounce for a glass of milk in a restaurant than for a gallon of milk at the supermarket.

# CREDIT RECORDS

## How to Establish a Credit Record

**Q. How can I get credit if I never previously had it?**

**A.** First-time borrowers soon realize that in order to get credit they must have a credit history. There are several ways to start building a good, solid credit history. For example, you may:

- open a checking or savings account; when credit grantors see such accounts they can judge whether you have adequate money and know how to manage it;

- apply for limited credit from a large, local department store and use it (If you want to build a credit history, remember that some small local retailers, travel-and-entertainment cards, credit unions, and gasoline card companies do not report your credit performance to a credit bureau);

- obtain a secured credit card (discussed earlier in this chapter on page 246); or, deposit money in a bank, savings and loan association, or savings bank and then borrow against it;

- have someone co-sign the loan with you; that person must have a favorable credit record and will be liable for the debt if you cannot pay. With your first loan based on someone else's credit, it will be easier to get credit on your own after you pay back the loan. If you are asked to co-sign for another person's loan, be very careful; if that person fails to pay, the debt will be your responsibility.

**Q. Should I get credit in my own name, even though I am married?**

**A.** Yes, if you have your own sources of income, you should establish a credit history in your own name in case you become divorced or your spouse dies. This is also especially important if your spouse has a poor credit record and you do not want your credit records tarnished with his or her payment performance. However, many divorced or widowed persons do not have credit histories separate from their former spouses. In these cases, credit grantors must look at the credit history of any accounts held jointly with the former spouses. The non-earning spouse may be able to obtain credit by showing with checks, receipts, or other records that he or she is worthy of credit. If their former spouses had poor credit records, non-earning spouses may show that the records do not reflect whether they deserve credit by producing previous explanatory letters sent to credit grantors, copies of contracts signed only by the spouse, receipts, or other evidence.

**Q. What is a credit bureau?**

**A.** Credit bureaus (sometimes called credit reporting agencies or consumer reporting agencies) maintain computer files of your financial payment histories, public record data, and personal identifying data. Your credit record does not contain information on your medical history. There are three competing major credit reporting systems: TRW Information Services, Equifax Credit Information Services, and Trans Union Credit Information Company. You can find the bureaus serving your area by looking for credit reporting companies in the yellow pages of your phone book. Activities of credit bureaus are governed by a federal law: the Fair Credit Reporting Act (FCRA).

Credit bureaus do not make credit decisions. Instead, they provide data to credit grantors for use in making credit decisions. How does this work? Credit grantors provide information on their customers' debts and payment habits to credit bureaus, usually on a monthly basis. The data are stored on computer and then made available, sometimes on an "on-line" basis, to other credit grantors to whom you apply for credit. For this reason, a good credit record is very important to your ability to obtain credit to purchase goods and services, to rent an apartment or to buy a home. Credit reports may also be used when you apply for insurance or for employment. The law punishes unauthorized persons who lie to obtain a credit report, or credit bureau employees who supply a credit report to unauthorized persons. These people may receive fines of up to five thousand dollars or prison terms for one year, or both, if they are proven guilty. In addition, they may face civil liability as well, in the form of money damages a court may impose on them.

Since your credit record is critical to your obtaining credit it is very important that you assist the credit bureaus in assuring that each item in your credit record really reflects your credit history and not that of another person. Whenever you apply for credit you should use the same name. Thus, if you are James R. Jones, Jr., always append the "Jr.," and do not sometimes use J. Randall Jones and other times use J.R. Jones. Finally, you will typically be asked for your social security number on a credit application. If so, provide it. The request is not to invade in your privacy but to assure that your credit records do not get mixed in with those of some other James Jones.

## How to Check Your Credit Record

### Q. May I look at my credit record?

**A.** Yes, you have the right to know the content of credit files that contain information on you, and many consumer credit experts suggest that you examine these credit files about once a year. A periodic checkup will enable you to find out what the credit bureaus will report to those businesses with a legitimate reason to check your credit record. Whenever you ask to learn

of the contents of your file, you should be sure to provide adequate identification to the credit bureau so you will receive your report and not that of someone with a similar name.

The FCRA allows you to review your file at any time, and it is particularly important for you to do so if you plan to apply to rent an apartment or apply for a job or a home mortgage loan or other major loan or credit purchase. The credit bureau is permitted to charge you a reasonable fee for providing this service unless your inquiry is after adverse credit action is taken against you. Currently, credit bureaus that are members of the industry's trade association, Associated Credit Bureaus (ACB), charge no more than eight dollars for an individual report or sixteen dollars for a joint report. Some members offer consumers one free report each year upon request.

As noted earlier, a creditor may turn you down or take other adverse credit action because of a report from a credit bureau. If so, the law requires that the credit grantor give you the bureau's name and address. You are allowed to request information about the data from the credit bureau by phone, mail, or in person. If a credit grantor has denied you credit within the past thirty days because of data supplied by a credit bureau, the bureau may not charge you for the information. As a matter of practice ACB members will provide a free report within sixty days from the date your credit application was declined. Although federal law requires only that the credit reporting agency disclose the "nature and substance" of the report, most credit bureaus disclose all of the information in the report, although in a more "consumer friendly" form than the computerized report used by credit grantors.

The FCRA requires the credit bureau to tell you the names of the creditors who provided the data and the name of everyone who has received a report on you in the last six months (or within the past two years for employment reports). The credit bureau also must help you interpret the data.

## Q. What does a credit report look like?

**A.** A sample composite report is shown on page 258. This is the basic format used by members of the ACB and comes from a publication, *Building a Better Credit Record*, produced by the Federal Trade Commission in cooperation with ACB, the National Foundation for Consumer Credit and the U.S. Office of Consumer Affairs. Observe the major types of information:

- Identification and employment data: Your name, birthdate, addresses (present and former), employment history, home ownership, income, and similar data for your spouse, since this is a joint report.

- Payment history: Your account record with different credit grantors, showing how much credit has been extended and how you have repaid it. The first column, labeled "Whose," shows whether the debt listed is joint "2," while the "1" indicates that the person named has sole responsibility for the debt. The revolving credit card account with Big City Department Store is labeled "3," since one person is responsible for payment, but both spouses may use it. Note that they are thirty to fifty-nine days past due on their Super Credit Card.

- Inquiries: While none are shown on this credit report, credit bureaus maintain a record of all credit grantors who have checked your credit record within the past six months. Credit bureaus typically do not include credit prescreening inquiries in credit reports, but will provide them to consumers as a part of disclosure. Prescreening occurs when, for example, issuers of credit cards develop mailing lists to make pre-approved offers of their credit cards.

- Public record information: Events that are a matter of public information related to your creditworthiness, such as bankruptcies, foreclosures, or tax liens, will appear in your credit report. In this instance, you will note at the bottom a record of a dispute between the consumer and an appliance dealer that was settled in a small claims court. To set the record straight, the consumer has exercised the right in the FCRA to have the dispute reinvestigated and the report corrected, or, if there is still a dispute, to provide an explanation of his or her side of the dispute.

## Q. What does the law allow me to do if the credit bureau will not cooperate?

**A.** Under the Fair Credit Reporting Act, you may bring a lawsuit against any credit bureau or credit grantor who violates any provisions of the Act. This includes any credit reporting agency that fails to observe the restrictions about who may access your credit file and any credit bureau that does not properly reinvestigate and correct inaccurate data in your file that you have disputed. However, if the agency has followed reasonable procedures, it has obeyed the law. If you win the lawsuit, you deserve to receive actual damages (which might be lost wages for a job you did not get), as well as punitive damages if you prove the violation was intentional. If you are successful, you also will receive court costs and a reasonable amount for attorney's fees.

### How to Maintain a Good Credit Record

## Q. What may I do if I believe the credit bureau has incorrect information in my file?

**A.** If you find that information in the credit report is inaccurate, incomplete, or outdated, you may challenge its accuracy or completeness by notifying the credit bureau. Toll-free numbers are available: TRW (800-682-7654) and

| FOR | FIRST NATIONAL BANK ANYTOWN, ANYSTATE 12345 | | **Date Received** 5/11/89 | **CONFIDENTIAL** crediscope® REPORT |
|---|---|---|---|---|
| | | | **Date Mailed** 5/11/89 | |
| | | | **In File Since** APRIL 1970 | Member Associated Credit Bureaus, Inc. |
| | | | **Inquired As:** JOINT ACCOUNT | |

| REPORT ON: LAST NAME | FIRST NAME | INITIAL | SOCIAL SECURITY NUMBER | SPOUSE'S NAME |
|---|---|---|---|---|
| CONSUMER | ROBERT | G. | 123-45-6789 | BETTY R. |

| ADDRESS: CITY | STATE: | ZIP CODE | SINCE: | SPOUSE'S SOCIAL SECURITY NO. |
|---|---|---|---|---|
| 123 ANY ST. ANYTOWN | ANYSTATE | 12345 | 1973 | 987-65-4321 |

COMPLETE TO HERE FOR TRADE REPORT AND SKIP TO CREDIT HISTORY

| PRESENT EMPLOYER: | POSITION HELD: | SINCE: | DATE EMPLOY VERIFIED | EST. MONTHLY INCOME |
|---|---|---|---|---|
| XYZ CORPORATION | ASST. DEPT. MGR. | 10/81 | 12/81 | $ 2500 |

COMPLETE TO HERE FOR EMPLOYMENT AND TRADE REPORT AND SKIP TO CREDIT HISTORY

| DATE OF BIRTH | NUMBER OF DEPENDENTS INCLUDING SELF: 4 | [X] OWNS OR BUYING HOME | [ ] RENTS HOME | OTHER: (EXPLAIN) [ ] |
|---|---|---|---|---|
| 5/25/50 | | | | |

| FORMER ADDRESS: | CITY: | STATE: | FROM: | TO: |
|---|---|---|---|---|
| 4321 FIRST AVE. | ANYTOWN | ANYSTATE | 1970 | 1973 |

| FORMER EMPLOYER: | POSITION HELD: | FROM: | TO: | EST. MONTHLY INCOME |
|---|---|---|---|---|
| ABC & ASSOCIATES | SALES PERSON | 2/80 | 9/81 | $1285 |

| SPOUSE'S EMPLOYER: | POSITION HELD: | SINCE: | DATE EMPLOY VERIFIED | EST. MONTHLY INCOME |
|---|---|---|---|---|
| BIG CITY DEPT. STORE | CASHIER | 4/81 | 12/81 | $1200 |

CREDIT HISTORY (Complete this section for all reports)

| WHOSE | KIND OF BUSINESS AND ID CODE | DATE REPORTED AND METHOD OF REPORTING | DATE OPENED | DATE OF LAST PAYMENT | HIGHEST CREDIT OR LAST CONTRACT | PRESENT STATUS BALANCE OWING | PAST DUE AMOUNT | NO. OF PAYMENTS | NO. MONTHS HISTORY REVIEWED | 30-60 DAYS ONLY | 60-90 DAYS ONLY | 90 DAYS AND OVER | TYPE & TERMS (MANNER OF PAYMENT) | REMARKS |
|---|---|---|---|---|---|---|---|---|---|---|---|---|---|---|
| 2 | CONSUMER'S BANK B 12-345 AUTOMTD | 2/6/89 12/88 | 1/89 | 1200 | 1100 | | -0- | -0- | 2 | -0- | -0- | -0- | INSTALLMENT | $100/MO. |
| 3 | BIG CITY DEPARTMENT STORE D 54-321 MANUAL | 2/10/89 4/81 | 1/89 | 300 | 100 | | -0- | -0- | 12 | -0- | -0- | -0- | RELVOLVING | $ 25/MO. |
| 1 | SUPER CREDIT CARD N 01-234 AUTOMTD | 12/12/88 7/82 | 11/85 | 200 | 100 | | 100 | 1 | 12 | 1 | -0- | -0- | OPEN 30-DAY | |

PUBLIC RECORD: SMALL CLAIMS CT. CASE #SC1001 PLAINTIFF: ANYWHERE APPLIANCES AMOUNT $225 PAID 4/4/82

ADDITIONAL INFORMATION: REF. SMALL CLAIMS CT. CASE #SC1001--5/30/82 SUBJECT SAYS CLAIM PAID UNDER PROTEST. APPLIANCE DID NOT OPERATE PROPERLY.

## UNDERSTANDING YOUR CREDIT REPORT

*Contrary to popular belief, a credit bureau neither tracks all aspects of your personal life nor explicitly evaluates credit applications, though the "risk score" summary that credit grantors can ask for does suggest the probability of bankruptcy or serious delinquency in the future. Credit bureaus are simply organizations that collect and transmit four principal types of information: identification and employment data; payment histories; credit-related inquiries; and public record information.*

*A good credit report is vital to your access to credit. Therefore, it is important for you to understand and find out what your credit report contains, how to improve your credit report and how to deal with credit problems.*

Equifax (800-685-1111). Unless it believes that your request is "frivolous or irrelevant," the credit bureau must either verify the facts within a reasonable period of time or delete the information from its files. The "frivolous-or-irrelevant" provision is there in part to deal with some credit repair clinics (see below), who challenge all negative information, whether there is a basis for the challenge or not. As a matter of practice, ACB bureaus reinvestigate the complaint within thirty days. If your complaint is justified, the credit bureau will auto-matically notify the other bureaus of the change and, if you request it, notify any creditor that has checked your file in the past six months (two years for employment reports).

If reinvestigation of disputed information by a credit bureau does not resolve the matter, you may file your version of the story in a statement of up to one hundred words. The credit bureau must include your statement, or a clear and accurate summary of it, in all future credit reports containing the disputed item. You also may ask the credit bureau to mail copies of your statement to anyone who received a report containing the disputed item during the last six months. This time period is two years for employment reports.

### Q. How does the passage of time affect my credit report?

**A.** Under the FCRA most negative information (such as late payments, accounts charged off) may be maintained on your credit record for only seven years, unless the information is used when you apply for $50,000 or more in credit, for a life insurance policy with a face amount of $50,000 or more, or for a job paying at least $20,000 a year. Records of bankruptcies may be reported for ten years. The fact that negative information remains on your credit report for such a long time emphasizes the importance of maintaining a good credit record.

### Q. What is the story behind companies that advertise their abilities to repair faulty credit histories? They sound too good to be true.

**A.** These "credit repair clinics" can help you review and update your credit record and report. However, their fees could be as high as one thousand dollars, and you can deal directly with a credit bureau on your own. If your credit report has an error, you may correct it yourself for free or at very little cost. If the information in your credit report is accurate, only better management of your debts can offset the negative record and only the passage of time can remove it. Be very suspicious and careful if a credit repair clinic promises that it can remove accurate records of bankruptcy and bad debts from your credit record or if it promises to get you credit. In general, if a credit program sounds too good to be true, it probably is.

## HOW TO CORRECT CREDIT MISTAKES

### Billing Errors

**Q. Why should I keep a sales receipt when I buy an item on credit?**

**A.** One reason is so that you may return the item in case it is defective or damaged or the wrong size or color. Another reason to keep sales slips is to correct billing errors. Most creditors do not provide a sales slip with the monthly statement. Under this billing procedure, the statement usually gives only the date and amount of purchase and the store and department from which you bought the item. Therefore, you need to keep all sales slips, at least until you have checked them against the monthly billing statements.

**Q. Will my credit rating suffer if my bill contains an obvious error?**

**A.** Yes, if you don't bring the error to the attention of the creditor. The Fair Credit Billing Act requires credit grantors to correct errors promptly without damaging your credit record.

**Q. What exactly is a billing error?**

**A.** The law defines a billing error as a charge:
- for something that you didn't buy, or for a purchase made by someone not authorized to use your account;

---

**CREDITORS MAKE MISTAKES TOO**

*After you have established credit, the best way to remain in good standing is to repay your debts on time. However, what happens if the credit grantor makes an error on your bill? What if you are billed for an item that you did not buy or for a product that you returned as defective? If you just don't pay the bill, the creditor will hurt your credit record by reporting it as delinquent to the credit bureau. This section discusses what to do to correct creditors' mistakes.*

- that is not properly identified on your monthly statement, or that is for an amount different from the actual purchase price; or
- for something that you refused to accept on delivery because it was unsatisfactory or that the supplier did not deliver according to your agreement.

Billing errors also may include:
- errors in arithmetic;
- failure to reflect a payment that you made or other credit to your account;
- failure to mail the billing statement to your current address (if the credit grantor received notice of that address at least twenty days before the end of the billing period);
- extension of credit about which you request additional clarification.

## Q. *What should I do if my bill seems wrong?*

**A.** If you think your bill is incorrect, or if you simply want more details about it, take the following steps:

1. Technically, you should notify your creditor of the potential billing error in writing in order to preserve your legal rights. However, most creditors readily handle billing complaints over the phone, and it is a lot faster and easier than writing a letter. Be prepared to provide your name, address, account number and description of the error. If you aren't satisfied with the results of your phone call, note the name of the person that you talked to and send a letter to the address your credit grantor has supplied for this purpose so that it receives the notice within sixty days after it mailed the bill. If you don't do this, you may lose your rights under the Fair Credit Billing Act. The sixty-day period is very important.

2. The letter should contain your name, address, and account number. State that you believe your bill contains an error, specify the error and why you believe it is wrong, and include the date and the suspected amount of the error.

## Q. *What happens after I notify the credit grantor about the possible billing error?*

**A.** The law requires the credit grantor to acknowledge your letter within thirty days. (This does not apply if the credit grantor can fix the billing error in less time.) The credit grantor must correct your account within two billing periods. It should never take longer than ninety days from the time the credit grantor receives notice of your dispute. If the credit grantor does not correct the error, it must tell you why it believes the bill is not wrong.

If the credit grantor does not find an error, it must promptly send you a statement showing what you owe. The credit grantor may include any finance charges that accumulated and any minimum payments you missed while questioning the bill.

## Q. *Must I pay finance charges on the contested amount?*

**A.** There are two possible outcomes. If the bill is not correct, you do not have to pay the finance charges on the amount in dispute or the amount that was improperly billed to your account. If you have already paid these amounts, the credit grantor should refund them. If the bill is correct, you must pay the amounts owed, including finance charges.

## Q. *While I am trying to solve a billing problem, may a credit grantor threaten my credit rating?*

**A.** Not because you fail to pay the disputed amount or related finance or other charges while you're trying to resolve a billing dispute. Once you have taken the steps described above by writing down your question and sending it to the credit grantor, the law prohibits your credit grantor from reporting the account as delinquent because of the disputed amount or related finance or other charges. Until the credit grantor answers your complaint, the law forbids it from taking any action to collect the amount in dispute. You must, however, continue paying any undisputed amounts.

## Q. *What happens after the credit grantor has explained that my bill is correct?*

**A.** Then the credit grantor may take action to collect if you do not pay and may report you to the credit bureau as overdue on the amount in question.

### Q. What if you still disagree with the credit grantor?

**A.** Notify the credit grantor of your views in writing. Then, the credit grantor must report to the credit bureau that you have challenged the bill and give you written notice of the name and address of each person who has received information about your account after the dispute arose. When you settle the dispute, the credit grantor must report the outcome to each person who has received information about your account.

### Q. What happens if the credit grantor does not follow all the rules within the proper time limits?

**A.** The law does not permit the credit grantor to collect the disputed amount or related finance charges up to $50. This is true even if it is money you truly owed. In addition, the creditor is subject to remedies available for violating federal law.

## Defective Goods or Services

### Q. May the law help me if I bought a product on credit that is defective or not provided, or if there is a billing error or if the merchant has breached a contract with me?

**A.** Yes, if you use a store credit card to purchase shoddy or damaged goods or poor quality services, the Fair Credit Billing Act may help. If you have not already paid off the balance, it allows you to withhold payment that is still due for the disputed transaction when you first notify the card issuer or merchant of your claim or defense, as long as you have made a real attempt to solve the problem with the merchant. A "real attempt" could be demonstrated by a letter or by notes on a phone call to the complaint department of the retailer—a note on the date of the call and the name of the person with whom you spoke.

You have this right even if you bought the goods or services with a bank card such as Visa or MasterCard, or a travel or entertainment card. Thus, if you purchase a tour or an air travel ticket using your bank credit card, you may be in a good position to recover the cost from the bank that provided the credit for your purchase if the tour or airline goes bankrupt. However, when you use your bank credit card, the law limits your right to withhold the payment to purchases totaling more than $50 that took place in your home state or within one hundred miles of your home address. These restrictions do not apply to store credit cards.

If you refuse to pay because the goods or services were defective, the creditor might sue you for payment. If the court finds the goods or services to be truly defective, you probably won't have to pay. Also, during the dispute period, the card issuer cannot report the amount as delinquent to a credit bureau.

## Lost or Stolen Credit Cards

### Q. Am I liable for all the bills that may arise if I lose my credit card or someone steals it?

**A.** No, the Truth in Lending Act (TILA) limits your liability on lost or stolen credit cards. However, it is very important that you notify the credit-card company as soon as you notice the loss or theft of your card or cards. You do not have to pay any unauthorized charge made after you notify the company of the loss or theft of the card. Under the TILA, the most you will have to pay for any unauthorized charges made before that time is $50 on each card.

### Q. How should I prepare for the possibility of losing a credit card or having it stolen?

**A.** As noted in the earlier section on credit cards, it is a good idea to keep a list of all your credit cards showing their account numbers and how to notify the credit-card issuers of theft or loss. Since you may lose credit cards when traveling, always take a copy of the list with you and keep it separate from your credit cards. And be sure to keep the list itself in a safe place, since someone with the numbers may be able to make purchases on your account.

## HOW MUCH DEBT CAN YOU HANDLE?

**Q. What are the costs to me or my family of becoming over-indebted?**

**A.** First, as we have learned from the section on credit reports, your creditors will report your delinquencies to the credit bureaus. As a result, you will have difficulty in obtaining more credit or keeping the lines of credit that you now have on your credit cards. Some may be canceled or not renewed on their renewal dates. If you are already over-indebted, that result may not be entirely bad. But when you really need a good credit record to rent an apartment, to get a home mortgage loan, or to get a new job, having a bad or even a weak credit report can hurt.

Also, as you will see in the next section, you will be the target of vigorous collection efforts, from your creditors and ultimately from professional collection agencies. These people want to recover the money that you owe and will write you and telephone you frequently.

Finally, there is the ultimate possibility of bankruptcy, which is discussed in the next chapter. Regardless of what you might be told by others, that is not a pleasant experience. Moreover, the record of your having filed for bankruptcy stays on your credit record for ten years, and can handicap your access to various forms of credit for much of that period of time.

**Q. What guidelines are there for how much debt I can handle?**

**A.** As a rough guideline, one long-standing rule is that if your monthly payments on debts, excluding your home mortgage payment, exceeds 20 percent of your after-tax or take-home pay, you most likely have reached your debt limit. Or, to put it another way, a roughly equivalent debt limit for those same credit payments is 30 percent of your pretax income. Since less than 3 percent of American families find themselves with payments at 30 percent or more of their gross income, you can see that relatively few families permit their debt burdens to reach or exceed that limit.

**Q. Are there danger signs that I am heading for debt troubles?**

**A.** Aside from the ratio of payments to take-home pay or gross income, there are some very reliable danger signs:

---

### PREVENTING CREDIT PROBLEMS

*It is a lot easier to prevent credit problems from starting in the first place than it is to dig your way out once you have more debt than you can handle. Even if you do finally pay off an overload of debt, your credit record will be tarnished, making it difficult to obtain low-priced credit in future years. This section points out some warning signs of debt overload and some methods that you can use to attack the problem before it grows larger.*

- you are making only minimum monthly payments on your credit card accounts;
- you have to use credit for expenditures that you once paid cash for;
- you have used a series of consolidation loans, home equity loans or other types of loans to pay overdue bills;
- you are borrowing from one lender to pay another; for example, you take a cash advance on your bank card to pay amounts owed other banks or retailers;
- you begin to run a few days late on critical payments, such as your rent or mortgage payment, or you are consistently late with all your bill payments so that late fees are piling up;
- you dip into savings for normal living expenses.

### Q. So, what do I do when I see one or more of these danger signs?

**A.** The first step is to slow down on use of credit. If you are going shopping, take only the one credit card that you will need, or try using cash instead of credit cards. Cut up excess credit cards and return them to the creditor asking that the credit bureaus be notified that you have closed the account.

Next, find out where your money is going by keeping track of family purchases for just two weeks. If you start out the day with thirty dollars in cash and end with five dollars, where did the twenty-five dollars go? To the twenty-five dollars add any credit card slips from credit purchases during the two weeks. Keep track of these money outflows for just a couple of weeks and then have a family conference to discuss how those outflows can be reduced. Now is the time to begin financial training for teenagers and even younger children.

Once you have a good understanding of where the money is going, you may find it useful for the family to prepare a cash budget that will

show the highest monthly payments you can afford on your debts. A rough outline is shown below; it can be as fancy or simple as you want it.

A few comments on this budget may be helpful. It is easy to overlook annual expenditures and then be hit with a cash crisis when an insurance bill comes due. Also, it is easier to decide on a budget for clothes, recreation and such on an annual basis and then divide the total by twelve to get a rough estimate of acceptable monthly outlays. The trick is not to spend the annual budget in the first two months.

Note that savings are budgeted as a monthly expense. If we don't budget it, we won't save. Savings are for two purposes. First, to set up an emergency fund in case somebody is laid off or becomes ill. A rule of thumb is that an emergency fund in the form of savings or other readily accessible assets should equal three to five months of after-tax income. Second, once you have set up an adequate emergency fund, the saving is for retirement, to build a college tuition fund and to meet other long-term goals that the family may have. These rules, however, should take into account any sick leave and retirement programs you have through work.

You may have wondered why the section for payments on "Income already committed to monthly payments" did not include payments on your credit cards. Expenditures on credit cards have already been included in the budget allowed for clothes, entertainment, and the other expenditures for which you use your credit cards. If you live within your budget for those expenditures, you will be able to make those payments.

Finally, many families may find that the difference between the amount on line D: "Monthly income available for payments on debts" is less than the amount on line E: "Committed income." This result means that income must be increased or expenditures cut.

Go back and look at a two-week record of cash outflows and see where you can cut spend-

## Family Cash Budget

You and your spouse's monthly take-home pay          _____
Other income                                         _____

    **A. Total monthly income**                                    _____

*Your monthly expenses:*
  Food                                               _____
  Rent or mortgage payments                          _____
  Utilities                                          _____
  Telephone                                          _____
  Transportation (gasoline, mass transit costs)      _____
  Itemize other major categories                     _____
  Regular monthly savings                            _____

    **B. Total outlays**                                           _____

*Your annual expenses:*
  Taxes                                              _____
  Insurance (not paid monthly)                       _____
  Medical and dental bills                           _____
  School costs                                       _____
  Entertainment                                      _____
  Clothing                                           _____
  Itemize other major categories                     _____
*Total annual expenses*                              _____

    **C. Total annual expenses divided by 12**                     _____

    **D. Monthly income available for payments on debts:**         _____

    **(A – B – C)**

*Income already committed to monthly payments:*
  Personal loans                                     _____
  Auto loans                                         _____

    **E. Committed income**                                        _____

**Discretionary income (D – E)**                                   _____

ing, so that you can free more money to meet your monthly bills. Add up all of the costs of going bowling once a week or pursuing some other hobby. Consider writing letters rather than making long-distance calls. Adopt the industry approach of "zero-based budgeting." Show a real need for any expenditure above zero. In addition to cutting cash outflows, you may be able to improve cash inflows. For example, a spouse or teenager might take a part-time job.

If you are not able to meet your monthly payments, you may want to approach one or more of your creditors and try to reduce or defer monthly payments without having to pay a penalty. Simply be honest in explaining your cash flow problem and ask the creditors if they can help you get back on your feet. While there is no guarantee that creditors will agree to this arrangement, the worst thing that you can do is to try to avoid them or to make promises to pay that you don't keep. If these self-help efforts don't do the job, you may want to contact a consumer credit counseling service that can help you set up a new budget. These are discussed at the end of this chapter.

## DEBT COLLECTION AND THE LAW

### Q. What can happen to me when I don't pay a debt?

**A.** As noted earlier, creditors are very likely to report your delinquencies to one or more credit bureaus, thus harming your credit record. In many states they may seek a judgment and court order to garnish your wages; that is, an order to your employer to pay directly to the credit grantor some portion of your wages. Federal law sets a limit on what portion may be taken, and many state laws are even more protective. But if you have a good income, the probability is that some of it is subject to garnishment.

## WHAT IF YOU DON'T PAY DEBTS AS PROMISED?

*The law allows credit grantors various ways of collecting unpaid debts, some of which depend upon the law of the state in which you live. They may be able to seize part of your wages or the car that you purchased on credit. Or, they may rely on debt collectors. The law attempts to balance the rights of the credit grantor who provided the credit and the rights of consumers who used it but did not fully pay for it. If you have successfully managed your finances as explained in the previous section, you can skip this section.*

For a car, truck, home appliance or other durable good purchased on credit, your creditor probably has a lien on the item that you purchased. Having a lien means that, if you fail to pay as agreed, the creditor may recover (repossess) the item that you purchased with credit. Many state laws require that the creditor notify you, say two weeks in advance, of its intent to repossess so that you may have a last chance to pay your outstanding debt on the item. Remember, most agreements specify that when you are in default, the entire debt, not just the monthly payment, is immediately due. Nor does repossession of your car, for example, end your obligation to the creditor. If your unpaid balance and accumulated, unpaid finance charges, plus the creditor's costs of repossessing the car, are less than the net amount that the creditor obtains from the sale of the car, you are still legally liable to the creditor for the shortage. If the creditor thinks that you may be able to pay something towards the shortage, the creditor can ask a court to assess a deficiency judgment against you for the shortage. A few state laws prevent deficiency judgments in some cases, but you should not count on being able to avoid this problem.

### Q. Who is a debt collector?

**A.** Under the federal Fair Debt Collection Practices Act (FDCPA), a debt collector is someone, other than a creditor, who regularly collects debts for others. This federal law does not cover creditors, although your state laws in many cases may govern them. Thus, a retailer who attempts to collect unpaid debts owed to it would not be covered by the FDCPA, but may be covered by the laws of the state where the delinquent consumer resides. These laws usually are similar to the federal Fair Debt Collection Practices Act. The rest of this section is based on the federal act.

### Q. How may a debt collector contact me?

**A.** A debt collector may contact you by mail, in person, or by telephone or telegram during convenient hours. Unless you agree in writing (or a court specifically grants permission), a collector may not contact you at inconvenient or unusual times or places. Examples of poorly chosen times are before 8:00 a.m. or after 9:00 p.m. Also, a debt collector is not permitted to contact you at work if the collector knows or has reason to know that your employer forbids employees from being contacted by collectors at the workplace. You can tell the debt collector what times and places are inconvenient for you to receive calls.

Also, a debt collector is forbidden from contacting you if he or she knows that you are represented by a lawyer.

### Q. How can I stop a debt collector from contacting me?

**A.** By notifying a debt collector by mail not to contact you. After that, the attempts at contact must stop. There are two exceptions to this. The debt collector may tell you that there will be no more contact, and that some specific legal or other action may be or will be taken. However, debt collectors may state this only if they actually plan to take such action.

Debt collectors also must stop trying to contact you if you notify them, by mail within thirty days after they first contact you, that you dispute all or part of the debt or that you are requesting the name and address of the original creditor. However, debt collectors are permitted to begin collection activities again if they send you proof of the debt, such as a copy of the bill, or the information you requested about the original creditor.

### Q. What does the law require the debt collector to tell me about my debt?

**A.** Within five days of your first contact, a debt collector must send you a written notice stating:

- the name of the credit grantor to whom you owe the money;
- the amount of money you owe;
- that the debt collector will assume the debt is genuine unless you challenge all or part of it within thirty days, and what to do if you believe you do not owe the money;
- that if you ask for it, the debt collector will tell you the name and address of the original creditor, if different from the current creditor.

### Q. Whom may a collector contact about my debt?

**A.** A debt collector may contact any person to locate you. However, in doing so, the collector usually may not talk to anyone more than once or refer to the debt when talking to that person. If debt collectors use the mail to contact you or another person, they may not send letters in envelopes identifying themselves as bill collectors. They also may not send a postcard. Once collectors know that you have hired a lawyer, they may communicate only with your lawyer.

### Q. What types of debt collection practices does the law permit?

**A.** When your debt is secured by an asset, such as your car, the creditor may repossess your car. In some states, the creditor must give you an advance notice of his intent to repossess. But if you do not have a legal excuse for not paying, you may have your car repossessed. The creditor may not breach the peace when repossessing your car. For example, he may not seize it by force or break into your garage to seize the car.

If it is repossessed, your car may then be sold at auction by the creditor and, if the proceeds of the sale are less than the amount you owe, you are liable to the creditor for the difference, plus the costs of repossessing the car. If the amount is large enough, the creditor may go to court to obtain a deficiency judgment against you for the balance owing. You can, of course, avoid the costs and unpleasant experience of repossession by voluntarily turning the car over to the creditor once you realize that you cannot meet the monthly payments.

In some states creditors may garnish your wages if you fail to pay your debts. You will always have a chance to appear in court to defend yourself before the garnishment is approved. If the garnishment is approved, the creditor will then notify your employer to subtract a given amount from your paycheck each payday and pay that amount to the creditor until the debt is satisfied. Your employer may not fire you because of the garnishment. The maximum amount of the garnishment is also set by state law.

### Q. What types of debt collection practices does the law prohibit?

**A.** A debt collector may not harass, oppress, or abuse any person. For example, a debt collector may not:

- use threats of violence to harm you, your property, or reputation;
- use obscene or profane language;
- repeatedly use the telephone to annoy you;
- make you accept collect calls or pay for telegrams; or
- publish a "shame list" or other roster of individuals who allegedly refuse to pay their debts (though the debt collector can still report you to a credit bureau).

A debt collector may not use false statements when trying to collect a debt. For example, a debt collector may not:

- misrepresent the amount of the debt;
- falsely imply that the debt collector is a lawyer;
- tell you that your property or wages will be seized, garnished, attached, or sold, unless the debt collector or the credit grantor intends to do so and it is legal.

### Q. What may I do if the debt collector breaks the law?

**A.** If the collection effort is being made by a credit grantor (for example, a retailer or bank), check with the consumer protection office of your state attorney general's office and write that office a letter detailing your complaint (with a copy to the offending credit grantor). If the collection effort is from an independent debt collector, write the nearest office of the Federal Trade Commission or the office in Washington,

D.C. (See page 272 for addresses.) The FTC has been active in pursuing violators and may fine them heavily or even put them out of business.

In addition, if debt collectors violate the Fair Debt Collection Practices Act, you may sue them in a state or federal court. However, you may do so only within one year from the date they violated the law. You may recover money for the actual damage you suffered. In addition, the court may award up to one thousand dollars for each violation for an individual suit and as much as five hundred thousand dollars in a class action suit. (The latter is a suit brought by a group of people who claim that the illegal debt collection practice injured all of them. In other words, it injured them as a class.) You also may recover court costs and attorney's fees. However, consumers found acting in bad faith against a debt collector may have to pay for court costs.

## CREDIT COUNSELING

### Q. Are all financial counseling services the same?

**A.** No, there are nonprofit and for-profit financial counseling centers. The National Foundation for Consumer Credit provides leadership for about 800 nonprofit Consumer Credit Counseling Services (CCCS) throughout the United States. CCCS offices get most of their fees from credit grantors, but will typically charge consumers a small fee for setting up a budget plan. Hence, the costs to you may be lower than those of for-profit centers, which must cover all their costs from charges to consumers who use the centers' services. However, it is possible that, because of the source of their funding, nonprofit centers may favor arrangements that benefit creditors the most. While many for-profit financial counseling centers provide worthwhile services, some may exaggerate the benefits that they promise.

**WHERE TO GET CREDIT COUNSELING**
*You can get credit counseling from several sources. These include credit unions, lawyers, and university-sponsored programs. The personnel offices of some firms also offer the service, as do those of some of the armed forces. Nonprofit and for-profit specialized financial counseling services are also available. The major problem is not so much finding a source of credit counseling services, but in being willing to admit that there is a problem and share the problem with a stranger.*

### Q. What kinds of services can I get from a credit counseling center?

**A.** Most specialized counseling offices provide two types of services. First, they can help you set up a realistic budget so that you can manage your debts better. Second, if you still have trouble paying your debts on time, the center will contact your creditors and arrange a repayment plan based on your budget. You will make a single payment each month to the office, which will then distribute the payment among your creditors until it pays all your debts in full. Most creditors prefer this type of plan (since they eventually will get most of their money) rather than "straight" bankruptcy. While many credit grantors agree to such arrangements with CCCS offices, some will not work with for-profit counseling offices.

Under a repayment plan through a CCCS, you may still have to pay finance charges on your debts. However, many creditors will waive (not require payment of) finance charges and delinquency fees after you have agreed to repay your debts through a CCCS.

**Q.  *How can I find a CCCS or a for-profit counseling center?***

A. Check the yellow pages of your phone book for "Credit & Debt Counseling Services."

To find a nonprofit counseling CCCS near you, call toll-free 1-800-388-2227, or write and send a self-addressed, stamped envelope to:

National Foundation for Consumer Credit, Inc.
8611 Second Avenue
Silver Spring, MD 20910

## WHERE TO RESOLVE DISPUTES AND GET MORE INFORMATION

What if you believe that you have been treated improperly by a credit grantor? Resolving the problem involves a sequence of four possible steps—each one more aggressive than the other. Disputes can almost always be settled long before the third and fourth steps.

1. Check to be sure that you have the correct information regarding your rights under the law and the credit grantor's obligation to you under the law. In addition to the information included in this chapter, this section provides other sources that you may wish to review.

2. If you are reasonably confident that your complaint is well-founded, contact the creditor by phone or, if the matter is quite serious, by letter. Be sure to provide your name, address, account number and a statement of your concern. If your initial contact is by telephone, get the name of the person with whom you talked. To compete effectively, most credit grantors wish to keep good customers by settling complaints fairly and quickly. Nonetheless, create a "paper trail" by keeping a written record or log of all of your contacts with the creditor.

3. If you are not satisfied with the settlement offered by the creditor, based on your study of your rights under the law, the next step is to contact any state or federal agency that regulates your creditor. It is best to write the appropriate agency and to supply a copy of the written record that you have maintained. By sending a copy of the letter to your creditor, you may focus attention on your complaint. While the regulatory agency may require some time to get to your problem, it will often be able to arrange a solution that will be satisfactory to you. A description of the various regulatory agencies that might be involved and their addresses are included in this section.

4. If the regulatory agency fails to satisfy you, you can hire your own attorney to pursue the matter. However, if you do not win, you are likely to be liable for your attorney's fees. In some cases that may be true even if you win.

The first part of this resource section relates to step three. It provides lists of the major federal laws and the agencies responsible for enforcing those laws. First, determine the federal act that applies to your complaint. Second, identify the type of credit grantor against whom you have a complaint. Then look up the address of the agency so you can write to make your complaint. If you need more help, call your local consumer protection office. For its telephone number, look in your local telephone directory under the listings for your local or state government.

The second part of this resource section lists various low-cost or no-cost federal publications that will help you obtain and use credit more effectively. The office of consumer protection (often found in your state's attorney general's office) may also have useful publications.

### Federal Laws on Credit and Debt Collection

The Truth in Lending Act (TILA) requires all credit grantors to provide you with the annual percentage rate (APR), costs and terms, and other relevant information on the credit sought and obtained. Typical credit grantors are banks, department stores, credit-card issuers, finance companies, and oil companies, among others.

The Equal Credit Opportunity Act (ECOA) prohibits discrimination against a credit applicant and debtor because of age (except for capacity to contract), sex, marital status, race, color, religion, national origin, receipt of public aid, or exercise of certain legal rights.

The Fair Credit Reporting Act (FCRA) sets up a procedure for correcting mistakes on your credit record and requires that the record be kept confidential.

The Fair Credit Billing Act (FCBA) sets up a procedure for promptly correcting errors on a credit account and prevents damage to your credit rating while you are settling a dispute.

The Consumer Leasing Act (CLA) requires disclosure of information that helps you compare the cost and terms of one lease with another. It also orders firms that offer leases to reveal facts that help you compare the cost and terms of leasing with those for buying on credit or with cash.

The Fair Debt Collection Practices Act (FDCPA) applies to people and firms that regularly collect debts for others. It prohibits them from performing abusive collection practices and allows consumers to dispute a debt and to halt unreasonable collection activities.

### Where to File Your Complaint

You should file complaints about consumer credit reporting agencies or debt collection agencies with the Federal Trade Commission (FTC). The same goes for complaints about violations of the Truth in Lending Act and other federal laws involving credit issued by retail stores, department stores, and small loan and finance companies and for credit-related complaints about oil companies, public utility companies, state credit unions, or travel and entertainment companies that issue cards. Mail your complaint to:

Federal Trade Commission
Correspondence Branch
6th Street and Pennsylvania Avenue, NW
Washington, DC 20580

Instead of contacting the FTC's national headquarters at the address shown above, you can send your complaint to one of the FTC Regional Offices listed below:

Suite 1000
1718 Peachtree Street, NW
**Atlanta,** GA 30367
(404) 347-4836

Suite 2900
1405 Curtis Street
**Denver,** CO 80202-2393
(303) 844-2271

Suite 810
101 Merrimac Street
**Boston,** MA 02114-4719
(617) 424-5960

Suite 13209
11000 Wilshire Blvd.
**Los Angeles,** CA 90024
(310) 575-7575

Suite 1860
55 East Monroe Street
**Chicago,** IL 60603
(312) 353-8156

Suite 1300
150 William Street
**New York,** NY 10038
(212) 264-1207

Suite 520-A
668 Euclid Avenue
**Cleveland,** OH 44114
(216) 522-4207

Suite 570
901 Market Street
**San Francisco,** CA 94103
(415) 744-7920

Suite 500
100 N. Central Expressway
**Dallas,** TX 75201
(214) 767-5501

2806 Federal Building
915 Second Avenue
**Seattle,** WA 98174
(206) 220-6363

If a financial institution has violated a federal law discussed in this chapter, the regulatory agency that oversees that category of institutions might be able to help you. The following information will help you decide which agency to contact.

*National bank.* If the word "National" appears in the bank's name, or the initials N.A. or N.T.S.A. appear after its name, write to: Comptroller of the Currency, Consumer Affairs Division, 250 E Street, SW, Washington, DC 20219. (202) 622-2000.

*State-chartered bank.* A bank that is a member of the Federal Reserve System, FDIC insured. It will display two signs on the door of the bank or in the lobby. One will say "Member, Federal Reserve System." The other will state "Deposits Insured by the Federal Deposit Insurance Corporation." For complaints of violations, write to: Federal Reserve System, Division of Consumer and Community Affairs, 20th and Constitution Avenue, NW, Washington, DC 20551. (202) 452-3000. Or you can write the **Federal Reserve Bank** serving the area in which the state member bank has its office.

104 Marietta Street, NW
**Atlanta,** GA 30303-2713
(404) 521-8500

600 Atlantic Avenue
**Boston,** MA 02106
(617) 973-3000

P.O. Box 834
**Chicago,** IL 60690-0834
(312) 322-5322

P.O. Box 0387
**Cleveland,** OH 44101
(216) 579-2000

2200 N. Pearl
**Dallas,** TX 75201-2272
(214) 922-6000

925 Grand Blvd.
**Kansas City,** MO 64198
(816) 881-2000

250 Marquette Avenue
**Minneapolis,** MN 55401-2171
(612) 340-2345

33 Liberty Street
**New York,** NY 10045
(212) 720-5914

10 Independence Mall
**Philadelphia,** PA 19105
(215) 574-6116

P.O. Box 27622
**Richmond,** VA 23261
(804) 697-8000

P.O. Box 7702
**San Francisco,** CA 94120
(415) 974-2000

P.O. Box 442
**St. Louis,** MO 63166
(314) 444-8444

For violations of state laws, write to your state banking department. For the address and telephone number, consult the state government listings in your local telephone directory.

*State-chartered bank,* insured by the Federal Deposit Insurance Corporation (FDIC), but *not* a member of the Federal Reserve System. The bank will display a very conspicuous sign that says "Deposits Insured by the Federal Deposit Insurance Corporation." However, there will not be a sign saying "Member, Federal Reserve System." Write to: Federal Deposit Insurance Corporation, Office of Bank Customer Affairs, 550 17th St., NW, Washington, DC 20429. (202) 393-8400.

The FDIC maintains a toll-free telephone hot line for consumers. It allows the public to ask questions or offer views and complaints about consumer protection or civil rights matters involving FDIC-supervised banks. These include about 8,700 state-chartered banks that are not members of the Federal Reserve System. The toll-free number is 1-800-424-5488. It is in daily service, Monday through Friday, from 9:00 a.m. to 4:00 p.m. Eastern Time. In the Washington, DC, area the consumer information number is (202) 898-3536. The toll-free number also reaches a telecommunication device for the deaf (TDD). You can reach the device in the Washington area by calling (202) 898-3537.

***Federally chartered*** or ***federally insured savings and loan association.*** The word "Federal" usually appears in the name of the savings and loan association. Write to the **Office of Thrift Supervision** in your region. (If you choose the wrong region, your complaint will be forwarded to the appropriate office.)

**Northeast Region**
10 Exchange Place Centre
18th Floor
Jersey City, NJ 07302
(201) 413-1000

**Southeast Region**
1475 Peachtree Street, NE
Atlanta, GA 30309
(404) 888-0771

**Central Region**
Suite 800
111 East Wacker Drive
Chicago, IL 60601
(312) 540-5900

**Midwest Region**
Suite 600
122 W. John Carpenter Freeway
Irving, TX 75030
(214) 281-2000

**Western Region**
P.O. Box 7165
1 Montgomery Street
San Francisco, CA 94120
(415) 616-1500

***Federally chartered credit unions.*** The term "Federal credit union" appears in the name of the credit union. Write to: National Credit Union Administration, 1775 Duke Street, Alexandria, VA 22314-3428; telephone (703) 518-6300.

***State-chartered, federally insured credit unions.*** They will display a sign indicating that the NCUA (National Credit Union Administration) insures the deposits. Write to your state agency that regulates credit unions or to the Federal Trade Commission.

## PUBLICATIONS

You can find the addresses and telephone numbers for consumer protection offices in your local telephone directory. You also can find them in the *Consumers Resource Handbook*, available free by writing to: Handbook, Consumer Information Center-N, P.O. Box 100, Pueblo, CO 81009; telephone (719) 948-3334.

## Publications from the Federal Reserve

You can obtain various publications without charge from:

Board of Governors of the Federal Reserve System
Publications Services
Mail Stop 138
20 C Street, NW
Washington, DC 20551

These publications include:

*Consumer Handbook of Credit Protection Laws* (This 44-page booklet explains how to use the credit laws to shop for credit. It also tells you how to apply for credit, keep up your credit ratings, and complain about an unfair deal.);

*How to File a Consumer Complaint;*

*A Guide to Business Credit for Women, Minorities, and Small Businesses;*

*When Your Home Is on the Line: What You Should Know About Home Equity Lines of Credit.*

The Federal Reserve banks, listed above, also have many excellent publications.

## Publications from the Federal Trade Commission

The Federal Trade Commission (FTC) publishes many popular consumer publications in English or Spanish. For a listing, get a copy of "FTC Best Sellers." For it and all FTC publications, write to: Public Reference, Federal Trade Commission, 6th and Pennsylvania Avenue, NW, Washington, DC 20580. Many of these also are available from: Consumer Information Center, Pueblo, CO 81009. You can write there for a *Consumer Information Catalog.*

Some FTC publications include:

*A New Credit Identity: A New Credit Repair Scam*
*Advance Fee Loan Scams* *
*Building a Better Credit Record*
*Car Ads: Low Interest Loans and Other Offers*
*Co-signing a Loan* *
*Credit and Charge Card Fraud*
*Credit and Older Americans*

*Credit Billing Blues*
*Credit Practices Rule\**
*Credit Repair Scams*
*Electronic Banking*
*Equal Credit Opportunity\**
*Fair Credit Billing\**
*Fair Credit Reporting*
*Fair Debt Collection\**
*Fix Your Own Credit Problems*
*Getting a Loan: Your Home as Security*
*How to Resolve Consumer Disputes*
*Lost or Stolen: Credit and ATM Cards*
*Refinancing Your Home*
*Scoring for Credit*
*Second Mortgage Financing*
*Solving Credit Problems\**
*Women and Credit Histories*

\*Available in Spanish

# Consumer Bankruptcy

## CONTENTS

# INTRODUCTION

BEING IN OVER YOUR HEAD FINANCIALLY is frightening. If you find yourself in this unhappy position, several kinds of help are available. Bankruptcy is one of the alternatives for financial distress. You need to examine the options available to you for dealing with your financial problems and decide which course of action is best for you.

Some people in financial trouble can improve their situation by negotiating directly with creditors. Others get help from a local financial counseling program or a consumer credit counseling service with experience in negotiating with creditors and in budgeting plans. For some people, some form of bankruptcy may be the only realistic alternative.

The choice of a remedy is not always easy. As a first step, consider the pros and cons of filing for bankruptcy and selecting one of the two basic types of consumer bankruptcy: "Chapter 7" ("straight bankruptcy") or "Chapter 13" (sometimes called "wage earner bankruptcy"). The purpose of this chapter is to provide you with information that will help you make informed choices and to provide references to other sources of information if you wish. Also, see the "Family Law" chapter beginning on 51 for topics regarding bankruptcy and marriage and the chapter on consumer credit for bankruptcy-related discussions.

If after you have reviewed this material you decide to seek protection in bankruptcy, you should select a lawyer who is familiar with bankruptcy laws.

## ALTERNATIVES TO BANKRUPTCY

### Q. Right now, I cannot pay my debts. Besides bankruptcy, do I have any options?

**A.** Yes, there are alternatives that you may use to take care of debts that you cannot pay. Creditors might be willing to settle their claim for a smaller cash payment, or they might be willing to stretch out the loan and reduce the size of the payments. This would allow you to pay off the debt by making smaller payments over a longer period of time. The creditor would eventually receive the full economic benefit of its bargain.

Occasionally, you may "buy time" by consolidating your debts; that is, by taking out a big loan to pay off all the smaller amounts of debts that you owe. The primary danger of this approach is that it is very easy to go out and use your credit cards to borrow even more. In that case, you end up with an even larger total debt and no more income to meet the monthly payments. Indeed, if you have taken out a second mortgage on your home to obtain the consolidation loan, you might lose your home as well.

### Q. Is there anybody in particular I should contact about these options?

**A.** Yes. If you are behind on your payments, the collectors for each of your creditors may already be calling or writing you. You might be more successful if you phone each creditor, ask for the collection department, ask and note the name of the person you talk to, and explain your intent to repay the account and your need to stretch out the number of monthly payments and reduce their size. You might offer to come to the collection department office to discuss your situation. Ask each creditor to agree to a voluntary plan for the repayment of your debts.

### Q. I owe money to many creditors. What should I do?

**A.** The problem of dealing with many creditors is that some of them might not want to give you more time to pay without knowing what the other creditors are willing to do. Unless your debts are very large, it will be difficult for you to arrange for a meeting of your creditors and negotiate a reduction in your monthly payments or the amount of your debt. You can seek the help of a lawyer to negotiate an arrangement with your creditors. Some universities, local courts, military bases, credit unions, and housing authorities have credit counseling programs, but may not have the ability or experience to negotiate with your creditors to gain their consent to reduce your monthly payments. Your best bet may be to seek the help of a profit or nonprofit consumer credit counseling service (CCCS). As noted in the chapter on consumer credit, you can find the nearest CCCS by calling 1-800-388-2227. These centers charge a small monthly service fee. However, creditors provide most of the support for financial counseling services.

The repayment plans arranged through credit counseling centers enable you to make monthly payments which are then re-distributed by the program among creditors until all your debts are paid in full. Creditors usually prefer this kind of plan, since they will eventually get more of their money with this approach than they will under "straight" or "Chapter 7" bankruptcy.

Under a repayment plan through a financial counseling service, you still might have to pay interest charges on your debts. However, many creditors will waive interest charges and delinquency fees.

## BANKRUPTCY DEFINED

### Q. What exactly is bankruptcy?

**A.** Bankruptcy is a legal process through which people and businesses can obtain a fresh financial start when they are in such financial difficulty that they cannot repay their debts as agreed. The fresh start is achieved by eliminating all or a portion of existing debts or by stretching out the monthly payments under the protection and supervision of a court. The process is also designed to protect creditors, because general unsecured creditors share equally in whatever payments the debtor can afford to make.

### Q. What is the process of filing for bankruptcy?

**A.** Filing for bankruptcy is a very personal decision. Most people file when they have made a good-faith effort to repay their debts, but see no way out other than to file for bankruptcy. Such people and businesses may declare bankruptcy by filing a petition with the U.S. Bankruptcy Court; that is, a request that the court provide protection and relief under the Bankruptcy Code. In addition to that request, the petition provides information about the debtor's assets, liabilities, income and expenditures. Often, debtors have a lawyer prepare and file the petition for them, but some debtors represent themselves.

### Q. What are the advantages of filing for bankruptcy?

**A.** There are several advantages to filing for bankruptcy, many of which are unique to the United States.

By far the most important advantage is that debtors may obtain a fresh financial start. As we shall see below, consumers who file for Chapter 7 may be forgiven most unsecured debts and even some secured debts. In a number of European countries, consumer debts are

**USE BANKRUPTCY
WITH CAUTION**

*Bankruptcy may be the best, or only, solution for extreme financial hardship. However, it should be used only as a last resort, since it always has long-lasting consequences. The record of a bankruptcy remains in your credit files in credit bureaus for as long as ten years, which is a long time in today's economic system that is so dependent on having good credit. Moreover, there are limits on how often you can use certain forms of bankruptcy. Study the pros and cons carefully before resorting to bankruptcy as a means of solving your economic troubles.*

never forgiven; the "fresh start" principle exists in only a handful of the world's countries.

You may be able to keep (that is, exempt) many of your assets, although state laws vary widely in defining which assets you may keep.

Collection efforts must stop. As soon as your petition is filed, there is by law an automatic stay, which prohibits most collection activity. If a creditor continues to try to collect the debt, the creditor may be cited for contempt of court or ordered to pay damages. The stay applies even to the loan that you may have obtained to buy your car. If you continue to make payments, it is unlikely that your creditor will do anything. However, if you miss payments your creditor will probably petition to have the stay lifted in order either to repossess the car or to renegotiate the loan.

You cannot be fired from your job solely because you filed for bankruptcy.

### Q. What are the disadvantages of filing for bankruptcy?

**A.** As you might suspect, there is a cost to obtaining a fresh financial start. Since your bankruptcy filing will remain on your credit record for up to ten years, how will that affect your future finances?

- In general, creditors will be less likely to grant you credit. However, you may be able to obtain some new lines or sources of credit. A study by the Credit Research Center at Purdue University has shown that about one-third of consumers who filed for bankruptcy had obtained new lines of credit within three years of filing; one-half obtained new lines within five years of filing. Even these new lines of credit are likely to reflect your record of bankruptcy. Thus, whereas you might have been eligible for a bank card with a 14 percent rate before bankruptcy, the best card that you can get after bankruptcy might carry a rate of 20 percent— or you might have to rely on a card secured by a deposit that you make with the credit card issuer.

- The study cited above also showed that consumers who filed for bankruptcy had a hard time renting an apartment. It was also much more difficult to obtain a mortgage loan or insurance.

### Q. Is there more than one type of bankruptcy?

**A.** Yes, there are specific chapters of the Bankruptcy Code, a federal statute. Proceedings under Chapter 7 (straight bankruptcy) involve taking most of the borrower's nonexempt assets, as explained later. A bankruptcy trustee is appointed in every Chapter 7 case to liquidate (sell off) the nonexempt assets (if any) and distribute the cash among the creditors. Proceedings under Chapter 13 (wage earner's bankruptcy) require the debtor to propose a

## GENERAL COMPARISON OF CHAPTER 7 AND CHAPTER 13 BANKRUPTCY

| Feature | Chapter 7<br>Straight Bankruptcy Liquidation | Chapter 13<br>Payment Plan for People with Regular Income |
|---|---|---|
| Basic operation | File bankruptcy petition with court. Trustee appointed to administer bankruptcy. All non-exempt assets sold. Debtor retains only exempt assets. Money is split among creditors, according to priority established by the Bankruptcy Code. | File bankruptcy petition and proposed payment plan with court. Payment plan makes payments over a period of three to five years. Payments are made from disposable income (i.e., whatever is left over after necessities [food, shelter, etc.] have been allowed for), while debtor retains assets. |
| Limitations on availability | No monetary limitations. Discharge not available if debtor was discharged in bankruptcy within past six years. | For debtors owing less that $100,000 in unse-cured debt and less than $350,000 in secured debt. |
| Percentage of consumer filings under Bankruptcy Code | About 80 percent. | About 20 percent. |
| Availability | Can be used only if not used during previous six years. | Can be used repeatedly. |
| Effect on debts | With exceptions noted in text, most debts are dis-charged (extinguished) upon bankruptcy. Liability to creditors ends with discharge order from court. | All or a portion of debts paid off over a period of time under a specific plan. With exceptions noted in text, debts are discharged. Liability to creditors ends when plan successfully completed. |
| Effect on home | Home may be preserved under homestead exemp-tion or marital ownership law. | Home will be preserved if plan successfully com-pleted. If not, home may be preserved under homestead exemption of marital ownership law. |
| Effect on automobile | Auto might be taken by creditors (unless necessary for work and arrangements are made to pay off lien). | Auto will be preserved if plan successfully com-pleted. If not, it might be taken by creditors (unless arrangements are made to pay off lien). |
| Effect on non-exempt assets | All non-exempt assets will be sold. | No effect if plan successfully completed. If not, non-exempt assets can be sold to pay creditors, as in Chapter 7 bankruptcy. |
| Time to repay | Not applicable. | Usually up to three years, sometimes up to five years. |
| Payments | Most forms of debt discharged; however, other debts, such as taxes and child support, will have to be paid. | All "disposable income" is available for pay-ments; that is, whatever remains after necessi-ties (food, shelter, etc.) are taken care of. |
| Portion of debt repaid | Will depend on the value of non-exempt assets sold to pay off debts. | May allow payments for less than actual debts. |
| Result at conclusion of bankruptcy proceedings | Bankruptcy court enters a discharge order, ending enforceability of all debts that can be discharged in bankruptcy. | Borrower is no longer liable for most debts if plan successfully completed. |
| Requirement for bankruptcy pro-ceedings to end | Court must have entered a discharge order. | Borrower must have made all payments in accordance with court-approved plan. |
| Effect on credit | Record of bankruptcy may remain on credit record for up to ten years. | Record of bankruptcy may remain on credit record for up to ten years. Creditors may prefer to see this form of bankruptcy, since successful completion of plan may pay more debts than will be paid under Chapter 7 filing. |

plan for repaying all or a portion of the debt in installments from the debtor's income. Chapter 11 of the federal Bankruptcy Code covers businesses that are restructuring while continuing operations and generally is not used by consumer debtors. While an individual may file for Chapter 11 bankruptcy, such proceedings are more expensive and complex, so that consumer debtors normally use Chapter 7 or Chapter 13.

Under any chapter, once the bankruptcy case ends, most borrowers are no longer liable for most of their pre-petition debts. (The bankruptcy court enters a discharge order relatively early in a Chapter 7 case; in Chapter 13 cases the borrower makes full or partial payment to creditors under a court-confirmed plan over a three- to five-year period and then receives a discharge.) This means the court has discharged the borrower from having to pay most debts. (It should be noted, however, that in a Chapter 7 case, the discharge does not wipe out a creditor's lien.) The borrower then starts over again with a clean financial slate—except that the record of the bankruptcy will remain on the borrower's credit record for up to ten years.

**Q. How would I find a lawyer to represent me in a bankruptcy action?**

**A.** Some states certify attorneys as bankruptcy specialists when they have had significant experience in the field. Ask an attorney that you know well to recommend a specialist. Suggestions from a friend, relative, neighbor, or associate who has had a good experience with a particular lawyer also may help. Bar associations and groups operated for people with special needs, such as the elderly or persons with disabilities, often provide referral services. You might also find a lawyer by looking in the yellow pages of your telephone directory and advertisements in your local newspaper.

Of course, it is legal and proper to file your own bankruptcy petition, though the more complicated your debt situation, the more risky it is to represent yourself.

**Q. How would I evaluate lawyers who might represent me in a bankruptcy action?**

**A.** Be careful in your selection. Satisfy yourself that your lawyer is familiar with bankruptcy law and procedures, and has a good reputation. When you have an initial talk with a prospective attorney, does he or she seem to understand your problems and have solutions—or are you in a "factory" that merely processes paper? Remember that you can, and should, discuss your lawyer's fees in advance. This will give you as clear an idea as possible of what the bankruptcy procedure will cost. For more details, see the first chapter—"When and How to Use a Lawyer"—in this publication. Under certain circumstances, you can pay the lawyer from the assets of your estate administered by the court in the bankruptcy case. Depending upon the complexity of your case, your legal fees might range from $500 to $1,500.

## STRAIGHT BANKRUPTCY: CHAPTER 7

**Q. What does Chapter 7 bankruptcy involve?**

**A.** Straight bankruptcy under Chapter 7 is available if less drastic methods will not solve your financial problems. It allows you to discharge (extinguish) most debts. A section below describes the types of debts that you cannot avoid in any form of bankruptcy. Just over 70 percent of all consumer bankruptcy filings nationwide are under Chapter 7.

**Q. How does a Chapter 7 bankruptcy case begin?**

**A.** It starts when you file a petition with the U.S. Bankruptcy Court asking it to relieve you (or you and your spouse) from your debts. As of the date you file the petition, your assets will be under the protection of the court. In addition, most collection efforts against you must stop. However, if someone has co-signed a loan for you, your automatic stay does not stop creditors from seeking payment from your co-signer.

When you file the petition, you also must file a Statement of Financial Affairs and schedules that, among other things, describe your personal background and financial history, and list your income, all of your debts and your assets. These schedules are quite detailed:

*Your liabilities:*

- your priority debts (such as taxes);
- your secured creditors (auto dealers, home mortgages, and so on);
- your unsecured creditors (department store credit cards and the like).

Be sure that you list all your creditors and their correct names and addresses. If you omit some, or provide incorrect addresses, you might not be discharged from those debts.

*Your assets:*

- all your real property (real estate and so forth);
- all your personal property (such as household goods; clothing, cash, retirement funds, accrued net wages);
- all other assets that you did not list on other schedules.

### Q. Will I lose some of my assets if I file for Chapter 7?

**A.** Under Chapter 7, you might well have to turn over many, if not all, of your nonexempt assets. What happens depends upon the classification of the asset:

*Assets pledged as collateral on a loan.* When you have borrowed to buy a car, boat, household furniture, appliance, or other durable item, the seller commonly has a lien (legal claim)

on that property to secure the debt until the loan is fully repaid. If you cannot make the required payments (and also catch up on any back payments), the creditor has a right to take back the collateral after having the automatic stay lifted. However, you may be able to keep your car, boat, or other durable item by redeeming it or reaffirming your debt (as explained later in this section) or by continuing to make payments.

*Exempt assets.* These are assets that you must list on your Statement of Financial Affairs and schedules and which you may shield from your creditors. The assets that you may protect in this way are defined by federal and state law. In a few states you may choose either of the two laws, while in most states you may use only the state exemptions. Exemptions vary widely among the states. For example, under the federal statute a couple filing jointly may exempt a total of $15,000 in equity in their home. Thus, if the home is worth $50,000 and has a $30,000 mortgage, creditors can claim only $5,000 (the difference between the equity of $20,000 and the $15,000 exemption). As a matter of practice, the couple would probably keep their home rather than have it sold for the benefit of the creditors. In contrast, Florida allows a homestead exemption that protects from creditors a debtor's home and property so long as it does not exceed half an acre in a municipality or 160 acres elsewhere. Thus, an investment banker who filed bankruptcy has been able to retain a beach-front home reportedly valued at $3.25 million. In Georgia the homestead exemption is limited to $5,000. Similar variations among the states are found concerning a broad array of other exempt assets such as autos, jewelry, household furnishings, books and tools of the debtor's trade.

*Nonexempt assets.* The Bankruptcy Code requires that you give all your nonexempt assets to the bankruptcy trustee. The trustee will then liquidate (sell off) these nonexempt assets for the benefit of your creditors. However, in actual practice, about 95 percent of

Chapter 7 filings are "no-asset filings"—that is, there are no assets left for unsecured creditors after the exempt assets have been claimed.

### Q. How may I keep certain possessions that I do not want the trustee to sell?

**A.** If you are required to surrender some nonexempt property that you wish to keep—for example, a car—you may arrange to buy it back from the trustee. (Recall that the property that is exempt from seizure by creditors in a Chapter 7 bankruptcy is defined by state or federal law.) However, the property may still be subject to a lien by a creditor (for example, a bank or a finance company), or it might be property that the trustee has decided that it would not be worthwhile to seize. Since the market value or liquidation value of the property is almost always less than the amount you owe, you may pay the creditor only that value and redeem your furniture or car. For example, if you owe $3,000 on your car, but its market value is only $1,200, you can recover the car by paying $1,200 to the creditor. In the real world, of course, it may be very hard to come up with $1,200.

Alternatively, you may reaffirm some debts, if the creditor is willing. By reaffirming these debts, you promise to pay them (usually but not always in full), and you may keep the property involved.

You have the right to cancel a reaffirmation agreement within sixty days after such agreement is filed with the court or prior to the discharge, whichever occurs later. Reaffirmation is not always in the best interest of the debtor, especially when the reaffirmed debt relates to property worth far less than the debt reaffirmed. Most reaffirmations relate to mortgage loans and the retention of personal property—car, boat, etc.—valued by the debtor.

Finally, as for personal property securing a loan, you may simply continue to make payments. The law in this area is not particularly clear, but as a practical matter lenders will often not take action if they continue to receive full payment.

### Q. Can I protect some assets, such as a vacation home, by transferring title to relatives prior to filing for bankruptcy?

**A.** No. You will be asked whether or not you have transferred property within a year prior to filing. The trustee can cancel the transfer and recover the property for your bankruptcy estate. If the trustee discovers that you tried to conceal the transfer, you may be denied discharge and face charges of committing a fraudulent act.

### Q. What happens after I submit all the above information to the court?

**A.** The bankruptcy court clerk will notify your creditors that you have filed a petition. A trustee will be appointed, usually a local private lawyer who does this kind of work in the normal course of practicing law. After the clerk has notified your creditors of your petition, the creditors must stop most efforts to collect the debts you owe.

You will be required to appear at a first meeting of creditors, where the trustee will examine you under oath about your petition, Statement of Financial Affairs, and schedules. Later he or she will determine whether to challenge any of your claimed exemptions or your right to a discharge. If you disagree with the trustee's decision, you may protest to the court, which will make the final decision.

After determining your exemptions, the trustee will assemble and liquidate your nonexempt assets (if there are any). Then the trustee will first pay the entire amount of any priority claims, such as certain taxes or money owed to secured creditors (secured creditors will generally be paid up to the value of their collateral). Next, the trustee will pay your gen-

## DANGERS OF SUBSTANTIAL ABUSE OF BANKRUPTCY CODE

*There are numerous exceptions to the general rule concerning the discharge of debts through bankruptcy. Major exceptions involve a last-minute spending binge for luxury goods or services or taking out cash advances on your credit card. Luxury purchases exceeding five-hundred dollars for each creditor—such as jewelry or a fur coat—within forty days of bankruptcy or cash advances within twenty days above one thousand dollars may not be dischargeable. A pattern of running up debts in contemplation of bankruptcy could result in denial of any discharge of your debts.*

eral unsecured creditors on a *pro rata* (proportionate) basis. Say, for example, that the proceeds from the sale by the trustee of your nonexempt assets equal 20 percent of your remaining debts. Then the trustee will pay each unsecured credit grantor 20 percent of what you owe. In return, the court will discharge you from paying any remaining balance on your general unsecured debts.

### Q. May I use bankruptcy to get rid of all my debts?

**A.** No, bankruptcy does not discharge all types of debt. Besides the exceptions for luxury purchases and cash advances close to bankruptcy, exceptions include some tax claims, alimony, child support, most student loans, fraud debts, and debts from a drunk driving problem. Chapter 7 bankruptcy also will not release you from claims for punitive damages for "willful and malicious" acts such as assaulting another person. You may still be responsible for these debts, even after you declare bankruptcy.

### Q. Should husbands and wives file jointly for bankruptcy?

**A.** They are permitted to, but whether it is to their advantage depends on many factors, such as how closely entwined their finances are and whether they live in a community property or separate property state (see the chapter, "Family Law," beginning on page 51.) They're best advised to seek the counsel of a bankruptcy lawyer well versed in the law of their state. If they both file bankruptcy at the same time, only one case filing fee ($160) will have to be paid to the court in a Chapter 7 or 13 case.

## CHAPTER 13 OF THE BANKRUPTCY CODE

### Q. What does a Chapter 13 bankruptcy case involve?

**A.** Chapter 13 allows individuals who have steady incomes to pay all or a portion of their debts under protection and supervision of the court. Under Chapter 13, you file a bankruptcy petition and a proposed payment plan with the U.S. Bankruptcy Court. The law requires that the payments have a value at least equal to what would have been distributed in a Chapter 7 liquidation case. An important feature of Chapter 13 is that you will be permitted to keep all your assets while the plan is in effect and after you have successfully completed it.

Chapter 13 is available only to those borrowers who have less than $100,000 in unsecured debts (such as credit cards) and less than $350,000 in secured debts (such as mortgages and car loans). Anyone with greater debts usually must declare bankruptcy under Chapters 7 or 11 of the Bankruptcy Code. Congress is currently considering a proposal to substantially raise the limit on secured debts, thereby making Chapter 13 more widely available than at present.

### Q. What is a proposed payment plan?

**A.** Under the rules for a Chapter 13 filing, if a creditor or the trustee objects to your plan, your payments must represent all your disposable income for a three-year period; that is, whatever is left over from your total income after you have paid for taxes and necessary living expenses. If there is no objection, the plan may be more flexible. The plan that you prepare for review by your lawyer should show your income from all sources and then a list of your necessary expenses. What is left from your income after paying living expenses will be available for disbursement to your creditors. Your plan must provide for payment in full of all priority claims, such as taxes, although you can arrange to pay them over the life of the plan (usually three to five years).

You submit your plan to the court and a Chapter 13 trustee, who is appointed by the United States Trustee to handle Chapter 13 cases. The trustee will verify the accuracy and reasonableness of your plan and distribute your proposal to the creditors. They will have the opportunity at a hearing to challenge your proposal if they believe that it is unreasonable. With that in mind, the trustee will want to be sure that your plan provides enough for you to live on, but will also challenge expenses that are unreasonably high. The issue is whether you are making a "good faith" effort to repay your debts, even if it means a reduction in your living standards—such as cutting your entertainment expenses down from five hundred

dollars per month. Since the trustee's recommendation will carry considerable weight with the court, it pays to be honest and open with the information that you provide. Once the payment plan is approved by the court after the hearing, you make regular monthly payments to the trustee, who in turn splits up the money among your creditors according to the plan. A Chapter 13 discharge is granted after completion of the payments in the plan. If the payments are not completed, there are some circumstances under which a more limited discharge may be granted.

The role of Chapter 13 trustees varies among judicial districts. Some trustees work with debtors to help them learn to manage their finances, and may arrange for automatic payroll deduction of the monthly payments to be credited directly to the trustee's account for disbursement to the various creditors. A small part of the monthly payments goes to the trustee for these service.

A repayment plan under Chapter 13 normally extends your time for paying debts. The permitted repayment period is usually up to three years or, with special permission of the court, up to five years. Typically, the amount that you repay under a Chapter 13 plan is determined by the total of your planned monthly payments over three years, given your good faith effort to do the best that you can. A Chapter 13 repayment plan often results in your repaying less than you owe.

### Q. Compared with straight bankruptcy, are there any advantages to filing for Chapter 13?

**A.** Yes, there are several advantages.

First, you will be able to retain and use all your assets as long as you make payments to the trustee as agreed. There is an important difference between the treatment under Chapter 13 of two types of your secured creditors: those who have a lien on your car, for example, and those who have a lien on your home. Take the first group of secured creditors. Say that you have an unpaid balance on your car loan of $8,000, but that the car is worth only $5,000. In that case, the court will approve the "cram down" of the loan to $5,000 as the secured claim, with your monthly payments reduced to reflect the lower loan balance. (If the car were worth $10,000, you would need only pay the $8,000 balance outstanding on the loan. If you cannot make the required monthly payments on your car, you must return it, unless the creditor agrees otherwise.)

However, the story is quite different for your home mortgage. Even if the market value of your home has fallen below the unpaid balance on your mortgage, the court generally cannot "cram down" the amount you owe on your mortgage to the market value of your home. While you can put accumulated past delinquent mortgage payments (with interest to account for your delay) under the Chapter 13 plan, you must make future monthly payments on your home mortgage loan, or turn your home over to the lender.

Second, under Chapter 13, if you had people co-sign any of your loans or other credit, your creditors cannot collect from these co-signers until it is clear that the Chapter 13 plan will not pay the entire amount owed to the creditors. In contrast, if you file a straight bankruptcy (Chapter 7) petition, your creditors have the right to demand payment from your co-signers immediately.

Third, the discharge of debts under Chapter 13 is broader than it is under Chapter 7. Once you successfully complete a repayment plan under Chapter 13, individual creditors cannot require you to pay them in full, for example, even if you gave them false financial information when you applied for the credit, or if you used some other fraudulent means to get credit. (However, if you only partially complete a plan and the court discharges you anyway, you can be held liable for the full amount of fraudulent

debts, even under Chapter 13.) The story is different if you file for straight bankruptcy. Then any credit grantor to whom you gave false or fraudulent information may object to discharging you from repaying the debt you owe it. Congress is considering applying the same principle to Chapter 13.

Fourth, you have some flexibility in making payments to the trustee under a Chapter 13 plan. For example, if you have an accident that causes you to lose time from work temporarily, you may be able to arrange a moratorium to miss a payment and catch up later. Further, if there is a major permanent reduction in your income, for example, from lost hours due to a chronic illness, your trustee may support a modification in the plan. This might call for stretching out payments, reducing them, or giving up some asset for which you are making payments. As an alternative, if the default in your payments has resulted from circumstances for which you "could not justly be held accountable," and if the unsecured creditors have received as much as they would have received under Chapter 7, you might apply for a hardship discharge, which would provide for a Chapter 7-type discharge of your remaining unsecured debts, but not your payments on secured debts, such as your mortgage payments. Indeed, if the situation is very serious, you may file at any time under Chapter 7 and receive such a discharge, so long as you have not filed for Chapter 7 within the preceding six years. (Of course, in a Chapter 7 filing you risk having to surrender your nonexempt assets.)

Fifth, you may file under Chapter 13 more often than under Chapter 7. The law forbids you from receiving a discharge under Chapter 7 more than once every six years. However, Chapter 13 allows you to file repeatedly, although each filing will appear on your credit record and all Chapter 13 plans have to be filed in good faith. Note, however, that after you have been discharged under Chapter 13, you must wait six years before filing under Chapter

7, unless you have paid your unsecured creditors at least 70 percent of their allowed claims and the Chapter 13 plan was proposed by you in good faith and was your best effort.

Sixth, having filed for Chapter 13 may make it easier for you to obtain credit later, since potential creditors might prefer to see a Chapter 13 filing in your credit record instead of a straight Chapter 7 bankruptcy. Chapter 13 often results in the eventual repayment of a larger portion of your debts than would have happened in straight bankruptcy. Creditors have no legal duty, however, to give you any special consideration on this basis. You would have to discuss it with them when the time comes.

**Q.** *What happens if I can't keep up my payments under Chapter 13?*

**A.** If you fail to make your payments as agreed, any of the creditors may seek to have the case converted to Chapter 7 or simply to have the Chapter 13 case dismissed, whichever is best for the creditor. If the case is dismissed, the collection calls will begin again and you may have your car, for example, repossessed or your home foreclosed upon.

**Q.** *It is very important that we keep our home. To summarize, what are the relative merits of Chapter 7 and Chapter 13 for this objective?*

**A.** First, under either type of filing, you will be able to keep your home only if you continue to make the required monthly payments on your mortgages. If you file for Chapter 7, you must make arrangements acceptable to your mortgage lender to catch up on any delinquent payments; if you file for Chapter 13, you may be able to include the delinquent payments in the payment plan and pay those off over, for example, three years, while maintaining ongoing monthly mortgage payments. As will be seen below, a willingness to make monthly pay-

ments on the mortgage will not assure that you can keep your home. But *not* making monthly payments in the future will assure that you will *not* keep your home.

*Chapter 7*

A willingness to continue making the agreed monthly payments may not prevent you from losing your home if you file for Chapter 7. Under a Chapter 7 filing, your unsecured creditors may also have an interest in your home if it is worth more than the total of the mortgage debt and your homestead exemption. The trustee may take possession of your home and sell it for the benefit of the creditors; that is, it may become part of the collection of your assets taken by the trustee for the benefit of your creditors. Whether the trustee will actually take your home will depend upon two basic factors:

- *The homestead exemption.* Most states allow you some ability to retain an equity interest in your home, but how much varies a great deal among the states. Typically, the exemptions are termed homestead exemptions—"homestead" being simply your home and the lot that it sits on. Most states put a dollar limit on the amount of your equity in the homestead that you can shield from creditors. As noted earlier, under the federal code, the amount a husband and wife can jointly protect is $15,000. However, since thirty-seven states have replaced the federal exemptions with their own limits, you are more likely to be governed by a state statute. (The other thirteen states allow a choice between the federal and state exemptions.) To illustrate, assume that the market value of your home is $80,000, and you have a mortgage of $55,000. Your equity is the difference between those two figures, or $25,000. If your homestead exemption were $20,000 (as in Colorado), the creditors could seek to claim the $5,000 left over from your exemption. As a practical matter, the trustee would probably not go to the expense and trouble of taking over the property and selling it for the benefit of the unsecured creditors, but you could be called upon to pay the $5,000 to the trustee.

In a few states there is no dollar limit on the homestead exemption, only a limit on the acreage that can be shielded from creditors. This means some very valuable property can be shielded from creditors. As noted earlier, in Florida there is no dollar limit on the value of the homestead. In Texas unsecured creditors cannot seek payment from a homestead, so long as it is not more than one acre in a city or 200 acres elsewhere, *regardless of the value of the property*. However, the homesteader will still have to make the required monthly payments to the bank that is financing his $2 million townhouse in downtown Dallas or his home in Palm Beach.

• *The difference between the value of your equity and your homestead exemption.* The greater the spread between the market value of your home and your equity, the more likely is it that the trustee will find it worthwhile to take over your home and sell it for the benefit of creditors. Take the example given above, but assume that the market value is $180,000, not $80,000. Now, if the house is taken over by the trustee and sold for the benefit of the bankruptcy estate, the funds available for unsecured creditors would amount to $105,000:

| | |
|---|---|
| Selling price | $180,000 |
| Less: Mortgage loan | 55,000 |
| Value of your equity | 125,000 |
| Less: Homestead exemption | 20,000 |
| Available for unsecured creditors | $105,000 |

To add a touch of irony, say that you bought the house a few years ago for $70,000, but are now having it sold for $180,000. Your Chapter 7 estate faces the possibility of a tax on the capital gain of $110,000 the trustee has "realized."

*Chapter 13*

Under a Chapter 13 plan, your basic choice is either (a) to agree to continue your lender's lien on your home and to make the required ongoing monthly payments, in addition to curing the default, or (b) to turn the property over to the lender. A lender who recovers less from the sale of the house than the amount that you owe will have an unsecured claim against you for the difference. It is possible that if housing values are greatly depressed, a lender might be willing to lower the monthly payments in order to gain some income and keep the house occupied. But don't count on it.

## AN ALTERNATIVE FOR FARMERS: CHAPTER 12

### Q. Does the law offer farmers a special type of bankruptcy?

**A.** Yes, farmers have the option of a special type of bankruptcy under "Chapter 12" of the Bankruptcy Code. It is one of a series of special farm-aid provisions enacted to help farmers survive periodic economic slumps. Chapter 12 allows farmers with a lot of real-estate debts to avoid foreclosure by pledging part of the profits from their future crops to pay off the debts. Meanwhile, the farmers temporarily pay creditors an amount similar to the fair-market rent. Only farmers acting in good faith have the right to file a Chapter 12 petition. In order for a petition to proceed quickly, as in other chapter filings, the debtor must submit to the bankruptcy court a list of creditors, a list of assets and liabilities, and a Statement of Financial Affairs. The farmer-debtor usually will require legal help.

## IN CONCLUSION

### Q. What results from bankruptcy?

**A.** Fortunately, there are no longer debtors' prisons, but neglecting your bills, getting in debt over your head, or bankruptcy may hurt your credit history for many years. Federal law protects your right to file for bankruptcy. For example, you cannot be fired from your job solely because you filed for bankruptcy. However, creditors may deny you credit in the future. Remember, most unfavorable information in your credit file stays there for seven years and a bankruptcy stays for ten years. So long as your credit record has unfavorable information, you may have credit problems. This means that you may have trouble renting an apartment, getting a loan to buy a car, or a mortgage for a house. You also may find it difficult to obtain certain types of jobs for which financial responsibility is an important qualification.

Nonetheless, declaring bankruptcy is sometimes your only reasonable choice. People who file bankruptcies are usually doing so because of financial difficulties. These may have resulted from the loss of a job or from a serious illness or accident. Whatever the reason, you have a legal right to file for bankruptcy. A lawyer or other professional who specializes in bankruptcy can help you decide what is best for you.

## WHERE TO GET MORE INFORMATION

The resources for bankruptcy and credit are quite similar, since both topics deal with consumer economics. For this reason, if you need further details or assistance, see the "Where to Get More Information" section on page 270 at the end of the chapter on consumer credit, which precedes this chapter. More specialized resources are listed below:

John Ventura, *The Bankruptcy Kit* (Chicago: Dearborn Financial Publishing, Inc., 1991).

Henry Sommer, *Consumer Bankruptcy Law and Practice* (Boston: National Consumer Law Center, 1993). This is a book mostly for lawyers, but is of use to consumers as well.

# CHAPTER NINE

# Contracts and Consumer Law

# INTRODUCTION

RECOGNIZING WHAT CONSTITUTES A CONTRACT is the key to understanding many legal questions. Very often a dispute centers not on whether someone has violated a contract, but whether there was a contract in the first place. Other disputes center on whether a change in circumstances has made the contract unenforceable.

This chapter contains five sections. The first section, "A Contract Defined," outlines what contracts are and how people form them. The second section, "What a Contract Is Not," looks at cases where the necessary parts of a contract are missing, and discusses your defenses to other people's claims that they have a contract with you. The third section, "Practical Contracts," focuses on contracts in daily life and highlights issues of interest to consumers. The fourth section, "Special Types of Contracts," discusses leases, warranties, advertising, door-to-door sales, and other special types of contracts. The fifth section, "Breaches and Remedies," discusses ways to deal with disputes arising out of contractual relationships.

## A CONTRACT DEFINED

### Q. What is a contract?

**A.** A contract consists of voluntary promises between competent parties to do, or not to do, something that the law will enforce. These are binding promises, which may be oral or written. Depending on the situation, a contract could obligate someone even if he or she wants to call the deal off before receiving anything from the other side. The details of the contract—who, how, what, how much, how many, when, etc.—are called its provisions or terms.

In order for a promise to qualify as a contract, it has to be supported by the exchange of something of value between the participants or parties. This something is called consideration. Consideration is most often money, but can be some other bargained-for benefit or detriment (as explained more fully below). The final qualification for a contract is that the subject of the promise (including the consideration) may not be illegal.

Suppose that a friend agrees to buy your car for $1,000. That is the promise. You benefit by getting the cash. Your friend benefits by getting the car. Since it is your car, the sale is legal, and you and your friend have a contract.

It is common for the word "contract" to be used as a verb meaning "to enter into a contract." We also speak of contractual relationships to refer to the whole of sometimes complex relationships, which may comprise one or many contracts.

### Q. May anyone enter into a contract?

**A.** No. In order to make an enforceable contact, people have to be able to understand what they're doing. That requires both maturity and mental capacity. Without both of these, one party could be at a disadvantage in the bargaining process, which could invalidate the contract.

### Q. What determines enough maturity to make a contract?

**A.** In this sense, maturity is defined as a certain age a person reaches—regardless of whether he or she is in fact "mature." State laws permit persons to make contracts if they have reached the age of majority (the end of being a minor), which is usually age eighteen.

## Q. Does that mean minors may not make a contract?

**A.** No, minors may make contracts. But courts may choose not to enforce some of them. The law presumes that minors need to be protected from their lack of maturity, and won't allow, for example, a Porsche salesman to exploit their naiveté by enforcing a signed sales contract whose real implications a young person is unlikely to have comprehended. Sometimes this results in minors receiving benefits (such as goods or services) and not having to pay for them, though they would have to return any goods still in their possession. This would apply even to minors who are emancipated—living entirely on their own—who get involved in contractual relationships, as well as to a minor who lives at home but is unsupervised long enough to get into a contractual fix.

A court may require a minor or the minor's parents to pay the fair market value (not necessarily the contract price) for what courts call necessaries (what you would likely call "necessities"). The definition of a "necessary" depends entirely on the person and the situation. It probably will always include food and probably will never include CDs, Nintendo cartridges or Porsches. Minors who reach full age and do not disavow their contracts may then have to comply with all their terms. In some states, courts may require a minor to pay the fair value of goods or services purchased under a contract that minor has disavowed.

## Q. When does mental capacity invalidate a contract?

**A.** While the age test for legal maturity is easy to determine, the standards for determining mental capacity are remarkably complex and differ widely from one state to another. One common test is whether people have the capacity to understand what they were doing and to appreciate its effects when they made the deal.

Another approach is evaluating whether people can control themselves regardless of their understanding.

## Q. May an intoxicated person get out of a contract?

**A.** Very often someone who is "under the influence" can get out of a contract. The courts don't like to let a voluntarily intoxicated person revoke a contract with innocent parties this way—but if someone acts like a drunk, the other party probably wasn't so innocent.

On the other hand, if someone doesn't appear to be intoxicated, he or she probably will have to follow the terms of the contract. The key in this area may be a person's medical history. Someone who can show a history of alcohol abuse, blackouts, and the like, may be able to void the contract, regardless of his or her appearance when the contract is made. This is true especially if the other party involved knows about the prior medical history. The reasoning goes back to mental capacity, and whether a person is able to exercise self-control.

## Q. Do I need a lawyer to make a contract?

**A.** If you satisfy the maturity and mental capacity requirements, you don't need anyone else (besides the other party). But it probably is a good idea to see a lawyer before you sign complex contracts, such as business deals or contracts involving large amounts of money.

## Q. Must contracts be in writing?

**A.** Many types of contracts don't have to be written to be enforceable. An example is purchasing an item in a retail store. You pay money in exchange for an item that the store warrants (by implication, as discussed later) will perform a certain function. Your receipt is proof of the contract. And, in fact, with some important exceptions (discussed below) virtu-

## CAPACITY

*We've discussed the fundamental requirements for competence to make a contract—maturity and mental capacity. Of course, it should go without saying that there's an even more fundamental requirement: that both parties be people. In the case of a corporation or other legal entity, which the law considers a "person," this could be an issue. A problem in the formation or status of the entity could cause it to cease existing legally, thus making it impossible to enter into a contract. In that case, however, the individuals who signed the contract on behalf of the legally nonexistent entity could be personally liable for fulfilling the contract.*

*Historically, the law has had other criteria for capacity. Slaves, married women and convicts were at one time not considered capable of entering into contracts in most states. Even today, certain American Indians are regarded as "wards" of the U.S. government for many purposes, and their contract-law status is similar to that of minors.*

ally any transaction agreed to orally could be enforceable.

As with a written contract, the existence of an oral contract must be proved before the courts will enforce it. But as you can imagine, an oral contract can be very hard to prove—you seldom have it on video. An oral contract is usually proved by showing that outside circumstances would lead a reasonable observer to conclude that a contract most likely existed. Even then, there is always the problem of what the terms of the oral contract were. The courts typically look only to unrefuted (uncontested) testimony to help them "fill in the blanks," and are hesitant to add words or terms to any written document.

### Q. Are there any advantages to putting a contract in writing?

**A.** Although most states recognize and enforce oral contracts, the safest practice is to put any substantial agreement in writing. Get any promise from a salesperson or an agent in writing, especially if there already is a written contract—even an order form, printed receipt, or a handwritten "letter of agreement" or "understanding"—covering any part of the same deal. Otherwise that order form or other paper probably will be regarded by the law as a complete statement of all understandings between the parties. Anything not in that written contract would be deemed not to be part of the deal.

Writing down the terms of a good-faith agreement is the best way to ensure that all parties are aware of their rights and duties—even if no party intends to lie about the provisions of the agreement.

### Q. Which contracts have to be in writing?

**A.** Under statutes (laws passed by legislatures) in most states, the courts will enforce certain contracts only if they are in writing and are signed by the parties who are going to be obligated to fulfill them. In most states, these contracts include:

- any promise to be responsible for someone else's debts—often called a surety contract or a guaranty; one example would be an agreement by parents to guarantee payment of a loan made by a bank to their child;
- any promise, made with consideration, to marry (though this rule has been eliminated in many states);
- any promise that the parties cannot possibly fulfill within one year from when they made the promise;
- any promise involving the change of ownership of land or interests in land such as leases;
- any promise for the sale of goods worth more than $500 or lease of goods worth more than $1,000;
- any promise to bequeath property (give it after death);
- any promise to sell stocks and bonds.

Some states have additional requirements for written contracts. These statutes are designed to prevent fraudulent claims in areas where it is uniquely difficult to prove that oral contracts have been made, or where important policies are at stake, such as the dependability of real estate ownership rights.

### Q. What are the rules regarding signatures?

**A.** A signature can be handwritten, but a stamped, photocopied, or engraved signature is often valid as well, as are signatures written by electronic pens. Even a simple mark or other indication of a name may be enough. What matters is whether the signature is authorized and intended to authenticate a writing, that is, indicate the signer's execution (completion and acceptance) of it. That means that you can authorize someone else to sign for you as

well. But the least risky and most persuasive evidence of assent is your own handwritten signature.

### Q. Do contracts have to be notarized by a notary public?

**A.** In general, no. Notary publics or notaries, once important officials who were specially authorized to draw up contracts and transcribe official proceedings, now act mostly to administer oaths and to authenticate documents by attesting or certifying that a signature is genuine. Many commercial contracts, such as promissory notes or loan contracts, are routinely notarized with the notary's signature and seal to ensure that they are authentic, even where this is not strictly required. Many technical documents required by law, such as certificates of incorporation, must be notarized if they are going to be recorded in a local or state filing office.

### Q. What is an offer?

**A.** Offer and acceptance are the fundamental parts of a contract, once capacity is established. An offer is a communication by an offeror of a present intention to enter a contract. (The offeror is the person making the offer.) It is not simply an invitation to bargain or negotiate. For the communication to be effective, the offeree (the one who is receiving the offer) must receive it. In a contract to buy and sell, for an offer to be valid, all of the following must be clear:

- Who is the offeree?
- What is the subject matter of the offer?
- How many of the subject matter does the offer involve (quantity)?
- How much (price)?

Let's say you told your friend, "I'll sell you my mauve-colored Yugo for one thousand dollars." Your friend is the offeree, and the car is the subject matter. Describing the car as a mauve Yugo makes your friend reasonably sure that both of you are talking about the same car (and only one of them). Finally, the price is $1,000. It's a perfectly good offer.

### Q. Is an advertisement an offer?

**A.** No. Courts usually consider advertisements something short of an offer. They are an "expression of intent to sell" or an invitation to bargain. The section on special types of contracts later in this chapter discusses this further.

### Q. Does an offer stay open indefinitely?

**A.** Not unless the offeree has an option, an irrevocable offer for which the offeree bargains (discussed below). Otherwise, an offer ends when:

- the time to accept is up—either a "reasonable" amount of time or the deadline stated in the offer;
- the offeror cancels the offer;
- the offeree rejects the offer;
- the offeree dies or is incapacitated.

An offer is also closed, even if the offeree has an option, if:

- a change in the law makes the contract illegal;
- something destroys the subject matter of the contract (see below).

### Q. What is an option contract?

**A.** An option is an agreement, made for consideration, to keep an offer open for a certain period. For example, in return for a fifty-dollar consideration today, you might agree to give your friend until next Friday to accept your offer to sell her your Yugo for $1,000. Now you have an option contract, and you may not sell the car to someone else—even for $1,200—

> **GIVE AND TAKE**
> *A contract can only come about through the bargaining process, which may take many forms. This section discusses the definitions of consideration, offer, and acceptance. A later section will look at contracts that involve less give and take. But all the principles discussed here will have to be present, in some form, in any contract.*

without breaching that contract. Selling an option puts a limit on your ability to revoke an offer, a limit that the optionee (the option-holder) bargains for with you.

### Q. What constitutes the acceptance of an offer?

**A.** Acceptance is the offeree's voluntary, communicated agreement or assent to the terms and conditions of the offer. Assent is some act or promise of agreement. An easy example of an assent might be your friend saying, "I agree to buy your mauve Yugo for one thousand dollars."

Generally, a valid acceptance requires that every term is agreed to be the same as in the offer. Thus, if the offer requires acceptance by mail, you must accept by mail for the offer to be effective. If there's no such requirement, you just have to communicate your acceptance by some reasonable means (not by carrier pigeon or smoke signals but by telephone, mail, or maybe facsimile). On the other hand, an assent that is not quite so specific but is crystal-clear would also suffice—such as, in the Yugo example, saying, "It's a deal. I'll pick it up tomorrow." Once again, the standard is whether a reasonable observer would think there was an assent.

## Q. Can silence make up an acceptance?

**A.** In most cases, the answer is no. It isn't fair to allow someone to impose a contract on someone else. Yet there are circumstances where failure to respond may have a contractual effect. Past dealings between the parties, for example, can create a situation in which silence constitutes acceptance. Suppose a fire insurance company, according to past practice to which you have assented, sends you a renewal policy (which is, in effect, a new contract for insurance) and bills you for the premium. If you kept the policy but later refused to pay the premium, you would be liable for the premium. This works to everyone's benefit: If your house burned down after the original insurance policy had expired but before you had paid the renewal premium, you obviously would want the policy still to be effective. And the insurer is protected from your deciding not to pay the premium only after you know what claims you might have.

## Q. Can acts make up an acceptance?

**A.** Yes. Not only words, but any conduct that would lead a reasonable observer to believe that the offeree had accepted the offer qualifies as an acceptance. Suppose you say, "John, I will pay you fifty dollars to clean my house on Sunday at nine o'clock a.m." If John shows up at nine o'clock a.m. on Sunday and begins cleaning, he adequately shows acceptance (assuming you're home or you otherwise would know he showed up).

To take another example, you don't normally have to pay for goods shipped to you that you didn't order (a later section will discuss this in more detail). But if you were a retailer and you put them on display in your store and sold them, you would have accepted the offer to buy them from the wholesaler and you would be obligated to pay the invoice price. You otherwise would only have to allow them to be taken back at no cost to you. Sometimes this is called an implied (as opposed to an express) contract. Either one is a genuine contract.

## Q. When is the acceptance effective?

**A.** The contract usually is in effect as soon as the offeree transmits or communicates the acceptance—unless the offeror has specified that the acceptance must be received before it is effective, or before an option expires (as discussed previously). In these situations, there's no contract until the offeror receives the answer, and in the way specified, if any.

## Q. What is the "meeting of the minds"?

**A.** This term describes an offer that the offeree accepts in all its critical or material terms. This phrase also implies that both parties understand (or reasonably should understand) these terms in the same way. The "meeting of the minds" is a useful phrase to help determine in your own mind whether you ever got past the bargaining stage of negotiations.

## Q. Is an "agreement to agree" a contract?

**A.** Generally not, because it suggests that important terms are still missing. Rarely will a court "supply" those terms itself. An agreement to agree is another way of saying that there has not yet been a meeting of the minds, although the parties would like there to be.

## Q. Can a joke be the basis for a contract?

**A.** It depends on whether a reasonable observer would know it's a joke, and on whether the "acceptance" was adequate. In our Yugo example, you probably couldn't get out of the contract by saying, "How could you think I'd sell this for one thousand dollars? I meant it as a joke!" On the other hand, if someone sued

## THE REASONABLE PERSON

*Throughout this and any other law book, the word "reasonable" will appear many times. Very often you'll see references to the "reasonable man" or the "reasonable person." Why is the law so preoccupied with this mythical being?*

*The answer is that no contract can possibly predict the infinite number of disputes that might arise under it. Similarly, no set of laws regulating liability for personal or property injury can possibly foresee the countless ways human beings and their property can harm other people or property. Since the law can't provide for every possibility, it has evolved the standard of the "reasonable" person to furnish some uniform standards and to guide the courts.*

*Through the fiction of the "reasonable person," the law creates a standard that the judge or jury may apply to each set of circumstances. It is a standard that reflects community values, rather than the judgment of the people involved in the actual case. Thus a court might decide whether an oral contract was formed by asking whether a "reasonable person" would conclude from people's actions that one did exist. Or the court might decide an automobile accident case by asking what a "reasonable person" might have done in a particular traffic or hazard situation.*

you because you "backed out" on your "promise" to sell her France for fifteen dollars, the joke would be on her—no one reasonably could have thought you were serious.

### Q. What is a condition?

**A.** People often use the word "condition" to mean one of the terms of a contract. A more precise definition is that a condition is an event that has to occur if the contract is to be performed. In our earlier example, your friend might have said, "I'll buy your mauve Yugo for one thousand dollars only if you can deliver it to me by tonight." At this point, you are still negotiating; there is no contract. But if you reply, "It's a deal—I'll be there tonight," you have a contract, with a condition of delivery by tonight. If you fail to deliver the car by tonight, you have breached the contract. (Breaches of contract and what you can do about them are covered later.)

Conditions can be after the fact, too. You may make the payment for decorating a room in your house conditional on your complete satisfaction. If the contract didn't state that, though, it would only guarantee you normally acceptable work.

Neither party is required to agree to a condition that comes up during the bargaining, and the one who wants it may have to pay extra for it. When a condition is put into negotiations, you have to decide whether it's worth it to you, considering the risks and costs of not having it. In this respect, a condition is the same as any other term, such as price or quantity.

The most common conditions include those in real estate sales contracts requiring that the sale be conditional on the buyers obtaining financing or selling their present home, or on an acceptable home inspection report.

### Q. How much consideration, or payment, must there be for a contract to be valid?

**A.** There is no minimum amount. A price is only how people agree to value something, so there's no absolute standard of whether a price is fair or reasonable. The courts presume that people will only make deals that they consider worthwhile. So if you want to sell your car to your friend for one dollar instead of $1,000, you can do it. (But don't sell it for $1,000 and just report a one dollar sale to the state to avoid paying the full sales tax. Many states have systems in place to check for just such abuses.) The exception is something that would "shock the conscience of the court." The idea of unconscionability will be discussed later in this chapter, on page 307.

### Q. Does consideration have to be money?

**A.** No. Consideration is any promise, act, or transfer of value that induces a party to enter a contract. Consideration is a bargained-for benefit or advantage, or a bargained-for detriment or disadvantage. A benefit might be receiving $10. First dibs on Super Bowl tickets might be an advantage. A disadvantage may involve promising not to do something, such as a promise not to sue someone. For these purposes, even quitting smoking, done with the reasonable expectation of some reward or benefit from someone else, is a detriment: Even though it's good for your health, it took effort that you otherwise would not have made.

For example, you could agree to give your car to your friend in exchange for his promise that he'll stop letting his schnauzer out late at night. Your friend is giving up what is presumably his right to let his dog out any time he wants. In return, you are giving up your car. Other types of valid considerations include a promise to compromise on an existing dispute.

### Q. Do both sides have to give consideration?

**A.** Yes. There's a crucial principle in contract law called mutuality of obligations. It

> **IN CONSIDERATION...**
> The doctrine that consideration is a central element of a contract is of relatively recent origin. Until the last few centuries, elaborate formality rather than consideration was the chief requirement to form a contract. The necessary formalities were a sufficient signed writing, a seal or other attestation of authenticity, and delivery to whomever would have the rights under the contract. A seal could be an impression on wax or some other surface, bearing the mark of a notary public or other official. The vestiges of the seal remain in some contracts, where the initials "L.S." (for the Latin locus sigilli, "place of the seal"), or simply the word "seal" is printed to represent symbolically the authentication of the contract's execution. Even today, traditional Jewish wedding contracts are made on these formal bases: a writing, an attestation by witnesses, and delivery.

means that both sides have to be committed to giving up something. If either party reserves an unqualified right to bail out, that person's promise is merely illusory: It's no promise at all.

### Q. Does the consideration have to be a new obligation?

**A.** Yes, because someone who is already obligated to do something hasn't suffered any detriment. Suppose you agree to have a contractor paint your house this Thursday for $500. Before starting, though, his workers strike for higher wages. He tells you on Wednesday night that he settled the strike but now the job will cost $650. You need the house painted before you leave for the North Pole on Friday, and there's no time to hire another contractor, so you agree to the new price. But the new agreement is not enforceable by him. He already had to paint your house for $500. He should have figured the possible increased costs into the original price. You didn't get anything of benefit from the modified contract, since you already had his promise to paint the house. Therefore, you only owe $500.

### Q. Does that mean I can't renegotiate a contract?

**A.** No, it only means that no one can force you to renegotiate by taking advantage of an existing agreement. In the previous example, you might have decided that the painter deserved more money than you had originally bargained for. More realistically, you might have agreed that he would do some work not included in the original contract. You could want to use the contractor later, or you might feel that he does the best job at any price. (Considerations like these allow many sports stars to renegotiate their contracts.)

Keep in mind that whenever you get involved in a deal, you are taking a risk that it might be less beneficial for you than you

planned when you agreed to the contract terms. The other party doesn't have to ensure your profit, unless the two of you included that in your bargain.

### Q. Is a promise to make a gift a contract?

**A.** Not if it truly is only a promise to make a gift, because a gift lacks the two-sided obligation discussed above. But if the person promising the gift is asking for anything in return, even by implication, a contract may be formed. The key, again, is consideration.

### Q. What if someone makes a promise without consideration, but I rely on it?

**A.** Remember that consideration may be a disadvantage to one party. From that idea, the law has developed the concept of promissory reliance—that a contract may be formed if one party reasonably relies on the other's promise. That means that he does more than get his heart set on it. He has to do something he wouldn't have done, or fail to do something he would have done, but for the promise. If that reliance causes some loss, he may have an enforceable contract.

Suppose that rich Uncle Murray loves your kids. On previous occasions he has asked you to buy them expensive presents and has reimbursed you for them. This past summer, Uncle Murray told you he would like you to build a swimming pool for the kids, and send him the bill. You did so, but moody Uncle Murray changed his mind. Now he refuses to pay for the pool, and claims you can't enforce a promise to make a gift. The pool, however, is no longer considered a gift. You acted to your detriment in reasonable reliance on his promise, by taking on the duty to pay for a swimming pool you would not normally have built. Uncle Murray has to pay if you prove that he induced you to build the pool, especially if this understanding was consistent with many previous gifts.

Remember, however, that you still have to live with your Uncle Murray.

### Q. May someone else make a contract on my behalf?

**A.** Yes, but only with your permission. The law refers to such an arrangement as agency. We couldn't do business without it. For example, when you buy a car, you bargain and finally cut a deal with the salesperson. But she doesn't own the car she's selling you. She might not even have a car. She is an agent, someone with the authority to bind someone else—in this case, the car dealership—by contract. The law refers to that someone else as the principal.

To take another common example, real-estate brokers typically act as your agent when you sell a home. As the principal, you generally establish the terms or range of terms he is authorized to accept. (For example, "I'll sell if they will come up to one hundred thousand dollars and agree to close the sale by July.") Then your agent goes into negotiations on your behalf.

As long as agents do not exceed the authority granted them by their principals, contracts they make bind their principals as if the principals had made the contracts themselves. If something went wrong with the contract, you would sue the principal—not the agent—if you couldn't resolve the dispute in a friendly manner. An agent normally does not have any personal obligation.

While acting on behalf of principals, agents are required to put their own interests after those of the principal. Therefore, they may not personally profit beyond what the principal and agent have agreed to in their agency contract. That means they cannot take advantage of any opportunity which, under the terms of the agency, is meant to be exploited for the principal.

### Q. What happens when an agent does exceed the authority granted by a principal?

**A.** That depends on the circumstances. Suppose an agent exceeds her authority, but the person she's dealing with reasonably doesn't understand that she's exceeding it. If the principal knew (or reasonably should have known) that the agent has exceeded her authority in similar circumstances, but has done nothing about it, the principal may be bound by the contract negotiated by the agent. On the other hand, if the principal is not aware of the agent's actions exceeding her authority, they will only be enforceable against the principal if it was reasonable for the other person to believe the agent was acting within her authority.

For example, suppose the teenage boy wearing a service station uniform who fills your gas tank and checks your oil—and who appears to be an agent, to some limited degree, of the service station—offers to sell you the whole service station in trade for the sleek mauve Yugo you are driving. It's not reasonable for you to assume he has that power when common sense tells you he can only sell you his boss's gasoline and oil for a fixed price.

In contrast, if an insurance agent wrote you an insurance policy from his company that exceeded the policy amount he was authorized to write, but the insurer never told you this, you would be acting reasonably to assume he was authorized, and you probably could collect on a claim above his limit.

### Q. May I transfer my duties under a contract?

**A.** Yes, unless the contract prohibits such a transfer. The law refers to a transfer of duties or responsibilities as a delegation. If, however, someone contracts with you because of a special skill or talent only you have, you may not be able to transfer your duty. Such cases are quite rare. There are arguably no car mechanics who are so good at tuning an engine that they

**AGENTS WHO EXCEED THEIR AUTHORITY**

*On occasion, while making a contract, an agent might exceed the authority granted by the principal. An example might involve an automobile salesperson who signs a contract on behalf of a car dealer which, without the dealer's authority, gives the customer a warranty for 40,000 extra miles. In that case, the dealer might very well be bound by the contract.*

may not delegate someone else to do it for them—unless they specifically promise to do it themselves. On the other hand, if you hire well-known entertainers to perform at your wedding, they may not send other entertainers (no matter how talented) as substitutes without your permission.

### Q. May I delegate my rights?

**A.** A delegation or transfer of rights, called an assignment, is more flexible than a transfer of duties. For example, you may wish to transfer the right to receive money from a buyer for something you have sold. Generally, a contract right is yours to do with as you wish, as long as you didn't agree in the contract not to assign the right. You can sell it or give it away, though most states require you to put an assignment in writing, especially if it is a gift.

There are exceptions to the rule that assignments may be made freely. If an assignment would substantially increase the risk, or materially change the duty of the other party to the contract, the contract may not be assignable, even if its terms contain no explicit agreement to the contrary. Such an assignment would be

regarded as unfairly upsetting the expectations the other party had when he or she entered the contract.

For example, suppose you made a contract for fire insurance on a garage for your Yugo. Then a notorious convicted arsonist and insurance cheat contacted you upon release from prison and asked you to sell the garage and assign your rights under the garage's fire insurance policy to the arsonist. You would probably be in for a disappointment, even if the insurance policy didn't prohibit assignment. Since the insurer made its decision to insure in part based on your solid citizenship, insuring the arsonist would greatly increase its burden by taking on a risk it never anticipated.

## WHAT A CONTRACT IS NOT

### Bars to a Contract

### Q. May someone make a contract to do or sell something illegal?

**A.** No. The courts will not help someone collect an illegal gambling debt, or payment for illegal drugs or prostitution. The law treats these contracts as if they never existed—they are unenforceable or void. This is the contract defense of illegality.

Similarly, some contracts that are not specifically outlawed nonetheless will not be enforced if a court determines that enforcement would violate public policy. An example would be a contract to become a slave, which may not be prohibited by any specific statute but offends the law's view of what kinds of contracts society will permit.

### Q. What if the contract became unenforceable because something made it illegal after the people agreed to it?

**A.** Generally speaking, the Constitution forbids lawmakers from passing laws that would impair the rights people bargain for in contracts. Therefore, a contract is usually considered by courts in light of the law that applied at the time the contract was made—*unless the change in the law involves a compelling public policy.*

For example, a contract between a railroad and a property owner who leased a right-of-way to the railroad provided that the railroad was not responsible for any fire damage to the property caused by locomotives. Later, the state legislature made it illegal to fail to take certain precautions against fire damaging an adjoining property. The court held that, even if the new law would have made the old contract illegal (because it didn't include the newly required precautions), because it was passed after the contract was made it did not affect the contract.

Typically, however, courts say that because of a change in *public policy* as a result of the change in the law, they will not enforce the old contract. Obviously, a contract to sell someone a slave could not be enforced after slavery became illegal; neither could you enforce a contract to purchase a banned assault rifle that was made before the ban went into effect. This works both ways: a contract that was illegal when made usually will not be enforced, even though it would be legal if entered into today. One case involved a contract that violated wartime price-controls, entered into when those controls were in effect, which one of the parties wanted enforced after the war. The court ruled that a contract that was so damaging to the public good when made (and when no change in the law was anticipated) should never be enforced. To do so would have been to provide an incentive to enter into illegal contracts in the hope that they will someday be enforceable—a bad prescription for effective public policy.

## Q. Does the same hold true for a contract to do something immoral?

**A.** The courts will only enforce a moral code that the law (or "public policy") already

reflects, such as laws against prostitution or stealing. You may feel that X-rated movies or fur coats are immoral, but as long as they're legal, they can be the subjects of enforceable contracts.

## Q. May a contract that I am a party to but that was made against my will be enforced against me?

**A.** No. A contract that someone agrees to under duress is void in most states. Duress is a threat or act that overcomes someone's free will. The classic case of duress is a contract signed by someone "with a gun to his head." Since this kind of duress is very rare—and often very hard to prove—the defense of duress is rarely successful.

Duress goes beyond persuasion or hard selling. Persuasion in bargaining is perfectly legal. It also isn't duress when you say, "I would never pay that much for a Yugo if I had a choice." You do have a choice—to buy a nice Taurus instead. But if you want that mauve Yugo, you "have to" pay what the owner demands. In contrast, duress involves actual coercion, such as a threat of violence or imprisonment.

## Q. Are there other kinds of duress besides physical threats?

**A.** Duress is a suspension of your free will. Besides being done by threats of physical violence, it may be duress to threaten to abuse the court system to coerce your agreement.

There is also economic duress. That was alluded to earlier when the contractor demanded more money after his workers went on strike and you needed your house painted before you left the country. This isn't the same as "driving a hard bargain." Rather, the contractor had already made a deal. When the contractor threatened to withhold his part of the deal, he left you with no practical choice but to agree. The classic case is where the supplier of a

## IS IT OR ISN'T IT A CONTRACT?

*The principles discussed will go a long way toward determining if people have formed a contract. You now know that a contract has to be made between willing, competent parties. Also, the contract must concern a legal subject matter. The preceding section also discussed many aspects of consideration.*

*Applying these principles isn't always easy. Sometimes special protections in the law complicate matters. If successfully invoked, only one of these may be needed to provide a complete defense against someone claiming you owe him or her money or something else you supposedly promised. It would prompt a court to resolve the dispute as if there never were a contract. Since the contract is void, neither party may enforce its terms in court against the other.*

*Other contracts are voidable, but not automatically void. What's the difference? A contract produced by fraud is not automatically void. People who are victimized by fraud have the option of asking a court to declare that contract void, or to reform (rewrite) it. On the other hand, if they went along with the contract for a substantial period of time, they could lose their right to get out of it. This is called ratification, and is based on the idea that they have, by their actions, made it clear that they are able to live with the terms.*
*A checklist of contract defenses appears in this section.*

necessary ingredient or material threatens, on short notice and at a critical time, not to deliver it—in violation of an existing contract—unless he or she gets more favorable terms. Courts have set aside contracts made under such economic duress.

### Q. What should I do if someone forces me to sign a contract under duress?

**A.** Once you get out of danger, see a lawyer who can tell you how to protect yourself. The lawyer can help you determine whether you have assumed any obligation, and what legal rights you might have besides disavowing the contract. It's important to act quickly. The courts are especially skeptical of a claim of duress made long after the danger has passed.

### Q. Are there other uses of unfair pressure, less severe than duress, that void a contract?

**A.** There is a contract defense called undue influence, which doesn't involve a threat. Rather, it's the unfair use of a relationship of trust to pressure someone into an unbalanced contract. Undue influence cases usually involve someone who starts out at a disadvantage, perhaps due to illness, age, or emotional vulnerability. The other person often has some duty to look out for the weaker one's interests.

An example would be a court-appointed guardian who "persuades" his twelve-year-old charge to lend him $25,000 from his trust fund, free of interest. The loan contract would be unenforceable because of undue influence, regardless of whether the minor otherwise had the capacity to make a contract.

## Q. What is fraud?

**A.** A contract can be canceled by a court because of fraud when one person knowingly made a material misrepresentation that the other person reasonably relied on and that disadvantaged that other person. A material misrepresentation is an important untruth. In many states, it doesn't have to be made on purpose to make the contract voidable.

Consider our earlier example involving a car sale. You offered to sell your Yugo to a friend. Suppose you knew it had no transmission, and you knew she wanted it for the usual purpose of driving it. You told her it was working fine, and she relied on your statement. Then the contract you made may be set aside on the grounds of fraud.

Here, there is no issue of the statement being merely the seller's opinion, or exaggerated "sales talk" puffery which people know not to believe literally. You didn't merely say it was a great car when really it was a mediocre car. Saying it's "great" is just an opinion, while fraud requires an outright lie, or a substantial failure to state a material fact about an important part of the contract. For that reason—and because corrupt people often know well the fine line between fraud and puffing—actual fraud that will invalidate a contract is a lot less common than people think.

## Q. If I enter into the contract under a mistaken impression, does that affect the contract's validity?

**A.** Probably not, assuming the other party didn't know about your mistake. This defense, unilateral mistake, is almost impossible to prove, even if the mistake is about the most important terms of the contract. If allowed liberally, it would lead to a lot of abuse. People would claim they made a mistake in order to get out of a contract they didn't like, even though they had no valid legal defense. Therefore, courts hardly ever permit such a defense, and even then, only in specialized business cases.

## Q. When is unilateral mistake ever a defense?

**A.** Courts have permitted a mistake defense most commonly if there has been an honest error in calculations. The calculations must be material to the contract, and the overall effect must be to make the contract unconscionable (discussed below), that is, unfairly burdensome. Such mistakes often happen when a unit of government puts public work out for bid. If a contractor mistakenly bids five million dollars to construct a bridge and a road, when the true cost to build the bridge alone was five million dollars, he or she might be able to raise this defense. Even then, however, if several months have elapsed and the government has materially relied on the mistaken figures before the mistake is discovered (for example, by taking a number of steps to move the process

### WHEN SOMEONE FORCES YOU TO SIGN

*Between the defenses of duress and undue influence, you should never have to fear a court holding you liable for a contract that someone forces you to sign. Both concepts are hard to define, though, and people often use them interchangeably. Also, their limits vary from one state to another. If you think either might apply to an agreement you want to get out of, see a lawyer.*

forward), then it would be unfair to the government to cancel the deal, and the defense would probably fail. (But see the discussion of reformation in the section on remedies, pages 334–335.)

Of course, if you explicitly state your mistaken idea, the other party has a duty to correct you. Then the issue is no longer one of mistake but of fraud. In our car-sale example, suppose the car's heater worked, but not too well, and you, the seller, knew that. Under contract law, if you and your friend hadn't discussed it, you probably wouldn't have to tell your friend about it. But suppose your friend told you, "The best thing about this car is that it's so hard to find a Yugo with a perfect heater." Then you would be obliged to tell your friend that the heater was faulty. If you didn't, many states would permit your friend to set aside the contract, or would allow your friend to collect damages for repairs required on the heater.

Having said this, the best defense is a good offense. Don't assume anything important or questionable. Ask the questions now—before you sign.

**Q.  *What if both sides make a mistake?***

**A.** Then you don't have the "meeting of the minds" discussed earlier. Or perhaps more accurately, the minds aren't meeting with the facts. Then, in order to avoid injustice, the court will often set aside the contract, under the theory of a mutual mistake.

The classic case of mutual mistake occurred when someone sold a supposedly infertile cow for eighty dollars. It turned out soon afterward that the cow was pregnant, which made her worth $800. The court ruled that since both parties thought they were dealing with a barren cow, the contract could be set aside.

**Q.  *Does that mean that contracts always have a built-in guarantee against mistakes?***

**A.** No. As you can imagine, this is a very tricky and unpredictable area. After all, many people make purchases on the understanding that the object is worth more to one person than to the other. You wouldn't pay $80 for a cow if she were not worth at least $80.01 to you. That is, you figure you're somewhat better off with the cow than with the $80. (Economists call this amount the "marginal benefit.") Similarly, the seller would not sell her if she were worth more than $79.99 to the seller. Both people have to be getting some benefit to agree to the sale. In the case of the cow, both buyer and seller understood clearly—but mistakenly—that the cow could not get pregnant. It's as if they made the contract for a subject that turned out not to exist.

Various courts draw the line between $80.01 and $800 at different places, if they are willing to draw it at all. Competent legal advice about the law in your state is crucial if you are considering voiding a contract because of a mistake.

**Q.  *What are statutes of limitations?***

**A.** These are laws setting time limits during which a lawsuit can be brought. The typical deadline for bringing a contract action is six years from the time the breach occurs. The idea of this policy is that everyone is entitled, at some point, to "close the book" on a transaction. It encourages people to move on and reduces the uncertainty that, for example, businesses would face if they could be sued for breaching contracts that no one alive in the organization remembers.

### Changing Situations

**Q.  *What if it becomes physically impossible to perform a contract?***

**A.** Suppose that you hire a contractor to paint your house on Thursday, and it burns down Wednesday night through no fault of your own. Then the contract will be set aside, because there's no way to perform it. You won't have to pay the painter, under the doctrine of impossibility of performance. Both of you are out of luck. The same is true if the contract covers a specific kind of product, and it becomes unavailable because of an act of God, such as an earthquake or blizzard. Courts usually will not enforce such a contract.

For example, suppose you contract to deliver one hundred barrels of a specific grade of oil from a specific Arabian oil field by a certain date. Then an earthquake devastates the oil field, making recovery of the oil impossible. You're probably off the hook under these circumstances.

This doctrine is also known as impracticability of performance, which reflects the fact that it may apply even if performance is not literally impossible, but is still seriously impractical.

### Q. What if changing circumstances make it much more costly to fulfill the contract, but it's still possible to do what the contract promised?

**A.** The courts probably would enforce the contract, on the grounds that the new circumstances were foreseeable, and that the possibility of increased costs was or could have been built into the contract. For instance, suppose again that you contract to deliver one hundred barrels of Arabian oil. This time, fighting breaks out in the Persian Gulf, interrupting shipping and greatly increasing the cost of the oil. When a court considers these facts, it's likely to say that you should have foreseen the possibility of fighting and built that risk into the price. The contract will stand.

### Q. What if the contract can be performed, but to do so would be pointless?

**A.** Sometimes a change in conditions doesn't make performance impossible or impractical, but it does make performance meaningless. The legal term for this is frustration of purpose. One famous case decided around the turn of the century involved a party that rented an apartment in London to view the processions to be held in connection with the coronation of the King of England. Because of the King's illness, the coronation was canceled. The court excused the renter from paying for the room. Through no fault of his own, the whole purpose of renting it—which the people who owned the room knew—had disappeared. Such cases, though, are rare indeed. More typically, you take your chances when you make a contract in expectation of some third party's or outside force's action; many contracts have a term to that effect built in.

There are three important criteria for a contract to be set aside for frustration of purpose. First, the frustration must be substantial—nearly total, and with almost no chance at improved benefit. Second, the change in circumstances must not be reasonably foreseeable. Third, the frustration must not have been your fault.

### Q. May someone have a contract set aside because it simply isn't fair?

**A.** It is possible, but not likely. Courts have a powerful weapon called unconscionability (from the word "conscience") at their disposal. Unconscionability means that the bargaining process or the contract's provisions "shock the conscience of the court." For example, selling $10,000 worth of rumba lessons to a ninety-five-year-old widow living on social security would probably be held unconscionable. An unconscionable contract is grossly unfair. Its terms suggest that one party took unfair advantage over the other one when they negotiated it. The courts are reluctant to use this weapon, but consumers have a better chance with it than anyone else, especially in installment contracts.

The important thing to remember is that you shouldn't rely on unconscionability in

## SHOULD THE BUYER STILL BEWARE?

*The well-known Latin maxim caveat emptor—"let the buyer beware"—is a strict rule placing the risk in a transaction with the buyer. Under this rule each party is protected only by inspecting and analyzing a potential transaction, because there is no remedy if there is a hidden problem. In fact, this "ancient" law really predominated only in the 19th and early 20th centuries, when the idea of "the sanctity of the contract" reigned. More common are the principles of "just prices" and fair dealing in transactions. They are part of rabbinic law, medieval law, and more recently statutory law—particularly the consumer fraud acts prohibiting unfair or deceptive acts and practices. Having said that, every buyer should recognize that the first line of defense is common sense, and not depend on a sympathetic judge to save him or her from a bad deal.*

## PRACTICAL CONTRACTS

### Q. Are form contracts worth reading?

**A.** Believe it or not, it pays to read them. Failure to read a contract is virtually never a valid legal defense. In most states the courts have held that people are bound by all the terms in a contract, even if they didn't read the contract before signing it (unless the other party engaged in fraud or unconscionable conduct). Don't trust the other party to tell you what it means; even if his intentions are good, he could be mistaken himself. Also, be suspicious if the salesperson urges you to "never mind, it's not important." (Ask the salesperson, "If it's not important, is it okay to cross out the whole paragraph?") Where a substantial amount of money is at stake, take the time to sit down with the form, and underline parts you do not understand. Then find out what they mean from someone you trust.

At the same time, you have to be realistic about exercising your right to read a form contract. At the car rental counter at the airport, you probably don't have time to read the contract and get an explanation of the terms you don't understand. Even if you did take the time, with whom would you negotiate? The sales clerk almost certainly doesn't have the authority to change the contract (but see the discussion on page 311 on contracts of adhesion).

### Q. What if all the time I take to protect my legal rights results in my losing a great bargain?

**A.** Rarely will a truly great bargain not be there tomorrow. For all the great deals that work out fine, the one you will remember is the one that went sour—where they socked you with the fine print you didn't bother to read. A great bargain won't fall into your lap, anyway. It requires a lot of footwork, research, and com-

making a contract. Though courts sometimes will void contracts on these grounds, the application of unconscionability is uncommon and uneven. Make the effort to understand all the terms of a contract. After all, it's also "unconscionable" to let someone take advantage of you.

## FILL IN THE BLANKS

*There are many kinds of form contracts. One is the kind you simply have to sign if you want to get insurance or a loan, or if you're financing a car. These are called contracts of adhesion—if you want the deal, you have to "adhere" or stick to the terms.*

*Another common kind of form contract is one with numerous blanks on it, which can be filled in with the names of the parties, the monetary terms, dates, etc. These are used commonly for the sale of homes and for leases on real estate. There are two main points to be aware of regarding these forms, which can be purchased at stationery stores:*

*First, while they may be standardized, there's no such thing as a "standard contract." Many innocuous-looking forms are available in several different versions, each fulfilling the same function—for example, an apartment lease—but each subtly different. One might be a "landlord's" contract, where the preprinted terms are more favorable to the landlord, while a nearly identical one is a "tenant's" contract. In any event, don't let anyone tell you it's "standard." Insist on crossing out or changing any term you don't like. If the other party refuses to accept changes that are important to you, then don't sign the contract. In today's economy, there is usually more than one source for the product or service you want.*

*Second, fill in all the blanks! A contract with your original signature but containing blank spaces can be like a blank check if altered unscrupulously. Be sure all blanks are filled, either with specific terms or straight lines to indicate that nothing goes there. And insist on your own copy with the other side's original signature.*

parison shopping. If you've done all that, it's unlikely that someone else is right behind you who has done it also.

#### Q. What is a rider?

**A.** A rider is a sheet of paper (or several pages) reflecting an addition or amendment (change) to the main body of a contract. Often

it's simpler to put changes in a rider, which supersedes any contradictory parts of the main contract, than to try to incorporate the changes on the original form.

#### Q. What can be so dangerous in fine print?

**A.** Very often the fine print contains terms that could greatly affect your personal finances

## GETTING OUT OF A CONTRACT

*A contract may be set aside if competent parties have not made it voluntarily. It also may be set aside if there was grossly insufficient consideration. In addition, certain contracts must be in writing, or they are also unenforceable. Here is a list of other contract defenses:*

- *illegality;*
- *duress;*
- *undue influence;*
- *fraud;*
- *mistake;*
- *unconscionability;*
- *impossibility of performance;*
- *frustration of purpose.*

*If you can prove any of these, the contract will probably be deemed void or voidable. In either case it is practically as if there never were a contract. If either party paid money, it would have to be returned.*

*Later, the section on remedies, page 329, goes into more detail.*

beyond what the actual deal would lead you to believe. It may contain details about credit terms, your right to sue, and your right to a jury in a lawsuit.

### Q. What should I do about the fine print?

**A.** First, try to read it. Often if you sit down with it, sentence by sentence, you'll find that you can understand a lot more than you expect, especially in states that have passed "plain English" laws requiring that consumer contracts use nontechnical, easy-to-understand words. You will at least, by expending the effort, identify which terms raise questions for you. The trick is not to be intimidated by the salesperson or the fine print in the contract.

### Q. If I understand it but don't like it, must I accept the contract?

**A.** No. You never have to accept a contract. Every part of a contract is open for negotiation, at least in theory. Just because the salesperson gave you a form contract doesn't mean that you have to stick to the form. You can cross out parts you don't like. You can write in terms that the contract doesn't include, such as oral promises by a salesperson. (Make sure that all changes to the form appear on all copies that will have your signature; initial altered but unsigned pages and have the other party do the same.)

## READ THE FINE PRINT

*Perhaps the most unpleasant part of making contracts comes after negotiating your best deal. It occurs when a salesperson presents you with a form contract, which is often one or two pages of tiny print that you might not understand even if you could read it. Even many law school graduates don't know what everything in these pages means. But the law usually assumes that you read and, to a reasonable extent, understand any contract you sign.*

That doesn't mean the other side has to agree to your changes. You have no more power to dictate terms than they do. But if you get a lot of resistance on what seem to be reasonable issues, take a hard look at with whom you are dealing—especially if they resist your request to put oral promises in writing.

**Q. What if I come across "legalese" that I just can't figure out?**

**A.** Until you understand every term in a substantial contract, don't sign it. Legalese most often occurs in contracts that include some type of credit terms, such as when you buy something on installment payments. The parts of this book on consumer credit and automobiles explain many of these terms. If you still have questions, ask someone you trust (not the salespeople) to explain the terms to you. That could be someone experienced with the kind of contract you are considering, a state or local consumer agency, or a lawyer. (See "Where to Get More Information" on page 337 at the end of this chapter.)

**Q. Are there any laws that protect consumers against the use of confusing language?**

**A.** Yes. Many states now require plain-English consumer contracts, with potentially confusing sections or clauses in precise, standard terms that nearly anyone can understand. Federal and state truth-in-lending laws require providers (or grantors) of credit to furnish specific information about credit contracts in clearly understandable form. Finally, the legal doctrine regarding contracts of adhesion may protect you.

**Q. What are contracts of adhesion?**

**A.** As mentioned briefly earlier, these are contracts that give you little or no bargaining power, as is often the case in many of the form contracts discussed above, such as loan documents, insurance contracts, and automobile leases. The consumer has some protection, however. Courts generally assume that such contracts have been drafted to provide maximum benefit to lender, lessor, or insurance company. So when a dispute arises over terms or language, the courts usually interpret them in the way most favorable to the consumer.

**GET IT IN WRITING**

*When dealing with a written contract, a court will almost always treat the contract's terms as the final, complete contract. The court usually will not even consider oral promises that are not in the contract. The main exception to this is when oral promises are used fraudulently to induce one party into signing the contract in the first place. That is, the party is persuaded by the fraudulent oral promise to enter into a contract he or she otherwise would have avoided. The general rule prohibiting evidence of oral promises in all other cases protects both parties, since they know that once they sign the contract, they have clearly and finally set the terms.*

*Don't be swayed if the salesperson orally promises you an extended warranty or a full refund if you're not completely satisfied. Get it in writing.*

In one case, for example, a woman tried to collect on an airline trip insurance policy she had purchased. The insurance company held that the policy applied only to a trip on a "scheduled airline" and that "technically" under some obscure regulations the woman's flight was not "scheduled," even though she had every reason to believe that it was. The court held in favor of the woman, saying the ordinary insurance buyer's understanding should apply.

This doesn't mean that the consumer gets the benefit of the doubt on any question about any terms of a contract of adhesion; it only applies to confusing or unclear clauses. To some extent, though, even contracts that are not contracts of adhesion are interpreted or construed to favor the party who didn't draft them.

Like the doctrines of unconscionability and fraud discussed earlier, this rule isn't something to depend on prior to signing a contract. Rather it's a strategy that you and your lawyer may choose if a problem arises.

---

## SPECIAL TYPES OF CONTRACTS

### Leases and Surety Contracts

**Q. Is a lease a contract?**

**A.** Yes. A lease has all the elements of a contract explained earlier: It involves something someone lets you use for a specified time, for a specified fee. There are two main kinds of leases. The first involves real estate, such as a lease for an apartment (discussed more fully in the "Renting Residential Property" chapter). The second includes all other kinds of property, such as leases for office equipment and vehicles, for example.

**Q. What should I look for in a lease for equipment or a vehicle?**

**A.** These leases, usually on preprinted forms with very few blanks, often offer little room for bargaining. Hence, it is very important that you understand the terms and are sure you'll be able to meet them, especially where there's an option to buy. Make sure that the lease states the price at which you'll be able to buy the item. The lease may specify the price as a dollar figure or as a percentage of some amount that you should be able to figure out easily. Obviously, be sure that at least from where you stand now, it's a price worth paying. If you have no intention of buying, of course, then there's no problem—but you should be able to get a less expensive deal by not including an option to buy in the contract.

**Q. Why would I lease something instead of buying it?**

**A.** Leasing doesn't usually require you to invest as much of your money up front as buying because you are not paying for ownership of the item. You must return the item to the owner at the end of the lease period. A lease also cushions you from the risk of owning a piece of equipment that may become obsolete in a few years. The drawback is that your payments never add up to equity (an ownership interest) in the property. Leases also normally come with service contracts of some sort (a later section will discuss these contracts more fully).

**Q. Are there laws designed to protect renters under residential leases?**

**A.** Yes. Most states have laws that protect people who lease their homes. The chapter on rental property discusses them fully. Many states also have laws that require special disclosures (information statements) and other protection for people who enter into other types of consumer leases. These laws may even cancel out what the contract states.

### Q. What are surety contracts?

**A.** A surety contract is an agreement where one party, called the surety, accepts the responsibility for someone else's contractual obligations. For example, you might agree to pay back your son's bank loan if he does not. Usually a surety is bound with the other person (the principal) on the same promise, often on the same document; under such an arrangement the surety is sometimes called a co-signer. A guaranty contract is similar, but with a guaranty the person who's vouching for the principal—called the guarantor—makes a separate promise and is liable only if the principal breaches and it is impossible to collect from him or her. In many cases, the terms "surety" and "guaranty" are used interchangeably, since their practical effects are nearly identical.

## Warranties

### Q. Is there any difference between a guarantee and a warranty?

**A.** In law, there is a very fine difference. But for consumers the two terms mean essentially the same thing. Both words have the same root, which means "to protect." Each represents obligations taken on by the provider or imposed on the provider by law. Some warranties deal with the quality of the goods: Will they do a specific job or meet certain specifications? Are they reasonably fit for their intended purpose? Other warranties might deal with the ownership of the goods: Does the seller have good title or ownership rights that may be lawfully transferred to the buyer?

A federal law, the Magnuson-Moss Act, covers written warranties for consumer goods costing more than a few dollars. It does not require that merchants make written warranties. If they do make such a warranty, however, it must meet certain standards. The warranty has to be available for you to read before you buy. It must be written in plain language, and must include the following information:

- the name and address of the company making the warranty;
- the product or parts covered;
- whether the warranty promises replacement, repair, or refund, and if there are any expenses (such as shipping or labor) you would have to pay;
- how long the warranty lasts;
- the damages that the warranty does not cover;
- the action you should take if something goes wrong;
- whether the company providing the warranty requires you to use any specific informal (out-of-court) methods to settle a dispute;
- a brief description of your legal rights.

Consider all these warranty terms when you shop. The terms of a warranty are seldom negotiable, especially the length of the warranty, whether it covers only parts or certain problems, and what you must do to use your rights. But some elements, such as the price of an extended warranty, may be negotiable. Many companies offer such extended warranties (sometimes called service contracts) for varying lengths of time and for varying amounts of money (see below).

Some states have warranty laws that provide consumers with greater protection than the Magnuson-Moss federal warranty law.

## Q. What is the difference between a full warranty and a limited warranty?

**A.** Magnuson-Moss requires all written warranties for consumer products costing more than a few dollars to be designated as either a "full" warranty or a "limited" warranty. A full warranty is a promise that the product will be repaired or replaced free during the warranty period. State and federal laws require that if the warrantor (the company making the warranty) will repair the item, it must be fixed within a reasonable time and it must be reasonably convenient to get the item to and from the repair site. Many stores will offer a short full warranty of their own (thirty to ninety days), above what the manufacturer offers, and some premium credit cards will double a warranty for up to a year for products purchased with the card. Repairs or replacement during the extended warranty period become the responsibility of the card issuer after the manufacturer's warranty expires.

A limited warranty is much more common. Not surprisingly, it covers less—usually only parts, and almost never the cost of labor.

## Q. What are express and implied warranties?

**A.** Express warranties are any promises to back up the product that a warrantor expresses either in writing or orally. Suppose your friend bought your Yugo and you said, "I guarantee you'll get another ten thousand miles out of this transmission." That's an express warranty. It isn't an opinion about quality or value, such as, "This Yugo is the best mauve used car for sale in town." Rather, it's a specific statement of fact or a promise.

A warrantor does not state implied warranties at all—they're automatic in certain kinds of transactions. There are two main types of implied warranties: The implied warranty of merchantability and the implied warranty of fitness for a particular purpose.

**WARRANTY SENSE**
*The best-made products usually have the best warranties, because they're less likely to need them. Thus the manufacturer can guarantee a long period with little risk. A warranty is a statement about the maker's confidence in its products; because it involves the manufacturer's pocketbook, it's a statement you should take seriously. Try to figure the value of a warranty into the price of a product and make it part of your formula for buying.*

## Q. What is the implied warranty of merchantability?

**A.** When someone is in the business of selling or leasing a specific kind of product, the law requires that the item must be adequate for the purpose for which it is purchased or leased. This is a general rule of fairness—that what looks like a carton of milk in the supermarket dairy case really is drinkable milk and not sour or unusable. The implied warranty of merchantability wouldn't apply, however, to someone buying your car, unless you were in the business of selling cars.

## Q. What is the implied warranty of fitness for a particular purpose?

**A.** It means that any seller or lessor (even a nonprofessional) is presumed to guarantee that an item will be fit for the purpose for which you are getting it—as long as you make that purpose known. Even when you sell your used Yugo to your friend you make this warranty as far as your general understanding of her purpose

This is a multiple warranty that is part full and part limited. The initial two-year full warranty spells out that the customer has a right to a refund or a replacement. The remainder of the warranty is limited because it covers only parts and not labor.

# Full Two Year Warranty on the Black Star 2001 Clothes Washer

**What is Covered:** Any defect in your 2001 Clothes Washer.

**For How Long:** Two years after the date you bought your 2001 Clothes Washer.

**What Black Star Will Do:** Repair, or if repair is not possible, either replace your 2001 Clothes Washer, or refund the purchase price, whichever you prefer.

# Limited Warranty on Parts for the Third through Fifth Years

**What is Covered:** Any defect in your 2001 Clothes Washer.

**For How Long:** From the start of the third year after you bought your 2001 Clothes Washer until the end of the fifth year.

**What Black Star Will Do:** Provide free new or rebuilt replacement parts, but not labor to install the parts. Any servicer you choose can do service during this period.

**How to Get Service:** Contact any Black Star Dealer or any Authorized Black Star Service Center. See the Yellow Pages under "Appliance Repair" for the name of a Black Star Servicer near you, or call 800-111-1111.

**Your Rights Under State Law:** This warranty gives you specific legal rights, and you may also have other rights which vary from state to state.

SOURCE: Federal Trade Commission

(basic transportation). Suppose your friend told you she needed a car that could tow a trailer full of granite up steep mountains in the snow. When you sell the Yugo to your friend with this knowledge, you make an implied warranty that it can do that. When the car fails in that purpose, your warranty will have been breached. On the other hand, if your friend tells you she's buying your car only because she needs spare Yugo parts, you can sell your Yugo to her—even if it's sitting out back on cinder blocks—without breaching a warranty of fitness for the intended purpose.

### Q.  How long do warranties last?

**A.** It depends on the type of transaction and warranty involved, and the applicable law. In

This part full and part limited multiple warranty is a pro rata warranty—one which provides a refund or credit that decreases during the life of the product according to a formula. Notice that the formula is carefully spelled out. The warranty specifies that during the initial period of full coverage the customer has a right to a replacement or a refund. The remainder of the warranty is limited because the customer can get only a partial credit.

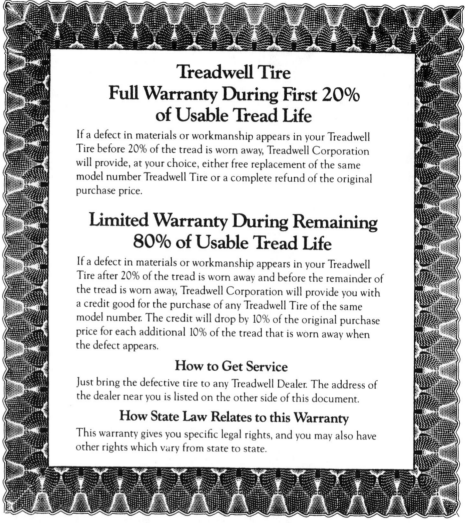

### Treadwell Tire
### Full Warranty During First 20% of Usable Tread Life

If a defect in materials or workmanship appears in your Treadwell Tire before 20% of the tread is worn away, Treadwell Corporation will provide, at your choice, either free replacement of the same model number Treadwell Tire or a complete refund of the original purchase price.

### Limited Warranty During Remaining 80% of Usable Tread Life

If a defect in materials or workmanship appears in your Treadwell Tire after 20% of the tread is worn away and before the remainder of the tread is worn away, Treadwell Corporation will provide you with a credit good for the purchase of any Treadwell Tire of the same model number. The credit will drop by 10% of the original purchase price for each additional 10% of the tread that is worn away when the defect appears.

### How to Get Service

Just bring the defective tire to any Treadwell Dealer. The address of the dealer near you is listed on the other side of this document.

### How State Law Relates to this Warranty

This warranty gives you specific legal rights, and you may also have other rights which vary from state to state.

SOURCE: Federal Trade Commission

most states, you have up to four years to enforce an implied warranty after the start of the transaction. In cases involving written warranties the period may be much shorter. A written warranty will disclose how long it lasts. It may be as short as ninety days for a portable radio. A warranty on a new car, on the other hand, may last several years or many thousand miles.

### Q. May a merchant disclaim a warranty?

**A.** Not after you've made the purchase. But before you buy, unwritten express warranties and (in most states) implied warranties of merchantability or fitness may be excluded or disclaimed if the contract or disclaimer is in writing and the relevant language is obvious. The word "merchantability" may have to

This is an example of a limited warranty. It is limited because there are requirements that the customer pay labor and postage charges, and that the customer return a registration card.

# Magnifisound Corporation

## Limited Warranty

**What Does This Warranty Cover?** This warranty covers any defects or malfunctions in your new Magnifisound hearing aid.

**How Long Does The Coverage Last?** This warranty lasts as long as you own your Magnifisound aid. Coverage terminates if you sell or otherwise transfer the aid.

**What Will Magnifisound Do?** Magnifisound will replace any defective or malfunctioning part at no charge. You must pay any labor charges.

**What Does This Warranty Not Cover?** Batteries, or any problem that is caused by abuse, misuse, or an act of God (such as a flood) are not covered. Also, consequential and incidental damages are not recoverable under this warranty. Some states do not allow the exclusion or limitation of incidental or consequential damages, so the above limitation or exclusion may not apply to you.

**How Do You Get Service?** In order to be eligible for service under this warranty you **MUST** return the warranty registration card attached below within 30 days of purchasing the aid.

If something goes wrong with your aid, send it postage paid with a brief written description of the problem to:

Magnifisound Corp.
Box 10000
Auditory, Ohio

We will inspect your aid and contact you within 72 hours to give the results of our inspection and an estimate of the labor charges required to fix the aid. If you authorize repairs, we will return the repaired aid to you COD within 72 hours. You must pay any labor charges upon receipt of the repaired aid.

If you inform us that you wish us to provide necessary parts to you but you wish to have repairs performed elsewhere, we will return the aid and replacement parts to you within 72 hours.

There is no charge for inspection.

**How Does State Law Apply?** This warranty gives you specific legal rights, and you may also have other rights which vary from state to state.

SOURCE: Federal Trade Commission

appear for a such a disclaimer of an implied warranty to be valid, or it may have to state that a product is sold "as is." In contrast, the implied warranty of fitness for a particular purpose may be disclaimed merely by a less communicative written statement. In any event, a person may not disclaim an express warranty that's written in the contract.

---

## READ WARRANTIES BEFORE YOU BUY

*Don't wait until a product needs repair to find out what's covered in any written warranty you get. Compare the terms and conditions of the warranty before you buy and look for the warranty that best meets your needs.*

*There are several points to consider. How long is the warranty, and when does it start and end? Will the warranty pay 100 percent of repair costs? Does it cover parts but not labor? What kinds of problems are covered? What do you have to do to enforce your warranty rights? And when do you have to do it? Are regular inspections or maintenance required? Do you have to ship the product to the repair center? If so, who pays for shipping? What about a loaner? Who offers the warranty—the manufacturer or the retailer? How reliable is each?*

---

**Q. Is disclaiming a warranty common?**

**A.** It cannot be done on a consumer product that carries a written warranty. If there is not such a warranty, a disclaimer is common. In many cases of consumer products, a warranty will be stated and the contract you sign will state a specific remedy if the product fails. This avoids having to give no warranty while still protecting the seller or lessor to some extent. For example, the contract may provide that the seller will repair or replace the merchandise, if necessary, but that the customer has no right to get back any money. This protects the seller against the worst-case scenario (having to give your money back) while still protecting the buyer.

**Q. Does the law ever overrule the guarantees contained in a warranty?**

**A.** Yes. Lemon laws provide a good example. Many states have these laws, which provide extra guarantees to people who have been unlucky enough to buy new cars so bad that they fit the statutory definition of a "lemon." (See the "Automobiles" chapter on page 351 for details on lemon laws.)

**Q. Most warranty limitations exclude some forms of consequential damages. What are consequential damages?**

**A.** Consequential damages are losses caused by the product's defect, including your lost time and expense that result from the defect and repair costs. If, for example, your new computer crashes and destroys weeks of work, you may get a new computer. But under the terms of the wording in the warranty that came with the computer (as well as the disks), the warrantor will almost certainly not reimburse you for the lost time, work or software—much less a lost job or client. At some point, the law expects you to protect yourself, in this case by backing up your computer files. However, you usually may recover damages in cases of personal injury that result from a product's defect.

### Q. What about extended warranties or service contracts?

**A.** Both of these will cost you extra. Take a hard look and ask if the benefits are worth the cost. Consider how the extended warranty or service contract enhances your regular warranty. Find out where you'll have to send the product for repairs. Also look, especially in service contracts, at whether there's a deductible amount. For example, the contract might not cover repairs costing less than fifty dollars. The deductible amount, or a per-repair flat fee that you agree to pay, can add up to erase all the expected savings. Sometimes it pays to wait until after the warranty has expired before deciding to buy a service contract, if you can. Then you have a sense of a product's reliability.

Be sure to take a good look at who is backing up the contract or warranty. Is it a well-known manufacturer? The store where you got it? Or a company you have never heard of with only a post-office box for an address?

Ultimately, don't be pressured by a salesperson into taking one of those contracts. They're frequently a major source of profit on the transaction. Ask the salesperson why you should be so concerned about insuring yourself for repair costs if the product is well made.

### Q. How can I protect my warranty rights?

**A.** First, keep your receipts through the warranty period. They are your proof of when the warranty period starts and ends, and are more important than the warranty return card. (That card is often just a marketing device to learn more about you.)

Also remember that any violation of the manufacturer's operating and service instructions probably will void the warranty.

If a problem arises, try the store where you got the item. It may be able to "go around" the warranty process, especially if it's very soon after your acquisition. If you end up contacting the manufacturer, do so only as instructed in the warranty. Keep a list of the people with whom you have spoken or letters you have written. It's a good idea to contact the manufacturer in writing, keeping copies of all correspondence, at the address specified in the warranty. That's especially true if you aren't getting quick responses. Your correspondence file will protect your warranty rights near the end of the coverage period. For more details, see the section on contract remedies later in this chapter, on page 331.

## Advertising

### Q. An earlier section said that store advertisements are not usually offers. Are there any exceptions to this?

**A.** Yes. Suppose a store advertises that it will give a free gift or a special discount to "the first one hundred customers" or to a person who has made some other special effort. If so, the store has made an offer. You can accept it by making the special effort successfully. (In fact, a major department store recently got into hot water by carelessly advertising: "Be among the first 1,000 shoppers at our store tomorrow to win a $1,000 shopping spree." The wording suggested that all 1,000 would win.)

### Q. What is false advertising?

**A.** False advertising is an unfair method of competition forbidden under federal law and in most states, notably under the consumer fraud laws (discussed below). The advertiser's intent isn't important. The overall impression conveyed is what counts.

False advertising misleads about a product's place of origin, nature or quality, or maker. An example of misleading about a product's place of origin is putting French labels on sweaters made in Arkansas. Promising first-quality socks and delivering irregulars or seconds is misleading about an item's nature or quality. Claiming a Yugo is a Lexus is misleading about a product's maker. As for services, false advertising would mislead you into thinking that someone has qualifications (such as being a master carpenter) that he or she does not actually have.

### Q. How exact do advertisements have to be?

**A.** They must be accurate about material aspects of the product or service in the offer. It's no crime to sell a dress that looks better on the fashion model in the ad than on a normal person. It also is legal to prepare a food product in a special way to make it look more tempting on television than it will be at home. If an advertisement led you to expect green spark plugs and you got gray ones, the ad did not materially mislead you. But if the ad said the plugs would last a long time and they failed early on, you were probably misled.

### Q. What about contests and investment schemes?

**A.** The rule is this: Any contest or get-rich-quick scheme that requires you to part with money probably is a losing proposition. Often these are "pyramid schemes." Someone may contact you by mail or over the phone, promising you some huge return on your money and telling you of real people who made a bundle in the scheme. That part is true, actually. Some did get a lot of money. But they did it illegally—by inducing people like you to pony up. The only way you could do the same is to con a large number of people to make the same mistake you did. The courts have held these scams—and any promotion that promises an unrealistic return—to be false advertising; if they involve mail, they are postal violations. Some cases might involve violations of securities laws. One good rule of thumb is that no legitimate speculative investment will ever promise or even strongly suggest a specific return to you.

If you are contacted by mail regarding what seems like a fraudulent scheme, contact the office of the U.S. Postal Service Inspector General. Otherwise, report such a pitch to your state or city's consumer protection office or state attorney general. Virtually all states now provide a way for shutting down these scams and recovering victims' money, but the process may be long and may not always be successful.

### Q. What is "bait and switch"?

**A.** The bait is an advertisement luring you with the promise of an unbeatable deal on an appliance or auto. The switch occurs when you walk into the store and the salesperson tells you that the advertised model isn't available or is "not for you," but a more expensive model is. The salesperson has "switched" you from the one you wanted to buy. This practice is illegal in most states if the advertised model was never available in reasonable quantities. You have a right to see the model that appeared in the newspaper ad. If the store is "fresh out of them," it also may be guilty of false advertising. You're allowed to be persuaded, but keep up your guard, and don't let someone talk you into buying a model you can't afford. If insisting on your rights gets you nowhere, keep the ad, get the salesman's name (and that of anyone else you spoke to) and report the matter to the state or local consumer protection office.

## Door-to-Door Sales

**Q. What are the problems in door-to-door sales?**

**A.** Most people feel secure in their homes. Ironically, that feeling makes them especially vulnerable to door-to-door salespeople. That's particularly true of homebound people, such as the elderly or invalids. You have few facts by which to judge a door-to-door salesperson. There is no manager, no showroom, and no immediate way to assess the company that the salesperson represents (if there is one).

**Q. Do any laws protect purchases made as a result of door-to-door sales?**

**A.** Federal law now requires a three-day "cooling-off period" for door-to-door sales. During that time, you can cancel purchases you make from someone who both solicits and closes the sale at your home.

You don't have to give any reason for changing your mind, and the three days don't start until you receive formal notice of your right to cancel. You can cancel almost any sale not made at a fixed place of business, such as sales made at your home, someone else's home, or a hotel. Federal law extends this cooling-off period to both credit and noncredit sales. It also forbids the company to charge you any cancellation fee.

The federal law will apply to most such cases, and many states have similar laws that fill in the gaps.

**Q. What if you do buy from a door-to-door salesperson?**

**A.** Federal and state laws usually require such salespeople to provide you with the following details on your receipt:

- the seller's name and place of business;
- a description of the goods and services sold;
- the amount of money you paid, or the value of any goods delivered to you;
- your cooling-off period rights (see above).

Also, if the salesperson makes the sale in Spanish or another language, you may have the right to all the above details in that language.

**Q. What happens if I cancel my order during the cooling-off period?**

**A.** State law usually will require the salesperson to refund your money, return any trade-in you made, and cancel and return the contract. The salesperson has ten business days to do this under federal law. You must make the goods available to be picked up during that period. Under federal law, if the salesperson waits longer than twenty calendar days, you may be allowed to keep the goods free.

**Q. What about door-to-door home repair sales?**

**A.** Tell anyone who supposedly has some leftover asphalt, shingles, or other material from a nearby job, and offers you a sweet deal to fix your driveway, roof, or whatever, to go somewhere else. Make your home repairs when you're ready, and only with contractors you know. (See the section below on home repairs, page 324.)

## Buying by Mail

**Q. How long does a mail-order company have to deliver goods that I ordered?**

**A.** Under federal law, the goods must be in the mail within thirty days of your order. If they

you keep them, though, you have to pay their usual price, unless the company offers them for less. Pick up a pen or the telephone and try to negotiate. Since mail-order firms depend on goodwill more than other companies do, a reputable company should be able to strike an acceptable deal with you.

**Q. What about unordered merchandise I receive in the mail?**

**A.** Federal law requires the sender of an unordered item sent through the mail to mark the package "Free Sample." (The law permits charities to send you Easter Seals, Hanukkah candles, and the like, and ask for a contribution.) Consumers who receive unordered merchandise in the mail should consider it a gift. They have no obligation to pay for the merchandise, and they may keep it. Sending you a bill for such merchandise may be mail fraud, which is a federal crime. Report such practices, or any harassment or threats to force you to pay the bill, to the Postal Service and your state consumer protection bureau. But first make sure you, or a family member, didn't actually order the item in question.

**Q. Does the same rule about unordered goods apply to merchants?**

**A.** A merchant who receives unordered merchandise from a supplier doesn't have to pay for it, but the sender must be allowed to arrange for its return. If, however, the merchant does something that shows that he or she is willing to buy the merchandise, such as selling or displaying it, then the merchant must pay for it.

aren't, you must at least have received a letter informing you of the delay and of when to expect delivery. The seller also has to offer you a refund within one week if you don't want to wait any longer. The exception is goods that you understand not to be available until a certain time, such as magazines or flower seeds. Many states have laws that protect you even further than the federal law.

**Time-shares**

**Q. May the company send substitute goods to me?**

**A.** Yes, but you don't have to accept them. You can send them back and ask for a refund. If

**Q. What should I be aware of when buying a time-share?**

**A.** Time-shares are a period of time, maybe a week or so per year, that you can buy for a specific property (usually a residence at a resort), during which the right to use the property belongs to you. The idea is that you benefit by "prepaying" for a vacation place rather than renting it, as you otherwise might do. The profit that would have gone to the owner supposedly stays in your pocket.

One problem is that the savings are often offset by expenses. If, like most people, you finance your time-share purchase over time, the interest costs alone may eat away that supposed profit. Even if you pay cash, you lose the interest you could otherwise have earned on that money.

And unlike renters, who have the option of coming or not from season to season as a resort becomes more or less desirable, time-share owners are generally locked in. In some cases they may be able to exchange their property, but that involves a formal exchange program and costs money. They usually cannot sell the property except at a substantial loss.

Furthermore, your time-share contract will make you responsible to pay any increases in taxes, maintenance or repairs. If you think any of these amounts are going to decrease, you're in for a big surprise.

### Q. If I don't like the time-share deal, though, can't I just sell it?

**A.** In theory, yes. Practically speaking, though, many people who bought time-shares in the 1980s—when any investment involving real estate looked like a winner—are finding themselves with white elephants on their hands. You may have to unload the time-share for much less than you paid, if you can find a buyer at all. You may be stuck agreeing with the sponsors that they will take back the time-share during the payment period and you will be off the hook for the rest of the term. You would get nothing back for what you've already paid in (which might be several times what you would have paid in rent) but you would have no further obligations.

### Q. Don't time-shares eventually "break even"?

**A.** Time-share sellers will often point out that, notwithstanding these problems, once you pay off the time-share you will have "free" vacationing, so at some point you will break even with the cost of renting and eventually be in the black. But that break-even point, which takes in account all of your costs, including interest, may not come for ten to twenty years. Ask yourself whether you are prepared to vacation in the same place every year for the next decade so you can eventually save on your vacation expenses.

## Pets

### Q. What may I ask about a pet before I buy it?

**A.** You may ask anything. You have a right to know about the pet's health, family history or pedigree, training, and medical care, both normal and unusual.

### Q. Do states have pet laws that cover an owner's rights?

**A.** Many states do have such laws. If your state doesn't, then general warranty laws apply.

### Q. What should I do if I am dissatisfied with my pet purchase?

**A.** Immediately notify the seller in writing, keeping a copy for yourself. Keep all contracts, papers, and even the original advertisement, if there was one. If you have not received a replacement or refund within thirty days, consider filing a small-claims lawsuit. Don't worry about becoming an expert on pet law. The judge will probably base a decision on the fairness of the case, not on technicalities.

**BUYING SICK OR INJURED PETS**

*Suppose you buy a pet, and it turns out that it's sick or injured. Legally, what can you do? The answer may depend on whether you bought the pet from a pet shop or a private owner. It also may depend on whether you had a written contract, and what express and implied warranties exist under your state's laws. It also matters whether you bought this pet for a specific purpose, such as breeding it for competition. In general, it's best for you and the seller to sign a written agreement about your pet which will clarify most of a new owner's questions.*

*Another way of avoiding problems is to ask the seller for the name of the pet's veterinarian. Ask the vet for an opinion on the pet's health, which may alert you to potential problems before you complete the purchase.*

### Home and Home Appliance Repairs and Improvements

**Q. Does the law protect consumers who contract for home repairs or improvements?**

**A.** Yes. The Federal Trade Commission and federal truth-in-lending laws police this area. To a certain extent, the states regulate home repairs, too. Generally, as in any other contract, home-repair contractors may not mislead you in any way to get the job. Be aware of these tricks:

- promising a lower price for allowing your home to be used as a model or to advertise their work;
- promising better quality materials than they will use (beware of "bait and switch" here as well);
- providing "free gifts"—find out when you will receive them, or try to get a price reduction instead;
- not including delivery and installation costs in the price;
- starting work before you sign a contract, to intimidate you;

- claiming that your house is dangerous and needs repair;
- claiming that the contractor works for a government agency;
- offering you a rebate or referral fee if any of your friends agree to use the same contractor.

**Q. How may I protect myself?**

**A.** Get several written estimates. Check into a contractor's track record with other customers before you sign a contract. Don't pay the full price in advance, and certainly not in cash. Don't sign a completion certificate or receipt until the contractor finishes the work to your satisfaction—including cleanup.

**Q. Are there special things to look for in a home-improvement contract?**

**A.** Yes. Be sure the contract has all the details in writing. Too often a contract of this type will read "work as per agreement." Instead it should specify who will do the work, and include a detailed description of the work, the materials to be used, and the dates of starting and completion. It also should contain all charges, including any finance charges if you are paying over a period of time. In addition, the contract should include the hourly rate on which the total cost is to be based. Be sure any "guarantee" is in writing.

Be especially wary of any mortgage or security interest the contractor takes in your home, which means that you may lose your home if you don't meet the payments for the work. (If the contractor takes a mortgage or security interest, federal law gives you three days to change your mind and cancel.)

Consider having a lawyer look at the contract, especially if there's a security agreement. If problems do arise that threaten your rights to own your home, see a lawyer immediately. (For more on this topic, see the chapter on home ownership.)

### Q. What about appliance repairs?

**A.** Much of what the "Automobiles" chapter discusses about car repairs (see page 363) applies to home appliance repairs. You can best protect your rights by getting a written estimate. At least make sure you get an oral estimate before work begins, telling how the repair shop will figure the total charge, including parts and labor. Also, tell the repair shop to get your approval before beginning work. It will then be able to give you a better idea of how much the repair will cost.

### Q. How can I determine whether it is no longer worth fixing a major appliance?

**A.** When deciding whether to repair or replace, consider these points:

- the appliance's age and likely life span after this repair, compared with that of a new appliance;

- how the repaired appliance will compare with a new appliance in operating costs and efficiency;

- the length of the warranty on the repair, compared with the warranty on a new appliance;

- the price of a new appliance compared with the cost of the repairs.

## Buying Clubs

### Q. What is a buying club?

**A.** There are several different types of buying clubs. One of the more popular kinds is a compact disc (CD) or music club. It offers five or ten CDs or tapes to you for an initial nominal price. You might pay only a nickel or a dollar, plus postage and handling. In return, you agree to buy a certain number of CDs or tapes at the "regular club price" over a period of time. The "regular club price" is much higher than the initial price, and is often higher than normal retail store prices, especially with postage and handling. In fact, though, the average price including the introductory deal usually works out to your benefit. (Remember that there are costs involved in getting to a store downtown or at the mall, too.)

The problem with these clubs is that they automatically send you a CD or tape every month or so. Before shipping the item, the club sends you a notice of the upcoming shipment. The only way to prevent the automatic shipment is to return the notice before the date it specifies. Book clubs operate on a similar basis. Other clubs, such as those that sell children's books or science books, don't send you any notice—they assume you want the whole "library."

### Q. So should I avoid these clubs?

**A.** Not necessarily. You may want to meet your additional obligation quickly and then

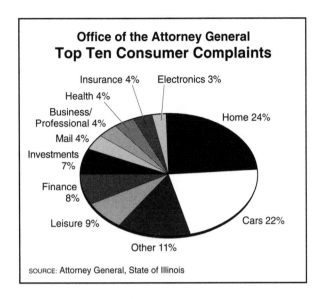

**Office of the Attorney General**
**Top Ten Consumer Complaints**

Insurance 4%
Electronics 3%
Health 4%
Business/Professional 4%
Mail 4%
Investments 7%
Finance 8%
Leisure 9%
Other 11%
Home 24%
Cars 22%

SOURCE: Attorney General, State of Illinois

resign your membership. Also, the clubs do offer many incentives to try to keep you as a member, which may be worthwhile to you. But if you forget to return the monthly notice, you will receive unwanted CDs or tapes, and you will be obligated to pay for them or to return them, sometimes at your own expense.

### Q. *What about merchandise clubs?*

**A.** The idea behind these is that you pay a fee in order to qualify for discounts. The club presumably obtains these discounts because of its volume buying power. Before joining one of these, take a good look at what it promises. Will it limit you to certain manufacturers? Are catalogs easily accessible? Shady clubs often appear on lists put out by the offices of state attorneys general and consumer protection agencies. Check with them first.

### Funeral Homes

### Q. *What is the Funeral Rule?*

**A.** This Federal Trade Commission rule, which has the effect of federal law, requires mortuaries or funeral homes to give you prices and other information you request over the telephone. The intention is to prevent corrupt funeral home operators from requiring you to come to their showrooms, where they can prey on your weak emotional state.

### Q. *Does the Funeral Rule require anything else?*

**A.** If you visit a funeral home, it must give you a written list with all the prices and services offered—including the least expensive. You can keep this list. You have the right to choose any service offered, as long as it does not violate state law. The funeral home must give you a copy of that state law. The funeral home must reveal any fees charged for outside items, such as flowers, and may not charge a handling fee for purchases of caskets from third parties. The home may not falsely state that embalming is required by state law, and must give general information about embalming options. The Funeral Rule also entitles you to an itemized list of all charges you incur. The general idea of the Funeral Rule is that the funeral home must inform you of your options every step of the way. (For more details, see "Where to Get More Information" at the end of this chapter, on page 337.)

### Travel

### Q. *Is overbooking by hotels a violation of my contract?*

**A.** It is if you have paid in advance. Otherwise, the reservation is just a "courtesy." Therefore, it is often worth it to pay for a hotel reservation by credit card when you make it. If you cancel within a couple of days before the reservation date, you probably will get a complete credit, depending on the credit card company's arrangement with the hotel. Also, many premium credit card companies guarantee their

## THE TOP TEN CONSUMER PROBLEMS

*The State of New Jersey's Office of Consumer Protection has published a list of the ten most troublesome consumer problems in that state, which unfortunately exist in every state. The list also includes basic advice for handling each problem.*

- *Fly-by-night home repair contractors (as discussed previously in this chapter).*

- *Telephone solicitations. Always ask the caller to send written information. Also, determine your total obligation before agreeing to anything. Don't give credit-card information to strangers over the telephone.*

- *Furniture delivery delays. Do not take "ASAP" (as soon as possible) as a delivery date in a sales contract. Get an exact date. If the merchandise doesn't show up by that date, you would then have the right to cancel.*

- *Free vacation offers. An example is the postcard telling you about a "free vacation" you have won: Just call a toll-free number and "confirm" your credit card number. Later the vacation is not as free as you thought. Play it safe—book your travel arrangements through a reliable agent or directly with travel carriers.*

- *"Bait and switch" tactics (see the section above on advertising).*

- *Mail-order rip-offs. When shopping by mail, you're always taking a risk. When the offer sounds too good to be true, it probably is.*

- *Work-at-home schemes. Usually aimed at young mothers and the disabled, these schemes promise to help you "earn money in your spare time." They'll ask you for twenty dollars in "start-up" costs. What you'll get is information about how to rip someone else off the way they just cheated you.*

- *Detours around contract cooling-off periods (see the section above on door-to-door sales). Federal law only protects you if you sign the contract in your home or somewhere other than the normal place of business. Even at home, don't depend on a cooling-off period—think before you sign.*

- *Health spa memberships. Most complaints center on high-pressure sales tactics. A year's membership can cost quite a bundle—make sure that you'll use it, and that all "understandings" and assurances are in writing.*

- *Time-share lures. People often buy time-sharing vacations on impulse. Be sure you're ready to go to the same place during the same period of time for years to come. If the time-sharing resort (or condominium or whatever) is not fully built, make sure all occupancy dates are in the contract and review these contracts with a lawyer. (High-pressure time-share sales pitches have led to a federal law giving consumers some protections. The federal Interstate Land Sales Full Disclosure Act gives you the right, in some circumstances, to get out of a time-share contract.)*

cardholders' hotel rooms through the evening if the rooms are reserved with the card. (Contact the credit card company if the hotel doesn't honor your reservation.)

If your room is unavailable even after you speak to the manager, you could have a contract

**MORE TOP SCAMS**

*A listing of the "top scams" compiled by the Better Business Bureau of Mainland British Columbia (Canada) adds the following:*

- *phony invoices that look authentic but are really solicitations;*
- *advertisements offering "big money" overseas jobs that are really selling nearly worthless listings;*
- *look-alike postal notices asking for payment to release unsolicited merchandise held at a warehouse in the recipient's name;*
- *offshore lotteries implying that you've won even before you buy your tickets;*
- *loan brokers who charge hefty up-front fees but seldom deliver;*
- *solicitation for "charities" that are really businesses.*

*The Better Business Bureau can usually help consumers only before they commit. It maintains information on the reliability of businesses throughout the continent, but it is not a government agency and has no power to enforce contracts or penalize wrongdoers.*

claim. But it probably won't be worthwhile to pursue it legally because of the cost. Perhaps the best advice is to request firmly that the hotel arrange suitable alternate accommodations for you.

### Q. What about an airline bumping me off my flight?

**A.** Generally, even if you have paid in advance, you do not have a contract to go at a certain time. You only have a contract for a ticket for transport (or carriage) to a certain city. You do, however, have certain rights if you check in on time and have a confirmed ticket. Federal regulations require that if you get bumped against your wishes, the airline must give you a written statement, describing your rights and explaining how the airline decides who gets on an oversold flight and who does not.

Travelers who don't get on the flight are often entitled to an on-the-spot payment as compensation. The amount depends on the price of their ticket and the length of the delay. There's no compensation if the airline can arrange to get you on another flight that is scheduled to arrive at your destination within one hour of your originally scheduled arrival time. If, however, the substitute transportation is scheduled to arrive more than one hour but less than two hours after your original time of arrival, the airline must pay you an amount equal to the one-way fare to your final destination, up to $200. You're entitled to up to $400 if your substitute transportation will not arrive within two hours (four hours for international flights).

These rules have exceptions and conditions. "Fly-Rights" is a pamphlet published by the U.S. Department of Transportation. It contains a full discussion of this and other areas of airline law, and is available from the Superintendent of Documents, Order Department, U.S. Government Printing Office, Washington, D.C.

20402, telephone (202) 783-3238. The order number is 050-000-00513-5.

If you're just delayed, not bumped, ask the airline staff what services it will provide. Ask about meals, telephone calls, and overnight accommodations.

You can complain to the U.S. Department of Transportation if you think an airline has abused you. But write to the airline first. In these competitive times for the travel industry, airlines often are responsive to consumer complaints.

### Q. How can I protect myself when paying for charter tours?

**A.** Your money often takes a twisting route to the tour operator. This leaves you vulnerable to many different stops that exist in between. The best approach is to pay by credit card, and receive the protections of the Fair Credit Billing Act, discussed on page 333. If you pay by check, the tour operator's brochure usually will specify the name of an escrow bank account where all payments eventually go. Make out your check to that account. Also, if possible, put the destination, dates, and other details on the face of the check, which should guarantee that the payment goes where it should go. That may help you get your money back if the tour is canceled or if the tour operator or travel agent goes out of business. Your contract is with the tour operator.

U.S. Department of Transportation regulations require that you be shown and sign an operator/participant contract, which describes your rights, before your payment is accepted. Demand it if it is not offered to you.

Some operators carry bonds to reassure their customers, rather than using escrow accounts. If an operator doesn't have an escrow account, ask whether it is bonded and how you would be reimbursed in case of a default.

Often, the travel agent will insist that the check be made out to the travel agency, because it is the policy of some agents to write a single check to the tour operator themselves. That's fine, but insist on a written guarantee from the tour operator and the agency, and make sure that the agency's check is made payable to the tour operator's escrow account. Reputable agents and operators should be willing to stand behind the tour.

You also can protect yourself by getting trip insurance. This guards you if you have to cancel the trip because of your illness or an illness in the immediate family. Various types of trip insurance, as well as message relaying and referrals to overseas legal and medical help, are also provided free by many premium credit cards.

---

## WHAT IF SOMETHING HAPPENS?

*Now you know how contracts should work, and how to avoid the more troublesome kinds of contracts. But what happens when something goes wrong?*

*A significant violation of a contract is a breach. A remedy is how you can go about repairing a breach, or getting compensated for the loss it causes. This section discusses breaches and remedies.*

---

## BREACHES AND REMEDIES

### Breach of Contract

### Q. What is a breach of contract?

**A.** A breach of contract—also called a default—is one party's failure, without a legally valid excuse, to live up to any of his or her

# SAMPLE COMPLAINT LETTER

(Your address)
(Your city, state, zip code)
(Date)

(Name of contact person)
(Title)
(Company name)
(Street address)
(City, state, zip code)

Dear (contact person):

- Describe your purchase
- Name of product, serial numbers
- Include date and location of purchase

On (date), I purchased (or had repaired) a (name of the product, with serial or model number or service performed). I made this purchase at (name of store, location, date, and other important details of the transaction).

Unfortunately, your product (or service) has not performed well (or the service was inadequate) because (state the problem).

- State the problem
- Give the history

- Ask for specific action
- Enclose copies of documents

Therefore, to resolve the problem, I would appreciate your (state the specific action you want). Enclosed are copies (copies, not originals) of my records (receipts, guarantees, warranties, canceled checks, contracts, model and serial numbers, and any other documents).

I look forward to your reply and a resolution to my problem, and will wait (set time limit) before seeking third-party assistance. Please contact me at the above address or by phone at (home and office numbers, with area codes).

- Allow time for action or response
- Include how you can be reached

Sincerely,

(Your name)
(Your account number)

* Keep copies of your letter and all related documents

SOURCE: U.S. Office of Consumer Affairs

responsibilities under a contract. A breach can occur by:

- failure to perform as promised;
- making it impossible for the other party to perform;
- repudiation of the contract (announcing an intent not to perform).

### Q. What qualifies as a failure to perform?

**A.** One party must not have performed a material part of the contract by a reasonable (or stated) deadline. Suppose your friend promised to buy your Yugo for $1,000, and to pay you "sometime early next week." It would be a material breach for your friend never to pay you, or to pay you six months later. If your friend paid you on Thursday of next week, however, it probably would not be a breach. You did not explicitly make time an essential part of the contract—the source of the phrase "time is of the essence."

### Q. How is a contract breached by making performance impossible?

**A.** Suppose you hire a cleaning service to clean your house on Sunday at a rate of ninety dollars for the day. Early Sunday morning you go out for the day, neglecting to make arrangements to let the cleaning people into the house. You've breached by making performance impossible, and would owe the money since the cleaning service was ready and able to clean your house and presumably turned down requests to clean for other clients.

### Q. What if someone partially breaches a contract?

**A.** That happens when the contract has several parts, each of which can be treated as a separate contract. If one of those parts is breached, you could sue for damages even though there isn't a total breach. An example of this would

be a landowner hiring a contractor to perform a construction project within certain deadlines. These deadlines have already been missed, but overall the project is going well. As long as the delay (the breach) is not material, the owner can continue the contractual relationship but sue for whatever damages were suffered as a result of the delay (for example, canceled leases). On the other hand, if the delay is material—so damaging to the project that it seriously undermines its value—the breach strikes at the heart of the contract and is total. The owner may terminate it and pursue remedies against the builder while hiring someone else to finish the job.

### Q. What is a breach by repudiation?

**A.** Repudiation is a clear statement made by one party before performance is due that the party cannot or will not perform a material part of that party's contract obligations. Suppose that on the day before your friend was to pick up the Yugo that you promised to sell to her, you sent her a message that you decided to sell the car to someone else. That would be a repudiation. It's not repudiation if one party will not perform because of an honest disagreement over the contract's terms.

## Remedies for Breach of Contract

### Q. What are the main types of remedies for a breach?

**A.** When someone breaches a contract, the other party is no longer obligated to keep its end of the bargain, and may proceed in several ways:

- urging the breaching party to reconsider the breach;
- if it's a contract with a merchant, getting help from local, state, or federal consumer agencies;

- bringing the breaching party to an agency for alternative dispute resolution;
- suing for damages or other remedies.

### Q. What's the point of asking the breaching party to reconsider?

A. One advantage is that it's cheap. Often the only cost is the price of a telephone call and a little pride. The breaching party may have breached the contract because of a misunderstanding. Perhaps the breaching party just needs a little more time. Or maybe you could renegotiate. That would almost certainly leave both of you better off than if you went to court. If you do hire a lawyer, the first thing that lawyer is likely to do is try to persuade the breaching party to perform.

### Q. Should I keep records of my communications with a breaching party?

A. Yes. Once you see you're in for a struggle, make a file. Keep copies of any letters you send and move all receipts, serial numbers, warranty cards, and the like to this file.

### Q. Assuming the breaching party does not budge, what else can I do?

A. If the dispute is between you and a merchant, you might want to contact the manufacturer of the product. If it involves a large chain of stores, contact the management of the chain. This goes for services, too.

If that doesn't help, contact a consumer protection agency, either in your city or state. The Federal Trade Commission is less likely to get involved in small disputes. If, however, the FTC believes that what happened to you has occurred to many people nationwide, it might be interested. The FTC's involvement carries a lot of weight. The same goes with your state attorney general or local consumer agency. Another resource is your local post office, where you can report any shady business practices that took place through the mail.

### Q. If these methods don't work, what else can I do short of filing a lawsuit?

A. The first and second chapters of this book discuss many different types of alternative dispute resolution systems, such as arbitration. Note that the contract itself may include a specific type of alternative dispute resolution that you must use. You may have already agreed not to go to court to resolve disputes.

### Stopping Payment

### Q. What if I want to cancel a contract or void a purchase that I made, but I already paid with a check?

A. First, you should call the seller and ask for a cancellation of your contract and the return of your check. If the seller won't do this, you may call your bank and "stop payment" on that check. Remember, you're still liable for the purchase price, and you may be sued by the seller for its amount, unless you have a legal excuse not to pay. Also be aware that when you stop payment, you raise the stakes and diminish the chance of a settlement—merchants don't take kindly to this technique.

### Q. Isn't stopping payment on a check a criminal act?

A. No. It's not the same as having insufficient funds to cover the check, which may carry criminal penalties. Stopping payment on a check is your legal right.

### Q. How do I stop payment on a check?

A. Call your bank and tell them the relevant information about the check. The bank will then send you a form to confirm your instructions in writing, which you must return within a certain number of days for the bank to honor your original request. If you don't provide all the information your bank requires, your stop-payment order might not be good. The bank's charge for this service will usually be ten to thirty dollars or even more.

Don't try to avoid the fee by reducing your bank balance so the check won't clear. The bank can't read your mind, so other checks you've written may not be paid, or the bank might even pay the check you don't want paid, in an attempt to accommodate you. More important, you will have gone from exercising a legal right (stopping payment) to committing a legal wrong (passing a bad check).

**Q. Is there anything else that I should do after I place the order to stop payment?**

**A.** You could inform the seller of your action, but you don't have to.

**Q. What if the seller has already deposited the check in a bank account?**

**A.** If the check has not cleared your account, your bank may still put through the stop-payment order. If your bank has paid the check, you'll have to try to void the contract and get your money back in other ways discussed here.

**Q. What if I'm dissatisfied with goods or services that I've paid for with a credit card?**

**A.** Then the Fair Credit Billing Act may protect you. Under the Act, products that you rightfully refuse to accept on delivery or that aren't delivered according to an agreement are regarded by the law as billing errors which the card issuer must investigate and may correct by granting you a credit. The same is true of shoddy or damaged goods or poor service. The

Act may allow you to withhold payment or, if you've already paid, to get back your money. See the "Consumer Credit" chapter, page 260, for more details.

### Suing for a Breach of Contract

**Q. What's the most common legal remedy for a breach of contract?**

**A.** The usual legal remedy is a suit for damages, usually compensatory damages. This

> ## GETTING OUT OF A CONTRACT
> *This chapter has tried to emphasize that it is more important to recognize when you have actually made a contract than to worry about a breach of contract. Sometimes, though, someone will breach a contract with you. Or you'll find yourself in a position where you have to breach a contract. Breaching a contract isn't always a bad thing to do, as long as you're ready to take your lumps. Sometimes the price you pay through a remedy for breach is less damaging than performing a contract that has just become a big mistake.*
>
> *Remember, though, that a contract is your pledge. If you want to be known for keeping your word, you'll take your contract commitments seriously—even if you don't profit each time.*

is the amount of money it would take to put you in as good a position as if there had not been a breach of contract. The idea is to give you "the benefit of the bargain."

### Q. What's an example of compensatory damages?

**A.** Suppose you hired a contractor to paint your house for $500. This job could cost as much as a $650, but you're a good negotiator. Now the contractor regrets agreeing to the $500 price and breaches. If you can prove all the facts just stated, you can recover $150, or whatever the difference is between $500 and what it ultimately cost you to have your house painted.

### Q. What other kinds of damages are there?

**A.** The most common ones are:

- Nominal damages, awarded when you win your case but you have not proved much of a loss. The court may award you a small amount as a matter of course.

- Liquidated damages, an amount that is built into the contract. Although one or both parties have effectively breached the contract, this term will stand, as long as it fairly estimates the damages. In contrast, the courts will not enforce a penalty clause, an amount of liquidated damages that is way out of line with the actual loss.

- Consequential damages, as discussed in the section on warranties. These are rarely available in a contract suit, unless they are provided for in the contract.

- Punitive damages, available if the breaching party's behavior was offensive to the court. Punitive damages are virtually never recovered in a suit for breach of contract, but it may be possible to get punitive damages or some form of statu-

tory damages (legal penalties) under a consumer fraud law or in a suit for fraud.

### Q. Are there other remedies in a contract suit besides damages?

**A.** Yes. The main one is specific performance, a court order requiring the breaching party to perform as promised in the contract. Courts are reluctant to award this because it is awkward to enforce. They will impose specific performance only if there is no other remedy available because of the contract's unique subject matter, such as real estate or a unique piece of personal property.

### Q. What else can a court do?

**A.** A court may rescind (cancel) a contract that one party has breached. The court may

---

## LAWSUITS AS REMEDIES

*This section will discuss the different kinds of relief you can ask a court for, considering what you already learned about contract defenses.*

*Remember: Any time one side can prove one of the contract defenses discussed in the second section, there's no breach of contract because there's no enforceable contract. Then the party that does not or cannot perform merely has to pay back any money or return any goods transferred in the agreement.*

## WHEN IN ROME...

*Why are there so many foreign legal terms? Many legal concepts trace their roots to Roman legal principles, though the classical Anglo-American judge-oriented legal system—the common law—has less in common with Roman law than does the European "code" system. (The code system is also used in Louisiana, where the Napoleonic code took hold before the territory became part of the U.S.) Also, much of the infamous redundant language of the law—such as "cease and desist," "open and notorious"—is a result of the introduction of Norman French terms alongside Anglo-Saxon ones in legal procedure after the Norman conquest of England in 1066. (English legal proceedings were carried on in the French language until the late 14th century.) Numerous French terms are still in common use, such as petit and grand juries.*

*With the decreased knowledge of classical languages and the trend away from elitism, fewer and fewer non-English terms have remained in use over the years. Any lawyer who tries to impress you with his proficiency in Latin legalisms should be taken with what the great Roman advocate and orator Cicero would have called cum grano salis—with a grain of salt.*

then order the breaching party to pay the other side any expenses incurred; it could also order the return of goods sold. Or, the court could reform the contract. That involves rewriting the contract according to what the court concludes, based on evidence at trial, the parties actually intended. Although these have traditionally been rare remedies, they are being used increasingly under the provisions of many states' consumer fraud laws (discussed below).

### Q. What are consumer protection or consumer fraud acts?

**A.** Laws prohibiting unfair and deceptive trade practices in consumer transactions have been enacted in every state. They apply to almost all consumer transactions and are both extremely flexible and very potent—often providing for treble (triple) damages where a viola-

tion is found. Generally requiring lower legal hurdles than traditional fraud remedies—for example, intent to deceive is usually not a requirement—these laws usually provide both for state action and recovery by private lawsuits. These laws are the ultimate legal reaction to *caveat emptor*. Their use involves numerous technicalities, though, and competent legal advice is absolutely necessary to take advantage of them.

### Q. If I have a contract for services or goods with a company that goes out of business, what can I do?

**A.** If another firm bought the company, as in a corporate merger, usually the new company must take responsibility for the contract obligations of the old company. If, however, the company went through the bankruptcy process,

## MORE ON REASONABLENESS

*Earlier we discussed the "reasonable person." There are two principles that extend that fictional person's capacities into the practical realm. One is the concept of the "reasonable observer," a reasonable person who sets the standard of whether an action or statement would reasonably suggest, for example, an offer or acceptance, or a repudiation. This person is not an eagle-eyed expert, but stands for common sense.*

*Closely related is the concept of "knew or should have known." If parties to a contract are considered to know, or be "on notice" of something—say, that their offer has been accepted—it is not enough to ask whether they actually knew it. If it were, we would have only their word as really reliable evidence that they knew or didn't know. The law will not allow parties who should have known something through the reasonable exercise of their senses and intelligence to fail to use them. Thus it isn't enough to say, "I didn't know the Yugo I sold you had no engine." That's something that someone selling a car reasonably should know.*

your contract could legally be disavowed, though any debt owed to you might not be.

If the company has ceased doing business, or is under the protection of the bankruptcy laws, your chances of recovering anything of value are small. If you have a contract that still is in force with a troubled company, you may have to get the rest of your contract needs filled by another company if the one you have a contract with can't come through. Then you may have a damages claim against the first company. If the company is in bankruptcy, you may be contacted by the bankruptcy court, or you may need a lawyer's help to put in your claim. If your claim isn't substantial, though, it's usually not worth the trouble.

**Q. I realize that I may have to get goods from another company. What about any money the first company may owe me under the contract?**

**A.** If the company is in bankruptcy, you can file a claim against it through the bankruptcy court. You'll have to "stand in line" with the other creditors, and you may get only a small percentage of what the company owes you, if you recover anything at all. If the business is a corporation that's dissolving under state law, you can file a claim against the corporation through the state agency (usually the secretary of state) for any losses you have accumulated. Whatever assets remain will be divided according to the number of claims filed and their amounts.

**Q. If the financially troubled company is holding goods for me on layaway, can I still get my goods?**

**A.** Most companies that go out of business will notify people that they are closing; often they want you to come in and finish the purchase because they need the cash. If they've tried to contact you and you haven't responded, they may sell those goods, and you'll have no way to recover the merchandise, although the law still entitles you to any money you paid toward the purchase.

**Q. If the merchandise is gone and I've paid money, how can I recover that money?**

**A.** If the store is still open, it probably will pay you when you present your receipt for payments made toward the purchase price. If the store has closed, you might need to file a claim in the bankruptcy court or with the proper state agency, as described above.

**Q. What do I do about merchandise that was under warranty? Who'll cover it now that the seller has gone out of business?**

**A.** If you've purchased a national brand of goods, there probably will be a service center or a licensed warranty center in your area. It may not be as convenient for you as the seller's store. Almost all manufacturers will stand behind their products regardless of where you purchased them. The only drawback is that you may need to present an original receipt to show that the manufacturer's warranty still covers the product.

**Q. I also purchased an additional retailer's warranty when I bought my goods which extended the manufacturer's warranty. What will this extra retailer's warranty cover?**

**A.** Retailers usually offer this warranty to extend parts and labor for a much longer period of time than the manufacturer offers. Unfortunately, the retailer's warranty is useless if the place that made the promise is now out of business, unless its obligations have been taken over by another company.

## CONCLUSION

This chapter has discussed how to make a contract and how to find out if you have unknowingly made a contract. It also covered some special consumer contract issues, how to identify a breach of contract, and what to do about a breach. Yet this has merely scratched the surface of this highly complex area of law. It has not even dealt in detail with the millions of contracts made every day between merchants and other businesses, or investment-related contractual relationships. While many common contracts don't require the services of a lawyer, be aware of when legal assistance may help avoid serious problems in the future.

## WHERE TO GET MORE INFORMATION

In most states, a state agency, often the attorney general, has an office of consumer affairs and protection. (In some states this office is under the secretary of state's authority.) These offices are good starting points both for filing complaints and for free literature on consumer protection, and appear in your telephone directory under the state government listings, or you can call any state government information number.

Also consider contacting federal agencies, such as the Federal Trade Commission, if you think you have been subjected to a deceptive practice. (See consumer credit section for the FTC's national and regional offices.)

State and local bar associations often publish free pamphlets and handbooks on legal problems, and can provide lists of lawyers who handle consumer cases. (See pages 705–707 for a list of state bars.)

The local Better Business Bureau can be helpful.

Some television and radio stations or newspapers have "action lines" that follow up on complaints. They often get results in exchange for being able to use your complaint on the air or in the paper.

The federal government publishes helpful handbooks for consumers. They are available for little or no charge from the Consumer Information Center-N, P.O. Box 100, Pueblo, CO 81002, telephone (719) 948-3334.

Scores of other publications on everything from credit to cars and from weight-loss programs to food products are available from the federal government. For lists of some of these publications, write to the Federal Trade Commission, 6th Street and Pennsylvania Avenue NW, Washington, DC 20580.

## CONTENTS

# INTRODUCTION

S O, YOU PLAN TO BUY A CAR. The thought might excite you, or maybe it makes you anxious. But no matter how you feel about it, the bottom line is that you are about to make a major purchase—to part with a substantial amount of hard-earned dollars for an item that is going to be around for a while.

## BUYING A NEW CAR

As with any other big-ticket item, it is important to do your homework—decide in advance what kind of car you need, and how much you can afford to spend. Think about size—a big family car or a jazzy sports car? Think about options—do you care if you have power everything, or do you mind cranking open your windows yourself? Do you prefer cloth, vinyl, or leather seats? What features are important to you?

After you have analyzed your needs and your finances, you are ready to being looking. Before you start pounding the pavement, check out some of the consumer-oriented publications that have information on cost, reliability, comfort factors, and other features of many cars. Your local library and bookstores should have many of these references. Also, see the "Where to Get More Information" section at the end of this chapter.

### Advertising/Sales Practices

**Q. What information should an automobile ad include?**

**A.** This is an area largely regulated by statute, and it varies from state to state. In some places, the ad must state the number available of that type of vehicle. Other items that may be required include price, dealer and factory-installed options and warranty terms. In addition, if the vehicle is "on sale," the ad should state the date the sale ends.

## "BAIT AND SWITCH" ADS

*"Bait and switch" is advertising a vehicle that the dealer does not intend to sell. Usually this is done to lure the unsuspecting customer toward buying an unadvertised, often higher-priced vehicle. The ad draws the customer into the showroom, but the advertised car is not available at that time or stated price.*

*If you suspect that you have been the victim of such advertising, contact the consumer protection division of your state attorney general's office. If they have received a number of reports about this kind of advertising, they may file a claim against the dealer on behalf of all of the duped customers. If they find that yours is an isolated incident, they may still help you pursue an individual claim. In either case, it may be possible to hold the dealer to providing the vehicle at the publicized price.*

# Worksheet for Buying a New Car

To help you negotiate the price of your next car, you may want to use this worksheet to establish your bargaining room before you talk with a dealer.

**Model** _____          **Base Price** _____

*Options:*                                     *Invoice Price\**          *Retail Price*

| | | |
|---|---|---|
| Transmission: ............................ | _____ | |
|    Automatic ................................... | _____ | |
|    Stick ................................... | _____ | |
| Air Conditioning .......................... | _____ | |
| Engine: ................................... | _____ | |
|    Size ................................... | _____ | |
|    Diesel ................................... | _____ | |
| Sound System: ........................... | _____ | |
|    AM-FM ................................... | _____ | |
|    AM-FM Cassette ....................... | _____ | |
| Brakes: ................................... | _____ | |
|    Anti-lock ................................... | _____ | |
|    Power ................................... | _____ | |
| Air Bag(s) ................................... | _____ | |
| Power Steering ........................... | _____ | |
| Power Locks ............................... | _____ | |
| Power Seats ............................... | _____ | |
| Rear Window Wiper/Washer ........... | _____ | |
| Rear Window Defogger .................. | _____ | |
| Tires: ................................... | _____ | |
|    Full-Size Spare ......................... | _____ | |
|    Steel Belted Radials .................. | _____ | |
| Mirrors: ................................... | _____ | |
|    Dual ................................... | _____ | |
|    Dual Remote ............................ | _____ | |
|    Passenger Visor ....................... | _____ | |
| Other: ................................... | _____ | |
| **Totals** .................... | _____ | |

\*You can get the invoice price by looking at the dealer's invoice or by reviewing new car publications.
SOURCE: Federal Trade Commission

## Q. *What if the ad omits details?*

**A.** If the dealer knows of important facts about the vehicle, but fails to reveal them, the law may consider that as a deceptive act that could enable you to cancel the deal and even recover damages in court. Clearing up the missing facts later does not erase the dealer's deceitful act. (For more information, see the "Lemon Laws and Other Consumer Protection Statutes" section that appears later in this chapter on page 351.)

## The New Car Contract

### Q. *Must a car contract be in writing?*

**A.** Yes, according to the Statute of Frauds of the Uniform Commercial Code (UCC). The UCC, which is in effect in some form or another in every state but Louisiana, regulates sales of goods and securities and governs many kinds of commercial transactions. Since it has been adopted, with minor variations, by every state legislature except Louisiana's, it governs most auto transactions in the country, and it will be referred to often in this chapter.

The UCC says any sale of goods of $500 or more must be in writing and signed by the party against whom enforcement is sought. If the contract is challenged, the courts will not be permitted to enforce it unless it is in writing.

### Q. *Who signs the contract?*

**A.** Besides you, either an authorized salesperson or a supervisor or manager signs it. *Before* you sign, make sure you understand and accept all the contract terms, because you'll probably have to abide by a contract you have signed, even if you have not read it. Read the contract carefully. Ask questions. Cross out blank spaces to avoid any additions after you sign. Make sure that the dealer's promises appear in the contract. Do *not* sign until the contract satisfies *you*. The contract you sign binds you, and escape from the contract is both difficult and expensive.

### TERMS THAT THE CONTRACT SHOULD INCLUDE

*The sales contract should describe the car and include the vehicle identification number (VIN). You can find it on the driver's side of the dashboard near the windshield. The contract also should state whether the car is new, used, or has had a previous life as a demonstrator, rental car, or taxicab. In addition, the contract should include price terms consistent with your oral agreement, and details on any trade-in you will supply, including mileage and the dollar amount credited. Insist on a cancellation provision that enables you to get your deposit back. The contract should state the warranty terms very clearly. (See the "Warranties" section of this chapter on page 355.) The contract's financing terms should state price, deposit, trade-in allowance, annual percentage rate of interest (APR), and length of term.*

## Q. May I change a seller's preprinted contract?

**A.** Yes, if the seller agrees. If you do change terms, cross out the unwanted language, and write or type in the substitute terms. Both you and an authorized dealer representative should initial the changes. Handwritten or typed changes to a printed contract overrule printed terms.

## Q. May I cancel the contract even after I sign it?

**A.** It depends. If you were a minor when you signed it (under eighteen in most places), and you contracted with an adult, you can dodge the agreement at any time for any reason while you are still under age, or within a reasonable time after reaching the age of majority, as long as the car is not considered a "necessary" akin to food or clothing. For example, if you are a minor but you are out on your own, and you must have the car in order to get to the work that supports you, the car will be considered a necessary, and your youth will not be an acceptable excuse for you to cancel the contract. The law protects inexperienced young people from being bound by bad deals with tricky adults. Most car dealers know this rule, however, so they will avoid contracting with a minor. These dealers will insist that the car be bought by, or in the name of, a financially responsible adult.

## Q. How else may I get out of the contract?

**A.** If, for example, the car you buy is not what the dealer promised, the dealer may have breached its warranty. (See the "Warranties" section in this chapter on page 355.) If so, then you might attempt to cancel the contract because of the breach. Or you might try canceling for no reason. However, you risk losing your deposit. The dealer also might file a lawsuit to

> ## WHAT HAPPENS TO YOUR DEPOSIT IF YOU CANCEL THE CONTRACT?
>
> *If you cancel the sales contract, what happens to your deposit depends on the stage of the transaction and on the contract terms you signed. The earlier in the deal, the more likely the dealer will refund your deposit and the less likely you will be sued. Some states entitle you to a refund if, for example, you decide to cancel before the dealer representative signs the contract. Some states also allow you to get a refund if you cannot get financing, despite your best efforts, provided the contract is subject to getting financing.*

recover lost profits, for time spent with you and on your car, and other damages.

## Q. If we wind up in court in a contract dispute, may I offer information in addition to the contract?

**A.** The court, under the "parol evidence rule," may ignore any additional routine terms that don't appear in your original document. Consistent additional terms that explain or supplement, but don't change the contract's meaning, may be considered by the court. Generally, though, the court confines itself to the "four corners" of the document that you present. The court assumes that both parties read and understood the contract before signing it, and disallows prior inconsistent terms that vary or contradict the contract. You may be able to present evidence of an oral agreement made after the written agreement. Also, you may admit outside facts to prove that there actually was no contract or to prove that fraud induced you to sign.

### Q. *What if I want to add something after I sign the contract?*

**A.** Ask the dealer to write a contract addendum (a supplement), or write it yourself. Both parties should sign it. Make sure that whoever signs for the seller has the legal power to do so. Mention the original contract in the addendum, state that everyone should consider it an inseparable part of the original contract and that the addendum overrides any inconsistent terms in the two documents. This will help you avoid the parol evidence rule discussed above.

Bank Loan Versus Dealer Financing

### Q. *What if I do not have enough cash to buy my new car, even after my trade-in?*

**A.** Then you need financing. Banks, credit unions, loan companies, and car dealers are all potential funding sources. Interest rates will vary among these options. Shop around for the best deal by comparing the various loan terms and annual percentage rates (APRs). The APR is the actual interest you will have to pay on the unpaid balance of the loan, and may depend partially on your credit history. For further information on comparing terms and APRs, see pages 241–243 of the "Consumer Credit" chapter.

### Q. *What must the creditor tell me?*

**A.** The creditor (the person or institution to whom you will owe money) must inform consumers of:

1. the annual percentage rate (this must be conspicuous, for example, printed in red or in much larger type than the rest of the document);
2. how the creditor sets the finance charge;
3. the balance on which the creditor computes the finance charge;

> ## MAKING SURE A CREDITOR TREATS YOU RIGHT
>
> *The Truth in Lending Act (TILA) protects consumers. Congress passed it in 1969 to ensure that consumers get enough facts to enable them to make an informed decision about financing. It applies to consumers who seek credit for money, property, or services for personal, family, or household purposes. (TILA does not cover business, commercial, and agricultural credit. It applies to financing for personal, family, or household uses.) Creditors, either people or organizations, who regularly extend consumer credit that is payable in more than four installments are subject to the Act, as are creditors who require (or may require) a finance charge.*

4. the dollar amount of the finance charge (this also must be conspicuous);

5. the amount to be financed (the loan);

6. the total dollar amount that will be paid (loan plus finance charge); and

7. the number, amount, and due dates of payments.

### Q. What if the creditor does not follow the rules?

**A.** Creditors who disobey the rules may have to pay you any actual damages that you have sustained. For example, if you paid more than you should have, you may be able to recover the excess. They may also have to pay your court costs and lawyer's fees, as well as a fine to the state. In a class action lawsuit with many complainants, the penalty paid to the government could be much larger.

### Q. What is the maximum APR that I have to pay?

**A.** That depends on the laws of the state in which you live or where the deal occurs. The states allow different maximum APRs, depending on their "usury" laws. Remember, an APR is negotiable, though a creditor may not exceed an upper limit.

### Title

### Q. When do I get title to my car?

**A.** In most states, in any sale of a car, new or used, title passes when the previous owner endorses the certificate of title or ownership over to the new owner. Check with your local Department of Motor Vehicles for the law in your state.

### Q. Suppose I sign the contract, but do not yet have title. What if something happens to the car?

**A.** The answer depends on who has the risk of loss. Usually, the party who possesses the vehicle bears the risk and is more likely to have insurance against the loss. Under the Uniform Commericial Code (UCC), which is discussed in detail on pages 342–344, 345–347, and 355–359 if the seller is a merchant (for example, a car dealer), the risk of loss passes to buyers when they receive the car.

If the seller is not a merchant, as in a private sale of a used car, the risk passes to the buyer on "tender of delivery."

### Q. What is "tender of delivery"?

**A.** Tender of delivery occurs when the seller actually tries to deliver the car, or makes

---

**THE RIGHT TO REPOSSESSION**

*When you buy a car on credit, you may have to give the creditor rights in your property (the car) that are superior to the rights of your other creditors. When you are loaned the money, you sign a "security agreement," which gives the creditor a "security interest" in your car (the collateral). You are agreeing to give the creditor a lien on the car. If you don't pay, the creditor may try to get the car back and apply its value toward your debt.*

the vehicle available for a pick-up arranged by a contract.

### Q. What if I have title but the dealer still has the car?

**A.** A merchant seller who keeps physical possession may bear the risk of loss long after the title has passed and after the dealer has received payment.

### Q. May the risk of loss move from the seller to me?

**A.** Yes, the Uniform Commericial Code (UCC) provision governing risk of loss allows this. A sales contract that specifies when the risk of loss passes will override the standard UCC provision.

### Q. How may I lose title?

**A.** You may lose title if you fail to make your payments as they become due. The creditor is then permitted to repossess your car.

### Q. So if I don't pay, can the secured creditor just come and take my car away?

**A.** Afraid so. The only limitation on automobile repossessions is that the repossessor does it without breaching the peace. In many states, the creditor does not even have to sue the debtor, or notify the debtor of the default before reclaiming the vehicle.

### Q. What is a breach of the peace?

**A.** A breach of the peace generally is any act likely to produce disorder or violence, such as an unauthorized entry into your home. If you protest strongly enough when a repossessor appears, it may create a breach of the peace, and any repossession may be invalid.

### Q. What happens after the repossession?

**A.** Eventually, the creditor has the right to resell. However, before that happens, the debtor has the right to buy back the car (in legal terms, redeem the collateral).

### Q. How does redemption work?

**A.** The debtor must pay the entire balance due, plus any repossession costs and other reasonable charges. Watch out for consumer credit contracts containing acceleration clauses. These force the debtor to pay the entire outstanding debt, not just the amount of overdue payments. Because a default and repossession have already occurred, it is unlikely that the debtor will have enough money to pay the entire balance. Redemption rarely takes place.

### Q. What if I do not redeem the car?

**A.** The UCC gives the creditor two choices. First, it may sell the car to satisfy the debt. If the profits from the sale are not enough to pay expenses and satisfy the debt, you would be liable for the difference. The only limitation placed on the creditor by the UCC is that the sale be "commercially reasonable." As the UCC is applied in some states, that means first getting court permission to hold a sale. The sale may be public or private. However, the creditor must give you reasonable notice of the time, place, and manner of the sale. If it is a public sale, you have the right to take part (bid on the car). If the sale produces too much money, the creditor must pass that along to you. For example, if the amount of debt and expenses totals $5,000, and the creditor gets $5,600 from the sale of the car, the overage of $600 is due to you and the UCC obliges the creditor to refund the money to you.

## Q. *What is the second choice?*

**A.** The creditor may keep the car to satisfy the debt fully. The law refers to this as "strict foreclosure." There is no duty to return excess money in a strict foreclosure. Creditors seldom use it, because dealers want to sell, not keep, cars.

---

## BUYING OR SELLING
## A USED CAR

## Q. *What is a used vehicle?*

**A.** It is a vehicle that was driven farther than the distance necessary to deliver a new car to the dealer or to test drive it.

### Dealer Versus Private Sale

## Q. *Should I buy from a dealer or a private seller?*

**A.** Go with whoever gives you the best deal and with whom you are most comfortable. Some experts believe you may be better off buying from a private seller. They think a private seller may give a more accurate description of the car's faults based on personal knowledge, and you may get a lower price from a private seller. Private sellers, however, seldom give warranties, which dealers sometimes offer. (See the "Warranties" section in this chapter on page 355.) Also, some states have regulations governing used car sales that may apply only to dealers.

## Q. *Do I need a written contract if I buy from a private seller?*

**A.** If you are paying more than $500, you should have a written contract. Courts cannot enforce an oral contract to sell a car for over $500

**USED VEHICLES**
*Buying and selling a used car has some unique features, but it is similar to buying a new car. The advertising rules are largely the same, so you must still beware of "bait and switch" ads that look too good to be true.*

*Basically, the law about forming and executing the contract for purchase or sale is the same for new and used cars, and the car's title transfers via the same mechanism. Lenders may examine the purchase a little more closely to ensure they receive adequate collateral for their money, but the procedure for getting the money does not change. As with a new car, if you fail to pay, you lose it to the "repo man."*

under the Statute of Frauds. Even under $500, it is always best to put the contract in writing if you are not going to conclude the deal immediately with a Bill of Sale (see next question).

## Q. *Do I need to get anything else in writing?*

**A.** You should have a Bill of Sale. Many states require you to present a Bill of Sale to register your car. A Bill of Sale also may serve as a receipt. The Bill of Sale should contain the:

- date of the sale;
- year, make, and model of the car;
- Vehicle Identification Number (VIN);
- odometer reading;

- amount paid for the car, and in what form (cash, check, and the like); and
- buyer's and seller's names, addresses, and phone numbers.

The seller should sign and date the Bill of Sale, and both you and the seller should get a copy.

**Q. What is the Buyers Guide, and what must it say?**

**A.** Information contained on the Buyers Guide includes:

- whether or not the car comes with a warranty. If there is a warranty, the specific coverage must be outlined;
- whether the vehicle comes with implied warranties only, or is sold "as is," that is, with no warranties at all;
- a statement that you should request an inspection by an independent mechanic before you buy;
- a statement that you should get all promises in writing; and
- what some of the major problems are that may happen in any car.

If you do buy a used car from a dealer, you are entitled to receive a copy of the actual Buyers Guide that was posted in your car. If you have negotiated any changes in the warranty, it should be noted on the Buyers Guide. The Buyers Guide becomes part of your contract, and its terms override any conflicting terms in that contract.

**Q. Are there other facts that a seller must tell the buyer?**

**A.** The seller, whether a dealer or a private individual, should be truthful about the car. If the buyer is disappointed because it is not as described or does not perform as it was sup-

> ## SPECIAL RULES FOR USED CAR DEALERS
>
> *The Federal Trade Commission has issued a Used Car Rule for dealers. Under the rule, "dealers" are those who sell six or more used cars in a twelve-month period. The rule forbids used car dealers from misrepresenting the mechanical condition of a used car or any warranty terms, and prohibits them from representing that a car comes with a warranty when none exists. They must make available the terms of any written warranty they provide, and they must post a "Buyers Guide" on the side window of the car.*

posed to, a breach of warranty action may arise against the seller who has deceived the buyer. If possible, the seller should provide the buyer with the car's complete service records.

**Q. Does the seller have to tell the buyer the car's mileage?**

**A.** Yes, federal law entitles the buyer of a used car to receive a mileage disclosure statement from the seller, even if the seller is not a dealer. On request, the seller must give a signed written statement to the buyer stating the odometer reading at the time of transfer. The statement also should certify the odometer's accuracy, to the seller's knowledge. If the seller knows it is incorrect, the seller must admit it. Refusal to provide such a statement, or illegally tampering with the odometer, exposes the seller to stiff penalties.

# Example of Completed Buyers Guide

## BUYERS GUIDE

IMPORTANT: Spoken promises are difficult to enforce. Ask the dealer to put all promises in writing. Keep this form.

Chevrolet          Cavalier          1983          IGIAD27P6DJI23456
VEHICLE MAKE       MODEL             YEAR          VIN NUMBER

_____
DEALER STOCK NUMBER (Optional)

WARRANTIES FOR THIS VEHICLE:

## ☐ AS IS - NO WARRANTY

YOU WILL PAY ALL COSTS FOR ANY REPAIRS. The dealer assumes no responsibility for any repairs regardless of any oral statements about the vehicle.

## ☒ WARRANTY

☐ FULL    ☒ LIMITED WARRANTY. The dealer will pay _100*_% of the labor and _100*_% of the parts for the covered systems that fail during the warranty period. Ask the dealer for a copy of the warranty document for a full explanation of warranty coverage, exclusions, and the dealer's repair obligations. Under state law, "implied warranties" may give you even more rights.

| SYSTEMS COVERED: | DURATION: |
|---|---|
| Engine | 90 days or 3000 miles, whichever |
| Transmission + Drive Shaft | comes first. |
| Differential | |

MANUFACTURER'S WARRANTY STILL APPLIES. The manufacturer's original warranty has not expired on the vehicle. Consult the manufacturer's warranty booklet for details as to warranty coverage, service location, etc.

☒ SERVICE CONTRACT. A service contract is available at an extra charge on this vehicle. Ask for details as to coverage, deductible, price, and exclusions. If you buy a service contract within 90 days of the time of sale, state law "implied warranties" may give you additional rights.

PRE PURCHASE INSPECTION: ASK THE DEALER IF YOU MAY HAVE THIS VEHICLE INSPECTED BY YOUR MECHANIC EITHER ON OR OFF THE LOT.

SEE THE BACK OF THIS FORM for important additional information, including a list of some major defects that may occur in used motor vehicles.

SOURCE: Federal Trade Commission

**Below is a list of some major defects that may occur in used motor vehicles.**

**Frame & Body**
Frame-cracks, corrective welds, or rusted through
Dogtracks—bent or twisted frame

**Engine**
Oil leakage, excluding normal seepage
Cracked block or head
Belts missing or inoperable
Knocks or misses related to camshaft lifters and
push rods
Abnormal exhaust discharge

**Transmission & Drive Shaft**
Improper fluid level or leakage, excluding normal
seepage
Cracked or damaged case which is visible
Abnormal noise or vibration caused by faulty
transmission or drive shaft
Improper shifting or functioning in any gear
Manual clutch slips or chatters

**Differential**
Improper fluid level or leakage excluding normal
seepage
Cracked or damaged housing which is visible
Abnormal noise or vibration caused by faulty
differential

**Cooling System**
Leakage including radiator
Improperly functioning water pump

**Electrical System**
Battery leakage
Improperly functioning alternator, generator,
battery, or starter

**Fuel System**
Visible leakage

**Inoperable Accessories**
Gauges or warning devices
Air conditioner
Heater & Defroster

**Brake System**
Failure warning light broken
Pedal not firm under pressure (DOT spec.)
Not enough pedal reserve (DOT spec.)
Does not stop vehicle in straight line (DOT spec.)
Hoses damaged
Drum or rotor too thin (Mfgr. Specs)
Lining or pad thickness less than 1/32 inch
Power unit not operating or leaking
Structural or mechanical parts damaged

**Steering System**
Too much free play at steering wheel (DOT specs.)
Free play in linkage more than 1/4 inch
Steering gear binds or jams
Front wheels aligned improperly (DOT specs.)
Power unit belts cracked or slipping
Power unit fluid level improper

**Suspension System**
Ball joint seals damaged
Structural parts bent or damaged
Stabilizer bar disconnected
Spring broken
Shock absorber mounting loose
Rubber bushings damaged or missing
Radius rod damaged or missing
Shock absorber leaking or functioning improperly

**Tires**
Tread depth less than 2/32 inch
Sizes mismatched
Visible damage

**Wheels**
Visible cracks, damage or repairs
Mounting bolts loose or missing

**Exhaust System**
Leakage

*Reliable Used Cars*
DEALER
*1000 Downtown Expressway*
ADDRESS
*Lakeside, KS 01243*
*Stan Jones, General Manager, 202-916-4554*
SEE FOR COMPLAINTS

**IMPORTANT: The information on this form is part of any contract to buy this vehicle. Removal of this label before consumer purchase (except for purpose of test-driving) is a violation of federal law (16 C.F.R. 455).**

### INSPECTION BEFORE THE SALE

*Not only are you allowed to take the car to your mechanic before the sale is final but you should. The Buyers Guide sticker, which applies to used car dealers, urges you to do so. If the seller, whether a dealer or a private party, will not allow your mechanic to inspect the car, do not buy it unless it is such a good deal that you will not mind paying for car repairs later.*

## Seller Withdrawing from the Deal

**Q. May I get out of a contract to sell my used car?**

**A.** The same contract laws that govern a new car purchase also cover a used car purchase. Again, it depends on the stage of the contracting process and on the contract's language.

**Q. May a court force me to sell my car to a buyer after I have decided I do not want to sell?**

**A.** Probably not. In legal jargon, courts try to "leave the parties as they find them," and usually will not force a buyer to make a purchase or a seller to sell an item. If the car is an antique or unique in some way, however, the court might order the seller to perform the contract (specific performance). In cases like this, money damages might not suffice to satisfy a buyer who wants your specific car. Because the buyer cannot reasonably find a substitute for *this* car, the seller will have to take the money, and the buyer will get the car.

## LEMON LAWS AND OTHER CONSUMER LAWS

**Q. What must I do to make lemon laws work for me?**

**A.** First, you must notify the manufacturer, and, in some states, the dealer about the defect. Second, you should keep a copy of *every* repair or service receipt you are given. This serves as your record that the required number of repair attempts has been made, and is especially important if your car's defect had to be repaired at another garage or in another city because it was physically impossible to drive the car back to the seller's repair location.

Most states require that you go through an arbitration procedure before you can get a replacement or refund. Some states sponsor arbitration programs, which may be more objective than those run by manufacturers. Arbitration is usually free, and results often are binding only on the manufacturer; if you don't like the result, you can still take the manufacturer to court. Some states require arbitration only if the manufacturer refuses to give you a satisfactory replacement or a refund. You also may have the option of bypassing arbitration and going directly to court.

If you successfully pursue a lemon law claim, you may get a refund of what you paid for the car, as well as reimbursement for things like taxes, registration fees, and finance charges. If you choose, you may get a replacement car. Be sure that it is of comparable value to the lemon it is replacing, and that it satisfies you completely.

**LEMON LAWS**

*What can you do if the car you just bought is a real "lemon"? What if the car you purchased is in the repair shop almost as much as in your garage? To protect consumers from such situations, most states have passed some form of "lemon laws," which usually apply to new cars purchased for personal, family, or household use. These laws entitle you to a replacement car or a refund if your new car is so defective that it is beyond satisfactory repair by the dealer. You must, however, give the dealer a reasonable opportunity to repair the car.*

*How do you know if the law considers your car a lemon? States vary in their specifics. However, a lemon normally is a car that continues to have a defect that substantially restricts its use, safety, or value, even after reasonable efforts to repair it. This often means four repair attempts on the same problem or a directly related problem within six months or one year (the time period varies by state). Or, it might mean the car is out of commission for more than thirty nonconsecutive days during either: (1) The year after the dealer sold it; or (2) the duration of any express warranty, whichever is shorter.*

**Q. Do lemon laws cover used cars?**

**A.** Yes, they cover used cars in a growing number of states.

In some places, the law applies both to dealer and private seller purchases.

The laws may have a connection with the safety inspection sticker requirement. (See the "Inspections" section later in this chapter on page 363.) These sticker laws usually protect you if two conditions occur. First, the car must fail inspection within a certain period from the date of sale. Second, the repair costs must exceed a stated percentage of the purchase price. Then you are permitted to cancel the deal within a certain period. You probably will have to notify the seller in writing of your intention to cancel, including your reasons. You must return the car to the place of sale even if it requires towing. If the seller offers to make repairs, you can decide whether to accept the seller's offer or get your money back.

**Q. What if the car passes the safety inspection but still turns out to be a lemon (by requiring costly repairs or repeated repair attempts for the same problem)? Is it still considered a lemon?**

**A.** It might pass the safety inspection and still be a lemon. Some state laws define "lemon" for used cars the same way they do for new cars: by using a formula of repair attempts/time spent in the shop. These laws protect buyers of used lemons in much the same way as buyers of new lemons. (See the previous questions and answers for details.)

**Q. May I drive the car while we are deciding whether or not it is a lemon?**

**A.** Yes, you may drive the car (if it is drivable), but be aware that, if the car does indeed turn out to be a lemon, the law usually allows the seller to deduct a certain amount from your

# Lemon Laws

Sometimes, despite our best efforts, we buy a car that just doesn't work properly. There may be little problem after little problem, or perhaps one big problem that never seems to be fixed. Because of the bad taste that such cars leave in the mouths of consumers who buy them, these cars are known as "lemons."

In the past, it has been very difficult to obtain a refund if a car turned out to be a lemon. The burden of proof was left to the consumer. Because it is hard to define exactly what constitutes a lemon, many lemon owners were unable to win a case against a manufacturer. But things are changing. As of 1994, all states have passed "Lemon Laws." Although there are some important state-to-state variations, all of the laws have similarities: They establish a period of coverage, usually one year from delivery or the written warranty period, whichever is shorter; they may require some form of noncourt arbitration; and, most importantly, they define a lemon. In most states a lemon is defined as a new car, truck, or van that has been taken back to the shop at least four times for the same repair or is out of service for a total of 30 days during the covered period.

This time does not mean consecutive days. In some states the total time must be for the same repair; in others, it can be based on different repair problems.

Be sure to keep careful records of your repairs since some states are now requiring only one of the three or four repairs to be within the specified time period.

While some vehicles, such as tractors and motor homes, are not covered by these laws in some states, the laws listed below do apply to all vehicles discussed in this book.

Specific information about laws in your state can be obtained from your state attorney general's office (c/o your state capital) or your local consumer protection office. The following table outlines the laws in five of the biggest states and what you need to do to set them in motion.

| | |
|---|---|
| **California** | **Qualification:** 4 unsuccessful repairs or 30 calendar days out of service within shorter of 1 year or 12,000 miles. Notification/Trigger: Written notice to manufacturer and delivery of car to repair facility for repair attempt within 30 days. *State has certified guidelines for arbitration.* |
| **Florida** | **Qualification:** 4 unsuccessful repairs or 30 calendar days out of service within shorter of 18 months or 24,000 miles. Notification/Trigger: After 3 unsuccessful repair attempts or 15 calendar days notice by registered or express mail to manufacturer who has 10 calendar days for a final repair attempt after delivery to designated dealer. *State-run arbitration program is available.* |
| **New York** | **Qualification:** 4 unsuccessful repairs or 30 calendar days out of service within shorter of 2 years or 18,000 miles. Notification/Trigger: Certified notice to manufacturer, agent or dealer. *State-run arbitration program is available.* |
| **Pennsylvania** | **Qualification:** 3 unsuccessful repairs or 30 calendar days out of service within shorter of 1 year, 12,000 miles, or warranty. Notification/Trigger: Delivery to authorized service and repair facility. If delivery impossible, written notice to manufacturer or its repair facility obligates them to pay for delivery. |
| **Texas** | **Qualification:** 4 unsuccessful repairs when 2 occurred within shorter of 1 year or 12,000 miles, and other 2 occur within shorter of 1 year or 12,000 miles from date of 2nd repair attempt; or 2 unsuccessful repairs of a serious safety defect when 1 occurred within shorter of 1 year or 12,000 miles and other occurred within shorter of 1 year or 12,000 miles from date of 1st repair; or 30 calendar days out of service within shorter of 2 years or 24,000 miles and at least 2 attempts were made within shorter of 1 year or 12,000 miles. Notification/Trigger: Written notice to manufacturer. *State-run arbitration program is available.* |

SOURCE: Adapted, with permission, from *The Car Book*, by Jack Gillis, with Karen Fierst and Jay Einhorn.

refund based on the miles you have driven. This applies to both new and used car sales.

## Other Consumer Protection Laws

### Q. What is an unfair or deceptive practice?

**A.** The Federal Trade Commission (FTC) defines "unfair conduct" as that which, although not necessarily illegal,

- offends public policy as established by statute, common law, or other means;
- is immoral, unethical, troublesome, or corrupt; and
- substantially injures consumers (or competitors or other businesspeople).

"Deceptive conduct" is behavior that could have caused people to act differently than they otherwise would have acted. It does not have to involve the product's qualities, but it might include any aspect that could be an important factor in deciding whether to buy the goods. An example would be stating that the engine has six cylinders when it really has four. The quality may be fine, but the buyer may have been seeking a car with a six-cylinder engine. The FTC regulations are the basis of many states' laws.

### Q. Must the unfair or deceptive act be intentional?

**A.** No, in most states, the seller does not even have to know about the deception. Rather, the court considers the effect that the seller's conduct might possibly have on the general public or on the people to whom the seller advertised the product.

### Q. What must I do in order to use an unfair and deceptive practices statute?

**A.** In many states, you must make a written demand for relief before you sue. The law allows the seller one last chance to make good.

## ADDITIONAL PROTECTION FOR CAR BUYERS

*Other statutes protect car buyers besides lemon laws:*

- *the federal Anti-Tampering Odometer Law prohibits acts that falsify odometer mileage readings;*

- *the federal Used Car Law requires that dealers post Buyers Guides on used cars;*

- *the federal Automobile Information Disclosure Act requires manufacturers and importers of new cars to affix a sticker, called the "Monroney label," on the windshield or side window of the car. The Monroney label lists the base price of the car, the options installed by the manufacturer, along with their suggested retail price, how much the manufacturer has charged for transportation, and the car's fuel economy (miles per gallon). Only the buyer is allowed to remove the Monroney label.*

*By far, the statutes providing the strongest protection are those prohibiting unfair and deceptive acts and practices. Every state has enacted such laws. Car buyers may recover from the seller (the dealer and/or the manufacturer), regardless of who might have done the deceiving.*

If you have to sue, many states require proof of "injury" before you may recover. Loss of money or property is enough to prove this. You should be able to show that the seller's actions actually caused the injury. For example, only if you were determined to buy the car no matter what the seller said would you have a hard time showing that the seller's conduct caused you injury or loss. If you based your decision to buy on what the seller told you, or if you were coerced into buying something that you didn't

really want, then you may be able to use the statute.

Remember to begin the procedure before the statute of limitations expires. This time limit varies by state, but is typically three or four years.

**Q. What happens if I win?**

**A.** Many states permit you to recover double or triple damages, and lawyer's fees. The purpose of these harsh penalties is to discourage sellers from committing unfair or deceptive acts in the future.

---

## VIOLATIONS OF UNFAIR AND DECEPTIVE PRACTICE LAWS

*Each statute differs about what actions could violate unfair and deceptive practices statutes. The most common violations include:*

- *hiding dangerous defects;*
- *failing to state that service is not readily available;*
- *not revealing that the dealer advertised the car at a lower price;*
- *odometer tampering;*
- *failure to reveal that the dealer is charging excessive preparation costs; and*
- *withholding facts about the car's previous use as, for example, a racing car. Generally, a dealer's failure to disclose any important facts about the car, or an attempt to make such facts too hard to see, is illegal, and could lead to your recovery under your state's unfair and deceptive practices law.*

---

## WARRANTIES

### Uniform Commercial Code (UCC)

**Q. What is a warranty?**

**A.** It is a guarantee of the product's quality and performance. A warranty may be written or oral. Three kinds of warranties could be given by a car seller under the UCC. These are an express warranty, an implied warranty of merchantability, and an implied warranty of fitness for a particular purpose. A seller may also sell a car "as is."

**Q. How does a seller create an express warranty?**

**A.** Whenever a seller makes any declaration of fact, description, or promise on which the buyer relies when deciding to make the purchase, the seller creates an express warranty. A seller may create an express warranty orally, in writing, or through an advertisement.

**Q. What about the seller's opinion of the car?**

**A.** An opinion or recommendation does not form an express warranty. Sales talk, called "puffing," will not create an express warranty. An example is "This car runs like a dream." Statements such as "This car needs no repairs," or "This car has a V-8 engine," however, will create an express warranty.

### Q. When does the implied warranty of merchantability arise?

**A.** It occurs automatically if the seller is a merchant, such as a car dealer. It requires that the car be of a quality that would pass without objection in the trade, and be fit for the ordinary purposes for which the buyer will use it. This warranty essentially provides for the overall quality of the car, and means that the car will do what it is supposed to do.

Most people agree that the implied warranty of merchantability is part of a new car purchase. All states provide for implied warranties for used cars bought from dealers, unless the warranty is disclaimed specifically, in writing, by words like "as is" or "with all faults."

### Q. How does someone create the implied warranty of fitness for a particular purpose?

**A.** Suppose that you tell the seller that you need the vehicle for a special purpose, such as towing a trailer, and the seller recommends a specific vehicle. You buy it, relying on the seller's skill or judgment. This creates an implied warranty that the vehicle can do what you told the dealer you needed it to do.

### Q. What if I bought my car "as is"?

**A.** Then you accepted the car with all its faults. Any postsale defects are your problem. A car may be sold "as is" through a dealer or a private person. The implied warranty of merchantability does not automatically arise in "as is" purchases. Some states do not permit "as is" sales for used cars.

### Q. Do I get these warranties every time I buy a car?

**A.** Not necessarily. A seller may disclaim or change warranties. Obvious language that mentions merchantability may exclude or modify the implied warranty of merchantability. An obvious disclaimer in writing may exclude the implied warranty of fitness for a particular purpose. Language such as "sold as is" cancels implied warranties. If the seller has given you an express warranty, however, courts will not uphold any attempted disclaimer that is inconsistent with or cancels the express warranty.

### Q. What if the seller gives me express and implied warranties that are inconsistent?

**A.** According to the Uniform Commercial Code, the parties' "mutual intention" decides which warranty takes priority. If there is no way to decide this, the following rules determine priority:

1. Specific or technical language usually wins over descriptive language that is inconsistent and general.

2. Express warranties override inconsistent implied warranties of merchantability.

3. Implied warranties of fitness for a particular purpose survive other inconsistent warranties.

## Remedies for Breach of Warranty

### Q. What are my options if the seller will not honor its warranties?

**A.** If you have not already accepted the car, reject it. You may reject only within a reasonable time after delivery of the car. What constitutes a "reasonable time" is a question of fact to be decided by the court, if it goes that far. You must give the seller specific information about what is wrong. You need only show the car's

## SECRET WARRANTIES

*Strictly speaking, a "secret warranty" is not a warranty at all. Rather, it is more in the nature of a deceptive practice that is secret because it is an unpublicized policy. A secret warranty develops when a manufacturer knows that many cars have the same problem, but tells dealers to charge customers for the repairs unless they complain. Unlike a recall (discussed later in this chapter on page 359), the manufacturer is not required to notify owners of the problem. By hiding what it knows about the defect, the manufacturer makes a lot of money from unsuspecting consumers.*

*If you suspect that a warranty should have covered your car repair or that the defect is widespread, complain to the dealer. Perhaps the dealer will fix your car without charging you. Follow up with a complaint to the consumer protection division of your state attorney general's office. If they find that a secret warranty exists, the manufacturer may be required to notify owners, to pay for repairs, and to reimburse those owners who have already paid to fix the problem.*

nonconformance in *any way* to the contract; the defect need not be major. You have the option of allowing the dealer to attempt to remedy ("cure") the defects within a reasonable time. Once you reject the car, behave as if you are no longer the owner—do not drive it, except to return it. You may hold the car for the seller to reclaim, or you may return it yourself.

These steps should enable you to reject the car. However, to take the next step and force the seller to live up to its warranties, you may need to consult a lawyer.

**Q. How do I know if I have already accepted?**

**A.** Unfortunately, sometimes the law considers just driving the car off the dealer's lot as acceptance, as long as you had a chance to inspect the car, even if you do not discover the defect for some time. At most, you have a week or two to reject the car. Acceptance may also occur if you take possession of the car despite knowing about its defects.

**Q. What may I do if I have accepted a car that proves to be defective?**

**A.** First, once you have accepted, you must continue to make your car payments; for the time being, at least, you are considered the car's owner, and are responsible for its costs. (You may be able to get your money back later.) You may not reject a car already accepted, unless you accepted it based on the assumption that the seller would repair the defect within a reasonable period. Your option now is to *revoke* your acceptance. You must give the seller notice of the defect, and show that it *substantially* impairs the value of the car to you.

Revocation involves a higher standard than rejection, and different states have various standards. Generally, the defect will have to be major to allow revocation. After revoking acceptance, you must act as if you had originally rejected the car. Leave the car in your driveway until the seller reclaims it, or return it yourself.

### Q. Can I get my money back if I reject or revoke acceptance?

**A.** You should be able to recover your money. If your written demand for a refund is denied, you will have to sue the seller. The seller has the right to deduct an amount per mile driven from your refund. If your rejection is found to be wrongful, the seller may recover damages against you.

### Q. May I simply use lemon laws and consumer protection statutes instead of warranties?

**A.** You may use them all. If you can prove seller fraud or deception, the unfair and deceptive practices statute in your state will help. You could invoke the lemon laws by showing that you tried to get the defect fixed the required number of times, or that your car was in the shop longer than the legal minimum before you rejected or revoked acceptance. This requires you to keep your records and receipts.

### Q. What is the difference between "limited" and "full" warranties?

**A.** If a dealer offers a full warranty, it is promising:

- to replace a defective car or part for free, within a reasonable time;
- that the owner will not have to do anything unreasonable to get the repairs done;
- that the warranty applies to anyone who owns the car during the warranty period;
- a refund or free replacement part, including installation, if the dealer cannot fix a car or part after a reasonable number of attempts.

## THE MAGNUSON-MOSS WARRANTY ACT

The federal government protects consumers through laws like the Magnuson-Moss Warranty Act, passed in 1975. It applies to all cars manufactured after 1975 that dealers sell and warrant in writing, and provides that you have the right to see a copy of the dealer's warranty before you buy. The information provided in the warranty will be more detailed than that provided on the Buyers Guide, and includes an explanation of how to obtain warranty service. The Magnuson-Moss Warranty Act also provides remedies for breach of warranty. An aggrieved consumer can sue based on breach of express warranties, implied warranties, or a service contract. If you win, you can recover attorney's fees and your court costs. Under the Act, if a written warranty is given, then implied warranties may not be disclaimed. However, the duration of any implied warranties can be limited. The Act mandates that if the seller does give you written warranties, they must be conspicuously labeled as either "limited" or "full."

Note that the Magnuson-Moss Act does not apply to "as is" sales, or to cars bought from private sellers.

A limited warranty is anything else. At least one of the above promises is missing. Most car dealers do *not* give full warranties on the entire car, but may do so on a specific part, such as the battery. Most used car warranties are limited.

---

## RECALLS

### Q. What is the recall system?

**A.** The recall system identifies defective automobiles that are already on the road, by notifying car owners about how to get them fixed.

### Q. What defects does the recall process include?

**A.** Generally, it includes defects that affect the car's safety, cause it to fall below federal safety standards, or both, and that are common to a group of the same kind of cars or equipment. The defect can be in performance, construction, components, or materials found in the car or in related equipment, such as child safety seats.

### Q. How does the recall process begin?

**A.** Many recalls result from the manufacturer's response to owner complaints. However, the National Highway Traffic Safety Administration (NHTSA) influences and orders many of the recalls. The NHTSA receives safety-related complaints through letters and its telephone toll-free hot line. (This hot line number is listed at the end of this chapter, under "Where to Get More Information" on page 390.) When the NHTSA registers enough complaints, NHTSA engineers perform an engineering analysis. Then the NHTSA engineers contact the automobile's manufacturer. The manufacturer must either remedy the defect or launch its own defect investigation.

### Q. How is a defect investigation conducted by the automobile's manufacturer?

**A.** It begins with a press release, and opening a public file to receive comments and information. If this confirms the defect and the manufacturer still will not voluntarily recall the vehicle, agency engineers recommend an initial determination of a safety defect to the NHTSA administrator. If approved, this results in a public hearing and notification to the manufacturer of the basis for the finding. After the hearing, the NHTSA decides if a final defect determination and recall is proper. Occasionally, the NHTSA administrator first seeks the transportation secretary's approval.

### Q. How effective are recall campaigns?

**A.** Usually about 60 percent of the vehicles targeted by the recall receive repairs.

---

**WHAT HAPPENS IF THE NHTSA ORDERS A RECALL**

*If the manufacturer refuses to obey voluntarily and challenges the recall in court, it faces a huge fine unless the court overturns the NHTSA order. Once the recall campaign begins, the NHTSA assigns a campaign number and file. During the campaign's first six quarters (year and a half), the manufacturer must report its completion rate based on the number of vehicles actually repaired. The NHTSA may verify these figures.*

**Q. Who pays for the recall—the automobile's manufacturer or the owners?**

A. The manufacturer must remedy the defect for free. This does not apply when the first buyer bought the car more than eight years earlier. In comparison, the standard for tires is three years.

**Q. What must the manufacturer do?**

A. The manufacturer has the option of repairing the defect, replacing the car, or refunding the purchase price. If it refunds the money, the manufacturer may deduct a certain amount for depreciation (loss in value). The manufacturer reimburses the dealer who makes the repairs. If the manufacturer chooses to repair the defect, it must do so within a reasonable time. Otherwise the manufacturer must replace the vehicle or refund the purchase price.

## AUTOMOBILE LEASING AND RENTING

### Requirements

**Q. What are the prerequisites if I want to rent or lease a car?**

A. First, you must have a valid driver's license. Increasingly, you may be required to show a good driving record. In several states, the major car rental companies have electronic links to government computers and are obtaining driver records (motor vehicle reports) when someone wants to rent a car. They refuse a rental contract if the driver has had too many accidents or violations on his or her record. Some of the major rental and leasing companies set a rental age minimum of eighteen and require a major credit card. Other companies rent only to credit card holders aged twenty-five or older. The company may waive the age requirement if you have an account number in

> **LEASE OR BUY?**
> *Whether it is better to lease or buy a car depends on many factors. A car lease means lower monthly payments. After all, your installment payment depends on the purchase price minus the car's estimated value at the end of the lease term. Thus, your installment payment does not depend on the full value of the car. Leasing usually avoids a down payment and sales tax. There may also be tax advantages if you lease mainly for business use. On the other hand, a leased car does not gather any equity (cash value). Buying a car on credit does. Finally, when your lease is up, you must return the car.*

your name through a motor club or other association, or if you have a rental account through your business. You must sign a contract when you rent or lease a car.

**Q. How does leasing differ from renting?**

A. A lease is essentially a long-term rental. Leases usually have a one-year minimum. Rentals may last one day.

### Car Lease Contracts

**Q. Are there different kinds of leases?**

A. Yes, several forms exist. Under the "closed-end" lease contract, sometimes called a "walkaway" lease, the car's value when you

# Checklist for Comparing Leasing and Purchasing Costs

After you have selected a new vehicle, you might wish to use this checklist to help you compare the costs of leasing against the costs of purchasing through a conventional loan. In making such rough comparisons, you will need to consider three categories of costs: initial, continuing, final. However, when deciding whether to lease or purchase, you may not want to base your decision solely on total costs, but also may wish to consider when (or if) any large cash outlays are required.

## Initial Costs

| *Leasing* | | *Purchasing* | |
|---|---|---|---|
| Security deposit | ———— | Downpayment | ———— |
| Capitalized cost reduction, if applicable | ———— | | |
| First periodic payment | ———— | | |
| Last periodic payment, if applicable | ———— | | |
| Total amount of fees (license, registration, and taxes) | ———— | Total amount of fees (license, registration, and taxes) | ———— |
| Insurance | ———— | Insurance | ———— |
| Trade-in allowance, if applicable | ———— | Trade-in allowance, if applicable | ———— |
| | $ ———— | | $ ———— |

## Continuing Costs

| *Leasing* | | *Purchasing* | |
|---|---|---|---|
| Periodic payment (expressed as monthly) | ———— | Monthly payment (including finance charge)* | ———— |
| Insurance (expressed as monthly) | ———— | Insurance (expressed as monthly) | ———— |
| Estimated monthly maintenance and repair costs considering warranty coverage | ———— | Estimated monthly maintenance and repair costs considering warranty coverage | ———— |
| | $ ———— | | $ ———— |

## Final Costs

| *Leasing*\*\* | | *Purchasing* | |
|---|---|---|---|
| Maximum end-of-lease payment based on estimated residual value\*\*\* | ———— | Balloon payment, if applicable | ———— |
| Excessive mileage/wear charges | ———— | | |
| Disposition charge | ———— | | |
| Total amount of fees (license, registration, and taxes) | ———— | Total amount of fees (license, registration, and taxes) | ———— |
| Insurance | ———— | Insurance | ———— |
| Trade-in allowance, if applicable | ———— | Trade-in allowance, if applicable | ———— |
| | $ ———— | | $ ———— |

\*Finance charges are no longer deductible if you itemize your tax return.

\*\*If you have a purchase option, you may wish to consider the amount of the option price in your comparison.

\*\*\*For open-end lease only.

SOURCE: Federal Trade Commission

return it does not matter unless you have put extreme wear on the car. You return the car at the end of the term and "walk away." Payments are higher than under an open-end lease because the lessor (the leasing company) takes the risk on the car's future worth. An "open-end" lease involves lower payments. However, you gamble that the car will be worth a stated price, the "estimated residual value," at the end of the lease. If its appraised value at the end of the term equals or exceeds the specified residual value, you owe nothing and may be refunded the difference, if your contract provides for a refund. However, if it is worth less, you pay some or all of the difference, often called an "end of lease" payment.

### Q. What will a lease cost me?

**A.** You probably will have to pay a security deposit and lease fee for the first month and possibly the last. You may have to pay an initial "capitalized cost reduction." This is similar to a down payment when you buy a car. By paying a large amount up front, you could, in effect, reduce your monthly payments. But by doing this, you lose one of the advantages of leasing: lower upfront costs. Other expenses may include sales tax, title, and license fee, though the lessor may pay them. A lease may include insurance. If not, you must provide your own. You might have to pay for repairs and maintenance after any warranty period expires, unless the lessor agrees to pay in your contract. At the end of the lease term, you may have to pay an excess mileage cost if you have a closed-end lease. (Under an open-end lease, the final appraised value of the car will reflect any excess mileage.) Excessive wear and tear may also cost you.

### Q. May I renew or extend my lease at the end of the term?

**A.** Yes, if your lease contained this option or you negotiated for it. Such an option may reduce your initial costs.

### Q. May I escape my lease early?

**A.** You have signed a binding contract that obligates you to make payments for a stated term. However, your contract may contain an early termination clause. This usually requires a minimum number of monthly payments before you may cancel, and may require you to pay a penalty.

### Q. What is a purchase option?

**A.** It allows you to buy the car when your lease term ends. The lessor must state the purchase price or the basis for setting this price in the initial lease contract. Purchase options are more common in open-end leases than in closed-end leases.

## Car Rental Contracts

### Q. What should my car rental contract include?

**A.** It should list the base rate for the rental car and any extra fees. The length of the rental period should also appear.

### Q. What extra fees could there be?

**A.** The rental company might offer you the Collision Damage Waiver (CDW) option. The rental company covers damage to your rented car if you accept CDW. However, coverage does not include personal injuries or personal property damage. Before accepting this expensive option, make sure your own automobile, medical, and homeowner's insurance policies do not already protect you in an accident involving a rented car. If traveling on business, your company's insurance policy might cover you. Sometimes, charging rentals on certain credit cards automatically covers you.

Other additional fees might include dropoff fees, if you leave the car in a different city than where you picked it up. More costs might be fuel charges, extra mileage fees, and fees for renting equipment like child safety seats or ski racks.

## INSPECTIONS

States have an interest in your car beyond collecting taxes. They care equally about vehicles meeting minimum safety standards. As a result, many states have an inspection sticker requirement. The number of inspections required in a year vary from state to state.

### Q. What exactly does the state inspect?

A. It varies. Most states check the car's lights, brakes, windshield wipers, and horn. Some inspect the tires, windows, body and seat belts. Many states also test the emission levels, taking into account the automobile's make, model, and age.

### Q. What if I am buying the car?

A. A new car should pass inspection easily. Someone other than the seller should inspect a used car. In many states, a used car sale is not final until the car passes inspection. In other states, failing inspection cancels the sale at the buyer's option. Contact your state Department of Motor Vehicles for further information.

### Q. Where do I get my car inspected?

A. States often authorize certain private repair shops and car dealers to make inspections. A few states have government-operated inspection stations.

### Q. What will happen if my car does not pass the state's safety inspection?

A. Procedures vary, but you may get a "failed" sticker attached to your windshield. You have a grace period either to make repairs or get your car off the road. If you do neither, you could be subject to fines and other penalties.

## REPAIRS

### Dealer or Mechanic?

### Q. Where should I take my car for repairs?

A. You can take it to a car dealer, which warranty terms may require. Other choices include an independent garage, a franchise operation specializing in specific repairs, or repair-

### MECHANIC QUALIFICATIONS

To help determine whether a mechanic is qualified, ask if the National Institute of Automotive Service Excellence (NIASE) has certified the mechanic. A certified mechanic has taken one or more written tests in areas such as engine repair and electrical systems. The NIASE certifies a mechanic who passes all the tested areas as a General Automobile Mechanic.

Of course, certification is not everything. Often, you can discover the best mechanics from friends' recommendations and word of mouth.

ing it yourself. Each option has its advantages and disadvantages.

### Q. What if I choose a dealer?

**A.** Dealers may charge more. However, they are more familiar with your make of car than other repair shops, and may have new and better equipment to service your car. Manufacturers want to ensure that dealerships run quality repair operations, so they invest in training mechanics.

### Q. What if I bring my car to a service station?

**A.** This is a good option for nonwarranty work if the mechanics have adequate training and test equipment. Parts might cost more, but labor might be less expensive than dealer repairs. If you often use the service station, the mechanics get to know your car. Then they might spot potential problems early.

### Q. What about the highly advertised repair chains?

**A.** Specialty shops may repair one part of a car, such as brakes or mufflers. Or, they may advertise complete car care services. Sheer size and volume means lower costs than dealers and independent mechanics. If you know what repairs your car needs, franchise shops can be a good deal.

## The Repair Contract

### Q. What should appear in a repair contract?

**A.** The repair contract, often called the repair order, is essential for getting a satisfactory repair job done on your car. The repair order describes the work to be done, and, once signed, creates a contract authorizing the mechanic to make the described repairs.

---

**REPAIR WARRANTIES**

*The law may entitle you to some repair warranties. If the repair shop makes an express warranty, you are protected as long as you abide by the terms of the warranty. Likewise, if a manufacturer's warranty covers the car or part, you should not have to pay as long as you satisfy warranty conditions. Some state courts have held that the implied warranty of merchantability covers car repairs.*

*Beware of "unconditional" guarantees offered by many franchise repair shops. There are always some limitations on written guarantees. Be sure to read the fine print; there may be special procedures that you are required to follow in order to obtain the benefits of the warranty.*

---

The repair order should contain:
- the make, model, and year of your car;
- the repair date;
- an accurate description of the problem;
- a list of parts to be used and their charges;
- the amount of labor estimated to be needed (time to be spent fixing your car);
- the rate to be charged, either per hour or the flat rate to do the work; and
- your name, address, and telephone number.

The mileage and repair date are important. They verify warranty terms and simplify service records. Also, your telephone number is critical should unexpected problems arise. If the mechanic cannot reach you, the mechanic has to decide whether or not to proceed, and you may have to live with the results of that decision.

Note that in many states, if you do not sign the repair order, you do not have to pay for any services done by the mechanic.

#### Q. Must I receive a cost estimate for the repairs before work actually begins?

**A.** It is a good idea, and a required practice in some states. In those states, the final cost must not exceed a certain percentage or dollar value of the original estimate without the customer's consent. Repair shops generally have the right to charge for making estimates, but you must receive advance notice.

### False and Deceptive Repair Practices

Most drivers don't understand how cars work. To protect consumers against fraudulent practices, mechanic incompetence, and overcharging, many states have enacted statutes specifically governing car repairs, or have included car repairs in their unfair and deceptive practices statutes.

#### Q. How do the state unfair and deceptive practices statutes protect me from a repair shop rip-off?

**A.** As discussed earlier, they usually require price estimates and repair orders. Also, many states give you the right to keep or examine replaced parts, and require repair shops to prepare a detailed invoice, which must state the labor and parts supplied, warranty work done, guarantees, and installation of any used or rebuilt parts. In some states, you may have the right to same-day repairs, unless you agree to a

longer period or the delay is beyond the shop's control. Shoddy repair work must be corrected at no charge, especially in states where the implied warranty of merchantability has been extended to repair work. Finally, many states require repair shops to post price lists conspicuously.

If you think a repair shop has intentionally cheated you, you should notify your state attorney general's office and call your lawyer to discuss possible legal action.

#### Q. What can I do if the automobile mechanic makes unauthorized repairs?

**A.** First, you may wish to complain to your state attorney general's office, or the local branch of the Better Business Bureau, or even to the Chamber of Commerce. For many mechanics, their business depends on a good reputation, and they will take care to maintain that reputation. If you do not get satisfaction, you may wish to sue if, for example, the shop made unneeded repairs or reinstalled the original part rather than a replacement. If the shop tried its best to correct the fault by fixing something that *was* broken, though *not* the problem's ultimate cause, you should pay the shop. After all, the repair shop *did* fix one of your car's problems.

### The Mechanic's Lien

#### Q. What if I do not pay for the repairs?

**A.** In most states, if you refuse to pay for completed repairs, the shop may keep your car. For example, if you have authorized extensive work, but decide that the car isn't worth that much after the shop completes the work, the shop obtains a "mechanic's lien" on your car. The car's actual value, and the actual cost of the repairs, do not matter. If you abandon your car in this manner, the mechanic may ultimately sell your car so that it can recover as much of the cost of repairs as possible.

In states that require written estimates and repair authorization, the mechanic's lien does not attach if the repair shop has not complied with these requirements.

Of course, if you do pay for the repairs, the repair shop must return your car.

---

## HOW A SERVICE CONTRACT DIFFERS FROM A WARRANTY

*Unlike a warranty, a service contract may not come from the manufacturer. Service contracts are optional and expensive, and often coverage overlaps the warranty protection. Also, a service contract often contains more limitations and exclusions than a warranty, may require you to pay a deductible fee, and might not cover all parts and labor or routine maintenance. If a service contract is available on a used car, the appropriate box must be checked on the Buyers Guide.*

*Finally, if you believe that your service contract has been breached, in addition to any state remedies available to you, you may be able to sue under the Magnuson-Moss Warranty Act, and recover your attorney's fees and court costs, as well as your damages.*

---

## Service Contracts

**Q. What is a service contract?**

A. A service contract specifically covers car repairs and maintenance for a set period of time. Manufacturers, contract companies, insurance companies, and car dealers offer service contracts.

**Q. Should I purchase a service contract on my automobile right away?**

A. If you buy one at all, you should consider waiting until your warranty period expires. After all, why pay extra for duplicate coverage?

---

## YOUR AUTO AND THE POLICE

Although the area of automobile law is in constant flux and the degree of protection offered by states widely variant, there are some fundamental points to remember if your vehicle is stopped by the police.

### The Stop

**Q. What should I do once I realize that the officer is signalling me to pull over?**

A. Pull over to the side of the road as quickly and safely as possible. Remain in your vehicle until the officer otherwise directs you. Get ready to produce your license and registration, because you may be asked to do so.

**Q. The officer is at my window. Now what?**

A. Stay composed and politely ask why you were stopped. If you have any doubt that you were stopped by a real police officer—if, for example, you were pulled over by an unmarked vehicle—politely ask to see the officer's photo identification, not just his or her badge. If you are still not certain that he or she is a real police officer you may ask that a supervisor be called to the scene or request that you follow the officer to a police station.

### The Search

**Q. Suppose the officer wants to search my car?**

**A.** Ask why the officer wants to conduct a search. If you have absolutely nothing to hide, expediency might dictate that you let the search proceed. If you don't want the search to proceed, you do not have to consent. Usually, the officer is not permitted to conduct the search unless you consent, the officer has probable cause (see below), or the officer reasonably believes that he must search the auto for his or her own protection. Ask courteously whether the officer has a search warrant or if you are under arrest. If the officer replies that you are under arrest, ask for an explanation.

**Q. What if the officer insists on searching my car?**

**A.** Don't interfere. You can always challenge the legitimacy of the search later in court.

**Q. Can the police legitimately search my vehicle without a warrant?**

**A.** That depends on the circumstances. The police would not usually have the right to search your automobile when you are stopped only for a minor traffic offense such as speeding, but if the violation requires that you be taken into custody (for example, a "Driving Under the Influence" [DUI] arrest or driving with a suspended license), the search would generally be permitted. If the officer has arrested you, the officer does not need a warrant to pat down your body in searching for weapons.

In general, when an arrest is not involved, the police have more latitude to search a vehicle than to search a home. The U.S. Supreme Court recognizes an automobile exception to the Fourth Amendment's protection against warrantless searches. The Court has held that a person expects less privacy in an automobile than at home. (No one ever said "A man's Chevy is his castle.") The rationale for permitting warrantless searches of cars is that the mobility of automobiles would allow drivers to escape with incriminating evidence in the time it would take police to secure a search warrant. For a warrantless search to be valid, however, the officer *must* have probable cause. (See the "Criminal Justice" chapter on pages 544–549 for more details on this topic.)

**Q. What is probable cause?**

**A.** Probable cause, in this context, is a reasonable basis for the officer to believe that the vehicle contains incriminating evidence, so that the officer is legally justified in searching it.

**Q. What part of the vehicle may the police search if they have probable cause?**

**A.** Generally, the police officer may search the immediate area at the driver's command, that is, under and around the front seat. The law is always changing. Sometimes state constitutions offer greater protection against searches than the U.S. Constitution. Therefore, if you have questions about a search the police have made of your vehicle, it is best to consult a lawyer in your state.

**Q. May the officer search in my glove compartment?**

**A.** Yes, the Supreme Court has held that such a warrantless search is permissible. The reason is that the glove compartment is within the arrested driver's reach.

**Q. May the officer search a closed container inside my car?**

**A.** Police are permitted to search containers or packages found during a *legitimate* warrantless search of a vehicle. The container must be one that might reasonably contain evidence of a crime for which the officer had probable cause to search the vehicle in the first place. In 1982, the Supreme Court ruled that the police do not need a warrant to search closed containers found in the passenger compartment of an automobile whose occupant is under arrest.

**Q. May the police search my car without a warrant after they have impounded it?**

**A.** The police do not need a warrant to undertake a routine inventory of an impounded vehicle. The reason is that such an inventory protects the driver's possessions against theft, and also protects the police against claims of lost or stolen property. Such an inventory also protects the holding facility from dangerous materials that may be in the impounded vehicle, and it may aid in the identification of the arrested person.

**Q. Suppose the officer sees a packet of marijuana on the backseat?**

**A.** When the police can see evidence readily from a place in which they have a right to be, the law does not consider it a search. Rather, it is a plain-view seizure. As long as the officer has a legitimate reason to be standing by the car and easily sees what the officer has probable cause to believe is evidence of a crime, the officer can make the seizure. Then the officer probably could conduct a warrantless search of the rest of the passenger compartment of the vehicle and possibly the trunk (if probable cause exists to believe the trunk may contain evidence).

**Q. Can the police pull me over in a roadblock and demand to check my license and registration?**

**A.** The U.S. Supreme Court has said that such roadblocks do not constitute an unreasonable search as long as police stop all the cars passing through the roadblock or follow some neutral policy, such as stopping every fourth car. The police can't single out your car unless they have an articulable suspicion that you don't have your driver's license, your vehicle is unregistered, or that you or your car are otherwise seizable for violating the law.

**Q. Is it legal to design a roadblock to catch drunk drivers?**

**A.** Yes, provided the selection of vehicles to be stopped is not arbitrary and it minimizes the inconvenience to drivers. Courts have upheld such roadblocks as constitutional. States' legislatures disagree, however, about whether the prosecution needs to show that a roadblock is the least intrusive way to enforce drunk driving laws. Also, some states require that the ranking police officer who supervised a roadblock testify at the offender's trial.

**Q. I got stuck in a speed trap. What can I do about it?**

**A.** If the speed limit was clearly marked and you were exceeding it, grit your teeth and pay the fine. If you think you've been unfairly prosecuted, you might report the trap to your auto club or state authorities to spare other drivers the same expense.

**Q. I was stopped for speeding by a radar gun. Do those things work?**

**A.** Courts today regularly take judicial notice of the ability of radar to measure accurately vehicular speeds. That doesn't mean that

Table: Driving Under the Influence (DUI/DWI) Laws by State

| STATE | Admin. Per Se Law / BAC Level | Mandatory Susp./Revoc. Per Se 1st | 2nd | 3rd | Mandatory Prelim. Breath Test | Admin. Susp./Revoc. BAC Test Refusal 1st | 2nd | Illegal Per Se BAC Level | BAC Test Req. Traffic Fatalities/Serious Injuries | Lower BAC for Youth | Drug Alcohol Postponement | Open Container Law | Anti-Consumption Law | "Happy Hours" Prohibition | Dram Shop |
|---|---|---|---|---|---|---|---|---|---|---|---|---|---|---|---|
| Alabama | ○ | – | – | – | ○ | S - 90 Days | S - 1 Year | .10% | ○ | | ○ | ○ | | ● | S |
| Alaska | ● /.10% | R - 30 Days | R - 1 Year | R - 10 Years | ● | R - 90 Days | R - 1 Year | .10% | ○ | | | ○ | | ● | S |
| Arizona | ● /.10% | S - 30 Days | S - 90 Days | S - 90 Days | ● | S - 12 Mos. | S - 12 Mos. | .10% | ○ | 0% | | ○ | | ● | S |
| Arkansas | ○ | – | – | – | ● | S - 6 Mos. | S - 1 Year | .10% | ● | | | ○ | | ● | S |
| California | ● /.10% | S - 30 Days | S - 1 Year | S - 1 Year | ● | S - 1 Year | R - 2 Years | .10% | ● | | | ○ | | ● | S |
| Colorado | ● /.10% | R - 3 Mos. | R - 1 Year | R - 2 Years | ● | R - 1 Year | R - 1 Year | .10% | ○ | .05% | | ○ | | ● | S |
| Connecticut | ● /.10% | R - 3 Mos. | R - 1 Year | S - 2 Years | | R - 6 Mos. | R - 1 Year | .10% | ○ | | | ○ | | ● | ○ |
| Delaware | ● /.10% | – | R - 6 Mos. | R - 18 Mos. | ● | R - 12 Mos. | R - 18 Mos. | .10% | ● [1] | | | ● | | ● | C |
| District of Columbia | ● /.10% | – | – | – | ○ | S - 12 Mos. | S - 12 Mos. | .10% | ○ | | | ● | | – | C |
| Florida | ● /.08% | – | S - 1 Year | S - 1 Year | ○ | S - 1 Year | S - 18 Mos. | .10% | ○ | | | ○ | | – | S |
| Georgia | ○ | N/A | S - 120 Days | S - 2 Years | ● | S - 1 Year | S - 1 Year | .10% | ○ | .09% | | ○ | | – | C |
| Hawaii | ● /.10% | R - 30 Days | R - 1 Year | R - 2 Years | ○ | R - 1 Year | R - 2 Years | .10% | ○ | | | ● | | – | S |
| Idaho | ● /.10% | S - 30 Days | S - 90 Days | S - 1 Year | ○ | S - 180 Days | S - 1 Year | .10% | ○ | | | ○ | | – | S |
| Illinois | ● /.10% | S - 180 Days | S - 180 Days | S - 90 Days | ● | S - 1 Year | S - 1 Year | .10% | ● [1] | | | ● | | – | S |
| Indiana | ● /.10% | – | R - 180 Days | S - 180 Days | ● | R - 1 Year | R - 360 Days | .10% | ○ | | | ○ | | – | S |
| Iowa | ● /.10% | S - 180 Days | R - 1 Year | R - 1 Year | ● | R - 240 Days | R - 1 Year | .10% | ○ | | | ○ | | – | S |
| Kansas | ● /.09% | R - 30 Days | R - 1 Year | R - 1 Year | ● | S - 1 Year | S - 1 Year | .08% | ○ | | | ○ | | – | S |
| Kentucky | ● /.10% | – | – | – | ● | – | – | .10% | ○ | | | ● | | – | S |
| Louisiana | ● /.10% | S - 30 Days | S - 365 Days | S - 365 Days | ● | S - 90 Days | S - 545 Days | .10% | ○ | .02% | | ● | | – | S |
| Maine | ● /.08% | S - 45 Days | R - 1 Year | S - 2 Years | ● | S - 90 Days | S - 1 Year | .08% | ○ | .02% | | ● | | – | S |
| Maryland | ● /.10% | R - 30 Days | R - 1 Year | R - 2 Years | ● | S - 120 Days | S - 1 Year | .10% | ● [2] | | | ● | | – | C |
| Massachusetts | ● /.10% | – | – | – | ● | S - 120 Days | S - 120 Days | .10% | ○ | | | ● | | – | C |
| Michigan | ○ | – | – | – | ● | S - 1 Year | S - 1 Year | .10% | ● [3] | 0% | | ● | | – | S |
| Minnesota | ○ | R - 15 Days | R - 90 Days | R - 90 Days | ● | R - 90 Days | R - 180 Days | .10% | ○ | | | ● | | – | S |
| Mississippi | ● /.10% | S - 30 Days | S - 365 Days | S - 90 Days | ● | S - 90 Days | S - 90 Days | .10% | ○ | | | ● | | – | S |
| Missouri | ● /.10% | R - 90 Days | R - 1 Year | R - 1 Year | ● | R - 1 Year | R - 1 Year | .10% | ○ | | | ● | | – | S |
| Montana | ○ | – | – | – | ● | R - 1 Year | R - 1 Year | .10% | ○ | | | ● | | – | S |
| Nebraska | ● /.10% | R - 90 Days | R - 1 Year | R - 90 Days | ● | R - 1 Year | R - 1 Year | .10% | ● [4] | | | ● | | – | ○ |
| Nevada | ● /.10% | R - 90 Days | R - 90 Days | R - 90 Days | ● | R - 3 Years | R - 3 Years | .10% | ● [5] | .04% | | ○ | | – | ○ |
| New Hampshire | ● /.08% | S - 6 Mos. | S - 2 Years | S - 2 Years | ● | S - 6 Mos. | S - 2 Years | .08% | ○ | .01% | | ● | | – | S |
| New Jersey | ○ | – | – | – | ● | S - 6 Mos. | S - 2 Years | .10% | ○ | .02% | | ○ | | – | S |
| New Mexico | ● /.08% | R - 90 Days | R - 1 Year | R - 1 Year | ● | R - 1 Year | R - 1 Year | .08% | ○ | | | ● | | – | S |
| New York | ○ | R - 10 Days | R - 10 Days | R - 10 Days | ○ | R - 6 Mos. | R - 12 Mos. | .10% | ● [6] | 0% | | ● | | – | S |
| North Carolina | ● /.08% | S - 30 Days | S - 365 Days | S - 120 Days | ● | R - 6 Mos. | R - 2 Years | .08% | ○ | 0% | | ○ | | – | S |
| North Dakota | ● /.10% | S - 15 Days | S - 365 Days | S - 180 Days | ○ | R - 1 Year | R - 2 Years | .10% | ○ | .02% | | ○ | | – | S |
| Ohio | ● /.10% | R - 15 Days | S - 30 Days | R - 180 Days | ● | R - 90 Days | R - 1 Year | .10% | ● [7] | | | ○ | | – | C |
| Oklahoma | ● /.10% | – | R - 1 Year | R - 18 Mos. | ● | R - 90 Days | R - 1 Year | .10% | ○ | 0% | | ○ | | – | S |
| Oregon | ● /.08% | S - 30 Days | S - 1 Year | S - 1 Year | ○ | S - 90 Days | S - 1 Year | .08% | ○ | | | ○ | | – | S |
| Pennsylvania | ○ | – | – | – | ● | S - 12 Mos. | S - 12 Mos. | .10% | ○ | .04% | | ○ | | – | S |
| Rhode Island | ● /.10% | S - 3 to 6 Mos. | S - 1 to 2 Years | S - 2 to 3 Years | ○ | S - 3 Mos. | S - 1 Year | .10% | ○ | | | ○ | | – | C |
| South Carolina | ● /.10% | S - 6 Mos. | S - 1 Year | S - 2 Years | ● | S - 6 Mos. | S - 90 Days | .10% | ○ | | | ● | | – | C |
| South Dakota | ○ | – | – | – | ○ | S - 1 Year | S - 90 Days | .10% | ● [8] | | | ○ | | – | S |
| Tennessee | ○ | – | – | – | ● | – | – | .10% | ○ | .02% | | ○ | | – | S |
| Texas | ○ | S - 90 Days | S - 90 Days | S - 90 Days | ● | R - 1 Year | R - 1 Year | .10% | ○ | .07% | | ○ | | – | S |
| Utah | ● /.08% | S - 90 Days | S - 120 Days | S - 120 Days | ● | S - 1 Year | S - 18 Mos. | .08% | ○ | .00% | | ● | | – | S |
| Vermont | ● /.08% | S - 90 Days | S - 18 Mos. | S - 2 Years | ● | S - 6 Mos. | S - 6 Mos. | .08% | ○ | .02% | | ● | | ○ | C |
| Virginia | ○ | – | – | – | ● | S - 6 Mos. | S - 1 Year | .10% | ○ | | | ○ | | ○ | C |
| Washington | ○ | – | – | – | ● | R - 30 Days | R - 2 Years | .10% | ○ | | | ○ | | ○ | C |
| West Virginia | ● /.10% | R - 30 Days | R - 1 Year | R - 1 Year | ○ | R - 90 Days | R - 1 Year | .10% | ○ | 0% | | ● | | ○ | C |
| Wisconsin | ● /.10% | – | – | – | ● | R - 30 Days | R - 30 Days | .10% | ● [6] | 0% | | ○ | | ○ | C |
| Wyoming | ● /.10% | – | S - 90 Days | S - 90 Days | ○ | S - 6 Mos. | S - 8 Mos. | .10% | ○ | | | ● | | ○ | S |

BAC Test Required for Drivers in Traffic Fatality or Serious Injury: 1) A driver, based on probable cause for DWI, may be required to submit to a chemical test for drunk driving law violatic regardless of whether there was a death or serious injury; 2) only in fatal crashes; 3) a person arrested for an injury-related DWI offense may be compelled to submit to a chemical (blood) test; 4) a driver may be required to submit to a chemical test if he/she is involved in a DWI-related crash regardless of whether there has been a death or if; 5) a test for any DWI offense, also, a BAC test shall be made on an automobile driver who has survived a traffic crash fatal to another; 6) a person may be compelled to submit to a chemical (blood) test in traffic crash situations where the person has been cited for a traffic offense; 7) a chemical test is required for a third DWI offense regardless of whether it is injury or death related. (Note: A third DWI offense is a felony); 8) possible

Dram Shop:    S = Suspension    C = Case (Common) Law

● = Yes    ○ = No

SOURCE: American Automobile Association Traffic Safety and Engineering

you can't try to prove that the particular radar gun in your case was poorly maintained or that its operator misread the results or was inadequately trained to use the device, but it is an uphill fight.

**Q. Aren't "fuzzbuster" devices the best way to avoid speed traps and radar guns?**

**A.** Depends where you drive. Some states have declared them illegal, subjecting drivers who use them to fines.

### The Arrest

**Q. What should I do if the police arrest me?**

**A.** Better to discuss what you *shouldn't* do. Do not:

- speak to anyone about your case;
- answer police queries or waive your right to advice of counsel;
- submit to a lineup or any kind of tests without your lawyer;
- dodge news photographers or cover your face (looks guilty); or
- be impolite to the police.

Some people cooperate with the police by making statements in the hope that the officer will let them go. Remember that once you have been arrested you *will* be charged with an offense, and any statements you make, if incriminating, will be used against you.

**Q. What do I tell my lawyer while I'm in custody?**

**A.** Be prepared to tell your attorney where the police have taken you, where the arrest occurred and if it was made by uniformed or plainclothes police, the charges against you, and the amount of bail you can afford.

## DRIVING UNDER THE INFLUENCE

*Statistics indicate that at least one-third of all drivers involved in fatal accidents were alcohol impaired at the time. Groups such as Mothers Against Drunk Driving and legislators are spearheading a nationwide crackdown on drunk drivers that includes passage of tougher laws, including every state hiking the legal drinking age to twenty-one. Although it is a traffic offense, drunk driving is classified as criminal in the ordinary sense of prohibited conduct willfully undertaken.*

**Q. If the police arrest me and issue a citation, can I dispose of the case in a noncriminal way?**

**A.** No. Once you've been arrested, you must go through the criminal process.

**Q. How come police never say "you're under arrest for drunk driving"?**

**A.** Different states call the offense different names. These include driving under the influence (DUI), operating under the influence (OUI), and driving while intoxicated (DWI).

**Q. Does the language really matter?**

**A.** Yes, "operating" jurisdictions (those charging OUI), for example, do not require that the vehicle be in motion. In most states a person may be charged with OUI if he or she is in actual physical control. Actual physical control may be shown when the person is seated in the driver's seat, in possession of the ignition key, and capable of starting the motor.

## Q. What does "drunk driving" mean?

**A.** The elements of the offense vary from one state to another. However, the Uniform Vehicle Code says proof is necessary that the person is under the influence of alcohol or drugs. Most states agree that a person is under the influence if he or she is less able, either physically or mentally, to exercise clear judgment and to operate a vehicle with safety. As noted above, the person must be driving or in actual physical control of a vehicle. If a particular state's statute includes language such as "on a public highway" or "intoxicating liquor," the state also must prove that point. Some states treat "driving while impaired by alcohol" as a lesser offense of DWI.

## Q. How does the state prove its DWI case?

**A.** The prosecution relies heavily, sometimes solely, on the arresting officer's testimony about the offending vehicle's operation and the defendant's behavior (observations of the defendant's appearance, speech, and an odor of alcohol), and results of field sobriety tests and chemical tests (breath, blood, or urine). The officer might say, "The car was weaving over the center line of the highway," or "The driver had slurred speech, heavy odor of alcohol, glassy bloodshot eyes, and could not walk straight."

## Q. May the police force me to give a sample of my blood or my breath?

**A.** Every state has "implied consent" laws for chemical testing of intoxication. The law views people who have a driver's license as automatically agreeing to submit to blood, breath, or urine tests to determine whether they are sober. In 1983, the U.S. Supreme Court ruled that a driver may be forced to submit to a blood alcohol test without the driver's consent or a warrant and without violating the driver's right against self-incrimination if the driver has already been arrested for another offense, such as vehicular homicide; the driver's blood has already been taken for another purpose, such as medical care; and such action is permissible under the state's implied consent law.

While police generally will not compel you to submit to a blood test, the Supreme Court decision discussed in the previous paragraph permits a blood test taken by force so long as the officer has probable cause to believe that you are under the influence.

If you can refuse to take the test, should you? There is no hard and fast answer to that question.

On the one hand, unless you are certain that you have had fewer than three or four drinks in the past hour, or fewer than five drinks in the past several hours, common wisdom holds that it is a good idea to refuse the tests. It is generally more difficult to convict a driver of drunk driving if no field sobriety or chemical tests are taken.

On the other hand, if you refuse to take a breath-testing-device test, your driver's license probably will be suspended automatically for a long period of time. In Illinois, for example, it will be suspended for six months, but only three months if you take and fail the test (if you are a first offender).

## Q. What are field sobriety tests?

**A.** Every police department has its own preferred tests. The police may ask you to do several things after you have gotten out of the vehicle, such as standing on one foot for a specified time or walking a straight line. The police also may ask you to touch your nose with your index finger with your eyes closed and head back, and have you stare at a flashlight or a pen so that the officer can see how your eyes respond.

### Q. Suppose I fail the tests?

A. It is not like school. You cannot promise to study harder next time. A skilled lawyer, however, may challenge whether the police administered the tests properly, or whether the tests effectively measure what they intend to. In addition, a lawyer may present qualifying evidence. For instance, a chronic knee injury may prevent you from supporting your weight on one foot.

### Q. How does a breath-testing device work?

A. The person blows into the machine, which measures the percentage of alcohol in the person's body. The law considers a standard measure as legally intoxicated. This measure might be .10 (one-tenth of one percent blood-alcohol concentration), or .08, depending on the state. The rules vary from one state to another. However, the law often entitles the defendant to two breath tests that must measure within .02 (or some other percentage) of each other.

### Q. If the breath-testing device hits .10, am I in serious trouble?

A. Probably, but a lawyer may show that the machine's operator received inadequate training, the operator's certification has lapsed, or the operator did not maintain the machine well. Other factors may also affect the breath-testing device reading and may be established through an expert witness. Diabetics, for example, have high levels of ketone (a naturally occurring chemical), which could yield false results when diabetics are tested. However, in most cases the result of a breath test will be allowed into evidence.

### Q. May I change my mind after declining to take a blood or breath test?

A. There is no right for a person to change his mind once he or she has refused. The law still considers a change of heart as a refusal so far as it concerns a license suspension. It is a good idea to call a lawyer while you are thinking over a decision, if the police allow you to do so. However, unless you have a statutory right to a lawyer in your state, which could delay the test for several hours while the attorney is en route to the police station, you will have to decide whether to submit to the test fairly soon after being asked to do so. In some states (for example, Illinois) you must decide immediately.

### Q. What kind of penalty am I likely to get for DWI?

A. Consult a lawyer in your state because penalties vary widely and depend on several factors, such as whether you are a repeat offender. Sixteen states require minimum penalties for first-time offenders, for example, which might involve enrollment in an alcohol treatment program and a license suspension of a month or so. A second-time offender might suffer a two-year license suspension or revocation of license. Some states impound the license plates or vehicles of habitual drunk drivers, and others revoke the licenses of habitual offenders.

This is an extremely volatile area of the law. Jail terms for first offenders are more common than they used to be. Community service and enrollment in mandatory alcohol programs, as well as heavy fines, are doled out by courts in various combinations with regularity as a result of changing public perceptions about drunk driving and the efforts of highly visible groups such as Mothers Against Drunk Driving.

## License Suspension/Revocation

### Q. Suppose the police stop me and I've forgotten my license at home?

A. Driving a motor vehicle on a public street or highway without a license is an

# THE NATIONWIDE CRACKDOWN ON DRUNK DRIVING

*Tragic stories of victims killed by drunk drivers proliferate in the news media; the ranks of groups, such as Mothers Against Drunk Driving (M.A.D.D.) and Students Against Drunk Driving (S.A.D.D.), continue to swell; and state legislatures introduce harsh new drunk driving laws at a dizzying clip. Society is no longer satisfied with giving offenders a slap on the wrist when it comes to drunk driving.*

*The legal drinking age is twenty-one in every state in the Union. In addition, the majority of our states have enacted so-called "per se" laws, which prohibit a person from driving an automobile if the person has a blood-alcohol reading of a certain amount or more. When the per se law is used, the prosecution need not show that the person is under the influence. Rather, the prosecution need only prove that the person was driving and showing a blood-alcohol reading of the certain amount or more at the time. A blood alcohol reading of .10 remains the legal presumptive level of intoxication in some states, but a growing number of states (including California, Florida, Kansas, New Hampshire, New Mexico, North Carolina, Maine, Oregon, Utah, and Vermont) have lowered their per se limit to .08.*

*Another trend nationwide among legislatures is to pass laws that create harsher penalties for higher breath-testing device results. New Hampshire provides for enhanced penalties for blood alcohol readings of .20 and higher. Other states, such as New York, have created lesser offenses, such as driving "impaired," with a blood alcohol level of .07.*

*In civil courts throughout the country, "dram shop" cases and "social host" cases are gaining wider acceptance, and expanding the liability for negligence. Taverns, restaurants, and individuals who furnish alcohol to intoxicated persons knowing that they are likely to drive are liable to third persons who are injured as a result of the conduct of the intoxicated individual.*

offense in most states. Often, a person accused of failing to have a license in his or her possession can avoid conviction if able to produce a license in court that was valid at the time of the police stop.

**Q. What is the difference if the state suspends, cancels, or revokes my license?**

**A.** Suspension involves the temporary withdrawal of your privilege to drive. The state may

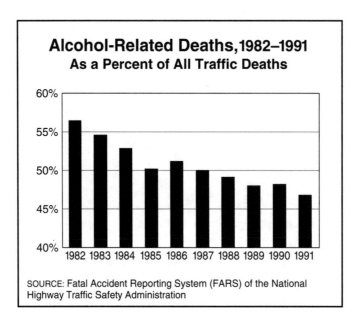

**Alcohol-Related Deaths, 1982–1991**
As a Percent of All Traffic Deaths

SOURCE: Fatal Accident Reporting System (FARS) of the National Highway Traffic Safety Administration

## DRIVING WITH A SUSPENDED OR REVOKED LICENSE

*The police probably will arrest you for driving with a suspended or revoked license. This usually is a serious misdemeanor that carries with it a stiff fine and possibly some time in the local jail. In some states, however, it may be a felony that lands the offender in state prison or with a significant amount of community service to work off, particularly if the suspension or revocation was based upon a DUI.*

*If you are stopped while driving with either a revoked or suspended license, you can expect to be arrested and taken to the police station to post bond. If you cannot raise the required amount of bond money, you will be taken to court for a bond hearing (usually within twenty-four hours), where a judge, in his or her broad discretion, will set bond.*

*You will remain in jail until the bond is posted. The bond you will need to post depends on the crime you are alleged to have committed and on your previous driving record. A monetary bond might be set, or you might be released on a personal recognizance bond, which requires only your signature and promise to return to court as ordered and not to violate any other laws.*

reinstate that privilege after a designated time period and payment of a fee. You may also restore the privilege by remedying the underlying cause of the suspension, such as buying automobile insurance.

Cancellation involves voluntarily giving up your driving privilege without penalty. Cancellation allows you to reapply for a license immediately.

Revocation aims both to discipline the driver and protect the public. Revocation involuntarily ends your driving privilege. Revocation generally is permanent until you are eligible after a minimum period set by law to apply for a new license. The state may conduct a reinstatement hearing. You may have to retake a driver's license examination.

### Q. If State A has suspended/revoked my license, but I have a valid license in State B, can I drive in State A?

A. Under the law of some states, a valid driver's license from another jurisdiction does not enable you to drive on the highways of a state that has cancelled, suspended, or revoked your license. However, other states have held that a license properly issued by a foreign state under the Driver's License Compact ends the suspension or revocation of a motorist's original license.

### Q. What are the grounds for license suspension?

A. They vary by state. A local lawyer will be able to give you details about your state laws. Generally, however, a state might provide that three moving violations within one year warrant a three-month suspension. Refusal to submit to a field sobriety or breath testing device test also will result in suspension.

### Q. What are the grounds for license revocation?

A. They are based on violating specific laws, such as habitual reckless driving, drunken driving, nonpayment of your motor vehicle excise tax, using a motor vehicle to commit a felony, and fleeing from or eluding the police. Again, they vary by state.

### Q. Does the law entitle me to notice and a hearing before the state revokes my license?

A. Barring an emergency, due process under the Fourteenth Amendment generally requires notice and a chance to be heard before the state ends a person's license privileges. However, for certain serious offenses, the state may simply rely on the court conviction to revoke the person's license without the need for any hearing.

### Q. What if the state charges me with an offense that requires a license suspension?

A. Unless another law says otherwise, no notice is necessary before a state may suspend your license under the mandatory provisions of a law. As a driver, you are presumed to know the law.

### Q. If the state does notify me, what should the notice say?

A. The time, place, and purpose of the hearing should appear on the notice of a hearing to suspend or revoke your license.

### Q. Does the law entitle me to a jury?

A. No. A suspension/revocation hearing is an administrative, not a judicial proceeding. You are entitled, however, to confront and cross-examine witnesses against you at such a hearing. You are well advised to be represented by counsel at such a hearing.

### Q. What must the state prove before a court can convict me of driving on a suspended or revoked license?

**A.** The law varies from one state to another. The state, however, usually has to show that:

- the accused's license or privilege to drive was revoked or suspended on the occasion in question; and
- the accused was driving a motor vehicle on a public highway at the time of the offense.

### License Renewal

### Q. Must I take another examination to renew my license?

**A.** Check with your state's division of motor vehicles. A handful of states permit renewal by mail. Most states require a vision test, and in some instances, a new photograph for renewal. Utah, Michigan, Kansas, and Hawaii require a written test. California tops the list of prerequisites for license renewal, including a vision test, written test, thumbprint, signature, and photograph. Some states impose additional requirements if a driver has amassed a number of traffic convictions or if the driver is of a certain age or has certain physical problems. Illinois, for example, requires a road test for drivers seventy-five years old or older prior to renewal.

### Q. May a physical or mental affliction prevent me from driving legally?

**A.** Yes. A few states require doctors to report physical and mental disorders of patients that could affect driver safety.

### Seat Belt Laws

### Q. My kids hate wearing seat belts. Must they wear these?

**A.** All fifty states and the District of Columbia require children to be restrained while riding in motor vehicles. State laws vary, however, concerning the age of the child subject to the child restraint law. Seat belts are desirable when one considers that approximately 700 children under the age of five die in passenger vehicles annually and that 45 percent of the deaths of children between ages one and fourteen are caused by car accidents.

### Q. Do I have to wear a seat belt?

**A.** It depends where you live. In 1984, New York became the first state to enact a mandatory seat belt law for adults. If you hate wearing seat belts, live, in, or at least confine your driving to, the Dakotas and New Hampshire, which have not passed seat belt regulations. Maine and Massachusetts only require children up to a certain age to wear seat belts. Kentucky has no statewide seat belt regulation, but some counties have enacted regulations requiring restraints. The remaining states have seat belt laws, which are enforced through fines, though some states merely require front-seat passengers to wear them.

### Q. May I still recover payment for my injuries if I am in an accident and not wearing my seat belt?

**A.** Yes. Most states reject the so-called "seat-belt defense," and will not permit evidence that plaintiffs did not buckle up as proof that they were negligent in a way that contributed to the injuries. In some jurisdictions, however, evidence of the plaintiff's failure to use a seat belt may reduce the amount of damages awarded to the plaintiff.

## CHILD RESTRAINT LAWS

| State | Children Covered | May Substitute Adult Safety Belts |
|---|---|---|
| Alabama | Up to 6 years | 4 to 6 years |
| Alaska | Up to 16 years | 4 to 16 years |
| Arizona | Up to 5 years[2] | No |
| Arkansas | Up to 5 years | 3 to 5 years |
| California | Up to 4 years[2] | No |
| Colorado[1] | Up to 4 years[2] | No |
| Connecticut | Up to 4 years | 1 to 4 years (rear seat) |
| Delaware | Up to 4 years[2] | No |
| DC | Up to 16 years | 3 to 16 years |
| Florida | Up to 6 years | 4 to 6 years |
| Georgia | Up to 5 years | 3 to 5 years |
| Hawaii | Up to 4 years | 3 to 4 years |
| Idaho[1] | Up to 4 years[2] | No |
| Illinois | Up to 6 years | 4 to 6 years |
| Indiana | Up to 5 years | 3 to 5 years |
| Iowa | Up to 6 years | 3 to 6 years |
| Kansas | Up to 14 years | 4 to 14 years |
| Kentucky[1] (own car) | Up to 40 inches | No |
| Louisiana[1] | Up to 5 years | 3 to 5 years (rear seat) |
| Maine | Up to 19 years | 1 to 4 years[3] |
| Maryland | Up to 10 years | 4 to 10 years (over 40 lbs.) |
| Massachusetts | Up to 12 years | All children |
| Michigan | Up to 4 years | 1 to 4 years (rear seat) |
| Minnesota | Up to 4 years | No |
| Mississippi | Up to 2 years | No |
| Missouri | Up to 4 years | All children (rear seat) |
| Montana[1] (own car) | Up to 4 years[2] | 2 to 4 years |
| Nebraska[1] | Up to 5 years | 4 to 5 years (over 40 lbs.) |
| Nevada | Up to 5 years[2] | No |
| New Hampshire | Up to 12 years | All children |
| New Jersey | Up to 5 years | 1½ to 5 years (rear seat) |
| New Mexico | Up to 11 years | 1 to 5 years[4] (rear seat) |
| New York | Up to 16 years[5] | 4 to 16 years |
| North Carolina | Up to 6 years | 3 to 6 years |
| North Dakota | Up to 11 years | 3 to 11 years |
| Ohio | Up to 4 years[2] | 1 to 4 years[6] |
| Oklahoma[1] | Up to 6 years | To 4 years (rear seat)[7] |
| Oregon | Up to 16 years | 1 to 16 years |
| Pennsylvania | Up to 4 years | 1 to 4 years (rear seat) |
| Rhode Island | Up to 13 years | 3 to 13 years |
| South Carolina | Up to 6 years | 1 to 6 years (rear seat)[7] |
| South Dakota | Up to 5 years | 2 to 5 years |
| Tennessee | Up to 4 years | No |
| Texas[1] | Up to 4 years | 2 to 4 years |
| Utah | Up to 8 years | 2 to 8 years |
| Vermont | Up to 13 years | 1 to 5 years (rear seat)[4] |
| Virginia | Up to 4 years | No |
| Washington | Up to 5 years | 1 to 5 years |
| West Virginia | Up to 9 years | 3 to 9 years |
| Wisconsin[1] | Up to 4 years | 4 to 8 years |
| Wyoming | Up to 3 years[2] | 1 to 3 years |

[1] Law applies only to residents of the state.
[2] Law covers children of ages specified or up to 40 pounds, except in Wyoming where law covers children of ages specified or up to 40 inches.
[3] Only drivers who are neither parents nor guardians may substitute regular adult safety belts for children age 1–4. All children older than 4 years may be placed in adult safety belts.
[4] Children older than 5 years may use adult safety belts in front or rear seat.
[5] Law covers children 16 years old in the front seat, to 10 years old in the rear seat.
[6] Children younger than 4 years who are traveling in parents'/guardians' car must be in special infant carriers or child safety seats. In other vehicles, this applies to children younger than one year.
[7] In Oklahoma and South Carolina, adult safety belts may also be used for 4–6 year olds in front seats.

Information obtained from the Insurance Institute for Highway Safety.

SOURCE: *AAA Digest of Motor Laws* (58th Ed. 1993)

## Speeding and Other Offenses

This chapter cannot possibly discuss the many traffic offenses and statutory variations that exist among the fifty states. Generally, minor infractions are those in which a first offense is likely to yield a fine and no jail time. Examples include parking offenses, speeding, failure to keep to the right of the center line, driving an unregistered car, and driving a vehicle with defective equipment. More serious offenses carry stiffer fines and the possibility of a jail sentence. These include reckless driving, leaving the scene of an accident, and driving after a license revocation.

**Q. How could I have received a speeding ticket when I was being careful?**

A. A lack of due care is not an element of the charge of speeding. Simply because you were not in an accident does not prove that you were driving at a reasonable speed.

**Q. What are the elements of a speeding charge?**

A. It depends on whether your state bases its speeding laws on "absolute/fixed maximum limits" or "prima facie limits." It is a violation to exceed a fixed maximum limit regardless of the circumstances at any time. On the other hand, prima facie limits allow drivers to justify the speed at which they were driving by considering traffic and road conditions and visibility.

**Q. Does the type of speed limit change the nature of the complaint against me?**

A. Yes. The complaint and notice or summons to appear for a fixed maximum violation will specify both your alleged speed and the maximum speed allowable within the locality. In contrast, in prima facie jurisdictions, driving above the posted speed limit is not the

## State Safety Laws

| | Seat Belt Law | Adult Helmet Use Laws | Mandatory Motor Vehicle Safety Inspection | Commercial License Required | Two License Plates | Adminis. per se Laws | Studded Tires | 65 MPH Speed Limit |
|---|---|---|---|---|---|---|---|---|
| Alabama | YES | YES | NO | YES | NO | NO | NO* | YES |
| Alaska | YES | NO* | NO | YES | YES | YES | YES | YES |
| Arizona | YES | NO* | NO | YES | NO | YES | YES | YES |
| Arkansas | YES | YES | YES | YES | NO | NO | YES | YES |
| California | YES | YES | NO | YES | YES* | YES | YES | YES |
| Colorado | YES | NO | NO | NO | YES* | YES | YES | NO |
| Connecticut | YES | NO* | NO | YES | NO* | YES | YES | NO |
| Delaware | YES | NO** | YES | YES | YES | YES | YES | NO |
| District of Columbia | YES | YES | YES | YES | NO | YES | YES | YES |
| Florida | YES | YES | NO | YES | NO | NO | YES | YES |
| Georgia | YES | YES | YES | YES | YES | YES | NO | NO |
| Hawaii | YES | NO* | NO | YES | YES | NO | YES | YES |
| Idaho | YES | NO | NO | YES | YES | YES | NO | YES |
| Illinois | YES | NO* | NO | YES | NO | YES | YES | YES |
| Indiana | YES | NO | NO | YES | YES | YES | YES | YES |
| Iowa | YES | NO* | NO | YES | NO | YES | YES | YES |
| Kansas | NO | YES | NO | YES | NO | NO | YES | YES |
| Kentucky | YES | YES | YES | YES | NO | YES | NO | YES |
| Louisiana | NO | ♦ | YES | YES | YES | YES | YES | YES |
| Maine | YES | NO* | NO | YES | YES | YES | NO** | NO |
| Maryland | NO | NO* | YES | NO | NO | NO | YES | YES |
| Massachusetts | YES | YES | NO | YES | NO | NO | NO | YES |
| Michigan | YES | NO* | NO | YES | YES | YES | NO | YES |
| Minnesota | YES | YES | NO | YES | NO | YES | NO | YES |
| Mississippi | YES | YES | YES | YES | YES | YES | NO | YES |
| Missouri | YES | YES | YES | YES | YES | NO | YES | YES |
| Montana | YES | NO* | NO | YES | YES | YES | YES | YES |
| Nebraska | YES | YES | NO | YES | YES | YES | YES | YES |
| Nevada | YES | YES | NO | YES | YES | YES | YES | YES |
| New Hampshire | NO | NO* | YES | YES | YES | NO | YES | NO |
| New Jersey | YES | YES | YES | YES | YES | YES | YES*** | YES |
| New Mexico | YES | NO* | NO | YES | NO | NO | YES | NO |
| New York | YES | YES | YES | YES | YES | YES | YES | YES |
| North Carolina | YES | YES | YES | YES | NO | YES | YES | YES |
| North Dakota | NO | NO* | NO | YES | YES | YES | YES | YES |

| | | | | | | | |
|---|---|---|---|---|---|---|---|
| Ohio | YES | NO* | NO | YES | YES | YES | YES |
| Oklahoma | YES | NO* | YES | YES | YES | YES | YES |
| Oregon | YES | YES | NO | YES | YES | YES | YES |
| Pennsylvania | YES | YES | YES | YES | NO | YES | NO |
| Rhode Island | YES | NO◆ | YES | YES | NO | YES | NO |
| South Carolina | YES | NO*** | YES | YES | YES | YES | NO |
| South Dakota | NO | NO* | NO | YES | NO | YES | YES |
| Tennessee | YES | YES | NO | YES | NO | YES | YES |
| Texas | YES | YES | YES | YES | YES | YES | YES |
| Utah | YES | NO* | YES | YES | YES | YES* | YES |
| Vermont | YES | YES | YES | YES | YES | YES | YES |
| Virginia | YES | YES | YES | YES | NO | YES | YES |
| Washington | YES | YES | NO | YES | NO | YES | YES |
| West Virginia | NO | YES | YES | YES | YES | YES | YES |
| Wisconsin | YES | NO* | NO | YES | YES | YES | YES |
| Wyoming | YES | NO** | NO | YES | YES | YES | YES |

Adult helmet use laws:

\* = Helmet use required for drivers under 18

\*\* = Helmet use required for drivers under 19

\*\*\* = Helmet use required for drivers under 21

◆ = Helmet use required for drivers under 16

◆◆ = Helmet use required for passengers only

Two license plates:

\* = Non-reflectorized

Studded tires:

\* = Soft studs only

\*\* = Except in western counties

\*\*\* = Only for safety reasons

SOURCE: *AAA Digest of Motor Laws* (58th ed. 1993)

offense. The police must charge you with driving above a speed that was reasonable and proper given the existing conditions. One example might be driving fifty miles per hour in a school zone.

Speeding laws vary greatly from state to state. Therefore, it is a good idea, for legal and safety reasons, to get into the habit of reducing your driving speed whenever you approach a railway crossing or intersection, drive around a curve, or encounter special hazards, such as severe weather.

### Q. Are there any excuses I can offer that might prevent a police officer from writing up a speeding ticket?

**A.** If you are taking a pregnant or sick person to the hospital, you might be spared a speeding citation, and you might even get a police escort to the hospital. Sometimes a court emergency (be sure to display the court papers to the officer), or a broken speedometer (be prepared to give the officer a test ride) may succeed—but only, of course, if they are truthful reasons.

### Q. What kind of information is included on a traffic ticket?

**A.** The color, model, and registration of your vehicle, and the date, time, and place of the alleged offense is provided on the ticket. Also, the specific violation charged (if it's a parking meter offense, the meter number as well), the officer's name and badge number, the fine schedule, and a notice of your ability to have a hearing to contest the ticket will probably be on a ticket as well. However, each jurisdiction has its own form. If the officer includes incorrect information in writing the ticket, such mistakes may provide you with a defense against the citation.

### Q. What does "leaving the scene of an accident" mean?

**A.** Consult a lawyer about your state's law. Generally, drivers of vehicles involved in an accident in which personal injury or property damage occurs must stop and identify themselves and their vehicles. Drivers must also notify police, and help any injured persons. Neither the driver's intent nor the ownership of either vehicle involved in the collision are elements of the offense. (See the "Accidents" section immediately following this section.)

### Q. What are the defenses to such a charge?

**A.** It is a complete defense if no personal injury or property damage resulted from the accident, or if you had no knowledge that an accident had occurred. On the other hand, claiming that you left intending to drive directly to the police station to report the accident probably would not be a good defense.

### Q. What is "reckless driving"?

**A.** The language varies from jurisdiction to jurisdiction, but increasingly, states are following the Uniform Vehicle Code, which defines it as "willful or wanton disregard for the safety of persons or property." Essentially, the prosecution must show that reckless drivers were indifferent to the probable harmful results of their driving, and that the reckless drivers should have realized that such driving posed a hazard.

### Accidents

### Q. According to the law, how safely must I drive?

**A.** You have to use reasonable care under the circumstances. Negligence—the failure to exercise such care—is the most common basis for liability. However, ordinary negligence does not mean you are guilty of reckless driving in the criminal sense. For such driving to be unlawful, it must be willful or wanton as defined above.

### Q. Do I owe a higher standard of care toward pedestrians?

**A.** No, the same standard applies. Motorists must exercise reasonable care under the circumstances toward pedestrians. In practical terms, this means keeping a careful lookout for them, and maintaining control over your vehicle to avoid injuring them. You must also sound your horn to warn of your approach when you believe that the pedestrian is unaware of the danger. In some states, you must stop if you see a pedestrian anywhere in a crosswalk.

The law does not, however, expect you to anticipate a pedestrian darting out into the roadway.

### Q. Do I owe the same duty of care toward my passengers?

**A.** Generally, yes, although it may change based on your passengers' relationship to you. However, as in all accidents, you will not be liable if a passenger sustains injury through no fault of your own.

### Q. To what standard of care am I held if someone else is driving my car in which I am a passenger?

**A.** The law in some states will assume you still have "control" over the vehicle. Other states require the owner to take steps to stop the negligent driving as soon as the owner becomes aware of it. In other words, as a car owner, you can be liable for more than just your own negligent driving.

## WHAT YOU SHOULD DO IF YOU HAVE AN ACCIDENT

*If possible, park on the shoulder of the road and do not obstruct traffic. Use your car's flashers or flares to warn approaching motorists of the accident. If asked, give your name, address, vehicle registration certificate, and proof of insurance to the other driver. Get the same information from the other driver. Write down the names and addresses of all passengers and possible witnesses. Also, get the names and badge numbers of any police officers who respond to the scene. If you have a camera handy, photograph damaged cars, skid marks, and the accident scene. Draw a diagram of the accident and make notes about the weather, lighting conditions, and road conditions. Most important, help any persons who are injured.*

*Do not make any statements about who you believe was at fault. Also, do not admit blame to the other parties or witnesses. As soon as possible after the accident, notify your insurance company. If you sustained any personal injury, seek medical attention promptly. Consult an attorney if you intend to file suit.*

### Q. Am I legally responsible even if I am not in the car if an accident occurs?

**A.** Possibly. You still might be liable for property damage, injuries, and even death if you permit someone else to operate your defective vehicle, or if you allow an inexperienced, habitually intoxicated, or otherwise incompetent person to drive your car. The law refers to this conduct as "negligent entrustment."

### Q. What if my child is driving my car and an accident occurs?

**A.** Some jurisdictions recognize the "family purpose doctrine," under which the "head" of the family who maintains a car for general family use may be held liable for the negligent driving of a family member who was authorized to use the vehicle. The fewer than twenty states that adhere to this doctrine treat the family member as an agent of the vehicle owner, who is presumed to be better able to satisfy property damage and injury claims.

### Q. If I am involved in an accident, must I identify myself to other involved parties?

**A.** In the past, common law did not require you to give your name before leaving an accident scene. Modern laws that require you to identify yourself after an accident in which someone is hurt or killed have survived court challenges. You should identify yourself to a police officer (see below), and show your license and proof of insurance coverage if asked. Otherwise, you do not have to, and probably should not, say anything. Specifically, do not reveal how much insurance coverage you have, or admit liability.

### Q. If I collide with a parked car, am I required to do anything?

**A.** The law requires you to try to find the owner. Alternatively, you are permitted to attach a written note to the parked car identifying yourself and your vehicle. You should also notify the police.

### Q. Must I tell the police if I am in an accident?

**A.** Alert the police immediately if someone is hurt or killed. Generally, if the accident involves a death, personal injury, or property damage above a specific amount that varies among states, you must notify the police and file a written accident report immediately, or within a short time span, usually five to ten days. Often, states require you to file the report with the bureau of motor vehicles or similar state authority. Some states do not require you to report an accident if no one is injured or if property damage is less than a certain dollar amount. Other jurisdictions require a report only if no police officer responded to the accident scene.

### Q. What if I do not fill out an accident report?

**A.** Failure to file a written report is a misdemeanor in most states. Some states may suspend your driver's license until you file the report. Remember, by completing an accident report, you are verifying that the report contains a recital of all important facts known to you. Providing false information in a written report is illegal, and typically is punished by a fine.

### Q. Should I contact an attorney after the accident? What should I tell the lawyer?

**A.** If you are filing a lawsuit against the other driver, you will hire your own lawyer. If the other driver is suing you, your insurance company will provide a lawyer for you. At the initial client interview, supply information about:

- your family status and employment situation;

# Accident Report Filing Requirements

All states require the filing of a report if an accident results in personal injury or death.

| State | Property Damage in Excess of | Days to File Report | State | Property Damage in Excess of | Days to File Report |
|---|---|---|---|---|---|
| Alabama | $250 | 10 | Montana | $400 | 10 |
| Alaska | $500 | 10 | Nebraska | $500 | 10 |
| Arizona | $500 | 5 | Nevada | $350 | 10 |
| Arkansas | $250 | 30 | New Hampshire | $500 | 5 |
| California | $500 | 10 | New Jersey | $500[7] | 10 |
| Colorado | $1,000[1] | 10 | New Mexico | $250 | 5 |
| Connecticut | $1,000 | 5 | New York | $600 | 10 |
| Delaware | $500[2] | Immediately | North Carolina | $500 | Immediately |
| District of Columbia | $250 | 5 | North Dakota | $600 | Immediately |
| Florida | $500[3] | 5 | Ohio | $400 | 30 |
| Georgia | $250 | 10 | Oklahoma | $300 | 10 |
| Hawaii | $300 | 1 | Oregon | $400 | 3 |
| Idaho | $250 | Immediately | Pennsylvania | $200[8] | 5 |
| Illinois | $250 | 15 | Rhode Island | $500 | 10 |
| Indiana | $750 | 10 | South Carolina | $400 | 15 |
| Iowa | $500 | 3 | South Dakota | $500 per person or $1,000 per accident | Immediately |
| Kansas | $500[4] | Immediately | | | |
| Kentucky | $200 | 10 | Tennessee | $400 | 10 |
| Louisiana | $500 | 10 | Texas | $500[9] | 10 |
| Maine | $500 | 5 | Utah | $400 | 5 |
| Maryland | see note[5] | 15 | Vermont | $500 | 3 |
| Massachusetts | $1,000 | 5 | Virginia | $750 | 5 |
| Michigan | $200[6] | Immediately | Washington | $500 | 1 |
| Minnesota | $500 | 10 | West Virginia | $250 | 5 |
| Mississippi | $250 | 10 | Wisconsin | $500 | 10 |
| Missouri | $500 | 30 | Wyoming | $500 | 10 |

**Notes:**

[1]State law also requires a police officer to submit an accident report (regardless of the amount of property damage) if one of the participants cannot show proof of insurance.

[2]The filing of an accident report is required if it appears that an alcohol-impaired driver was involved in the accident.

[3]State law stipulates that a driver need not submit an accident report if a police officer submits the report.

[4]State law requires that drivers shall report accidents to a police officer, who then shall submit the accident report. It also stipulates that the Division of Vehicles may require drivers to submit a written report to satisfy certain provisions of the law.

[5]No accident reports are required if: (1) the accident results in property damage only; (2) a police officer files a report; or (3) a person is physically unable to make a report.

[6]Accident reports are to be submitted to the investigating police officer who then shall forward the report to the Director of the State Police.

[7]State law requires the filing of proof of financial responsibility if a driver is involved in an accident resulting in injury, death, or property damage greater than $200 to one person.

[8]Pennsylvania law is a combination of financial responsibility, compulsory liability, and no-fault insurance reparative systems.

[9]The law requires the filing of proof of financial responsibility if a driver is involved in an accident resulting in injury, death, or property damage greater than $1,000 to one person.

SOURCE: National Association of Independent Insurers

- the accident, including witnesses' names and addresses; and
- your injuries.

If you are filing suit, tell the lawyer about all your out-of-pocket expenses, such as doctors' bills, ambulance and hospital costs, automobile repairs, rental car costs, and any lost income.

### Q. What might happen if I believe the collision is at least partly my fault?

A. You may not be in the best position to determine how the accident happened. Defective equipment in your vehicle, a malfunctioning traffic signal, or the other driver's intoxication are among the many possible causes of the accident. Accepting blame and apologizing to the other driver may be used as evidence against you at trial. Leave it to the judge or jury to decide who is at fault.

### Q. If the accident is partly my fault, may I still receive payment for my injuries?

A. The answer depends on whether you live in a contributory negligence, comparative negligence, or no-fault jurisdiction. (See the discussion of no-fault insurance in the "Insurance" section of this chapter below.)

### Q. What is contributory negligence?

A. Essentially, contributory negligence bars you from recovering money for your injuries if your own negligence in any way contributed to the accident's occurrence. The other driver must prove that you were negligent.

### Q. What is the logic behind this legal doctrine?

A. The reasons behind contributory negligence range from punishing you for your own misconduct to discouraging you from acting

negligently again. Only six states still accept the concept of contributory negligence, which once was widely supported.

### Q. What does "comparative negligence" mean?

A. Adhered to in forty-four states, comparative negligence divides the damages among the drivers involved in an accident based on their degree of fault. In "pure" comparative negligence states, you can receive payment for your injuries regardless of how much of the blame you carry for the accident, as long as the other driver is at fault to some degree. In "modified" comparative fault states, you may recover payment only if your own fault is below a certain threshold, such as 50 percent.

### Q. How does comparative negligence work?

A. As an example, you are involved in an accident in which you were driving ten miles above the posted speed limit on an icy road. You believe, however, that the accident occurred because the other driver ran a red light.

In a comparative negligence state, it is up to the fact-finder, be it judge or jury, after hearing your case, to assign the degree of fault for each of you in terms of a percentage. Suppose the fact-finder decides that your speeding was responsible for 20 percent of your injuries, and the other driver's going through the red light contributed the remaining 80 percent. If the total amount of damages were $100,000, you would only recover $80,000.

## INSURANCE

### Q. Does my bank have a say in the amount of insurance I buy?

A. Possibly. Many states allow lenders from whom you borrowed to buy a car to protect their collateral by requiring you to purchase insurance options such as "collision," which pays for damage to your car regardless of fault, and "comprehensive," which pays for damage to your car caused by theft, fire, and vandalism.

### Q. What is a deductible?

**A.** A deductible is the amount of each claim that you agree to pay for by yourself. The higher the deductible you choose, the lower your annual insurance premium, though you need more cash on hand to pay for damages when you select a high deductible. Typical deductibles are $50, $100, $250, and $500.

### Q. May my insurance agent force me to pay my premium in a lump sum?

**A.** Check your particular state's law. Some states limit the amount an agent may demand before renewing your insurance to a certain percentage of the premium. If you have not paid your premium payments in the recent past, however, an insurance agent may legally ask you to pay your entire premium before renewing your policy.

### Q. May my insurance agent charge me a service fee for issuing or renewing a policy?

**A.** Consult your state's law. Some states, such as Massachusetts, forbid agents from charging service fees for issuing or renewing auto insurance policies, and do not require you to pay for services that your agent performs without your consent.

### Q. How are insurance rates determined?

**A.** A classification system based on objective criteria helps actuaries to determine the risk of an accident and thereby set the varying rates that drivers pay. Criteria include your age, sex, marital status, and geographic location; the age, make, and model of the car; and the car's primary use (cars used for recreation are statistically less likely to be involved in an accident than a vehicle used for commuting). In some states, the insurance rates are set by the state's insurance commission, which regulates insurance companies.

If you have been involved in several accidents over a short period of time, you are a high risk, so insurance companies would add a surcharge to the basic premium you pay. On the other hand, insurance carriers might offer safety discounts if your vehicle is equipped with automatic safety belts, anti-lock brakes, or air bags. States have varying regulations governing safety discounts, ranging from Massachusetts, which does not permit discounts for air bags, to New York, which mandates safety discounts for air bags.

Insurance companies will offer other types of discounts as well, such as for senior citizens, "good students," if you join a car pool, or if you insure multiple vehicles with the same carrier.

### Q. My teenage son's insurance premium is much higher than mine. Is it unconstitutional to discriminate based on age?

**A.** No. Actuaries cite research that persons under age 21, especially males, have the highest rate of car accidents. This is the justification for the disparity in rates between adults and minors.

### Q. Will my insurance premium automatically increase if I have an accident?

**A.** Not necessarily. If the insurance carrier has to dole out $300 to $500 or more in claims, you are likely to see a premium increase. If you have been accident-free for the previous three years, the surcharge, if any, might still be less than your costs to pay for the repairs out-of-pocket. If you are on your third accident and just getting warmed up, prepare yourself for a 20 percent to 50 percent premium hike.

## WHO PAYS THE MOST FOR CAR INSURANCE?

*Following are the states that have the highest average automobile insurance premiums for the year 1991.*

| STATE | AMOUNT |
|---|---|
| New Jersey | $1081 |
| Hawaii | 999 |
| Washington, D.C. | 981 |
| Rhode Island | 939 |
| Connecticut | 928 |
| Massachusetts | 913 |
| California | 904 |
| New York | 841 |
| Alaska | 810 |
| Delaware | 783 |
| National Average | 686 |

SOURCE: *The Boston Globe, 6/16/93*

### Q. Do I have to buy uninsured motorist coverage?

**A.** It depends on where you live. Twenty-two states now require drivers to purchase such coverage, which enables you to collect from *your* insurer if you are injured in an accident caused by an uninsured driver. The insurance carrier, in turn, receives subrogation rights against the uninsured wrongdoer; that is, the carrier takes your place (and your rights) as the legal claimant against the uninsured driver. Skyrocketing hospital costs, combined with a tight economy that has forced people to inadequately insure their vehicles, if at all (where not required by the state), make this coverage desirable, even if not mandated by your state.

### Q. How do I collect on my uninsured motorist coverage?

**A.** Generally, you must prove both that the other driver was at fault and without liability insurance to compensate you. An uninsured motorist may actually have no coverage, or may be "uninsured" if underage, unlicensed, or otherwise ineligible for protection under the policy covering the vehicle that caused the accident, as, for example, when the driver at fault used the vehicle without the owner's permission. Practically speaking, if the insurance carrier of the driver at fault denies coverage, you are dealing with an uninsured motorist.

### Q. How much can I recover on an uninsured motorist claim?

**A.** Check your state's law. Some states, for example, prohibit adding together the liability limits for two policies to determine how much coverage is available to injured persons.

### Q. How does underinsured motorist coverage work?

**A.** Underinsured motorist coverage, which exists in a majority of states, provides indemnification from the injured person's insurer in a sum equal to or greater than what the injured insured person could have realized had the driver at fault carried the statutorily prescribed liability insurance minimum. If, for example, you have underinsurance coverage with a "trigger" provision in the amount of $100,000, and the other driver who injured you has only $50,000 in bodily injury coverage, but you have $70,000 in damages, once you recover from the other driver's carrier, you can look to your own insurer, up to a maximum $50,000, to cover the excess damages.

### Q. Do underinsured motorist policies differ?

**A.** Yes. A minority of those states that recognize this insurance option weigh the insured accident victim's damages against the driver at fault's liability coverage, compensating the injured person only if the driver at fault's liability coverage is less than the damages the victim suffered or was entitled to receive. Other states examine the injured person's uninsured motorist coverage and the driver at fault's liability insurance, with the insurance carrier paying out only when the driver at fault's liability insurance limit is less than the victim's underinsured motorist coverage. Most policies enable the insurer to deduct ("set-off") the amount the victim receives from the driver at fault from the sum it pays to the victim carrying the underinsured motorist protection.

### Q. What is no-fault insurance?

**A.** Under this type of insurance, which is usually compulsory, insurance carriers compensate their own policyholders for medical and other costs associated with automobile accidents. This type of insurance is designed to protect you, any passengers in your car, and any pedestrian you may injure, without having to enter a court of law to determine who is at fault for the accident. Most no-fault statutes apply only to bodily injury claims, and do not encompass property damage claims.

Massachusetts was the first state in the nation to pass a no-fault statute. At one time, more than twenty states passed no-fault statutes, though the current trend among states— most recently, Connecticut—is to repeal such laws.

### Q. What are the pros and cons of no-fault?

**A.** The purported advantage of no-fault is that the injured party is reimbursed relatively promptly by his or her insurance company, sav-

> ## THE AUTO INSURANCE JUNGLE
> *"No-fault," "choice," "financial responsibility"—most drivers would rather drive cross-country, nonstop, in a Yugo, than attempt to decipher the mysteries of automobile insurance. Virtually each state has its own insurance regulations, yet not every state has mandatory insurance. A detailed analysis of the issues and options associated with automobile insurance is beyond the scope of this chapter, but here's a quick guide to some of the major issues.*

ing the party from a protracted court case. On the debit side, no-fault laws restrict the injured person's right to sue the other driver for general damages. For example, often a dollar "threshold" in medical expenses and damages must be satisfied before an injured party can bring suit against a negligent driver. Some states, such as Michigan, have a so-called "verbal threshold," which uses words—not figures—to determine when a suit may be filed. A typical statute precludes an individual injured in a car accident from initiating a tort action unless his or her injuries resulted in death, permanent serious disfigurement, or serious impairment of a body function. Under this verbal threshold, sprains, strains, and other so-called "soft tissue" injuries, which are most common in automobile accidents, would not be compensable. Critics also lambaste no-fault for: 1) not providing an incentive to drive safely, because both the careless driver and the innocent victim are entitled to the same compensation, and, 2) for not resulting in reduced insurance premiums, as promised by insurance companies.

## Q. What are choice statutes?

**A.** These laws enable drivers to choose between a no-fault policy that limits the driver's right to sue the other party to an accident but allegedly carries with it a lower premium, and a straight tort-based negligence plan, at a supposedly higher premium, that gives drivers a broader right to sue. Choice proposals have recently been rejected in Rhode Island, Connecticut, and Arizona, and one is on the drawing board in Massachusetts.

## Q. What are "financial responsibility" laws?

**A.** These laws require drivers either to have insurance or post a bond or have a sum of money in cash. "Security-type" financial responsibility laws require, following an accident, that each driver demonstrate an ability to pay damages that might be assessed against the driver in subsequent litigation. Another type of financial responsibility law involves a minimum requirement of financial responsibility covering death or injury of a person, death or injury of more than one person, and property damage.

## Q. What are "compulsory insurance" statutes?

**A.** These laws mandate that drivers file proof of financial responsibility as a condition of receiving their vehicle registration. Many states require drivers to purchase certain insurance options, such as "collision," which pays you for damage to your car irrespective of who was at fault, and "comprehensive," which pays you for damage done to your car caused by theft, fire, and vandalism.

---

## WHERE TO GET MORE INFORMATION

The following list is a starting point for getting more details or registering various types of complaints.

### Manufacturer/Dealer Associations

The Motor Vehicle Manufacturer's Association (MVMA) publishes *Motor Vehicle Facts and Figures* annually. It also publishes a complete *Directory of Motor Vehicle Related Associations*. For details on how to obtain these publications, call (313) 872-4311 or write to:

Motor Vehicle Manufacturer's Association
7430 Second Avenue, Suite 300
Detroit, MI 48202

The Automobile Importers of America is the foreign-car counterpart of the MVMA. For details, call (703) 416-1577 or write to:

Automobile Importers of America
1725 Jefferson Davis Highway
Arlington, VA 22202

The National Automobile Dealers Association is a major trade association of U.S. automobile dealers. It publishes a number of brochures for consumers on topics such as automotive safety. For details, call (703) 821-7000 or 1-800-252-6232 or write to:

National Automobile Dealers Association
8400 Westpark Drive
McLean, VA 22102

The Recreational Vehicle Industry Association is a national trade association representing manufacturers of motor homes, travel trailers, truck campers, multi-use vehicles, and component part suppliers. It publishes brochures offering hints for buyers, tips for campers, and safety and driving tips, among other topics. For details, call (703) 620-6003 or write to:

Recreational Vehicle Industry Association
1896 Preston White Drive
Reston, VA 22090

The Rubber Manufacturers Association offers information on tires and other rubber products. For details, call (202) 682-4800 or 1-800-325-5095 or write to:

Rubber Manufacturers Association
1400 K Street, NW
Washington, DC 20005

For information and publications on using certified car technicians for repairs, contact:

Automotive Service Excellence
13505 Dulles Technology Drive
Herndon, VA 22071
(703) 713-3800

You also can call the car manufacturers' headquarters or their regional offices directly. Ask your local dealer for details.

## Consumer and Government Groups

Almost every state has a Better Business Bureau (BBB). Every local BBB has a hot line for automobile-related complaints, particularly regarding warranties. The BBB arranges arbitration hearings for participating manufacturers. Check your local telephone directory or write to:

Council of Better Business Bureaus, Inc.
4200 Wilson Boulevard, 8th Floor
Arlington, VA 22203
(703) 276-0100

The Federal Trade Commission (FTC) has many pamphlets related to automobiles. It has regional offices, which are listed in the "Where to Get More Information" section of the "Consumer Credit" chapter. You also can call the FTC's Bureau of Consumer Protection at (202) 326-2222 or write to:

Federal Trade Commission
Bureau of Consumer Protection
6th and Pennsylvania Avenue, NW
Washington, DC 20580

The National Highway Traffic Safety Administration (NHTSA) provides information on car recalls and defect investigations. You can also report safety-related defects. The NHTSA offers a toll-free auto safety hot line. In the D.C. area, you can call this hot line at (202) 366-0123. In the continental U.S., call the hot line at 1-800-424-9393. Or write to:

National Highway Traffic Safety Administration
400 7th Street, SW
Washington, DC 20590

Ralph Nader's automobile consumer protection organization is the Center for Auto Safety. It provides information on automobile defects for various models of cars and may follow up on consumer complaints: Write to:

Center for Auto Safety
Suite 410
2001 S Street, NW
Washington, DC 20009

The United States Consumer Product Safety Commission is a federal agency that offers safety-related information on most, but not all, products available to the consumer market. In Maryland, call (301) 504-0580 and ask for the "Public Affairs Department." In the rest of the United States, call 1-800-638-2772.

Or you can write to:

U.S. Consumer Product Safety Commission
Washington, DC 20207

Other automobile-related organizations include:

Consumer Federation of America
1424 16th Street, NW, Suite 604
Washington, DC 20036
(202) 387-6121

National Safety Council
1121 Springlake Drive
Itasca, IL 60130
(708) 285-1121

National Transportation Safety Board
490 L'Enfant East, SW
Washington, DC 20594
(202) 382-6600

For additional assistance with automobile-related problems or questions, you also can contact your state attorney general's offices or your state Department of Consumer Affairs. Some states have separate bureaus that handle only motor vehicle problems. Your state or local Department of Motor Vehicles also may be helpful. Check your local telephone directory.

## Insurance

For information designed to help consumers understand state laws and insurance, contact:

Insurance Information Institute
110 William Street
New York, NY 10038
(212) 669-9200

The Insurance Information Institute not only has many useful pamphlets, but it also has state and regional counterparts.

## Publications

The American Automobile Association (AAA) annually publishes an updated edition of the *Digest of Motor Laws*. It is a summary of laws and regulations governing passenger cars in each state. It also covers each U.S. territory and each Canadian province. Copies are available from your local AAA club or from:

Traffic Safety
American Automobile Association
1000 AAA Drive
Heathrow, FL 32746
(407) 444-4700

The Consumer Information Center has various booklets that might be of interest to you. Call or write: Consumer Information Center-N, P.O. Box 100, Pueblo, CO 81002; telephone (719) 948-3334

■

# Law and the Workplace

# INTRODUCTION

THE LAW AFFECTS JUST ABOUT EVERY ASPECT OF WORK. Federal and state laws regulate the hiring process, terms and conditions of employment, and the circumstances under which employees can be fired.

The law helps shape the relationship between employer and employee. The law does not address every issue that can arise in the employment relationship, but a basic understanding of what the law does require can help both the employer and employee anticipate problems and avoid trouble.

Understanding your legal rights does not mean that those rights can only be enforced by a lawsuit in court. A lawsuit should be viewed as a last resort, not as a starting point. Lawsuits are costly and time-consuming. Rather, employers and employees should first try to discuss their differences. Such discussions are easier and more productive when both sides understand how the law affects the situation. Many employers try to anticipate problems before they occur, and solve problems when they do arise.

This chapter can help both employees and employers understand how the law affects their rights and obligations at work. It explains the laws and suggests places to turn for further details. Each section in this chapter briefly explains a specific area of law and then answers commonly asked questions.

**Q. Is there a single law of the workplace?**

**A.** No, there is no single "law of the workplace." Today's workplace law consists of federal and state laws, civil service rules, collective bargaining agreements, contracts, company personnel handbooks, and employer practices.

**Q. Will this chapter answer specific questions for the employee or employer?**

**A.** No, you should view it as a basic road map. This chapter will help employees determine if the law provides redress for a problem they encounter at work and it will help employers determine if their policies or practices are consistent with the law. It will tell you where to find more information, and which government agencies can provide help in dealing with certain workplace issues. After reading this chapter, you will be in a better position to decide whether to seek legal advice for a particular problem. This chapter cannot, however, cover every situation or offer advice on your specific problem.

**Q. Does it matter if a person works for a government instead of a private employer?**

**A.** Yes, it makes a big difference. Generally, labor contracts and federal and state laws regulate the relationship between a private sector employee and employer, such as a retail business or a manufacturer. The public sector employer, however, works for government and is subject not only to the labor contracts and laws but also to the restrictions imposed by federal and state constitutions. For example, the First Amendment restriction on government interference with free speech prohibits a governmental employer from disciplining a worker who speaks out on issues of public concern. The First Amendment, however, generally does not apply to a private sector employer and thus does not prohibit a private sector employer from discharging such an employee. In addition, most governmental employment is also regulated by civil service rules.

### Q. What is the legal significance of a union contract?

**A.** When employees select a union as their bargaining representative, the union negotiates a contract (collective bargaining agreement) with the employer containing the terms and conditions of employment for all employees. Individual employees cannot negotiate separate deals with the employer. If there is no union contract, the employee deals directly with the employer and negotiates his or her own terms of employment.

### Q. Does this chapter cover independent contractors?

**A.** No. Workplace law deals with the regulation of the relationship between employers and employees. As a matter of law, independent contractors are not considered to be employees. Generally speaking, where an employer controls, directs and supervises the individual in the performance of his or her work, that individual is considered to be an employee. But, where the employer merely specifies the result to be achieved, and the individual uses personal judgment and discretion in the means used to achieve that result, then that individual is considered to be an independent contractor. Other indications of employee status are payment on a salary or wage basis rather than a per project basis and the furnishing by the employer of the equipment used in the performance of the work. For example, ABC Company hires Jill to construct a fence around its property, and agrees to pay her $1000. ABC does not supervise Jill's work; it does not tell her how to build the fence or what time to report to work. The company cares only about getting the fence built. Jill's income is based on the profits she makes on the job after subtracting for the cost of buying the fencing materials. Her relationship with ABC ends when she finishes the job. Jill is an independent contractor, not the employee of ABC.

### Q. Does this chapter cover state laws as well as federal laws?

**A.** While this chapter discusses both federal and state laws, it does not detail the laws of each specific state. There will be references to state law and there will be a general discussion concerning how state law impacts the work relationship. However, no two states have laws exactly alike, so discussion of state law issues will not provide guidance as to how a specific state's laws affect the workplace.

## FEDERAL LAWS REGULATING THE WORKPLACE

Throughout this chapter there will be continuous reference to federal law. Many of these laws impact not just one aspect of the employment relationship, but the entire spectrum of rights and responsibilities within the workplace. Thus, as a matter of convenience to the reader, and to avoid unnecessary duplication of information, some of the major federal laws are listed below with a short description of their content.

### Q. What is Title VII of the Civil Rights Act?

**A.** Title VII (29 U.S.C. Section 2000e–2000e-17) is a federal law that prohibits discrimination in employment based on race, color, religion, sex, and national origin.

### Q. What types of employers are regulated under Title VII?

**A.** Public sector and private sector employers that employ at least fifteen employees are

# A CHECKLIST OF OTHER FEDERAL LAWS REGULATING PRIVATE SECTOR EMPLOYMENT

*Besides those laws listed in the accompanying questions and answers, there are other federal laws that impact the employment relation. The following provides an introductory checklist of these laws, which will be discussed in more detail later in this chapter.*

## Unions

*RAILWAY LABOR ACT, 45 U.S.C. Sections 151–188: this law regulates union activity in the workplace and prohibits discrimination in employment based on union activity. The airlines and railways are the only employers subject to the provisions of this law.*

## Wages and Hours

*DAVIS-BACON ACT, 40 U.S.C. Section 276a–276a-7; SERVICE CONTRACT ACT, 41 U.S.C. Sections 351–358; WALSH-HEALY PUBLIC CONTRACTS ACT, 41 U.S.C. Sections 35–45: these statutes require employers with certain types of federal government contracts to pay their employees a minimum wage as determined by the Secretary of Labor.*

*EQUAL PAY ACT, 29 U.S.C. Section 206(d): requires employers to pay equal wages to male and female employees who are performing substantially equivalent work.*

## Workplace Safety

*OCCUPATIONAL SAFETY AND HEALTH ACT, 29 U.S.C. Sections 651–678: requires employers to furnish a workplace free from hazards likely to cause death or serious injury and to comply with safety and health standards promulgated under the statute.*

*MINE SAFETY AND HEALTH ACT, 30 U.S.C. Sections 8-01–8-78: requires mine operators to comply with safety and health standards promulgated under the statute.*

## Pensions

*EMPLOYEE RETIREMENT INCOME SECURITY ACT, 29 U.S.C. Sections 1001–1461: establishes eligibility and vesting rights for employees in company pension plans; establishes administrative, fiduciary, funding and termination requirements for pension plans.*

## Immigrant Workers

*IMMIGRATION REFORM AND CONTROL ACT, 8 U.S.C. Sections 1324a–1324c: prohibits employers from hiring illegal aliens; requires employers to verify the work eligibility status of applicants; prohibits discrimination in employment based on citizenship status against lawfully admitted aliens.*

## Other Terms Of Employment

*VETERANS' REEMPLOYMENT RIGHTS ACT, 38 U.S.C. Sections 2021–2026: requires employers to reinstate to their former jobs, upon completion of their military duty, employees who have served in the armed forces.*

*WORKER ADJUSTMENT AND RETRAINING NOTIFICATION ACT, 29 U.S.C. Sections 2102–2109: requires employers to give sixty days' advance notice of plant closing or mass layoff to workers, unions, and state and local governments.*

*EMPLOYEE POLYGRAPH PROTECTION ACT, 29 U.S.C. Sections 2001–2009: prohibits employers from requiring employees or applicants to submit to polygraph examinations.*

*FAMILY AND MEDICAL LEAVE ACT, 29 U.S.C. Sections 2601, 2611–2619, 2651–2654: requires employers to grant employees up to twelve weeks of unpaid leave during any twelve-month period because of the birth or adoption of a child, because the employee has a serious health condition, or because the employee has to care for a parent, spouse, or child with a serious health condition.*

*JURY SYSTEM IMPROVEMENTS ACT, 28 U.S.C. Section 1875: prohibits the discipline or discharge of an employee because of federal court jury duty.*

*DRUG-FREE WORKPLACE ACT, 41 U.S.C. Sections 701–707: requires government contractors and grantees to establish a drug-free awareness program for their employees.*

covered by this federal law. Unions and employment agencies are also covered under Title VII. It should be remembered, however, that employers with fewer than fifteen employees may be covered under state law prohibiting discrimination in employment.

**Q. Is there a federal agency responsible for enforcement of Title VII?**

**A.** Yes. The Equal Employment Opportunity Commission (EEOC) is charged with the responsibility for enforcing Title VII.

**Q. *What is 42 U.S.C. Section 1981?***

**A.** This is a federal statute that prohibits employment discrimination based on race or ethnicity.

**Q. *What types of employers are regulated under 42 U.S.C. Section 1981?***

**A.** All public and private sector employers, regardless of size, are covered by this statute.

**Q. *Is there a federal agency responsible for enforcement of 42 U.S.C. Section 1981?***

**A.** No. This statute is enforced solely by private individuals filing lawsuits.

**Q. *What is the Age Discrimination in Employment Act?***

**A.** The ADEA (29 U.S.C. Sections 621–634) prohibits discrimination in employment based on age. For purposes of this statute, age is defined as at least forty years of age or older. Thus, it would not be a violation of the ADEA for an employer to refuse to hire an individual because that person was twenty-five years old. However, some state laws that prohibit age discrimination have a broader definition of the protected class; for example, Oregon prohibits age discrimination against any individual eighteen years of age or older.

**Q. *What types of employers are regulated under the ADEA?***

**A.** Public and private sector employers employing at least twenty employees are covered by this federal law. Unions and employment agencies are also covered by this law. It should be remembered, however, that employers with fewer than twenty employees may be covered under state law prohibiting age discrimination.

**Q. *Is there a federal agency responsible for enforcing the ADEA?***

**A.** Yes, the EEOC has enforcement authority under the ADEA.

**Q. *What is Title I of the Americans with Disabilities Act?***

**A.** The ADA (42 U.S.C. Sections 12101–12118) prohibits discrimination in employment against persons with disabilities, both physical and mental.

**Q. *What types of employers are regulated under the ADA?***

**A.** Public and private sector employers employing at least fifteen employees are covered. Unions and employment agencies are also regulated by the ADA. It should be remembered, however, that employers not covered under the ADA may be subject to regulation under state law prohibiting disability discrimination.

**Q. *Is there a federal agency responsible for enforcing the ADA?***

**A.** Yes, the EEOC has enforcement authority under the ADA.

**Q. *What is the Rehabilitation Act?***

**A.** The Rehab Act (29 U.S.C. Sections 706(8), 791, 793–794a) prohibits discrimination in employment against persons with disabilities, both physical and mental.

**Q. *How is the Rehabilitation Act different from Title I of the Americans with Disabilities Act?***

**A.** The main difference between these two statutes is in the types of employers to which

# Required Workplace Posters

Practically all federal and most state employment laws have some notice-posting requirement. Such notices must be posted conspicuously and in enough places so employees can see them as they enter and exit the workplace. In order to ensure that they will remain prominently posted as required, and not get frayed, defaced, or lost, it is a good idea to hang them in glass or clear plastic cases, near time clocks and at the various entrances to the facility.

The federal government has consolidated some of its posters to simplify posting problems. Some of the official posters can be obtained in Spanish as well as English, but regulations don't require other than the English-language poster.

## Posters Required

| Statute | Coverage | Basic Requirements | Official Form |
|---|---|---|---|
| Age Discrimination in Employment Act | Employers engaged in interstate commerce with 20 or more employees | Prohibits employment discrimination on the basis of age 40 or over | "Consolidated EEO Poster" (FEP 441)* |
| Americans with Disabilities Act | Employers with 15 or more employees engaged in interstate commerce; also employment agencies | Prohibits employment discrimination on basis of disability | "Consolidated EEO Poster" (FEP 441) |
| Civil Rights Act of 1964 (Title VII) | Employers engaged in interstate commerce with 15 or more employees | Prohibits employment discrimination on the basis of race, color, religion, sex, or national origin | "Consolidated EEO Poster" (FEP 441) |
| Davis-Bacon Act | Employers with public construction contracts for $2,000 or more | Requires payment of prevailing minimum wage in area | "Notice to Employees" (WH 99) |
| Employee Polygraph Protection Act | All employers engaged in commerce or in production of goods for commerce | Bars lie detector tests to screen job applicants; limits employers' use of lie detector tests for current employees | "Notice of Protection" (PM 201, generally sent to employers by the Federal Employment Standards Administration; FEP 441) |
| Equal Pay Act of 1963 | Employers engaged in interstate commerce | Requires equal pay for substantially equal work regardless of sex | "Consolidated EEO Poster" (FEP 441) |
| Executive Order 11246 as amended | Federal government contractors/subcontractors; also, contractors under federally assisted construction contracts | Prohibits employment discrimination on the basis of race, color, religion, sex, or national origin | "Consolidated EEO Poster" (FEP 441) |

* FEP 441, advising employees of their rights under several different laws, is available from: U.S. EEOC, Publishing and Information, 1-800-669-3362.

SOURCE: Business & Legal Reports, Inc. (SNA)

## THE MEANING OF THE TERM "DISABILITY"

*Both the ADA and the Rehabilitation Act protect individuals with disabilities. The definition of the term "disability" is the same for both laws. An individual with a disability is one who:*

1. *has a physical or mental impairment that substantially limits a major life activity; or*

2. *has a record of having such a physical or mental impairment; or*

3. *is regarded as having such an impairment.*

*The term is defined broadly to include any physiologically based impairment or any mental or psychological impairment, but it does not include mere physical characteristics or cultural, economic, or environmental impairment. For example, an individual with dyslexia has a disability but an individual who is illiterate does not; an individual who is a dwarf has a disability but a person who is short does not.*

*The impairment must cause a substantial limitation to a major life activity. Temporary conditions, such as a broken leg or a cold, would not be considered substantial limitations.*

*The second meaning of the term includes individuals who no longer have a disability but have a record of a disability, such as a person who successfully recovered from tuberculosis, or an individual who was diagnosed as having cancer but in fact did not have or no longer has cancer.*

*The third meaning of the term includes individuals who have a condition that does not substantially limit their activity but which the employer believes substantially limits their activity. For example, a worker who has high blood pressure is denied a promotion because the employer believes that the stress of the job would cause a heart attack.*

the statute applies. Whereas the ADA applies to employers who employ at least fifteen employees, the Rehabilitation Act applies to employers who are contractors or subcontractors of the federal government or who receive federal funds.

**Q. Is there a federal agency responsible for enforcing the Rehabilitation Act?**

**A.** Yes. The Office of Federal Contract Compliance, Department of Labor, enforces the Rehabilitation Act.

## Q. What is the National Labor Relations Act?

**A.** The NLRA, also called the Wagner Act and the Labor-Management Relations Act (29 U.S.C. Sections 141–197), deals with the role of unions in the workplace and prohibits discrimination in employment based on union activity.

## Q. What types of employers are covered under the NLRA?

**A.** The coverage of the NLRA is limited to private sector employers that have an impact on interstate commerce. Specifically excluded from coverage are public sector employers, railway and airline employers, and individuals who are employed as agricultural laborers. Generally, whether or not an employer has an impact on interstate commerce is determined according to the dollar volume of business generated by the company. For example, a retail or service establishment with annual gross receipts of at least $500,000 is covered. Manufacturing companies that ship at least $50,000 worth of goods across state lines, or that purchase at least $50,000 worth of goods from out of state, are covered. The conduct of labor unions is also regulated under the NLRA. It should be remembered, however, that an employer that is not covered under the NLRA may be covered by a state law that provides similar protections and regulations regarding unions in the workplace.

## Q. Is there a federal agency responsible for enforcing the NLRA?

**A.** Yes, the National Labor Relations Board is responsible for enforcement of the NLRA.

## Q. What is the Fair Labor Standards Act?

**A.** The FLSA (29 U.S.C. Sections 201–219) establishes minimum wage and overtime standards for employees and regulates the employment of children.

## Q. What types of employers are covered under the FLSA?

**A.** As a general rule, a private sector employer is covered by the FLSA if at least two employees are engaged in interstate commerce activities and if the annual volume of business is at least $500,000. Hospitals, educational institutions, and public sector employers are also covered. Moreover, individual employees who are engaged in interstate commerce activities are covered by the FLSA even if their employer does not gross $500,000 a year. It should be remembered that employers not covered by federal law may be covered by a state law regulating minimum wages, overtime, and child labor.

## Q. Is there a federal agency responsible for enforcing the FLSA?

**A.** Yes, the Wage-Hour Division, Department of Labor, is responsible for enforcing and administering the FLSA.

## THE HIRING PROCESS

There are several stages involved in the hiring of employees: solicitation and review of applications, interview of candidates, and selection of a candidate for hiring. The law impacts on each of these stages.

Federal antidiscrimination laws prohibit discrimination in employment, including the hiring process, based on race, color, religion, national origin, sex, age, disability, and union affiliation. At the state level, most states have laws duplicating the prohibitions contained in federal law. Moreover, many state laws forbid discrimination based on other types of classifications as well. For example, Wisconsin prohibits discrimination based on arrest and conviction records, sexual orientation, marital status, and the use of lawful products off employer premises during nonwork hours.

There are, in addition, some federal and state laws that regulate the use of certain types

# DETERMINING WHEN INDIVIDUAL EMPLOYEES ARE ENGAGED IN INTERSTATE COMMERCE

*The Wage and Hour Division of the Department of Labor has identified five general categories of employees who are considered to be engaged in interstate commerce for purpose of coverage under the FLSA.*

1. *Employees participating in the actual movement of commerce. For example, employees employed in the telephone, telegraph, television, transportation, banking, and insurance industries.*

2. *Employees doing work related to the instrumentalities of commerce. For example, employees who maintain and repair roads, bridges or telephone lines; or employees who work at warehouses, airports, or bus stations.*

3. *Employees who regularly cross state lines in the performance of their duties. For example, traveling salespersons or traveling service technicians.*

4. *Employees who produce or work on goods for commerce. For example, assembly workers in an auto plant, coal miners, shipping department employees, or clerical and administrative workers who do the support work necessary to produce goods for commerce.*

5. *Employees who are employed in a closely related process or occupation essential to producing goods for commerce. For example, employees who build tool and die machines used by auto plants.*

*As can be seen, the reach of FLSA coverage is extremely broad.*

of tests and screening devices in the hiring process. Also, state common law of torts imposes a duty on employers not to unnecessarily invade employees' privacy.

Finally, public sector employers are subject to additional restrictions imposed by the U.S. Constitution and civil service laws. Because of the constitutional guarantee to citizens of the right to freedom of association, government employers cannot discriminate in hiring based on political affiliation (except for high level, policy-making jobs). Civil service laws generally provide that hiring decisions be based on the "merit" of the applicant, which is usually determined by administering competitive examinations.

The ways in which these laws impact on the hiring process will be developed more fully in the following series of questions and answers.

**Q. What are the elements of a good job advertisement?**

**A.** The main idea is to avoid discrimination while at the same time targeting qualified candidates. Ads should avoid words suggesting a preferred race, sex, religion, national origin, or age. For example, use of the term "recent

# EMPLOYMENT OF DOMESTIC WORKERS

*The first issue to be determined when considering the employment of domestic workers is whether the individuals are employees or independent contractors. (See the question discussing the differences between employees and independent contractors on page 395). For example, if you contract with a landscaping company to mow your lawn and maintain the flower beds, the employees that the company sends out to perform the work are not your employees. If, however, you employ a cook/housekeeper whose work you control, then the worker is your employee.*

*The contractual relationship between an individual and an independent contractor is not governed by employment laws. However, if a domestic worker is an employee, then that relationship is regulated by certain federal employment laws. Examples of domestic workers who may be considered employees are: in-home child care workers, cooks, housekeepers, and babysitters.*

*You must make quarterly social security payments to the IRS for every domestic employee who earns more than $50 per calendar quarter. (At press time Congress was debating changes in these figures, so you should consult with your financial adviser if you are considering employing a domestic employee.) You must also pay federal unemployment taxes for every domestic employee who earns more than $1000 per calendar quarter. Consult your accountant for rules regarding withholding taxes from an employee's pay.*

*The FLSA applies to domestic employees, other than babysitters, who earn more than $50 during a calendar quarter and work for one or more employers for more than eight hours in any workweek. Any employee who meets this definition must be paid the federal minimum wage, and overtime for hours worked in excess of 40 during any one workweek for a single employer. Babysitters are generally covered by the FLSA if they work more than 20 hours per work as babysitters. If a domestic employee resides in your house, then the overtime provisions of the FLSA do not apply, but the minimum wage requirements do. See page 415 for federal laws governing the employment of aliens.*

### YOU NEED A LICENSE FOR THESE JOBS

*State rules limit some jobs to people who have licenses. Depending on the state, these might include cosmetologists, barbers, electricians, heating/air conditioning technicians, engineers, nurses, builders, lawyers, accountants, dental hygienists, and physicians. When considering such a career, contact your state licensing authorities to see what requirements apply.*

college grad," instead of "college degree required," could indicate a preference for young people and discourage older qualified applicants from applying. Or, using the term "salesman" instead of "salesperson" suggests only men should apply. The phrase "An Equal Opportunity Employer" in an ad means the employer will judge all applicants based on their qualifications for the job, without regard to race, sex, religion, national origin, age, or disability.

#### Q. Can an employer set basic job requirements and work standards?

**A.** Yes, as long as they do not discriminate. Qualifications listed for a job should be necessary for the performance of the job. Even neutral job requirements can cause discrimination. For example, requiring a college degree for a job on a factory assembly line would disproportionately screen out minority applicants vis-à-vis white applicants, since disproportionately fewer minority students attend college than white students. The minority applicants would be screened out based not on their ability to do the job but based on a factor (college education) unrelated to being a good assembly line worker.

#### Q. What are some other examples of neutral job requirements that can cause discrimination?

**A.** Refusing to hire single custodial parents may discriminate against women, since women are more likely to have physical custody of their children. Requiring applicants to speak fluent English for a job that does not require communication skills may discriminate against applicants whose nation of origin is not the United States. Height and weight standards can discriminate based on sex and national origin. Where neutral requirements have a discriminatory effect, the employer must be able to show that the requirements are related to job performance. Thus, requirements for job-related experience and specific job-related skills are usually valid.

#### Q. How does the ADA affect an employer's ability to establish basic job requirements and work standards?

**A.** Job requirements and work standards that would screen out an individual based on his or her disability must be job-related and consistent with business necessity. Under the ADA, in order to be job-related, a job requirement must be related to the essential functions of the job and not merely an incidental aspect of job performance. For example, a job description for a receptionist position states that typing skills are required; however, the employer has never required the receptionist to type. This requirement, therefore, is not an essential function of the job, and requiring typing skills could have the effect of screening out an individual with only one arm or an individual who is a paraplegic.

**Q. How can an employer identify the essential functions of a job?**

**A.** The EEOC regulations list several factors to consider in determining the essential functions of a job:

1. The position exists to perform the function; for example, a secretarial position exists to type letters and documents;

2. There are a limited number of other employees available to perform the function; for example even though the receptionist's main duty is not typing, there is only one secretarial employee at the company and when he is sick or on vacation the receptionist fills in for him;

3. The amount of time spent performing the function; for example, the secretary spends 75% of his time typing documents;

4. The effect of not requiring the person in this job to be able to perform the function; for example a firefighter may be called upon to carry a heavy person from a burning building only rarely, but her failure to be able to perform this function could cost a life;

5. The work experience of employees who have previously performed the job.

**Q. If an individual with a disability cannot perform an essential function of the job, can the employer refuse to hire him?**

**A.** Not necessarily. The question is whether the inability to perform the essential function of the job is due to lack of qualifications or due to the disability. If the employer is hiring for a secretarial position and the applicant cannot type, then the employer could refuse to hire her even though she suffered from epilepsy. (See sidebar discussion of "The Protected Class Under the ADA.")

If, however, the applicant possesses typing skills, then the question becomes whether, with a reasonable accommodation, she would be able to perform the essential function of the job. For example, an applicant for a secretarial position who is blind may be unable to use the word processor. However, if she is provided with a braille keyboard she can use the word processor and would thus be able to perform the essential function of the job.

**Q. How does an employer know if an applicant or employee needs an accommodation?**

**A.** Generally speaking, it is the responsibility of the applicant or employee to inform the employer of his need for an accommodation. The ADA does not require the employer to provide an accommodation if it is unaware of the need for one.

Also, the employer may ask for documentation of the need for an accommodation where the disability is not an obvious one.

---

## THE PROTECTED CLASS UNDER THE ADA

*The ADA protects "qualified individuals with a disability" from discrimination in employment. An individual with a disability is qualified if he "satisfies the requisite skill, experience, education and other job-related requirements." For example, in deciding whether a person with epilepsy is qualified to be a teacher, one would determine if she had a teaching certificate or a college degree in education. If not, then she is not qualified and is not a member of the protected class under the ADA.*

# EXAMPLES OF REASONABLE ACCOMMODATIONS

*The following are examples of the types of actions an employer may be required to take to provide a reasonable accommodation:*

- *making existing facilities readily accessible;*
- *job restructuring;*
- *part-time or modified work schedules;*
- *modifying equipment;*
- *providing readers or interpreters.*

*Employers are not required to provide equipment or devices primarily for personal use, such as corrective glasses, hearing aids, or wheelchairs.*

*Whether a particular employer is required to provide a specific accommodation will depend on whether providing it will cause undue hardship.*

**Q. Is an employer required to provide any accommodation necessary for the otherwise qualified individual with a disability to perform the job?**

**A.** No. The ADA only requires the employer to provide reasonable accommodations which do not cause undue hardship. The law specifically lists what factors should be considered in determining undue hardship:

1. the nature and cost of the accommodation needed;

2. the overall financial resources of the facility involved; the number of persons employed at the facility; the effect on expenses and resources of the facility; the impact on the operation of the facility;

3. the overall financial resources of the employer as a whole; the overall size of the business;

4. the type of operation of the employer, including the composition, structure and function of the workforce and the rela-

tionship of the facility in question to the employer as a whole.

Whether or not an accommodation causes an undue hardship is determined on a case-by-case basis.

**Q. Is it ever appropriate to indicate a preference for applicants of a specific sex or age?**

**A.** Rarely. Antidiscrimination laws require employers to consider applicants as individuals, not based on stereotypical assumptions. If a factory job requires a worker to lift forty pounds on a regular basis, an employer cannot express a preference for young male applicants based on the stereotyped notion that men are strong and older people and women are weak. Some women and older people can lift forty pounds, just as some young men cannot. Rather, the employer's job ad should state that the job requires "regularly lifting forty pounds."

In some rare circumstances, however, it is an objective fact that individuals who are mem-

**RELIGIOUS INSTITUTIONS EXPRESSING A PREFERENCE FOR EMPLOYEES OF A PARTICULAR RELIGION**

*Title VII expressly allows religious corporations and sectarian educational institutions to hire applicants of a particular religion. For example, a Catholic grade school could decide to hire a teacher because he is a Catholic rather than hire an applicant who is a Protestant. This exemption applies only to religion, however. The school may not discriminate in hiring teachers based on race, color, sex, national origin, age, or disability.*

bers of a protected class cannot perform the job in question. For example, a filmmaker may hire only men for male roles, or a kosher deli may hire only Jewish people as butchers. In both of these examples, sex and religion are bona fide occupational qualifications (BFOQ). Both Title VII and the ADEA allow employers to limit a job to applicants of a specific group where the employer can prove that sex, religion, national origin, or age is a BFOQ for the job in question. Race and color, however, can never qualify as a BFOQ.

### Q. Some employers find applicants through word-of-mouth, by talking to their current employees. Is anything wrong with this?

**A.** That depends on the make-up of the work force. Use of the "old boy" network generally results in applications mainly from other old boys. Where the workers are mainly white people, news about the job vacancy will be limited to their circle of acquaintances, who may be mostly white people as well. This has the effect of closing out minority applicants. An employer can avoid problems by disseminating news of job openings as widely as possible in order to reach a broad pool of applicants. Placing ads in newspapers and magazines with a widespread circulation base, and using employ-

ment agencies, can help in reaching a variety of qualified applicants.

### Q. What should employers be aware of in conducting job interviews?

**A.** By their very nature, job interviews are subjective experiences. Employers cannot help but form an assortment of impressions in judging an applicant's ambition, motivation, creativity, dependability, and responsibility. Realizing the inherently subjective nature of the process, employers should strive to make an interview as objective (fact-based) as possible. Concentrating on objective information helps to avoid decisions made on conscious or subconscious prejudice and focuses the hiring process on the issue of an individual's qualifications and employment experience.

Employers should also attempt to make job interviews as uniform as possible. The same set of questions should be addressed to all applicants for the same position. This allows for a better basis for comparison among applicants. It can also prevent discrimination in the content of a job interview. For example, asking one applicant "do you type" but not asking another applicant the same question, could indicate discriminatory stereotyping if the applicant who is asked the question is a woman.

# Preemployment Inquiries: Applicant Screening

Federal law requires employers to conduct the applicant screening and hiring process in a nondiscriminatory manner. Preemployment inquiries (on application forms, by telephone, in interviews) can be attacked if they screen out women or minorities. As a result, the Equal Employment Opportunity Commission (EEOC) cautions that inquiries concerning an applicant's race, color, religion, or national origin, either directly or indirectly, may be regarded as evidence of discrimination.

Exceptions. Preemployment inquiries are permissible if required by local, state, or federal law. Also excepted are those infrequent instances where religion and national origin are bona fide occupational qualifications (BFOQs), or where the employer can prove that the inquiry is justified by business necessity that is job-related.

# What can you ask?

The following chart is based on guidelines and other directives issued by the various antidiscrimination agencies. It summarizes the types of questions often asked of applicants and offers acceptable alternatives.

| Category | Question | Acceptable Alternative |
| --- | --- | --- |
| Age | How old are you? What is your date of birth? These questions may be asked if they are accompanied by a statement that federal and state law prohibits age discrimination. However, age-related questions may create the wrong impression and should be avoided unless there is a valid age-related rule in effect; e.g., bona fide apprenticeship programs are not subject to age discrimination prohibitions. | Do you meet the state minimum age requirement for work? Are you over 18? 16? |
| Arrests and convictions | Have you ever been arrested? As a general rule, this question should be avoided because it disqualifies a disproportionate number of minorities. | Have you ever been convicted of a crime? |
| Availability for work, availability for travel | Can you work Saturdays and Sundays? Do you have children? What are your child care arrangements? The first question may be interpreted as a sign of religious discrimination; the other two questions, as a sign of discrimination against women. | These are the hours of work—or— Our work sometimes requires overtime. Can you work such a schedule? Do you have any obligations that would keep you from work-related travel? |
| Birthplace, citizenship | Where were you born? | Are you legally authorized to work in the U.S.? |
| Clubs and associations | To what organizations do you belong? | Do you want to provide any additional information that relates to your ability to perform the job? |

*(Continued)*

# Preemployment Inquiries *(continued)*

| Category | Question | Acceptable Alternative |
|---|---|---|
| Disabilities | Do you have a disability? Do you have any health problems? Have you ever filed for workers' compensation? | Can you perform the essential functions of the job for which you are applying? Can you show me how you would perform those functions? |
| Economic status | Have you ever had your wages garnished? Do you own your own home? Have you ever filed for bankruptcy? Courts consider these types of questions to disproportionately disqualify women and minorities. | No questions. |
| Military service | What type of discharge did you receive? Have you served in another country's armed forces? | Are you a U.S. veteran? List experience and special education received in the military. |
| Name | Have you ever had your name changed? What is your maiden name? | Is there any additional information we need about your name to verify your employment/education record? |
| National origin | | No questions. |
| Physical characteristics, photographs | What color skin (hair, eyes) do you have? Before meeting with applicant, requesting that the applicant submit a photograph. | Only questions about height and weight are permitted if the characteristics are job related. No photographs until after hire. |
| Relatives | Who is the relative to be notified in case of emergency? | Is there someone we should notify in case of emergency? (best asked after hire) Do you have any relatives who work for this company? |
| Religion | | No questions. |
| Union membership | | No questions. |

SOURCE: Business & Legal Reports, Inc. (SNA)

## Q. *Does federal law prohibit any specific questions?*

A. Yes. The ADA prohibits an employer from asking an applicant whether he or she has a disability or inquiring into the nature or severity of a disability (though the employer may ask questions about the applicant's ability to do the job). The National Labor Relations Act (NLRA) prohibits employers from questioning employees about union membership or activities. Neither Title VII nor the Age Discrimination in Employment Act (ADEA) prohibit any specific questions. An employer, however, should not ask questions that may imply discrimination. Moreover, some state laws, such as those in West Virginia, expressly prohibit certain types of preemployment questions, such as questions about marital status or number of dependents.

## BONA FIDE OCCUPATIONAL QUALIFICATIONS

*Title VII allows an employer to make a hiring decision based on sex, religion, or national origin if the employer can prove that being a particular sex, religion, or national origin is a bona fide occupational qualification (BFOQ) for the job in question. The ADEA also allows the employer to make a hiring decision based on age if the employer can prove age is a BFOQ.*

*The employer must prove that his hiring decision falls within the very narrow limits allowed by the BFOQ defense. The employer must show both:*

1. *that all persons of the excluded class would be unable to perform the requirements of the job; and*
2. *the requirements of the job directly relate to the essence of the employer's business.*

*The evidence that the employer presents must be objective and not based on stereotyped beliefs about persons in the protected class.*

*Years ago some airlines tried to defend their decision not to hire men as flight attendants on the basis that males were unable to provide reassurance to anxious passengers or give courteous, personalized service. The court held that even if this were true, the ability to reassure and give courteous service did not relate to the essence of the employer's business, which was the safe transport of passengers.*

*The BFOQ defense applies in very limited circumstances, such as for actors or fashion models.*

### Q. What types of questions may imply discrimination?

A. Direct questions relating to an applicant's age, family background or religious affiliation may indicate discrimination. Also questions or comments based on stereotyped notions may also imply discrimination.

Generally speaking, interview questions should relate to the requirements of the job, the applicant's qualifications, work experience and history. Even when the information sought is related to the job, the interviewer must be careful that the way the question is asked does not imply discrimination. For example, an employer trying to determine whether a female applicant is going to stay with the company for the next few years should not ask, "Do you plan to get married?" or "Do you plan to have children?" or "What kind of birth control do you

## HOW EMPLOYERS CAN HIRE WITHOUT DISCRIMINATION

*It helps to use a standard application form that avoids irrelevant questions. Avoid asking about age, height, weight, marital status, education or arrest record unless they relate to the job. For example, questions about height and weight may reject women or members of some ethnic groups who are usually smaller. Asking about marital status may suggest sex discrimination. Asking about disabilities is prohibited.*

*Employers and prospective employees both benefit when job openings are clearly defined. Employers should prepare a detailed job description for each position, specifying what the work is and what qualifications the employer requires. If both sides come to the interview with a clear idea of what the job involves, the interview is more likely to focus on the qualifications essential for doing the job or that have predicted successful job performance.*

## GOVERNMENT CONTRACTORS AND HIRING POLICIES

*Executive Order 11246 imposes certain obligations on employers with a federal contract or subcontract. If a contract is worth at least $10,000, the employer is forbidden to discriminate in employment based on race, color, religion, sex, or national origin. The nondiscrimination requirement is essentially the same as that imposed under Title VII. If a contract is worth at least $50,000 and the contractor employs at least fifty employees, the employer must also develop and utilize an affirmative action plan.*

*The Rehabilitation Act prohibits federal contractors and subcontractors with contracts in excess of $2,500 from discriminating against individuals with disabilities and requires them to take affirmative action to employ individuals with disabilities.*

*The development and implementation of affirmative action plans will be discussed later in this chapter.*

use?" More direct, job-related questions seeking the same information might be:

- We are looking for employees who will make a commitment to the company. Is there any reason you might not stay with us for the next few years?

- What are your career objectives?
- Where do you see yourself in five years?

In the same way, suppose an employer is trying to determine a female job candidate's commitment to living in a particular area of the country. Then it is better to ask, "Do you intend

**DRUG TESTING REQUIREMENTS FOR CERTAIN OCCUPATIONS**

*The U.S. Department of Transportation (DOT) has issued regulations requiring drug testing of railroad employees and motor carriers who operate commercial motor vehicles in interstate commerce. Testing occurs in certain circumstances, such as preemployment, periodically and for reasonable cause. The U.S. Federal Aviation Administration (FAA) has also issued drug testing regulations, similar to those issued by the DOT, covering airline flight personnel. The Drug-Free Workplace Act, while not requiring drug testing, does require all federal contractors with contracts worth at least $25,000 or more, to establish a drug-free awareness program and communicate the program to all its employees. Some states also impose drug testing requirements for certain jobs— mainly jobs in the transportation industry.*

to stay in the area?" rather than "Is your husband's employer likely to transfer him?"

If attendance is the issue, questions like, "Does your husband expect you to be home to cook dinner?" or "What will you do if your children get sick?" are indirect and inefficient. It would be more direct to ask, "How was your attendance record with your prior employer?"

**Q. What is "need-to-know," and how does it apply to job interviews?**

**A.** Whether a question will be viewed as inappropriate often depends on whether there is an objective, job-related reason why the employer wants its applicants to answer it. Questions that would not run afoul of the antidiscrimination laws may still create problems. Some state tort law protects individuals from unwarranted invasions of personal privacy. Offensive inquiries into an applicant's personal life, unrelated to the requirements of the job, may subject an employer to liability for invasion of privacy.

Sometimes employers clearly must have certain information. For example, employers do need to make their job offers dependent on candidates' production of proper documentation of their citizenship or work authorization. However, asking about national origin may be viewed as discriminatory. Similarly, whether an applicant has ever been convicted of a crime may substantially affect the applicant's fitness for a specific job. The key to determining the appropriateness of an interview question is whether there is a legitimate business reason to inquire into the subject.

**Q. What should an applicant do if the interviewer does ask questions that seem inappropriate or discriminatory?**

**A.** The tactful applicant might answer by providing the information the interviewer "really wants to know." For example, "Oh— you're wondering whether I'll be able to work long hours. I can assure you that I will. My current boss can confirm that."

**Q. What should an employer consider in making hiring decisions?**

**A.** If the interview process was as uniform and impartial as possible, and if only job-related questions were asked, the employer should be

## DRUG TESTING AND THE CONSTITUTION

*The Fourth Amendment of the U.S. Constitution prohibits the government from engaging in unreasonable searches and seizures. This restriction acts as a limit on a public sector employer's ability to use a drug test on its employees. Generally speaking, courts have been reluctant to allow public sector employers to engage in random drug tests; they generally require the employer to show some reasonable suspicion of drug use, or some compelling evidence showing that public safety would be jeopardized if the employee used drugs.*

able to follow a checklist. This should allow the employer to rate applicants in an organized and consistent manner based on their respective qualifications for the job.

**Q. May an employer use a lie detector to find out if a job applicant or an employee is honest?**

**A.** The Employee Polygraph Protection Act (EPPA) prohibits employers from requiring employees or applicants to take a polygraph test. This federal law covers all private sector employers with at least two employees engaged in interstate commerce activities and an annual volume of business of at least $500,000. It does not apply to any public sector employer.

The statute provides an exception to the use of a polygraph in two situations. An employer is allowed to use a polygraph in connection with an ongoing investigation into theft. Employers engaged in providing security services can administer a polygraph to certain applicants, as can employers engaged in the manufacture of controlled substances.

Most states also have state laws that either prohibit or regulate the use of polygraph tests in employment. A few states, such as Massachusetts and Minnesota, prohibit all tests and devices purporting to determine honesty.

**Q. May an employer run a background check on an applicant?**

**A.** Background checks may be necessary for certain jobs. These include jobs involving security or trade secrets. Checks should be made fairly and without bias. They should concern only issues relating to performance of the specific job. Checks that unnecessarily pry into private information or which employ unreasonable methods of data gathering may subject an employer to tort liability.

**Q. May an employer run a credit check on an applicant?**

**A.** A credit check should be used only where the information is necessary for job-related purposes. Court cases under Title VII have held that requiring good credit as a condition of employment can have a discriminatory result, since disproportionately more non-whites than whites live below the poverty level. Even if a credit check is necessary for the job in question, the Fair Credit Reporting Act (a federal law) requires employers to notify applicants if they are not hired due to the information contained in a credit report. Moreover, some state laws, such as in Maine and New York, require employers to notify applicants when a consumer credit report is requested. See the "Consumer Credit" chapter for more details on credit reporting, page 255.

### Q. May an employer require applicants to undergo a physical examination?

**A.** Generally speaking, no. The ADA prohibits employers from requiring preemployment physical examinations. After offering an applicant a job, however, an employer may require the applicant to successfully undergo a physical exam under certain conditions:

1. all employees must be required to take a physical exam;

2. information obtained from the exam must be maintained in a separate medical file and kept confidential; and

3. the employer cannot use the information to discriminate against the employee because of a disability.

### Q. May an employer require applicants or employees to undergo drug screening tests?

**A.** There is no federal law which prohibits the use of drug screening tests. Several states, however, have placed certain restrictions on the use of drug testing. Iowa and Rhode Island, for example, require employers to have probable cause before they can test employees. Other states, such as Minnesota and North Carolina, have established guidelines that must be followed in administering drug tests.

Moreover, the method used by an employer in administering a drug test (such as direct observation of urination) could be considered outrageous and make the employer liable under tort law for invasion of privacy or intentional infliction of emotional distress.

### Q. May an employer use other types of tests (such as a skills test or an intelligence test) to screen applicants?

**A.** Yes, but they should be job-related. A test may have an illegal discriminatory result on a protected class, even if it seems fair. This may cause an employer to deny jobs to an unusually high number of minorities. For exam-

**THE AMERICANS WITH DISABILITIES ACT (ADA) AND THE ADMINISTRATION OF EMPLOYMENT TESTS**

*In administering tests, employers must be careful to ensure that the manner in which the test is administered does not screen out applicants based on a disability. Tests should be administered in a manner that accurately reflects the applicant's job-related skills rather than reflecting an applicant's disability. For example, an applicant with dyslexia or with a visual disability might fail a written test because he could not properly see the material and not because of a lack of knowledge. In such a circumstance, the employer may be required to provide a reader to help the applicant read the test instructions and materials. Similarly, oral tests may screen out applicants with a hearing disability. Usually, it is the responsibility of the applicant to inform the employer that an alternative method for administering the test is needed.*

ple, a test of English language skills might disqualify an unusual number of persons for whom English is a "second language." Unless the job requires English, the test may be illegal.

Extensive federal regulations govern the use of employment tests. A test has a discriminatory impact if the pass rate for a protected class is less than 80 percent of the pass rate for white men. If 50 percent of the white males pass the test, then 40 percent or more of black males must pass. If the pass rate is less than 80 percent, the test is considered discriminatory under Title VII unless the employer can prove that the test is directly related in a significant way to successful job performance. If the test is job-related, then the employer is allowed to use it.

### Q. Are there laws that govern the hiring of workers under eighteen years of age?

**A.** Yes. The Fair Labor Standards Act (FLSA) regulates the employment of minors. With few exceptions (such as newspaper delivery) children under fourteen years of age may not be employed. Children under the age of sixteen may only work in nonhazardous jobs and their hours of work are limited. During the school term, work hours are limited to a maximum of three hours a day and eighteen hours a week. Outside the school term, they may work up to eight hours a day and forty hours a week. In either case, children under sixteen years old may work only from seven o'clock a.m. to seven o'clock p.m. (nine o'clock p.m. in the summer). Workers who are sixteen and seventeen years old are not limited in the amount of hours of work, but are prohibited from working in hazardous jobs.

Many states have their own rules for youth employment. An employer must follow these if they are more restrictive than federal law. For example, many states require all minors to get work permits from school authorities.

### Q. Are there laws that govern the hiring of alien workers?

**A.** Yes. The Immigration Reform and Control Act (IRCA) prohibits all employers from hiring unauthorized alien workers. As part of the hiring process, employers must complete an eligibility form (Form I9) for each new employee. The purpose of this form is to ensure that the employer has verified the legal eligibility of the applicant to be employed in this country. Employers who hire unauthorized aliens are subject to fines and imprisonment.

Compliance or noncompliance with this law does not affect in any way the immigration or alien status of the employee or applicant. Whether or not an individual immigrant is legally in this country and is entitled to work is determined under other federal laws regulating immigration into the United States. The employment-related provisions of the Immigration Reform and Control Act are aimed solely at what steps an *employer* must take to ensure that it hires only those individuals eligible to work in the United States.

### HOW TO VERIFY THE EMPLOYMENT ELIGIBILITY OF AN APPLICANT

*The following documents are considered acceptable verification of authorization to work in the U.S.: a U.S. passport; a birth certificate showing birth in the U.S.; a naturalization certificate; a valid foreign passport with an endorsement authorizing employment in the U.S.; a resident alien card with photograph and authorization for employment in the U.S.; or a Social Security card and driver's license with photograph.*

**Q. Must an employer verify the employment status of current workers?**

**A.** The Immigration Reform and Control Act applies only to employees hired after November 6, 1986. An employer is not required to verify the employment eligibility of any workers hired before that date. However, if the employer has reason to believe that a worker hired before November 6, 1986, is an unauthorized alien, then the employer would be subject to penalties under the law if it did not verify the worker's status and, if the employee was not authorized to work, fire that worker.

## DISCRIMINATION IN THE WORKPLACE

**Q. Besides hiring, what other aspects of the employment relationship are regulated by the antidiscrimination laws?**

**A.** The laws regulate all aspects of work, including hiring, firing, promotions, job duties, wages, benefits, and reviews. Generally speaking, the laws do not require an employer to provide specific benefits or to institute job review procedures or to draw up job descriptions. Rather, the employer is allowed to establish its own policies so long as they are applied to all employees in a nondiscriminatory manner and so long as the policies do not have the effect of discriminating against a protected class.

**Q. What are the major federal antidiscrimination laws?**

**A.** Title VII prohibits discrimination based on race, sex, color, national origin or religion. The ADEA prohibits discrimination based on age (if over forty). Title I of the ADA prohibits discrimination based on disability.

Almost every state has antidiscrimination laws that mirror the protections found under

---

### SEXUAL ORIENTATION DISCRIMINATION

*The meaning of the term "sex" discrimination as used in Title VII refers to gender and does not include discrimination based on sexual orientation. There are some states, however, such as California, Hawaii, and Wisconsin, and some cities, such as Chicago, whose antidiscrimination laws prohibit discrimination based on sexual orientation.*

---

### SENIORITY SYSTEMS AND ANTI-DISCRIMINATION LAWS

*Bona fide seniority systems are immune from attack under Title VII and the ADEA. A seniority system is bona fide so long as it was not established for the purpose of discriminating against a protected class and is applied equally to all employees covered by the system.*

*A seniority system that has an adverse impact is considered a bona fide system. Thus, decisions as to who is laid off during a downturn in business based on who has the least seniority are legal, even though all the most recent hires (and therefore all the employees laid off) are female.*

**TIME LIMITS UNDER TITLE VII AND THE ADA**

*If you have been discriminated against, you must file a charge with the EEOC within 180 days from the date of the discriminatory act. There are regional offices of the EEOC in most major cities in the U.S. There is an exception to this time limit if the discrimination occurred in a state that has a state law prohibiting discrimination. In that case you must first file a charge with the state agency responsible for enforcing the state law. You must give the state agency at least sixty days to investigate your complaint. After sixty days you can then file a charge with the EEOC, but the charge must be filed within 300 days from the date the discrimination occurred or within thirty days after the state agency terminates its proceedings, whichever occurs first.*

*When the EEOC completes its investigation of the charge, it sends a letter to the person who filed the charge. The letter states whether the EEOC found reasonable cause to believe the law was violated and informs the charging party that he or she has ninety days within which to file a lawsuit in court. This letter is called a "right to sue" letter.*

federal law. Some states also have more expansive protection than federal law, for example, prohibiting discrimination based on marital status, sexual orientation, or weight.

### Q. How do I know if an action is discriminatory in violation of the law?

**A.** First, not all discriminatory actions are forbidden by law. The law only prohibits discrimination when it is based on a person's protected status—race, color, religion, national origin, sex, age, or disability under federal law.

Thus, if an employer makes a decision because of an employee's race, that employer has engaged in prohibited discrimination. Paying a worker lower wages than other employees because that worker is a black African-American violates Title VII. But paying a worker lower wages than other employees because that worker is performing different kinds of job

duties does not violate Title VII. The question is whether the reason for the difference in treatment is based on the employee's protected status. Different treatment based on protected status is called intentional discrimination or disparate treatment.

Title VII also prohibits conduct that has the effect of discriminating against individuals in a protected class even if the employer's reason for the different treatment is not based on protected class. For example, an employer may decide to hire only applicants who do not have custody of preschool-age children. On its face the reason for the employer's hiring decision is not a protected class reason. However, the effect of this policy is to disproportionately screen out women applicants as compared to male applicants because more women are custodial parents. This policy, therefore, would have a discriminatory effect, also called adverse impact. Adverse impact discrimination is also

**DISCRIMINATION BASED ON RACE**

*Federal law forbids job discrimination because of race. Executive Order 11246 also requires that employers doing business with the federal government not discriminate because of race and take affirmative steps to hire and promote racial minorities. Most states and many local governments have laws prohibiting racial discrimination in employment. These laws protect all races, including African-Americans, Hispanics, Asians, Native Americans, and Caucasians.*

forbidden by Title VII unless the employer can prove that the policy is required by business necessity and is significantly related to the requirements of the job.

The ADA defines discrimination not only in terms of disparate treatment and adverse impact but also in terms of a refusal to provide reasonable accommodation to an otherwise qualified individual with a disability. (The section of this chapter on page 401, entitled "The Hiring Process," discusses this concept in more detail.)

**Q. What should I do if I think I have been discriminated against in violation of the law?**

**A.** It is usually a good idea to bring your complaint directly to the attention of the employer and attempt to resolve the problem on an informal basis. The employer may not be aware that there are individuals within its organization who are discriminating, or the employer may want to address your complaint and fix the problem.

If, however, you want to pursue a legal remedy, you should get expert advice and act relatively quickly. Antidiscrimination laws have strict time limits for making a claim. The federal laws require employees to file a complaint first with the EEOC before filing a lawsuit in court. In some circumstances an employee is also required to file a complaint with the state agency charged with enforcing the state antidiscrimination laws.

Lastly, if fired or not hired for discriminatory reasons, you should look for another job. Do so even if it seems that you are entitled to the former job. If you do not actively seek other work, it appears as though you are not seriously interested in employment. This can weaken your claim and may limit any award of back pay.

**Q. Do the antidiscrimination laws protect only women and minorities?**

**A.** No. The antidiscrimination laws protect all workers from employment decisions based on protected status. Thus, if an employer pays a female worker better wages than a male worker performing the same job, that employer has discriminated against the male worker based on his sex in violation of Title VII. Similarly, if an Asian-American worker who misses three days of work is suspended but a Caucasian worker who misses three days of work is fired, then the Caucasian worker has been discriminated against based on his race.

**Q. What is an Affirmative Action Plan (AAP)?**

**A.** An AAP establishes guidelines for recruiting, hiring, and promoting women and minorities in order to eliminate the present effects of past employment discrimination. An employer analyzes its current employment practices and the make-up of its workforce for any indications that women and minorities are excluded or disadvantaged. If the employer identifies some problems, it then devises new or different polices and practices aimed at solving the problems. Lastly, the employer develops goals by which it can measure its progress in correcting the problems.

**Q. Are employers required to have Affirmative Action Plans?**

**A.** Neither Title VII, the ADEA, nor the ADA require Affirmative Action Plans (AAPs). Employers that have contracts with federal, state and local governments, however, are often required to develop AAPs. Executive Order 11246 requires federal contractors with contracts exceeding $50,000 and that employ at least fifty employees to develop an AAP. Many states, such as Iowa, California, and Pennsylvania, requires employers that have state contracts to implement AAPs. Governors, mayors and other public bodies may require public sector employers to adopt AAPs.

Some employers voluntarily adopt AAPs in order to eliminate the effects of past discrimination and more effectively utilize qualified workers who in the past may have been overlooked because of their race, sex, or national origin.

**Q. If an employer gives preferential treatment to a woman or minority employee pursuant to an AAP, isn't this reverse discrimination in violation of Title VII?**

**A.** Not necessarily. The U.S. Supreme Court has held that voluntary AAPs that remedy an obvious racial or sex imbalance in traditionally segregated job categories are lawful. The question involves balancing the interest of minority employees to be free from the effect of unlawful discrimination with the employment interests of nonminority employees.

## EQUAL WAGES AND THE EQUAL PAY ACT

*The Equal Pay Act (EPA) prohibits an employer from discriminating in wages on the basis of sex, where the employees are performing substantially equivalent work. This same type of discrimination is also prohibited under Title VII. Both statutes are enforced by the EEOC but there are some differences between the two. First, the EPA applies to all employers that are subject to the FLSA (at least two workers engaged in interstate commerce and $500,000 annual volume of business), whereas Title VII covers employers with fifteen or more employees. Second, the EPA prohibits wage discrimination based only on sex, whereas Title VII prohibits wage discrimination based on race, color, religion, national origin, and sex. Lastly, an employee who brings a lawsuit under the EPA may be entitled to recover twice the amount of lost wages, whereas under Title VII the employee may recover lost wages, as well as compensatory and punitive damages. In some circumstances, the total amount of damages awarded may be greater under Title VII.*

### Q. What factors do the courts consider in deciding the validity of an AAP?

**A.** The state of the law is still developing in this area, but the courts tend to focus on four factors. First, the AAP should be designed to eliminate obvious racial or sex-based imbalances in the work force.

Second, the plan cannot "unnecessarily trammel the interests" of nonminority (white or male) workers. It should not automatically exclude nonminority employees from consideration for the job in question. The minority employee favored by the AAP should be qualified for the job; employers should avoid favoring unqualified workers.

Third, the AAP should not adopt strict quotas. It should strive toward realistic goals, taking into account turnover, layoffs, lateral transfers, new job openings, and retirements. These goals should also take into account the number of qualified minorities in the area work force. Moreover, goals should be temporary in nature, designed to achieve, not maintain, racial balance.

Fourth, courts are more likely to validate AAPs that focus on recruiting, hiring, and promotion practices, rather than plans that give special treatment in the event of a layoff. The courts are more willing to protect an incumbent employee's interests in his current job than any speculative expectations an employee might have about a job that he doesn't currently hold.

### Q. Is an employer required to pay workers the same wage when they are performing substantially the same job?

**A.** No. Differences in wages are prohibited only when the reason for the difference is the race, color, religion, national origin, sex, age, or disability of the worker. An employer is allowed to pay workers different wages based on seniority, merit, or piece rate.

### Q. What is the difference between comparable worth and equal pay for equal work?

**A.** The basic concept behind comparable worth is to compare the value of different jobs to the employer. Each job is dissected to determine the types of skills the employee uses and the amount of effort and independent judgment involved. Those jobs that require the use of the same skills, etc. are said to be comparable. Thus, an assembly line job and a secretarial job could be comparable in worth to the employer. Proponents of comparable worth argue that where two jobs are comparable, the pay for the two jobs should be the same. Proponents claim that an employer's failure to pay equally for jobs of comparable worth is sex discrimination and violates Title VII. So far, most courts have rejected this legal theory.

The concept of equal pay is based on the Equal Pay Act of 1963. This federal law requires employers to pay the same wage rate to all workers doing jobs that are substantially identical. The focus here is on the actual job being done. If the job is the same, then the employer cannot pay different wages based on sex. However, differences in pay are allowed if they are based on seniority systems, merit systems, systems based on production quantity or quality, or any factor other than sex. Several states also have equal pay laws.

### Q. Some benefits cost more to provide based on an employee's age. Must an employer provide all employees with exactly the same benefits even if it has to pay more for some of the employees?

**A.** Generally speaking, the employer cannot discriminate in providing benefits based on age. However, the ADEA recognizes that age is actuarially significant in determining the cost of providing some benefits. For example, the cost of providing life insurance for a sixty-year-old employee may be more expensive for the employer than buying the same insurance for a twenty-year-old employee. So long as the employer pays the same amount in premiums for both the sixty-year-old and the twenty-year-old, it will not violate the ADEA even though the effect of paying the same premium is that the sixty-year-old will have less coverage than the twenty-year-old. However, where age does not have an actuarially significant effect on the cost of the benefit, the employer cannot discriminate based on age. For example, an employer could not grant three weeks vacation to all employees under fifty but only give two weeks vacation to all employees over fifty.

**Q. If an employer provides health insurance for its employees, must it offer coverage to employees with disabilities?**

**A.** Yes. Under the ADA an employer cannot deny employees with disabilities equal access to health insurance coverage.

**Q. Must health insurance cover all medical expenses of an employee with a disability?**

**A.** Not necessarily. Many insurance policies have preexisting condition clauses that disallow coverage for medical conditions that an individual had before being employed by his or her current employer. Such clauses are lawful so long as they are not used as a subterfuge to evade the purposes of the ADA. Many health insurance policies also limit coverage for certain procedures or treatments to a specific number per year. For example, some provide reimbursement for only twelve psychiatric treatment sessions per year. Such limitations are generally allowed. It is not clear, however, whether an employer could offer a health insurance policy that puts a cap on the amount of reimbursement for a specific disease, for example, a $5000 reimbursement limit for cancer, as opposed to a cap on the amount of reimburse-

ment that is available for any type of medical condition, for example, a $1 million lifetime limit.

**Q. Since actuary tables show that women live longer than men, can employers provide different retirement and pension plans for each sex?**

**A.** No. The United States Supreme Court has specifically held that pension plans cannot discriminate based on sex. Thus, in defined contribution plans, an employer must contribute the same amount for both males and females. In defined benefit plans, both males and females must receive the same benefits.

## Discrimination Based on Gender

**Q. Must an employer provide health insurance coverage for pregnancy?**

**A.** The answer depends on whether the employer provides any health insurance coverage at all. The antidiscrimination laws do not require an employer to provide any benefits, including health insurance coverage. However, if an employer does provide such benefits, they must be available to all employees without regard to sex, race, color, religion, national origin, age, or disability. Thus, if an employer provides health insurance it must include coverage for pregnancy and pregnancy-related conditions.

**Q. Must the employer's health insurance pay for abortions?**

**A.** No. The Pregnancy Discrimination Act expressly provides that employers do not have to pay health insurance benefits for abortion, "except where the life of the mother would be endangered if the fetus were carried to term, or

**DISCRIMINATION BASED ON PREGNANCY**

*In 1978 Congress passed the Pregnancy Discrimination Act, amending Title VII so that the prohibition against sex discrimination includes discrimination because of pregnancy, childbirth, and related medical conditions. Thus, an employer cannot base employment decisions on the fact that a worker is pregnant. Moreover, the employer must treat pregnancy the same as it would treat any other employee medical condition.*

except where medical complications have arisen from an abortion."

**Q. May employers provide dependent health care coverage to married male workers but deny it to married women workers?**

**A.** No. Title VII prohibits all discrimination in benefits based on sex. Thus, if the employer provides health insurance benefits to the spouses of male workers, it must provide the same coverage to the spouses of female workers. Moreover, the extent of the coverage provided for dependents must be equal. For example, if all medical expenses of female workers' spouses are covered, then all medical expenses of male workers' spouses must be covered, and that would include coverage for pregnancy.

**Q. Is there any exception under Title VII allowing the employer to take sex into account in providing fringe benefits?**

**A.** No.

**Q. May an employer refuse to hire an applicant because she is pregnant, or fire a worker who becomes pregnant?**

**A.** No. The Pregnancy Discrimination Act prohibits employment discrimination based on pregnancy.

**Q. May an employer require a worker to take a leave when she becomes pregnant?**

**A.** No.

**Q. When I take time off to give birth to a child, will I get my old job back?**

**A.** Under Title VII, the employer must treat time off from work due to pregnancy the same as any other medical condition. Thus, if an employer reinstates a worker who was absent from work because he or she had the flu, the employer must reinstate a worker after childbirth.

If your employer is covered under the terms of the Family and Medical Leave Act (see sidebar, page 424), then you are entitled to your old job back regardless of how the employer treats other workers.

**Q. Is an employer required to give workers maternity/paternity leave?**

**A.** If an employer is covered under the terms of the Family and Medical Leave Act, it is required to give workers maternity and paternity leave.

Title VII requires employers who grant leaves of absence for other types of personal nondisability reasons to grant maternity leave on the same terms. If there is a medical reason for an extended leave after childbirth, then the employer must treat the leave the same as it would treat any other request for medical or disability leave.

Some states, such as Washington and Minnesota, have laws requiring employers to grant parental leave to employees.

## Q. May employers fire female workers who get married?

**A.** Title VII does not protect workers based on their marital status. However, if the employer fires only female workers who get married but not male workers, the employer has violated Title VII by engaging in disparate treatment sex discrimination—it applies an employment policy only to women.

Some states, however, such as Wisconsin, Oregon, and Illinois, have laws that expressly prohibit employment discrimination based on marital status. In those states it would violate the law to fire married workers even if the employer applied its policy to both sexes.

## Other Protections for Workers

## Q. I'm in the army reserve and must attend training camp every year. Is my employer required to give me time off?

**A.** Yes. The Veterans' Re-employment Rights Act requires all employers to grant employees who are in military service unpaid leaves of absence to perform their military obligation. Upon completion of their military duties, employees are entitled to their previous job with such seniority, status, pay and vacation as if they had not been absent. The re-employment rights granted by this law apply to all types of military service—active or reserve armed forces and National Guard—whether the employee is drafted or enlisted.

---

### TIME OFF FOR JURY DUTY

The Jury System Improvements Act is a federal law that prohibits an employer from disciplining or discharging an employee because he or she has been called to serve on a federal jury. Additionally, approximately thirty-seven states have laws that prohibit an employer from firing a worker who is called to perform jury service in the state court system.

---

### TIME TO VOTE

There are approximately thirty states, including New York, Ohio, and Maryland, that have state laws requiring employers to grant employees time off from work to vote in elections. The purpose of the laws is to ensure that those employees whose work hours do not allow for sufficient time to vote while the polls are open can take some time off from work to vote. Thus, if an employee's work shift is from three o'clock until eleven o'clock p.m., the employer would not have to give the employee time off to vote. But, if the employee worked from eight a.m. until six p.m., the employer may be required to grant time off. Most of the laws apply to all elections, whether federal, state, or local, although a few are limited to particular types of elections. Most of the laws do not allow the employer to deduct wages for the time off.

# THE FAMILY AND MEDICAL LEAVE ACT

*The Family and Medical Leave Act is a federal law requiring employers to grant up to twelve weeks of unpaid leave with right to reinstatement to employees under certain conditions. The law applies to private sector employers that employ at least fifty employees and to all public sector employers. Employees are eligible for leave if they have worked at least 1250 hours for their employer for at least one year and if there are at least fifty employees at the employees' work site or there are at least fifty employees within at least seventy-five miles of that worksite.*

*The law requires employers to grant employees up to twelve weeks of unpaid leave during any twelve-month period for any one of the following reasons:*

1. *because of the birth of a child and in order to care for the child;*
2. *because of adoption or foster care placement of a child;*
3. *because of a serious health condition that makes the employee unable to perform his duties;*
4. *in order to care for a spouse, child, or parent with a serious medical condition.*

*If the employer provides health insurance coverage for its employees, it must continue that coverage during the leave of absence with no additional charge to the employee. At the end of the leave period, the employer is required to reinstate the employee to his or her previous position or to an equivalent position.*

*Employees can enforce their entitlement to the rights granted under the FMLA by filing a lawsuit.*

**Q.** *My employer wants me to work on Saturdays, but my religion requires me to attend services on Saturdays. Can the employer fire me for refusing to work on Saturdays?*

**A.** Title VII requires employers to accommodate the religious beliefs of their employees unless the accommodation would cause an undue hardship for the business. If another employee is willing to work your shift on Saturdays, and the employer would not have to pay him more than he would pay you, the employer would be required to accommodate you. However, if the accommodation would cost the employer additional money, or would cause a disruption in the business, accommodation would probably be considered unreasonable.

## Sexual Harassment

**Q. Is sexual harassment illegal?**

**A.** Yes. The U.S. Supreme Court has held that Title VII's prohibition against sex discrimination includes sexual harassment as a type of illegal sex discrimination. Moreover some states, such as Illinois, Michigan, and North Dakota, have laws expressly prohibiting sexual harassment. Most other states interpret their laws prohibiting sex discrimination to include sexual harassment.

**Q. How is sexual harassment defined?**

**A.** The EEOC defines sexual harassment as "unwelcome sexual advances, requests for sexual favors, and other verbal or physical conduct of a sexual nature . . . when . . . submission to or rejection of such conduct is used as the basis for employment decisions . . . or such conduct has the purpose or effect of . . . creating an intimidating, hostile or offensive working environment."

Thus, sexual harassment consists of two types of prohibited conduct: 1) *quid pro quo*—where submission to harassment is used as the basis for employment decisions; and 2) hostile environment—where harassment creates an offensive working environment.

**Q. What is quid pro quo *harassment?***

**A.** This occurs when a job benefit is directly tied to an employee submitting to

---

**RACIAL, RELIGIOUS, AND ETHNIC HARASSMENT**

*Title VII also forbids words and conduct that vilify and denigrate individuals based on their race, religion, or national origin. Severe and pervasive racial, religious, and ethnic slurs can create a hostile work environment. This concept is very similar to the concept of sexual harassment caused by a hostile work environment, and the employer's liability for this conduct is based on similar principles.*

---

**WHAT VICTIMS OF SEXUAL HARASSMENT CAN DO**

*Employees subjected to sexual harassment should immediately notify their supervisor. If the supervisor is the harasser, the worker should go to the supervisor's superiors. Employers cannot solve the problem if they do not know about it. If there is a grievance procedure, employees should use it.*

*Victims should keep a written record of all incidents of harassment, detailing the place, time, persons involved, and any witnesses. Victims can also express their disapproval of the conduct to the perpetrator and tell him or her to stop.*

*An employee can file a claim with the EEOC. If the state in which the employee lives prohibits sexual harassment, the worker should contact the proper state agency.*

## EXAMPLES OF SEXUAL HARASSMENT

*Sexual harassment can take many forms. It can consist of vulgar or lewd comments, or forcing workers to wear sexually revealing uniforms. It can involve unwanted physical touching or fondling, or suggestions to engage in sexual conduct. Even obscene, or sexually suggestive, cartoons and posters can be sexual harassment. Occasional inappropriate touching, off-color jokes, or repeated sexual references can be sexual harassment. It depends on the circumstances. Courts consider the nature and frequency of the conduct as well as the conditions under which the conduct occurred.*

unwelcome sexual advances. For example, a supervisor promises an employee a raise if she will go out on a date with him, or tells an employee she will be fired if she doesn't sleep with him.

Only individuals with supervisory authority over a worker can engage in *quid pro quo* harassment, since it requires the harasser to have the authority to grant or withhold job benefits.

### Q. If a worker "voluntarily" has sex with a supervisor, does this mean that she has not been sexually harassed?

**A.** Not necessarily. In order to constitute harassment, sexual advances must be "unwelcome." If an employee by her conduct shows that sexual advances are unwelcome, it does not matter that she eventually "voluntarily" succumbs to the harassment. In deciding whether the sexual advances are "unwelcome," the courts will often allow evidence concerning the employee's dress, behavior and language, as indications of whether the employee "welcomed" the advances.

### Q. Is an employer liable for quid pro quo harassment engaged in by its supervisors?

**A.** In general, an employer is held to be strictly liable when a supervisor engages in *quid pro quo* harassment.

### Q. What is hostile environment harassment?

**A.** This occurs when an employee is subjected to comments of a sexual nature, offensive sexual materials, or unwelcome physical contact as a regular part of the work environment. Generally speaking, a single isolated incident will not be considered hostile environment harassment unless it is extremely outrageous and egregious conduct. The courts look to see whether the conduct is both serious and frequent.

Supervisors, managers, co-workers and even customers can be responsible for creating a hostile environment.

### Q. Is an employer liable for hostile environment harassment?

**A.** It depends on who has created the hostile environment. When supervisors or managers are responsible for the hostile environment, the EEOC has taken the position that if the employer has an established policy against sexual harassment with an effective enforcement mechanism, the employer will not be liable unless it is aware of the problem and does not take appropriate action to stop the harassment.

When co-workers or customers have created the hostile environment, an employer will not be liable unless he has knowledge that the

## HOW EMPLOYERS CAN PREVENT SEXUAL HARASSMENT

- *Develop a written policy dealing with sexual harassment, indicating that sexual harassment is against the law and also violates company policy. The employer can contact the EEOC in Washington, D.C. for its guidelines on sexual harassment. These will help the employer formulate its policy.*
- *Develop an effective complaint procedure for workers subjected to sexual harassment. Provide a mechanism for employees to bypass their supervisor when the supervisor participates in the harassment or fails to take proper action. The complaint procedure should encourage a prompt solution to the problem.*
- *Promptly and effectively respond to sexual harassment complaints. Undertake a complete and confidential investigation of any allegations of harassment and impose appropriate disciplinary action.*
- *Prevent sexual harassment before it occurs. Circulate or post the company antiharassment policy and the EEOC rules on sexual harassment. Express strong disapproval of such conduct and tell employees of their right to be free from harassment.*

harassment has occurred and fails to take proper corrective action.

## Age Discrimination

### Q. Can employers force workers to retire?

**A.** Generally speaking, no. The ADEA prohibits mandatory retirement based on age. If an employee can no longer perform his or her job duties, however, the employer is allowed to discharge that person.

There are some exceptions to the general rules against forced retirement. Executives or high level policy makers can be forced to retire at age sixty-five if they are entitled to receive retirement benefits of at least $44,000 a year, exclusive of social security. Firefighters, police officers, and prison guards employed by state and local governments can also be forced to retire if required to do so by state or

local law and pursuant to a bona fide retirement plan.

### Q. Can employers offer voluntary retirement incentives?

**A.** Yes, so long as they are truly voluntary, and the decision whether to accept the incentives and retire is up to the employee.

## PRIVACY IN THE WORKPLACE

### Q. Are there any federal laws that protect the confidentiality of workplace records?

**A.** The ADA requires employers to keep any medical records regarding employees confidential and separate from employee personnel files. The law states that the only persons who may be informed about an employee's medical conditions are:

**FILING A COMPLAINT UNDER THE ADEA**

*If you believe you have been the victim of age discrimination, you may file a complaint with the EEOC. There are regional offices of the EEOC in most major cities in the U.S. If you are in a state that has a state law prohibiting age discrimination, you may also file a complaint with the state agency charged with enforcing the state law.*

*The time limit for filing a charge with the EEOC is 180 days after the discrimination happened; or, if you are in a state with a state age law, 300 days after the discrimination occurred, or thirty days after the state agency terminates proceedings, whichever happens first.*

*When the EEOC completes its investigation it issues a right to sue letter. The charging party must file any lawsuit within ninety days of receipt of the right to sue letter.*

- first aid or safety personnel if the medical condition may require emergency treatment; and
- government officials investigating compliance with the ADA.

The employer may also inform supervisors and managers about restrictions on work duties or necessary accommodations required by a disability.

The Privacy Act (5 U.S.C. Section 552a) forbids federal government employers from disclosing any information contained in employee files without the written consent of the employee in question.

**Q. Do state laws protect the confidentiality of workplace records?**

**A.** Some states have statutes prohibiting the disclosure of certain employee information. Several states, including California, Florida, and Pennsylvania, prohibit disclosure of employee medical records. At least one state, Connecticut, prohibits disclosure of any employee personnel information without the written consent of the employee in question.

Unnecessary disclosure of information in which the employee has a reasonable expectation of privacy may result in employer liability in tort for invasion of privacy or intentional infliction of emotional distress.

**Q. Do employees have a right of access to their personnel files?**

**A.** The Privacy Act allows federal government employees to have access to their records and to make a copy of any portion of the documents. It also provides for a procedure by which federal employees can challenge the information contained in their files.

Several other laws apply to the private sector. OSHA requires private-sector employers to give employees access to medical records that the law requires employers to maintain when employees are exposed to potentially toxic materials at work.

The NLRA imposes on the private-sector employer a duty to disclose to unions information that is necessary and relevant for collective bargaining purposes, which can include access to employee personnel files. There is, however, no duty to disclose such information directly to the employee.

Approximately fifteen states, including California, Massachusetts, Michigan, and Wisconsin, grant employees access to their personnel files. Some of the statutes also provide for procedures by which employees can challenge information in their files.

### Q. Can employers listen to employee telephone calls?

**A.** Title III of the Omnibus Crime Control and Safe Streets Act (18 U.S.C. Sections 2510–2520) prohibits employers from eavesdropping on, or wiretapping, telephone calls. There is a large exception allowing employers to listen in on an extension telephone used in the ordinary course of business. A second big exception allows employers to monitor telephone calls where employees have been expressly notified that their telephone conversations will be monitored. Some courts have indicated, however, that once the private nature of a telephone conversation is determined, any continued eavesdropping would not be in the ordinary course of business and may subject the employer to liability.

An employer violating the law can be sued for money damages.

### Q. Can employers use video cameras to monitor workers?

**A.** The NLRA prohibits employer surveillance of employee union activity, discussions about unions or union meetings. Some state laws regulate the extent to which an employer can monitor workers. For example, Connecticut prohibits surveillance or monitoring "in areas designed for the health or personal comfort of the employees or for the safeguarding of their possessions, such as rest rooms, locker rooms or lounges." Moreover, state tort law may protect employees against highly offensive intrusions upon privacy in a place where a person has a reasonable expectation of privacy. For example, monitoring an employee bathroom may be considered an invasion of privacy.

### Q. Can employers search workers or their possessions?

**A.** Within limits, such searches are usually allowed by law. However, a collective bargaining agreement might restrict or prohibit such conduct. (For a discussion of the constitutional restrictions on public employers see section in this chapter titled "Special Rights of Public Sector Employees" on page 432.)

It is extremely important, however, that employers are careful about the manner in which they conduct searches so as to avoid tort liability for assault, battery, false arrest, intentional infliction of emotional harm or invasion of privacy.

First, employers should have a work-related reason for the search, although they do not have to prove probable cause to conduct a search. Second, any search should be conducted by the least intrusive means possible. Third, employers should inform employees that searches might be conducted. Fourth, employers should not physically harm employees in the course of the search or threaten employees with physical harm. Fifth, the employer should not attempt to prevent employees from leaving the premises by threat of harm or other coercive means, although they are usually allowed to tell employees that they will be disciplined or discharged if they leave.

### Q. Can employers impose dress and grooming codes?

**A.** Generally speaking, employer dress and grooming policies are allowed. There are a few instances, however, in which such policies may run afoul of Title VII. Some employers, for example, impose a dress code on female employees but not male employees. This could be a violation of Title VII for disparate treatment based on sex. Or a grooming code may impact more severely on members of a particular protected class, thus having an adverse impact under Title VII. For example, a rule requiring employees to be clean-shaven may adversely impact on members of certain religious groups. In that case, the employer would have to show a business necessity in order to enforce the policy.

### Q. Can employers require employees to speak only English while at work?

**A.** The EEOC has interpreted Title VII to prohibit the promulgation of an English-only rule unless it can be justified by business necessity. Requiring employees to speak only English may have an adverse impact on persons of certain ethnic or national origin. Thus, an employer may be able to justify an English-only rule when its employees are dealing with customers but could not enforce such a rule in the employee lunchroom.

### Q. Can employers prohibit smoking in the workplace?

**A.** Yes, unless there is a collective bargaining agreement which allows for smoking in the workplace.

### Q. Can employers base employment decisions on employee off-duty conduct?

**A.** It depends. There are at least four states—Illinois, Minnesota, Montana, and Nevada—that prohibit an employer from taking adverse action against an employee because that employee uses lawful products off employer premises during nonworking time. Thus, in those states an employer could not refuse to hire, or fire, a worker who smoked off duty or drank alcohol. Moreover, a majority of states prohibit employers from refusing to hire, or firing, employees because they use tobacco products off employer premises during non-working time.

A collective bargaining agreement may require the employer to justify employment decisions based on just cause. As a general rule, in order to satisfy a just cause requirement, the employer would have to show that the employee's off-duty conduct somehow implicates the employer's legitimate business interests.

Some state anti-discrimination laws prohibit employers from discriminating in terms and conditions of employment based on marital status, arrest and conviction records, or sexual orientation. The federal bankruptcy law prohibits an employer from discriminating against an individual solely because that individual has filed for bankruptcy.

### Q. What are the legal implications of providing employee references to prospective employers?

**A.** Approximately twenty states prohibit employers from engaging in blacklisting. Blacklisting consists of intentionally taking action aimed at preventing an individual from obtaining employment. Truthful statements concerning an individual's ability to perform the job in question are not considered to be blacklisting.

The manner in which a reference is made and its content can give rise to employer liability under state tort law relating to defamation, intentional interference with a prospective employment contract, intentional infliction of emotional distress, or negligent misrepresentation.

Defamation occurs when one person's false statement injures the reputation of another person. However, most states recognize a qualified privilege defense to defamation for references to prospective employers given in good faith. Providing false information to a prospective employer with the intent of causing an applicant to lose the job constitutes intentional interference with prospective employment contract. Disclosure of private personal matters unrelated to work can result in an invasion of privacy or intentional infliction of emotional distress. Lastly, a false statement which causes a loss of money can be grounds for negligent misrepresentation.

To be safe, an employer should limit the number of individuals authorized to provide references on its behalf. Second, statements based on hearsay or gossip should be avoided. Third, only items which have a direct bearing on an individual's work performance should be discussed.

### Q. Must an employer provide an employee with a reference?

**A.** Generally speaking, no. There are, however, at least four states—Indiana, Missouri, Texas and Washington—which require an employer to provide, upon request, a service letter to the employee. A service letter contains the nature of the employee's job while employed by the employer, the duration of the employment, and the reason for the separation.

## AIDS IN THE WORKPLACE

The medical information in this section comes from a report by the New York State Department of Health entitled *100 Questions and Answers, AIDS.* You can get a copy by calling their AIDS hotline at (212) 447-8200. The U.S. Centers for Disease Control (CDC) in Atlanta, GA, also has information for employers and employees. Guidelines for the workplace are of particular value. They are available by calling (404) 639-3534 or by writing to the Centers for Disease Control, Public Inquiries Office, Building 1, Room B46, 1600 Clifton Road NE, Atlanta, GA 30333.

### Q. What is AIDS?

**A.** Acquired immune deficiency syndrome (AIDS) is a disease complex characterized by a collapse of the body's immune system. This makes AIDS patients vulnerable to one or more unusual infections or cancers. These infections or cancers are not a threat to anyone whose immune system works normally. The cause of AIDS appears to be a specific virus.

### Q. How contagious is AIDS?

**A.** AIDS is unlike most communicable diseases, such as colds and the flu. Sneezing, coughing, or eating or drinking from common utensils cannot spread AIDS. Merely being around infected people for a long time cannot transmit AIDS. The vast majority of scientific evidence appears to indicate that AIDS can be spread only by sexual contact or any exchange of infected blood, semen, or vaginal fluids.

Medical experts have studied AIDS for roughly fifteen years. It is evident that casual contact with AIDS patients does not threaten others. Scientists have not found any AIDS cases due to casual (nonsexual) contact with a household member, relative, co-worker, or friend. Health workers and others who care for AIDS patients have contracted AIDS only when they have pricked themselves with contaminated needles or in other ways been directly contaminated by the patient's blood, semen or vaginal fluids. No health worker has ever contracted AIDS from casual contact with an AIDS patient.

### Q. May employers fire workers because they have AIDS?

**A.** No. The ADA prohibits employment discrimination against individuals with AIDS. Moreover, almost every state has a law prohibiting discrimination against individuals with a disability, and most of those laws interpret disability to include AIDS.

It is not clear at this time whether the protection against disability discrimination would include those individuals who tested HIV-positive. However, to the extent that an employer would regard an individual who was HIV-positive as having a disability, then that person would be protected since the definition of disability under both the ADA and the Rehabilitation Act includes individuals regarded as having a disability.

Some laws target the AIDS problem directly. For example, laws in California, Wisconsin, and Florida prohibit using the results of certain blood tests to make employment decisions. Public health laws that encourage AIDS testing usually require that the test results be kept secret.

### Q. What can an employer do about AIDS?

**A.** First, the employer should make someone responsible for informing management about current events. The Center for Employment Relations and Law (CERL) offers a series of four videotapes entitled "AIDS and the Workplace." You can order them from CERL, College of Law, Florida State University, Room 218, Tallahassee, FL 32306; telephone (904) 644-4287.

Second, consider hiring a medical consultant familiar with AIDS. As an alternative, get advice from the state or local health officer in charge of AIDS.

Third, consider developing company policies about AIDS. The U.S. Centers for Disease Control (CDC), your state health authority, or other companies or organizations may already have established guidelines. It might help to write to the proper health authorities in New York, California, or Florida.

Fourth, educate your employees. Public health officials and the CDC have materials that you can distribute to your employees.

Fifth, do not overreact if an employee of your company develops an AIDS problem. Seek expert legal and medical advice about the proper action that you should take. Keep the information you obtain on specific employee medical problems confidential. The ADA

requires that medical histories be kept confidential. Moreover, unnecessary disclosure of such information may leave the employer liable to a lawsuit for invasion of privacy or intentional infliction of emotional distress.

## SPECIAL RIGHTS OF PUBLIC SECTOR EMPLOYEES

Most of the anti-discrimination laws which have been discussed in this chapter apply to public sector employers as well as private sector workers. Moreover, even though the NLRA expressly excludes public sector employers, the federal government and most states have collective bargaining laws patterned after the NLRA which give public sector employees the right to be represented by labor unions and negotiate collective bargaining agreements.

Because public sector workers are employed by the government, they have additional protections not normally available to private sector employees. These protections, found in the civil service laws and the federal and state constitutions, apply only to governmental employers.

### Q. What are civil service laws?

**A.** Civil service laws establish employment policies for public sector employees based on the merit principle. The purpose behind establishing civil service laws was to eliminate political considerations in the employment process. The elements of a civil service system generally include guidelines for recruiting applicants, testing programs for screening applicants, impartial hiring criteria, job classifications based on duties and responsibilities, and protection against arbitrary discipline and discharge. A commission is usually established to ensure that the public sector employer is following the civil service rules. The particulars of civil service laws and the role and operation of the commission varies from state to state.

### Q. What type of protection does the U.S. Constitution afford public sector employees?

**A.** The most important protections afforded by the U.S. Constitution (which are not duplicated by anti-discrimination laws already discussed) are the rights to freedom of association, freedom of speech, the right to be free of unreasonable searches and seizures, and due process protections in the event of discharge from a job.

### Q. How does freedom of association protect a public employee?

**A.** Basically, a public sector employer cannot base employment decisions on the fact that an individual belongs to certain types of clubs or associates with particular people. Thus, a public sector employer can't refuse to hire an applicant just because he is a Republican, or belongs to a motorcycle club, or is a member of the American Civil Liberties Union.

### Q. How does freedom of speech protect a public employee?

**A.** When a public employee speaks out on issues of public concern, his employer cannot discipline or discharge him for his comments. For example, if a school teacher writes a letter to the newspaper criticizing the curriculum developed by the school board, the school board could not discharge that teacher for her criticism. However, if the comments of the employee relate to matters of purely private concern, such as the teacher complaining that she did not get a day off when she requested it, the principle of freedom of speech would not protect her in the employment arena.

### Q. How does freedom from unreasonable search and seizure protect a public employee?

**A.** An employee may have a reasonable expectation of privacy in certain places at work, such as a desk or filing cabinet which is not shared with other workers. In those areas where the employee has such a reasonable expectation of privacy, an employer may conduct a work-related noninvestigatory search, as well as an investigatory search for work-related misconduct, only if there are "reasonable grounds for suspecting the search will turn up evidence that the employee is guilty of work-related misconduct, or that the search is necessary for a noninvestigatory work-related purpose such as to retrieve a needed file."

Although the law on this point is unsettled, public sector employers would likely need probable cause to suspect workplace misconduct before they could search personal items such as a briefcase, luggage or purse which an employee brings into the workplace.

As for searches relating to drug testing, see sidebar on Drug Testing and the Constitution on page 413 of the section of this chapter entitled "The Hiring Process".

### Q. How does due process protect a public employee?

**A.** Where an employee has a property interest in his job, he or she cannot be discharged without due process. In determining if a property interest exists, the courts look to whether there is a written or implied contract granting the employee a property interest in his job; whether past practice of the employer shows that the employee has a property interest in his job; or if a statute gives the employee a property interest in his job. For example, a teacher with tenure is considered to have a property interest in his or her job, because there is the express or implied understanding that a teacher cannot lose that job without just cause.

Due process requires that the employee be given notice of the reason for being discharged, a hearing at which to contest the decision, and a decision by an impartial third-party decision-maker.

## UNIONS IN THE WORKPLACE

The role of unions in the workplace is to act as the representative of the employees in dealing with the employer concerning workplace issues. Thus, instead of each worker negotiating separately with the employer regarding wages, health insurance coverage, etc., the union bargains with the employer on behalf of all the workers. The NLRA, which regulates union-employer relations at work, is premised on the notion that individual employees have very little leverage in bargaining with their employer, and that in practice the employer unilaterally sets wage and benefit levels without any discussion with the workers. If the workers pool their individual bargaining power, however, and negotiate collectively through a union, the result will more likely be a produce of true give-and-take where the workers will have an effective voice concerning workplace issues.

**UNION-MANAGEMENT RELATIONS IN THE AIRLINE AND RAILWAY INDUSTRIES**

*The Railway Labor Act regulates union-management relations in the airline and railway industries. It is very similar to the NLRA regarding the types of employee activities protected and the types of employer conduct regulated. One of the major differences between the two statutes is in the enforcement mechanisms provided. The Railway Labor Act is enforced by the National Mediation Board and the National Railroad Adjustment Board.*

**Q. What kinds of employees are covered by the NLRA?**

**A.** Initially, an employee must be employed by an employer subject to the jurisdiction of the NLRA, which includes private sector employers engaged in interstate commerce, but excludes railroad, airlines and public sector employers. (For more details see section in this chapter entitled "Federal Laws Regulating the Workplace" on page 395.)

Secondly, even if one is employed by a covered employer, there are certain categories of workers who are not protected by the statute: domestic employees of a family, farm workers, persons employed by a parent or spouse, independent contractors, supervisors and managers.

**Q. Who is a supervisor or manager?**

**A.** Supervisors are defined as individuals who have the authority to hire, fire, discipline, promote or adjust the grievances of other employees or to effectively recommend such action. Managers are generally high level employees who use independent judgment in formulating and effectuating company policies.

**Q. How does the NLRA regulate the union-employer relationship?**

**A.** First, the NLRA gives employees certain rights and prohibits employers and unions from interfering with those rights. Second, the NLRA sets up a mechanism by which employees can vote on whether or not they want a union to represent them in the workplace. Third, it requires employers and unions to engage in collective bargaining and regulates certain types of employer and union tactics which may occur during the course of collective bargaining.

## UNION-MANAGEMENT RELATIONS IN THE PUBLIC SECTOR

*Although the NLRA does not apply to public sector employees, there are separate federal and state laws which regulate the role of unions in government employment. Title VII of the Civil Service Reform Act (5 U.S.C. Sections 7101-7135) grants federal employees the right to be represented by a union for purposes of collective bargaining and prohibits discrimination in employment based on union activity. This statute also sets up the Federal Labor Relations Authority and the Federal Services Impasse Panel to enforce the rights and duties contained in the law.*

*As of 1990 there were forty-one states with statutes covering collective bargaining and union representation of public sector employees. These statutes are generally modeled after the provisions of the NLRA with one significant difference—there is usually some type of restriction or modification on the right of public sector employees to engage in a work stoppage.*

## EMPLOYEE ACTIVITY ON COMPANY PROPERTY

*While employees have the right to discuss work issues and union issues with their co-employees and to distribute leaflets and pamphlets talking about unions, these rights can be limited when the employees are on company property.*

*As a general rule, employers can prohibit discussions during working time, that is, during those periods of the workday when employees are required to work. Thus an employer could prohibit discussions while employees are working at their machines, but could not prohibit discussion while employees are taking their rest breaks or lunch break.*

*As for the distribution of literature, employers are allowed to prohibit it during working time and in work areas at all times. Thus, employees can be prohibited from passing out leaflets on the shop floor but not in the lunchroom.*

### Q. What rights do employees have under the NLRA?

**A.** The NLRA gives employees the rights to: join unions; engage in conduct aimed at promoting or helping unions; choose a union to represent them in collective bargaining with their employer; and engage in group conduct which has as its purpose collective bargaining or helping each other regarding workplace issues (this includes the right to strike). The law also says that employees have the right *not* to do these things if that is their desire.

### Q. What are some examples of how employees might use these rights?

**A.** Attending union meetings, talking to co-employees about unions or other workplace issues, passing out union literature, wearing union buttons, campaigning for union office, circulating petitions advocating workplace improvements, or engaging in a work stoppage or picketing are some examples of exercising NLRA rights.

### Q. Must there be a union in the workplace in order for employees to be able to use their rights?

**A.** No. Employees have these rights regardless of whether or not a union represents them in the workplace. For example, a group of workers in a non-union workplace can circulate a petition asking the employer for a wage increase.

### Q. Can an employer fire workers who engage in one of their rights under the NLRA?

**A.** No. The NLRA prohibits an employer from discharging, disciplining or otherwise discriminating against employees who exercise their rights. Prohibited discrimination includes demotion, lay off, wage cuts and denying a promotion.

### Q. What other types of restrictions does the NLRA place on employer conduct?

**A.** The NLRA prohibits an employer from interfering, restraining or coercing employees in the exercise of their rights. Employers cannot threaten employees with discipline or other adverse actions because they have used their rights. For example, an employer who tells employees they will lose their jobs or have their

## SOME EXAMPLES OF EMPLOYEE ACTIVITIES WHICH ARE NOT PROTECTED BY THE NLRA

*Even if employees are exercising a right under the NLRA, the manner in which they conduct themselves may remove them from the protection of the law. Slowdowns, violence, sabotage or vandalism of company property are not protected by the law.*

*Also, the NLRA generally protects activities only if they involve a group. For example, one worker asking the employer to institute health insurance coverage is not engaged in protected conduct. However, if the worker was acting as a spokesperson for other employees, or if the employees went as a group to ask the employer for health insurance coverage, then the law would protect that group. A single employee attempting to organize colleagues would also be protected.*

wages reduced if they vote for a union has violated the NLRA.

Neither can an employer promise employees benefits in order to get them to vote against a union, such as promising a wage increase if the employees reject the union.

## SOME EXAMPLES OF EMPLOYER CONDUCT PROHIBITED BY THE NLRA

*If a group of employees asks the employer for a raise and the employer fires them for asking, the employer has violated the NLRA— the employees were engaged in group conduct for the purpose of dealing with a workplace issue. An employer who refuses to promote an employee because that employee had spoken with her co-workers about union representation has also violated the NLRA. Similarly, an employer who suspends a worker for handing out union leaflets in the locker room during lunch has violated the NLRA.*

## FILING A COMPLAINT UNDER THE NLRA

*If workers believe their rights under the NLRA have been violated, they can file a charge with the National Labor Relations Board (NLRB). There are regional offices of the NLRB in most major cities in the U.S. The time limit for filing a charge is 180 days from the date of the unlawful action. The NLRB will investigate the charge and decide whether or not the law has been violated. If it decides there was no violation, it will dismiss the charge. A worker whose charge has been dismissed does not have the right to file a lawsuit in court.*

*If the NLRB decides the charge has merit, it will hold a hearing at which evidence is taken and arguments are made. An administrative law judge will then decide whether or not the law was violated. The decision of the administrative law judge can be appealed to the NLRB in Washington D.C. The decision of the NLRB can be appealed to the federal circuit courts of appeal.*

As a general rule, employers cannot question employees about their union activities, ask them whether other employees support a union, or ask them what happened at a union meeting.

**Q. How does a union come to represent a group of workers?**

**A.** A union organizing campaign can start either because the employees in the workplace have contacted the union or the union on its own seeks to organize the workers.

The first step in an organizing campaign is to determine whether the employees have any interest in having a union represent them. The union asks the employees to show their interest by signing an authorization card. This card indicates that the employee is interested in union representation. If at least 30 percent of the workers sign cards, then the union can ask the NLRB to hold a secret ballot election.

Before the election is held, there is usually time for both the union and employer to campaign among the workers, discussing the pros and cons of union representation. The election itself is usually held at the employer's place of business so that it is easy for the workers to vote. The NLRB monitors the election.

If the union wins the election it becomes the bargaining agent for the employees and negotiates a collective bargaining agreement with the employer. If the union loses the election the status quo prevails.

The key point is that it is up to the employees to decide whether or not they want a union; it is their choice to make.

**Q. If the union wins the election, which workers does the union represent?**

**A.** If a union is voted in to represent the workers, it doesn't necessarily represent every worker employed by the company. The union election is held among those employees who are considered to have a "community of interest" at the workplace. These employees form a bargaining unit, which will be the group of workers who will be represented by the union in the event the union wins the election.

Employees have a community of interest where they share similar working conditions, jobs, hours of work and supervision. For example, employees who work on an assembly line probably do not have a community of interest with office workers, whereas salespersons in a department store would probably share a community of interest even though they worked in different departments and sold different types of goods.

**Q. If a worker voted against the union in the election and the union wins, does the union represent that worker?**

**A.** Yes. The law requires the union to represent all employees in the bargaining unit, fairly and nondiscriminatorily, regardless of whether or not they supported the union.

## RELIGIOUS AND POLITICAL OBJECTIONS TO UNIONS

*An individual whose religion prohibits him from supporting a labor union is exempt from the requirement of paying dues and fees to a union pursuant to a union security clause. An alternative requirement can be imposed on such an individual—he or she must pay an amount equivalent to union fees and dues to a non-religious, non-labor charitable organization. Both the NLRA and Title VII require that such an accommodation be made to employee religious beliefs.*

*Individuals whose political views conflict with those of the union which represents them can object to the payment of dues or fees which are used for political purposes. The objector is entitled to have the financial obligation imposed by the union security clause reduced by that proportion of union dues money spent on activities unrelated to collective bargaining and representation of workers. The burden is on objectors to notify the union of their political objection.*

**Q. If a union wins the election, must the workers join the union?**

A. No. Just as the NLRA gives employees the right to join unions, it also gives employees the right to refuse to join a union. The NLRA prohibits both employers and unions from forcing employees to join a union.

However, employees can be forced to pay for the work which the union performs on their behalf. Most collective bargaining agreements contain a "union security clause." In effect, this clause requires workers to pay the dues and fees that union members are required to pay. If a worker refuses to pay dues, he or she can be fired.

Because the law requires the union to represent all the workers in the bargaining unit, regardless of whether or not they are members of the union, the law allows the union to "tax" the workers for the benefits they receive from union representation. Some states, however (mostly located in the South and Western mountain regions), do not allow contracts to have union security clauses.

**Q. What is a collective bargaining agreement?**

A. A collective bargaining agreement is the contract which the employer and the union negotiate. When a union wins an NLRB election, the law requires the employer to sit down and bargain in good faith with the union in an attempt to agree on the terms of a contract. This contract will cover the wages, hours, terms and conditions of employment which govern the employees in the bargaining unit. While this contract is in effect (usually a term of three years) the employer must live up to its terms and cannot make any changes in working conditions unless those changes are agreed to by the union.

**Q. What is covered in a collective bargaining agreement?**

A. Most collective bargaining agreements cover the basic terms and conditions of employ-

ment. These include rates of pay, hours of work, health insurance, pension benefits, vacations, seniority rights, job assignments, work rules, and procedures for promotions, layoffs, recalls and transfers. Most contracts also contain a provision allowing the employer to discipline or discharge employees only if there is "just cause."

**Q. What happens if the employer fails to live up to the terms of the collective bargaining agreement?**

A. Most union contracts contain grievance procedures. If the union believes that the employer has violated the contract it can file a complaint through the grievance procedure. This procedure has several steps during which the union and employer can attempt to settle the dispute between themselves. If they are unsuccessful, the complaint may be submitted to an arbitrator for an impartial decision. At a hearing, the arbitrator will listen to evidence and arguments from both sides and decide whether or not the contract was violated. In most instances the decision of the arbitrator is final.

**Q. What is the union's responsibility in representing the workers?**

A. The union has two major duties toward the employees. First, the union is required to represent the workers in bargaining with the employer. Second, the union has a duty to fairly represent all workers in its dealings with the employer.

**Q. What does the duty to fairly represent the workers entail?**

A. In carrying out its responsibilities, the union has to make many decisions. It has to decide whether to ask the employer for better wages or better pension benefits. It has to decide whether an employer's decision to discharge a worker violated the contract or was based on just cause. The basis on which the union makes its decision on these and other issues affecting the workers cannot be arbitrary, discriminatory or in bad faith.

For example, a worker is discharged for tardiness and he complains to the union. The union has to decide whether it should file a complaint under the contract's grievance procedure to protest the discharge or whether the employer was within its rights to discharge the worker. If the union decides not to file a grievance because the worker is not a union member, or because he is African-American, it has violated its duty to fairly represent the worker. That decision is based on a discriminatory reason. If, however, the union decides not to file the grievance because the worker was tardy for fourteen days in a row and this violated a known company rule, then the union has not violated its duty to fairly represent the worker.

### Q. What are the legal consequences of engaging in a strike?

**A.** That depends on what caused the strike. If the reason for the strike is to protest workplace conditions or to support union bargaining demands, it is called an economic strike. Economic strikers can be permanently replaced by the employer. If the employer replaces the strikers, it is similar to being laid off. When the strike ends, if the replacement worker is still employed, then the striker is not entitled to be reinstated to his job. However, as soon as a vacancy occurs, the striking employees have the right to be reinstated to their jobs.

If the reason for the strike is to protest the fact that the employer has violated the NLRA, it is called an unfair labor practice strike. Unfair labor practice strikers cannot be permanently replaced and they have the right to be immedi-

ately reinstated to their jobs when the strike ends.

In neither event is an employer allowed to discharge, discipline or otherwise discriminate in terms or conditions of employment because an employee engaged in a strike.

### Q. Are all strikes legal?

**A.** No. Although the NLRA grants employees the right to strike, not all strikes are protected. If a collective bargaining agreement contains a no-strike clause (the union agrees not to go on strike while the contract is in effect), a strike during the life of the contract would not be protected. The strikers could be fired.

The NLRA requires health care workers to give ten days notice before they go on strike. If these workers strike without giving notice, then they are not protected and can be fired.

Sitdown strikes and intermittent strikes are also unprotected. An example of an intermittent strike is when employees engage in a five-hour work stoppage one day, then two days later engage in another five-hour work stoppage, and then two days later do it again.

---

## WAGES AND HOURS

The FLSA sets the minimum wage that a covered employer must pay all its workers; it also establishes overtime payment requirements. Even if the employer itself is not covered (because, for example, it does not gross $500,000 annually) it will still be required to pay the minimum wage and overtime to all of its employees who are engaged in the interstate commerce. (See discussion of coverage under the FLSA in section in this chapter titled "Federal Laws Regulating the Workplace," on page 395.) Finally, even if an

## GOVERNMENT CONTRACTORS AND FEDERAL WAGE LAWS

*An employer performing a contract for the federal government involving the manufacture or furnishing of materials, supplies, articles or equipment in excess of $10,000 is covered by the Walsh-Healy Act. This statute requires that the employer pay all employees the prevailing minimum rate for similar work performed in the locality. This prevailing minimum rate is determined by the Secretary of Labor. Employers are also required to pay all employees who work in excess of forty hours a week "time and a half" pay for overtime.*

*The Davis Bacon Act requires that federal contractors performing work valued in excess of $2000 on federal construction projects pay their employees the prevailing area wage and fringe benefit rate. The prevailing area wage is determined by the Secretary of Labor.*

employer and its employees are not subject to the FLSA, many states also have minimum wage and overtime laws which will apply to all employers doing business within the state.

The minimum wage laws deal solely with wage rate issues; they do not require employers to provide any other type of employment benefit, such as health or life insurance.

### Q. What is the minimum wage?

**A.** The federal minimum wage under the FLSA is $4.25 an hour. The majority of states which have minimum wage laws peg their minimum wage to the federal minimum. There are approximately eight states, including Colorado, Georgia and Indiana, which have set their state minimum wage below the federal limit. Another seven states have set minimum wage rates which are higher than the federal rate. For example, both Alaska's and Oregon's minimum wage is $4.75, and Hawaii's is $5.25.

In those states which have a minimum wage above the federal rate, all employers, even those covered by the FLSA, must pay the higher state rate. In those states where the state minimum rate is below the federal level, those employers covered by the FLSA must pay the higher federal rate.

### Q. How is an employee's minimum wage rate determined?

**A.** The minimum wage is paid for every hour worked in any workweek. Thus, an employee covered under the federal minimum wage of $4.25 who works twenty hours a week must be paid at least eighty-five dollars for that week's work.

### Q. What does the law consider as an "hour worked?"

**A.** Generally speaking, hours worked include all the time spent by employees performing their job duties during the work day. When a worker's job requires him to travel during his work day, such as a service technician who repairs furnaces at customer's homes, the time spent traveling is considered "hours worked." Preparatory time spent prior to the start of the work day which is required in order to perform the job is considered hours worked. For example, workers who have to sharpen

**ENFORCING EMPLOYEE RIGHTS UNDER THE FLSA**

*Employees who believe they are not being paid in accordance with the requirements of the FLSA can file a complaint with the Wage and Hour Division of the U.S. Department of Labor. There are regional offices of the Division in most major cities in the U.S. The Division will investigate to determine whether or not the FLSA has been violated.*

*Employees can also file a lawsuit themselves in state or federal court to collect double the back wages and overtime pay owed.*

**EMPLOYER RECORD-KEEPING REQUIREMENTS UNDER THE FLSA**

*Employers are required to maintain and preserve certain wage records in order to show their compliance with the FLSA. Employers must maintain employee payroll records for three years containing such information as employee names, hours worked each workday and workweek, wages paid, deductions from wages, straight-time wages and overtime paid. The employer must also retain for a two-year period records which provide documentation in support of the payroll records, such as time cards, work schedules, and order and billing records.*

their knives at a meat processing plant, or workers required to wear special protective clothing at a chemical plant would have to be compensated for the time spent sharpening their knives or changing their clothes. Mandatory attendance at lectures, meetings and training programs is considered hours worked. Also included in hours worked are rest periods and coffee breaks shorter than twenty minutes.

The following are examples of activities which are generally not considered hours worked for purposes of minimum wage compensation:

- commuting time to work;
- lunch or dinner breaks of at least thirty minutes;
- changing clothes when done for the benefit of the employee;

- on-call time away from the employer's premises and which the employee can use for his or her own purposes.

**Q. Must the minimum wage be paid in money, rather than benefits?**

**A.** Yes, but an employer is allowed to take a credit for the cost of providing certain non-cash benefits to employees from the minimum wage owed.

**Q. What types of credits is an employer allowed to take from the minimum wage owed?**

**A.** The employer can credit the reasonable cost of board, lodging and other facilities cus-

# Fair Labor Standards Act complaint form

**Employment Information Form**

**U.S. Department of Labor**
Employment Standards Administration
Wage and Hour Division

This report is authorized by Section 11 of the Fair Labor Standards Act. While you are not required to respond, submission of this information is necessary for the Division to schedule any compliance action. Your identity will be kept confidential to the maximum extent possible under existing law.

OMB No. 1215-0001

**1. Person Submitting Information**

A.  Name (Print first name, middle initial, and last name)

Mr.

Miss

Mrs.

Ms.

B.  Date

C.  Telephone number:
(Or No. where you
can be reached)

D.  Address: (Number, Street, Apt. No.)

(City, County, State, ZIP Code)

E.  Check one of these boxes

☐ Present employee
of establishment

☐ Former employee
of establishment

☐ Other _____
(Specify:  relative, union, etc)

**2. Establishment Information**

A.  Name of establishment

B.  Telephone Number

C.  Address of establishment: (Number, Street)

(City, County, State, ZIP Code)

D.  Estimate number of employees

E.  Does the firm have branches?

☐ Yes    ☐ No    ☐ Don't know

If "Yes", name one or two locations: _____

F.  Nature of establishment's business: (For example; school, farm, hospital, hotel, restaurant, shoe store, wholesale drugs, manufactures stoves, coal mine, construction, trucking, etc.)

G.  If the establishment has a Federal Government or federally assisted contract, check the appropriate box(es).

☐ Furnishes goods    ☐ Furnishes services    ☐ Performs construction

H.  Does establishment ship goods to or receive goods from other States?

☐ Yes    ☐ No    ☐ Don't know

**3. Employment Information**  (Complete A, B, C, D, E, & F if present or former employee of establishment; otherwise complete F only)

A.  Period employed (month, year)

From: _____

To: _____
(If still there, state present)

B.  Date of birth if under 19

Month _____ Day _____ Year _____

C.  Give your job title and describe briefly the kind of work you do

(Continue on other side)

Form WH-3
Rev. 10/89

D. Method of payment

$ _____ per _____
   (Rate)        (Hour, week, month, etc.)

E. Enter in the boxes below the hours you usually work each day and each week (less time off for meals)

| M | T | W | T | F | S | S | Total |
|---|---|---|---|---|---|---|-------|
|   |   |   |   |   |   |   |       |

F.  **Check the appropriate box(es) and explain briefly in the space below** the employment practices which you believe violate the Wage and Hour laws. (If you need more space use an additional sheet of paper and attach it to this form.)

☐ Does not pay the minimum wage

☐ Does not pay proper overtime

☐ Does not pay prevailing wage determination for Federal Government or federally assisted contract

   Approximate date of alleged discrimination

   _____

☐ Discharged employee because of wage garnishment (explain below)

☐ Excessive deduction from wages because of wage garnishment (explain below)

☐ Employs minors under minimum age for job

☐ Other (explain below)

_____

_____

_____

_____

_____

_____

_____

_____

_____

_____

_____

_____

_____

**(Note:  If you think it would be difficult for us to locate the establishment or where you live, give directions or attach map.)**

**Complaint Taken By:**

_____

_____

_____

### Public Burden Statement

We estimate that it will take an average of 20 minutes to complete this collection of information, including time for reviewing instructions, searching existing data sources, gathering and maintaining the data needed, and completing and reviewing the collection of information. Send comments regarding this burden estimate or any other aspect of this collection of information, including suggestions for reducing this burden, to the Office of Information Management, U.S. Department of Labor, Room N1301, 200 Constitution Avenue, N.W., Washington, D.C. 20210; and to the Office of Management and Budget, Paperwork Reduction Project (1215-0001), Washington, D.C. 20503.

## TIPPED EMPLOYEES AND THE FLSA

*Employers are allowed to credit tips received by tipped employees against the minimum wage owed to those employees under certain circumstances. In order to qualify for the credit, the tipped employee must be engaged in an occupation in which he or she customarily receives more than thirty dollars per a month in tips, for example a waiter or a beautician. The maximum credit for tips allowed against minimum wage is 50 percent of the amount owed. Of course, the employer is allowed to credit only that amount the employee actually receives in tips. Thus, if the employee receives less than 50 percent of the minimum wage in tips, the employer could not take credit for 50 percent of minimum wage. The employee must always receive at least the minimum wage when wages and tips are combined.*

*For example, a waitress works 40 hours in a week during which time she earned $80 in tips, which is $2 per hour in tips. The employer is allowed to take $2 per hour as credit against the $4.25 minimum wage. Thus, the employer is required to pay the waitress at least $90 for that week's work ($4.25 - $2.00 tip credit = $2.25 x 40 hours).*

*Employers may not take the tip credit unless the employer informs the workers about it. Employers must also be able to prove that the employee actually receives tips equal to the tip credit taken by the employer.*

tomarily provided to employees. In order to credit the cost of such non-cash benefits, they must be furnished for the employee's convenience and they must be voluntarily accepted by the employee. Examples of non-cash items whose fair value can be credited to the minimum wage owed are: meals furnished at the company cafeteria, housing furnished by the company for residential purposes, and fuel or electricity used by the employee for non-business purposes.

Employers who have a policy of requiring employees to pay for breakage or cash shortages cannot take such amounts as credit toward the minimum wage owed. Neither are employee discounts allowed as credits toward minimum wage.

### Q. Can the employer take deductions from an employee's paycheck?

**A.** The employer is required to deduct taxes and amounts which have been garnished from an employee's paycheck. (See sidebar discussion of garnishment).

An employer is allowed to deduct certain items from an employee's paycheck if the employee has authorized the deduction. Examples of such deductible items are union dues, charitable contributions, or insurance premiums. These deductions are allowed even if the amount received by the employee after deduction falls below the minimum wage.

Certain types of items cannot be deducted from employee paychecks if the deduction would cause the amount received by the employee after the deduction to fall below the minimum wage. Examples of such items are: cost of uniforms used for work, cost of cleaning uniforms used for work or employee breakage or cash shortage debts.

**Q. When is a worker eligible for overtime pay?**

**A.** The general rule is that employees must be paid overtime for all hours worked over forty hours in any workweek.

**Q. Are all employees entitled to overtime pay?**

**A.** No. There are several categories of workers who are exempt from the overtime requirements. The most common employee exemptions are:

- executive, administrative and professional employees who are paid at least $250 a week;
- retail commission salespeople whose regular rate of pay is more than one and a half times the minimum rate and for whom more than half of their wages comes from commissions;
- taxicab drivers.

**Q. What is the overtime pay rate?**

**A.** The FLSA requires employers to pay employees one and a half times (150 percent) their regular rate of pay for each hour, or fraction of an hour, over forty hours in any workweek.

**Q. How is the overtime pay rate computed?**

**A.** The main issue is to determine the regular rate for the employee in question. When an

## GARNISHMENT OF WAGES

*A garnishment is an order issued by a court requiring that the earnings of a worker be withheld from the worker's paycheck and paid to a third party to whom the worker owes a debt. The Consumer Credit Protection Act (15 U.S.C. Sections 1671-1677) is a federal law which limits the amount of money which may be withheld from a paycheck pursuant to a garnishment order. The general rule is that the maximum amount which can be garnished from a paycheck is the lesser of 25 percent of an employee's take-home pay or that part of take-home pay exceeding thirty times the federal minimum wage. The law permits a larger amount to be deducted where the debt owed is for child-support payments, bankruptcy, or back taxes.*

*The Consumer Credit Protection Act also prohibits an employer from discharging an employee because his or her wages have been garnished once.*

employee is paid an hourly rate, the employee's regular rate and hourly rate are the same. For example, an employee who is paid $6.00 an hour and who worked 43 hours in the last work week, would be owed $27 in overtime pay.

($6.00 regular rate x 1½ = $9.00 overtime rate; $9.00 x 3 (hours worked in excess of 40) = $27).

The employee's salary for that week would be $267 ($6 x 40 hrs. = $240 + $27 (overtime) = $267).

When an employee is paid a salary or commission, the employee's compensation must be converted to an hourly rate. This conversion is accomplished by dividing the employee's compensation for the week by the number of hours worked in that week. For example, an employee who was paid $225 a week, and worked 45 hours the last week, earned a regular rate of $5.00. The employer, therefore, would owe the employee an additional $37.50 for the 5 hours of overtime worked in that last week ($5.00 x 1½ = $7.50 x 5 (hours worked in excess of 40) = $37.50). The employee's salary for that week would be $262.50.

## WORKPLACE SAFETY

The Occupational Safety and Health Act (OSH Act) is a federal law whose purpose is to "assure so far as possible every working man and woman . . . safe and healthful working conditions." The statute is administered and enforced by the Occupational Safety and Health Administration (OSHA).

The OSH Act applies to all private sector employers engaged in a business affecting commerce. The courts have broadly interpreted the phrase "affecting commerce," such that almost every business in the country with at least one employee is covered by the Act. The OSH Act does not apply to public sector employers.

States may also regulate workplace health and safety in two ways. First, they may have regulations covering workplace conditions that are not dealt with by OSHA standards. Second, they may adopt a state safety and health plan that duplicates the requirements of the OSH Act, and if approved by OSHA, the state would then be responsible for enforcing safety and health regulations within its borders. In the absence of approval by OSHA, however, a state may not regulate any safety

### WORKING WITH HAZARDOUS CHEMICALS

*OSHA requires that employees who work with hazardous chemicals be informed of the types of chemicals they are working with and be trained in their handling. Chemical manufacturers and distributors are required to label containers identifying any hazardous chemicals and give appropriate hazard warnings.*

*Employers who use such hazardous chemicals in the workplace are required to develop a written hazard communication program for their employees. As part of this program the employer must compile a list of all hazardous chemicals used in the workplace; identify the physical and health hazards associated with these chemicals; state precautions to be used in handling the chemicals; and indicate emergency and first aid procedures to be used in the event of a problem. This information must be made available to the employees.*

*Employees must also receive training in detecting the presence of chemicals in the workplace and protecting themselves from hazards.*

# REQUEST FOR HEALTH HAZARD EVALUATION
U. S. DEPARTMENT OF HEALTH AND HUMAN SERVICES
U. S. PUBLIC HEALTH SERVICE
CENTERS FOR DISEASE CONTROL
NATIONAL INSTITUTE FOR OCCUPATIONAL SAFETY AND HEALTH

Form Approved
OMB No. 0920-0102
Expires Nov. 30, 1995

## ESTABLISHMENT WHERE POSSIBLE HAZARD EXISTS

Company name: _____

Address: _____

City: _____ State: _____ Zip Code: _____

What product or service is provided at this workplace?

_____

Specify the particular worksite, such as building or department, where the possible hazard exists:

_____

How many people are exposed? _____ Duration of exposure (hrs/day)? _____

What are the occupations of the exposed employees; what is the process/task?

Occupations: _____

Process/task: _____

To your knowledge, has NIOSH, OSHA, MSHA, or any other government agency previously evaluated this workplace? YES ____ NO ____

Is a similar request currently being filed with, or is the problem under investigation by any other local, state, or federal agency? YES ____ NO ____

If either question is answered yes, give the name and location of each agency.

_____

_____

Which company official is responsible for employee health and safety?

Name: _____ Title: _____ Phone: _____

_____

## DESCRIPTION OF THE POSSIBLE HAZARD OR PROBLEM

Please list all substances, agents, or work conditions which you believe may contribute to the possible health hazard. (Include chemical name, trade name, manufacturer or other identifying information, as appropriate.)

_____

_____

In what physical form(s) do(es) the substance(s) exist? ____Dust ____Gas ____Liquid ____Mist ____Other

How are the affected employees exposed (route of exposure)? _____Breathing _____Skin contact

_____Swallowing _____Other (please list) _____

**What health problem(s) do employees have as a result of these exposures?**

_____

_____

**Use the space below to supply any additional relevant information.**

_____

_____

**REQUESTER'S SIGNATURE:** _____ **DATE:** _____

Typed or print name: _____

Address: _____

City: _____ State: _____ Zip code: _____

Business phone: _____ Home phone: _____ Best time of day to call: _____

**CHECK <u>ONLY ONE</u> OF THE FOLLOWING:**

_____ I am an <u>employer representative</u>.

_____ I am an authorized representative of, or an officer of the <u>union</u> or other organization representing the employees for collective bargaining purposes. <u>Name and address of this organization:</u>

_____

_____ I am a <u>current employee</u> of the employer, and an <u>authorized representative of two or more other current employees</u> in the workplace where the exposures are found. Signatures of the authorizing employees are below:

Signature: _____ Phone: _____

Signature: _____ Phone: _____

_____ I am <u>one of three or fewer employees</u> in the workplace where the substance, hazard, or health problem exists.

**Please indicate your desire:**     _____ I do not want my name revealed to the employer.
                                     _____ My name may be revealed to the employer.

STATEMENT OF AUTHORITY:
Sections 20(a)(3-6) of the Occupational Safety and Health Act (29 USC 669(a)(6-9)), and Section 501(a)(11) of the Federal Mine Safety and Health Act (30 USC 951(a)(11)). Confidentiality of the respondent requester will be maintained in accordance with the provisions of the Privacy Act (5 USC 552a). The voluntary cooperation of the respondent requester is required to initiate the Health Hazard Evaluation.

**SEND COMPLETED FORM TO:**

**National Institute for Occupational Safety and Health
Hazard Evaluations and Technical Assistance Branch
4676 Columbia Parkway, Mail Stop R-9
Cincinnati, Ohio 45226
Phone: (513) 841-4382     FAX: (513) 841-4488**

This form is provided to assist in requesting a health hazard evaluation from the U.S. Department of Health and Human Services. Public reporting burden for this collection of information is estimated to average 12 minutes per response. Send comments regarding this burden estimate or any other aspect of this collection of information, including suggestions for reducing this burden to PHS Reports Clearance Officer; ATTN: PRA, Hubert H. Humphrey Bldg, Rm 721-B; 200 Independence Ave., SW; Washington, DC 20201, and to the Office of Management and Budget; Paperwork Reduction Project (0920-0102); Washington, DC 20503.

## EMPLOYEE PROTECTION FOR EXERCISING RIGHTS UNDER THE OSH ACT

*The law expressly protects employees from discharge or discipline under two circumstances. First, the employer cannot discriminate against an employee because that employee has filed a complaint with OSHA, asked OSHA to inspect the workplace, talked to the OSHA inspector during the walk-around, or otherwise assisted OSHA in the investigation.*

*Second, the law also protects the worker who refuses to perform a job that is likely to cause death or serious injury. As a general rule the employee does not have a right to refuse to perform work and normally the employer could discipline or discharge the employee for such a refusal. However, a worker cannot be discharged or disciplined for such a refusal if all the following circumstances apply:*

- *the reason for the employee's refusal is a good faith belief that there is a real danger of death or serious injury;*
- *a reasonable person in the employee's position would conclude there is a real danger of death or serious injury;*
- *there is insufficient time to eliminate the danger through the regular OSHA channels;*
- *the employee has unsuccessfully asked the employer to fix the problem.*

and health issue that is already regulated by the OSH Act.

### Q. What obligations are imposed on employers under the OSH Act?

**A.** The Act imposes three obligations on employers. First, employers are required to furnish a workplace "free from recognized hazards that are causing or are likely to cause death or serious physical harm" to employees.

Second, employers are required to comply with the safety and health standards promulgated by OSHA. Third, employers are required to keep records of employee injuries, illnesses, deaths, and exposures to toxic substances, and to preserve employee medical records.

There are some exemptions from certain requirements imposed by the law for employers with ten or fewer employees. These small companies do not have to maintain certain types of records, and they are exempt from certain types of penalties and enforcement activities; however, they are still required to provide a safe workplace and comply with OSHA standards.

### Q. What types of workplace conditions do the health and safety standards address?

**A.** The standards regulate such issues as: the safety of working areas such as ladders, scaffolding, stairs and floors; provision of sufficient entry and exit ways; exposure to noise, carcinogens, radiation and other types of harmful substances;

fire protection systems for the workplace; safety devices for machines and equipment used in the workplace; and the provision of medical and first aid services. There are literally hundreds of standards covering all aspects of the workplace.

### Q. What should an employee do if he or she thinks there is a safety or health hazard at work?

**A.** There are two methods of addressing safety and health problems. The employee can notify his or her supervisor or company safety director and discuss the problem. An employee can also contact OSHA and request a safety inspection.

### Q. How does an employee initiate a request for an OSHA inspection?

**A.** There are OSHA regional and area offices located in cities throughout the U.S. An employee can either make an oral complaint to OSHA or file a formal written complaint. In either case, the employee should indicate what workplace conditions he or she believes constitute a safety or health hazard. OSHA will decide, based on the information received, whether there are reasonable grounds for believing a violation of the law exists. OSHA will then either send the employer a letter regarding the alleged violation and how to correct the problem, or send an inspector to the workplace to conduct an on-site safety inspection.

### Q. What happens during an OSHA inspection?

**A.** The OSHA inspector will meet with the employer and explain the nature of the inspection and review employer documents pertaining to workplace injuries and hazards. Then the inspector will "walk-around" the plant and physically inspect the workplace. The employer and a representative of the employees are allowed to accompany the inspector on the walk-around. The inspector will also talk with employees and ask them questions. At the end of the inspection, the inspector will informally tell the employer of any possible violations that may have been uncovered during the inspection.

### Q. What are the penalties for violating the OSH Act?

**A.** First, an employer is required to correct any hazards that violate the law. The employer can also be fined a monetary penalty, the amount of which is determined by the seriousness of the violation. An employer can also be subject to criminal liability and imprisonment for willful violation of an OSHA standard that results in an employee's death.

---

## WORKPLACE INJURIES

### Workers' Compensation

The workers' compensation laws provide monetary compensation to pay for medical expenses and to replace income lost as a result of injuries or illnesses that arise out of employment. The employee is not required to prove that the injuries were caused by some negligence of the employer in order to recover under the workers' compensation laws. These laws impose strict liability on employers for injuries suffered at the workplace.

Each state has its own law providing workers' compensation benefits. While the dollar amounts recoverable and certain procedural or coverage details vary among the states, the general requirements of the laws are similar. There are separate federal workers' compensation laws covering federal government employees, and employees of the railroad and maritime industries.

The cost of providing workers' compensation is borne solely by the employer, usually through the purchase of a workers' compensation insurance policy from an insurance company. The cost of providing this insurance cannot be deducted from the employee's wages.

### Q. Are all employees covered by workers' compensation?

A. Most employees are covered. Some state laws exempt certain categories of workers, such as casual employees, agricultural employees, domestic employees, and independent contractors. Moreover, a few states require coverage only if an employer employs a minimum number of employees, for example Alabama, where coverage is compulsory only if an employer has at least three employees.

### Q. What types of injuries are compensated under workers' compensation?

A. Injuries and illness that "arise out of and in the course of employment" are compensable. This means that there must be some connection between an employment requirement and the cause of the injury. An automobile accident that occurs during the commute to work is not compensable, but a traveling salesperson who is in an accident while on her way to a sales call would be compensated. Some examples of compensable injuries are injuries caused by defective machinery, fires or explosions at work, repeated lifting of heavy equipment, or slipping on an oily floor surface at work.

Illnesses that are caused by working conditions, where the job presents a greater risk of contracting the illness than the normal risks of everyday life, are also compensable. A clerical worker in an office with co-workers who smoke, and who contracts emphysema from secondhand smoke, would probably not be compensated for the illness, because there is nothing peculiar about her job that increased the risk of contracting emphysema. However, a coal miner who contracts black lung disease would be eligible for compensation.

### Q. If a workplace injury causes death, is compensation provided to the worker's survivors?

A. Yes, death benefits are generally provided to the spouse until remarriage, and to the children until they reach majority. Death benefits consist of a burial allowance and a percentage of the deceased worker's weekly wage. There may also be a maximum cap on benefits receivable.

### Q. How much compensation is paid for an injury or illness?

A. Workers receive a fixed weekly benefit based on their regular salary. The percentage of regular salary received varies from state to state but is generally in the 50 to 66 percent range. This wage payment is made for the period during which the employee is temporarily unable to work due to the injury.

Workers' compensation also pays for all medical expenses associated with the injury or illness. Most state laws also provide some compensation for the costs associated with medical and vocational rehabilitation.

Employees who suffer a permanent disability, whether partial or total, are also eligible for a payment to compensate for the decrease in earnings attributable to the permanent nature of the disability. The amount payable may be determined by a schedule (a list that specifies wage loss for specific disabilities, for example, $8,910 for loss of an index finger), or by percentage of weekly wage.

### Q. What must a worker do to obtain compensation for a work-related injury?

A. First, the worker should notify the employer as soon as possible after an injury occurs. Usually the employer will have claim forms available for the employee to fill out. The documents are then submitted by the employer to the insurance company and the state workers' compensation agency. Should the employer not have claim forms available, the employee should contact the state workers' compensation agency.

If a claim is not challenged by the employer, payment for medical bills and wages will be made by the insurance company to the employee. If the employer contests a claim, a hearing is scheduled and evidence relating to the circumstances of the injury and the extent of the injury is presented. The resulting decision as to whether, and how much, compensation is owed can be appealed by either the employer or the employee.

As a general rule, the exclusive means for being compensated for workplace injuries or illness is by filing a claim under workers' compensation. Only where an employee or employer is not covered by workers' compensation can the employee sue in court to collect damages for the injuries suffered. In those suits the employer is held liable if the injury was caused by its negligence.

### Social Security Disability Insurance

The Social Security Disability Insurance system differs from workers' compensation in that the cause of the injury is irrelevant for purposes of social security. Whereas in order to be compensable under workers' compensation an injury must arise out of employment, the main issue for purposes of compensation under social security is whether the injury prevents a person from being able to work regardless of the cause of the injury. Thus, while the automobile accident on the commute to work is not compensable under workers' compensation, a worker may be eligible for social security benefits if the injuries resulting from the accident prevent the worker from earning a living.

**Q. Can an injured worker receive social security benefits?**

**A.** Yes, if the employee is in a job covered by social security, and if the injury or illness is considered to be "disabling."

**Q. What types of injuries are considered "disabling"?**

**A.** A "disabling" medical condition is one that can be expected to last at least twelve months and causes a worker to be unable to engage in gainful employment anywhere in the country. The Social Security Administration has published a list of impairments that are considered disabling, such as severe epilepsy and loss of vision or hearing. A medical condition that does not appear on the list may still be considered disabling if the worker can show that the condition is the medical equivalent of a listed impairment—that it is equal in severity and duration to a listed impairment.

**Q. What if workers do not suffer from a medical equivalent of a listed impairment?**

**A.** These employees would be eligible for benefits only if they could prove by another means that they had a disabling medical condition. They would have to show that their condition or disease is so severe that it prevented them from doing their former job or other similar work. It is not easy to prove this.

**Q. Can a disabled worker's spouse and children receive social security benefits for a worker's disability?**

**A.** If the spouse and children meet the requirements for the worker's social security retirement benefits, they should qualify for disability benefits.

**Q. Where can workers apply for social security disability benefits?**

**A.** Workers should file a claim at the local Social Security Administration office; there are offices in most large cities in the U.S. The following documents should be submitted with the application: a medical history along with a detailed statement from a doctor concerning the cause of the disability; a detailed work history; and information concerning educational background. These documents help the Social Security Administration decide whether the condition is disabling. Statements from family and friends may also be submitted.

**Q. What happens if the Social Security Administration rejects an application for benefits?**

**A.** There is an appeals process for rejected applications. This process is explained in a later section on social security retirement benefits, on page 588 of the chapter titled "The Rights of Older Americans."

## EMPLOYMENT TERMINATION

In the United States, most employees are considered employees "at will." This means that they have no written contract that governs the length of their employment or the reasons for which they may be terminated from employment. The employer is free to lay off or fire such employees with no notice and with no reason.

Not all employees, however, are employees at will. Those employees who are represented by unions and covered by a collective bargaining agreement usually cannot be fired "at will." Their contracts normally provide that they can be terminated only for "just cause." Moreover, the grievance mechanism contained in most collective bargaining agreements provides a process by which union employees can challenge their firing. (For a fuller discussion of

### ENFORCING RIGHTS AND EMPLOYER RETALIATION

*Effective enforcement of the federal laws regulating employment relies heavily on information and help provided by employees. Employees are in the best position to know whether or not their rights have been violated. Employees can also, however, be subjected to pressure from their employers not to make complaints for fear of adverse employment actions. Because of this potential problem, almost all federal employment laws expressly prohibit employers from taking adverse actions against employees because they have filed a complaint to enforce their rights or cooperated in an investigation conducted by a federal agency enforcing the law. The Worker Adjustment and Retraining Notification Act, the Veterans Reemployment Rights Act and 42 U.S.C. Section 1981 do not expressly protect against retaliation.*

union protections, see the section in this chapter titled "Unions in the Workplace," page 434.)

Also, public sector workers are protected by civil service laws that normally require the employer to have "just cause" in order to terminate employment. Civil Service Commissions provide a mechanism by which public sector employees can appeal any decision to discharge them. (For further discussion of civil service laws, see the section in this chapter titled, "Special Rights of Public Sector Employees," on page 432.)

**Q. Are there any statutory limitations on an employer's ability to fire at-will employees?**

A. Yes, the NLRA, Title VII, the ADEA, and the ADA all prohibit an employer from firing an employee where the reason for the decision to fire is based on the employee's union activity or membership in a protected class, that is, race, sex, religion, national origin, color, age, or disability. Most of the federal laws regulating the workplace also prohibit employers from retaliating against workers who assert their rights under federal law. (See following sidebar.)

Moreover, many state antidiscrimination laws protect a broader class of workers from discrimination in firing. For example, Wisconsin prohibits firing based on weight, height, or sexual orientation. (For further discussion of the antidiscrimination laws, see the section in this chapter titled "Discrimination in the Workplace," on page 416.)

There is one state, Montana, that expressly requires an employer to have good cause in order to terminate or lay off a worker.

Finally, there are several states, such as New Jersey and California, that have passed laws to protect "whistleblowers" from being fired.

**Q. What is a whistleblower?**

A. A whistleblower is an employee who reports to a government agency the fact that he has reasonable cause to believe that there is a violation of state or federal law occurring in his workplace. The "whistleblower" statutes prohibit employers from firing a worker who is a

**PLANT CLOSING AND MASS LAYOFFS**

*The Worker Adjustment and Retraining Notification Act is a federal law requiring employers to provide workers, their unions, and state and local government officials sixty days' advance notice of any plant closing or mass layoff. The law applies to private sector employers with one hundred or more employees. A mass layoff is defined as a reduction in force that results in the layoff of at least 33 percent of the workforce and at least fifty employees, or at least 500 employees. Failure to give the sixty days' notice subjects an employer to liability for back pay and benefits under an employee benefit plan for each day that the notice was not given. Employees can enforce the law by filing a lawsuit in federal court.*

whistleblower and also prohibit employers from firing employees who participate in government investigations and hearings relating to violations of law at the workplace.

**Q. Have the courts recognized any exceptions to an employer's ability to fire at-will employees?**

A. Yes. In approximately forty states, such as Oregon, Illinois, Wisconsin, and Michigan, the courts have held that an employer cannot fire a worker for reasons that conflict with, or undermine, a state's public policy. This is known as the public policy exception to employment at will.

### Q. In what circumstances would firing a worker conflict with, or undermine, a state's public policy?

**A.** Generally speaking, public policy of a state can be found in the state statutes and constitution. There are four categories of discharge that have been determined by the courts as undermining public policy.

1. Firing a worker because he refuses to perform an act that state law prohibits. For example, an employer tells the worker to dump toxic waste into the city sewer system. The worker refuses and is fired.

2. Firing a worker for reporting a violation of the law. For example, a worker reports to the state agriculture department that his employer is selling contaminated meat, and is fired.

3. Firing a worker for engaging in acts that public policy encourages. For example, an employee is called to sit on a jury and the employer fires her for missing work.

4. Firing a worker for exercising a statutory right. For example, an injured worker files a claim under the state worker's compensation law and the employer fires him.

### Q. I have no written contract, but my employer told me that as long as I perform my work well I have a job. Can my employer fire me even if I am performing my job well?

**A.** It depends. A number of state courts, such as those in Michigan, will enforce an oral promise by the employer under certain circumstances. Generally speaking there must be clear, unequivocal evidence that a promise was made; there must be evidence that the employer and employee specifically discussed the issue of job security and reasons for termination; evidence of the employer's past practice that it fires employees only for cause is helpful; and evidence that the employee turned down other job offers or left a job in reliance on the promise made can help to persuade the court to enforce the oral promise.

Other courts, however, will not enforce such an oral promise.

### Q. My employer's handbook states that employees will only be fired for just cause. Can my employer still fire me at will?

**A.** It depends. Over thirty states, such as Wisconsin, Michigan, and California, will enforce specific terms contained in an employment handbook or personnel manual under certain conditions. First, the handbook or manual must have been given to the employee. Second, the language of the manual must be specific. For example, "all employees will be treated fairly" would be considered too vague to be enforced; whereas "employees will only be fired for just cause" is specific enforceable language.

Handbooks or manuals, however, that contain clear and express disclaimers informing employees that the information contained therein is not meant to create a contract and can be changed or revoked at any time will probably not be viewed as enforceable contracts by the courts.

### Q. Must an employer provide notice to an employee prior to discharge?

**A.** Generally no. If the employee has a written contract requiring notice, or if there is a collective bargaining agreement with a notice requirement, then the employer must provide notice. The law requires notice only in a very specific situation—if there is a mass layoff or plant closure.

**Q. Is an employer required to pay severance pay when it fires a worker?**

**A.** There is no law requiring employers to pay severance pay. If the employee has a written contract guaranteeing severance pay, or if there is a collective bargaining agreement providing for severance pay, then the employer will be required to pay severance. Otherwise, the employer is under no obligation to pay it.

**Q. My employer offered me severance pay if I agreed to sign a waiver of my right to sue the company. What is the legal effect of signing such a waiver?**

**A.** Generally speaking, a knowing and voluntary waiver is enforceable and as such would prevent an employee from being able to sue the employer for anything that occurred while he was employed. Whether or not a waiver is knowing and voluntary depends on the circumstances. The courts usually consider several factors in deciding whether a waiver is knowing and voluntary:

- Is the waiver written in a manner so that it can be understood by the employee?

- Did the employee receive a benefit in exchange for the waiver that he or she was not already entitled to receive?

- Did the employee have a reasonable time to consider the offer?

The ADEA specifically contains a list of requirements that must be met in order for a waiver of employee rights under the ADEA to be effective. Included among those requirements is that the employee be advised in writing to consult with an attorney before signing the waiver and that the employee be given at least twenty-one days to consider the waiver before signing.

Lastly, the courts will not enforce a waiver of any claims that arise under the FLSA.

# UNEMPLOYMENT INSURANCE

The Unemployment Insurance (UI) system is administered by the states for the purpose of providing workers and their families with weekly income during periods of unemployment. When unemployed due to plant closures, layoffs, natural disaster, or other acts or circumstances that are not the worker's fault, an employee may receive UI benefits.

The system is funded by state and federal taxes paid by employers. Subject to certain federal guidelines, each state determines the

## LOSING YOUR JOB DOESN'T MEAN LOSING YOUR HEALTH INSURANCE

*The Consolidated Omnibus Budget Reconciliation Act (COBRA) provides that workers who lose their jobs will not automatically lose their health insurance coverage. This federal law requires companies with at least twenty employees carrying group health insurance to offer terminated employees the opportunity to purchase at group rate continued participation in the company's health insurance plan for up to eighteen months. The employee may be required to pay no more than 102 percent of the cost of the premium. Usually 102 percent of the premium cost at group rate will be less than the premium for an individually purchased policy.*

## MOVING OUT OF STATE AND COLLECTING UNEMPLOYMENT

*If workers move to another state to look for work, they can still collect UI benefits, because all states belong to the Interstate Reciprocal Benefit Payment Plan. This Plan allows workers to register for work and file for UI benefits in a state different from the one in which they previously worked. The law of the state in which the employee previously worked, however, is the applicable law for determining eligibility for benefits. The workers must satisfy that state's requirements in order to receive UI benefits in the new state.*

scope, coverage, and eligibility requirements for UI benefits.

### Q. *What workers are covered under the UI system?*

**A.** Most workers are covered, but there are some exceptions. Categories of workers generally excluded from coverage are: self-employed individuals, independent contractors, casual employees and agricultural workers.

### Q. *If a worker is covered under UI, is he automatically entitled to receive benefits if he is unemployed?*

**A.** No. In order to receive benefits, a covered worker must meet the eligibility require-

ments and not be otherwise disqualified from receiving benefits.

### Q. *What are the eligibility requirements for UI?*

**A.** The eligibility requirements vary from state to state but most states look at four criteria, all of which have to be met:

1. applicant earned a minimum amount of wages within a specified period and/or worked for a minimum period in recent past (for example applicant worked at least twenty weeks at average weekly wage of at least twenty dollars);
2. applicant registered for work with the state unemployment office;
3. applicant is available for work; and
4. applicant is actively seeking employment.

### Q. *What will disqualify a worker from receiving UI benefits?*

**A.** As a general rule, a worker is disqualified if he voluntarily quits without good cause or was fired for misconduct. In some states, even if a worker's conduct disqualifies him, the disqualification will last only for a specific length of time, after which the employee will be eligible to receive UI benefits.

The meaning of good cause varies greatly among the states. Some states consider certain types of personal reasons as good cause, such as having to care for a sick relative or following a spouse who has found work in another state. Most states, however, require that good cause be due to the employer's actions. For example, working conditions that are so bad they would cause a reasonable person to quit would be considered good cause in some states. The "reasonable person" perspective is very important to a determination of good cause. It is not enough that a situation is intolerable to a specific worker; the conditions must be such that a reasonable person, in the same position as the employee, would feel compelled to quit.

The meaning of misconduct also varies by state, but generally incompetence alone is not considered misconduct. Violations of known company rules and insubordination are examples of employee behavior normally deemed to be misconduct.

### Q. Can a worker refuse a job offer and still collect UI benefits?

**A.** It depends on why the worker refused the job offer. If the job is not suitable work, then the refusal is allowable. A job is not suitable if the worker has no experience in it, if it is more hazardous than the worker's previous job, or if the physical condition of the worker prevents him from accepting it. States also consider travel costs and time, bad working hours, community wage levels, and compelling personal problems in deciding if a job may be rejected. Finally, workers usually cannot lose benefits for refusing a job that is available because the current workforce is on strike.

If the wages and conditions of a new job are below those of the worker's previous employment, he may not have to accept it. For example, a skilled craftsperson is permitted to refuse a job as a janitor. After a certain period of time, however, most states require the worker to "lower his sights" and accept a lesser job.

### Q. Are workers who are on strike entitled to collect UI benefits?

**A.** It depends on the specific state law. A few states allow workers to collect UI if the strike is caused by an employer's violation of the NLRA or an employer's breach of the collective bargaining agreement. Some states allow workers to collect UI if the employer has "locked out" the workers.

Most states, however, do not permit workers on strike to collect UI benefits. The period of disqualification varies by state—in some states the disqualification lasts for the duration of the strike; in other states the disqualification lasts for a fixed period of time. If a striker is permanently replaced, however, the worker may then be eligible for UI benefits.

### Q. How does a worker apply for UI benefits?

**A.** Employees file claims for UI benefits at their local state unemployment office. The claim should be filed as soon as possible after unemployment begins, since benefits will not be paid until all the paperwork is processed and eligibility for benefits is verified.

Employees should take the following documents with them to the unemployment office to help verify their eligibility: social security card, recent pay stubs, and any documentation relating to the reason for the job loss.

After filing the initial claim, employees are usually required to report on a regular basis to the unemployment office to verify their continued eligibility for benefits. Failure to report when required can result in a loss of benefits.

### Q. How is the amount of UI benefits determined?

**A.** While the amount varies by state, the general formula is 50 percent of the employee's weekly wage, not to exceed a statutory cap on amount paid. The cap is based on a percentage of the state's average weekly wages for all workers. Because of the cap on maximum benefits, most workers receive much less than 50 percent of their weekly wage.

### Q. How long are UI benefits paid?

**A.** The usual duration for UI benefits is twenty-six weeks. In times of extended high unemployment, however, benefits may be paid for an additional thirteen weeks and sometimes longer.

**Q. Can an unemployed worker receive other benefits or earn extra money while collecting UI benefits?**

**A.** Some states ignore small amounts of money earned. Usually, however, income received is deducted from UI benefits. Most states reduce or stop UI benefits for weeks in which an unemployed worker received disability benefits, severance pay, and other types of income.

## PENSION PLANS

**Q. Does the law require employers to provide pensions?**

**A.** No, but if an employer does offer a pension plan, the federal Employee Retirement Income Security Act (ERISA) probably covers it. ERISA applies to private sector employers whose plans are "qualified" under the federal tax laws and/or whose business affects interstate commerce. The tax laws provide important advantages to companies whose plans "qualify," so most pension plans are regulated by ERISA. (For further information on pensions, see the chapters titled "The Rights of Older Americans," on page 571, "Estate Planning," (many references; chapter begins on page 651) and "Family Law," on page 51.)

**Q. What are the participation provisions of pension plans?**

**A.** ERISA provides that where an employer offers a pension plan, most workers must be allowed to participate if they meet the following requirements: they must be at least twenty-one years of age and have completed one year of service to the company. ERISA defines one year of service as a twelve-month period during which an employee has worked 1,000 hours or more.

**Q. How does a worker accrue benefits under a pension plan?**

**A.** Benefit accrual is the process of building up benefits once an employee qualifies for the pension plan. Normally, employees start accumulating benefits as soon as they begin participation in the plan. How benefits accrue depends on the type of pension plan.

A defined-contribution plan establishes a separate retirement account for each participant. The employer (and sometimes the employee) makes a contribution to the account. The benefit due to the worker upon retirement depends

### THE PURPOSE OF ERISA

*ERISA (29 U.S.C. Sections 1001–1461) protects workers who participate in pension plans. It also covers the beneficiaries of such workers. This federal law preempts almost all state laws covering pensions and other types of benefit plans.*

*ERISA deals with the following aspects of pension plans: 1) participation; 2) benefit accrual, vesting, and breaks-in-service; 3) funding; 4) administration of funds; 5) reporting and disclosure; 6) joint and survivor provisions; and 7) plan termination.*

*ERISA sets legal minimums that a pension plan must provide. However, an employer may provide more liberal terms in its pension plan.*

on the amount of money in the account and the payout method selected. Benefits accrue based on a predetermined amount that the employer at least annually pays into the account.

A defined-benefit plan promises a worker a specific level of payment upon retirement. The employer pays money into a fund, whose investment gains are used to pay the retirement benefit. Benefits accrue to workers based on total years of participation in the plan and usually their final salary or their average salary for their last several years of employment.

### Q. When do benefits vest in the worker?

**A.** Vesting refers to the point after which the employee's accrued benefits cannot be taken away; they must be paid to the worker upon retirement. If a worker leaves his place of employment before his pension vests, he loses any benefits that he accrued under the pension plan. Once the benefits vest, however, the worker is entitled to a retirement benefit even if he subsequently quits that job.

ERISA provides two different methods for vesting. One method requires that after five years of service employees are eligible for 100 percent of their retirement benefit. A second method provides for a graduated system of vesting: after three years of service employees are eligible for 20 percent of their pension benefit; after four years, 40 percent; after five years, 60 percent; after six years, 80 percent; and after seven years, 100 percent.

### Q. What happens if there is a break-in-service before pension benefits become vested?

**A.** A break-in-service occurs when employment is interrupted. If a break-in-service occurs before benefits become vested, the worker loses any entitlement to those benefits. When an employee works fewer than 500 hours in a

---

## FIRING WORKERS TO AVOID PAYING PENSIONS

*Employers may not fire employees to avoid making benefit payments or to prevent benefits from vesting. Neither may employers force workers to quit for these reasons. However, a worker can lose nonvested benefits if fired for other reasons, or if he or she voluntarily quits.*

---

## HOW CHANGING JOBS BEFORE RETIREMENT AFFECTS PENSIONS

*If you change jobs before retiring, ERISA provides that you are entitled to all your vested benefits. Any benefits that are not vested at the time of the job change are forfeit. These vested funds may be put into an individual retirement account or may be transferred to your new employer's pension plan. You can also take the vested funds as a lump sum payment. However, if you do this, the money will most likely be subject to an income tax. You can avoid the tax consequences if you "roll over" (quickly transfer) the vested pension funds into an individual retirement account or another qualified pension plan.*

year for the employer, a break-in-service has occurred.

## Q. What are ERISA's funding requirements?

A. Generally, the law requires that the employer (and employee, depending on the type of pension plan) contribute enough money to cover pension payments when they become due, as determined actuarially. Funding provisions aim to strengthen pension funds and prevent abuses. The employer and the fund's administrators are obligated to ensure that the funding requirements are met.

## Q. How does ERISA prevent misuse of pension funds?

A. Those who manage pension funds are considered to be fiduciaries who are obligated to act with "care, skill, prudence, and diligence" in conducting the affairs of the pension plan. This means that the assets of the pension plan must be diversified among a group of investments so as to minimize the risk of large losses. Plan administrators are prohibited from using pension assets to invest in funds or property in which they have a financial interest. ERISA prohibits a plan administrator from borrowing money from the fund for personal use or making loans with pension money to the employer. It also gives pension plan participants the right to sue administrators who breach their duty and violate ERISA.

## Q. How do I file a claim for benefits?

A. Each pension plan specifies the claims procedure. Generally, a vested participant is eligible for payments from a pension fund when he or she reaches the age of sixty-five (or the normal retirement age specified in the plan) or upon leaving the company. Most pen-

sion plans require the participant to file a written claim in order for payments to begin. Within ninety days, the plan administrators must either begin payment to the participant or notify the participant in writing that the claim is denied.

If a claim is denied, the participant is entitled to request a review of the decision. If, upon review, the claim is still denied, the participant can appeal that decision. Some plans provide for arbitration as a means of appeal. When arbitration is required, the participant must use the mechanism. The denial of a claim can eventually be challenged in court by filing a lawsuit under ERISA.

## Q. If a plan participant dies before a spouse, can the spouse still collect the pension?

A. Under ERISA, a pension plan must provide for payment of vested pension benefits to the spouse if a plan participant dies before retirement. This is known as the survivor's benefit. The survivor's benefit is automatically provided unless the spouse consents in writing to waive the benefit.

ERISA also provides that a plan must provide for continuation of retirement benefits to a spouse when a plan participant dies after he begins to receive retirement benefits. This is called the qualified joint and survivor annuity benefit. It is automatically provided under the terms of the pension plan unless the spouse consents in writing to waive the benefit.

## Q. If a plan participant gets divorced, is the ex-spouse entitled to a share of the pension?

A. This depends on state law. Most states consider a pension to belong jointly to a participant and the participant's spouse. If a state court decree orders that part of a participant's vested benefits be paid to an ex-spouse or child,

ERISA requires the plan administrator to honor the court decree.

## Q. How can I find out about the specific terms of my pension plan?

**A.** ERISA requires the employer to give a summary plan description (SPD) and a summary of the annual financial report to every participant in the pension plan. The SPD is a nontechnical explanation of how the plan works and how benefits are paid out. It explains the benefit accrual rules, vesting requirements and procedures for filing a claim for benefits. The summary of the annual financial report is a nontechnical explanation of the financial data relevant to the operation of the plan contained in the annual report. ERISA also requires that the employer make available to the plan participants, upon request, copies of the plan itself and the annual report.

## Q. Does an employer have the right to terminate a pension plan?

**A.** If the pension plan was instituted pursuant to a collective bargaining agreement, then the employer cannot terminate the plan without bargaining with the union over the issue. ERISA itself does not prohibit an employer from terminating a pension plan.

ERISA does, however, provide some protection if a plan is eliminated. The law established the Pension Benefit Guaranty Corporation (PBGC). ERISA requires defined-benefit pension plans to pay insurance to the PBGC. In return, the PBGC guarantees the vested benefits of participants in the fund, up to a certain limit.

The PBGC provides this protection only for certain benefits in specific types of funds. Thus, the PBGC may not protect your benefits if you do not participate in a defined-benefit plan, if your benefits have not vested, or if your plan provides medical and disability benefits.

## WHERE TO GET MORE INFORMATION

This chapter is a basic road map to make you aware of the laws governing employment. If you have questions about your rights and duties, or if you want more details, the agencies listed below can provide additional information. The federal agencies are listed by their main office addresses in Washington, D.C. Most federal agencies, however, have regional offices located in major cities throughout the U.S. To find a federal agency, look in your local telephone directory under "United States Government."

### Discrimination

For more information about workplace discrimination and equal employment, contact:

Equal Employment Opportunity Commission (EEOC)
1801 L Street, NW
Washington, DC 20507
(202) 663-4900
1-800-669-3362 for publications

Your state may also have its own civil rights agency that handles employment discrimination. The EEOC has information on state agencies.

If you work for, or are, a federal contractor, you can receive information about additional legal requirements imposed on contractors and about Affirmative Action Programs from:

Employment Standards Administration
Office of Federal Contract Compliance Programs
200 Constitution Avenue, NW
Washington, DC 20210
(202) 219-9475
(202) 219-9434 (for publications)

## Family and Medical Leave Act (FMLA)

The Women's Legal Defense Fund has a fact sheet explaining FMLA. Write to 1875 Connecticut Ave., NW, Ste. 710, Washington, DC 20009.

9 to 5, National Association of Working Women, has a job-problem hot line staffed 10–5 in the Eastern time zone. Information is offered to the public on job counseling and professional advice, and to members there is a legal referral list on jobs and problems. Call 1-800-522-0925.

The National Institute of Business Management has published *The Employer's Guide to the Family and Medical Leave Act*. Call 1-800-762-4924 for information or write to P.O. Box 25287, Alexandria, VA 22313.

## Union-Management Relations

For information regarding rights and responsibilities under the National Labor Relations Act (NLRA), contact:

National Labor Relations Board
1099 14th Street, NW
Washington, DC 20570
(202) 273-1991

## Wages and Hours

Contact the Wage and Hour Division of your local U.S. Department of Labor office for details on laws affecting wages and working conditions. They offer many publications. The main office is located at:

Wage and Hour Division
U.S. Department of Labor
Room S302
200 Constitution Avenue, NW
Washington, DC 20210
(202) 219-8305

## Workplace Safety

Inquiries concerning job-related safety issues can be directed to the Occupational Safety and Health Administration (OSHA). It can answer your questions and send literature about the OSH Act.

U.S. Department of Labor
Occupational Safety and Health Administration (OSHA)
Suite 3647
200 Constitution Avenue, NW
Washington, DC 20210
(202) 219-8151

## Workers' Compensation

Since the individual states manage these programs, write to your state department of labor for additional information.

## Social Security Disability Insurance

The local Social Security Administration can provide details and literature on your benefits. The main office for the Social Security Administration is located at:

Social Security Administration
Baltimore, MD 21235
1-800-772-1213

## Unemployment Compensation

Contact the local office of your state's employment security or unemployment department or the state job service.

## Pensions

For information about ERISA and your rights under a pension plan, write to:

Pension and Welfare Benefits Administration
U.S. Department of Labor
200 Constitution Avenue, NW
Washington, DC 20210
(202) 219-8233
(202) 219-8920 (for information and materials)

## Government Publications

The federal government publishes hundreds of pamphlets about employment. These range from "how to" books for teenagers looking for jobs to statistics on the number of OSHA claims in a specific year. To find out if there is a pamphlet about your specific problem, check the government bibliographies. They cover subjects such as employment and occupations, retirement, and civil rights, listing all the government publications available under that heading.

The following is a list of the bibliographies about employment issues:

Handicapped—SB37
Employment and Occupations—SB-4
Labor-Management Relations—SB-4
Women—SB-11
Workers' Compensation—SB-08
Veterans Affairs & Benefits—SB-0
Personnel Management, Guidance, and Counseling—SB-02
Civil Rights and Equal Opportunity—SB-07
Occupational Safety and Health—SB-13

The bibliographies listed above are available without charge from the Superintendent of Documents, U.S. Government Printing Office, Washington, DC 20402. The telephone number is (202) 783-3238.

The federal government's Consumer Information Center also distributes free or inexpensive booklets on the law of the workplace. They are available from Consumer Information Center-N, P.O. Box 100, Pueblo, CO 81002, telephone (719) 948-3334.

## Still Have Questions?

The law of the workplace is complex. Your decisions and actions may have far-reaching consequences. It is often worthwhile to consult with a lawyer trained to deal with these matters. Government agencies often advise people with questions to retain a lawyer to represent their unique interests. Contact your state or local bar association for details on lawyers in your area. Many of these organizations have a lawyer referral service. The first chapter in this publication ("When and How to Use a Lawyer," which begins on page 1) can help you find a lawyer.

# Forming and Operating a Small Business

# INTRODUCTION

THIS CHAPTER DEALS WITH the legal and other issues that have to be resolved when forming and operating a small business. It contains six sections. The first section discusses issues that are common to all small businesses, regardless of their legal structure. Section two explores the various types of business organizations that exist in the United States, comparing their strengths and weaknesses and discussing the taxation of each type of business organization. Section three discusses the considerations that must be taken into account when selecting a form of business organization. Section four examines the steps that must be taken to get a new business organized. Section five explores the legal problems that commonly arise during the life cycle of a business, such as changing the legal format or otherwise reorganizing the business and buying, selling, or liquidating the business. Section five also provides a brief summary of what happens when a business experiences financial difficulty or becomes involved in bankruptcy proceedings. The sixth and final section explains where you can go to get help and additional information about your business.

The material in this chapter is written from the perspective of a small business, such as one owned and operated by you and a few other family members or other individuals. The rights of the employees and customers of the business and transactions with your business by third parties, such as landlords or banks, are considered only with respect to the impact they have on the legal structure of the business and your exposure to personal liability for claims they may have against the business. The rights of employees, customers, and third parties are dealt with in more detail in other chapters of this book. See the chapter on "Law and the Workplace" for more information on employer/employee rights and responsibilities. The chapter on "Contracts and Consumer Law" includes details on customer rights, seller responsibilities, and warranties.

## GETTING STARTED

This section deals with some of the major issues that you must resolve before becoming involved in owning or operating a small business.

### Q. What are the first steps that should be taken?

A. There are four preliminary steps that should be taken before deciding to start or buy a business: development of sound business ideas, market research, financial planning, and deciding whether to have co-owners.

### Q. How can market research help?

A. Because the failure rate for new businesses is so high it is important to determine whether a market exists to purchase your service or product, and, if so, the best way to sell it. One important issue to be decided is the location of the business. You may not want to open up a greeting card shop across the street from another greeting card shop in a small town. But two greeting card stores located in a different part of a major shopping center might both be successful. In addition, if your market is specialized or has particular needs, market research will help you to understand what your customer

---

## GETTING A SOUND BUSINESS IDEA

*A sound business idea is a venture that makes economic sense, generally based on your experience and background. You will generally want to choose a type of business with which you are familiar and have some experience. It would not be advisable, for example, for an individual who has no experience in food service operations to open up or buy a restaurant. Because operation of a successful business requires hard work and expertise, prior experience in the same or a similar business will save you the time and expense of developing the background and knowledge of what the particular business requires to be successful.*

---

wants and how to communicate that your business can meet that need.

### Q. How do I develop a financial plan?

**A.** Inadequate or unwise financing is one of the principal reasons why so many new businesses fail. The financial requirements of businesses vary greatly. Trade associations are often a good source of information about the capital needs of a particular business. The local office of the federal Small Business Administration (SBA) and the equivalent state offices can also assist with financial planning for a new business. If the business is going to be run as a franchise operation, the franchisor will probably have a great deal of useful information about the financial resources the franchisee will need. Franchise operations will be discussed in more detail later in this chapter. Finally, banks and private business consultants can help with financial planning. Once you have gathered this information, you are in a position to develop a financial plan.

### Q. How do I secure financing?

**A.** There are, as a general rule, three potential sources of capital for a new business:

1. contributions made by the investors who will be actively involved in the management of the business;

2. loans from banks and other financial institutions; and

3. capital raised from other individuals and institutions.

Capital contributions from the management investors will frequently be insufficient to meet the needs of the business. Loans from financial institutions are a possibility for additional working capital, though the long-term effect of paying off the debt has to be taken into account. Most rates of profit are under 10 percent, making the assumption of an interest-paying burden a severe strain on a beginning business.

If you do decide to borrow capital, the business must have collateral to secure the loan. Financial institutions will also generally require personal guaranties and collateral from the owners of the business, which means that you might have to risk losing your home or other valuable property to get funding. The federal Small Business Administration has loan and lease guarantee programs that are designed to encourage banks and other financial institutions to lend money to small businesses. Many states also have special loan or guaranty programs or financial assistance packages and tax relief plans for small businesses. Information about these programs can be obtained from the local SBA office or the office of the equivalent state or local agency charged with the responsibility of assisting small businesses.

## Q. What are consequences of bringing others into the business?

**A.** The fourth preliminary step is to decide whether you are going to own the business by yourself or have other investors who will have an ownership interest in the business.

The decision to bring others into the business can affect its legal structure. For example, you must have two or more owners to operate a business as a partnership. Partnerships and the other legal forms of business will be discussed in the next section of this chapter. The decision to have co-owners can trigger the applicability of federal and state securities laws, if the co-owners are not going to be actively involved in the operations of the business.

Obtaining capital from other individuals and institutions is a possibility but, because of the potential applicability of federal and state securities laws, must be pursued with caution. The securities laws apply to the sale of any ownership interest in a business where the profits are expected to come from the efforts of others. Under this broad definition, virtually all types of equity or debt ownership interest in a small business sold to persons may be securities. For this reason, you should not contact anyone about investing in a business without fully reviewing your investment plans with a securities lawyer. This includes stock, debentures, and other similar corporate debt instruments, limited partnership interests, and even general partnership interests, where one or more of the general partners does not have the expertise (or authority) to participate in the management of the business.

Assuming a particular type of ownership interest is a security, the antifraud provisions of the securities acts automatically apply. In addition, unless an exemption is available, a prospectus, which is a very technical and complex disclosure document, must be prepared and the securities must be registered with the federal Securities and Exchange Commission and the equivalent state administration office in every state where the securities will be sold. Failure to comply with the prospectus and registration requirements will trigger a variety of administrative and private remedies, including money damages, and, in extreme cases, criminal sanctions.

In most cases, the particular ownership interest will qualify for an exemption from federal and in some cases state registration requirements. An exemption is a statute or regulation that says certain types of securities can be sold to the public without the expense of a prospectus, so long as other specific requirements are met. There is an exemption from federal registration requirements, for example, for a company issuing securities all of which are sold to persons in one state. There are also several exemptions designed primarily for small businesses. These exemptions, many of which are incorporated into what is known as Regulation D, have limitations on the number of purchasers or the total dollar amount of the offering. These exemptions restrict or prohibit advertising of the offering and also restrict resales of the acquired securities. Another complicating factor is that the applicable state securities laws are frequently inconsistent with the federal securities laws, and compliance with both is required.

Needless to say, no one should attempt to issue any securities without the assistance of a lawyer, accountant, and other experts. All the exemptions, however, have very technical requirements with which you must strictly comply. Compliance is also expensive, although complying with the exemptions is less expensive than complying with the full registration requirements.

## Q. Besides these four steps, what other issues need to be considered before going into a new business?

**A.** The remainder of this section will discuss issues other than the legal format of the business. These include the location of your business, insurance, various licenses and permits, tax identification numbers and tax registration, protection of any patents, trademarks, and copyrights that will be owned or licensed by the business, whether to operate your business as a franchised operation, and employer-employee problems.

It is important that you carefully review all of these issues, even if it ultimately turns out that some of them are not applicable to your particular business. Some businesses, for example those that are involved in health care or food service, are subject to complex regulation by numerous federal, state, and local agencies. Other businesses, on the other hand, may only be subject to minimal regulation. The size of the business can also affect the extent of the regulations. The laws of most states, for example, exempt businesses with fewer than four or five employees from having to carry workers' compensation insurance covering injuries to employees. Even if your business is exempt, you might still decide to carry workers' compensation insurance because of the protection it would give both you and your employees in the event one of your employees is injured while working in the business.

### Q. Why is the location of a business so important?

**A.** There is an old adage that goes something like this: What are the three most important reasons for the success of a business? The answer is location, location, and location. The location of the business vis à vis your competitors has already been discussed in connection with the need to conduct market research for your business. Location is important for other reasons as well.

### Q. What are these other reasons?

**A.** One is the necessity of being located in an area that is convenient for your customers and clients. Your market research should help you to find a suitable location for your business; but that's not the only decision you have to

make. Another important decision is whether to own or lease the building where the business is to be located.

### Q. What are some of the most important issues involved in a commercial lease?

**A.** A detailed discussion of commercial leases is beyond the scope of these materials, but four important issues to look for should be mentioned—the amount of the rent, an option to renew, an option for additional space and protection against competitors.

### Q. How do you determine the rent?

**A.** In most cases the rent in a commercial lease will be expressed as so many dollars per

---

**BUY OR LEASE YOUR PLACE OF BUSINESS?**

*Unless you already own a suitable building, this can be a difficult decision. Buying or building a new building generally involves a larger capital outlay than a lease, but if the building is mortgaged, the term of the mortgage will frequently be longer than the term of a lease of similar space. On the other hand, commercial leases are generally much longer and more complex documents than residential leases and should be reviewed by your lawyer before you sign the lease agreement. Your lawyer should, of course, also review all the documents involved in the purchase or construction of any building you buy or build.*

square foot. This is the annualized price for the unit, so the monthly rent is determined by multiplying the rent per square foot by the total number of square feet in the unit and dividing by twelve months. For comparative purposes with other suitable rental units, you need to know whether the rent includes or excludes taxes, insurance on the building, and utilities. To the extent it excludes them, you will have to pay for these items in addition to the rent.

Sometimes rent escalation clauses permit the owner to raise the rent because of inflation or when taxes or utilities go up during the year. Finally, many retail and restaurant leases will include clauses that require the tenant to pay either a flat monthly rental or a rental based on a set percentage of sales in the store or restaurant, whichever is higher.

### Q. What is an option to renew?

**A.** A second important issue in commercial leases involves an option to renew the lease at the end of the lease term for an additional term. Without an option to renew, you may be forced to move or to pay an extraordinarily high rent to remain where you are just at the time the business is becoming very profitable. To provide maximum protection, the rent, or at least a formula for determining the rent during the renewed period, should be specified.

### Q. What is the significance of an option for additional space?

**A.** A third issue that needs to be investigated is an option to lease additional space and the rent for that space. That option allows the new business to lease only the amount of space it needs, with the protection of being able to increase the amount of space when and if it is needed. The advantage of an option is that you are not obligated to rent the additional space unless you want to.

### Q. Can the lease protect my business from competitors?

**A.** A fourth issue involving commercial leases that can be important in some types of business is a provision prohibiting the lessor from leasing space to a competitor, or if the lessor will not agree to this, a provision stating that space leased to any competitor must be located on a different floor or in a different wing of a shopping center.

### Q. What about operating a business out of my home?

**A.** For some types of businesses, especially those where you visit your customers rather than being dependent on their coming to your place of business, this is fine. In some situations, you may be able to deduct the rental value of the space you use for your business operations on your income tax return. To qualify for the deduction, however, your home office must, as a general rule, be your principal place of business, be located in a separate structure not attached to your house, or be used on a regular basis by your clients or customers.

One of the most prevalent types of businesses operated from homes is a day care center. Many states have special license requirements for day care centers. In some states the licensing and other requirements for day care centers in private homes having only a few children are less rigorous than larger group day care centers. Finding out what regulations apply is important for this and every type of business.

### Q. What types of licenses and permits are required for a business?

**A.** It depends on the type and location of the business. All states have statutes and regulations that require tests, proof of financial responsibility, and compliance with other requirements to obtain a license to engage in a particular business or profession. A state license to operate a day care center is one example. Doctors, lawyers, and even barbers have to be licensed by the state before they can practice their profession. The types of businesses subject to these licensing requirements vary from state to state.

Some businesses exempt from state licensing regulations are required to obtain a license or permit from a county or city to perform certain operations. Building contractors, for example, have to get a city or county building permit to build a house or commercial building.

Most cities and many counties require businesses located in their jurisdiction to have a business license. In reality, this is a tax based generally on the gross receipts of the business rather than a regulatory license designed to protect the public against shoddy work and incompetence. Avoiding this tax can be an important factor in choosing the location of a business.

### Q. What kinds of insurance will I need?

**A.** As is the case with most of the other issues discussed in this section, it depends to some degree on the type and size of the business. The exemption from workers' compensation insurance for small businesses with very few employees is an example of this principle. Another is employee fidelity bonds, which are a form of insurance to protect against embezzlement. Some businesses are required to have fidelity bonds for employees such as bookkeepers who handle money. Most businesses, however, can choose whether to bond all or some of the employees.

Some of the other types of insurance a typical small business will want to consider include:

- business interruption insurance (often referred to as business continuation insurance) to offset losses if the business is forced to shut down for a substantial period because of a fire, flood or other catastrophe;

- liability insurance, including product liability insurance, to protect against damage claims filed by third parties injured on the premises, by delivery trucks or other company vehicles, or by a product produced by the business;

- malpractice and errors and omissions insurance for professional businesses;

- director and officers (D & O) liability insurance to pay the expenses and damage awards against corporate executives as a result of suits filed against them by shareholders of the corporation;

- medical insurance covering the owners and the employees of the business;

- disability insurance, which pays a portion of the salary of an employee or owner who has a long-term disability and cannot work;

- life insurance that will provide a death benefit to the families of the owners and the employees and possibly provide funds to compensate the business for the loss of one of the owners (often called "key man" insurance) and funds to purchase the equity interest of a deceased owner;

- unemployment insurance, which is really a tax based on the payroll of a business used to pay benefits to all long-term unemployed workers in a state.

### Q. What tax registration and identification numbers, tax forms and the like are required for a new business?

**A.** There are several federal and state requirements. The Internal Revenue Service (IRS) publishes a pamphlet entitled "Your Business Tax Kit," which is available at any IRS office. It contains a great deal of helpful information on the various federal taxes that apply to a business. Many state tax commissions have similar publications describing the state taxes that apply to a business. Both types of publications contain samples of the tax registration and other forms that must be filed.

All businesses must obtain a Federal Employer Tax Identification Number before beginning to operate. Each state also requires tax registration by a new business. In most cases the state will use the Federal Employer Tax Identification Number (see sidebar). All states that have sales taxes also require any business that is not exempt from the tax to register with the appropriate state agency. The business is required to collect and remit to the state on a regular basis (monthly or more frequently) the applicable sales tax.

Every business is required to withhold from employee wages federal and state income taxes and FICA (social security and Medicare) taxes and regularly remit these funds to the IRS (in the case of federal withholding and FICA) and the applicable state tax agency. Businesses whose total federal payroll tax liability for the prior year is $50,000 or less must deposit payroll taxes in a special account once a month. Businesses whose payroll taxes for the prior year exceeded $50,000 must deposit the tax money two times each week. The total deposits must then be paid to the IRS at the end of each quarter. The state

requirements may or may not be the same as the federal deposit requirements. It is important to know the requirements and follow them, as there may be heavy penalties for late payment.

Most states require registration or at least periodic filing with the state agency that administers the state unemployment insurance tax, which is a tax based on the businesses payroll. A business must also pay the federal Unemployment Insurance Tax, which is also based on its total payroll, on a periodic basis.

In addition, all businesses must file annual federal and state income tax returns. The applicable forms vary with the type of business. Partnerships, "S" corporations, limited liability companies, and other businesses that as a general rule pass the tax consequences of their operations to their owners file a different type of return from that of businesses that are operated as "C" corporations. The differences in the way various types of business organizations are taxed will be discussed in the next section of this chapter. "S" and "C" Corporations are terms that are applied to different types of corporations for tax purposes. The characteristics of these designations are described on page 491.

---

## GETTING AN EIN

*The EIN, as the Federal Employer Tax Identification Number is known, is obtained by filing an IRS form SS4, which can be obtained from any office that has IRS forms. If the form is mailed, the EIN will be issued in four to six weeks. Alternatively, the SS4 can be faxed to 816–926–7988 and the number will be issued within 24 hours, or the applicant can call direct (816–926–5999) and receive the EIN number verbally. If the latter method is used, the applicant must place the number on the SS4 and mail the form to the IRS for processing.*

## Protection of Patents and Other Intellectual Property Rights

**Q. How can patents, trademarks, trade secrets, trade names, and copyrights owned or licensed by an investor or a business be protected?**

**A.** These types of property are generally referred to as intellectual property rights. Each type is subject to special legal and tax rules, which will be briefly described below. Because of the highly technical nature of intellectual property rights, it is essential that competent legal counsel be consulted as soon as possible once it becomes evident that such a right exists, in order to maximize the protection of the developer or owner of the right.

**Q. What kinds of inventions are patentable and what is the advantage of obtaining a patent?**

**A.** Not every invention is patentable. By statute, the invention must fall into at least one of four classes: process (for example, manufacturing of chemicals or treating of metals), a machine, an article of manufacture, or composition of matter (for example, mixtures of chemicals). In addition, based on existing technology (known technically as prior art), the invention "would not have been obvious at the time the invention was made to a person having ordinary skill in the art to which said subject matter pertains." This is usually referred to as the "unobviousness" test. Not only must the invention meet the foregoing criteria, it must have some utility and not be frivolous or immoral, and there must be proof that it can be made operative. Moreover, a patent will not be issued if the invention has been described in any printed publication anywhere in the world or was in public use or offered for sale anywhere in the United States for more than one

year prior to the time an application for a United States patent is filed. Assuming all these conditions are met, the patent may still not be issued because of existing valid conflicting patents. Even if it is not possible to obtain a patent, however, it may be possible to provide basic protection for the owners of the invention through the trade secret doctrine, or in the case of a design invention by means of a trademark or copyright. These and other possibilities, such as an unfair competition claim against unauthorized users of the invention, should be explored with the client's patent counsel.

The application for a patent is filed with the Patent and Trademark Office in Washington, D.C. The grantee of a patent has nonrenewable exclusive monopoly in the United States to use or assign rights to use the patent for seventeen years from the date of issue. A patent issued in the United States does not provide any protection in another country, however. For such protection, additional patents must be obtained. In order to have maximum protection in all other countries that are signatories to various treaties and conventions establishing reciprocal priority rights, foreign patent applications must be filed in this country. Since patents in many other countries are subject to onerous taxes and in some cases compulsory licensing within the country, it is often advisable not to seek foreign patents, or to seek them only in countries where it will be economically worthwhile to do so.

The time involved in pursuing all the procedural steps in obtaining a final decision on a patent may take several years. Since the seventeen-year life of a patent begins to run only from the date of issue and an infringement claim can cover the period between the filing of the application and the issuance of the patent, however, the inventor's rights are not prejudiced by the delay, assuming a valid patent is ultimately issued.

### Q. What are the tax consequences of patents?

**A.** For tax purposes, marketing an invention involves two stages. The first is the research and development stage, when the invention is refined and reduced to practice. The expenses incurred in this stage are generally deductible. The second stage involves the tax consequences of sale or license of the patent once it is issued. Self-exploitation of a patented invention has no particular tax consequences. The sale or license of rights in an invention, however, can produce either ordinary income or capital gains, taxable at a lower rate than ordinary income under current law. The Internal Revenue Code has very stringent requirements, however, for obtaining capital gains treatment, and it is very important to seek the early assistance of a lawyer who is familiar with the tax consequences of patents. This is particularly true if there is any possibility the patent will be transferred to a business with the expectation that the owners of the business will receive capital gains treatment on the royalties generated by the patent. For this plan to work, the invention must be transferred to the business prior to the time the invention has been tested and successfully operated or has been commercially exploited, whichever is the earlier. It is often difficult to determine when an invention has been reduced to practice.

If a patent is going to be transferred by the inventor to a business in which the inventor has an ownership interest, it is generally easier to achieve favorable tax treatment if the business is a partnership or limited liability company than if it is a corporation.

### Q. What are trade secrets?

**A.** A trade secret, sometimes referred to as "know-how," is generally defined as an aggregation of data or information not generally known in the industry that gives the user an advantage over competitors. Common examples of "know-how" are formulas, manufacturing techniques and processes, designs, patterns, programs, systems, forecasts, customer lists, specifications, and other technical data. A trade secret is not patentable, nor can it be registered as a trademark. Trade secrets are recognized legally as proprietary rights and are protected against unauthorized use by the courts. However, for information to continue its status as "trade secrets," its owner must take appropriate steps to protect it from disclosure and maintain its confidentiality.

### Q. How are trade secrets taxed?

**A.** Trade secrets are not specifically covered anywhere in the Internal Revenue Code. Nevertheless, the tax treatment of trade secrets and "know how" is fairly well established by the courts.

---

## USING A PATENT TO GENERATE INCOME

*An inventor can maintain total control of a patent and manufacture and market goods employing a patent as a sole proprietorship. Alternatively, the inventor can sell or license the patent to others on an exclusive or nonexclusive basis in return for a payment called a royalty. One option is for the inventor to sell or assign the invention to a new or existing business in which the inventor is an investor with the expectation that the business will develop and market the patented product. These various methods of marketing a patent have different tax consequences.*

The expenses incurred in developing a trade secret can be either amortized or deducted. There are no other tax consequences associated with trade secrets unless they are transferred, for example, as part of the sale of all the assets of a business. In some situations, the amount allocated to the trade secrets may qualify for capital gains treatment.

### Q. What are trademarks and trade names and how are they protected?

**A.** A trademark is generally defined as any work, name, symbol, or device used by a manufacturer or distributor to distinguish its goods from those manufactured or sold by others. A related property right is a service mark that is basically the same as a trademark except that it relates to services rather than goods. Certification marks, such as seals of approval and collective marks used to indicate membership in an organization, are also related concepts. Applications for registering a trademark are filed with the Commissioner of Patents and Trademarks, Crystal Park Building, 2121 Crystal Drive, Arlington, VA 22202, telephone (703) 305–8600.

A trade name is generally the name that the business uses for advertising and sales purposes that is different from the name in its articles of incorporation or other officially filed documents. Most states authorize the protection of a trade name by filing in that state. Drawing the line between a trademark and a trade name can sometimes be difficult. Is "McDonald's" or "Holiday Inn" a trade name, a trademark, or both? It is often advisable to seek protection under both sets of statutes in these situations.

Your lawyer will help you search to discover whether there is an existing trademark or copyright that may conflict with yours.

### Q. How are trademarks and trade names taxed?

**A.** The cost of developing and registering a trademark or trade name must be capitalized.

The advertising and promotional expenses incurred in marketing goods and services subject to a trademark or trade name, are, however, deductible as selling expenses.

The sale of a trademark or trade name can generally result in capital gains treatment. Instead of an outright sale, a trademark or trade name is frequently licensed to one or more third parties, often as part of a franchise agreement. (Franchises are discussed in the next section of this chapter.) The income received from this licensing arrangement will generally be treated as ordinary income rather than capital gains.

### Q. How are artistic efforts protected by copyrights taxed?

**A.** An individual who creates an artistic work, unlike the inventor of a patentable product, is unable to obtain capital gains treatment upon the sale or transfer of the rights to the work. However, capital gains tax treatment is possible when the creator of the artistic effort is a corporation or business entity taxed as a partnership. Thus, sales of films produced by a corporation, partnership, or limited liability company can, under some circumstances, qualify for favorable capital gains tax treatment.

## Franchises

### Q. Is operating a business as a franchise something I should consider?

**A.** Franchising is essentially a method of marketing and distributing products and services that usually involves the licensing of an established trademark or trade name or both. There are well over 500,000 franchised outlets in this country in virtually every type of business. Franchises employ several million employees and generate several hundred billion dollars of receipts each year. In many industries, franchising is the dominant form of distri-

## ART THAT IS PROTECTABLE BY A COPYRIGHT

*Seven types of artistic endeavors can be copyrighted:*

*1. literary works;*

*2. musical works;*

*3. dramatic works;*

*4. pantomimes and choreographic works;*

*5. pictorial, graphic, and sculptural works, including fabric designs;*

*6. motion pictures and other audio visual works; and*

*7. sound recordings.*

*Copyright protection is obtained by placing the symbol © and the name of the copyright holder on every publication of the material and filing a copyright application for the artistic work with the Federal Copyright Office, Copyright Information Office, Library of Congress, 101 Independence Avenue, SE, Room #LM 401, Washington, D.C. 20540, telephone (202) 707–9100.*

bution. For example, most automobile and truck dealerships and soft drink bottlers are franchisees.

### Q. What are the advantages of franchising?

**A.** From a manufacturer's or distributor's point of view, the logic behind franchising is simple: it requires a great deal less capital to distribute goods and services by use of franchises than by operating company-owned units, and additional income is generated from licensing trademarks and trade names and from other services provided by the franchisor to the franchisee. The major benefits to the franchisee are the use of the good will of the franchisor's trademarks and trade name, and expert guidance in such matters as site selection, training of employees, bookkeeping and other managerial services. These items are particularly valuable to the inexperienced business person who desires to own his or her own business but

wants to minimize the risk of failure. These services also make franchising an attractive vehicle for encouraging minority-owned businesses.

### Q. What kinds of fees and costs must a franchisee pay to the franchisor?

**A.** Typically, the franchisee will pay a franchise fee, which can often be spread out over a period of years, for the right to use the trademarks, trade names, and trade secrets of the franchisor and for managerial services involved in getting the franchise established. Frequently, a franchisee will also be required to purchase all its initial equipment, including signs and trade fixtures, from the franchisor. The franchisee may also be required to purchase many of its supplies from the franchisor or from franchisor-approved sources. In addition, a franchisee will normally pay the franchisor a royalty, which is usually based on a percentage of the gross receipts from the franchised goods or services. The royalty covers such items as advertising and continuing managerial services as well as a licensing fee for use of the franchisor's trademark and trade names. If the franchisor owns the franchised location, the franchisee will obviously have to pay rent for the building to the franchisor.

### Q. What type of business form should a franchisor or franchisee use?

**A.** The determination by a franchisor or franchisee to operate as a proprietorship, partnership, corporation or limited liability company is essentially the same as for any other business. The size and financial success of the business, tax considerations, and the potential exposure of the investors to liabilities from the operation of the business are the principal factors that influence the choice of business form.

In this connection, a franchisor may, in some circumstances, be held liable for the debts, torts, or taxes of a franchisee. Increasingly, franchisors are being held liable for product liability claims based on defective products manufactured or distributed to franchisees and ultimately sold by the franchisees in retail sales. In many states the doctrine of privity, which at one time would have barred any damage or injury claim directly against the manufacturer and any intermediate distributor, has been abolished or curtailed. In addition, the Magnuson-Moss Warranty Act authorizes a direct suit against a manufacturer in any case involving express written warranties made by the manufacturer in connection with sales of consumer products. Franchisors are also vulnerable to a variety of claims asserted by their franchisees.

### Q. What legal protection does a franchisee have?

**A.** Considerable evidence suggests that historically the franchise marketing system has been abused by both franchisors and franchisees, particularly by the former. This abuse has prompted a considerable amount of litigation and remedial legislation in recent years both on the state and federal level. Many states, for example, have statutes that regulate the sale, termination and transfer of franchises.

The most significant federal regulation of franchising is the Federal Trade Commission (FTC) rule entitled "Disclosure Requirements and Prohibitions Concerning Franchising and Business Opportunity Ventures."

### Q. What does the FTC franchise disclosure rule require?

**A.** Essentially the FTC rule requires that a franchisor give a potential franchisee a disclosure statement (on twenty different topics) that is similar to a securities registration statement. Detailed information about the business and financial history of the franchisor and its principals, the franchise agreement, and financial obligations of the franchisee are required by this rule. Provisions regulating statements by the franchisor concerning potential profitability are also included in the rule. These projections must be related to the geographic area where the franchisee is to operate, and the franchisor must disclose the factual basis of the projections. The disclosure statement, which must be updated within ninety days after the close of the franchisor's fiscal year, and a copy of the franchise agreement, must be given to a prospective franchisee before any person-to-person meeting between the franchisor and franchisee, or at least ten business days before the franchisee signs any binding agreement to purchase the franchise or makes any payment for the franchise, whichever date is the earlier. Violation of the rule is an unfair trade practice subjecting the franchisor to a cease and desist order, damages, and fines of up to $10,000 for each violation.

## PRECAUTIONS BEFORE SIGNING A FRANCHISE AGREEMENT

*In addition to careful study of the disclosure statement and all proposed contract documents, the FTC recommends that before investing in a franchise you take the following precautions:*

1. *consult with an attorney and other professional advisors before making a binding commitment;*

2. *be sure that all promises made by the seller or its salespersons are clearly written into the contracts you sign and be sure the franchisor provides training programs for new franchisees;*

3. *talk with others who have already invested in the business and find out about their experiences; and*

4. *if you are relying on any earnings claims or guarantees, study the statement giving the basis for the claims and find out the percentage of past investors who have done equally well.*

**Q. How can a lawyer help an individual or group considering a particular franchise?**

**A.** There are a number of areas in which an attorney can provide valuable services to a client considering a franchise. For example, though some state laws make it difficult to make major changes in a franchise agreement, the franchisee's lawyer can often help negotiate the critical terms of the franchise agreement with the franchisor. It is sometimes possible to work out an agreement to reduce the initial fee, to spread out payment of the initial fee over a longer term than originally proposed, or to require a rebate of a portion of the initial fee if the franchise is terminated before the expiration of the contract term. Additional protection of the franchisee against excess competition from the franchisor or other franchisees can also frequently be negotiated. Rights of the client to additional franchises in the area should be explored. Another important area of negotiation concerns the circumstances under which the franchisor can terminate or refuse to renew the franchise and the amount of the franchisor's control over the price and other terms of any sale or other disposition of the franchise. Although franchisors have traditionally resisted any changes in their standard printed agreements, there is evidence that they are becoming more flexible in their willingness to negotiate terms and to remove from their standardized franchise agreements provisions that have resulted in successful claims of overreaching and antitrust violations.

Besides negotiating the terms of the franchise agreement, the franchisee's lawyer can also provide valuable counseling services, for example, by assisting the client in obtaining additional information on the franchisor from financial services companies such as Dun and Bradstreet, Better Business Bureaus, and other franchisees, and in evaluating the economic risks of the particular venture compared to other similar franchised and nonfranchised ventures. The amount of initial fees and royalties and uses of the royalty income vary significantly even among franchisors in the same line of business. Careful investigation may uncover improper hidden charges and kickbacks. Frequently the franchisee will not be experienced in financial matters, including knowledge of necessary start-up costs, working capital needs, and available financing sources. The information provided a prospective franchisee under the FTC Disclosure Rule and from other sources is of no real value if the client is unable to evaluate it properly. A lawyer can also negotiate the business's lease and other related agreements.

## Employer-Employee Relations

### Q. How are employer-employee relations regulated?

**A.** There are numerous federal and state statutes that regulate employer-employee relations. Most of these statutes have been enacted in the past thirty years. A list of some of the most important federal legislation in this field includes the following:

- The Norris-LaGuardia Act and the Labor Management Relations Act, which regulate labor unions.

- The Fair Labor Standards Act, which primarily regulates minimum wages, maximum hours, and overtime.

- The Equal Pay Act, which prohibits sex-based pay differentials for equivalent work.

- Title VII of the 1964 Civil Rights Act, the principal statute that prohibits employment discrimination based on race, color, sex, religion, or national origin. Title VII also established the Equal Employment Opportunity Commission, which is the main administrative body with responsibility to enforce employment antidiscrimination legislation.

- The Age Discrimination in Employment Act, which prohibits discriminatory practices in hiring, firing, compensating, and setting terms of employment of individuals forty years of age or over.

- The Occupational Safety and Health Act of 1970, administered by the Occupational Safety and Health Administration (OSHA), which sets safety and health standards for production plants and machinery.

- The Americans with Disabilities Act, which requires removal of barriers to persons with disabilities by all businesses "providing public accommodations," a term that is much broader than it sounds and includes restaurants, theaters, and even doctors' offices.

- The Employee Retirement Income Security Act of 1974, referred to as ERISA, which establishes substantive and procedural rules for employee pension and welfare benefits, such as medical coverage.

- The Family and Medical Leave Act, enacted in 1993, which requires employers to allow individuals up to twelve weeks of unpaid leave per year to care for a child or other family member without fear of dismissal or other penalty.

In addition to these statutes, there are a number of federal statutes that affect private businesses only if they receive federal financial assistance. Examples are the Comprehensive Employment and Training Act of 1973, which prohibits discrimination in special employment incentive programs that receive federal assistance, and Titles VII and VIII of the Public Health Service Act, which prohibit discrimination in health training programs that receive federal assistance.

There are also many state statutes that regulate employment relations. Some of these

## PREVENTIVE LAW TO THE RESCUE

*Because of the differing exemptions, the overlap between the various applicable statutes and the involvement of various federal and state administrative agencies, there are many problems in complying with all the regulations (many of which are inconsistent) and developing case law. Moreover, the law in this area is developing and changing so rapidly that it is advisable for businesses to invite employment law specialists to visit the business on a regular basis to review recent legal developments and any existing and potential employment law problems the firm has. This "preventive law" approach can help to reduce the incidence of employment law problems and the severity of any problems that do arise.*

state statutes parallel and often overlap federal statutes. Others, however, deal with issues not dealt with in federal statutes. The most prominent of these are the state workers' compensation statutes, which compensate employees for job-related injuries on a no-fault basis.

### Q. Is every one of these acts applicable to small businesses?

**A.** Almost all businesses are subject to one or more of these statutes. Some small businesses may, however, be exempt from one or more of the acts, because of their size. For example, Title VII of the Civil Rights Act covers only employers having fifteen or more employees, and the Age Discrimination in Employment Act covers only businesses having twenty or more employees. On the other hand, the Fair Labor Standards Act, the Equal Pay Act and the Americans With Disabilities Act cover virtually all nongovernmental employers.

### Q. Can compliance with these regulations be avoided by the use of temporary workers and independent contractors?

**A.** The answer is generally yes, assuming the contractual relation creating the arrangement is bona fide. The use of temporary workers, including leased-employee arrangements, part-time employees, and independent contractors, has been growing rapidly in recent years. By using these kinds of workers instead of full-time employees, a business may be able to qualify for an exemption from many of the federal and state statutes that regulate employers. Moreover, having very few employees saves on health insurance premiums and makes it less costly for a business to have generous fringe benefit plans for the principal executives.

These cost savings must, of course, be borne by the company that provides the temporary employees and the independent contractors providing services for a business, which in turn may increase the amount the business must pay for these services. These companies, however, can often provide compliance more efficiently and cost effectively than most small businesses.

The downside for companies using temporary and leased employees is the considerable risk of lower morale on the job, reduced quality and productivity, and the need to be seeking and training workers constantly. When figuring in these factors, many companies have concluded that the cost savings are illusory and they're better off with experienced, full-time employees.

## TYPES OF BUSINESS ORGANIZATIONS

There is a wide variety of basic legal formats for structuring a business. Each type has its own special characteristics, uses, and limitations. The proprietorship, partnership, and corporation are the most popular and well-known. A newer but increasingly popular form of business organization is a limited liability company. The principal characteristics of all these types are described in this section.

### Q. What is a sole proprietorship?

**A.** A sole proprietorship is an unincorporated business that is owned by one person. If there is more than one owner or the business is incorporated as a corporation, a process that is described later in this chapter beginning on page 486, it cannot be a proprietorship.

A proprietorship can have employees, however, and, except for a few restrictions that vary from state to state, can operate any type of business. If you conduct a business without co-owners and take no legal steps to become another form of business, then you are a sole proprietor with respect to that business even if you are not aware of this fact. A person who, for example, on a part-time basis paints pictures in her home which she exhibits and sells is a sole proprietor with respect to her paintings and therefore must comply with all applicable tax, licensing and other regulations.

Sole proprietorships are the most prevalent form of business in this country. Recent published statistics indicate that there are over 14 million proprietorships compared to 3.5 million corporations and 1.6 million partnerships.

### Q. What are the advantages and disadvantages of a proprietorship?

**A.** The sole proprietorship is an inexpensive and informal way of conducting a small business. Its drawbacks are full personal liability for the owner (explained below) and the danger of liquidation at the death of the proprietor.

The principal advantage of the sole proprietorship is that it is the simplest form of business organization. No statutes similar to those applicable to corporations and partnerships govern its organization or operation, though, as explained in the section of this chapter on getting organized, if the person uses a name other than his or her own, he or she may need to file a "Doing Business as Certificate" or "Assumed Name Certificate." The sole proprietorship provides an entrepreneur with an opportunity to own his or her own business without the formalities and expense of incorporation or the

### WHEN THE PROPRIETOR DIES

*The single-ownership principle combined with the lack of separate entity status creates severe problems at the death of the proprietor. Legally a sole proprietorship ceases to exist at the proprietor's death. Unless the executor is authorized to continue the business during the administration of the estate, a new owner is found, or the business is incorporated, the proprietorship will have to be liquidated with the consequent loss of the going concern value. For the same reasons, providing an optimum estate plan for a sole proprietor is more restricted than with the other forms of business organizations.*

necessity of sharing control of the business with others, as is the case in a partnership or in a corporation having more than one shareholder.

The fact that the assets and obligations of a sole proprietor are not separate from those of the proprietor results in the proprietor's being fully liable for the debts and other liabilities of the proprietorship, and avoids a separate level of taxation on the business. The taxable income, credits, and deductions of the business must be reported by the proprietor on his or her individual income tax return.

A proprietorship also has the least flexibility of all the business forms with respect to raising capital. No ownership interests can be sold to other persons; and the ability to borrow money for the business is dependent on the net assets of the sole proprietor.

## Q. What are partnerships?

**A.** A partnership is an unincorporated association of two or more persons who carry on a business for profit as co-owners. A partnership exists if these conditions are met, even though the persons involved do not know or intend that the business be a partnership. If a husband and wife, for example, are jointly operating an unincorporated retail shoe store, unless it is clear from their financial records that one of them is the true owner and the other is merely an employee (in which event the company would be classified as a sole proprietorship), the business will be a partnership and both the husband and wife will be considered as partners and co-owners of the business.

## Q. What kinds of partnership exist and what are the differences between them?

**A.** There are two types of partnerships recognized in the United States: general partnerships and limited partnerships. The fundamental distinction between the two types is that in a limited partnership, there must be at least one limited partner and at least one general partner. The advantage of being a limited partner is that if the business is unsuccessful, the limited partner may lose the amount of money invested in the partnership, but has no other financial risk. In this sense a limited partner bears the same risk of loss as a shareholder in a corporation or a member of a limited liability company. General partners, including general partners in a limited partnership, on the other hand, can lose not only whatever money or other property they have put into the partnership, but in addition their personal assets can be used to satisfy the unpaid claims of the partnership's creditors. This is why general partners are said to have unlimited liability whereas limited partners are said to have limited liability.

The following are the primary differences between general and limited partnerships: first, only limited partners have limited liability; second, limited partners can lose their limited liability if they take part in control of the business and third parties believe them to be general partners; third, a change in the number or composition of limited partners is not potentially as disruptive as the retirement, death, or disability of a general partner; and fourth, there are in general more legal formalities connected with limited partnerships, including the necessity of filing limited partnership certificates in one or more places, keeping them up to date, and maintaining certain records. With the exception of compliance with state and local assumed name statutes, there are no mandatory filing requirements for general partnerships in most states.

## Q. What are the advantages of partnerships?

**A.** The principal advantage of partnerships is the ability to make virtually any arrangements defining their relationship to each other that the partners desire. There is no necessity, as there is in a corporation, to have the ownership interest in capital and profits proportionate to the investment made; and losses can be allocated on a different basis from profits. It is also generally much easier to achieve a desirable format for control of the business in a partnership than in a corporation, since the control of a corporation, which is based on ownership of voting stock, is much more difficult to alter.

Because it is possible to sell equity interests in a partnership, the ability to raise capital in a partnership is greater than in a proprietorship. However, as a result of the greater familiarity with the corporate form, and the potential of personal liability or lack of participation in control in a partnership, a corporation may have a greater ability to raise capital than a partnership.

With careful advance planning, a partnership can avoid some of the problems inherent in a proprietorship when an owner dies, retires, or becomes disabled. In fact, many believe that a limited partnership is an ideal vehicle to provide for continuity and succession in a family business.

The mechanics of succession vary with the situation. If you want to pass your share of the business to other family members (usually a spouse or children), it is relatively simple to transfer your interest to them, perhaps by leaving the family members enough cash (possibly through life insurance proceeds) to buy out the others and thus avoid conflicts. (In a small corporation, you could leave voting stock to family members who will operate the business, and leave nonvoting stock to others.)

Things get slightly more complicated if you decide to pass ownership on to people who are not beneficiaries of your will. If your business is a partnership, you will usually want your partners to remain in operational control. A "buy-sell agreement" is the most common device for transferring ownership of a business on the death of a partner. Under such an agreement, the remaining partners agree to purchase your interest when you die. This allows the business

to continue running smoothly with the same people in charge, minus one.

Buy-sell agreements typically provide that at the owner's death, his or her interest in the business will be acquired by the remaining partners or shareholders, or by the business itself, leaving the deceased owner's relatives with the proceeds of the sale. Life insurance is usually the vehicle used to finance these arrangements, which lets the business avoid a drain on its cash. The partners buy life insurance on each other's lives, and the proceeds go to the surviving spouse, children, or other designated beneficiaries, in return for the deceased owner's share of the business.

Partnerships are taxed on a conduit or flow-through basis under subchapter K of the Internal Revenue Code. This means that the partnership itself does not pay any taxes. Instead the net income and various deductions and tax credits from the partnership are passed through to the partners based on their respective percentage interest in the profits and losses of the partnership, and the partners include the income and deductions in their individual tax returns.

### Q. What are the disadvantages of partnerships?

**A.** The major disadvantages of a partnership, as with a proprietorship, stem primarily from the fact that a partnership is not as stable as a corporation. This results from the fact that a general partnership technically dissolves whenever a general partner dies, files for bankruptcy, resigns, or otherwise ceases to be a partner (dissociates). A general partnership and a limited partnership dissolve on the dissociation of a general partner unless either a remaining general partner continues the business or all the partners (or under some statutes, a majority) agree to continue in business. Upon dissolution, a partnership will normally be required to be liquidated, but in most large professional general partnerships, the partners agree to continue the business. However, a corporation, under most statutes, continues forever until some affirmative action is taken to dissolve it.

It may be more difficult in a partnership than in a corporation to have a hierarchy of management and to raise capital from outside sources. Careful planning and drafting, however, can minimize or eliminate most of these and other supposed disadvantages of a partnership, through agreements providing for a specific governance relationship and desired variations in capital ownership in a partnership. This is particularly true with respect to limited partnerships.

### Q. What are corporations and how do they differ from other types of business organizations?

**A.** A corporation is a legal entity that is formed by filing what is known as articles of incorporation or a certificate of incorporation with the secretary of state in your state along with the required filing and license fees.

One or more persons can form a corporation. Thus, a sole proprietor can incorporate if he or she wants to. Although there are some exceptions (doctors and lawyers are prohibited by ethical and regulatory constraints from operating in certain types of corporations), corporations can generally operate any type of business.

The person or persons who file the articles or certificate of incorporation are called incorporators. The equity ownership interest in a corporation is called stock and the owners of shares of stock are called shareholders or stockholders. There are two types of stock, common stock and preferred stock. They differ in that dividends generally must be paid on the preferred stock before the common stock receives dividends. Another difference is that upon liquidation, the owners of the common stock are paid the amount of the corporation's assets left over after paying all the creditors and the amount due the holders of the preferred stock (which usually includes accrued but unpaid dividends and the par value or redemption value allocated to the preferred stock). In short,

## THE BASIC CHARACTERISTICS OF A CORPORATION

*Acceptance of a corporation as a separate legal entity evolved during the 19th century. It is now well established that a corporation has a legal status that is independent of its shareholders. Partnerships and limited liability companies are also legal entities for some purposes. The separate entity status of partnerships is, however, less complete than in corporations. The entity status of limited liability companies, on the other hand, is virtually the same as corporations.*

*The corporation's independent existence as an entity undergirds the basic corporate attributes of limited liability, perpetual existence, free transferability of shares, and the ability to own property, bring suit, and be sued in the corporate name. It also accounts for the tripartite system of corporate management, consisting of shareholders, directors, and officers.*

the common stock is entitled to the residual value of the corporation. That is why the value of the common stock fluctuates with the success of the corporation. If the corporation is successful, the value of the common stock will increase to the extent the net profits are not paid out in the form of dividends. On the other hand, if the corporation loses money, the value of the common stock will decrease in order to reflect those losses. There are instances in which the value of stock will increase even if the corporation is not showing a profit. This is particularly true in start-up companies in which there are no profits available for reinvestment but the business is growing or developing.

### Q. What is the advantage of corporate limited liability?

**A.** Shareholders generally are at risk only for the amount of money or other property they invest in the corporation, though some state laws impose shareholder liability for unpaid wages in small corporations. Creditors of the corporation whose claims are greater than the assets of the corporation cannot satisfy their excess claims against the personal assets of the shareholders, unless the shareholders have previously obligated their personal assets by personal guarantees or co-signing a note or other obligation in their individual capacity. This ability to shield personal assets from the creditors of a corporation has long been the principal reason why investors have been more willing to invest in a corporation than any other type of business organization. As was pointed out earlier, sole proprietors and general partners are personally liable for all the debts and other obligations of a business they own. Given a choice, an investor will always choose limited liability to unlimited liability.

It is now possible to achieve at least some form of limited liability in most other types of business organizations. Limited partners, for example, have limited liability. So do all of the

members in a limited liability company. Moreover, the shareholders of a corporation that is a general partner also have limited liability, though the corporate general partner itself is liable. Nevertheless, the corporate-style limited liability is generally thought to be more complete and to provide more flexibility than in other types of business organizations. Limited partners, for example, lose their limited liability if they take part in the control of the partnership in a manner not permitted by the state's governing statute, provided that creditors are led to believe by that control that the limited partner is a general partner. Corporate shareholders do not, however, lose their limited liability by exercising control rights. In fact, one of the most important attributes of share ownership is that shareholders control the corporation through their voting rights.

When shareholders of a corporation guarantee its debts, co-sign its notes in their individual capacity, or pledge their own assets as security for loans to the corporation, which frequently occurs because of creditors' demands, the shareholders waive their limited liability with respect to those debts, notes or assets. But this is a limited waiver. The shareholders in question still have limited liability with respect to any other debts or obligations of the corporation.

The following example will help to illustrate this distinction. Suppose the sole shareholder in a corporation personally guarantees payment of a $20,000 bank loan that is used to purchase a new delivery truck for the corporation. Subsequently the corporation ceases doing business and is liquidated. At the time of liquidation the corporation has $50,000 of assets and the creditors of the corporation other than the bank that made the truck loan have valid claims of $75,000. Assume further that the unpaid balance on the bank note is $15,000. The bank can recover the $15,000 owed it directly from the shareholder because of the personal guarantee. The other creditors, however, can recover only

**THE IMPORTANCE OF PERPETUAL EXISTENCE**

*When a general partner ceases for any reason to be a partner, the partnership will end up being dissolved and liquidated unless the remaining partners agree to continue the business. Getting necessary consent from the partners to continue the business can be very difficult and may be impossible. Yet liquidation may result in significant losses to all the partners. This risk of dissolution and liquidation is one of the principal drawbacks of operating a business as a partnership. In a corporation, on the other hand, if a shareholder leaves, there is no risk of liquidation (unless that departing shareholder has a contractual or voting right to force a liquidation) because the life of a corporation is indefinite. Thus, perpetual existence gives a corporation permanence, and this in turn is thought to make investments in a corporation somewhat safer and less risky than investments in business organizations that have less inherent permanence.*

*A reasonable form of perpetual existence can be obtained in both partnerships and limited liability companies through buyout agreements and other contractual arrangements, but these agreements must be carefully crafted to meet various legal and tax requirements.*

$50,000 from the corporation. They cannot recover the additional $25,000 they are owed from either the corporation, because it does not have any more assets, or from the shareholder, because his other assets are protected by the limited liability doctrine.

### Q. Is the ability to freely transfer shares of a corporation important?

**A.** In large corporations with many shareholders, the answer is yes. Being able to freely transfer shares to anyone at any time gives an investor the right to liquidate his or her investment at any time. This right to transfer makes shares of the stock very marketable, provided, of course, there is someone who wants to buy them. The shares of all the corporations whose stock is registered with a stock exchange like the New York Stock Exchange are, for example, freely transferable.

But in a small corporation with only a few shareholders, free transferability of stock can often be a detriment. Assume, for example, that one of the three founding shareholders of a corporation that operates a camera store wants to sell his or her shares to someone the other two shareholders intensely dislike. Assume further that in order for the camera store to be successful, it is necessary for all three of the shareholders to work in the store on a regular basis without undue friction between them. If the shareholder who wants to sell can freely transfer his or her shares to anyone, and the other two shareholders cannot prevent the sale, disastrous results may ensue. In many states, a complete prohibition against the transferability of stock is not possible, and that is the reason why in most small corporations, the shareholders will enter into what is known as a shareholders' agreement or a share transfer restriction agreement, which, subject to case law and statutory requirements, will impose restrictions on the sale of stock. Legal counsel is needed to draft the terms of such an agreement.

Restricting the free transferability of the shares, however, can produce its own set of problems, one of which is that the shareholder who wants to sell may not be able to find a buyer acceptable to the other shareholders. To counteract this illiquidity problem, the shareholders may want to enter into what is known as a redemption or cross-purchase agreement, under which the corporation or the other shareholders agree under certain specified conditions to buy the stock of a shareholder who wants to liquidate his or her investment in the corporation.

### Q. How does the separate entity status of a corporation affect its right to own property, bring suit, or be sued in its corporate name?

**A.** A corporation as a separate legal entity has the right to own and dispose of property in its own name and to sue and to be sued in its own name. This facilitates commerce by not requiring action by all shareholders.

While partnerships for some purposes are not considered as entities, all states have statutes that allow them to own and convey property in their own name. Moreover, most states now have statutes that allow partnerships to sue and be sued in their own name. Suits by and against partnerships used to be a significant problem, however, until these statutes were enacted.

A limited liability company, like a corporation or a partnership, may own property and commence and defend lawsuits in its own name. A proprietorship, on the other hand, does not have separate entity status, but this does not cause any practical problems because there

is only one person, the sole proprietor, in whose name title to property belonging to the proprietorship is taken. Moreover, suits by and against a proprietorship must be in the name of the sole proprietor, even if the proprietorship operates under a name different from that of the proprietor.

### Q. How are small corporations managed?

**A.** The tripartite management scheme works well in a large corporation. But it can cause difficulties in a small corporation having only a few shareholders. In a corporation with one shareholder, for example, it is burdensome to go through the mechanics of having that shareholder elect himself or herself as a director and then in a subsequent meeting elect himself or herself to various offices. Yet that is what is

---

### A DISTINCTIVE MANAGEMENT STRUCTURE

*There are three levels of management in a corporation. The shareholders, as previously discussed, own the equity stock and vote on fundamental issues affecting the corporation. One issue of vital importance is the right of the shareholders to elect the directors of the corporation. The directors are by statute in charge of managing the corporation. They in turn select the officers, who run the corporation on a day-to-day basis and as the agents of the corporation implement the policies established by the board of directors.*

required by the corporate statutes in most states.

Voting is based on number of shares, not number of shareholders. Consider a situation where one of three shareholders in a corporation owns 67 percent of the stock and the other two own the remaining stock. Because directors are elected by a majority of the stock, the 67 percent shareholder can nominate and elect all the directors, and the directors in turn will elect all of the officers. Because the holders of two-thirds of the shares under corporate statutes can approve any action that shareholders are entitled to vote on, the 67 percent shareholder can vote to merge with another corporation or to liquidate the corporation, regardless of the wishes of the two minority shareholders.

It is possible to give the minority shareholders in the above example some protection through various special provisions that have been incorporated into state corporate statutes in recent years. One way is to have cumulative voting, where if three directors are to be chosen, shareholders can use their votes for one director, rather than vote for each candidate. Another way to enhance the rights of the minority shareholders would be to create two classes of shares and allow each class to elect an equal number of directors. Since the directors elect the officers, a slate of officers acceptable to the minority shareholders would have to be proposed in order to elect any officers. Each class voting separately would also have to approve any fundamental change in the corporation, such as a merger or liquidation. Thus, the minority shareholders would, in effect, have equal management rights in the corporation even though they own only one-third of the stock.

### Q. How does the managment structure of a corporation compare with that of a general partnership?

**A.** The management structure of a general partnership is very different. Unless the part-

ners otherwise agree, each partner has one vote, and action in the ordinary course of business requires approval by a majority of the partners. Extraordinary action, however, requires unanimous consent of all the partners. Thus, in a general partnership with three partners, one of whom has 67 percent of the capital and profits, the 67 percent partner can be outvoted on all ordinary course of business decisions by the other two partners. The 67 percent partner could, however, prevent the partnership from merging with another partnership.

Another difference between general partnerships and corporations is that in most partnerships the partners perform every management function in their capacity as partners. Therefore, you do not need to have the three levels of management that exist in a corporation. In a large partnership, however, for the sake of convenience and efficiency, the partners will often select one or more managing partners to run the business on a day-to-day basis. In this type of arrangement the managing partners are like the board of directors and officers of a corporation, and the other partners function somewhat like the shareholders in a corporation.

### Q. Is the management structure of limited partnership different?

**A.** A limited partnership has a management structure that is a hybrid between a general partnership and a corporation. The general partners are like the managing partners in a general partnership. The limited partners are like passive nonmanagement shareholders in a corporation. However, they lose their limited liability if they take part in the control of the business with respect to people who are misled by such participation in control into believing that a limited partner is a general partner.

In a limited partnership, voting rights of the partners, including the general partners, may be modified by the agreement of the partners. In the absence of such an agreement, decisions are

> **SIMPLE AS CAN BE**
> *The management structure of a proprietorship is quite simple. The sole proprietor is the only person who has management power so there are none of the complexities that exist in the other forms of business organizations.*

made by the general partners on a per capita basis, as is the case in a general partnership.

### Q. What is the management structure of a limited liability company?

**A.** The management structure of a limited liability company has features of both partnerships and corporations. Unless management is delegated to designated managers, the investors in a limited liability company, called members, exercise all management rights. This is the same basic scheme as exists in a general partnership. The various limited liability statutes differ, however, with respect to whether the members have per capita voting rights, as in a general partnership, or voting rights based on the respective percentage of total capital.

### Q. How are corporations taxed?

**A.** There are two subchapters in the Internal Revenue Code that govern corporations. One is Subchapter S, which corporations meeting designated criteria can elect. The other is Subchapter C, under which the majority of corporations operate.

### Q. How are corporations that elect to be under Subchapter S taxed?

**A.** S corporations, as they are commonly called, are taxed in a manner similar to partnerships, although there are important differences between S corporations and partnerships. Except in a limited number of circumstances, an S corporation does not itself pay any taxes. Rather, the income and deductions generated by the S corporation are passed through to the shareholders, who report their proportionate share on their individual tax returns. The requirements for qualifying to elect to be taxed as an S corporation are discussed later.

### Q. How are corporations taxed under Subchapter C of the Internal Revenue Code?

**A.** A corporation which has not made an election to be taxed as an S corporation must pay a tax on its net taxable income, and then the shareholders must pay a second tax on any of the corporation's net earnings that are distributed in the form of taxable dividends. In many cases, the total of these two taxes, plus the tax on any money received by a shareholder as a salary for working in the corporation, will be more than if the same income was subject to only one level of taxation—as is the case with S corporations, proprietorships, partnerships, and limited liability companies, which are taxed on the conduit or flow-through theory. Although the corporation's income is taxed when earned, a shareholder is not taxed until property or cash is distributed to the shareholder in an operating distribution, redemption of the shareholder's shares, or liquidation.

The double taxation of C corporation taxable income is definitely disadvantageous when the combined taxes payable by the corporation and its shareholders exceed the total taxes payable if the business were operated as a partnership, proprietorship, limited liability company, or S corporation. With respect to fringe benefits, however, C corporations enjoy a distinct tax advantage over the other forms. Shareholders who are employed by a corporation in some capacity—unlike sole proprietors, partners, and the members of a limited liability company, who are regarded as self-employed—can qualify as employees of the company and, therefore, are eligible for special life and medical insurance programs and other fringe benefits offering advantageous tax results. For the most part, however, these fringe benefits must not discriminate in favor of any highly paid corporate executives and therefore involve significant costs to the business. The overall tax savings derived from these fringe benefits is usually marginal, and in most situations it will not constitute a significant factor in deciding whether to incorporate a new business.

### Q. What is a business corporation?

**A.** A business corporation is a corporation, generally organized for profit, that is formed under a state's corporation act or business corporation act. If a general business corporation, (including a professional corporation or a close corporation) does not qualify or elect to be an S corporation, it will be treated as a C corporation and subject to double taxation under Subchapter C of the Internal Revenue Code. Shares of stock in a business corporation are securities subject to state and federal registration unless they or the transactions in which they are sold are exempted from such laws.

### Q. What is a close corporation?

**A.** A close corporation is one in which, as a general rule, all or most of the shareholders are actively involved in managing the business. Many state corporation statutes have special provisions that are designed to meet the needs of close corporations. These special statutes vary from state to state but generally provide that the shareholders may manage the corporation directly rather than through directors or officers and that the shareholders may make other agreements for management which are not available to other corporations.

The term "close corporation" is applied not only to corporations formed under close corpo-

> **SEVERAL TYPES OF CORPORATIONS**
>
> *As is evident from the prior discussion of taxes, there is more than one kind of corporation, just as there is more than one kind of partnership. The various types of corporations, however, are not as distinct as are general and limited partnerships. From a nontax perspective there are three principal forms of corporation: the general business corporation and two specialized derivatives of the general business corporation, the close corporation and the professional corporation. For federal income tax purposes any of these corporations may be subject to double taxation (a C corporation) or, if the corporation otherwise qualifies and elects to be taxed as such, an S corporation.*

ration statutes, but also to those with a small number of shareholders, who are generally actively involved in the management of the corporation. Using this criterion, most corporations qualify as close corporations. A study made several years ago concluded that 95 percent of all corporations in the United States had ten or fewer shareholders.

### Q. What is a professional corporation?

**A.** This kind of corporation is limited to the practice of one or more professions with licensed professionals as its shareholders. Tax advantages are now marginal, but protection from malpractice on the part of other shareholders remains an important motive for incorporation rather than practicing a profession as a sole proprietorship or in a partnership, although under some state laws these corporations do not protect innocent shareholders from personal liability.

Historically, professionals such as doctors, lawyers, and accountants have been prohibited from conducting business in a corporate form. The main rationale advanced for this policy is the necessity of preserving full individual liability for professional malpractice and the fact that only individuals could be licensed. Under traditional corporate law, the separate entity doctrine would theoretically protect a professional doing business as a corporation from personal liability for malpractice committed by his or her associates, even though a judgment in excess of the corporation's assets is recovered by a claimant.

A professional corporation is a business corporation and may be a close corporation with a fancy name. The major differences are that:

1. most of the professional corporation statutes limit the purposes of a professional corporation to the practice of a single profession;

2. only licensed professionals employed by the professional corporation can be shareholders or directors—a requirement that necessitates a mandatory buy-out plan if the professional retires, dies, or has his or her license to practice suspended or revoked;

3. although a professional is individually liable for his or her own malpractice, in most states there is no liability for the malpractice of other professionals in the professional corporation; and

4. either the term "professional corporation" or "professional association," or one of their abbreviations, must be used in the corporate name and included on all letterheads, contracts, and advertising material.

Several states in the past few years have enacted statutes, included as part of their general partnership statutes, that protect partners against malpractice liability to the same extent as, and in some cases provide more complete protection than, professional corporation statutes. Partnerships electing this status are called limited liability partnerships.

Because of the decrease in the tax advantage once enjoyed by professional corporations and the advent of limited liability partnerships, there are likely to be fewer new professional corporations founded in the future than in past years.

### Q. What is an S corporation?

**A.** An S corporation is a business corporation (including a professional corporation, a close corporation or both) that has elected to be taxed in a manner similar to a partnership under Subchapter S of the Internal Revenue Code rather than according to the provisions of Subchapter C, the normal corporate tax section. As previously explained, the principal distinction between S and C corporations is that S corporation income for the most part is not subject to double taxation at both the corporate and the shareholder level. Recent federal tax legislation that has liberalized the eligibility requirements for S corporations and changed the maximum rates on taxable income has dramatically increased the number of S corporations. At the present time, approximately one-third of all corporations are S corporations.

The basic eligibility requirements are that the corporation be a domestic corporation and not have:

1. more than one class of stock;

2. more than thirty-five shareholders;

3. or own 80 percent or more of the stock of another corporation.

All of the shareholders must be individuals (some trusts and estates can qualify, however), and must be U.S. citizens or resident aliens. Any corporation, including a professional corporation and an existing C corporation, can elect to be taxed under Subchapter S if the eligibility requirements can be met. If it appears it may be advantageous at some point to be an S corporation, however, it is generally advisable, because of some very complex potential adverse tax consequences, to start off as an S corporation rather than converting from a C to an S corporation sometime after incorporation.

### Q. How does does a corporation choose to be taxed as an S corporation?

**A.** The election to be taxed as an S corporation is made by filing a Form 2553, which must be signed by all the shareholders. The Form 2553 must be filed not later than two months and fifteen days after the beginning of the taxable year in which it is to be effective. For newly formed corporations that wish to have subchapter S apply from their inception, the taxable year begins when the corporation has shareholders, acquires property, or begins doing business, whichever occurs first. This technicality can be a trap for the unwary. For example, the period for filing the Form 2553 begins to run from the day the corporation enters into a lease, even though it is not at that time conducting any business operations and even though the incorporation process is incomplete and no shares have been issued to the shareholders. If the Form 2553 is filed after the two-month, fifteen-day period, the subchapter S election will not be effective until the corporation's second taxable year, and it will be taxed as a C corporation for its first taxable year. Therefore, it is important that the Form 2553 be filed as soon as possible after the articles of incorporation have been filed.

### Q. What is a limited liability company?

**A.** A limited liability company (LLC) is an unincorporated business organization that pro-

## HOW STATES TAX S CORPORATIONS

*The taxation of S corporations under state tax laws varies from state to state. For the most part, S corporations are taxed the same under state law as they are under the Internal Revenue Code. Some states, however, exact a special tax on S corporations that is similar to the state's income or franchise tax on C corporations. The differences in state taxation of S corporations can also cause technical difficulties for shareholders who are residents of states other than the state where the S corporation has its principal place of business. These are issues that shareholders should discuss with a lawyer and accountant before deciding whether to elect subchapter S status.*

vides the same flexibility of organization as a general partnership, the same limited liability protection for its owners, called members, as is provided to the shareholders of a corporation, and, generally, the same pass-through taxation as a partnership. The combination of flexibility, limited liability and the avoidance of the two-tiered tax on C corporations makes an LLC very attractive to investors.

There are two other features of LLCs that make them attractive. First, the members may have full management rights without the prohibition against taking part in the control of the business that applies to limited partners in a limited partnership and the cumbersome three-tiered management structure of shareholders, directors, and officers of a corporation. Second, although a member can, unless otherwise agreed, freely transfer his, her, or its financial rights in an LLC, under many of the statutes rights to participate in the governance may not be transferred without the consent of the remaining members. This protects the remaining members against unacceptable transferees becoming involved in the management of the business.

Moreover, there are no restrictions on the number or type of persons who can be members of an LLC or the types of interests. Consequently, LLCs can be used in far more situations than S corporations, which can have no more than thirty-five shareholders, all of whom, with the exception of certain types of trusts and estates, must be U.S. citizens or resident aliens. An LLC, for example, can have a nonresident alien, corporation, partnership, or another limited liability company as a member.

### Q. Aren't limited liability companies fairly new?

**A.** Yes. The first LLC statute in this country was enacted in 1977 by Wyoming. Florida adopted a similar act in 1982. Very few LLCs were formed, however, until after 1988 when the Internal Revenue Service ruled that they would be taxed as partnerships rather than as C corporations as long as they met certain requirements. The two principal requirements are that the membership interests not be freely transferable and that the limited liability company not have the same type of continuity of existence as a corporation. These requirements are relatively easy to meet under the existing LLC statutes.

Over two-thirds of the states now have LLC statutes, and in all probability every state will have enabling legislation within the next few years. The existing statutes differ greatly,

however, and these differences can create uncertainty. Moreover, the legal status of LLCs that do business in states that do not have enabling legislation is uncertain. State taxation of LLCs also varies. A majority of the states tax them as partnerships. Some states, for example Florida, tax them as corporations, and others impose a high annual license or franchise fee on LLCs. In addition, many technical federal and state tax issues are still being resolved. As these and other uncertainties, caused primarily by the newness of this type of business organization, are being resolved, an increasing number of businesses are being formed as LLCs, and this trend is expected to continue. Some experts predict that in time LLCs will supersede partnerships and S corporations as a preferred form of business entity, but in all probability, LLCs will provide an alternative to existing business structures, to be used only in appropriate circumstances.

### Q. What kinds of businesses operate as limited liability companies?

**A.** LLCs can be used for virtually any type of business. The types of businesses where they have been used most frequently have been those where taxation as a partnership produces advantageous tax consequences. LLCs are widely used for real estate ventures; extraction of oil, gas and minerals; high-tech ventures, for example, a company formed to exploit a patent; corporate joint ventures; as a vehicle for acquisitions; agriculture; and venture capital companies. Because of their corporate-style limited liability, LLCs are also becoming more widely used as a form of business organization by professionals such as doctors, lawyers, and accountants. Some states, however, do not as yet allow certain professionals to practice as an LLC.

The following summary chart compares the essential features of the eight forms of businesses discussed in this section.

# Characteristics of Business Forms

| Characteristics | Proprietorship | General Partnership | Limited Partnership | Regular Corporation |
|---|---|---|---|---|
| Limited Liability | No | No | No, general partners; Yes, limited partners | Yes |
| Management Rights of Owners | All rights belong to sole proprietor | Yes, partners vote on a per capita basis unless agreed otherwise | Yes, general partners; No, limited partners, who can, however, have voting and other rights so long as no control | Holders of majority of voting shares elect directors who in turn select officers and other agents |
| Transferability of Ownership Interests | Freely transferable—but very limited market | Financial rights are transferable but transferee does not become a partner without the consent of all remaining partners | Same as general partnership unless agreement provides otherwise | Shares freely transferable and no distinction between financial and management rights as in partnerships and limited liability companies |
| Business Continuity on Dissociation of Owner | No | No—withdrawal of a partner generally results in a dissolution and liquidation unless all the partners agree that the business can continue | No—withdrawal of a general partner results in dissolution unless business continued by agreement of the remaining partners; withdrawal of a limited partner generally has no effect on continuity | Perpetual existence |
| Taxation | Single tax—owner taxed directly | Single tax—partners include their pro rata share of income and deductions on their individual tax returns | Same as general partnership | Double tax—income initially taxed at corporate level; shareholders pay additional tax on dividends and other distributions from the corporation |
| Distinctive Features | There is no legal distinction between the sole proprietor as an individual and the business | (1) Unlimited liability of the partners; (2) lack of continuity because of danger of liquidation when a partner leaves | (1) Unlimited liability of the general partners but limited liability of the limited partners; (2) the inability of the limited partners to take part in the control of the business | (1) Limited liability of the shareholders; (2) the three-tiered management scheme of shareholders, directors, and officers |

## CHOICE OF BUSINESS FORM

**Q. What are the principal nontax factors that should be considered?**

**A.** For obvious reasons most investors want limited liability. Investors in businesses where all or most of the owners will be actively involved in the management of the company will usually also want restrictions on the transfer of ownership interests and a simple management structure. In addition, most investors want to be able to continue the business even after one or more of them leave.

| S Corporation | Close Corporation | Professional Corporation | Limited Liability Company |
|---|---|---|---|
| Yes | Yes | Yes as to liabilities other than shareholders' own malpractice | Yes |
| Same as regular corporation | Same as regular corporation, but right to vary by agreement | Same as regular corporation, but right to vary by agreement | Yes—same as general partnership but most statutes specify that the members vote in accordance with % ownership of capital |
| Shares freely transferable but as a general rule transfers are restricted by share transfer restriction agreements to protect the remaining shareholders against unacceptable transferees | Same as S corporation | Same as S corporation, but only licensed professionals of the same profession can be transferees | Same as general partnership |
| Perpetual existence | Perpetual existence | Perpetual existence | Essentially the same as a limited partnership |
| Except in limited circumstances, single tax at the shareholder level basically similar to partnerships | Will be taxed as either a regular corporation or an S corporation | Same as close corporation | Same as partnership |
| (1) Limited liability of shareholders; (2) lack of flexibility because of restrictions on number and types of shareholders (individuals and some trusts) | (1) Limited liability; (2) ability to modify the management and free transferability characteristics of a regular corporation | (1) Exclusion of shareholder's own malpractice from limited liability; (2) only useful for those professionals who cannot have corporate limited liability because of ethical or statutory restrictions | Combination of the same limited liability as a corporation and the tax and nontax flexibility of a partnership |

All of these features can be achieved to a greater or lesser extent in most types of business organizations, although it is more difficult to obtain the desired results in some forms. For example, it is possible to have limited liability in a general partnership if all the general partners are corporations or limited liability companies. Similarly, corporate-style limited liability can be achieved in a limited partnership where all of the general partners are corporations or limited liability companies. This type of structure may not be desirable, however, for other reasons. Incorporating all the general partners can add unnecessary expense, especially when the alternatives of forming a corporation or limited liability company are available, and may adversely affect the tax consequences desired by the investors.

Restrictions on transfers and a simplified management structure, inherent characteristics of partnerships, can be obtained in corporations by carefully crafted agreements among the shareholders, although, except in close corporations, most formalities of the statutory management structure in state corporation codes will need to be observed.

Finally, in most situations business continuation agreements authorize the purchase of a departed owner's investment and allow the business to continue. These agreements, however, can be very complex and expensive.

Only a lawyer has the necessary training to analyze the deficiencies in a particular form of business and to be able to draft the proper agreements to overcome these deficiencies, to the extent it is possible to do so.

### Q. Are there any other nontax factors that should be taken into account when soliciting a business form?

**A.** There are always factors that at first appear to be insignificant, but may in the end turn out to be critically important. Therefore, it is important to be sensitive to the possibility that one or more of these factors may be present.

Organizational and administrative costs are an example. Proprietorships and general partnerships involve the least expense because no written documents or public filings (except possibly to comply with an assumed name statute) are legally required. It would be prudent, however, to have a written agreement or general partnership agreement defining the rights and obligations of the partners. Also, there are generally no annual fees to be paid. Written documents and various filing and annual fees are required for all the other business forms, however. The total of these expenses can be significant.

> ## CHOOSING THE BEST ORGANIZATIONAL FORM FOR YOUR BUSINESS
> *There are many tax and nontax factors that must be taken into account in making this critical decision. As a general rule, more than one form will be available. Choosing the best of the available forms is a complex task and requires expert assistance from your lawyer, accountant, and other advisors.*

When a business intends to do business in more than one state, the law of the various states where it expects to operate must be investigated to determine if any special problems exist. A limited liability company, for example, should probably not be used if a significant amount of a company's income is expected to come from sales in a state that does not have a limited liability company act.

If the business organization will borrow money in a state that has usury laws, these laws normally set maximum interest rates that can be charged for a loan, but provide exceptions for corporations, meaning that the corporation is permitted to give up the benefits of the usury law to obtain a loan. If a lender will only make a loan to the business at an interest rate in excess of this limitation, it may be necessary to form a corporation to borrow the money. Having to incorporate for this reason is less likely to occur today than in the late 1970s and early 1980s because general interest rates are relatively low. But interest rates are very cyclical and at some point in time rates will increase substantially above today's rates.

Finally, state law restrictions can limit the possible choices. A sole proprietor who wants both limited liability and basic partnership taxation, for example, can achieve these goals by incorporating as an S corporation, but because most limited liability company statutes require a minimum of two members, cannot operate the business as a limited liability company.

### Q. What are the principal tax factors that should be taken into account in selecting a business form?

**A.** The applicable tax factors are even more complex than the nontax factors, and changes in the tax statutes and regulations can dramatically alter the way taxes affect the various types of business organizations. Bearing this limitation in mind, four generalizations might provide some useful guidance.

First, under the present income tax structure, there is a presumption that a business should be formed as a proprietorship, partnership, limited liability company, or S corporation rather than as a C corporation.

Although the following chart indicates that except for taxable income between $75,000 and $140,000 the C Corporation tax rate for 1994 is less than the individual rates applicable to other types of businesses, tax rates per se do not tell the whole story.

As was previously explained (see page 491), C Corporation taxable income is subject to a double tax. First, a C corporation must pay taxes on its taxable income at the rates specified in this chart. In addition, the shareholders must pay taxes at the individual rates applicable to them for any income they receive from the corporation in the form of salaries or dividends. The combination of both these taxes can often be higher than the taxes that would be payable if the business was operated as an S corporation, partnership, or limited liability company. Even if the total taxes paid by the C corporation and its shareholders on taxable income generated by the corporation are less than if the business were operated in another form, the difference in most cases will not justify operating a small business as a C corporation. Moreover, there are other tax disadvan-

## Comparison of 1994 Individual Joint Tax Rates With C Corporation Tax Rates

| Dollar Amount | Individual | C Corp | Differential |
|---|---|---|---|
| Up to $38,000 | 15% | 15% | None |
| $38,000–50,000 | 28% | 15% | C Corp. + 13 |
| $50,000–75,000 | 28% | 25% | C Corp. + 3 |
| $75,000–91,850 | 28% | 34% | C Corp. –6 |
| $91,850–140,000 | 31% | 34% | C Corp. –3 |
| $140,000–250,000 | 36% | 34% | C Corp. + 2 |
| $250,000–10,000,000 | 39.6%* | 34%** | C Corp. + 5.6 |
| $10,000,000–15,000,000 | 39.6% | 35% | C Corp. + 4.6 |
| Over $15,000,000 | 39.6% | 35%*** | C Corp. + 4.6 |

* Includes 10% surtax

** +5% or $11,750, whichever is less

*** +3% or $100,000, whichever is less

NOTE 1: Professional Corporations that are C Corporations are taxed at a flat rate of 35%.

NOTE 2: The dollar levels for the various rates are adjusted each year based on increases in the consumer price index.

tages of operating as a C corporation, including the potential application of the higher corporate alternative minimum tax and the tax liabilities incurred in liquidating a C corporation or converting it to another business form, which more than offset the possibility of lower annual taxes based entirely on a tax rate structure that can be changed at any time. In this connection, it is worth noting that from 1986–1992, the tax rate for C corporations was higher than that of business forms for most levels of taxable income.

Second, as a general rule, if flow-through taxation is important, partnerships and limited liability companies provide more flexibility than S corporations because of the ability in partnerships to authorize special allocations of income and losses and to make distributions of capital without triggering adverse tax consequences.

Third, consider the possibility that at some point in the expected life cycle of the business it might be advisable to change the organizational format. For this reason it is important to remember that it is possible to go from a proprietorship to any other form, to convert a partnership to another form of partnership or to a limited liability company or corporation, and to convert a limited liability company to a partnership, all on a tax-free basis. It is also possible to convert an S corporation to a C corporation without adverse tax consequences. But it is not possible to convert any type of corporation into a proprietorship, partnership, or limited liability company, or to convert a C corporation into an S corporation without serious tax problems.

Finally, as is the case with nontax factors, be alert to special facts that may end up limiting the available choices. For example, if the business will have a corporate shareholder, then Subchapter S will not be available and a partnership or limited liability company will have to be used if pass-through tax treatment is desired.

## GETTING ORGANIZED

This section will describe in general terms the legal steps that must be taken to organize a new business and get it to the operational stage.

**Q. In which state should the business be organized?**

**A.** In the state where the business will have its principal place of business. This will generally also be the state where the principal investors live. Every state's laws have some shortcomings, but as a general rule these can be overcome by carefully drafted agreements.

**Q. What steps are involved in organizing a proprietorship?**

**A.** Very few, as a general rule. A sole proprietorship is the simplest form of business. The only legal requirements are usually a business permit or license and tax identification numbers. If the business is to operate in a name other than that of the proprietor, it may be necessary to comply with a state or local assumed name statute. No written documents will be necessary unless the proprietorship is buying or leasing property or will operate a franchise.

**Q. What steps are involved in organizing a general partnership?**

**A.** From a strictly legal point of view, the same as in a proprietorship. Although there is no requirement that a general partnership have any kind of written agreement, it would be foolish not to have one, if for no other reason than to provide concrete evidence of the partners' agreement.

A written partnership agreement will typically contain provisions relating to capital accounts and drawing accounts, partner salaries, reimbursement of expenses, vacations and fringe benefits, voting rights, the rights of the partners when one of them leaves the partnership, admission of new partners and what happens if the

## INCORPORATING IN A "FRIENDLY" STATE

*Some states have a reputation for having laws favorable to a particular form of business. This is true, for example, with respect to the Delaware Corporation Code. The features of the Delaware Corporation Code that are touted as being important reasons for incorporating there are for the most part applicable only to large corporations with hundreds of shareholders. For example, if a small corporation whose investors and business operations are in Oregon were to incorporate in Delaware, the corporation would have to qualify as a foreign corporation in Oregon. Moreover, annual fees and license taxes would have to be paid in both states and a lawyer admitted to practice in Delaware would have to be retained whenever a corporate law problem involving the business arises. These extra expenses are rarely justified.*

ment known as a certificate of limited partnership to be filed, together with a specified filing fee. While the information required to be in the certificate of limited partnership varies, all the statutes require the name of the limited partnership, the address of its principal place of business and the name and address of the agent for service of process, the name and business address of each general partner, and the latest date when the partnership will dissolve. Some of the statutes also require the business purpose to be specified and also the circumstances under which additional capital may be required. All the statutes also authorize the partners to include any other information they wish in the certificate.

**Q. What steps are necessary to organize a limited liability company?**

**A.** There are two documents that a limited liability company must have.

The first is a document generally referred to as "articles of organization" which must be filed in the office of the secretary of state in your state. The statutory requirements vary, but generally the articles of organization must contain the same type of information as is required in a certificate of limited partnership. One difference is that most of the limited liability company statutes require the articles of organization to specify whether the LLC will be member managed or manager managed (a situation similar to having managing partners in a partnership) and the names and addresses of the members or managers.

The second required document is generally referred to as an operating agreement. It is also sometimes called a member control agreement or referred to as "regulations." This agreement is similar in format and content to a partnership agreement. It does not have to be filed in any public office.

Every member of an LLC should have a copy of both the articles of organization and the operating agreement.

partnership liquidates. A well-drafted partnership agreement that is carefully tailored to the particular needs of the partners is a lengthy and very complex document.

**Q. Is organizing a limited partnership any different from a general partnership?**

**A.** Yes. The most significant difference is that limited partnership statutes require a docu-

### Q. What steps are required to form a corporation?

**A.** The legal formalities for a corporation are more complex than in the other forms of business organizations. Corporate codes require the filing of a document generally known as either "articles of incorporation" or a "corporate charter," bylaws, the issuance of share certificates, and an organizational meeting. In addition, in most situations other written documents designed to protect the rights of the investors will be advisable.

### Q. What are the requirements for the articles of incorporation?

**A.** The statutes vary, but generally corporate codes require the inclusion of the following information in the articles of incorporation: the name of the corporation, its duration, the corporation's business purposes, the amount of stock that will be authorized, certification that any required minimum capital has been paid into the corporation, the address of the registered office and the name and address of the registered agent, the names and addresses of the initial directors, and the names, addresses and signatures of the incorporators. Corporate statutes also authorize other information to be included in the articles of incorporation. Examples of the kind of optional provisions often included are share transfer restrictions and elimination or curtailment of the usual powers of the board of directors.

There are some differences between the articles of incorporation of regular corporations, close corporations, and professional corporations, but these differences are for the most part technical and not that significant.

### Q. What are bylaws?

**A.** The purpose of bylaws is to provide guidelines for regulating the internal affairs of a corporation. Typically corporate bylaws deal with the mechanisms of shareholder, director and committee meetings, the issuance of stock and dividends, and the appointment, duties, and removal of the officers.

### Q. What takes place at the organizational meeting?

**A.** Some state corporation codes require two organizational meetings, one by shareholders to elect the directors and a second by the directors to approve everything else. Most state statutes, however, require only one meeting, which will typically ratify all the actions taken by the promoters and incorporators, adopt the bylaws and the corporate seal, select and set the salary of the officers, authorize the issuance of shares, approve resolutions designating one or more banks as depositories and establishing check signing authority, approve contractual agreements among the shareholders or with third parties, approve resolutions authorizing the corporation to be taxed as an S corporation (assuming the shareholders want the corporation to be an S corporation), and authorize designated officers to take the appropriate action to complete the incorporation process, including, if necessary, qualification as a foreign corporation in another state.

### Q. What other documents are commonly advisable at the time a corporation is organized?

**A.** Because of gaps in most corporate statutes and the need to protect the rights of minority shareholders to a greater extent than is provided by statute, it is often advisable for the shareholders and the corporation to enter into one or more of the following documents: a shareholder voting agreement or voting trust, a long-term employment agreement for the investors who will become executive officers, a shareholder-management agreement, which in effect can create the same type of management scheme as exists in a partnership, a share transfer restriction agreement, and a buyout agree-

## STOCK CERTIFICATES

*Stock certificates are documented proof of share ownership. A share certificate is like the title certificate you receive when you purchase an automobile. State corporation codes contain detailed requirements for stock certificates. Unless a transfer restriction is clearly noted on them, stock certificates are freely transferable.*

ment providing for the purchase (under specified conditions) of the shares of a shareholder who leaves the employment of the corporation or for some other reason wants to liquidate his or her investment. These are very complex, technical documents that must be drafted by a lawyer.

Other contracts that will typically need to be reviewed or drafted include one or more leases, a franchise agreement, and loan agreement.

If the corporation is electing S corporation status, then a Form 2553 must be completed and filed with the Internal Revenue Service. The Form 2553 or a similar document must also be filed with the state tax commission of the state where the S corporation was incorporated. Other forms, such as a patent or trademark application or an application for a tax identification number, may also be necessary. (See the section at the end of this chapter on page 508 for ways to accomplish these applications or filings.)

In addition, applications for any required licenses and for assumed or trade names need to be filed. Most business licenses, however, are state and/or local, as are assumed and trade names filings. Consult a lawyer for what is required in your area.

## OPERATIONAL PROBLEMS AND ORGANIC CHANGES

This section will discuss the legal issues that commonly occur during the life cycle of a business. It is divided into three parts. The first deals with the normal kind of legal problems that an operational business encounters. The second part deals with the principal issues involved in buying and selling a business. The last part discusses the basics of a bankruptcy proceeding involving a business organization.

### Operational Problems

**Q. What legal problems does a business typically encounter after it is organized and operational?**

**A.** There are four general types:

1. major transactions such as a bank loan, or a purchase or lease of equipment or real estate that involves the drafting or review of various legal documents and the preparation of minutes authorizing the transaction;

2. changes in statutes and regulations that necessitate changes in the company's contractual documents and internal manuals;

3. ongoing regulatory compliance—for example, timely filing of corporate annual reports, assumed name refilings and the like; and

4. the necessity of periodically reviewing and updating the company's legal structure.

**Q. Must a business have a lawyer involved in all these transactions?**

**A.** At the very least a business should regularly consult a lawyer about major transactions and compliance problems. Even if the law firm

## TIMING YOUR ANNUAL LEGAL AUDIT

*The best time is a month or so before the end of the company's taxable year. This enables the audit to include year-end tax planning issues. Frequently, significant amounts of taxes can be saved by either completing a transaction this tax year or deferring the transaction until the next taxable year.*

*Many businesses have the audit done a month or so before the company's annual meeting and use the audit as a planning vehicle for action that needs to be approved at the annual meeting. Most small businesses, however, operate on a very informal basis and do not hold regular annual meetings. This informality is now built into the corporate statutes, which require an annual meeting but allow the requirement to be met by the use of consent minutes signed by all the shareholders and directors. Consent minutes ratify the action taken even though no meeting is held. Even though it is possible to legally avoid having an annual meeting, however, one should be held if for no other reason than to review the annual legal audit.*

representing a bank prepares the loan documents and the borrower has to pay for this work, which is customary, the borrower's attorney should review all of the documents before they are signed.

To provide adequate legal protection for a business, its general counsel needs to review all of the company's legal documents on a regular basis, preferably at least once a year. This annual legal audit can uncover omissions, such as the absence of corporate minutes and changes in documents necessitated by changes in statutes and regulations. The review of the annual audit with the client will also provide the lawyer with the opportunity to discuss with the client recent legal changes so that the executives and employees will be alerted to potential problems and better able to comply with the changes. As part of this process, the lawyer may uncover potentially serious legal problems at a time when they can be resolved in an efficient cost-effective fashion.

**Q. What kinds of issues should be dealt with in the annual legal audit?**

**A.** The following is a partial list of the issues to be reviewed:

- basic constituent documents, for example, articles of incorporation, bylaws and stock transfer records of a corporation; the articles of organization and operating agreement of a limited liability company; the partnership agreement, and in a limited partnership, the certificate of limited partnership;

- employment agreements;

- all leases, licensing agreements and other contracts with third parties, with particular emphasis on termination dates, renewal options and the like;

- insurance policies;

- all standardized contract forms used by the business, for example, purchase order forms, warranties, brochures and the like;

- internal policy and procedural manuals, for example, employee policy and procedure manual, antitrust compliance handbook;

- transactions that require additional documentation, such as official minutes;

- regulatory compliance, for example, environmental regulations, ERISA problems, Securities and Exchange Commission requirements;

- structural changes in the business organization, for example, conversion to another business form, adoption of a retirement plan or a fringe benefit plan;

- tax planning issues, for example, S corporation status, legal audit, alternative minimum tax review;

- filing of tax returns, licenses, and reports;

- pending and potential litigation involving the company; and

- recent legal developments affecting the business.

## Business Acquisitions

### Q. What are the ways in which one business can acquire another?

**A.** There are four basic acquisition methods: merger, consolidation, sale of assets, and exchange of ownership interests. Each type is briefly described below.

The distinctive feature of a merger is that one or more of the merging business entities disappears into the surviving business entity, which automatically becomes vested with all the assets and liabilities of the disappearing entities. For example, if the merger agreement among A, B, and C corporations calls for C to be the surviving corporation, A and B will be merged into C, and after the merger C will own all of the assets and will have to pay all of the liabilities of A and B, both of which no longer legally exist.

A consolidation is in essence a type of merger but differs from a typical merger in that *all* of the merging entities disappear into a *new* entity. Using the prior example, a consolidation would occur if A, B, and C were merged into D, a new entity, which was probably created and owned by A, B, or C or all of them.

A sale of assets differs from a merger or consolidation in several respects, the most important being that the acquiring company buys only the acquired company's assets and therefore is not legally responsible for payment of the acquired company's liabilities. The acquiring company can, however, be liable in some situations for some of the acquired corporation's liabilities, even if the acquired corporation stays in existence. The acquiring company, for example, may be liable for environmental clean-up costs caused by the acquired company under the Comprehensive Environmental Response, Compensation and Liability Act of 1980 (CERCLA). Moreover, a sale-of-assets transaction may, unlike a merger or consolidation, require consents from third parties to transfer leases, mortgages, franchises and the like, which may not be forthcoming.

An exchange of ownership interests, the final basic acquisition method, involves the owners of one business offering to purchase the ownership interest of another business or one business offering to pay cash or issue ownership interests for the outstanding ownership interests of the other business. All kinds of combinations can result from this type of transaction. The most typical is for the acquired company to be operated as a subsidiary of the acquiring company. For example, assume that corporation A agrees to purchase all of the outstanding stock of B corporation for cash. After the transaction A will own all of the stock of B, which will as a consequence be a subsidiary of A.

There is danger in the outright purchase of stock in a corporation. When such a purchase is made, all of the undisclosed liabilities of the corporation are purchased. As a preventive measure, it is common for an acquisition agreement to provide for a period of diligent investigation, and for the buyer's approval of the results of the investigation.

### Q. How do you determine which of these acquisition methods to use?

**A.** You determine which acqustion method to use with the advice of your company's legal counsel, accountants, and other experts. Every type of acquisition is complex and fraught with legal problems. As a general rule, more than one acquisition method will be available, and the acquisition can be structured as either a taxable or a nontaxable event, depending on which produces the best overall tax results.

Selecting the best method, however, is only one of the problems that must be resolved. The mechanics of the transaction can be incredibly complex. Corporate codes have detailed statutory provisions setting out the approval process and the rights of shareholders who vote against the acquisition (called dissenters' rights). These statutes are complex but at least provide some basic guidance. Very few partnership statutes, however, currently have any statutory provisions that describe the mechanics of a merger, and none of the partnership statutes deal specifically with sales of assets or exchanges. Moreover, the coverage of mergers and other acquisition techniques by limited liability companies is also incomplete, and the existing statutes are often confusing and inconsistent. An additional problem is that very few existing statutes deal with the possibility of a cross-entity acquisition, for example a merger between a partnership and a corporation or between a partnership and a limited liability company.

Regulatory compliance problems can also present difficult issues in any type of acquisition. Antitrust clearance is not a problem for most acquisitions but it is sometimes required by both the Federal Trade Commission and the Antitrust Division of the Department of Justice under the Hart-Scott-Rodino Act. Federal and state securities law compliance is also imperative, and environmental law compliance issues are becoming increasingly important. These are only a few of the compliance issues that must be reviewed.

In short, acquisitions are very complex transactions, and a company should consult a lawyer about a proposed acquisition in the initial planning stage and before any binding commitments about the method or tax consequences have been made.

## Bankruptcy

### Q. What happens if the business gets into financial difficulty?

**A.** Frequently, it is possible for the business to work out accommodations with its creditors on a voluntary basis that will enable the business to survive through a rough period. Banks and mortgage companies, for example, are often

> ### TWO KINDS OF BUSINESS BANKRUPTCY
> *If a business's difficulties cannot be resolved, bankruptcy may be the only viable option. There are two types of bankruptcy proceedings available to businesses. The first is a liquidation proceeding under Chapter 7 of the Bankruptcy Code. The second is a rehabilitation proceeding under Chapter 11, or in the case of proprietorships, Chapter 13 of the Bankruptcy Code.*

willing to refinance indebtedness, especially if they can be convinced that the business's financial difficulties are temporary. Trade creditors are also amenable to stretching out payments for the same reason. After all, the last thing a creditor wants is to foreclose on property securing a debt or reduce a debt to judgment. Everyone loses in that situation.

Even in these difficult straits, it is important for the company to continue paying its payroll taxes, since these are not dischargeable in bankruptcy and will become a personal liability of the owners.

### Q. What happens in a Chapter 7 liquidation proceeding?

**A.** Any type of business can file a Chapter 7 proceeding. It is also possible for creditors of the business to file a Chapter 7 proceeding, but this occurs infrequently.

Once the proceeding is filed, a trustee, who is appointed by the court and technically represents the creditors, is in charge of the debtor business and will proceed to sell all the business assets and distribute the net amount realized to the company's creditors in accordance with the priorities in the Bankruptcy Code.

### Q. What happens in a Chapter 11 or Chapter 13 rehabilitation proceeding?

**A.** These proceedings differ from a Chapter 7 proceeding in two fundamental respects. In a rehabilitation proceeding the ultimate objective is not the payment of the company's creditors out of the liquidation proceeds but rather to have the business continue in a reorganized form and to pay the creditors out of its future earnings. The second major difference is that in most cases the executives who were managing the business before the rehabilitation petition is filed can continue to manage the business during the bankruptcy proceedings. This conti-

nuity can be helpful in dealing with customers and creditors.

The business has the first option to submit to the court for approval a rehabilitation plan. If it is not approved, the creditors can submit their plan. If a plan is approved, the proceeding is dismissed and the business continues to operate under the provisions of the plan. If no plan is approved, the proceeding will be converted into a Chapter 7 liquidation proceeding.

### Q. When should the business seek legal advice about the possibility of bankruptcy?

**A.** At the first sign of serious problems. A lawyer can be very helpful in advising the business about its options and in assisting with negotiations with creditors. The timing of the bankruptcy filing can be very important because the filing of the proceeding results in an automatic stay of all legal actions against the debtor business. This means that no further action in the pending law suit can take place without the permission of the bankruptcy court. The ability to get the stay is often the primary reason for filing a petition, even in circumstances where the company is not currently unable to meet its ordinary debts as they become due.

Partnerships and limited partnerships present special problems under current law. Expert legal advice is, therefore, especially important for businesses operating in these formats. The difficulties with partnerships stem primarily from the personal liability of the general partners for the partnership's debts. The bankruptcy of the partnership will often force all of the general partners also to file bankruptcy petitions. Limited liability companies are so new that there is no case law resolving the questions that are bound to arise. It is not yet certain, for example, whether a limited liability company will be treated as a partnership or a corporation under the Bankruptcy Code.

# WHERE TO GET MORE INFORMATION

The best source for general information is the Small Business Administration (SBA), which has branch offices through the United States. Contact the SBA, Washington Office Center, 409 3rd Street, SW, Washington, DC 20416, telephone 1–800–827–5722.

The SBA offers many "free" and "for sale" management assistance publications to aid small businesses. Examples are: *Incorporating a Small Business*, *Checklist for Going into Business*, *The ABC's of Borrowing*, *Planning and Goal Setting for Small Businesses* and *Woman's Handbook*.

In addition, the SBA offices regularly offer workshops and counseling sessions for small businesses.

The SBA also has a number of financial assistance programs for small businesses. Information about these programs and applications can be obtained from any branch office.

The Internal Revenue Service publishes a pamphlet entitled *Your Business Tax Kit*, which contains helpful information about the various federal business taxes. Similar kits and pamphlets, many of which contain other useful information such as business license applications, are available in most states through the state's tax commission or other state administrative offices.

The secretary of state's office, located in your state capital, can provide you with a great deal of useful information about filing requirements for corporations, partnerships, limited liability companies and other business forms.

Most states have a state development board that provides various forms of assistance to businesses, particularly new businesses and existing businesses that are planning to move to the state. Some states also have regional development boards. Illinois, for example, has Small Business Development Centers located throughout the state.

Many states authorize special financial assistance for businesses, such as industrial revenue bonds. There will generally be one or more agencies or commissions that are in charge of administering these programs and can provide information about them.

Local and state chambers of commerce can be useful sources of information about businesses.

Trade associations are excellent sources of statistical information about a particular type of business.

The business section of the public library has directories, manuals, association lists, and statistical and demographic data on businesses. In addition, the Federal Trade Commission (FTC) has a number of manuals for business owners, informing them of how to comply with various laws. Included are: *How to Write Adverse Action Notices*, *Offering Layaways*, *Writing a Care Label*, *How to Write Readable Credit Forms*, *Writing Readable Warranties*, and *Road to Resolution: Settling Consumer Disputes*. For information about these publications, call or write the Federal Trade Commission, 6th and Pennsylvania Avenue, NW, Washington, DC 20580; telephone (202) 326–2222.

Small business incubators exist in many parts of the country. Their purpose is to provide consulting services, access to research, and rental space at favorable rental rates for new business.

For trade or service mark applications:

Commissioner of Patents and Trademarks
Crystal Park Building
2121 Crystal Drive
Arlington, VA 22202
(703) 305–8600

For tax information, contact your local IRS agency.

For the federal Securities and Exchange Commission:

Securities and Exchange Commission
450 5th St., NW
Washington, DC 20549
(202) 942–8642

For copyright information:

Copyright Office
Library of Congress
101 Independence Ave., SE
Rm LM 401
Washington, DC 20540
(202) 707–9100

Finally, in addition to lawyers who practice business law, accountants, insurance agents, bankers, and management consultants can be helpful sources of information and advice.

# Personal Injury

## CONTENTS

# INTRODUCTION

PERSONAL INJURY LAW, also known as tort law, is designed to protect you if you or your property is injured or harmed because of someone else's act or failure to act. In a successful tort action based on one of three theories—negligence, strict liability, or intentional misconduct—the one who caused the injury or harm compensates the one who suffered the losses.

Automobile accidents, the area in which the majority of personal injury actions arise, provide a good example of how the tort system works. You have a negligence claim in a "fault" state if you are injured by a driver who failed to exercise reasonable care, because drivers have a duty to exercise reasonable care any time they are on the road. When they breach that duty and your injury results, personal injury law says you can recoup your losses. (Note, though, that the system may be very different in states that have passed no-fault laws.)

Negligence reaches far beyond claims stemming from car accidents. It is the basis for liability in the majority of personal injury lawsuits, including medical malpractice.

An important and growing area of tort law is strict liability, which holds designers and manufacturers strictly liable for injuries from defective products. In these cases, the injured person does not have to establish negligence of the manufacturer. Rather, you need to show that the product was designed or manufactured in a manner that made it unreasonably dangerous when used as intended. Strict liability standards also apply in other areas of personal injury, such as workplace accidents. (Workplace injuries are further explained later in this chapter, as well as in the chapter on "Law and the Workplace," beginning on page 393.)

Finally, although they are not as frequently brought, claims for intentional acts that invade a legally protected interest of yours may be the basis for holding someone liable to you in tort. If someone hits you, for example, even as a practical joke, you may be able to win a suit for battery. Or if a store detective wrongly detains you for shoplifting, you may be able to win a suit for false imprisonment. While perpetrators of some of the intentional torts—assault and battery, for example—can be held criminally liable for their actions, a tort case is a civil proceeding in court brought by an individual or entity and remains totally separate from any criminal charges brought by the government.

Every tort claim, regardless of its basis, whether intentional, negligence, or strict liability, has two basic issues—liability and damages. Was the defendant liable for the damages you sustained, and, if so, what is the nature and extent of your damages? If you can prove liability and damages, our system of justice will award you compensation for your loss.

## PERSONAL INJURY CLAIMS

**Q. How do I know if I have a personal injury case?**

**A.** First and foremost you must have suffered an injury to your person or property. Second, was your injury the result of someone else's fault?

It is not always necessary to have a physical injury to bring a personal injury lawsuit, however. Suits may be based on a variety of nonphysical losses and harms. In the intentional tort of assault, for example, you do not need to show that a person's action caused you actual physical harm but only that it caused an expectation that some harm would come to you. (Assault is described in more detail later in this chapter, on pages 534–35.) You also may have an action if someone has attacked your reputation, invaded your privacy or negligently or intentionally inflicted emotional distress upon you.

**Q. If I have suffered a personal injury and think I have a case, how do I go about finding a personal injury lawyer?**

**A.** Contact a local bar association for referrals to lawyers who handle personal injury cases, talk with lawyers you know, or ask your friends about lawyers they know or have used. You can find the telephone number of the local bar association in your telephone directory. Most lawyers offer free consultations, so you are able to meet with as many as you like. Choose a lawyer you feel most confident about—and comfortable with—to handle your case.

**Q. Should I bring any documents with me to the consultation?**

**A.** Yes, you should supply any documents that might be potentially relevant to your case. Police reports, for example, contain eyewitness accounts and details about conditions surrounding auto accidents, fires, assaults and the like. Copies of medical reports from doctors and hospitals will describe your injuries. Information about the insurer of the person who caused the injury, is extremely helpful, as are any photographs you have of the accident or of your injury. The more information you are able to give your lawyer, the easier it will be for him or her to determine if your claim will be successful. If you haven't collected any documents at the time of your first meeting, don't worry. Your lawyer will be able to obtain them as well.

**Q. What kind of legal fees should I expect in a personal injury case?**

**A.** Personal injury lawyers generally charge their clients on a contingent fee basis. That means you pay your lawyer only if you win. Your lawyer is paid a percentage of the total amount recovered. You'll sign what is called a retainer agreement with the lawyer you choose to represent you, clarifying all fees and charges. Remember that even if you lose the case, you are likely to have to pay the expenses of investigating and litigating your case, such as court filing fees and payments to investigators, court reporters, and medical experts, as well as the expenses of securing medical records and reports.

**Q. What can I expect after the first consultation?**

**A.** If a lawyer believes your claim is one you can recover on—and you have signed the retainer—he or she will proceed with gathering information about your claim. In order to arrive at a figure for damages, your lawyer will need to determine the extent of your injuries, including pain and suffering, disability and disfigurement, the cost of medical treatment, and lost wages. Your lawyer then provides your damages figure to the insurer of the person who injured you. If the insurer considers it a valid claim, the case is likely to be resolved early on and won't have to be tried in court.

### Q. If I am not happy with my lawyer, do I have to keep him or her?

**A.** No. You have a right to hire and fire any lawyer at any time.

### Q. What does it mean to settle a case?

**A.** Settling a case means that you agree to accept money in return for dropping your action against the person who injured you. You'll actually sign a release absolving the other side of any further liability. To help you decide whether to accept the settlement offer, your lawyer will be able to provide a realistic assessment of whether a lawsuit based on your claim will be successful. (Settlement can also take place at any point in a lawsuit once it is filed, including before trial or even after a case has been tried but before a jury reaches a verdict.) The decision to accept a settlement offer is yours, not the lawyer's.

### Q. What happens if I file a lawsuit?

**A.** You become the plaintiff in the case and the person who injured you becomes the defendant. Lawyers for each side (and for the insurer) typically begin gathering facts through exchange of documents, written questions (interrogatories), or depositions (questions that are asked in person and answered under oath). This process is called discovery. After discovery, many cases get settled before trial. Only a small percentage of personal injury actions ever go to trial. Of the cases that do go to trial, most plaintiffs ask for a jury to hear their case, but personal injury actions can be decided by judges as well. That is known as a bench trial, as opposed to a jury trial.

### Q. What if more than one person has caused my injury?

**A.** You must bring an action against every person who caused your injury. The negligence of two drivers, for example, may have produced a collision in which you were injured. According to traditional legal principles, each one could be held 100 percent liable to you. In a more recent legal trend, however, many jurisdictions have abolished such "joint and several" liability and each defendant, known legally as a "joint tortfeasor," becomes responsible for only that portion of the harm he or she caused. This is the rule of comparative negligence, which exists in most states. (See the section titled "Automobile Accidents," on page 517 for more on comparative negligence.)

### Q. What will I get if I win my case?

**A.** If you win, a judge or jury awards you money, known as damages, for your injuries. That amount can include compensation for such expenses as medical bills and lost wages, as well as compensation for future wage losses. It can also compensate you for physical pain and suffering. In addition, you may receive damages for any physical disfigurement or disability that resulted from your injury. The money is intended to restore your loss, is not considered as income, and is not taxable as income by the federal government or the states.

Note that an award of damages does not necessarily translate into hard cash. You may have to take further legal steps to actually collect the money.

If a defendant against whom you have won a judgment does not pay it, collection proceedings can be initiated. If the defendant owns property, for example, you may be able to foreclose on it. Another option would be to garnish the defendant's wages. Your personal injury lawyer—or any lawyer you contact—would be able to help you in this regard.

# Nonvehicular Million-Dollar Verdicts

The following table identifies the number of total awards of one million dollars or more and the number of compensatory awards of one million dollars or more for categories of nonvehicular liabilities from 1987 to the present.

| Nonvehicular Liability | Total Verdicts of $1,000,000+ | Compensatory Verdicts of $1,000,000+ |
|---|---|---|
| Airline Negligence | 15 | 13 |
| Animal Attack | 5 | 3 |
| Assault | 68 | 48 |
| Bad Faith | 90 | 38 |
| Dental Malpractice | 2 | 2 |
| Discrimination | 15 | 12 |
| False Arrest | 19 | 13 |
| Libel/Slander | 24 | 18 |
| Medical Malpractice | 553 | 488 |
| Negligent Supervision | 10 | 9 |
| Nursing Home Negligence | 13 | 9 |
| Occupational Negligence | 63 | 47 |
| Premises Liability | 238 | 211 |
| Police Negligence | 48 | 46 |
| Professional Negligence | 64 | 51 |
| Products Liability | 451 | 381 |
| Road Design/Maintenance—Gov't | 59 | 52 |
| School Negligence | 18 | 15 |
| Work Accident | 241 | 211 |
| Wrongful Termination | 54 | 48 |

# Nonvehicular Recovery Probabilities

The following table identifies the plaintiff recovery probabilities for several nonvehicular liabilities from 1989 to 1991.

| Liability | 1989 | 1990 | 1991 |
|---|---|---|---|
| Airline Negligence | 69% | 68% | 58% |
| Animal Attack | 68% | 68% | 64% |
| Assault | 65% | 75% | 72% |
| Bad Faith | 62% | 62% | 73% |
| Dental Malpractice | 44% | 35% | 36% |
| Discrimination | 59% | 61% | 59% |
| False Arrest | 52% | 52% | 48% |
| Legal Malpractice | 78% | 80% | 76% |
| Libel/Slander | 74% | 73% | 66% |
| Malicious Prosecution | 73% | 68% | 76% |
| Medical Malpractice | 48% | 46% | 40% |
| Negligent Supervision | 61% | 60% | 50% |
| Nursing Home Negligence | 53% | 58% | 50% |
| Occupational Negligence | 61% | 59% | 60% |
| Police Negligence | 43% | 42% | 48% |
| Premises Liability | 52% | 55% | 50% |
| Products Liability | 59% | 55% | 50% |
| Professional Negligence | 55% | 50% | 64% |
| Road Design/Maintenance-Gov't | 53% | 49% | 46% |
| School Negligence | 46% | 53% | 45% |
| Sexual Harassment | 67% | 82% | 83% |
| Work Accident | 74% | 76% | 70% |
| Wrongful Termination | 59% | 57% | 60% |

SOURCE: Current Award Trends: 1993 Edition, LRP Publications, Horsham, PA

### Q. Will the person who caused my injury get punished?

**A.** No. Punishment comes from criminal cases, not civil cases. Defendants in civil actions for personal injury do not receive jail terms or stiff fines as punishment. Those are criminal sentences and personal injury cases are civil disputes. But juries and courts can award what the law calls punitive damages when the defendant's intentional acts have injured you. These awards are rather rare. Courts use them to punish people (and more often large corporations) who have behaved recklessly or against the public's interest. Courts also hope that ordering the payment of punitive damages will discourage such defendants from engaging in the same kind of harmful behavior in the future.

### Q. Does a personal injury lawsuit have to be filed within a certain amount of time?

**A.** Every state has certain time limits, called "statutes of limitations," that govern the period during which you must file a personal injury lawsuit. In some states, for example, you may have as little as one year to file a lawsuit from an automobile accident. If you miss the statutory deadline for filing a case, your case is thrown out of court. (As explained later in this chapter, limitations in medical malpractice cases are often calculated differently.) You see, then, why it is important to talk with a lawyer as soon as you receive or discover an injury.

### Q. What if a person dies before bringing a personal injury lawsuit?

**A.** It depends on whether a person dies as a result of the injuries or from unrelated causes. If a person injured in an accident subsequently dies because of those injuries, that person's heirs may recover money through a lawsuit. Every state has some law permitting an action when someone causes the wrongful death of another. And if a person with a claim dies from unrelated causes, the tort claim survives in most cases and may be brought by the executor or personal representative of the deceased person's estate.

## NEGLIGENCE

### Q. If someone causes an accident and I am hurt, on what basis will that person be responsible (liable)?

**A.** A person is liable if he or she was negligent in causing the accident. Persons who act negligently never set out (intend) to cause a result like an injury to another person. Rather, their liability stems from careless or thoughtless conduct or a failure to act when a reasonable person would have acted. Conduct becomes "negligent" when it falls below a legally recognized standard of taking reasonable care under the circumstances to protect others from harm.

### Q. Negligence law seems so confusing. It uses words such as duty and causation. What do they mean?

**A.** Negligence law can be complex and confusing even for people who are familiar with it. To understand it better, forget all the legal jargon and go back to the car accident example. A driver has a duty to use reasonable care to avoid injuring anyone he or she meets on the road. If a driver fails to use reasonable care and as a result of that failure injures you, then the driver is responsible (liable) to you for those injuries.

### Q. Who determines whether a defendant has acted reasonably?

**A.** After being presented evidence by your lawyer, a judge or jury will decide what an "ordinary" or "reasonable person" would have done in similar circumstances. In the example of an automobile accident, a judge or jury is likely to find a driver negligent if his or her conduct departed from what an ordinary reasonable person would have done in similar circumstances. An example would be failing to stop at a stop light or stop sign.

## AUTOMOBILE ACCIDENTS

**Q. I was in a car accident, but I think I can prove it was not completely my fault. Will this make a difference with regard to what damages ultimately are awarded?**

**A.** In the past the rule was that if you could prove the other driver contributed in any way to the accident, he or she could be totally barred from recovering anything from you. But now most states have rejected such harsh results and instead look at the comparative fault of the drivers. If a jury finds that you were negligent and that your negligence, proportionally, contributed 25 percent to cause the injury and that the defendant was 75 percent at fault, the defendant would only be responsible for 75 percent of your damages, or $75,000 if your damages totaled $100,000. In some states, a plaintiff may recover even if he or she were more negligent than the defendant, that is, negligent in the amount of 51 percent or more. (See page 380 of the "Automobiles" chapter for more on standards of negligence for car accidents.)

**Q. A neighbor who rides with me to work was injured when I got into a car accident. Do I have to pay her medical bills?**

**A.** In many states today, no-fault automobile insurance would protect you—and often passengers in your car—by compensating those injured up to a specified level, regardless of who was at fault in the accident. About half of the states currently have no-fault insurance.

Though there is a strong trend away from them, some states still have automobile "guest statutes" that make drivers liable for injuries to nonpaying—or guest—passengers only if the drivers were "grossly negligent" by failing to use even slight care in their driving.

In a guest statute state, if your neighbor can prove she was not a guest passenger—that both of you agreed to share expenses—then she possibly could recover from you under ordinary negligence principles.

Cases have also held a driver liable for the negligent operation of a car and for harm caused by known defects, but not for injuries caused by defects in the vehicle about which the driver had no knowledge.

**Q. I received an injury when the bus I ride to work was involved in an accident. Is the bus company at fault?**

**A.** It's likely. "Common carriers"—bus lines, airlines, and railroads—transport people for a fee, owe their passengers "the highest degree of care," and are held to have a special responsibility to their passengers. Common carriers must exercise extra caution in protecting their riders and do everything they can to keep them safe. Whether you win your case will depend on the circumstances of the accident. Did the driver pull out in front of a car and have to slam on the brakes? What were the road conditions? A jury will have to consider those factual circumstances to determine if your driver acted negligently. But as an employee of a common carrier, the driver must provide you with a high degree of care. (If the bus were hit by another car, the other driver may also be liable for your injuries.)

**Q. My car sustained damage when it hit a pothole on a city street. Can I recover from the city?**

**A.** Some cities have pothole ordinances, a form of immunity that releases them from any liability for pothole accidents, except where they had prior notice. Whether you can recover will depend on your city's law controlling liability and its immunities against suits.

**Q. I was in a car accident during my pregnancy and my baby was born with a deformity as a result of injuries from the accident. Does my child have any legal recourse?**

**A.** Many states today will permit an action by a child for the consequences of such prenatal (before birth) injuries. (In states with no-fault automobile insurance, your right to sue often is limited.) Most courts also will allow a wrongful death action if the baby dies from the injuries after birth.

**Q. Someone recently stole my car and then wrecked it, injuring passengers in another vehicle. Now one of those passengers is trying to sue me. Can they win? Am I responsible?**

**A.** Probably not, since the thief did not have your permission to use the car, although a lot would depend on the law in your state. Suppose you left your car unlocked with the keys in it, making it easy for the thief to steal. This could be negligence. Even then, most courts generally will not hold you liable if the thief later injures someone by negligent driving. That is because courts hold that you could not foresee that your actions ultimately would result in such injuries. In a few cases, though, courts have looked at whether your actions caused an unreasonable risk of harm to someone else. If you left your car parked with the engine running, for example, you might be liable if the car thief then injures children playing nearby.

## Vehicular Recovery Probabilities

The following table identifies the plaintiff recovery probabilities for several vehicular liability situations from 1989 through 1991.

| Liability | 1989 | 1990 | 1991 |
|---|---|---|---|
| Backing Collision | 49% | 44% | 50% |
| Bicycle/Vehicle Collision | 39% | 43% | 57% |
| Collision with Object | 62% | 59% | 55% |
| Disabled Vehicle | 46% | 46% | 63% |
| Head-On Collision | 74% | 74% | 69% |
| Intersection Collision | 70% | 69% | 62% |
| Lane Change Collision | 48% | 47% | 50% |
| Motorcycle/Vehicle Collision | 60% | 63% | 65% |
| Multiple Vehicle Collision | 78% | 74% | 74% |
| No Contact Accident | 40% | 64% | 48% |
| Parked Vehicle Accident | 63% | 65% | 60% |
| Parking Lot Accident | 42% | 44% | 58% |
| Passenger Suit | 69% | 67% | 74% |
| Pedestrian Accident | 56% | 53% | 53% |
| Railroad Crossing Accident | 63% | 57% | 67% |
| Rear-End Collision | 63% | 60% | 68% |
| Turning Collision | 56% | 53% | 68% |

The most frequently claimed vehicular liabilities in the analysis of 1991 cases were rear-end collisions, accounting for 21 percent of the cases; passenger suits, accounting for 18 percent of the cases; and intersection collisions, accounting for 15 percent of the cases.

SOURCE: *Current Award Trends, 1993 Edition*, LRP Publications, Horsham, PA

In a no-fault state, on the other hand, it might be difficult—if not impossible—for the passenger to sue you.

**Q. I was hit by a car driven by a drunk driver who was going home after a night out. What can I do, in addition to suing the drunk driver?**

**A.** If you live in a state that has a Dram Shop Act, you may be able to recover from the tavern owner where the drunk driver was served the liquor. Such acts usually come into play when intoxicated people served by the bar later injure somebody while driving. Some of those laws also make tavern owners liable when drunk customers injure others on or off the premises. But some courts say a tavern owner will not be liable unless the sale of the liquor itself was illegal.

**Q. My wife was injured when her car was hit by one being driven by some kids who had been drinking at the home of our neighbor. May I take any action against the neighbor, who supplied the liquor to the youths?**

**A.** Possibly. Courts have imposed liability against such neighbors or parents when they have served liquor to minors. Parents can be liable for negligent supervision of their children. But as a general rule, courts have said that social hosts are not responsible for the conduct of their guests, unless the hosts routinely allow guests to drink too much—or take illegal drugs—and then put them into their cars and send them out on the highway.

**Q. I was injured when my automobile collided with a truck driven by a deliveryperson. Can I recover damages from the driver or the employer?**

**A.** You may be able to recover from both. Under a form of strict liability, known as vicarious liability, you probably can recover from the deliveryperson's employer. Under the law, employers may be held liable to third persons for acts committed by employees within the scope of their job. Although the employer was not negligent, it becomes indirectly liable for the negligence of its employee. Was the employee making a delivery when the accident occurred? If so, the employer is liable, since deliveries clearly are part of the driver's job. But if the employee first stopped at a restaurant for drinks and dinner with friends, the employer may be able to escape liability.

**Q. A car ran over my dog. Can I recover from the driver?**

**A.** Yes, you might win a lawsuit. A dog is property, and you have suffered property damage. You will have to show that the driver was negligent.

## INJURIES AT YOUR HOME AND ON YOUR PROPERTY

Under traditional legal principles, your liability to people injured on your property changed according to the reason they came onto your property. Were they there to visit, to sell, to solicit, to fix something, or to trespass? A more recent trend, however, holds land or property owners to a general duty of care to prevent injury to anyone coming onto their property, unless the dangerous condition was open and obvious.

**Q. A furniture deliveryperson was injured when he tripped over an electrical extension cord in my living room. Can he recover damages from me?**

**A.** He could sue, though it is not certain that he would win. As noted above, until recently your liability for someone's personal injuries while at your home hinged on why he or she was there.

If people were doing work for you, the law held that you had a special duty to make your home reasonably safe. In those situations, a court would have asked if the cord was dangerous to anyone who came into your living room, or was it only dangerous if someone moved your furniture? Did you warn the deliveryperson to watch out for the cord? Courts would need the answers to such questions to decide if you are liable to the deliveryperson. A growing trend would make you liable for the injury only if you failed to exercise a general duty of care. By the way, homeowner's insurance policies generally protect homeowners in cases such as these.

**Q. A door-to-door salesperson tripped on our front steps, injuring himself. May he hold me responsible?**

**A.** Perhaps. A door-to door salesperson may expect that you will warn him about dangerous conditions on your property that may not be obvious. If your steps were in perfect condition and he merely lost his footing, a court would not hold you responsible. However, if he tripped because one of the stairs was wobbly and you knew about it, you should have repaired it or posted a warning sign.

**Q. What if a salesperson, or another passerby, falls on an icy sidewalk in front of my house?**

**A.** In some places, ordinances say that landowners whose property is next to a public sidewalk are responsible for keeping the sidewalk in repair and clear of ice and snow. But elsewhere owners have no duty to remove natural accumulations of ice and snow that have collected on adjacent public sidewalks. In fact, they may be liable for negligence if they undertake such a job and do not make the sidewalks safe. If landowners fail to take reasonable action to correct a dangerous condition on the sidewalk, other than a natural accumulation of ice or snow, that they knew or should have known about, however, they can be held liable.

**Q. Would I be liable if a trespasser gets injured on my property?**

**A.** You generally are not liable for any injury to a trespasser on your property. Suppose, however, that you know certain people continually trespass on your property, perhaps using it as a shortcut. Then a court might find that you should have notified these regular trespassers about any hidden artificial conditions of which you were aware could seriously injure them.

**Q. A group of eight-year-old children has been playing in a vacant lot that I own. Could I be liable if one of them gets injured?**

**A.** Yes, the law generally places a greater burden on landowners when injuries involve children. The reason is that children are too young to understand or appreciate danger in certain situations. Under a legal theory known as the attractive nuisance doctrine, owners who knew or should know about potentially dangerous artificial conditions on their lot must warn children who are playing there, or must take reasonable precautions to protect them. If, for example, there is machinery or other equipment on your vacant lot that could present an unreasonable risk to children, you should remove it. If you don't, you could very well be liable to the children for any injuries they suffer, even if they were trespassing. In some jurisdictions, the attractive nuisance doctrine is being replaced by a duty of reasonable care under the circumstances.

**Q. Our children's friends often come to swim in our backyard pool, even though we are not always able to be there. What if one of them gets hurt?**

**A.** You are liable because you have a legal duty to protect children from possible harm should they decide to play around a dangerous place on your property. You should make sure an adult is present when children are swimming, though this will not necessarily avoid liability. And warning the children that they should not swim without an adult present may not be enough to avoid liability if one of them gets injured. Also check with your state or city to find out its requirements for residential swimming pools. Under them, you may have a legal duty to erect barriers or such other protective features as an automatic pool cover, a tall fence with a good lock that you keep locked or an alarm on the sliding glass door from your home to the pool.

## INJURIES ON OTHERS' PROPERTY

**Q. What if I get injured while at the home of my neighbor, who invited me there for a party?**

**A.** As a social guest, you might be able to recover from your neighbor, depending on how your injuries happened. Homeowners must tell their guests about—or make safe—any dangerous conditions that the guests are unlikely to recognize. Suppose, for example, that your injury was caused when you tripped on a throw rug. You may be able to recover if you can prove that your neighbor knew other people had tripped over it and you were unlikely to realize its danger. Your neighbor probably should have warned you about it, removed it during the party, or secured it to the floor with tape or tacks.

**Q. I was walking on a public sidewalk next to a construction site when I tripped and fell on a brick from the site, spraining my ankle. May I recover damages from the construction company?**

**A.** In some circumstances, you will be able to recover damages from the construction com-

**IF YOU GET INJURED IN A STORE**

*Suppose you tripped and fell on a spilled can of paint in a hardware store where you were shopping, injuring your foot. Can you recover damages from the store? It depends on the facts of the case. Store owners must keep their premises reasonably safe for customers, inspecting and discovering any dangerous conditions. They also must keep all aisles clear and properly maintained. A judge or jury will look at whether the owner was aware that the paint can was in the aisle and how long it had been there. But a judge or jury also might find that you discovered the spilled paint and proceeded to walk right through it. Then the judge or jury might deny you damages or find you comparatively at fault, thus reducing your recovery.*

pany, which has a duty to take reasonable steps to keep sidewalks near its construction sites free from bricks and other debris. If the company fails to remove such obstructions and you trip and fall, the company may be liable for your injuries. Construction companies should tell pedestrians that they could get injured if they stray from the sidewalk. But posting a sign is not enough. If a company fails to place barriers or warning lamps by a building pit, for example, it may be responsible if anyone falls into it and gets injured.

**Q. I fell on a broken piece of a city sidewalk and injured my ankle. Do I have a case against the city?**

**A.** In many states, municipal immunity statutes prohibit recovery in many kinds of cases against a city or town. If there is not such a statute or ordinance, however, you may have a case. Municipalities have a duty to keep streets and sidewalks in repair. You might have a successful case against the city if you can show that it failed to maintain the sidewalk properly.

**Q. My son received an injury during basic training in the U.S. Army. May he recover damages from the federal government?**

**A.** No. People in the armed services who receive injuries during the course of their duties are not permitted to recover for their injuries. But the Federal Tort Claims Act of 1946 waives U.S. immunity for a "negligent or wrongful act or omission." So it would permit, under certain conditions, recovery in personal injury lawsuits against the U.S. government for torts committed by its employees. These actions are brought in the U.S. Claims Court. Some states have their own courts of claim. In other states, claims actions can be brought through other courts.

**Q. My son and his friends went snowmobiling on a nearby farm. When the vehicle ran into a fence, one of them got hurt. The farmer now says he is not liable. Is that true?**

**A.** If landowners know that others are using their land for snowmobiling, most states say they must warn snowmobilers about hidden dangerous conditions or remove them. Was the fence visible? Did the farmer recently build it? A few states, such as Michigan, have laws specifically dealing with liability when someone uses property for recreational purposes without permission. In those states, the farmer probably would not be liable if he did not authorize the boys to be on his land and did not act

recklessly. You might want to ask a lawyer about your state's law.

**Q. I got injured on a ski lift. May I recover against the ski resort?**

**A.** Possibly. Can you prove that the resort was negligent? Remember that some states have laws limiting the liability of resorts, saying there are certain risks that a person assumes when skiing. However, some states hold that ski lifts are common carriers, like buses. They have higher duties than others, so in one of these states you might have an excellent case.

**Q. My daughter, who plays on the local park's basketball team, brought home a note asking us to sign a form saying we won't hold the park district responsible for injuries. What is that?**

**A.** You are talking about a so-called waiver of liability that is intended to contractually release the organization of any liability should an injury occur. Your signature doesn't necessarily mean that you've signed away all of your rights. If you must either sign such a form or deprive your child of the chance to participate in the activity, a court may hold that your waiver is not really voluntary and thus not valid. And even in those states that recognize waivers, the waiver might not mean that you are giving up your right to sue entirely. If an injury results because of intentional or reckless behavior, you probably will be able to seek damages.

**Q. I was staying at a motel when there was a fire, but there was no water sprinkler system and no escape route posted in the room. Doesn't the hotel have to have those safety precautions?**

**A.** The motel management probably should have exercised reasonable care about the fire alarms and fire escapes. And they should have helped you escape. As in the case of the com-

## LANDLORD LIABILITY

*In recent years many states have required landlords to maintain residential property in "habitable" condition by imposing a warranty of habitability. A violation of that warranty could result in your suing the landlord for failing to maintain the property and thus violating the warranty. But negligence claims are also possible. If guests are injured when a back porch that is part of a unit collapses during a party, the landlord probably would be held liable, especially if he or she had been warned that the porch was sagging or was infested with termites but had not repaired it. Of course, the landlord may be able to argue that the porch collapsed because there were too many people on it.*

*Landlords also must maintain any "common area" of the building—including stairs, corridors and walkways—for both tenants and guests of the building. If a guest is injured when she trips over some loose carpeting in a corridor, for example, the landlord generally would be liable.*

*If you are a landlord, there are ways to reduce your chances of liability. Consider having your insurance company inspect the premises and then promptly repair any safety problems the inspector uncovers. If you inspect the premises yourself, look for unsafe wiring, loose railings, poor lighting, or similar flaws. You might also write tenants a letter each year asking them to point out hazards or needed repairs they may have noticed. If a tenant who lives in the building every day fails to notice a hazard, it is hard to argue that the landlord should know about it. But that still may not protect you in a suit by someone who is injured while visiting.*

mon carrier above, the law generally says that innkeepers, who have a special relationship with their guests, have a higher duty of care.

### Q. Someone attacked my daughter on the campus of the college she attends. May she hold the school responsible for this attack?

**A.** Your daughter might have a negligence action against the college. In a developing area of law known as premises liability, courts have found such entities as universities, motels, con-venience stores, and shopping malls liable for attacks because they did not exercise reasonable care in preventing victims from being harmed by a third person.

In a case that drew headlines in the 1970s, for example, a court awarded $2.5 million to singer Connie Francis for an attack at a Howard Johnson's Motor Lodge. The court found that the motel did not take proper and reasonable steps to prevent the attack. In general, a hotel must provide adequate security and not permit people to loiter.

## LIABILITY AT SPORTING EVENTS

*Suppose you went to a baseball game, and a ball that a player hit into the stands injured you. What can you do? Spectators at a baseball game know they may be injured by a fly ball. That is why courts generally say that spectators assume the risk of being hurt by a ball. The same usually holds true if a golf ball hits you while you are watching a golf match. Likewise, if a wheel from a car in an automobile race flies into the stands, you assume the risk of getting hurt. The legal term for this doctrine is assumption of the risk. It means that you agreed to face a known danger. But if there is a hole in a screen intended to protect spectators at the baseball park, you then probably could argue that it was negligence not to have it repaired.*

In your daughter's case, a court would look at the facts and ask whether similar attacks had occurred previously in the same area. If so, the court would ask what security precautions the college had taken.

**Q. I was attacked after withdrawing money from an automated teller machine (ATM). What can I do?**

**A.** Under the tort theory of premises liability, discussed above, customers have sued banks for failing to protect them from assault at ATMs. While there used to be no common law duty to provide security against such crimes, a duty has

been recognized in recent years. In such a case, a judge or jury would determine if there were past occurrences and if a likelihood of a crime was foreseeable. If so, they may hold that the bank had a duty to protect people using that machine and that the bank was liable.

**Q. Is there anything else victims may do?**

**A.** Yes. Most states have laws compensating victims of violent crimes for lost wages, counseling, and medical expenses. There also are several victim assistance programs. Check with your local prosecutor's office (possibly called the office of the state's attorney or district attorney).

**Q. I think my colleagues' smoking at work is making me sick. Since I'm a nonsmoker, do I have any recourse?**

**A.** In a growing area of interest, a recent Environmental Protection Agency report has linked "passive" tobacco smoke to lung cancer and other ailments. Some nonsmokers have filed workers' compensation claims saying they became ill in a smoke-filled workplace. Damage suits also have been filed against the employers, for allowing smoking, and directly against tobacco companies. The nonsmoker would have to show that the presence of smoke caused his or her illness.

## NEGLIGENT INFLICTION OF EMOTIONAL DISTRESS

**Q. We recently got a call from the hospital where someone had taken my mother. The hospital told us that she had died of a heart attack. However, it was not true. The hospital's false report devastated us. What can we do?**

**A.** The circumstances you describe are rare. Nonetheless, you may be able to recover from the hospital for the negligent infliction of emotional distress. That is, you may be able to sue the hospital successfully for negligently causing you to endure emotional pain. Courts generally have maintained that a person must have physical injuries to recover in such cases. But courts in some states have allowed recovery when there are no physical injuries. Other successful emotional distress suits have involved bystanders. For example, a court allowed a mother who saw her child fatally hit by a car to recover money damages.

**Q. The store where I bought my wedding gown failed to deliver it in time for the ceremony. What can I do?**

**A.** Although you no doubt suffered some distress, it is unlikely that you have a personal injury case. The store was negligent in failing to

---

### IF YOU GET INJURED AT WORK

*Workers' compensation laws, currently in place in all fifty states and the District of Columbia, cover most workers injured on the job. Under these laws, employers compensate you for your injuries, including medical expenses, lost wages (temporary disability) and permanent or temporary disability, regardless of who was at fault. All you have to do is file notice with your employer and a claim with the state's workers' compensation commission, or board. (See page 451 of the "Law and the Workplace" chapter for more details.)*

*Legislatures created the laws because they thought that liability for workplace accidents should be placed on the one most able to bear the loss—the employer. The statutes fall under strict liability principles, discussed below, so no employer or employee negligence or fault need be shown. In fact, the statutes prohibit employees from filing tort claims against their employers for conditions covered by the law. Instead, an employee gets paid according to a fixed schedule of benefits, regardless of who was at fault.*

*It is extremely rare that an employee is not covered by such a law, but if you are not, you may be able to recover from your employer on a negligence claim. To do so, you must show that your employer failed to exercise reasonable care in providing you with safe working conditions or that your employer failed to warn you of unsafe conditions that you were unlikely to discover. Other possible suits against your employer might include an action alleging an intentional injury or an intentional disregard of your safety. Or your spouse might sue for loss of consortium. (See pages 58–59 of the "Family Law" chapter for more details.)*

get your dress to you on time. Although it may have been traumatic for you, generally you would have to show a physical consequence of the injury. You may, however, have a case for breach of contract.

---

## MEDICAL MALPRACTICE

### Q. What is medical malpractice?

A. Medical malpractice is negligence committed by a professional health care provider—a doctor, nurse, dentist, technician, hospital, or hospital worker—whose performance of duties departs from a standard of practice of those with similar training and experience, resulting in harm to a patient or patients.

Most medical malpractice actions are filed against doctors who have failed to use reasonable care to treat you. The profession itself sets the standard for malpractice by its own custom and practice. Historically under the so-called "locality rule," a doctor was required only to possess and apply the knowledge and use the skill and care that is ordinarily used by reasonably well-qualified physicians in the locality, or similar localities, in which he or she practiced. But today the trend is toward abolishing such a rule in favor of a national standard of practice.

### Q. Hasn't there been talk about changing the way that malpractice cases are handled?

A. Yes. Especially in the 1980s, doctors and members of the insurance industry said there was a "malpractice crisis," with spiraling insurance premiums and unreasonably high jury verdicts. As a response to that, some states passed laws capping damage awards, limiting attorneys' fees and shortening the time period in which plaintiffs could bring malpractice suits. Some states instituted no-fault liability for malpractice claims, or developed arbitration panels to hear medical malpractice claims before they could be filed in court to be determined by a judge or jury.

Other "tort reforms" are often discussed, including reducing recovery for "pain and suffering" in malpractice lawsuits and reducing damages to take into account payments from insurance and workers' compensation.

## Medical Malpractice Verdicts and Ratios
## 1982–1991

| Year | Total verdicts | Million $ verdicts | Million $ verdicts as % of total verdicts |
|---|---|---|---|
| 1982 | 252 | 51 | 20.2 |
| 1983 | 341 | 77 | 22.6 |
| 1984 | 369 | 82 | 22.2 |
| 1985 | 272 | 107 | 39.3 |
| 1986 | 299 | 87 | 29.1 |
| 1987 | 367 | 81 | 22.1 |
| 1988 | 360 | 97 | 26.9 |
| 1989 | 423 | 107 | 25.3 |
| 1990 | 343 | 124 | 36.2 |
| 1991* | 147 | 58 | 39.5 |
| Total | 3,370 | 920 | 27.3 |

*1991 data are incomplete.
SOURCE: Jury Verdict Research, Inc.

### Q. What do I do if a think I have a medical malpractice claim?

**A.** Talk to a lawyer who specializes in such work. Tell the attorney exactly what happened to you, from the first time you visited your doctor through your last contact with him or her. What were the circumstances surrounding your illness or injury? How did your doctor treat it? What did your doctor tell you about your treatment? Did you follow your doctor's instructions? What happened to you? Answers to these and other relevant questions become important if you think your doctor may have committed malpractice. Like other personal injury claims, the case will either be settled or go to trial, usually before a jury.

### Q. How does a jury determine if a doctor's actions were within the standards of good medical practice?

**A.** A jury will consider testimony by experts—usually other doctors, who will testify whether they believe your physician's actions followed standard medical practice or fell below the accepted standard of care. In deciding whether your heart surgeon was negligent, for example, a jury will be told to rely on expert testimony to determine what a competent heart surgeon would have done under the same or similar circumstances. A specialist, like a heart surgeon, is held to a higher standard of care—that of a specialist—than would be expected of a nonspecialist.

### Q. I signed a consent form before my doctor performed surgery. What did it really mean?

**A.** It is common practice in hospitals for patients to sign a form giving the doctor their consent, or approval, to perform surgery. In the form, the patient usually consents to the specific surgery as well as to any other procedures that might become necessary. Before you sign it, your doctor should give you a full description of the surgery and the risks involved, and the ramifications of not getting such treatment. If you can prove that your physician misrepresented or failed to adequately inform you of the risks and benefits before surgery, your consent may be invalid. The only time the law excuses doctors from providing such information is in emergencies or when it would be harmful to a patient. But even if your doctor should have secured your consent and did not, you still may not automatically recover. You may still have to prove that, if adequately informed, a reasonable person would not have consented to the surgery.

### Q. If the consent form is considered valid, can I recover any damages in a malpractice action against my doctor?

**A.** Yes, you still may be able to recover damages. A consent form does not release from liability a physician who did not perform the operation following established procedures or who was otherwise negligent. You may also have a claim that the surgery the physician performed went beyond the consent you gave. Then the doctor might even be liable for battery.

### Q. What if I'm just not satisfied with the results of my surgery? Do I have a malpractice case?

**A.** In general, there are no guarantees of medical results. You would have to show an injury or damages that resulted from the doctor's deviation from the appropriate standard of care for your condition.

### Q. I got pregnant even though my husband had a vasectomy. Can we recover damages?

**A.** Yes, you may be able to win a case. A number of negligence cases have been permitted against physicians for performing unsuccessful

## SHOULD YOU STOP AND HELP SOMEONE IN AN EMERGENCY?

*Generally you do not have a duty to stop and help someone in an emergency. The law says that if you did not cause the problem and if you and the victim have no special relationship you need not try to rescue a person. But states have passed so-called Good Samaritan laws that excuse doctors—and sometimes other helpers— from liability for negligence for coming to the aid of someone in an emergency. In some states, if you injure someone while driving, you must help that injured person, regardless of who was at fault. Some courts look at the circumstances of the rescue. They say that if you know someone is in extreme danger that could be avoided with little inconvenience on your part, you must provide reasonable care to the victim. Of course, you are always free to go voluntarily to the aid of someone in trouble. But if you abandon your rescue efforts after starting them, you may be liable if you leave a victim in worse condition than you found him or her.*

vasectomies or other methods of sterilization that resulted in unwanted children. Courts increasingly allow a suit to be filed by the parents of a child born as a result of wrongful conception or wrongful pregnancy. Damages generally are limited to those associated with the pregnancy and birth and do not extend to support of the child.

**Q. I don't think it was necessary for me to have a cesarean section when I delivered my daughter. Is there anything I can do about it?**

**A.** Although most malpractice cases involving cesarean sections are brought against doctors who did not perform them when they should have, with resulting injuries to the mother or child, it is possible for a woman to win damages against her doctors for unnecessarily delivering her child by cesarean section. An expert would still be necessary to state that in doing the cesarean section, the delivering doctor deviated from the appropriate standard of care.

**Q. My doctor prescribed a drug for treatment but failed to tell me it was part of an experimental program. What can I do?**

**A.** This is quite a rare circumstance, but your physician had a duty to tell you that the drug was part of an experimental program. You had the right to refuse to participate in it. You now may have grounds for an action against your doctor.

**Q. May I recover medical and hospital bills from someone who caused an injury to me even though my insurance company has paid the bill?**

**A.** Yes. However, if you do recover payment from the person who injured you for those bills, some states require you to reimburse your insurance company. In those states, the law does not allow you to get a double recovery. Often the insurance policy contains a subrogation clause that does not permit double recovery.

### Q. My aunt discovered that a sponge left in her during an operation years ago was the source of stomach trouble. May she still sue?

**A.** Like other personal injury cases, medical malpractice lawsuits are subject to specific statutes of limitations (discussed earlier in this chapter, on page 516). Until recently, your aunt's suit may have been thrown out of court. In many statutes, time limits on filing began when the injury occurred—on the day of the operation. To alleviate such a harsh—and final—result, many states today have altered their laws, and the clock for filing a case does not begin to toll until people discover that they have suffered an injury, or should have discovered it. Even with the discovery rule, there are time limits, known as statutes of repose, that limit the time within which to file suit before or after discovery of the injury.

### Q. My father's job exposed him to asbestos. Now he has lung disease. Is it too late to file a claim?

**A.** It may not be too late. Many people who suffered injuries from toxic substances such as asbestos did not know at the time of exposure that the compounds were harmful. As a result, some states have enacted laws allowing people to file lawsuits for a certain amount of time from the date when the lung impairment or cancer begins, rather than from the date of exposure. A lawyer can tell you whether your father still has time within the statutes of limitations applicable in your state. In general, the area of workplace illnesses is covered by workers' compensation (discussed earlier in this chapter, on page 525, and in the "Law and the Workplace" chapter, on page 451).

### Q. What about malpractice actions against professionals such as lawyers? I recently hired a lawyer who seemed inexperienced and I was unhappy with the outcome of the case.

**A.** Like doctors, lawyers and other professionals must possess and apply the knowledge and the skills of other reasonably well-qualified professionals. Not only must they exercise reasonable care in handling your case, they also must possess a minimum degree of special knowledge and ability. That means that they will be liable to you if their skills do not meet the accepted standard of practice. You must also prove that the case your lawyer mishandled was likely to succeed. Lawyer malpractice usually results in property damage only. You cannot recover for the emotional distress of hiring a negligent lawyer.

In your case, you may have a malpractice action against the attorney if he or she was negligent in representing you. You'll have to show more than dissatisfaction with the outcome of the case. Did he or she fail to meet a deadline for filing for a court proceeding? Were all the crucial legal elements of the case fully explored? If you are unsure about a basis for a malpractice case, check with the state agency that regulates lawyers in your state. Your state bar association will be able to tell you the name of the agency.

## STRICT LIABILITY

### Q. Is there any other basis for liability besides negligence?

**A.** Courts hold some persons or companies strictly liable for certain activities that harm others, even when they have not acted negligently or with wrongful intent, a concept that will be discussed on page 534, later in this chapter. Persons or companies engaged in blasting, storing dangerous, toxic substances or keeping dangerous animals, for example, can be strictly liable for harm caused to others. The theory behind imposing strict liability on the part of those conducting such activities is that these activities pose an undue risk of harm to members of the community. Thus, anyone who conducts that activity does so at his own risk and is liable when something goes wrong—even innocently—and someone is harmed. The people who posed the risk are in the best position to pay for it. Holding manufacturers liable for injuries their products cause is a good example of strict liability.

**Q. I was opening a soft drink bottle when it exploded in my face, and flying glass cut me. Was somebody at fault?**

**A.** Yes, someone was at fault, since bottles ordinarily do not explode in a person's face. Courts often decide such cases under principles of strict liability, meaning that instead of having to prove that someone was negligent, a plaintiff would only have to prove that the bottle exploded and that he or she was injured by it.

Some courts continue to decide such cases under negligence principles, however. If the bottler sealed the bottle and it was handled carefully between the time it left the bottler's possession and the time of the explosion, some courts assume—or consider it circumstantial evidence—that the bottler was negligent.

**Q. We live near a site where a gasoline company stores its flammable liquids and worry about the possibility that an accident may occur. Would we be able to recover damages if an accident was to occur?**

**A.** Probably. Courts have found such storage to be an inherently dangerous activity. This means that the act is hazardous by its very nature, whether it is done well or badly. Courts normally are likely to impose strict liability

against the company for injuries that an accident may cause. Courts still might look at the location of the storage, however. If storage in the middle of a large city poses unusual and unacceptable risks, then courts might impose strict liability. The same holds true when a factory emits smoke, dust, or noxious gases in the middle of a town. But a company may not be held strictly liable if it conducts such activities in a remote rural area and is not doing the activity in any unusual manner.

**Q. What is the legal responsibility of a person who keeps wild animals?**

**A.** Most states impose strict liability against keepers of such wild animals as bears, lions, wolves, and monkeys, reasoning that merely keeping them exposes people to abnormal risks. If an injury occurs on the owner's premises and is caused by a confined or restrained animal, however, courts tend to deny strict liability. The courts reason that you assumed a risk by going there.

**Q. What if one of my animals escapes from our fenced-in yard and goes onto our neighbor's property?**

**A.** In most jurisdictions, keepers of all animals, including domesticated ones, are strictly liable for damages resulting from the trespass of their animals on another person's property.

But courts make exceptions for the owners of dogs and cats, saying they are not strictly liable for trespasses, absent negligence, except where strict liability is imposed by statute or ordinance.

**Q. Am I automatically liable if my dog, normally a friendly and playful pet, turns on my neighbor and bites her?**

**A.** It may depend on where you live. A number of jurisdictions have enacted dog bite statutes, which hold owners strictly liable for injuries inflicted by their animals. If there is no such law in your town, you still can be found liable under a common law negligence claim if you knew the animal was likely to cause that kind of injury and failed to exercise due care in controlling the pet. If, on the other hand, you did not know or have any reason to suspect that your dog had such a dangerous trait, courts have said owners generally are not liable.

It is important that you contact your local animal control department to find out about any regulations in your area.

**Q. Our neighbors have a vicious watchdog. We are scared to death that the dog will bite one of our children, who often wander into the neighbor's yard. What can we do?**

**A.** The situation you pose is a common one and, as in the example above, is precisely the reason a number of municipalities regulate dog ownership, especially of vicious dogs, through ordinances. A great deal would depend on the ordinance where you live. Unless your neighbor posts adequate warnings, he may be strictly liable for injuries caused by a vicious watchdog. (And there is a question of whether written warnings are sufficient if a child is injured.)

Even if the dog never bit before, such liability is imposed because of the mere fact that the dog is known to be vicious—or has certain dangerous traits.

## PRODUCT LIABILITY

Strict product liability, now the law in nearly every state, allows an action against a manufacturer that sells any defective product resulting in injury to a buyer or anyone who uses it. If you are injured by a defective product, you do not need to prove that a manufacturer was negligent, but only that the product was defective. A strict liability action can be brought against the parties that designed, manufactured, sold or furnished the product.

It is possible for plaintiffs to recover punitive damages in strict product liability actions, though such cases are relatively rare and usually deal with outrageous conduct. Punitive damages are money awards that go beyond an award for other damages. Punitive damages are intended to set an example and punish wrongdoers for intentional and outrageous conduct with evil intent.

Liability actions against manufacturers for products that injure consumers also may be based on negligence, a contractual breach of warranty or, sometimes, a manufacturer's intentional wrongful conduct.

**Q. Our brand-new power mower backfired and injured me. From whom may I recover damages?**

**A.** This is a typical product liability case. You may be able to prove that the manufacturer of the lawn mower made a defective product. Most courts today hold companies responsible for a defective product strictly liable to consumers and users for injuries caused by the defect. The product may have had a design flaw or a manufacturing defect. Another possibility may be that the producer or assembler failed to provide adequate warning of a risk or hazard or failed to provide adequate directions for a product's use.

**Q. A disclaimer that came with the lawn mower said the manufacturer did not warrant it in any way. Will that defeat our claim?**

**A.** While limited warranties are sometimes enforced by courts, full disclaimers often are not. Courts find such warranties invalid because you, as the consumer, are not in an equal bargaining position. They also rule that such clauses are unconscionable (grossly unfair) and contrary to public policy. (See the discussion of "contracts of adhesion" and unconscionability in the chapter on contracts and consumer law, on page 309.)

Most courts limit the effect of limited warranties to repairs. A limited warranty is not a waiver of liability for injuries.

**Q. A toy my grandson was playing with came apart, and he put one of the pieces in his mouth and started choking. Do we have any redress against the toy manufacturer?**

**A.** The manufacturers of toys are closely monitored by the federal Consumer Product Safety Commission (CPSC), but lawsuits against them are abundant as well. Like others that put products into commerce, toy manufacturers have a duty to consider any foreseeable misuse of their products. As in any strict liability action, several questions would need to be answered to determine the manufacturer's culpability. Did it have a duty to warn of the danger of the toy falling apart? If so, what was the likelihood that it would break into small parts that could be dangerous to a small child? Did it make a difference how the child was playing with the toy? Because toy manufacturers outside of the U.S. can be difficult to sue, you also might want to consider suing other parties in the toy's chain of

**BREAST IMPLANT LITIGATION**

In the past several years, there have been literally thousands of lawsuits filed by women who have undergone breast implantation and now allege that the implants contributed to a wide range of health problems, ranging from cancer and auto-immune diseases to joint pains and interference with cancer detection. In addition to saying that both silicone breast implants and other artificial implants were responsible for adverse-health effects in them, women in at least one recently filed suit against implant manufacturers have alleged for the first time that the implants also caused miscarriage and harmful effects in their children, some of them because they were breast-fed. The suits generally say that the manufacturers were negligent and that they knew the product was defective. Because this is such a new area of tort law, it is important to contact a personal injury lawyer if you think you may have a claim.

distribution—the toy store, for example, or perhaps a fast-food chain that distributed the toy as part of a promotion. Such retailers also can be liable for injuries.

**Q. I suffered a severe allergic reaction from some cosmetics I used and needed medical treatment. May I recover from the manufacturer?**

**A.** Perhaps. Did the manufacturer warn you that the cosmetic could cause such a reaction? Some courts normally will not hold the manufacturer liable for failing to warn you of the risk of an adverse reaction unless you can prove that an ingredient in the product would give a number of people an adverse reaction. You also must prove that the manufacturer knew or should have known this and that your reaction was because you were in that group of sensitive people, and not because you are hypersensitive. In addition, courts will determine whether you used the product according to the directions provided with it. Misuse is a defense recognized in strict liability. If the court does not find strict liability, you still might recover on a negligence claim.

**Q. My little boy contracted Reye's syndrome after I gave him children's aspirin for a respiratory ailment. Can we recover?**

**A.** Because of the known danger of contracting Reye's syndrome when a child takes aspirin, children's aspirin bottles contain warnings. But in one recent California case, an appellate court said a jury should decide whether a manufacturer was negligent in failing to supply a Spanish-language warning of the hazards associated with aspirins. The child's mother could only speak Spanish and was unable to read the warning in English on the aspirin bottle. The case is now before the California Supreme Court.

**Q. I got hepatitis from a blood transfusion. Is someone liable?**

**A.** In many states, laws protect suppliers against strict liability when people who receive blood transfusions contract an illness from contaminated blood. However, you may recover if you can show negligence by the supplier.

**Q. I was injured because of a brake defect in a used car I bought. May I recover from the dealer?**

**A.** At least one used car dealer has been subject to a negligence action for failing to inspect or discover such defects. But courts are split on whether dealers in used goods should be subject to strict liability. Holding them strictly liable appears to be a minority position.

## WHAT YOU SHOULD DO IF YOU ARE INJURED BY A PRODUCT

Keep the evidence. If a heating fixture ruptures and injures someone in your family, keep as many pieces of the equipment as you can find and disturb the site as little as you can. Make note of the name of the manufacturer, model, and serial number. Keep any packaging or instructions. Keep any receipts showing when and where the product was purchased. Take pictures of the site and of the injury. Make a record of exactly when the incident occurred and under what circumstances. Be sure you have accurate names and addresses for all doctors and hospitals treating the injured victim.

## INTENTIONAL WRONGS

### Q. Is a civil lawsuit based on liability for an intentional tort different from a lawsuit based on negligence or strict liability?

**A.** Not really. You may claim the same types of damages, but you must prove different elements. A person who is found liable for an intentional tort does more than just act carelessly, which might make him or her liable for negligence. The person committing the former tort is said to intend the consequences of his or her action. If you pick up a realistic model of an AK-47 and point it at another person out of the window of your car, you are going to scare that person. Under the law of intentional torts, you may be liable for an assault.

You do not have to intend to harm that person to be liable for an intentional tort, either; you may even be attempting to help that person. In one reported case, for example, a defendant was found liable for an intentional tort when, despite her protests, he proceeded to set the broken arm of a woman who had fallen. Unlike a negligence action, a plaintiff alleging an intentional tort does not need to show actual damages to recover.

### Q. I got a black eye in a fistfight with a man whose car accidentally bumped into mine while we sat at a red light. I would love to get even with him. Can I recover if I sue him?

**A.** Normally you could recover damages in a civil battery case against someone who hits you. But a court might hold that two people who get into a fistfight in effect agree to being hit by one another. If so, a battery case probably would fail. A lot would depend on the facts of the case. Who started the fight? Were you simply trying to defend yourself from his aggression? Were there witnesses? What would their testimony be?

### Q. Isn't battery a crime?

**A.** Yes, battery can be a crime but as a personal injury action it is a civil claim, as are all tort actions. The law considers torts to be wrongs against an individual, allowing the individual to sue for money damages. (For more on criminal assaults and batteries see the "Criminal Justice" chapter.)

As a tort, a battery is a harmful or offensive touching of one person by another. Anyone who touches you or comes into contact with some part of you—even your purse—when you do not agree to it may be liable to you for battery. The law does not require any harm or damage. You do not even have to know a battery is occurring at the time in order to bring a battery claim. The person committing the battery may have meant no hatred or ill will. In one case, for example, a plaintiff successfully recovered damages for an unwanted kiss. In another case, a court found a defendant liable for spitting at someone's face. Also, a court found a battery when a person forcibly removed a woman's hat. However, damages for technical batteries are small. After all, you were not actually hurt, so how much should you get?

### Q. What is the tort of assault?

**A.** An assault is a reasonable apprehension (expectation) of some harm that may come to you. Unlike a battery, you must know that an assault is occurring at the time it takes place. A court will look at what happened. A great deal will depend on the reasonableness of your own feelings when threatened. The court will consider whether the closeness of the physical threat should have subjectively upset, frightened, or humiliated you. Words alone usually are not enough to bring a case for assault.

**Q. My neighbor fired his shotgun to scare a solicitor whom he did not want coming to his door. The bullet grazed a passerby. Will my neighbor be liable?**

**A.** Under a legal doctrine known as transferred intent, your neighbor could be liable for a battery to the passerby. This is true even though the passerby was an unexpected victim whom your neighbor did not intend to harm. The solicitor also is likely to win an assault case against your neighbor. The firing of the gun placed the solicitor in reasonable apprehension of a battery, which is the legal definition of an assault.

**Q. A security guard in a store suspected me of shoplifting and detained me. I have heard about something called false imprisonment. Do I have an action for that?**

**A.** If the security guard was acting in good faith, most courts will allow the guard to detain you briefly on the store premises. A number of states by law have given shopkeepers a limited privilege to stop suspected shoplifters for a reasonable amount of time to investigate. Nonetheless, you may be able to recover damages for false imprisonment. Suppose the security guard genuinely restrained you against your will, intending to confine you. Damages for such an action generally include compensation for loss of time and any inconvenience, physical discomfort, or injuries. If the guard acted maliciously, you also may be able to receive punitive damages.

**Q. Someone broke into my house in the middle of the night and attacked me. It was dark and I could not see the intruder well. I chased and knocked down a teenager run-**

ning down the street because I thought he was the culprit, but I was wrong. Will I be liable to him?

**A.** If you reasonably believe someone broke into your house and attacked you, you have the right to defend yourself by injuring him, even though it turns out that the one you injured is not the same person who broke into your house. If you believe someone is about to inflict bodily harm, you may use nondeadly force to defend yourself. In this particular case, if the teenager already was running down the street, courts may say that there no longer was danger to you or your property. Then, outrageous as it sounds, you might well be liable. In situations where you believe an intruder is about to inflict death or serious bodily harm, courts allow you to use deadly force. The question then becomes whether the force you used was reasonable under the circumstances.

**Q. We got behind on our bills and a bill collector has been stopping by and calling us day and night. The bill collector intimidates us, calls us names and threatens to destroy our credit record. We are nervous wrecks. What may we do?**

**A.** You may be able to make a case that the collector's conduct is a tort, the intentional infliction of mental distress. Courts recently have begun to recognize such actions as extreme and outrageous conduct that someone else intentionally inflicts on you. For you to recover damages, you must show more than hurt feelings. Without aggravating (intensifying) circumstances, most courts have not allowed recovery if the collector was merely profane, obscene, abusive, threatening, or insulting. The collector would need to have used outrageous and extreme high-pressure methods for a period of time. If the collector touched you offensively without your consent, you might even want to consider adding claims

## FORMS OF DEFAMATION

*Defamation involves your reputation. If something is said or shown to a third person and is understood by that person to lower your reputation, or keep others from associating with you, you may have a defamation claim. Libel and slander are two types of defamation. To recover for defamation, you have to prove that the information is false—truth is a defense. Plaintiff's consent to the publication of defamatory matter concerning him is a complete defense as well.*

*Defamation generally is easier to prove if you are a private person. Courts treat public officials and figures differently from private persons in deciding whether someone has defamed them. Public figures must show that the speaker or publisher either knew the words were false or was negligent in saying them. Courts have established certain constitutional protections for statements about public officials. That is why they must show that the speaker or publisher made the statement knowing it was false—or seriously doubting its truth.*

for two other intentional torts—assault and battery. You also might want to consider a case against the collector's employer. Just as employers are vicariously (indirectly) liable for the negligent acts of an employee, employers can be liable for the intentional acts of an employee. (See page 266 of the "Consumer Credit" chapter for other legal protection against debt collectors.) A court would need to determine whether the collector's particular conduct fell within the scope of his or her job.

### Q. What is the difference between slander and libel?

**A.** A defamation action for slander rests on an oral communication made to another that is understood to lower your reputation or keep others from associating with you. Libel generally is considered written or printed defamation that does the same thing. Radio and television broadcasts of defamatory material today are nearly universally considered libel.

### Q. My late grandfather, who owned a textile factory, was called "unfair to labor" in a recent book about the industry. Is that libelous?

**A.** While it can be libelous to write that someone is unfair to labor—or is a crook, a drunk, or an anarchist—no defamation action can be brought for someone who is dead. If your family still owns the factory and the same accusation made against your grandfather was made against one of you, a defamatory action could be brought.

### Q. I have a tax-return preparation business, and a neighbor recently told a potential client that I did not know a thing about tax law. Isn't that slander?

**A.** You might have a case. If someone says something that affects you in your business, trade, or profession, you can recover in a slander action even without showing actual harm to your reputation or other damages. You can do the same in three other situations—if someone says that you committed a crime, that you have a loathsome disease, or that a specific female is unchaste (impure).

Of course, you can recover in other slander cases, but in those you must show that you were actually damaged.

### Q. Are there defenses to defamation?

**A.** There are several defenses that will defeat a defamation claim. As mentioned above, consent is one; truth is another. And certain persons and proceedings (such as a judge in his or her courtroom, witnesses testifying about a relevant issue in a case, and certain communications by legislators) are said to be privileged. They are protected from defamation claims.

## WHERE TO GET MORE INFORMATION

Tort law covers a broad spectrum of potential injuries to persons and property, but nearly all the cases involve insurable interests—your life, your health, your home, your property, and your car. For that reason, qualified insurance representatives might be the best place to start to get information about the insurance you would need to protect you if a claim were brought against you. Should a claim on your own behalf arise, you probably will need to contact a qualified personal injury attorney, following some of the suggestions set out earlier in this chapter.

There are several agencies that also might help you with certain kinds of claims. The federal Consumer Product Safety Commission (CPSC), for example, regulates many products put into commerce, including toys, and could be helpful if you believe a product is defective. The federal Food and Drug Administration (FDA) regulates drugs and other items, like breast implants, that have been subject to recent litigation.

In addition to making a tort claim, you might want to pursue other methods of complaint. Consumer protection agencies can be found in every state. State attorney generals' offices offer information and accept complaints. You also can contact state boards that regulate the conduct of lawyers, doctors, veterinarians, and even barbers. Check the government listings in your telephone directory for the numbers of these agencies.

# Criminal Justice

# INTRODUCTION

FOR MANY PEOPLE, the criminal justice system may seem intimidating. Most people have never even seen the inside of a courthouse, let alone a jail. Their only experience with police officers may have been a quick stop on the highway for a speeding ticket. For people who have never been charged with a crime, facing criminal charges can be disturbing. However, our system of justice was carefully designed to prevent people from being unfairly convicted by guaranteeing many legal rights to anyone charged with a crime. This chapter will discuss those rights, provide you with a basic understanding of the steps in the criminal justice system, and suggest where you can look for more help.

It is important to be informed about the criminal law in your state. Most crimes are punishable under state, rather than federal, laws. Although all states must comply with certain federal constitutional minimums, there are considerable variations from one state to another. For example, some state constitutions provide a higher degree of personal and procedural rights to the criminally accused than others. Therefore, the information in this chapter will generally be true in most states, but may not be true in all.

## THE BASICS OF CRIMINAL LAW

### Q. How do civil and criminal law differ?

**A.** Both criminal and civil cases involve a dispute over the rights and responsibilities of the people involved. In civil matters, the issue is usually money. In a criminal case, however, the defendant might be ordered to pay a fine or sentenced to probation, jail or prison, or even death. It is the possibility of losing life or liberty that distinguishes criminal from civil penalties.

### Q. What is a citation?

**A.** A citation or summons (ticket) is the penalty for the least serious offenses. While most jurisdictions have decriminalized these offenses, in some municipalities a citation could result in a short jail sentence. The normal penalty is a fine, which may range from under twenty dollars to several hundred dollars. Police typically give citations for such offenses as minor traffic violations (for example, speeding, parking in a no-parking zone, or jaywalk-

ing). If the police cite you for such an offense, they will issue a ticket to you. You have the option of not contesting the citation by mailing in the ticket with the specified payment. Or if you feel the police have wrongly given you a ticket, you have the right to contest the citation at a hearing.

Not all traffic violations are citable offenses, however. The most serious traffic violations, such as driving while intoxicated, are criminal offenses. The law classifies them as misdemeanors or felonies.

### Q. What distinguishes a misdemeanor from a felony?

**A.** Each state has a body of criminal law that categorizes certain offenses as felonies and others as misdemeanors. These offenses generally appear in the state's "penal code," the vehicle code, or the health and safety code (for drug offenses).

Felonies are more serious crimes than misdemeanors. Robbery, kidnapping, rape, and murder are examples of felonies. Public drunkenness,

# What Are the Characteristics of Some Serious Crimes?

| *Crime* | *Definition* |
|---------|--------------|
| Homicide | Causing the death of another person without legal justification or excuse, including crimes of murder and nonnegligent manslaughter and negligent manslaughter. |
| Rape | Unlawful sexual intercourse with a female by force, without consent, or when she is underage. |
| Robbery | The unlawful taking or attempted taking of property that is in the immediate possession of another, by force or threat of force. |
| Assault | Unlawful intentional inflicting, or attempted inflicting, of injury upon the person of another. Aggravated assault is the unlawful intentional inflicting of serious bodily injury or unlawful threat or attempt to inflict bodily injury or death by means of a deadly or dangerous weapon with or without actual infliction of injury.<br>Simple assault is the unlawful intentional inflicting of less-than-serious bodily injury without a deadly or dangerous weapon or an attempt or threat to inflict bodily injury without a deadly or dangerous weapon.<br>Many states have separate categories of assault for child victims. |
| Burglary | Unlawful entry of any fixed structure, vehicle, or vessel used for regular residence, industry, or business, with or without force, with the intent to commit a felony or larceny. |
| Larceny-theft | Unlawful taking or attempted taking of property other than a motor vehicle from the possession of another by stealth, without force and without deceit, with intent to permanently deprive the owner of the property. |
| Motor vehicle theft | Unlawful taking or attempted taking of a self-propelled road vehicle owned by another, with the intent of depriving him or her of it, permanently or temporarily. |
| Arson | The intentional damaging or destruction or attempted damaging or destruction by means of fire or explosion of property without the consent of the owner, or of one's own property or that of another by fire or explosives with or without the intent to defraud. |

SOURCES: U.S. Department of Justice, Office of Justice Programs, Bureau of Justice Statistics, Federal Bureau of Investigation, *Crime in the United States*, 1985.

resisting arrest, and simple battery are misdemeanors. However, the same offense might be either a misdemeanor or a felony, depending on its degree. Petty larceny (stealing an item worth less than a certain dollar amount) is a misdemeanor. Over that amount, the offense is grand theft (a felony). Similarly, the first offense of driving while intoxicated may be a misdemeanor. After a certain number of convictions for that same offense, the state may prosecute the next violation as felony drunk driving.

The federal government and most states classify felonies as all crimes that carry a maximum sentence of more than one year. Misdemeanors are offenses punishable by a sentence of one year or less. Some states, however, draw the line based on the place of possible confinement. If incarceration is in the state prison, the offense is a felony. If the offense is punishable by a term in jail (usually a county facility), it is a misdemeanor.

## THE POLICE AND YOUR RIGHTS

### Q. How do the police investigate crimes?

**A.** When the police receive a report of a crime (such as a home burglary in progress), they send investigating officers to the scene as soon as they can. If the officers arrest a suspect, they will transport that person to the police station for booking. The officer will write an arrest report, detailing when and why the officer went to the scene, along with any observations, and why the officer arrested the suspect. The officer also will fill out a property report, detailing what items (for example, drugs or cash) the police found on the suspect during booking. The officer also will list any items of evidence found at the scene, such as tools the suspect might have used to gain access to the home.

### HOW TO REPORT A CRIME

*Call the police and say that you wish to report a crime. If you have observed a crime or know that a crime took place, the law considers you a witness. If somebody has committed a crime against you, the law regards you as a victim. In either case, the police will want to talk to you to determine what you know about the incident so they can decide whether to investigate further. If you were in any way involved in the crime, the law might consider you a suspect. In this instance it is a good idea to call the local public defender or a lawyer in private practice before you talk to the police. A lawyer, or possibly a public defender, will be permitted to accompany you to the police station and be present to protect your interests during police questioning. Many people believe that what they say to the police is not admissible unless written down, recorded on tape, or said to a prosecutor or judge. That is not true. To be on the safe side, you should assume that anything you say to anybody but your lawyer could be used against you at trial.*

If the crime is complex or serious, the police then assign an investigating officer (usually a detective) to the case. That officer will make a

## The Sequence of Events in the Criminal Justice System

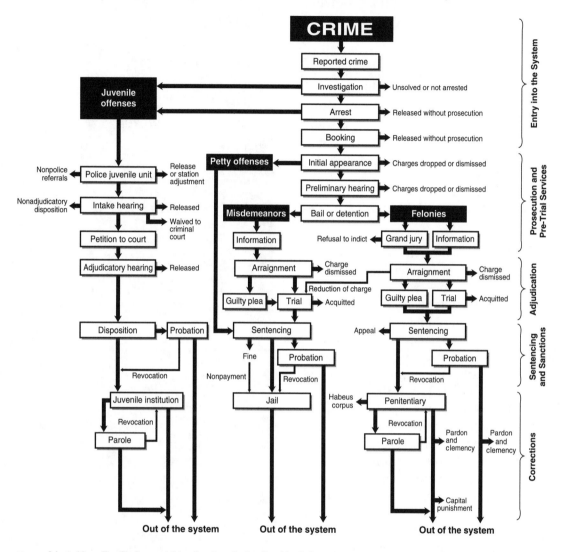

SOURCE: Adapted from *The Challenge of Crime in a Free Society.* President's Commission on Law Enforcement and Administration of Justice, 1967.

return visit to the crime scene, look for more evidence, and interview any other witnesses. If the police have not arrested anyone, the detective will analyze the evidence and try to narrow down the list of suspects. The detective will question suspects and sometimes will obtain a confession.

### Q. How long may police hold suspects before filing charges?

**A.** If the police have probable cause to believe a person has committed a crime but have not yet brought formal charges, they may detain him or her in custody only for a short period of time (generally up to 48 hours). Probable cause is defined as facts sufficient to support a reasonable belief that criminal activity is probably taking place or knowledge of circumstances indicating a fair probability that evidence of crime will be found. It requires more than a mere "hunch," but less than proof beyond a reasonable doubt.

After this short period the police must release the person or bring formal charges and take him or her before a judge. However, he or she may be rearrested at a later date if the police obtain sufficient evidence.

**Q. Do the police have the right to tap my telephone?**

**A.** Yes, if they can show the court that they have probable cause that intercepting your telephone conversations is necessary to help solve certain crimes (such as treason, narcotics trafficking, wire fraud, and money laundering).

However, the law considers wiretapping to be very intrusive. Therefore, federal law closely regulates it. A court will permit wiretapping only for a limited period. The authorities (usually FBI agents) who listen to your telephone calls must make efforts to minimize this intrusion by limiting the number of intercepted calls that do not involve the investigation. An example of this would be tapping a bookie's telephone only during the hours when bets likely will be placed. After the wiretap period has ended, the authorities must inventory the calls and reveal to the court the content of the conversations they intercepted.

A less intrusive form of electronic surveillance is the pen register. This device records every number dialed from your telephone. However, a pen register simply lists telephone numbers. It does not enable anyone to listen to your conversations.

**Q. May the police search me without a warrant?**

**A.** That depends on whether you are under arrest. If the police have lawfully arrested you,

## WHO EXERCISES DISCRETION?

*These criminal justice officials must often decide whether or not or how to:*

### Police

- *Enforce specific laws*
- *Investigate specific crimes*
- *Search people, areas, buildings*
- *Arrest or detain people*

### Prosecutors

- *File charges or petitions for adjudication*
- *Seek indictments or file informations*
- *Drop cases*
- *Reduce charges*

### Judges or magistrates

- *Set bail or conditions for release*
- *Accept pleas*
- *Determine criminal guilt or delinquency*
- *Dismiss charges*
- *Impose sentences*
- *Revoke probation*

### Correctional officials

- *Assign to correctional facility*
- *Award privileges*
- *Punish for disciplinary infractions*

### Paroling authority

- *Determine date and conditions of parole*
- *Revoke parole*

SOURCE: *Report to the Nation on Crime and Justice, second edition,* Department of Justice, Bureau of Justice Statistics, March 1988.

## STOPPING AND FRISKING SUSPECTS

*Do the police have the right to stop and frisk you? That depends on the circumstances. Suppose the police reasonably suspect that you are engaging in a criminal activity and that you may be armed and dangerous. Then they may stop you briefly to frisk you for weapons. For example, assume that the police observe you walking back and forth in front of a store after dark. They observe you looking around nervously and apparently "casing" the place to break into it. The police are permitted, under these circumstances, to stop you to conduct an outer clothing "pat-down" (also known as a "frisk") for weapons. If they feel a hard object in your pocket that might be a gun, they are permitted to reach in and remove it.*

*Suppose, however, that the police feel something soft in your pocket that could not possibly be a weapon. Under long-standing legal doctrine, the police have no right to seize such an item. Recently, the United States Supreme Court reaffirmed this doctrine. The Court held that a police officer conducting a pat down search for weapons was not entitled to seize an item that, based on the officer's sense of touch, bore no resemblance to a weapon.*

*The example above highlights weapons, but remember that the police can stop, briefly detain, and question a suspect based on reasonable suspicion of a crime, even if no weapons are suspected. In these brief detentions, police do not have to give Miranda warnings (see "The Miranda Rule" on page 550).*

they are permitted to search you. They also are allowed to search the area under your immediate control (also known as your wingspan, or where you can reach). In the example given in the sidebar "Stopping and Frisking Suspects," the police would have the authority to seize the cigarette pack containing drugs from your pocket if you were under arrest. They could then use that evidence against you in court.

If you are not under arrest, the police may need a warrant to search you, though they can do so without a warrant on probable cause, reasonable suspicion, or a wide variety of circumstances. You may consent to a search if you choose, but this is not wise because it limits the range of your defense in later proceedings. Your

consent, for example, will make it difficult to challenge the legality of the search at a pretrial suppression hearing. Many people feel they should consent to show the police they "have nothing to hide"—but what you consider insignificant, such as a piece of paper with a telephone number, may be incriminating evidence in the hands of the police to link you to a crime.

**Q. Does the law permit the police to search my home or items in it?**

**A.** You have greater rights in your home than you do in your car. (See page 366 of the "Automobiles" chapter for information on car searches.) That is because the courts have decided that the law entitles people to greater "privacy rights" in their home. Therefore, the police normally cannot search your home unless they have a warrant. The warrant must specify what the police are looking for and at what location they are likely to find it. The law limits the search to areas where it is reasonable to believe the item might be. You cannot look for a bazooka in a breadbox—it is not sensible to look for a large item in a container too small to hold it.

The police do not need a warrant to search your home if you agree to the search. Consent must be voluntary and must be given by someone who has the legal right to be in the home. Obviously, you can give consent to search your home or apartment. But you are not the only person whose consent would be valid. Your spouse could consent, as could an adult child living in your home. It is also important to note that, in seeking your consent, the police are not required to explain the consequences. For example, they need not tell you that any item in plain view or found during a search, if somehow connected to a crime, can be used against you or any other member of your household. Consent usually is not a good idea because the police may recover evidence you did not know was in your home or was linked to a crime. For example, say the police come to your home to arrest one of your relatives for a drug transaction. You knew nothing about his involvement in selling drugs, so you cooperate with the police and give them blanket permission to search your home. In your bedroom they find a large quantity of cash, which you use for your legal weekend flea market business. Despite your explanation, the officers may seize *your* cash under "asset forfeiture" laws and impound it as evidence of drug sales. You may lose your money—and worse, you may find yourself charged as a co-conspirator in the drug case.

Even if you do not agree to a search, the police are permitted to search your home without a warrant if there are sufficiently exi-

## WHEN MUST POLICE KNOCK BEFORE ENTERING

*The police must execute a search warrant promptly after the court has issued it. This requirement prevents a warrant from becoming "stale" and ensures that police will not conduct a search when there is no longer reason to believe evidence of crime is still present. Some jurisdictions have a "knock-notice" requirement. This means that the police must knock on the door and announce their presence and purpose before entering the premises to search for items in the warrant.*

*If there are sufficiently exigent circumstances, however, the police have a right to force entry without knocking to execute the warrant. For instance, the police may not need to knock if they have evidence that doing so would place them in danger. Also, some states are beginning to pass "no knock" laws for particular searches, like drug raids.*

gent circumstances—that is, if there is an emergency situation where the police have reason to believe someone's life is in danger, a suspect is about to escape, or you might destroy the evidence (flush illegal drugs down the toilet, for example) if they do not conduct the search immediately. In cases such as these when there is no time to get a warrant from the court, the police can search your home without permission.

A warrantless search is presumed invalid, so you have the right to challenge it in court. If the judge finds there was a valid exception to the warrant requirement, he or she will rule the evidence admissible.

On the other hand, if there was no such exception, the "exclusionary rule"—which prevents illegally obtained evidence from being introduced at the trial—will probably prevent the evidence from being used against you. The exclusionary rule has been applied in federal courts since 1914, and in state courts since 1961. It simply says that evidence that police have obtained illegally (for example, through an illegal search) cannot be used against the defendant at trial. The purpose of this judge-created rule is to remove police officers' incentive to conduct illegal searches, and so enforce the protections of the Fourth Amendment of the Constitution.

### Q. If the police stop me for drunk driving, what tests may they force me to take?

**A.** If the police observe you driving strangely or violating the rules of the road, they are permitted to stop your vehicle. If the police then smell alcohol on your breath or have other reason to believe you are driving while intoxicated or under the influence of alcohol, they have the right to ask you to take certain tests. The law refers to these as "field sobriety" tests. Typical tests involve walking a straight line heel-to-toe or touching your finger to the tip of your nose with your eyes closed.

If you do not perform these tests satisfactorily, the police will ask you to submit to a scientific test that shows how much (if any) alcohol is in your body. Many states will offer you one of three choices—give a blood sample, give a urine sample, or take a breathalyzer test. The breathalyzer involves blowing into a bal-

loon attached to a machine that measures the percentage of alcohol in your breath (breath-alcohol concentration, or BAC).

The police are not allowed to force you to take these tests. However, depending on the law in your state, they might use your refusal as evidence against you in court. Also, in many states, refusal to submit to such tests will result in automatic suspension or revocation of your driver's license.

### Q. After arresting me, may the police make me provide fingerprints, a handwriting sample, or a voice example?

**A.** Generally, yes, the police are permitted to force you to supply these. They will take your fingerprints during the "booking" procedure at the police station. The law considers handwriting samples and voice examples evidence of physical characteristics. Therefore, you may not claim that the police are forcing you to incriminate yourself through these identification procedures. The police may use these samples as evidence against you in court if they help prove that you committed a crime. For example, your handwriting may be compared to the signature on a forged check or to the writing on a note handed to a teller in a bank robbery.

### Q. What are my rights if the police put me in a lineup?

**A.** In a lineup, several people who look somewhat similar will be shown to victims or witnesses who observed the crime. The police will ask the witnesses if they can identify anyone in the lineup as the person who committed the crime.

If formal charges have been filed against you and the police put you in a lineup, you have a right to have an attorney present to protect your rights. A lineup is not supposed to be unfairly suggestive—that is, if the victim said her assailant was approximately six feet tall

## WHERE POLICE ARE PERMITTED TO MAKE ARRESTS

*Where the police are allowed to arrest you may depend on whether the police have a warrant for your arrest. The police make most arrests without a warrant. If you commit a misdemeanor in the officer's presence, that officer is permitted to arrest you without a warrant. If the officer has probable cause (the minimum level of evidence needed to make a lawful arrest) to believe that you committed a felony, the officer is allowed to arrest you without a warrant, even if he or she did not see you commit the crime. The law permits warrantless arrests in public places, such as a street or restaurant.*

*But to arrest you in a private place—your home or a friend's home, for example—the police must have a warrant or your consent unless there are exigent circumstances. There are two types of warrants: an arrest warrant and a search warrant. To arrest you in your own home, the police must have an arrest warrant. However, if they lack a warrant but have probable cause for a warrantless arrest, they are permitted to put your home under surveillance. They will then wait until you leave your home and arrest you in a public place. (When the police arrest you without a warrant, the law entitles you to a prompt hearing to determine whether there was probable cause for the arrest.) If the police wish to arrest you in someone else's home, they must name you as the "item" for which they will search.*

with a red beard, the lineup cannot include five short, cleanshaven, dark-haired men and only one tall bearded redhead.

Similarly, the police are not permitted to suggest to the victim that a certain person in the lineup is their main suspect—for example, they may not point to one person and ask, "Could that be the man who stole your purse?"

Neither are police permitted to make such a suggestion during photographic identifications, when a witness is asked to pick the criminal from six similar photographs on a card. (However, you do not have a right to have a lawyer present during a photographic identification.)

When you are in a lineup, the police have the right to ask you to speak if the witnesses feel they can identify you by your voice. The

law permits the police to have you speak the words used during the crime. They might ask you to say, for example, "Give me your money."

### Q. May the police use information from a confidential informant to obtain a search or arrest warrant?

**A.** The law allows police to use such information if it is reliable. Confidential informants are people who supply information to the police without having their identities disclosed. The police often use such information to obtain search warrants. For example, an informant might tell the police where someone has hidden evidence of a crime. The police will provide this and other information (such as the informant's prior reliability, how the informant obtained the information, and evidence obtained from other sources that confirms the informant's story) to a judge or magistrate (a type of court official). If the judge or magistrate determines there is probable cause to believe that this evidence will be found at the location specified, the magistrate will issue a search warrant.

### Q. What procedures must the police follow while making an arrest?

**A.** The police do not have to tell you the crime for which they are arresting you, though they probably will. They are not permitted to use excessive force or brutality when arresting you. If you resist arrest or act violently, however, the police are allowed to use reasonable force to make the arrest or keep you from injuring yourself.

While the police are arresting you, they might read you your *"Miranda"* rights (see "The *Miranda* Rule" on page 550). However, they do not have to read you these rights if they do not intend to interrogate you.

### Q. When am I in custody?

**A.** You might be in custody even if the police do not say, "You are under arrest." Generally, the law considers you in custody when you have been arrested or otherwise deprived of your freedom of movement in a significant way. This may occur when an officer is holding you at gunpoint or when several officers are surrounding you. Other examples are when you are in handcuffs or when the police have placed you in the back seat of a police car. The test is whether or not a reasonable person in the circumstances would have felt free to leave the scene. The most obvious example of being in custody, of course, is when the police say, "You are under arrest."

### Q. What is an interrogation?

**A.** An interrogation might be explicit questioning, such as the police asking you, "Did you kill John Doe?" Interrogation might also be less obvious, such as comments made by the police that they know are "likely to elicit" incriminating information from you. For example, in one actual case that made it all the way to the U.S. Supreme Court, the police knew that a murder suspect was deeply religious. To get the suspect to reveal where the body of a child was, they said that the only way for that girl to get a decent Christian burial is if her body is found before the snowstorm tonight. When the suspect gave an indication about where the body might be found in responding to the statement, he had undergone police interrogation. The law considers this to be indirect questioning or the "functional equivalent" of interrogation.

### Q. How do the police recommend that criminal charges be filed against someone?

**A.** Criminal cases go through a screening process before a defendant faces charges in court. This is a two-step process that begins with the police inquiry. The investigating officer (or another officer superior to the arresting officer) will review the arrest report. That officer will determine whether there is enough evidence to recommend filing charges against the arrested person. If the officer decides not to recommend filing charges, then the police will release the arrested person from jail.

If the officer decides to recommend that a charge be filed, a prosecutor (usually from the prosecuting or district attorney's office) will review the officer's recommendation. Based on the arrest report and any follow-up investigation, the prosecutor's office will decide whether to file charges and what criminal offenses to allege. These allegations will appear in a complaint (affidavit or information) filed in the court clerk's office.

## LAWYERS AND CRIMINAL LAW

**Q. If the police arrest a friend or relative, may I send a lawyer to the jail to offer help?**

**A.** Yes, but the right to counsel is personal to the accused. This means that the person who is under arrest must tell the police that he or she wants a lawyer. In some states, if your friend waives the right to counsel and agrees to talk to the police, the police do not have to tell your friend that you are sending a lawyer. Or, in some states, if your friend has not requested a lawyer the police are even permitted to turn away the lawyer upon arrival at the station without telling your friend. The best thing you can do (should your friend telephone you) is to say that a lawyer is on the way to offer help. Tell your friend to claim the right to counsel and urge him or her not to talk to the police until the lawyer arrives.

**Q. When do I have a right to an attorney— before or during police interrogation?**

**A.** You have a constitutional "right to counsel" (right to have an attorney's advice) before and during police interrogation. As soon as the police read your Miranda rights to you, tell them you want a lawyer. Do not answer any questions. Say nothing until your attorney arrives. If the police place you in a lineup, the

### THE *Miranda* RULE

Miranda *warnings are required because of a case called* Miranda v. Arizona. *When a person is in custody, some version of the Miranda* rights, *such as the following, is read to the individual before questioning:* "You have the right to remain silent. If you give up the right to remain silent, anything you say can and will be used against you in a court of law. You have the right to an attorney. If you desire an attorney and cannot afford one, an attorney will be obtained for you before police questioning."

*The Miranda* rule was developed to protect the individual's Fifth Amendment right against self-incrimination. Many people feel obligated to respond to police questioning. The Miranda *warning ensures that people in custody realize they do not have to talk to the police and that they have the right to the presence of an attorney.*

*If the Miranda* warning is not given before questioning, or if police continue to question a suspect after he or she indicates in any manner a desire to consult with an attorney before speaking, statements by the suspect generally are inadmissible. However, it may be difficult for your attorney to suppress your statement or confession in court.

*The best rule is to remain silent. You have the right to an attorney. Insist on it.*

law entitles you to have a lawyer present if you have been formally charged. This right continues at all your court appearances.

### Q. How do I find a lawyer?

**A.** If you have one, call your family lawyer immediately. If your family lawyer does not do criminal work, he or she may be able to recommend another lawyer who does. If you cannot afford an attorney, tell the police you wish to have a lawyer appointed on your behalf. A counsel for the defense—whether private, a public defender, or assigned—will be appointed on your behalf. Above all, say nothing else to the police until your lawyer arrives.

### Q. What should I tell my lawyer?

**A.** You should tell your attorney the truth. Your lawyer has to know exactly what happened in order to defend you effectively. Tell your lawyer as many details as you can remember. Anything you tell your attorney is confidential and will be kept secret. The law refers to this as the attorney-client privilege.

However, a lawyer also has an ethical obligation to the court. An attorney may not lie to the court for you or knowingly offer a false defense. In practical terms, that means that if you tell your attorney you did not commit the crime but were present when it happened, your attorney cannot bring in alibi witnesses who

## ADMISSIBLE CONFESSIONS

*A lot of people believe that only written, signed confessions are admissible as evidence. This is not true. Oral and unsigned written confessions are also admissible.*

*Whether you may withdraw a confession that you made before a lawyer arrived depends on whether you gave up your right to a lawyer and your right not to talk. If you voluntarily talked to the police after they read you your Miranda rights, you might have waived (given up) your right to counsel and protection against self-incrimination. The prosecution probably could use the confession against you in court.*

*However, if the police continued to question you after you told them you wanted a lawyer, your confession probably would not be admissible in court. In either case, your lawyer might be able to persuade the judge to suppress (exclude) the confession as evidence.*

*Remember that you are permitted to change your mind about wanting a lawyer. If you voluntarily begin to talk to the police, then tell them that you want a lawyer present, the questioning must stop immediately. Or if you have talked to the police once, you may refuse to talk to them a second time until a lawyer arrives.*

will falsely testify that you were with them in another state when the crime took place.

## Q. May I represent myself without a lawyer?

**A.** Just as you have a constitutional right to the assistance of counsel, you also have a constitutional right to represent yourself. The law refers to self-representation as *pro se*. If you request to proceed *pro se*, the judge will determine whether you are making a "knowing and intelligent" decision to give up your constitutional right to counsel. In particular, the judge will determine whether you are aware of the dangers and disadvantages of self-representation.

Those dangers are many. It is not a good idea for untrained people to try to represent themselves in criminal cases. The opponent will be a skilled prosecutor who has conducted many trials. The judge or jury will not necessarily be sympathetic toward you simply because you decided to "go it alone."

Some defendants choose to represent themselves because they feel they can do a better job than a lawyer whom the court has appointed to represent them free of charge. This simply is not true. First, any lawyer is sure to know more than you do about the legal system. Lawyers must complete a three- or four-year program in law school and pass a rigorous bar examination. Second, do not think that the public defender is an inadequate lawyer who could not get a "real job" in a law firm. Many top law students choose public-interest work because they want to help people.

In addition, most people charged with a crime are too close emotionally to their own problems. Therefore, they cannot maintain the clear, coolheaded thinking that is necessary in court. Even lawyers charged with a crime usually hire another attorney to represent them. This follows the old saying, "A lawyer who represents himself has a fool for a client."

By representing yourself, you are giving up a very important constitutional right: the right to counsel. If you represent yourself and are convicted, you cannot claim that your incompetence as a lawyer denied you effective assistance of counsel.

For these reasons, self-representation is a risk that most criminal defendants should not take. Remember that you have the right to dismiss your attorney for good cause. Then you could change lawyers or reconsider representing yourself, if the court will allow it (though the court may require you to proceed immediately with the case, without extra time for you or your new lawyer to prepare). However, once you have experienced the complexities of the legal process, you probably will realize that you need a professional at all times to protect your interests.

## CRIMINAL CHARGES

## Q. How are criminal charges brought against someone?

**A.** There are basically three ways in which formal charges may be brought: information, indictment, or citation. An information is a written document filed by a prosecutor (often the district or prosecuting attorney) alleging that the defendant committed a crime. The information may be based upon a criminal complaint, which is a petition to the prosecutor requesting that criminal charges be initiated.

An indictment is a formal charge imposed by the grand jury, which is a group of citizens convened by the court. Its function is to determine whether there is sufficient evidence to charge a person with a crime and to bring him or her to trial. The grand jury conducts its proceedings in secret and has broad investigative powers. The federal system and about half of the states use grand juries.

As noted earlier, a citation is issued by a police officer, most often for a misdemeanor or other minor criminal matter such as jaywalking, littering, or a minor traffic offense.

None of these mechanisms determine the guilt or innocence of defendants. Rather, they indicate that the issuing authority has determined that there is sufficient evidence to bring a person to trial.

### Q. What does it mean if I have been charged with an "attempt"?

**A.** An attempt means that you had the intent to commit the crime, but for some reason you did not complete it. Usually it means that you took a substantial step to commit the crime. Suppose you went into a bank and demanded money from a teller at gunpoint. Then an alarm rang, so you ran out of the bank before you could get the money. The police would recommend you be charged with attempted robbery. In many states, the punishment for an attempt is as severe as for the completed crime.

### Q. What is a conspiracy?

**A.** A conspiracy is an agreement between two or more people to commit a crime followed by any activity to carry out the agreement. The conspiracy itself is a separate crime. Therefore, the police are permitted to recommend that you be charged with conspiracy even if you did not complete the crime you intended to commit. Because conspiracy charges carry separate penalties, you can be convicted of both conspiracy and a crime that you or your fellow conspirators accomplished as a result of the conspiracy (the "substantive" count). You might receive two or more sentences as a result.

### Q. What is complicity or accomplice liability?

**A.** Complicity is the act of being an accomplice. An accomplice is someone who helps in, or in some states merely encourages, the commission of a crime. Courts sometimes refer to such a person as an aider or abettor. This person did not commit the crime, but his or her actions helped enable someone else to do so. Examples of complicity include supplying weapons or supplies, acting as a "lookout," or driving the getaway car. Other examples are bringing the victim to the scene of the crime or signaling the victim's approach. There are many other ways a person can serve as an accomplice—for example, conspirators are accomplices to all crimes committed during the life of a conspiracy to accomplish its purposes.

Accomplice liability means that anyone who helps in the commission of a crime is as guilty as the person who committed the crime and could be punished as severely if convicted.

## INITIAL CRIMINAL COURT PROCEEDINGS

### Q. How does a defendant appear in court?

**A.** After formal criminal charges have been brought against the defendant through information or indictment, he or she appears before the court. A defendant on pretrial release must come to court as ordered. If the defendant is in pretrial detention, jail officers will bring him or her to court. If a defendant has not yet been arrested or detained or fails to appear, the judge issues an arrest warrant if that person is not already in custody. A police officer locates the suspect and places him or her under formal arrest.

The defendant will then have a first appearance in court (it has different names from state to state). At this hearing, the defendant is usually represented by an attorney or the judge appoints one. During this brief appearance, a judge will explain the defendant's rights and the charges in the complaint. In most jurisdictions the accused can waive the initial appearance, but it usually is not a good idea to do so without consulting with an attorney. The purpose of the first judicial appearance is to ensure that the defendant is informed of the charges and made aware of his or her legal rights.

### Q. What happens next?

**A.** Generally, defendants charged with misdemeanors will be asked to enter a plea at the first appearance (see the section on arraignment on page 556 for more about pleas). For felony cases, the next step for defendants in most states will be the preliminary hearing (again, the name varies from state to state), a separate proceeding that occurs soon after the first appearance. This usually is a brief hearing during which the prosecutor will call only those witnesses necessary to show the judge that a crime happened and that there is a strong likelihood that the defendant committed it. Often there is just one witness, the police officer who investigated the crime or who arrested the defendant. The accused person must be present at the hearing, though the accused does not introduce evidence in his or her defense.

The preliminary hearing serves some of the functions of the grand jury, in that the judge determines whether there is enough evidence to charge the defendant with having committed a crime. (Remember that most defendants are not charged by a grand jury, but through some other mechanism.)

If the judge concludes that the state does not have sufficient evidence to support the charges, the judge will order the charges dismissed. If the judge believes the evidence is sufficient, as is usually the case, he or she may set the amount of the defendant's bail (or in some states, if the charge is serious, deny bail altogether), depending upon the nature of the crime and whether the accused is likely to flee.

### Q. How do I get out on bail until my trial?

**A.** Bail is money that you provide to ensure that you will appear in court for trial. If you do not have the money to post bail, a relative or friend can post bail on your behalf (or you can go to a bail bondsman, described below). After the trial ends, the court will refund the bail money, usually keeping a percentage for administrative costs.

The law does not automatically guarantee you the right to be released on bail. If the judge decides that the nature of your crime or other factors make you a danger to the public, the judge is likely to set a high bail amount or, in some states, deny bail. Then you would have to remain in jail until a judge or jury decides the case.

The judge also will consider whether you are likely to flee if the court releases you on bail. Points in your favor include strong family ties in the area, longtime local residence, and current local employment. The judge also will consider any negative information that appears about you in a pretrial release report.

If the judge decides bail is proper, the issue then becomes the amount of money that you must post for your release. Your bail may not be excessive (unreasonably high). However, there are no specific guidelines about what the amount of bail should be. Your attorney is permitted to make a request to the judge to reduce the bail or, possibly, set no bail. The term for that is releasing you on your own recognizance (often abbreviated "O.R." or "R.O.R."). This means you will not have to post any bail money. However, you will have made a binding promise to return to court on a date specified by the judge.

If the court grants you O.R. status or releases you on bail, you must reappear in court as agreed. If you do not appear, the judge could revoke your bail or O.R. status. The judge also could issue a bench warrant for your arrest. The police then will find you, take you into custody,

## Trial Progression of Criminal Actions

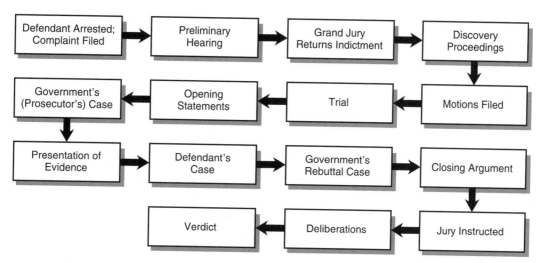

SOURCE: Understanding the Federal Courts

and place you in jail. And you will lose your bail money.

### Q. What role does a bail bondsman or surety play?

**A.** Many defendants cannot raise the entire amount of the bail. In some states, the court may release defendants after they pay 10 percent of the bail. In other states, defendants may arrange for their release through a bail bondsman. In that case, a defendant typically posts 10 percent of the total bail and signs over a lien on certain belongings to a bail bondsman or surety firm representative who guarantees to pay the remainder to the court if the defendant fails to appear for trial.

### Q. What is the next step in the proceedings?

**A.** For those charged with misdemeanors, the typical next step is to plead guilty or *nolo contendere* or go to trial. For those charged with felonies—assuming the judge has found enough evidence to support the charges—the case is generally then set for arraignment (called by a different name in some states). When defen-

dants appear for arraignment, the charges are read to them, their rights are explained, and they enter their plea. If the defendant pleads not guilty, the court will set a date for the next step in the process—the trial. (The plea of not guilty is often the first step in plea bargaining with the prosecutor.) If the defendant pleads guilty, a date will be set for sentencing, although probation, fines, or other sentences will be determined immediately for some minor crimes.

The vast majority of criminal cases eventually result in pleas of guilty or *nolo contendere.* Under either plea, you are guilty of the crime originally charged or of a lesser offense agreed to by the parties. *Nolo contendere* means "I do not contest [the charge]." On the other hand, a guilty plea is a specific admission of guilt. The practical effect is that the *nolo* plea avoids automatic civil liability. Let us say a nursing home operator is accused of the crime of abusing patients. If the operator pleads guilty, anyone who sues him or her for civil damages will not have to prove that the abuse occurred. However, if the operator pleads *nolo contendere*, the civil court will have to decide whether the acts alleged took place.

In a few jurisdictions, a defendant may elect to "stand mute" instead of making a plea. When the judge asks for a plea, the defense attorney would state, "my client stands mute." The court will enter a plea of not guilty. By standing mute, the accused avoids silently admitting to the correctness of the proceedings against him or her until that point. This leaves the defendant free to attack all previous proceedings that may have been irregular.

### Q. Must the judge accept my plea?

**A.** A plea of not guilty must be accepted. However, a judge cannot accept a guilty plea unless he or she ensures that you understand the rights you are giving up and that you are doing so of your own will (free from coercion or threats). In many states, the judge also must determine that there is a factual basis for your plea; in other words, that you actually are guilty of the offense. Should you decide to plead guilty, the judge will ask you a series of questions in open court to ensure that your guilty plea is valid.

### Q. What are plea bargains?

**A.** Plea bargains are legal transactions in which a defendant pleads guilty to a lesser charge or pleads guilty to the original charge in exchange for some other form of leniency. The rationale is based on the notion of "judicial economy" — plea bargains avoid the time and expense of a trial, freeing up the courts to hear other cases. The benefit to defendants is that the process is completed much sooner than it would be if they went to trial. Further, defendants are afforded a sense of certainty; they know what the outcome of their case will be, rather than taking their chances at trial.

Generally such offers are more generous in the early stages of prosecution as an incentive to the defendant to bring the case to an early conclusion. In many cases, the prosecution extends such offers at the time set for the arraignment. Such an early "disposition" of the case tends to be favored by the prosecution, the defense, and the judge because it eliminates several additional court appearances that would have been required had the case continued to trial.

In certain cases, the defense would be better off waiting to thoroughly investigate the case and consider a later offer or possible dismissal of the charges. For example, consider the case of a person charged with attempted murder because he allegedly uttered a death threat when he shot someone in the leg. An early offer might be to plead guilty to assault with a deadly weapon, which is a serious felony carrying a sentence of several years. However, after the victim testifies inconsistently at a preliminary hearing, the prosecutor realizes that he or she would not be a credible witness at trial. Rather than risk an acquittal at trial, the prosecutor may offer to plead the case down to a misdemeanor, such as negligent discharge of a weapon.

If you do not accept the offer when the prosecution first makes it, the prosecutor is allowed to reduce or withdraw the offer.

You do not have a right to have the prosecutor negotiate a plea with you or your attorney. However, prosecutors usually will offer a plea bargain to reduce their heavy caseloads. In most jurisdictions, the court has no obligation to adhere to the bargain the prosecution offers, but in many cases the judge will accept the plea if a legal basis for it is established in court (see the following section on the judge's role in plea negotiations).

Plea bargaining has become extremely commonplace. Today approximately 85 to 90 percent of all criminal cases are settled through plea bargains. The process, however, is not without its critics. Some "victims' rights" groups feel it is immoral for criminals to serve less time through plea bargaining than they would if convicted of actual crimes committed. In response to citizen pressure, some states, such as California, have passed laws severely restricting or even prohibiting plea bargaining in certain serious or violent crimes.

### Q. What role does the judge play in plea negotiations?

**A.** The judge is under no obligation to accept all terms of the plea bargain. Before accepting your guilty plea, the judge will explain the maximum time to which you may be sentenced and the maximum fine, if any, that may be imposed. That time may exceed the sentencing recommendation of the prosecution, or the judge could impose a shorter term in the interests of justice. If you do not accept at that point, your guilty or *nolo contendere* plea will not be entered and you will go to trial. Most often, however, the judge will honor the plea bargain reached between the parties unless he or she feels it is unfair.

### Q. Could the charges against me be dropped?

**A.** Yes. This is called "dismissal" of a case, which can occur for several reasons. For example, charges may be dismissed for insufficient evidence, which means the police either could not find enough evidence to link you to a crime or found evidence pointing to your innocence. Witness problems also prompt dismissals when those who observed a crime fail to appear, are reluctant to testify, or testify inconsistently. Sometimes cases are dismissed "in the interests of justice," a broad category that means the prosecutor does not feel the case is significant enough to pursue, such as minor property damage.

## EVIDENCE IN CRIMINAL CASES

### Q. How may I recognize and preserve evidence to help me at my trial?

**A.** Physical evidence—such as a gun or a piece of clothing—can be very important in helping a judge or jury piece together what actually happened. These people were not there when the alleged crime took place. The physical evidence can provide a way to show that your version of the facts is correct.

You should preserve any items that might be useful as evidence. In fact, it is against the law to destroy evidence, whether you think the evidence will help or harm your case. In any event, let your lawyer determine whether the

### TYPES OF IMMUNITY

*If you had some involvement in a crime with someone else, the prosecutor might agree to lesser charges against you (and thus a shorter stay in jail) if you agree to testify against your partner. Then the court will give you a "grant of immunity." This means that the information you reveal while testifying in court will not be used to prosecute you for your involvement in the crime. Once you accept immunity, you must testify.*

*Talk to your attorney before you accept immunity. Different types of immunity give different protections. "Use immunity" means the prosecutor is not permitted to use what you say to help prosecute you later. "Transactional immunity" gives far greater protection. It means the prosecution will never prosecute you for the crime, even based on evidence independent of your testimony.*

evidence is harmful. For example, you might believe that the prosecution will use a gun with your fingerprints as evidence against you in a shooting. However, your attorney might be able to show that the gun was too big or the trigger too hard to pull for someone of your size to have fired it. The only logical explanation then would be that you picked up the gun after the shooting. This may cause the jury to have a reasonable doubt about your guilt.

**Q. What kind of evidence may the prosecution use against me at the trial?**

**A.** The prosecution may use almost any type of legally admissible evidence that will help establish your guilt. This includes physical evidence, such as a murder weapon or items stolen during a burglary. Testimonial evidence is likely to be used as well. That involves testimony (oral statements) from a person on the witness stand. For example, the owner of a stolen car might testify that no permission was given to anyone to take the car on the day the crime occurred. The prosecution may also introduce circumstantial evidence of a crime, such as the fact that the defendant hurriedly packed and moved out of state within hours after the crime, circumstantially indicating a consciousness of guilt—or that a man charged with killing his wife took out a $100,000 life insurance policy the day before she was slain, circumstantially indicating motive.

If a lawyer asks a witness to testify about someone else's out-of-court statement, the opposing lawyer may object that the testimony is inadmissible because it is hearsay. The problem with hearsay is that the person who made the statement is not on the stand and is unavailable for cross-examination.

To decide whether the testimony would in fact be hearsay, the court must decide why the witness is being asked the question. If the witness's testimony about someone else's out-of-court statement is being introduced to prove

the truth of the out-of-court statement, it is hearsay. If it is only being introduced to prove that the out-of-court statement was made, it is not hearsay.

For example, assume Jane testifies that "John told me my husband was having an affair." If John's out-of-court statement ("Your husband is having an affair") is being introduced to prove that Jane's husband was in fact

**OVERLOOKED EVIDENCE**

*Some evidence is far less obvious than a gun. At a crime scene, tiny items such as rug fibers, hair, cigarette ashes, or matches may become important evidence in your defense. Therefore, if you are at the scene of a crime before the police arrive, leave everything undisturbed. Do not vacuum, move items, or touch anything. The police will secure the area and record everything to maintain what the law calls "crime scene integrity." Once evidence gets misplaced or damaged, a crucial link in winning your case may be lost. In addition, the judge or jury might view tampering with the evidence as an indication of your guilt.*

*The nature of the offense will determine the evidence to preserve. For instance, if the prosecution charges you with an economic crime such as fraud, you must preserve any important documents.*

having an affair, it would be hearsay. If, on the other hand, Jane is only testifying about what John said in order to explain why she slapped him in the face, her testimony would not be hearsay. Here the only issue is whether John made the statement, not whether the statement was true.

However, there are many exceptions to the rule against hearsay, so do not be surprised to hear such statements allowed during the trial.

## CRIME REQUIREMENTS

*Most crime requires both a criminal act (actus reus) and a criminal mind (mens rea). Even if you committed a criminal act (injuring someone, for example), you might not have had the required mental state, or wrongful purpose.*

*If the facts in your case show that you did not have this intent, you might not have committed a crime. Your lawyer will help you decide which defenses apply to your case.*

*On the other hand, sometimes you can be convicted even if you did not have intent to commit a crime. A person who kills another unintentionally has committed a crime if his or her actions were reckless or sufficiently negligent. For example, if an accident occurs while you were driving under the influence of alcohol or drugs, that is vehicular homicide, even if you had no intention of harming the victim.*

## WITNESSES

### Q. Who are witnesses? What makes a good witness?

**A.** Witnesses might be victims or defendants who are voluntarily testifying on their own behalf. Witnesses may be presented by both the prosecution and the defense. Or a witness might be someone testifying as an impartial eyewitness to a crime, or someone with information about it. In any event, the most important thing is to be honest. When you are

## EXPERT WITNESSES

*Expert witnesses are specialists in certain fields, such as narcotics, psychology, medicine, or engineering. The prosecution or the defense may call them to testify at a trial. Their testimony is another form of evidence that the judge or jury will consider. Usually, the experts' role is to offer an opinion of what they think the evidence means when lay people are unlikely to understand that evidence without help. For example, a narcotics expert might testify that the quantity of drugs seized and the way the defendant packaged them indicate a commercial drug operation. A fingerprint expert may compare the prints lifted from a crime scene to a fingerprint sample taken from the defendant and then give a professional opinion of whether the prints "match."*

on the witness stand, the law requires you to tell the truth. Answer the questions as completely as possible, but stick to the point. Do not add details that are not necessary to answer the question. If you do not understand the question, politely ask the lawyer to rephrase it. Do not answer any questions if you are unsure of the answer. If you do not know the answer, your answer should be, "I don't know." If you hear a lawyer say "objection" after a question is asked, do not answer the question. Wait until the judge rules on the objection. The judge will then tell you whether you may answer the question.

Testifying can be tiring and frustrating. Try to remain relaxed and keep a pleasant attitude. The worst thing you can do is to appear angry, lose your temper, or argue with the lawyer who is asking the questions. If the judge or jury disapproves of your behavior or attitude, they might not believe your testimony.

### Q. May the court force me to testify?

**A.** If you are a defendant, no. The Fifth Amendment of the U.S. Constitution gives you the right against self-incrimination.

If you are a witness or the victim of a crime, a subpoena compels you to testify, even if you "don't want to get involved." However, you may refuse to answer a question on the witness stand if you feel the answer might incriminate you, unless the district attorney has granted you immunity in exchange for your testimony—in that case, you must answer (see "Types of Immunity" on page 557).

Sometimes crime victims "get cold feet" and change their mind about testifying. This is especially true if the victim knows the defendant personally or is afraid of revenge. However, even if you reported the crime and later decide you want the charges dropped, the prosecutor might not agree. The prosecutor often considers a victim's wishes, but technically the injured person is only a witness. The "victims"

are the people of the state where the criminal committed the crime. Therefore, it is up to the district or prosecuting attorney to decide whether to proceed with the case and whether to subpoena a witness to testify.

### Q. Should I take the stand in my own defense?

**A.** Listen to your lawyer's advice. However, the final decision regarding whether to testify is yours. Many defendants do not testify. The judge will instruct the jury not to hold this against you because the Fifth Amendment gives you the right not to incriminate yourself.

Many defendants feel that they should testify because they are innocent and have "nothing to hide." However, any defendant who testifies is subject to tough cross-examination from the prosecutor, who may be able to put you in a very bad light. For instance, if you take the stand, the prosecutor may ask you whether you have had any prior felony convictions. You must answer truthfully. If you do not take the stand, nobody will reveal such information to the jury.

### Q. Are any resources available to help witnesses?

**A.** Most district or prosecuting attorney's offices have "witness assistance" departments that provide a number of services to simplify the process for witnesses. They will give you directions to court and even arrange transportation for you if necessary. If you must travel a distance to testify, these departments may provide you a per diem (daily allowance) for food and lodging. Witness assistance coordinators can help you with other necessary arrangements (such as child care) so you can testify.

If testifying puts you in danger, witness protection programs are available. The police will escort you between your home and court if necessary. If you are a confidential informant in fear for your life, steps will be taken to hide your identity.

## Q. Should I talk to the police if they want to question me about a criminal investigation?

**A.** If you are a witness to a crime, you should share your knowledge with the police. Without information from witnesses, police would be unable to solve crimes and prosecutors would be unable to convict guilty defendants in court. However, if you played a role in the crime or you think the police want to question you as a possible suspect, do not talk to the police. Tell them you want an attorney. Only after talking to a lawyer should you talk to the police.

## Q. What should I do if I receive a subpoena?

**A.** A subpoena or summons is a legal order to appear in court or to produce certain evidence. As soon as you receive a subpoena, you should take certain steps to protect your interests. First, be sure to preserve all related documents so that you will not risk being charged with obstruction of justice. Find an attorney and speak only to him or her about the subpoena. Do not confide in friends or contact others who may be in the same situation, since they may be cooperating with the authorities and could end up testifying in court against you.

If you receive a subpoena ordering you to appear in court at a certain date and time, you must obey or risk being held in contempt of court and receiving a fine or jail sentence. A contempt finding could also mean that you have to pay certain court costs for time lost because the case could not proceed.

The court might direct another type of subpoena at an item you possess, not at you. This "subpoena *duces tecum*" (SDT) orders you to produce certain evidence, usually in the form of documents. Before you obey this type of subpoena, call a lawyer. Depending on the content of the documents, you might be able to fight the

subpoena as forced self-incrimination. Or, based upon the items listed in the subpoena, your lawyer may be able to offer your cooperation to the authorities in an effort to show that no crime has been committed or that you were not part of it. Do not deal with the authorities yourself, however. Your attorney will need to ensure that your cooperation will not be used against you at a later date.

# DEFENSES AGAINST CRIMINAL CHARGES

## Q. What are my possible defenses?

**A.** One defense is an alibi. That is an explanation that at the time in question, you were not at the crime scene and could not have committed a crime there. For instance, if you were out of town on the date the crime happened, you can raise an alibi defense.

Depending on the nature of the crime, you might be able to offer the defense of entrapment. This means that in order to obtain evidence of a crime, the police induced you to commit (lured you into committing) a crime you had not been considering. This is a common defense in offenses involving the sale of drugs to an undercover agent. Precisely because it is a good defense, police work to counteract it by making sure that they file charges as a result of more than one sale.

They are also often careful about charging someone with an illegal purchase from an undercover agent. As a result of these precautions, the defense of entrapment does not often succeed in drug cases. As long as the prosecutors can show that the defendant was either predisposed to commit the crime or that the inducement (lure) was not outrageous, they probably will succeed over a defense of entrapment.

If the prosecutor charges you with a violent crime, you may be able to argue that you did it in self-defense.

There are many other possible defenses. These include intoxication (you were too drunk to be able to form the "specific intent" to commit a certain crime, such as first-degree murder), mistake (you thought the purse you took was yours), insanity (you committed the crime but are legally excused because you could not understand the wrongness of your act), defense of others (you shot an assailant to stop him from killing your wife), defense of property, and many more.

### Q. How does a defendant's mental health affect the legal process?

**A.** Under our system, it is unconstitutional to make anyone stand trial who is not mentally competent. This means defendants must be able to comprehend the nature of the charges against them and to assist properly in their own defense (such as explaining to an attorney what happened and which witnesses may be able to substantiate their account). When a defense attorney has reason to question a client's competency, he or she will ask the judge to order a psychiatric evaluation. Defendants who are found not competent may be committed to a psychiatric facility for treatment, where they will stay until they are competent to stand trial. In some states, the psychiatric patient must be released after a certain period.

### Q. Is incompetence the same as an insanity defense?

**A.** Being incompetent for trial differs from being incompetent ("insane") at the time of the offense. Insanity is a defense to certain crimes that require proof of intent. For example, it could be argued that one who is insane cannot commit first-degree murder because his or her mind is incapable of premeditating and deliberating (planning the crime).

A few states have abolished the insanity defense but allow psychiatric evidence at trial on the issue of intent. For example, a defendant in a drug case could not have formed the intent to sell an illegal substance if he was delusional and believed that he was a doctor dispensing medication.

Most states require formal notice of plans to raise the insanity defense. Such defendants enter a plea of not guilty and proceed to trial. If convicted, such an individual may be found guilty, not guilty by reason of insanity, or in a few states, guilty but mentally ill. Defendants found not guilty by reason of insanity are usually placed in a mental health facility until their mental condition improves so that they are no longer a threat to themselves or the community.

## PRETRIAL PROCEDURES

### Q. Does discovery take place in criminal cases as in civil cases?

**A.** "Discovery" is a process that allows the parties to learn the strengths and weaknesses of each other's case by, for example, obtaining the names and statements of witnesses the other side intends to call at trial. Because the defendant in a criminal case has certain constitutional safeguards (such as the right against self-incrimination), discovery in criminal cases is far more limited than in the civil context.

In most states, the defense's discovery power is much broader than the prosecution's. Some states, including California and Florida, have enacted reciprocal discovery laws, which allow the prosecution to ask the same questions of the defense. In all jurisdictions, however, the prosecution is required to produce all exculpatory material (that which is favorable to the defendant or tends to negate his or her guilt).

### Q. Do criminal cases involve interrogatories and depositions?

**A.** These common civil discovery procedures are rare in criminal cases. Interrogaries are written questions about the facts and background of the case, which the opposing party must answer in writing. Depositions involve the same types of questions, but are oral examinations conducted in a conference room without a judge present. Depositions are taken under oath and are transcribed. In a civil case, the parties must participate in depositions if requested by the opposing side; in a criminal case, because of the guarantees of the Fifth Amendment, it would be unconstitutional to force the accused to answer questions about the case (unless he or she elects to testify at trial). Criminal defendants must also be present at depositions in their cases (or waive that right) because of the Sixth Amendment right to be present and to confront witnesses.

## TRIAL

### Q. What happens at trial?

**A.** First the jury is selected (unless the defendant elects to have a trial by judge, commonly referred to as a "bench trial"). Once the jury has been impaneled (seated for the duration of the trial), the proceedings begin. Defendants have a constitutional right to a public trial.

Opening statements come first. The prosecutor addresses the jury first, explaining the nature of the case and what he or she intends to prove happened. Then the defense attorney may offer an opening statement, or may reserve opening statement until after the prosecution has rested its case.

Next the prosecution puts on its case in chief, which usually involves direct testimony by witnesses and the introduction of any physical evidence against the defendant, such as a gun or other implements of the alleged crime. Defense attorneys may cross-examine the prosecution witnesses by asking questions designed to negate the guilt of their client. After all prosecution witnesses have testified, the process repeats itself in reverse, with the defense putting on any witnesses it may have.

The defense, however, is not required to offer any witnesses, nor are defendants required to testify unless they so choose upon the advice of their attorney—the prosecution bears the burden of proving the defendant's guilt beyond a reasonable doubt.

When the defense has rested, the prosecutor will give a closing argument, summing up the evidence presented against the defendant. The defense attorneys will then make their own closing argument. The prosecutor has one last chance for a rebuttal argument, addressing the points made by the defense in closing. The judge then instructs the jury on the law to apply in deciding the case.

## TRIAL BY JURY OR JUDGE

*Should you exercise your right to a jury trial, or waive it in favor of a bench (judge) trial? This is a decision that you and your lawyer must make. In "nonpetty" criminal cases punishable by more than six months imprisonment, you have the right to be tried by a jury of your peers (fellow citizens). Your chances might be better with a jury, because the prosecutor often must convince each juror that you are guilty. However, juries are unpredictable. In some cases, you might stand a better chance of acquittal with a judge. Listen to your lawyer's advice.*

### Q. What is the role of a jury in a criminal case?

**A.** The jury weighs the evidence and finds the defendant guilty or not guilty. Juries are discussed more fully on page 39 in the chapter titled, "How the Legal System Works." It is important to understand that you have certain rights. First, you have a right to a jury trial in serious criminal cases (for example, for crimes punishable by more than six months' imprisonment). Second, you have a right to a jury that is chosen from a fair cross-section of the community and is not biased against you. Third, you have a right to a jury from which members of certain classes or groups (for example, African-Americans or women) have not been systematically excluded.

### Q. What are jury deliberations?

**A.** After closing arguments, the judge will charge the jury (give them instructions on how to apply the law to the evidence they have observed at trial). The jury then retires to a private room for deliberations, which involve discussion among the jurors as they review the evidence and attempt to reach a unanimous verdict. Deliberations are done in complete secrecy, to ensure fairness to the person on trial. If the jurors have questions, they may send a note to the judge, who will usually respond in writing to clear up any legal questions.

## SENTENCING OF CONVICTED CRIMINALS

### Q. If a judge or jury convicts me, how and when will the court sentence me?

**A.** Sentencing is a separate procedure, usually held several weeks or even months after a conviction. After the verdict is read, the judge will set a time and date for sentencing. The court will order a presentencing report from the probation department. It will examine your past record and will make recommendations about your sentence.

In most states the judge has some discretion in choosing your sentence. For misdemeanors, the judge usually chooses between a fine, probation, suspended sentence, or a jail term (or a combination of these). For felonies, the choice is often between imprisonment and probation, depending on the crime.

For state offenses, the criminal code often specifies the minimum and maximum sentences for each specific crime. Often these are designated as a range, such as three to five years. For federal offenses, the court follows the strict federal sentencing guidelines. (Similar strict guidelines have been adopted by some states, including Minnesota and Michigan.)

The federal guidelines involve a complex formula that calculates an offense level based on several factors, such as the nature and complexity of the crime, any injuries to victims and the defendant's "criminal history." It then results in a certain number of "points," which gives a range of incarceration (prison) time. In some very limited instances, a federal judge might be able to sentence you to a term that varies slightly from the required guidelines. If, for example, the judge finds that your criminal history score significantly underrepresents or overrepresents the seriousness of your actions, he or she can adjust your score upward or downward, affecting the length of time you would spend in prison.

### Q. Is the judge the only person who may decide the sentence?

**A.** In most states and in federal courts, the judge alone determines the sentence. Some states allow the jury to recommend a sentence, particularly in murder cases that carry the possibility of the death penalty. In such capital cases, the "penalty phase" becomes a minitrial of its own, with witnesses commonly testifying about the defendant's character and family upbringing, in an effort to show why he or she should be sentenced in a certain way.

## Q. What determines the sentence I will receive?

**A.** The primary factors are the sentencing range provided in the penal code and your prior convictions, if any. The judge may also consider any aggravating or mitigating factors. Aggravating factors, such as the violent nature of a crime or a high degree of sophistication in planning it, suggest a tougher sentence. Mitigating factors may be a good family history, a stable employment record or any benefits you have bestowed on the community (such as volunteer work at an organization for the disadvantaged).

In addition, before imposing your sentence, the judge usually must allow you to make a statement. You should discuss this with your lawyer in advance. Sometimes a plea for mercy or a promise to improve your behavior will be effective at this point. However, it depends on the judge and on whether the judge believes you.

## Q. Are there any alternatives to jail or prison sentences?

**A.** Yes. One option is monetary. The judge may order you to pay a fine as punishment, or to make restitution (repayment to a victim who lost money because of your crime). Another possibility is probation. When you are on probation, the court has released you into the community. However, you must obey the conditions set forth by the court. One example is submitting to periodic drug testing. If you violate these conditions, the court can revoke your probation and re-sentence you.

These alternatives are frequently combined. For example, a person on probation also may be required, as a term of release, to pay restitution (reimbursement) or perform community service.

A less restrictive sentence involves community service. The court could require you to donate a certain number of hours (usually hundreds or thousands) to doing service work at a community center. Often this involves working at youth facilities or lecturing at schools on the evils of your particular crime.

Another possibility is diversion, a program whose successful completion avoids a criminal conviction. Diversion programs usually are specialized alternatives, run by the prosecutor's office and agreed upon in exchange for a guilty plea. Diversion ordinarily involves your participation in a service program designed to rehabilitate you. For example, some states allow a first-time drug offender to attend a program such as Cocaine Anonymous instead of being tried and facing a prison sentence.

If the court requires you to remain in custody, you may be eligible for a residential program, such as a halfway house or a "boot camp." In a halfway house, you may be allowed to leave during the day to work at a job or go to school, but you must return to the building every evening. In a boot camp, you are housed at a prison facility and may not leave at all. However, you are segregated from the general prison population and are housed with "soft core" criminals, usually first-time offenders under the age of thirty-five. Your experience will be similar to a boot camp in the military—early morning rising and demanding physical labor during the day. You will also be allowed to attend educational or job-training classes and may receive counseling.

## Q. What are my rights as a prisoner?

**A.** The law entitles you to fair treatment as a human being. This means your jailers may not subject you to brutality and that you are entitled to food, water, medical attention and access to the legal system. Such access includes a law library in which to do legal research and typewriters on which to prepare legal motions if you are representing yourself *pro se*.

If your state laws provide for a right to parole (early release from prison), you can apply for parole when you become eligible. If the parole board denies your request for parole, you must be told why and you must be given an opportunity to be heard.

## APPEALS OF CRIMINAL CASES

### Q. May I appeal my conviction?

**A.** Usually a person convicted at a trial has the right to appeal the conviction at least once. (There are very few grounds for appeal if the defendant pleaded guilty.)

On appeal, the defendant can raise claims that mistakes were made in applying and interpreting the law during the trial. For example, the defendant might claim that the judge erroneously admitted hearsay testimony, gave improper jury instructions, should not have permitted the prosecution to use evidence obtained in violation of the defendant's constitutional rights, or permitted the prosecution to make improper closing arguments. If the appellate court agrees that there were significant errors in the trial, the defendant will get a new trial.

### Q. What if the law changes after a court convicts me?

**A.** If a court convicted you for something that is no longer a crime, you might be able to have your conviction overturned. This also might be possible if a trial court denied you a right that the U.S. Supreme Court later rules is guaranteed by the U.S. Constitution. However, your rights will depend on whether the new rule or law is retroactive, that is, applied to cases already decided. As a general rule, a change in the law would be retroactive to your criminal case if the case has been appealed but not resolved at the time the law is changed. If, on the other hand, your case on appeal has been resolved, the change in the law would not be retroactive to your case, unless the change is one that directly enhances the accurate determination of your guilt or innocence.

### Q. What is a habeas corpus proceeding?

**A.** Literally, *habeas corpus* means "to hold a body." A *habeas corpus* proceeding challenges a conviction based upon the grounds that you are being held in prison in violation of your constitutional rights. *Habeas corpus* is not an

### GETTING A LAWYER FOR YOUR APPEAL

*Because trial and appellate (appeals) work are two different types of legal practice, the lawyer who represented you at the trial will not automatically file or handle your appeal. You must ask your lawyer to do so, or find another one who will. In many states, the state public defender (or another assigned counsel) generally will handle the appeal for those unable to pay.*

*Trials require the skills of a lawyer who has experience in the courtroom and working before juries. Appeals involve a large amount of writing and legal research, as well as the ability to argue legal doctrines before a judge.*

appeal but a separate civil proceeding used after a direct appeal has been unsuccessful. A common constitutional challenge under *habeas corpus* is that defendants received "ineffective assistance of counsel" at trial, meaning that their lawyers did not do a competent job of defending them. Such a claim is difficult to prove and will require the defendant-appellant to find a different lawyer to argue the incompetence of the previous attorney. Legal arguments in a *habeas* case are generally done through written motions. An evidentiary hearing may be held as needed, however.

## THE RIGHTS OF VICTIMS AND JURORS

### Q. What are my rights as a victim?

**A.** You have a right to a reasonable amount of effort by the police in trying to find the person who committed the crime. If they find this person, you can tell the prosecutor whether you wish to have that person prosecuted. Often the prosecutor will consider the victim's wishes, though he or she need not.

As a victim, you may be entitled to *restitution*, which means that the judge will order the criminal to reimburse you for any financial damages. For example, a burglar who stole your television may be ordered to return it to you or to give you enough money to buy a replacement. Most states have laws allowing restitution, but such laws are enforced in only about half of the states. Restitution is required in federal courts, however.

If you were the victim of a crime that did not involve money, your concerns may focus more on your assailant's punishment. In about two-thirds of the states, victims are allowed to make oral "victim impact statements" to the judge about how the crime has affected them and what they believe should be the criminal's sentence.

In a serious or violent crime, victims may be afraid to testify. If the defendant or someone on the defendant's behalf has tried to threaten you into not testifying, tell the police. The law entitles you to police protection, and the police will protect you to the extent they can.

If the court releases the defendant from custody, the law still entitles the victim to protection. The court has the authority to order the defendant to stay away from you and your family if you so request. The police will try to ensure that the defendant obeys this order.

In almost all states, victims are notified when their assailants are being considered for parole (early release from prison). About half of the states notify the victim if the assailant escapes from prison.

Because of the variations among the state laws and the growing victims' rights movement, model legislation has been proposed for a uniform victims' rights act, which each state would have the option of adopting.

### Q. Will the court protect jurors against danger of threats or violence?

**A.** The law entitles jurors to such protection. Sometimes the court sequesters (houses in a hotel to isolate from outside influences) the jury throughout the trial. Police officers or court officials escort the jury to and from court. After the trial, the police will continue as best they can to ensure the safety of discharged jurors, at least for a time.

## JUVENILE CRIMINAL CASES

### Q. How do juvenile proceedings differ from adult criminal proceedings?

**A.** Because juveniles do not have a constitutional right to a jury trial unless tried as an adult, judges hear most juvenile cases. Juveniles also do not have a right to a public trial or to bail. However, the fundamental elements of due process apply in a juvenile proceeding as they do in the criminal trial of an adult. For example, a child charged in a juvenile proceeding is entitled to: notice of charges given in advance of any adjudication of delinquency; an attorney, including one paid for by the state if the family cannot afford one; the right to confront and cross-examine witnesses; and the right to assert his or her Fifth Amendment privilege against self-incrimination. Finally, the state is required to prove its charges beyond a reasonable doubt, just as in the trial of any adult on a criminal charge.

Under most state laws, juvenile offenders do not commit "crimes." They commit delinquent acts, which are acts that would constitute crimes if committed by an adult. The trial phase of a juvenile case is an adjudication hearing. This means that the judge hears the evidence and determines whether the child is delinquent. The court may then take whatever action it deems to be in the child's best interest. The purpose is to rehabilitate, not punish.

Juvenile courts usually hear cases involving persons between the ages of ten and eighteen. (The upper age may be lower in some states.) If the prosecution charges an older juvenile with a particularly serious or violent offense, the district or prosecuting attorney may request that an adult court try the juvenile as an adult. In some states, juveniles fourteen or older and charged with serious acts like murder, rape, or armed robbery are handled in adult courts unless the judge transfers them to juvenile court.

### Q. What is a parent's responsibility in juvenile cases?

**A.** Depending on the state where you live, you might be liable (legally responsible) for the acts of your child if you failed to supervise or control the child properly. For example, California recently passed a "gang parent" law that authorizes the arrest of parents of juvenile gang members who commit serious offenses. Similarly, if your teenage driver has an accident or commits a crime while driving the family car, the court may hold you responsible. One example of this is a teenager driving while intoxicated and causing injuries to another.

## ABUSE AND NEGLECT

### Q. Do I have a right to a lawyer if I am accused by the government of abusing or neglecting my children?

**A.** In some states persons may be charged with abusing or neglecting their children and may, if found guilty, lose custody of their children. In those states persons accused of those offenses are usually entitled to an appointed attorney if they cannot afford to pay for one. See page 71 of the "Family Law" chapter for more information on child abuse and neglect.

## WHERE TO GET MORE INFORMATION

Consult the "Where to Get More Information" sections at the end of the first two chapters for general information about lawyers and the legal system. Below are groups that might be of assistance to criminal defendants.

American Civil Liberties Union
132 West 43rd Street
New York, New York 10036
(212) 944-9800

The national organization can provide a variety of information on a range of issues and put you in touch with the state or local ACLU in your area.

National Association of Criminal Defense Lawyers
1627 K St., NW
12th Floor
Washington, DC 20006
(202) 872-8688

This organization can put you in touch with associations of criminal justice lawyers in your state. These groups are usually located in the state capital, with names such as Arizona Attorneys for Criminal Justice, Alabama Criminal Defense Lawyers' Association, or Arkansas Association of Criminal Defense Lawyers.

To find the Office of the Public Defender, look in the telephone book under "County Government" for state offenses or "Federal Government" for federal offenses.

■

# The Rights of Older Americans

# THE RIGHT TO A JOB

I N THE PAST, most of us viewed sixty-five as the age of retirement. Today, more people are choosing to continue working full or part-time well into their seventies or even eighties. Many even change their careers in later life. The contributions of older workers testify to their vitality.

## Age Discrimination in Employment Act

The Age Discrimination in Employment Act (ADEA) ensures that older workers receive equal and fair treatment in the workplace. It protects most workers forty years of age and older from arbitrary age discrimination while on the job. It also seeks to support the employment of older persons based on their ability rather than age. See page 398 in the chapter titled "Law and the Workplace" for a discussion of the ADEA.

**Q. Can I be forced to retire from my job when I reach a certain age?**

**A.** Not if you are at least forty years old and work for either: a private employer with twenty or more employees, or the federal government or any state or local government.

If you meet these criteria, you are protected by the Age Discrimination in Employment Act (ADEA) and cannot be forced to retire.

**Q. My employer says that I do not have to stop working at age sixty-five. However, I will have to accept a job with less responsibility and less pay. Is this legal?**

**A.** No, the ADEA also protects you in your present job situation. Your employer may not force you to take a less responsible job or accept a lower salary.

**Q. Are there exceptions to the rule that employees may not be forced to retire?**

**A.** Yes, the ADEA does not protect two categories of employees. One is government offi-

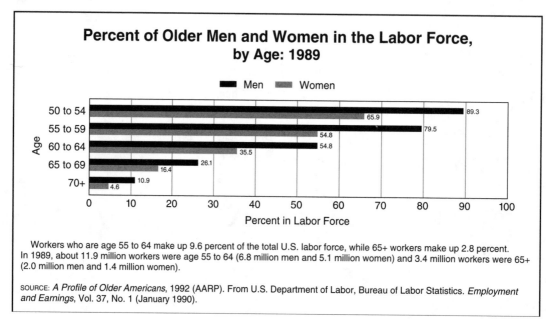

**Percent of Older Men and Women in the Labor Force, by Age: 1989**

■ Men  ■ Women

| Age | Men | Women |
|-----|-----|-------|
| 50 to 54 | 89.3 | 65.9 |
| 55 to 59 | 79.5 | 54.8 |
| 60 to 64 | 54.8 | 35.5 |
| 65 to 69 | 26.1 | 16.4 |
| 70+ | 10.9 | 4.6 |

Percent in Labor Force

Workers who are age 55 to 64 make up 9.6 percent of the total U.S. labor force, while 65+ workers make up 2.8 percent. In 1989, about 11.9 million workers were age 55 to 64 (6.8 million men and 5.1 million women) and 3.4 million workers were 65+ (2.0 million men and 1.4 million women).

SOURCE: *A Profile of Older Americans*, 1992 (AARP). From U.S. Department of Labor, Bureau of Labor Statistics. *Employment and Earnings*, Vol. 37, No. 1 (January 1990).

cials who are elected or appointed to a policy-making level. This exception includes the non-civil-service staff of these officials. The other is persons in bona fide executive or high policy-making positions whose retirement benefits (pension, profit sharing, savings, or deferred compensation) add up to at least $44,000 a year, not counting Social Security.

### Q. Must I retire if I become ill or disabled?

**A.** The law protects you only from being forced to retire because you have reached a certain age. If an illness or disability prevents you from doing your job satisfactorily, the ADEA does not prevent your employer from requiring you to retire, regardless of your age. However, other federal and state laws—including the 1990 Americans with Disabilities Act (ADA)—forbid discrimination against persons with disabilities or handicaps, including those associated with certain illnesses. So, if the ADEA does not cover you in these circumstances, you should consider whether you are being unfairly treated because of disability.

### Q. Are there any circumstances in which age discrimination by an employer is allowed?

**A.** Yes. If the employer can prove that age is a bona fide occupational qualification (BFOQ), discrimination is allowed. One obvious example of age as a BFOQ is a part in a movie requiring a child actor. The possibility of age as a BFOQ is most likely to arise in jobs directly involving public safety or public transportation personnel. However, the BFOQ exception is rare, difficult to prove, and the burden of proof is on the employer. The employer must show: first, that the job qual-ifications are reasonably necessary to the essence of the employer's business; and second, that substantially all persons over the age limit cannot perform the job safely and efficiently, or that it is impossible or highly impractical to assess fitness on an individualized basis.

## THE BREADTH OF AGE DISCRIMINATION IN EMPLOYMENT

*The ADEA does not offer a concrete definition of discrimination. Instead, the Act prohibits employers from doing anything that harms an older worker's status because of his or her age. This may range all the way from offensive age-related jokes to using age as a factor in hiring, firing, layoff, promotion, demotion, working conditions and hours, training opportunities, compensation, or benefits. Historically, most ADEA lawsuits have involved firings or layoffs of older workers.*

### Q. If I am part of a company division or class of employees being laid off, does the ADEA protect me?

**A.** Yes, if the employer considered age a factor in the layoff. Employers may make layoff decisions based on reasonable factors other than age. However, sometimes those factors merely mask age discrimination. For example, if an employer lays off only higher paid employees, it is possible that the employer is unlawfully discriminating against older employees. Higher pay is often synonymous with higher age.

### Q. Can my fringe benefits, such as employee insurance benefits, be reduced because I am older?

**A.** Normally no, although the law gives employers some flexibility in applying this rule. The general rule, with some exceptions,

**EMPLOYMENT AGENCIES AND UNIONS**
*The ADEA also applies to employment agencies and labor organizations. These organizations may not discriminate on the basis of age in referrals, notices, advertisements, or membership activities.*

requires employers to provide all age groups the same benefit, or alternatively, provide a benefit that costs the same for all age groups. For example, if a given life insurance benefit actually costs the employer more for older workers, then the employer may provide older workers a smaller insurance benefit, as long as the cost of the benefit to the employer is the same as that offered to younger workers.

As to health insurance, employers must cover older workers and their spouses under the same conditions as younger workers. Your benefits cannot be lowered just because you become eligible for Medicare. In fact, the employer's insurer must remain the primary insurer. Medicare will cover you as a secondary insurer.

**Q. Can I be denied new training that younger workers are receiving?**

**A.** No. Older workers must be given the same privileges of employment as younger workers. These privileges include training.

**Q. What are older workers' rights to promotions?**

**A.** Under the ADEA, older workers must be given the same chance to receive promotions as all other workers. But age does not entitle a person to a promotion; an employer may have a valid reason, apart from age, for promoting a younger person rather than an older one.

**Q. Can a change in job assignments be considered a form of discrimination?**

**A.** Yes. Employers cannot use terms or conditions of employment to discriminate against older workers. If a change in job assignments is used for this purpose, it is prohibited.

**Q. What if my age is only one of the reasons I was discriminated against?**

**A.** As long as age is a determining factor for the discrimination, you are protected by the ADEA. Age does not have to be the sole factor. Other unlawful forms of discrimination, based on factors such as race or sex, are covered by other laws.

**OVERQUALIFIED OR DISCRIMINATED AGAINST?**
*At some point, an employer may say that you are overqualified for a job. Is this legal? It depends. Sometimes it might be reasonable to deny you a job because you have too much experience or education. For example, it is reasonable to assume that someone with a Ph.D. in education is overqualified for a teacher's aide position that requires only two years of college education. In other cases, a court might decide that calling you "overqualified" is just an employer's pretext (excuse) to avoid hiring an older worker. Therefore, be wary if a potential employer says, "I'm sure that with your long experience, you wouldn't be interested in this entry level position."*

**Q. If I work in a foreign country, does the ADEA protect me?**

**A.** Yes, if you work for an American corporation or its subsidiaries and if the ADEA does not directly conflict with the law of the country you work in.

**Q. Can an advertisement state that only younger workers are wanted for a job?**

**A.** Not unless age is a bona fide occupational qualification (BFOQ). Except for this rare exception, advertisements are not allowed to exclude or discourage older workers from applying. Although courts differ as to which phrases are permissible and which are not, a general rule is that ads cannot imply that only certain age groups are wanted for the job.

### What to Do If You Are Discriminated Against

**Q. What can I do if I have been forced to retire, fired, or otherwise discriminated against because of my age?**

**A.** You should file a "charge" of age discrimination in writing with the federal Equal Employment Opportunity Commission (EEOC). If your state has an age discrimination law and enforcement agency (not every state has one), you should consider filing the charge with both the EEOC and your state agency. (The reason for hesitation is that in some states, filing a charge may prevent you from obtaining certain types of legal relief otherwise available to you. Before filing a charge, consult an elder law attorney in your state.)

In many cases, filing a charge with either the EEOC or the state agency is automatically treated as filing with both. To be on the safe side, you should usually take the initiative and file with both.

If you file a charge, your name will be disclosed to the employer. If you wish to remain anonymous, you can file a "complaint" instead. A complaint may start an EEOC investigation; however, the government gives complaints lower priority than charges. In addition, even if EEOC intervention leads an employer to correct its discriminatory practices, your own past unfair treatment may not be remedied if you filed only a complaint.

**Q. What is the EEOC?**

**A.** This federal agency has the power to investigate, the duty to mediate, and the option to file lawsuits in order to end practices of age discrimination. See pages 416–417 and following of the chapter titled "Law and the Workplace" for more about the EEOC.

**Q. Do I have to contact the EEOC with my claim, or can I file my own lawsuit?**

**A.** You must file a charge with the EEOC first. After sixty days, if the EEOC has not filed a lawsuit, you may do so.

**Q. What information should be included in my charge?**

**A.** You should include as much relevant data as possible. Be sure to include information about how to contact you, the name and address of the discriminating party, the type of discrim-

**FINDING THE CLOSEST EEOC OFFICE**
*EEOC offices are listed in the telephone directory under United States Government. You may also find the location of the office nearest you by calling a nationwide toll-free number: 1-800-669-4000.*

ination, relevant dates and witnesses, and specific facts. If pertinent, you might also include employment contracts, brochures or similar documents that demonstrate company policy. Before you file the charge, make sure you sign it.

### Q. How long do I have to file a charge with the EEOC?

**A.** Normally, you have 180 days from the date of the violation or reasonable notice of it (whichever occurs first). It is important to understand the time limits. If you are given notice of layoff on January 1, to take effect March 1, the time limit begins to run from the earlier date and not the date of layoff.

If your state has an age discrimination law and enforcement agency, the time limit may be extended to 300 days, but every effort should be made to act within the 180 days to be on the safe side. You may file your charge with your state's agency.

### Q. What happens once I file a charge with the EEOC?

**A.** The EEOC is required to contact the discriminating party and attempt conciliation between the parties. They also have the power to investigate charges and file a lawsuit to enforce your rights. However, the EEOC files lawsuits in only a small proportion of cases. It is important to realize that the EEOC does not make findings on your charge. Only a court can do that.

### Q. If the EEOC files a lawsuit on my behalf, can I still sue separately?

**A.** No. Once the EEOC begins a suit, private individuals are prohibited from bringing their own action.

---

**SPECIAL PROCEDURES FOR FEDERAL EMPLOYEES**

*Federal employees or applicants for employment who believe they have been discriminated against have these options:*

- *They may file a complaint with the EEOC or the federal agency they believe has discriminated against them.*

- *They may proceed directly to federal court by filing a "notice of intent to sue" with the EEOC within 180 days of the discriminatory action. The individual then has the right to file a lawsuit thirty days after filing the notice.*

---

**EARLY RETIREMENT INCENTIVE PROGRAMS**

*Early retirement incentive plans are frequently offered by employers to reduce their workforce. Generally, such plans are lawful if they are voluntary and otherwise comply with federal law. They often provide substantial benefits to employees willing to retire early. However, giving up employment also has great disadvantages, economically and personally. You should be given sufficient information and plenty of time to consider an early retirement offer. Review your options with a financial advisor if possible.*

## Q. If the EEOC does not file a lawsuit, is there a limit to how long I have to sue the discriminating party?

**A.** Yes. The statute of limitations is two years from the time you knew or should have known of the violation. If the violation was willful, you have three years to file a lawsuit.

Sometimes it is hard to determine when a person should have known of the violation. Other times, however, the exact date is easy to pinpoint. For example, suppose you receive a letter on March 12 from your labor union stating that you are expelled, and you do not open the letter. On April 12, when your union dues are not taken out of your paycheck, you call and discover your expulsion. March 12 is the date when you should have known of the violation, and so that is when the statute of limitations began to run.

## Q. Are state age discrimination laws identical to the ADEA?

**A.** Not necessarily, and not all states have such laws. It is important to check the applicable laws in your state. Some state statutes offer different protection or more protection against discrimination than the ADEA. If this is the case, you may be able to bring an action under a state law that you would not be able to bring under the ADEA.

## Q. How do I know if my state has an enforcement agency?

**A.** If you are unsure whether your state has an enforcement agency, contact your state's department of labor or an EEOC office in your area.

## Q. What should I consider in deciding whether to file a private lawsuit under the ADEA?

**A.** If you have suffered significant loss as a result of age discrimination and you are willing to invest substantial time and money, filing a

> ## WAIVING YOUR ADEA RIGHTS
> *Some companies ask employees who accept an early retirement offer or other exit incentive to sign a "waiver" of their rights under the ADEA, including the right to sue the employer. Waivers are legal only if they are "knowing and voluntary" and the employer follows specific procedures required by the Act. The required procedures involve extensive notices, disclosures of information, and time periods to ensure the employee has sufficient time to make a decision.*

private lawsuit may be worthwhile. The costs of such a lawsuit should be weighed realistically ahead of time. ADEA cases can involve a great deal of legal analysis, discovery, and effort. Generally, attorneys do not take ADEA cases on a contingency basis (that is, payment when and if the case is decided favorably). However, if your lawsuit is successful, the ADEA permits you to seek attorney's fees from the discriminating party.

## Q. What role will the EEOC play in my lawsuit?

**A.** If the EEOC files a suit either on its own or on your behalf, the Commission enforces your rights and you can no longer file a private lawsuit. If the agency does not file a suit, you may do so sixty days or more after the date you file a charge with the EEOC. Unlike other areas of civil rights law, you do not have to wait for a right-to-sue notice from the EEOC. Your own lawsuit will be a private one, and you must bear the court costs and attorney's fees. A big advan-

### YOUR RIGHT TO A JURY TRIAL

*In most lawsuits, the type of relief you seek can affect whether or not you will receive a jury trial. The ADEA, however, states all litigants under the Act are entitled to a trial by jury on any issue of fact, even if they seek only equitable (non-monetary) relief. A party wanting a jury trial must specifically ask for one. If not requested, a jury trial is automatically waived.*

tage of an EEOC suit on your behalf is that you would not be required to pay its costs.

**Q. What if my employer retaliates against me because I file a charge?**

**A.** The ADEA forbids such retaliation.

**Q. If there is already a lawsuit against my employer for age discrimination, can I join it?**

**A.** Yes. The ADEA allows class-action lawsuits. However, unlike many other class-action cases, you are not automatically part of the subject class. You must opt in by consenting in writing. By sending in the consent form, you can become part of the existing lawsuit against your employer.

**Q. What will happen if I win my case?**

**A.** The court will order the employer to make up to you what you lost through discrimination. This might include:

- the awarding of back-pay for salary you did not receive while unemployed;

- the awarding of future pay or "front pay" for a period of time has been recognized by some courts;

- compensation for lost benefits, or reinstatement of lost benefits—such as seniority rights, health or insurance benefits, sick leave, savings plan benefits, expected raises, stock bonus plan benefits, and lost overtime pay;

- reinstatement in your former job, with your former salary and benefits;

- double damages in cases of willful violations of the ADEA.

If you win your case, the company that discriminated against you may have to pay for your lawyer and other expenses, as well as for court costs.

## PENSIONS

**Q. Is my employer or union required to set up a pension plan?**

**A.** No. The law does not obligate an employer to have a pension plan. While many small companies do not have pension plans, most large employers and unions do. Most pensions are governed by rules of the Employee Retirement Income Security Act of 1974 (ERISA), which sets minimum standards for pension plans that already exist and new pension plans that are created. Small companies can set up simple pension plans for their employees called "SEPs." These plans require very little paperwork.

**Q. Does ERISA apply to all pension plans?**

**A.** No. It does not cover pension plans for federal, state, and local public employees, nor for church employees. Most ERISA provisions apply to plan years beginning in 1976. As a result, it does not protect workers who stopped working or retired before 1976. However, the terms of an employee's pension plan, as well as state law, do offer some protection.

### Q. What are the different types of pension plans?

**A.** There are two major kinds, and they are quite different. One kind, called a defined-benefit plan, guarantees you a certain amount of benefits per month upon retirement. For example, a defined-benefit plan might pay you ten dollars a month per year of service. Under that plan, a person who retires after ten years of service would receive $100 per month in pension benefits.

Under the other kind of plan, called a defined-contribution plan, the employer and/or the employee contribute a certain amount per month during the years of employment. The amount of the benefit depends on the total amount accumulated in the pension fund at the time of retirement. And that amount depends not only on how much you and your employer contributed, but on how much that money earned when it was invested.

Typically, pension trustees invest the fund's money in stocks, real estate, and other generally safe investments. If those investments do well over the years, the fund grows and your monthly benefits may be relatively high. But if the investments do poorly, the fund may not grow much or may even shrink. In that case, your monthly benefits may be far smaller. (See page 583 this chapter on the requirement that plans make prudent investments.)

Even in the defined-contribution plan, your benefit will be determined by some formula that takes into account your age, how long you worked for the employer, and how much you were paid.

The choice of defined-benefit or defined-contribution plan is not yours to make. The employer decides.

### Q. I am fifty-five years old and I want to retire now. Can I start collecting my pension at once?

**A.** Maybe. All pensions set a "normal" retirement age, often sixty-five. They usually set a minimum retirement age as well, perhaps fifty-five, sixty, or sixty-two. Check with your pension plan administrator. You may be able to collect benefits now or you may have to wait until you are older. Remember that benefits are usually calculated partly on the basis of your age. The younger you are when you retire, the smaller the benefits, but presumably you will get them for a longer period.

### Q. Do I get to choose how my pension will be paid to me?

**A.** Yes, to some extent.

The most common type of payment is called the joint and survivor annuity. It pays the full benefit to a married couple until one dies, then pays a fraction of the full benefit to the survivor as long as he or she lives. The fraction typically is one-half or two-thirds. The Retirement Equity Act of 1984 requires this kind of disbursement unless the worker's spouse signs a waiver. The waiver permits payment of a higher benefit, but only as long as the retired worker lives. When he or she dies, the benefits end and the surviving spouse gets no more.

The joint and survivor annuity may allow you some options. You might be able to have benefits guaranteed for a certain number of years. For example, if the guarantee is for fifteen years, benefits would be paid as long as one or both spouses are alive. But if both die before fifteen years have passed since retirement, benefits would continue to be paid to their beneficiary until the 15th year. Other guarantees might be for longer or shorter periods; the longer the guarantee, the lower the benefit.

There are some other kinds of pension disbursements as well. One pays a fixed amount

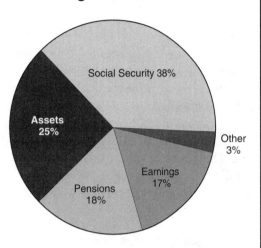

**Income Sources of Units
Age 65+: 1988**

- Social Security 38%
- Assets 25%
- Pensions 18%
- Earnings 17%
- Other 3%

Income from assets was the second most important income source for the elderly. In 1988, 25 percent of the income received by aged units was income from assets. In recent years, savings and other asset income have grown in importance as sources of income, increasing from 18 percent of total income in 1976, to 25 percent by 1988. However, income from financial assets was unevenly distributed among the elderly in 1988, with one-third (32 percent) of the aged units reporting no asset income, and one-fourth (27 percent) of those with asset income reporting less than $500 a year. Only 35 percent of those who had asset income received more than $5,000 a year from this source.

SOURCE: *A Profile of Older Americans*, 1992 (AARP). From Susan Grad, *Income of the Population 65 or Over*, 1988. Pub. No. 13-11871, Washington: U.S. Social Security Administration (June 1990).

for a fixed number of years, which means you could outlive your benefits and get nothing in your oldest years. Another pays all your benefits in a single lump sum when you retire, which could cost you a lot in income taxes.

**Q. Will my pension benefits rise over the years?**

**A.** Perhaps. Your union may negotiate cost-of-living increases with your employer. Or a nonunion employer may increase benefits voluntarily. But generally your benefits are frozen at the level they were when you retired. You will also probably be collecting social security benefits, however, and those benefits do rise with the cost of living.

**Q. What if I get sick after retiring? Will I still have health insurance?**

**A.** Companies are not required to continue to provide health insurance after retirement. But when they have promised to do so, some courts are requiring them to keep that promise. Under a 1985 federal law known as COBRA ("Consolidated Omnibus Budget Reconciliation Act"), you must be notified when you retire that you may continue coverage, but your employer may require you to pay the premiums. Coverage generally lasts for eighteen months after you stop working, but may be extended up to twenty-nine months if you are found eligible for social security disability or Supplemental Security Income (SSI) disability benefits. You will also be eligible for Medicare at age sixty-five or possibly earlier if you qualify for disability under social security or SSI.

**Q. Can my company's pension plan cover some employees but not others?**

**A.** Yes. Some companies establish pension plans only for certain kinds of workers. A plan might cover assembly line workers, for example, and not file clerks. There might or might not be a separate plan for the clerks. But a plan cannot discriminate against employees who are not officers, shareholders, or highly compensated. For example, a supermarket's plan could not include only the company's president and top executives while excluding the managers, baggers, and cashiers. The Internal Revenue Service (IRS) determines whether a plan is complying with these complicated "nondiscrimination" rules. You may call or write: Employee Plans Technical and Actuarial Division, Room 65256, Internal Revenue Service, 111 Constitution Ave., NW, Washington, DC 20224 (202) 622-8300 or (202) 622-5000.

### Q. What rules govern when an employee can participate in a pension plan?

**A.** ERISA sets up two criteria for when employers must permit workers to begin earning credit toward pensions. The employer must permit the earning of credit toward a pension if the worker is at least twenty-one years old and has worked for the employer for at least one year. ERISA calculates a year of employment as 1,000 or more hours of work in twelve months. Once employees satisfy these two requirements, they must be allowed to begin accruing credits that will affect the amount of their pensions.

Of course, as with all ERISA requirements, these are the minimums allowed by law. Individual pension plans can have more generous credit-earning policies. For example, they can permit beginning employees to start earning pension credits from their first day on the job, and they can permit workers younger than twenty-one to earn pension credits also.

### Q. Once I become a participant, how do I know what my rights are under the plan?

**A.** ERISA requires that participating employees be given detailed reports and disclosures. Within either ninety days of becoming a participant or 120 days of the plan's beginning, the employee must receive a summary plan description. This gives details of the employee's rights and obligations, gives information on the trustees and the plan's administration, sets conditions for participation and forfeiture, and outlines the procedure for making a claim and the remedies available to employees who appeal claims that are denied.

A summary of the plan's annual financial report must also be distributed. If you do not receive a summary, you should ask the plan's administrators for it. Or you can obtain one by contacting the Division of Public Disclosure, U.S. Department of Labor, Room N5507, Washington, DC 20210 (202) 219-8771.

### Q. How are years of accrual determined?

**A.** After you meet the participation requirements, each year you work for an employer counts as a year of accrual time. A year is defined as 1,000 or more hours of work in twelve months. You can work the 1,000 hours at any time during the twelve-month period; it need not be evenly distributed during the year. Days taken for sick leave or for paid vacation count toward the 1,000-hour minimum.

It is important to note that, depending on your company's policy, the first year you work for an employer does not have to count toward your years of accrual. Thus, your years of accrual will not always equal the number of years you worked for an employer.

### Q. If I stop working for an employer and later return, do I get credit for my previous years of service?

**A.** That depends on the length of this break in service. An employer can discount the years of your previous service if two conditions are met. First, your break lasts five or more continuous years. Second, your break is longer than the years you previously worked for the employer. If, for example, after six years of work, you took a seven-year break in service, you may be out of luck. However, an employer can have more lenient rules than the ones set out by ERISA. These rules on breaks in service are complex, so you should consult an expert if you think they apply to you.

### Q. Is my right to collect my pension guaranteed?

**A.** You always have the right to money you contributed to the pension fund. If you leave a company after only a few years, that money should be paid back to you in a lump sum. If you work for the employer long enough, you will have "a vested interest" in your pension, meaning your benefits cannot be denied even if you quit. However, if the total value of your pension is $3,500 or less, your plan can require that you take it as a lump-sum payment.

### Q. When are my pension rights vested?

**A.** Amendments to ERISA in 1989 changed the vesting rules. Now, your pension rights must either vest completely after five years— meaning that you have a right to 100 percent of the benefits you have earned—or partially after three years of service. Complete vesting after five years is called cliff vesting. If you work fewer than five years under cliff vesting, you are not entitled to any pension benefits. Partial vesting is called graded vesting. Under this system, your rights become 20 percent vested after three years of service, 40 percent vested after four years, and so on up to 100 percent vested after seven years.

With graded vesting, you have the right to 20 percent of your earned benefits after three years and 100 percent after seven years. Under the other system, you have no rights to benefits until five years, and then you have rights to collect full benefits.

You do not get to choose which vesting method applies. The employer decides.

### Q. I want to change jobs. May I take my pension benefits with me to my new job?

**A.** Generally, if you change jobs before your pension has vested, you usually lose all the benefits you built up in your old job, although your employer must refund money you put into the fund. If you change jobs after your benefits have vested, you are entitled to those benefits. You may put (or "roll over") those funds into an IRA or some other type of retirement program (to

**PROTECTION AGAINST BEING FIRED RIGHT BEFORE YOUR PENSION VESTS**
*ERISA prohibits an employer from firing you or otherwise treating you unfairly in order to stop the vesting of your pension rights. However, the burden is on you to show that you were not fired for legitimate reasons but because your employer did not want to guarantee you a pension.*

avoid taxation) or transfer the funds to the new employer's pension plan if possible. It is often not possible, though some unions have reciprocal agreements that allow you to change employers and transfer your benefits. There are also some state or nationwide pension systems that allow job changes with continued participation in a unified pension program (such as Teachers Insurance and Annuity Association, known as TIAA-CREF).

### Q. What if I join an employer at age sixty-two and retire at age sixty-five?

**A.** ERISA assures older employees that their rights will completely vest at normal retirement age, regardless of the number of years they have worked for an employer.

Also note that since 1988, employers have been required to make contributions to the plan for workers aged sixty-five and over.

### Q. If I retire and begin receiving my pension, can I still work?

**A.** Yes. You can retire, collect your pension, and work full- or part-time. However, if you work for the same employer that is paying your pension, you are limited to fewer than forty hours a month.

### Q. Can my employer change an existing pension plan?

**A.** Yes. ERISA permits an employer to change the way in which future benefits are accumulated. However, the employer may not make changes that result in a reduction of benefits which you have already accrued. In addition, ERISA specifically prohibits plan amendments that alter vesting schedules to the detriment of employees.

### Q. What protection does ERISA offer when my company is sold or taken over?

**A.** This area of law is not entirely clear. In a growing number of cases, "successor liability" is found and the company must continue the plan. If such liability is not found, your new employer is under no obligation to continue an existing pension plan. The new employer can go without a plan, set up a new plan, or continue the existing plan. If the new employer decides to continue the plan, however, ERISA requires that previous years of service be counted.

And you still have a right to all the benefits earned under the old employer. If the new employer abandons the plan, though, you will not continue to earn benefits.

### Q. Do I have a right to know how my pension plan is investing money?

**A.** Yes. You should receive a summary of the plan's annual financial report. Each year, a report summarizing the plan's financial operations must be made to both the Internal Revenue Service and the Secretary of Labor.

Also, ERISA requires that the people in charge of investing your plan's money use care, skill, and prudence and invest only in the inter-est of participants and beneficiaries. A require-ment for investment diversity minimizes the risk of losses. ERISA forbids several investment practices. For example, the pension directors cannot invest more than 10 percent of the fund in the employer's stock or real property. They cannot personally buy the fund's property or lend the fund's money to their friends.

### Q. What should I do if those in charge of investing my plan's money violate ERISA?

**A.** First, you should contact the nearest office of the U.S. Department of Labor. Then, if needed, ERISA permits you to file a lawsuit in federal court to enforce its rules.

### Q. I am worried about my pension plan going broke. Do I have any protection against such a disaster?

**A.** You might have some protection. ERISA established the Pension Benefit Guaranty Corporation (PBGC). If your company has a defined-benefit plan, it must pay insurance premiums to the PBGC. If the plan goes broke, the PBGC will pay vested benefits up to a certain limit, but it may not pay all you are owed. If the pension plan is still functioning but in danger of going broke, the PBGC will step in and take control. It will use the plan's remaining money and the insurance premiums paid by other plans to keep your benefits flowing.

Certain pension benefits are not covered, particularly for highly paid people and for those who retire before being eligible for social security.

If your plan is of the defined-contribution type, the PBGC will not get involved. If that plan goes broke, you may be out of luck. You should keep an eye on how the administrators are handling the fund's money, because ERISA requires that plan trustees act in the best interests of participants. Trustees can be sued by the Secretary of Labor or plan participants if they act improperly.

### Q. When must I begin to collect my pension?

**A.** Each plan sets a normal retirement age. However, if you choose to retire later, you must begin collecting your pension by April 1 of the year after you turn seventy and one-half years old.

### Q. Does the amount of social security payments I collect affect my pension benefits?

**A.** It might. Some pension plans allow a reduction of benefits depending on how much you receive from Social Security. You should check with your plan's administrators. Under federal law, plans subtracting social security payments from pension benefits must leave you with at least half your pension. However, the law applies only to years worked after 1988.

### Q. If I do not agree with the decision on my claim, how do I appeal?

**A.** The claims and appeal processes are regulated in ERISA. The plan summary must also contain information on the plan's appeal process. All plans must give written notice of the claim decision within ninety days of receipt of the claim. If the plan notifies you within ninety days that it needs an extension, one ninety-day extension is allowed. If you do not receive a written decision by the deadline, consider your claim denied.

If your claim is denied, the decision must give specific reasons for the denial. You then have sixty days to file a written appeal. The plan must make available important documents affecting your appeal, and you must be allowed to submit written support for your claim. The plan then has 120 days to issue a written decision on the appeal.

If you are still dissatisfied after going through this process, you have the right to sue in federal court to recover unfairly denied benefits. However, you may not get the opportunity to present additional evidence in court, so be sure to submit all relevant information and documentation in your appeal to the trustees. If you need to file a court case, the Pension Rights Center has referral lists of attorneys with expertise in this field. (See the resource list on pages 642–649 at the end of this chapter.)

### Q. What if I die before retiring? What are my spouse's rights to my pension?

**A.** If you are vested and if you have been married for at least a year, your spouse is entitled to pension benefits. Typically, he or she will receive an immediate annuity for the rest of his or her life. However, if you and your spouse have executed a written waiver of survivor benefits, your spouse will not be entitled to survivor benefits.

### Q. What are a divorced person's rights to an ex-spouse's pension benefits?

**A.** In order to be eligible, the divorced person must have been married to the worker for at least one year. The pension rights of divorced spouses are governed by state law. In most states, these benefits are part of the marital property divided during the divorce. If a divorced spouse

---

## CLAIMING YOUR PENSION

*Each individual plan establishes the procedure for submitting pension claims. To find out about your plan's filing procedure, check the plan summary provided by your employer. To claim your pension, follow the procedure. You should then receive a decision about your claim.*

is granted a share of pension benefits either through a property settlement or a court order, he or she can collect the appropriate sum when either:

- the worker has stopped working and is eligible to start collecting the pension (even if he or she hasn't yet applied for it); or
- the worker has reached the earliest age for collecting benefits under the plan and is at least age fifty.

## SOCIAL SECURITY

### Q. What types of social security benefits are available?

**A.** Qualified workers are eligible for old age and disability benefits. Benefits are also available for the spouse and dependents of a retired or disabled worker. When a worker dies, benefits can be collected by surviving family members who qualify.

Social security is the United States' most extensive program to provide income for older and disabled Americans. It is paid for by a tax on workers and their employers. The program is complicated, and the law and regulations change from time to time.

Contact your local office of the Social Security Administration (SSA) for literature about social security benefits or to ask specific questions about your own case. They are listed in the United States Government section of your telephone directory. Or, call 1-800-772-1213.

### Q. Who is covered?

**A.** Over 95 percent of American workers, including household help, farm workers, self-employed persons, employees of state and local government, and (since 1984) federal workers. Railroad workers are covered by a separate federal program, railroad retirement, that is integrated with social security.

### Q. Will my social security benefits be enough for me to live on?

**A.** You won't get as much as when you were working, so it is important to start financial planning for retirement early. Social security was not set up to be a complete source of retirement income, but rather to provide only a floor of protection. You will probably need other sources of income, such as a pension from your employer or union, a part-time job, or income from your life savings. Social security benefits do rise with the cost of living.

### Q. Who qualifies for social security?

**A.** Individuals must meet two fundamental qualifications to collect social security benefits. First, a worker must be "insured" under social security. The simplest rule-of-thumb is that ten years of work in covered employment will fully insure a worker for life. However, there are alternative measures of insured status that enable many workers with fewer than ten years of covered employment to be eligible, too. Second, you must meet the status requirement for the particular benefit (for example, age, disability, dependency on a worker, or survivorship).

### Q. Just how much money will I get when I retire?

**A.** That depends on how much money you have earned over your lifetime, your age at the time of retirement, and other factors.

The Social Security Administration will prepare an estimate, called a Personal Earnings and Benefit Statement, even if you are some years from retirement. Simply get a Personal Earnings and Benefit Statement Form from your local Social Security Administration office or by calling the Social Security Administration, toll free, at 1-800-772-1213. It's a good idea to request this every few years, not only to see how your benefits might change but to make sure your employers have been depositing to the Social Security Administration your share and theirs of the social security tax.

### Q. When can I retire?

A. The "normal" retirement age is sixty-five. But this age will be raised gradually starting in the year 2000. By 2002, you will have to be sixty-seven to retire and collect full benefits.

You can collect partial benefits as early as age sixty-two if you are fully insured. The benefits are reduced, because you potentially have more years of retirement to cover. Early retirement benefits will not be raised when you turn sixty-five, except for normal cost-of-living adjustments.

If you delay retirement until you are older than sixty-five, your benefits will be increased, because you will not have as many years of retirement in which to collect.

Of course, you can retire whenever you want or can afford to, but you will not receive social security retirement benefits until you are at least sixty-two.

### Q. I want to retire, but then take a part-time job. Will this affect my benefits?

A. Yes. If you are under age seventy and receiving benefits you may earn only a certain amount of wages before your social security benefits are cut. There are two cut-off points—one for workers age sixty-two through sixty-four, another for age sixty-five through sixty-nine. For retirees age sixty-two through sixty-four, one dollar of benefits is withheld for every two dollars you earn above the cut-off point. For retirees sixty-five through sixty-nine, one dollar of benefits is withheld for every three dollars you earn above the cut-off point. The cutoff point changes from time to time. Check with the Social Security Administration office to see what it is when you take your new job. If you are older than seventy, you may earn an unlimited amount and still receive your full retirement benefit. Note that the cut-off point applies only to wages. Your benefits will not be affected by any money you earn from savings, investments, insurance, and the like.

### Q. When the worker dies, who is eligible for benefits?

A. These family members qualify for benefits: a spouse who is at least sixty years old; a disabled spouse who is at least fifty; children who are under eighteen (or under nineteen if attending elementary or high school full-time) or are disabled; and parents who are sixty-two or older and who received at least half of their support from the worker at the time of his or her death.

### Q. When are spouses of retirees entitled to collect benefits?

A. Depending on the situation, a husband or wife may collect benefits based on the other's work record. A husband or wife need not prove that he or she was dependent on the other. In general, spouses qualify if they are at least sixty-two years old. They also qualify if they are under sixty-two but are caring for a worker's child who is either under sixteen years old or who has been disabled since before age twenty-two. The amount the spouse receives is usually one-half of what would have been paid to the worker. However, if the spouse is entitled to benefits based on his or her own work record, the spouse will receive the higher of the two benefits.

### Q. Are divorced spouses eligible?

A. Yes. As long as the divorced spouse is sixty-two or older, was married to the worker for at least ten years, and has not remarried. Divorced spouses who have been divorced for at least two years may draw benefits at age sixty-two, as long as the former spouse is eligible for retirement benefits; the former spouse does not actually have to be drawing benefits. A divorced spouse may also be eligible for survivor benefits if the worker dies while being fully insured or while receiving benefits.

### Q. Which children can receive benefits?

**A.** A deceased or disabled worker's unmarried children under eighteen years old are eligible. Children under nineteen who attend elementary or secondary school full-time can also collect. Also, a disabled child of any age can receive payments equal to approximately one-half of the worker's benefits, as long as the child became disabled before age twenty-two.

### Q. When should I file my claim to collect social security benefits?

**A.** If you are retiring, you should file two or three months before your retirement date. Then, normally, your first social security check will arrive soon after you quit working. It is important not to delay filing for either retirement or survivor benefits because you will get paid retroactive benefits only for the six months prior to the month you file your application, provided that you were eligible during those months. Retirement and survivor benefit applications take two to three months to process. Disability benefit applications, however, take longer.

### Q. What documents should I bring with me to apply for benefits?

**A.** A worker applying for retirement or disability benefits should bring his or her social security card or proof of the number; a birth certificate or other proof of age; W-2 forms from the past two years or, if you are self-employed, copies of your last two federal income tax returns; and, if applicable, proof of military service, since you may be able to receive extra credit for active military duty.

Spouses applying for benefits from the worker's account should also bring a marriage certificate. Divorced spouses should have a divorce decree.

### WHAT TO REMEMBER WHEN DEALING WITH THE SOCIAL SECURITY OFFICE

*As with any large government office, the best way to work with the Social Security Administration is to keep a full, organized account of your communications or conversations. Make a note of when you had each conversation, who you spoke with and what was said. When you file a claim, you are automatically assigned a SSA worker. Keep this person's name and telephone number handy in case you need to contact the SSA for any reason.*

*Before you submit any forms or documents to the SSA, make sure you keep copies for yourself. That way if anything is lost, you have a backup copy.*

*Since the SSA keeps records by social security numbers, all forms or documents you submit should have your social security number on the top of each page. Then if any page becomes separated, it will still be placed in your file.*

Children or their guardians seeking benefits need a birth certificate and evidence of financial dependence.

Dependent parents who want to collect benefits must bring some evidence of financial dependence.

Finally, spouses, children, or parents seeking death benefits need the worker's death certificate.

### Q. If I am filing for disability benefits, what other documents should I bring with me?

**A.** In addition to the documents listed above, you should try to bring a list, with addresses and telephone numbers, of the doctors, hospitals, or institutions that have treated you for your disability; a summary of all the jobs you have held for the past fifteen years and the type of work you performed; and claim numbers of any checks you receive for your disability.

### Q. What if I check on my benefits or file my claim and discover that the Social Security Administration has made an error in the number of quarters I worked or the amount of wages I was paid? Can I fix mistakes?

**A.** Yes. You have approximately three years from the year the wages were earned to fix mistakes. However, mistakes caused by an employer's failure to report your earnings have no time limit.

You will need proof to fix errors. A pay stub, written statement from the employer, or form OAR-7008 (Request for Correction of Earnings Record) are all acceptable types of proof.

## Disability

### Q. What if I am under sixty-five and become disabled? Am I entitled to benefits from social security?

**A.** Yes. Social security protects all workers under sixty-five against loss of earnings due to disability. However, you must meet certain strict requirements for the number of years employed, the age at which you became disabled and the severity of your disability.

### Q. How does the Social Security Administration define a disability?

**A.** A disability is defined as the inability to engage in substantial gainful activity by reason of any medically determinable physical or mental impairment which can be expected to result in death or which has lasted or can be expected to last for a continuous period of not less than twelve months. The disability must be medically certified. Some illnesses or handicaps are so serious that the Social Security Administration automatically treats them as disabilities, such as severe epilepsy or blindness; SSA has a list of such impairments. If you believe you are disabled but your impairment is not on the list, you will have to prove that it is just as severe and disabling as the ones on the list.

### Q. If I become disabled, how long may I get benefits?

**A.** Once you qualify for disability benefits, they will continue for as long as you remain medically disabled and unable to work. Your health will be reviewed periodically to determine your ability to return to work.

### Q. What about my family?

**A.** If you are disabled, your unmarried children under age eighteen (or nineteen, if still in high school full time) may be eligible for benefits from social security. In addition, unmarried children over eighteen who are themselves disabled before age twenty-two will also be eligible. If your spouse is caring for a child who is either under sixteen or disabled, he or she may be eligible, as is a spouse who is sixty-two or older. In some cases the disabled widow or widower or the divorced spouse of a deceased worker may become eligible for disability benefits. Check with your local Social Security Administration for specific eligibility requirements.

## Claims Decisions and Appeals

**Q. How will I know the outcome of my application for benefits?**

**A.** You should receive written notification informing you whether your claim has been approved or denied in sixty to ninety days.

If your claim is approved, you will be told how much your benefits will be and when to expect your first check. If, however, your claim is denied, your letter should list the reasons.

**Q. Can my social security benefits be reduced or terminated?**

**A.** Yes. Benefits may be terminated if: you leave the United States for more than six months; you are deported; you are convicted of certain crimes, such as treason and espionage; or, you are an alien.

Convicted felons cannot receive retirement benefits while in prison. Disability benefits can be terminated when the recipient recovers or refuses to accept rehabilitation efforts.

In any case, however, you should receive a letter notifying you of the reduction or termination before you receive your check.

**Q. If my claim is denied, or my benefits reduced or terminated, can I appeal?**

**A.** Yes. You have sixty days from the date on the written notification of denial to appeal. Make sure the SSA gives you a written denial; you cannot appeal an oral statement.

**Q. Should I bother to appeal?**

**A.** Since a large number of claim decisions are reversed on appeal, it is probably worth your time and effort. Also, if you do not appeal, the claim decision becomes final and you give up the chance to appeal later.

**Q. Do I need a lawyer to appeal?**

**A.** A lawyer is not required for an appeal. However, you should consider the complexity of your case and the amount of money you are seeking before deciding whether to hire one or not. If your appeal goes all the way to a federal court, you probably should have a lawyer to represent your interests. The fee of attorneys is limited to 25 percent of back benefits or $4,000, whichever is less, and the SSA must approve the fees. An experienced advocate who is not an attorney can also represent you.

**Q. If I cannot afford a lawyer but want legal representation, what should I do?**

**A.** You may be able to obtain legal representation through an agency that provides legal services to low-income or older persons. Check with your local agency on aging or bar association to see if such an agency exists in your area.

**Q. What if I just need some assistance in my appeal but do not want to hire a lawyer?**

**A.** Check with your state or local area agency on aging. They may be able to direct you to a community group that can provide help.

**Q. How do I appeal?**

**A.** The first step in the appeal process is to file a written request for reconsideration of your claim within sixty days of the notification of denial, reduction, or termination of benefits. This reconsideration is an examination of your paperwork by an SSA employee other than the one who first decided your claim. You may add more documents to your file if you think they will help.

You should receive written notice of the reconsideration decision within thirty days.

However, reconsideration of disability benefits will take longer, usually two to three months.

### Q. What is the next step?

**A.** If you are dissatisfied with the outcome of the reconsideration, your next step is to file a written request for an administrative hearing. You have sixty days after the reconsideration decision to make such a request. Normally, however, the hearing will not take place for several months.

### Q. Who acts as the judge at these administrative hearings?

**A.** An administrative law judge of the SSA's Office of Hearings and Appeals will preside over your case. The administrative law judge is a lawyer who works for SSA but has not been involved in your claim thus far.

### Q. What should I do to prepare for an administrative hearing?

**A.** Before the hearing you can, and should, examine your file to make sure it contains every document you have filed. At the hearing, you can represent yourself or be represented by a lawyer or nonlawyer advocate. You should provide evidence, such as documents or witnesses, about your medical condition and why you cannot work, and your own explanation of why the decision at the reconsideration level should be reversed.

The hearing will be a new examination of your case, conducted by an impartial judge.

### Q. What if witnesses refuse to appear on my behalf?

**A.** You can ask that witnesses be subpoenaed (ordered to appear before the judge). You must request subpoenas at least five days before the hearing.

### Q. Will the SSA be represented by a lawyer at the administrative hearing?

**A.** No, the office does not have a lawyer presenting its side of the case.

### Q. How long does it take to receive a decision from an administrative hearing?

**A.** You should find out within two to three months after the hearing. You will receive a written decision. If your claim is approved, you may be able to collect benefits dating back to when you filed your original claim.

### Q. Can I appeal an administrative hearing decision?

**A.** Yes. You have sixty days to file a written appeal with the SSA Appeals Council in Washington, D.C. The Council will review the file and issue its decision. You and your representative do not appear before the Appeals Council, but you can add additional information to your file. If you wish to appeal the decision further, you must sue the SSA in federal district court.

### Q. Should I file a federal lawsuit?

**A.** That depends. You must take into account the expense of filing a lawsuit, the amount of benefits you are claiming, and your chances of winning. And, although you are not required to have a lawyer, it is highly recommended that you do.

### Q. If I do want a lawyer, how do I find one who specializes in social security appeals?

**A.** You can contact your local legal services or Older Americans Act program (see page 640 in a later section of this chapter), your local bar association or the district Social Security Administration office, or call the National Organization of Social Security Claimants' Representatives toll-free at 1-800-431-2804.

## Q. What if I receive a notice from SSA that I have been overpaid?

**A.** If you disagree that you were overpaid, make a written request for a reconsideration of your claim. If you cannot repay the amount, first ask for a waiver within thirty days of notification of overpayment. You will be asked to fill out an "Overpayment Recovery Questionnaire." Try to show that the overpayment was not your fault, and that you are unable to repay the amount without hardship.

## Supplemental Security Income

## Q. I have virtually no money. I don't qualify for regular social security or disability benefits. Can social security help me anyway?

**A.** The Supplemental Security Income (SSI) program pays benefits to persons who are aged sixty-five or over, disabled, or blind, or who have very limited income and personal property. The SSI program is run by the Social Security Administration. However, it is supported with income tax dollars rather than social security taxes on workers' wages.

SSI benefits are not large and the eligibility requirements are strict. You must have very little income and own very little property. If you think you qualify, check with your local Social Security Administration office. One of the benefits of getting even a dollar in SSI is that in most states you become eligible for free medical care through Medicaid.

To apply you will need your social security number, proof of age, and a wide variety of financial information. You'll want to have a record of your mortgage and property taxes, records of your utility costs and food costs, payroll slips, income tax returns, bank books and insurance policies.

If you are applying because of disability or blindness, you will also need copies of your medical records. Be sure to have the names and

**GETTING YOUR CHECKS**
*Social Security checks are normally mailed on the first day of each month. But you may arrange with SSA to have your check deposited directly in your bank. This is safe and convenient. The money is available a day or two earlier than if you get a check in the mail. It's handy if you have trouble getting to the bank. And it makes it impossible for a thief to take the check out of your mailbox.*

addresses of physicians who have treated you and hospitals where you have been a patient. If you have worked with a social service agency, give the name of a worker who knows you.

## Q. I think my elderly father is eligible for SSI, but he is much too ill and confused to visit an office or complete an application. How can he receive benefits?

**A.** If you know someone who should be receiving SSI benefits but can't apply for himself, you can do it for him. However, you will still need to bring all the information described above.

## Q. If I am declared ineligible for SSI, are there any benefits I might be eligible for?

**A.** Yes. Even if you are not eligible for SSI, you may be able to have your Medicare premiums, deductible, and co-payments paid for you.

## Q. If I am denied benefits, can I appeal?

**A.** Yes, the appeals process is essentially identical to appealing a social security claim, as described above.

## YOUR RIGHT TO HEALTH AND LONG-TERM CARE BENEFITS

The federal government provides a program of basic health care insurance called Medicare. Practically everyone who has a work history and is sixty-five and older is eligible for Medicare, even those who continue working after age sixty-five.

The federal and state governments together also provide a comprehensive medical benefits program, called Medicaid, for qualified low-income people. Medicare and Medicaid are not the same, though some older people qualify for both. Medicaid coverage rules vary from state to state, but Medicare is the same all over the United States.

The questions that follow examine Medicare and Medicaid, as well as private "Medigap" insurance commonly used to supplement Medicare coverage. The section then turns to long-term care benefits under public programs and under private long-term care insurance.

Since Medicare and Medicaid came into being in 1965, they have been revised many times. More revisions are certain. Current information is available from your local Social Security Administration office. Other groups such as the American Association of Retired Persons, local legal services programs, senior centers, and area agencies on aging also provide useful information.

## Medicare

### Q. *What is the basic structure of the Medicare program?*

**A.** The Health Care Financing Administration, a branch of the U.S. Department of Health and Human Services, is the federal agency responsible for administering the Medicare program. Medicare has two main parts. The hospital insurance part, or "Part A," covers medically necessary care in a hospital, skilled nursing facility, or psychiatric hospital, home health care, and hospice care.

"Part B," or the medical insurance benefits part, covers medically necessary physician's services, no matter where you receive them, outpatient hospital care, many diagnostic tests, and a variety of other medical services and supplies not covered by Part A.

The exact coverage rules and limitations are complex. The actual coverage determinations and payments to providers of care are handled by insurance companies under contract with Medicare. These insurance companies are referred to as "fiscal intermediaries" under Part A and "carriers" under Part B.

Medicare beneficiaries also have the option of joining a Health Maintenance Organization (HMO) or other coordinated care plan that participates in Medicare. These organizations provide or arrange for all Medicare covered services and generally charge a fixed monthly premium and small or no copayments. They may also offer benefits not covered by Medicare, such as preventive care, for little or no additional cost.

### Q. *What does Medicare cost me?*

**A.** Part A coverage is provided free to all individuals sixty-five and older who are eligible for social security (even if they are still working). If you are not eligible for social security benefits, you can enroll in Part A after age sixty-five, but you will have to pay a sizable monthly premium.

Part B is available to all Part A enrollees for a monthly premium that changes yearly. The Social Security Administration office can tell you the cost of the current premium. Under both Parts A and B, beneficiaries must pay certain deductibles and coinsurance payments, depending on the type of service. "Deductibles" are payments you must make before Medicare coverage begins. "Coinsurance payments" are percentages of covered expenses that you are

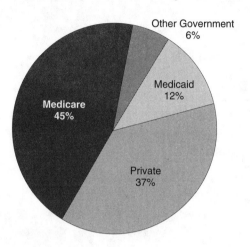

**Personal Health Care Expenditures for The Elderly, by Source of Payment: 1987**

Other Government 6%

Medicaid 12%

Medicare 45%

Private 37%

Private sources such as employer-paid insurance are the major source of health care payments for people under age 65. However, public funds are the major source for people 65+. In 1987, total public sector spending for the elderly's health care reached an estimated $102 billion.

SOURCE: *A Profile of Older Americans*, 1992 (AARP). From Daniel R. Waldo, Sally T. Sonnefeld, David R. McKusick, and Ross H. Arnett, III. "Health Expenditures by Age Group, 1977 and 1987." *Health Care Financing Review* Vol. 10, No. 4 (Summer 1989).

responsible for paying. These amounts can change from year to year.

If you meet certain income and resource tests, your state's Medicaid program will assist you in paying your share of Medicare costs. The income and resource tests are more generous than the limits for regular Medicaid eligibility, so even if you are not eligible for Medicaid, you may still be eligible for help as a "Qualified Medicare Beneficiary" (QMB) or a "Specified Low-Income Medicare Beneficiary" (SLMB).

**Q. I will turn sixty-five soon, but I do not plan to retire then. Am I still going to be able to receive Medicare benefits?**

**A.** Yes, but you must file a written application. This can be done in two different ways. Your "initial" enrollment period begins three calendar months before your sixty-fifth birthday month, and extends three months beyond your birthday month. You can enroll at any time during this seven-month period. Your benefits will begin on the first day of the month in which you turn sixty-five.

If you do not enroll during this time, you can enroll during the "general" enrollment period, which runs from January 1 to March 31 of each year. However, you will pay a higher monthly premium if you delay enrollment beyond your initial enrollment period.

If you are working and are covered by your employer's health insurance program, or if you are covered under your spouse's plan, Medicare is the secondary payer after the other insurance pays. If you haven't enrolled in Medicare and you lose the other insurance, you may sign up for the Medicare program during a "special" seven-month enrollment period which begins the month the other program no longer covers you.

To make sure you receive maximum coverage without penalty, talk to your employer's benefits office or your local Social Security Administration office.

**Q. Is Medicare only for older adults?**

**A.** No. In addition to older social security recipients, younger persons who have received social security disability benefits for more than

## PROTECTING YOUR RIGHTS WHEN YOU CONTACT PUBLIC AGENCIES

*Remember to note the name of the person with whom you speak, the date of your conversation, and the content of the conversation. This is useful if you later need to challenge the information provided.*

## SIGNING UP FOR MEDICARE

*Enrolling in Medicare is no problem for most people. Everyone who is turning sixty-five and applying for social security or railroad retirement benefits is automatically enrolled in Medicare Part A. If you are receiving these benefits before turning sixty-five, you should receive a Medicare card prior to the month you turn sixty-five. The Medicare benefits normally begin on the first of the month in which you turn sixty-five.*

*If you are under sixty-five and receiving disability benefits, your enrollment in Medicare will begin automatically as soon as you have been receiving benefits for twenty-four months.*

*If you are planning to work beyond age sixty-five and are covered by your employer's health insurance program, you must file a written application through your local Social Security Administration office.*

twenty-four months are eligible, as well as certain persons with kidney disease.

**Q. What does Medicare Part A (hospital insurance) cover?**

**A.** Medicare Part A helps pay for medically necessary hospital care, skilled nursing care, home health care, and hospice care as described below:

1. **Hospitalization**. This includes:
   - a semiprivate room and board
   - general nursing
   - the cost of special care units, such as intensive care or coronary care units
   - drugs furnished by the hospital during your stay
   - blood transfusions
   - lab tests, X rays, and other radiology services
   - medical supplies and equipment
   - operating and recovery room costs
   - rehabilitation services

   The coverage period for hospitalization is based upon a "benefit period." A benefit period begins the first time you receive inpatient hospital care. It ends when you have been out of a hospital and have not received skilled nursing care for sixty days in a row. A subsequent hospitalization begins a new benefit period.

   On the first day of hospitalization during a benefit period, the patient is responsible for a sizable inpatient hospital deductible ($676 during 1993). If you are hospitalized more than once during a benefit period, the deductible does not have to be paid for the other hospitalizations during the same benefit period. After the deductible, Part A pays for all covered services through the sixtieth day of hospitalization. From the sixty-first through ninetieth day, coverage continues but the patient is responsible for a daily coinsurance payment. After the ninetieth day, Medicare covers up to sixty extra days (called "reserve days") during the lifetime of the patient. The patient pays a sizable coinsurance payment during reserve days.

If psychiatric hospitalization is needed, Part A helps pay for a lifetime maximum of 190 days of inpatient care in a participating psychiatric hospital.

2. **Skilled Nursing Facility inpatient care following a hospitalization of at least three days.** Your condition must require on a daily basis skilled nursing or skilled rehabilitation services, which, as a practical matter, can only be provided in a skilled nursing facility. You must be admitted within a short time (usually thirty days) after you leave the hospital, and the skilled care you receive must be based on a doctor's order.

Most nursing home residents do not require the level of nursing services considered skilled by Medicare. *Consequently, Medicare pays for relatively little nursing home care.* In addition, not every nursing home participates in Medicare or is a skilled nursing facility. Ask the hospital discharge staff or nursing home staff if you are unsure of the facility's status.

The coverage period for skilled nursing facility services is limited to 100 days. In a benefit period, Medicare pays for all covered services for the first twenty days.

### SKILLED CARE OR CUSTODIAL CARE?

*Medicare helps pay only for "skilled" nursing home care. Medicare does not pay for "custodial" care. However, the distinction is often fuzzy, and many Medicare denials based on a finding of custodial care can be successfully appealed. Generally, care is considered custodial when it is primarily for the purpose of helping the resident with daily living needs, such as eating, bathing, walking, getting in and out of bed, and taking medicine. Skilled nursing and rehabilitation services are those that require the skills of technical or professional personnel such as registered nurses, licensed practical nurses, or therapists. Care that is generally nonskilled may nevertheless be considered skilled when, for example, medical complications require the skilled management and evaluation of a care plan, observation of a patient's changing condition, or patient education services.*

For days twenty-one through 100, the patient is responsible for a sizable coinsurance payment.

3. **Home Health Care.** Medicare covers part-time or intermittent skilled nursing care; physical, occupational, and speech therapy services; medical social services; part-time care provided by a home health

aide; and medical equipment for use in the home. It does not cover medications for patients living at home, nor does it cover general household services or services that are primarily custodial.

To be eligible for home health care services you must meet four conditions, presented in simplified terms here. First, you must be under the care of a physician who determines you need home health care and sets up a plan. Second, you must be homebound, although you need not be bedridden. Third, the care you need must include intermittent skilled nursing, physical therapy, or speech therapy. Finally, your care must be provided by a Medicare-participating home health care agency.

The coverage period for home health care is unlimited with no deductible or coinsurance payment (except for durable medical equipment) as long as you continue to meet all four conditions.

4. **Hospice Care**. A hospice is an agency or organization that provides primarily pain relief, symptom management, and supportive services to people with terminal illness. Hospice services may include physician or visiting nurse services, individual and family psychological support, inpatient care when needed, care from a home health aide, medications, medical/social services, counseling, and respite care for family care-givers.

To be eligible for hospice care, a patient must have a doctor certify that he or she is terminally ill (defined as a life expectancy of six months or less); the patient must choose to receive hospice care instead of standard Medicare benefits; and the hospice must be a Medicare-participating program.

The coverage period for hospice care consists of two ninety-day periods, followed by a thirty-day period, and when necessary, an indefinite extension. There

**FINDING A DOCTOR**
*Doctors and suppliers who agree to accept assignment under Medicare on all claims are called Medicare participating doctors and suppliers. You can get a directory of Medicare participating doctors and suppliers from your Medicare carrier. The directory is also available for your use in Social Security Administration offices, state and area agencies on aging, and in most hospitals.*

are certain coinsurance payments required under the hospice benefit, but no deductibles.

**Q. What does Medicare Part B (medical insurance) cover?**

**A.** Medicare Part B covers a wide range of outpatient and physician expenses regardless of where they are provided—at home, in a hospital or nursing home, or in a private office. Covered services include:

- doctors' services, including some services by chiropractors, dentists, podiatrists, and optometrists;
- outpatient hospital services, such as emergency room services or outpatient clinic care, radiology services, and ambulatory surgical services;
- diagnostic tests, including X rays and other laboratory services, as well as some mammography and pap smear screenings;
- durable medical equipment, such as oxygen equipment, wheelchairs, and other medically necessary equipment that your doctor prescribes for use in your home;

- kidney dialysis;
- ambulance services to or from a hospital or skilled nursing facility;
- certain services of other practitioners who are not physicians, such as clinical psychologists or social workers;
- many other health services, supplies and prosthetic devices that are not covered by Medicare Part A.

Part B will also cover home health services if you do not have Part A. Normally, Part A covers home health care as described previously.

Medicare does **not** cover:

- routine physical examinations;
- most routine foot care and dental care;
- examinations for prescribing or fitting eyeglasses or hearing aids;
- prescription drugs that do not require administration by a physician;
- most cosmetic surgery;
- immunizations except for certain persons at risk;
- personal comfort items and services;
- any service not considered "reasonable and necessary."

### Q. What is my share of the cost of Medicare Part B services?

**A.** For Part B benefits, you must pay a $100 annual deductible. Then Medicare generally pays 80 percent of Medicare-approved amounts for covered services for the rest of the year. You pay the other 20 percent of the approved amount. There is no limit on the patient's share of the cost. If you are a Medicaid recipient or a qualified medicare beneficiary (QMB), then your physician must accept assignment.

If a physician or other provider charges you more than the Medicare-approved amount, then your liability depends on whether the provider accepts assignment. "Accepting as-

> **SIGNING UP FOR MEDICARE PART B**
> *If you are receiving Part A coverage, you will automatically be enrolled for Part B coverage as well. If you don't want Part B coverage, you must notify the Social Security Administration. Also, anyone sixty-five and older can buy Part B coverage. Enrollment periods are similar to those for Part A. Your Part B premium will be deducted from your monthly social security check.*

signment" means that the provider agrees to accept the Medicare-approved amount as payment in full. This means that your liability is limited to the annual deductible and 20 percent copayment. If the provider does not accept assignment, generally you must pay for any excess charge over the Medicare-approved amount, but *only up to certain limits*. The government presently sets the limit on physician's charges at 115 percent of the Medicare-approved fee schedule. Doctors who charge more than these limits may be fined, and you should get a refund from the doctor.

Here is an example of the difference accepting assignment can make: Mrs. Jones sees Dr. Brown on June 1 for medical care. She has already paid her $100 annual deductible for covered Part B medical care this year. Dr. Brown charges $230 for the visit. The Medicare-approved amount for such services are $200. If Dr. Brown accepts assignment, Mrs. Jones must pay:

- $40 copayment (that is, 20 percent of the $200 approved).

If Dr. Brown does *not* accept assignment, Mrs. Jones must pay:

- $40 plus the $30 excess charge. Her Payment = $70.*

\* Note that Dr. Brown's actual charge ($230) is within 115 percent of the Medicare approved amount ($200) and is therefore permissible.

### Q. How are Medicare claims filed and paid?

**A.** For Part A benefits, the provider submits the claim directly to Medicare's fiscal intermediary (an insurance company). The provider will charge you for any deductible or coinsurance payment you owe.

For Part B claims, doctors, suppliers and other providers are required to submit your Medicare claims to the Medicare carrier (also an insurance company) in most cases, even if they do not take assignment. The provider will charge you directly for any deductible, coinsurance, or excess charge you owe.

If you belong to a Medicare participating Health Maintenance Organization (HMO), there are usually no claim forms to be filed, nor any deductible or copayment for any covered services, if the amount is small.

### Q. What if I disagree with a Medicare decision? How can I appeal?

**A.** You have the right to appeal all decisions regarding coverage of services or the amount Medicare will pay on a claim. If your claim has been denied in whole or in part, it is usually a good idea to appeal, especially if the basis of denial is unclear. A surprisingly high percentage of denials are reversed on appeal. In any case, the appeal will make clear the reason for the denial.

Medicare Parts A and B have different procedures for appealing and several steps in the appeal process. After the initial levels of review, Parts A and B both include the option of a hearing before an administrative law judge and even review by a federal court if sufficient amounts of money are at stake.

Key tips in appealing Medicare decisions:

- Denials by any Part A provider (hospital, nursing home, home health care agency, or hospice):

  Do not accept oral denials. You should be given a written notice of noncoverage from the provider explaining why the provider believes Medicare will not pay for the services. This is not an official Medicare determination. You should ask the provider to get an official Medicare determination. The provider must file a claim on your behalf to the Medicare fiscal intermediary if you ask for an official determination. If you still disagree, you may make use of several additional appeal steps if minimum threshold amounts of money are in dispute.

- Hospital coverage denials:

  Hospital coverage decisions are normally made by Peer Review Organizations (PROs). PROs are groups of doctors and other health care professionals under contract with the federal government to review care given to Medicare patients. When you are admitted to the hospital, you will receive a notice called *An Important Message From Medicare* which explains the role of PROs and describes your appeal rights. If you disagree with a PRO decision, the initial review will occur very quickly, usually within three days. You cannot be required to pay for hospital care until three days after you receive a written denial of Medicare coverage.

- Part B coverage denials:

  These decisions will be made by the Medicare carrier. After your doctor, supplier, or other provider sends in a Part B claim, Medicare will send you a notice called

*Explanation of Your Medicare Part B Benefits.* The notice tells you what charges were made and the amount Medicare approved and paid. It also shows the amount of any copayments, deductibles, or excess charges that you are responsible for paying. The notice gives the address and telephone number for contacting the carrier and an explanation of your appeal rights. You have six months from the date of the decision to ask the carrier to review it. If you still disagree, you may make use of several additional appeal steps if minimum threshold amounts of money are in dispute.

Always be conscious of time limits for filing appeals (normally sixty days from the date of the notice). You may lose your rights if you wait too long. You may want to get assistance with your appeal from a legal services office or a private attorney, particularly if large medical bills are involved. Nonlawyer volunteers and nonlawyer staff members of legal service programs help a number of people with benefit appeals without charging fees.

### "Medigap" Insurance

**Q. If I am covered by Medicare Parts A and B, do I need any other health insurance to supplement Medicare?**

**A.** Yes. Medicare provides basic protection against the cost of health care, but it leaves many gaps. Consequently, most seniors need to purchase a supplemental (or "Medigap") insurance policy from a private insurance company. Medigap policies are designed to cover some of the costs of care that are not covered by Medicare. These policies do *not* cover long-term care. Insurance for long-term care is discussed below under "Long-Term Care."

If you are covered also by Medicaid, you normally do not need a Medigap policy. If you already have Medigap insurance purchased on or after November 5, 1991, and you later become eligible for Medicaid, you can ask that the Medigap benefits and premiums be suspended for up to two years while you are covered by Medicaid. If you lose your Medicaid eligibility during the two years, your Medigap policy is automatically reinstated if you give notice and begin paying premiums again.

Even if you are not eligible for Medicaid, but your income is low, you may be eligible for the Qualified Medicare Beneficiary (QMB) program. If you qualify, the government may pay your Medicare Part B premiums and provide supplemental coverage equivalent to a Medigap policy.

If you get health coverage through a former employer or union, you *may* not need Medigap insurance. However, be aware that employer coverage may not provide the same benefits as

### EVALUATING A MEDIGAP POLICY

*Obtain a free copy of the booklet Guide to Health Insurance for People With Medicare from your local Social Security Administration or from the Consumer Information Center, Department 70, Pueblo, CO 81009 (719) 948-3334. This guide:*

- *explains how Medigap insurance works;*
- *explains the ten standardized plans;*
- *tells how to shop for Medigap insurance;*
- *lists addresses and phone numbers of state insurance departments and state agencies on aging. Most states offer free insurance counseling services.*

Medigap insurance and may not have to meet the federal and state rules that apply to Medigap. You should carefully examine the coverage, costs, and stability of your employer or union coverage to determine whether it is a better option than Medigap insurance.

If you belong to a Health Maintenance Organization (HMO), you probably do not need a Medigap policy, since HMO coverage is normally comprehensive.

### Q. How do I buy a good Medigap policy?

**A.** Effective in 1992, all Medigap insurance must conform to standardized benefit plans. There are ten possible standardized plans, identified as Plan A through Plan J. Plan A is a core package and is available in all states. The other nine plans have different combinations of benefits, including coverage of:

- Part A and B deductibles and copayments
- foreign travel emergencies
- at-home recovery (Short-term personal care services in the home)
- excess doctors charges
- preventive screening tests, and
- outpatient prescription drugs

To find out what standardized plans are available in your state, contact your state insurance department.

It is best to buy a Medigap policy at or near the time your Medicare coverage begins, because *during the six months immediately following the effective date of Medicare Part B coverage*, companies must accept you regardless of any health conditions you have, and they cannot charge you more than they charge others of the same age. However, during this open enrollment period, companies may still exclude "preexisting conditions" during the first six months of the policy. Preexisting conditions are medical conditions that were diagnosed or treated during the six months before the Medigap policy became effective.

### Q. If I already have a Medigap policy, should I consider buying a new one?

**A.** If you are satisfied with your present benefits and the company, there is no reason to change policies. If your policy is guaranteed renewable, you can keep it as long as you continue to pay the premiums. If you consider buying a new policy, remember that both state and federal laws strictly control the sales practices of Medigap companies and agents in order to prevent abusive or misleading sales practices. You only need one supplemental policy.

## Medicaid

### Q. What is Medicaid?

**A.** Medicaid is a medical assistance program for poor older or disabled persons whose income and assets fall below certain levels set by federal and state law. Unlike Medicare, which offers the same benefits to all enrollees regardless of income, Medicaid is managed by individual states, and the benefits and eligibility vary from state to state.

### Q. Is it possible to receive both Medicare and Medicaid?

**A.** Yes, if you qualify for both programs. Even if you do not qualify for Medicaid, the Medicaid program may still assist you in paying for all or part of the Medicare premium, deductibles and coinsurance payments if you meet the special income and resource tests under the "Qualified Medicare Beneficiary" (QMB) program or the "Specified Low-Income Medicare Beneficiary" (SLMB) program.

### Q. If I qualify for Medicaid, what sorts of services do I get?

**A.** Medicaid covers a broad spectrum of services. Certain benefits are mandated by federal law. They include:

## QUALIFYING FOR MEDICAID

*Medicaid programs in each state have different standards to determine whether needy individuals are eligible for assistance. All states require that older adults be at least age sixty-five, blind, or disabled, and that they meet income and asset tests. In most states, persons eligible for Supplemental Security Income (SSI) or Aid to Families with Dependent Children (AFDC) are automatically covered. Most states also cover some people whose income falls below a certain level after they "spend down" their income on medical bills. Medicaid eligibility rules are so complicated that it is advisable for older persons with low incomes or with high medical expenses to talk with someone with expertise in Medicaid—such as a legal services lawyer, paralegal, or social worker, or a private attorney experienced in handling Medicaid issues.*

- inpatient and outpatient hospital services
- doctors' and nurse practitioners' services
- inpatient nursing home care
- home health care services
- laboratory and X-ray charges

Other services may include private duty nursing; services from podiatrists, optometrists and chiropractors; mental health services; per-sonal care in your home; dental care; physical therapy and other rehabilitation; prescription medications; dentures; eyeglasses; and more. In all cases, you may receive these services only from a Medicaid-participating provider. As with Medicare, providers may choose whether or not to participate in Medicaid, and they must meet certain standards.

**Q. Does owning a home disqualify me from Medicaid?**

**A.** No. All states exempt your home as an asset as long as you or your spouse lives in it. If you must leave your home in order to receive nursing home care or other long-term care, the state may still exempt it, but state asset exemption rules differ from state to state and can be complex. Besides your home, all states allow you to keep a limited amount of cash and personal property.

**Q. What does Medicaid cost me?**

**A.** Medicaid does not require you to pay premiums or deductibles like Medicare, but can require copayments. Providers may not charge Medicaid patients additional fees beyond the Medicaid reimbursement amount. However, states are permitted to impose a nominal deductible charge or other form of cost-sharing for certain categories of services and prescription drugs. No Medicaid recipient may be denied services by a participating provider because of the patient's inability to pay the charge.

Individuals whose income or assets exceed the state's permissible Medicaid amount may be eligible for Medicaid only after "spending down" their income or assets to a poverty level by incurring medical expenses. These "spend down" amounts can be very high, especially for nursing home residents whose income far exceeds the Medicaid eligibility level but who face enormous monthly expenses for care.

## Q. *How do I apply for Medicaid?*

**A.** Contact the state or local agency that handles the Medicaid program. Its name will vary from place to place. It may be called Social Services, Public Aid, Public Welfare, Human Services, or something similar. You can also call your local agency on aging or senior center for information.

When you apply, you will have to document your financial need in detail, as well as your residency. The application form can be lengthy and complex, but the Medicaid agency can help you complete it. If you are homebound, a Medicaid worker can be sent to your home to help you apply. If you are in a hospital or other institution, a staff social worker should be made available to help you apply. Don't let inability to get to the public agency keep you from seeking assistance. Since the start of benefits is linked to your date of application, it is important to establish an application date as soon as you need Medicaid assistance. Almost any written request with your signature may be enough to establish your application date, even if you have not yet completed the full application form. The effective date can be retroactive, up to three months (except for QMBs and SLMBs).

## Q. *How are Medicaid claims filed and paid?*

**A.** Medicaid providers always bill Medicaid directly. The state Medicaid program reimburses providers according to the state's particular reimbursement formula. Providers cannot charge you additional amounts for covered services.

## Q. *If I disagree with a decision made by my Medicaid program, what can I do?*

**A.** You have the right to appeal all decisions that affect your Medicaid eligibility or services. When a decision about your Medicaid coverage is made, you should receive prompt written notice of the decision. This will include an explanation of how you can appeal the decision.

The appeal process includes a right to a fair hearing before a hearing officer. You may need a lawyer or public benefits specialist experienced in Medicaid law.

## Long-Term Care

## Q. *What federal programs will pay for long-term care in a nursing home?*

**A.** Medicare does *not* pay for a significant amount of nursing home care. Coverage of skilled nursing care, as described on page 595 above under "Medicare," is narrowly defined and limited to twenty days of full coverage and a maximum of eighty additional days with a large coinsurance payment.

Medicaid, on the other hand, pays a substantial portion of the nation's nursing home bill (over 40 percent). Medicaid, however, pays only when most other funds have been depleted. Medicaid will cover nursing home expenses if your condition requires nursing home care, the home is certified by the state Medicaid agency, and you meet income and other eligibility requirements to receive this benefit.

Many persons who normally are not eligible for Medicaid become eligible after a period of time in a nursing home. This happens because the high cost of nursing home care forces many individuals to spend down their assets and income to a level that qualifies them for Medicaid in many states. The rules and availability of this option vary from state to state.

The Department of Veterans Affairs (VA) pays for some nursing home care for veterans in VA facilities and private facilities, but the benefit is limited to the extent that resources and facilities are available. Priority is given to veterans with medical problems related to their military service, and to very old veterans of wartime service, and very poor veterans. Contact your local VA office for more information.

**Q. What if I don't want to live in a nursing home? Are home care services available under Medicare or Medicaid?**

**A.** Yes, but to a limited extent.

The home health care benefit under Medicare focuses mainly on skilled nursing and therapeutic services needed on a part-time or intermittent basis. The benefit is described on page 595 above under "Medicare."

Medicaid home health care is usually quite limited, too. But in addition to home health, several state Medicaid programs also provide some "personal care" services to Medicaid-eligible individuals who need help with normal activities of daily living, such as dressing, bathing, toileting, eating, and walking. Many states have also instituted Medicaid "waiver" programs that allow the state to use Medicaid dollars for home and community-based services that would not normally be covered under Medicaid. These waiver programs usually target persons who would otherwise have to live in a nursing home. Some of the services covered under Medicaid waiver programs include personal care, adult day care, housekeeping services, care management, and respite care. Respite care enables primary care-givers to take a break from their responsibilities. Check with your local office on aging or department of human services about the options available in your state.

**Q. What happens if my husband needs nursing home care but I am still able to live independently? Will all our income and assets have to be used for his support before Medicaid will help pay expenses?**

**A.** If your spouse resides in or may be entering a nursing home, Medicaid has special rules that allow the spouse remaining in the community (community spouse) to keep more income and assets than permitted under the regular eligibility rules. The specifics vary from state to state, but the general structure is as follows:

The community spouse can keep all income, no matter how much, that belongs *exclusively* to the community spouse. Joint income is another story. The state may require all or part of joint income to help pay nursing home expenses, depending upon the particular state's rules.

Most of the income of the nursing home spouse is considered available to pay for nursing home care. However, a portion of the nursing home spouse's income may be kept by the community spouse as a "minimum monthly maintenance needs allowance" if the community spouse's income is below a spousal allowance figure set by the state. States must establish a spousal allowance of at least 150 percent of the poverty level for a two-person household. (Thus, for 1993, this calculation results in a minimum spousal allowance of $1149 per month that could be kept by the community spouse.) States also permit the community spouse to keep a shelter allowance, if shelter costs (rent, mortgage, taxes, insurance, and utilities) exceed a specified amount.

Assets or resources are treated quite differently. The state applies a two-step rule. First, Medicaid counts all resources owned by either spouse. At the option of the couple, this inventory of resources will take place at the *time of entry into the nursing home or upon your subsequent application for Medicaid*. This inventory will exclude a few resources. The excluded resources are: your home, household goods, personal effects, an automobile, and a burial fund of up to $1,500.

Second, from the total countable resources, Medicaid permits the community spouse to keep one-half, as long as the one-half falls between a specified floor and ceiling amount, adjusted yearly. If the one-half falls below the floor (about $14,000 in 1993), the community spouse may keep more of the couple's resources up to the floor amount. If the one-half exceeds the ceiling (about $70,000 in 1993), the excess will be considered available to pay for the cost of nursing home care. Thus, the community spouse is permitted to keep no more than the ceiling amount even if it equals far less than half of the couple's assets.

Another special rule applies to your home. Even though your home is an excluded resource, the state, in limited circumstances, can place a lien against your home equal to the amount of nursing home expenses paid. The rules are complicated and vary by state; the advice of a lawyer experienced in Medicaid law is advisable. Moreover, almost all these rules have hardship exceptions in special circumstances.

**Q. If I have assets that exceed my state's Medicaid eligibility requirements, can I transfer these to my children or to a trust in order to qualify? After all, these are assets I intend to leave to my children when I die.**

**A.** The law on transferring assets before making a Medicaid application is complex. Such transfers can result in a period of ineligibility for Medicaid benefits. There are a number of legal, financial, ethical, and practical consequences to any such transfer of property. Anyone considering such transfer should seek advice from a lawyer experienced in Medicaid law.

**Q. Must children pay for parents in nursing homes?**

**A.** There is no legal obligation for children to pay for their parents' care. Only a spouse may be held legally responsible to help pay for the cost of nursing home care, and as a practical matter, the responsibility is often difficult to enforce against an unwilling spouse. If Medicaid enters the picture, the special rules for spousal responsibility described above will apply.

Children sometimes feel pressured to help pay for a parent's nursing home cost because of the shortage of nursing home beds, especially Medicaid covered beds. Some nursing homes give preference to admitting "private pay" patients over Medicaid patients because private-

## HOW MUCH HEALTH INSURANCE DO I NEED?

*Some people covered by Medicare think they need several additional policies to cover Medicare gaps, specific diseases, and long-term care. That is probably not a good idea. Chances are the policies would duplicate too many benefits to justify the cost. That is why insurance companies are no longer permitted to sell duplicate Medicare supplement policies. The consumer may purchase only one of the A-J policies.*

*The best recommendation for someone on Medicare, who is not also on Medicaid, is to purchase one good "Medigap" policy, and possibly one long-term care insurance policy if you can comfortably afford the cost of a good long-term care policy. Lower income persons are likely to qualify for Medicaid if they need long-term care, so purchasing private long-term care insurance may be a waste of money.*

pay rates are often considerably higher than the amount Medicaid pays. While admission priority for private pay patients is permissible in some states, it is illegal in others. In all states, federal law prohibits nursing homes from requiring a private payment from families, or a period of private payment, prior to applying for

Medicaid coverage. Federal law also prohibits nursing homes from requiring patients to waive their rights to Medicare and/or Medicaid.

### Q. What is long-term care insurance?

**A.** Long-term care insurance helps pay for nursing home care and usually home care services for a period of two or more years. Long-term care insurance is still a relatively new type of private insurance, so the features of this type of insurance change frequently. Most individual policies are available for purchase only to persons between ages fifty and eighty-four, and a medical screening of applicants is typically required. Not every older person needs or can afford a long-term care insurance policy. Policies are appropriate for those with substantial income and assets to protect, and who desire to buy this form of protection against the potential costs of long-term care.

Most long-term care policies are structured as indemnity policies. That is, they pay a pre-set amount for each day of covered nursing home care or home health care, or sometimes a per-visit amount for home care.

The specific provisions of these policies should be closely examined before purchasing one, since the possible conditions and limitations on coverage can be extensive and complex. For example, not all nursing home care may be covered. Some policies cover only "skilled" nursing home care as defined by Medicare, others cover lesser levels of care (sometimes called "intermediate" care) as well as custodial care. Likewise, home health care benefits may be defined to cover only skilled home health services, or more broadly to include some range of nonmedical, supportive services.

### Q. How are the costs of a long-term care policy determined?

**A.** The cost of the premium is determined in part by your age, the extent of coverage you purchase, and your health history. Age is clearly the single greatest factor because the risk of needing long-term care increases significantly with age. The premium for a seventy-five year old can be double or triple that for a sixty-five year old.

### Q. How do I evaluate a long-term care policy?

**A.** Compare more than one policy side by side. Your state's insurance department should have names of companies offering long-term care insurance. Many states are beginning to set minimum standards and consumer protection guidelines for these policies. Guides for evaluating long-term care insurance may also be available from the state insurance department or your state office on aging.

Keep in mind the following tips in evaluating policies:

- Make sure your policy will pay benefits for all levels of care in a nursing home, including custodial care.

- A good policy will pay benefits for home care, including in-home personal care. Personal care refers generally to help with activities of daily living, such as dressing, bathing, toileting, eating, and walking.

- Consider whether the amount of daily benefits will be adequate now and in the future. Many policies give you a range of daily benefit amounts to choose from. Make sure the policy has an "inflation adjustor" under which benefits increase by a certain percentage each year to keep pace with inflation.

- Do not assume that more years of coverage is always better. Some policies offer benefit options of six, seven, or more years. It is possible to buy too much coverage. The "right" amount depends in part on the amount of assets you have to protect.

- Avoid policies that exclude coverage of preexisting conditions for a lengthy period. Six months is considered a reasonable exclusion period for preexisting conditions.

- Better policies will allow payment of nursing home or home health benefits without requiring a prior period of hospitalization as a condition of coverage.

- Most policies impose waiting periods that restrict the starting time of benefits after you begin receiving nursing home care or home care—twenty to ninety days is a common waiting period. A longer waiting period will lower the premium cost. First day coverage will increase your premium.

- Be sure your policy covers victims of Alzheimer's disease and other forms of dementia. About half the residents of nursing homes suffer some form of dementia.

- Be sure that the premium remains constant over the life of the policy and that the policy is guaranteed renewable for life.

- Buy a policy only from a company that is licensed in your state and has agents physically present in your state. Out-of-state mail order policies often leave you powerless to remedy problems if anything goes wrong.

## HOUSING AND LONG-TERM CARE CHOICES

The range of housing options for older persons is enormous—from staying in your own home or apartment, to home sharing, to moving to a senior housing facility or development. The questions and answers that follow begin by exploring an important financial option (home equity conversion) that may help you stay in your home, and then end by describing the wide variety of housing choices that combine shelter with some combination of recreational and social opportunities or supportive services and health care. In all these areas, older persons need to be aware of the personal and financial risks and benefits involved, and, above all, their legal rights.

### Home Equity Conversion

**Q. I own my own home, and do not want to move, but I'm having trouble making ends meet. What can I do?**

**A.** Home equity conversion plans can help you add to your monthly income without having to leave your home. These plans fall into two broad categories: loans and sales. Loan plans permit you to borrow against the equity in your home. They include reverse mortgages and special-purpose loans on which repayment is deferred. They should not be confused with "home equity loans" and "home equity lines of credit," which require you to make monthly payments or risk losing your house.

**Q. How does a reverse mortgage work?**

**A.** A reverse mortgage lets you borrow against the equity in your home, receiving a lump sum, monthly installments, or drawing on a line of credit. The amount of the loan you will receive is based on your age, the value of your home and your equity, the interest rate, the term of the loan, and some other factors. Except for some special-purpose state plans, like those designed to pay for home repairs, there are no restrictions on how you use the money.

The loan usually does not have to be repaid until you sell, die or move from your home. In some new plans, you can continue to receive payments even if you move. When the loan does come due, the amount to be repaid cannot exceed the appraised value of the property.

**Q. Who is eligible for a reverse mortgage?**

**A.** A borrower must be at least sixty-two years of age, and own the property free and clear, except for liens or mortgages which can be paid off with proceeds from the loan. Unlike traditional loans or home equity lines of credit, the borrower's income is not considered. Only single family residences (including some condominiums) are eligible; mobile homes, multi-family dwellings (including duplexes), and cooperatives are not.

#### Q. Are reverse mortgages available in my area?

**A.** Reverse mortgages can be obtained in more than thirty-five states and the District of Columbia. The most common product is the federally insured Home Equity Conversion Mortgage, or HECM. Other products include state-subsidized home repair plans, lender-insured plans, and reverse annuity mortgages. A con-

sumer guide entitled *Home Made Money* and a list of reverse mortgage lenders is available from the American Association of Retired Persons, Consumer Affairs, 601 E. Street, NW, Washington, DC 20049, telephone (202) 434-2277.

#### Q. How will a reverse mortgage affect my other benefits?

**A.** The income from a reverse mortgage will not affect eligibility for social security, Medicare, or other retirement benefits or pensions which are not based on need. However, without careful planning, the income from a reverse mortgage could affect eligibility for Supplemental Security Income (SSI), Medicaid, food stamps, and some state benefit programs.

In general, reverse mortgage payments are considered to be a loan, and will not affect benefits if the money is spent during the month in which it is received. But if the money is not spent during that month, it will be counted as a resource, and may lead to termination of benefits. Be aware that payments received under the new reverse annuity mortgage plans will be considered income, even if they are spent in the month in which they are received.

#### Q. What about tax consequences?

**A.** There are two issues here. The first is whether the income from a reverse mortgage is taxed. So far, it has not been, under the assumption that it is a loan advance. Second is whether the interest can be deducted. Generally, interest cannot be deducted until it is paid. Since the interest on a reverse mortgage is not paid until the loan comes due, it cannot be deducted until that time.

#### Q. What other kinds of home equity conversion are available?

**A.** In addition to loan plans, you can generate income from the equity which you have acquired in your home through sale plans. Sale plans include sale-leasebacks, life estates, and charitable annuities.

### Q. What is a sale-leaseback, and how can I find someone who is interested?

**A.** In a sale-leaseback, you sell the equity in your home, but retain the right to continue living there, often paying a monthly rent. The buyer usually makes a substantial down payment to you. You act as a lender by granting the buyer a mortgage. You receive the buyer's mortgage payments; the buyer receives your rent payments. You remain in the home, and can use the down payment and the mortgage payments as income. The buyer can deduct the mortgage interest payment from his or her income, and will also benefit if the value of the property increases.

Be aware, however, that the IRS requires that both the sale price and the rental payments be fair market rate. Before 1986, the tax laws made sale-leasebacks good investments, especially for adult children. Today, however, there are fewer tax advantages, so finding an investor may be difficult.

### Q. What if I sell my house, and keep a life estate?

**A.** In a life estate, or sale of a remainder interest plan, you sell your home to a buyer, but keep the right to live there during your lifetime. The buyer pays you a lump sum, or monthly payments, or both. You are usually responsible for taxes and repairs while you live in the house. At your death, full ownership passes automatically to the buyer. This arrangement is most common within families, as part of an estate plan. As with a sale-leaseback, it might be difficult to find an outside investor.

Another way of remaining in your home while realizing income from it is a charitable remainder trust. This permits you to donate your home to a charitable institution in return for a lifetime annuity and possibly a tax de-duction. You keep a life estate, and you remain responsible for taxes and maintenance. When you die, your home becomes the property of the charitable institution.

### Q. What about a regular home equity loan?

**A.** A traditional home equity loan is very different from a reverse mortgage, and can be a risk for an older person on a fixed income. As with a reverse mortgage, you borrow against the equity you have built up in your home. But in a home equity loan, you must make regular monthly payments, or you may lose your home.

There may be some tax advantages, however. Since it is no longer possible to deduct interest on consumer goods such as car loans and credit card bills, many homeowners have turned to home equity loans. With such loans, you can borrow up to $100,000 on the equity in your first and second homes, use the money for any purpose, and deduct all the interest you pay. You can even deduct the interest on a home equity loan that exceeds $100,000 if you use the money for home improvements. If you're not going to use such a large loan for home improvements and still want to deduct the interest, you must be able to prove that your home equity, plus improvements, equals the amount of the loan.

### Q. Is home equity conversion the only way to increase my monthly income?

**A.** Not necessarily. If you find that your monthly income does not meet your expenses, you may be eligible for government benefits, such as Supplemental Security Income, food stamps, or Medicaid. (See pages 591 and 592 of the section on income security in this chapter). Some states also have property tax credit or deferral programs for which you may be eligible. To find out more about these programs, call your local agency on aging. You should consider all of the options available to you before you make your decision. If you are already receiving public benefits, you should make sure that the home equity conversion plan you choose does not affect those benefits.

**Q. I am not sure that I can continue to live in my own home, but I would like to stay in my community. What other choices do I have?**

**A.** You have several choices, depending on your current and future health needs, your financial circumstances, and your personal preferences, although not all may be available in your community. There are home-sharing programs, in which homeowners are matched with individuals seeking housing in exchange for rent or services; accessory units, which provide private living units in, or next to, single family homes; or assisted living, which combines a home-like setting with services designed to meet individual needs. These programs may be privately owned and operated, government supported, or sponsored by religious or other nonprofit organizations. For information, contact your local agency on aging.

### Retirement Communities

**Q. I have heard a lot about retirement communities that offer all kinds of different services and amenities. What types of retirement community are available today?**

**A.** In the last several years, there has been a large increase in the number of living options for the elderly as both the public and private sectors attempt to respond to the growing numbers of elders. The modern model of retirement community first sprung up in the 1950s in the sun-belt states with senior communities that offered independent living with a variety of social and recreational opportunities. Much has changed today. Between the extremes of independent living and nursing home care, a variety of alternatives now offer endless combinations of shelter plus services or amenities. Physically, facilities may range from single-family type housing, to high-rise or garden apartment buildings, to campus-like developments.

Facility definitions differ among states and sometimes even within states. For simplicity's sake, it is useful to distinguish three levels of community along a continuum of services. At one end of the continuum are independent living communities. These offer little or no health and supportive services, although they may have recreational and social programs. At the opposite end are "continuing care retirement communities" (CCRCs). These provide a fairly extensive range of housing options, care, and services, including nursing home services. In between are facilities that offer a wide variety of housing and health or supportive services but not nursing home care. These will be referred to as "assisted living" communities, but they include facilities variously called "housing with supportive services," "congregate care," "board and care," and "personal care" to list just a few.

**Q. Who sponsors and who regulates retirement communities?**

**A.** Most retirement communities are developed privately, although many are sponsored by nonprofit groups and agencies, including churches and charitable organizations. All states regulate one or more types of assisted living, and most states regulate continuing care communities, but the extent of regulation varies considerably among states.

**Q. What purchase or payment arrangements do retirement communities offer?**

**A.** Conventional independent living communities typically involve home ownership or rental arrangements that are no different from standard real estate purchases or rentals. Thus, these transactions are governed by local real estate or landlord-tenant law, and residents pay the costs of their mortgage or lease, and condominium or association fees if applicable.

In facilities that promise additional services, facilities, or health care, the payment arrangement includes some mechanism to pay for these added benefits. One may distinguish four basic types of contract, based on payment arrangement, although keep in mind that state regulations may categorize facilities differently:

1. **"Turnover of assets" or "total fee in advance" contracts *without* monthly fees.** These types of contracts are all but extinct today. They were common in the original continuing care communities, often called "life care" communities, developed by religious or fraternal organizations. Many communities using this model failed, because the assets received by the sponsors were not sufficient to keep up with rising health care expenses of residents over their lifetimes.

2. **Entrance fee *plus* monthly fee contracts.** Entrance fees, ranging from $15,000 to over $200,000, are charged by most continuing care retirement facilities today. An entrance fee may represent a partial prepayment for future services. It normally does not buy an interest in the real estate. Increasingly, CCRCs are providing greater refundability of entrance fees, even 100 percent refundability, although this usually results in higher monthly fees. Residency rights and obligations are governed by a long-term lease or occupancy agreement. Monthly fees are subject to periodic inflation adjustments, and, possibly, adjustments when the resident's level-of-care needs change.

3. **"Pay-as-you-go" contracts.** With no entrance fee, these contracts are essentially straight rental arrangements with a defined set of services available when needed for an additional charge. Most assisted living and an increasing number of continuing care facilities offer this arrangement. This type of contract involves the least initial investment, but is subject to greater changes in monthly fees, since the resident assumes all or most of the financial risk for services.

4. **Condominiums or cooperatives with continuing care contracts.** Retirement communities that offer an ownership interest to residents under a condominium or cooperative arrangement with a service package included are relatively new to the scene. These ownership/contractual arrangements are unavoidably complex and bring with them special advantages and risks.

**Q. *What sorts of things do I need to consider before moving into a continuing care community?***

**A.** This is a major financial investment, frequently using up most or all of an older person's financial resources, so consider it carefully and seek professional advice from a lawyer or financial advisor before you make a commitment. You may not be able to get your money back. Be sure to visit the facility at length and talk to both staff and residents.

The following checklist highlights key questions you should ask:

### *Solvency and Expertise of the Provider*

1. What is the provider's background and experience? The provider is the person or entity legally and financially responsible for providing continuing care. Some facilities may advertise that they are "sponsored" by nonprofit groups or churches that in reality may have no legal control or financial responsibility. Be wary if such illusory sponsorship is trumpeted in sales literature.

2. Is the provider financially sound? Have the facility's financial and operating statements reviewed by a professional. Determine whether the facility has sufficient financial reserves.

3. Are all levels of care licensed or certified under applicable state statutes regulating continuing care, assisted living, and nursing home care?

4. How does the facility ensure the quality of care and services provided? Is the facility accredited by any recognized private accrediting organization?

### Fees

5. What is the entrance fee, and when can you get all or part of it back? The facility should provide a formula for a *pro rata* refund of the entrance fee, based on the resident's length of stay, regardless of whether the facility or the resident initiates the termination. Some facilities offer the option of fully refundable entrance fees.

6. What is the monthly fee? When and how much can it be increased? What happens if fee increases exceed my ability to pay? Some facilities have a program that grants financial assistance to residents whose income becomes inadequate to pay increasing monthly fees and personal expenses.

7. Will fees change when the resident's living arrangements or level-of-care needs change (for example, transfers from independent living, to assisted living, to nursing care)?

8. What does my living unit consist of and to what extent can I change or redecorate it?

9. What happens if I marry, divorce, become widowed, or wish to have a friend or family member move into the unit?

### Services and Health Care

10. Exactly what services are included in my regular fees? Especially inquire about coverage, limitations, and costs of the following matters:

*Housing/Social/Recreational*
- meal services
- special diets/tray service
- utilities
- cable television
- furnishings
- unit maintenance
- linens/personal laundry
- housekeeping
- recreational/cultural activities
- transportation

*Health and Personal Care*
- physician services
- nursing care facility services
- nursing services outside a nursing unit (for example, assistance with medications)
- private duty nursing
- dental and eye care
- personal care services (that is, assistance with eating, dressing, bathing, toileting, etc.)
- homemaker/companion services
- drugs, medication, and medical equipment/supplies

11. If the facility provides a nursing unit, what happens if a bed is not available when you need it?

12. To what extent does the facility have the right to cut back, change, or eliminate services, or change the fees?

13. Does the facility limit its responsibility for certain health conditions or preexisting conditions? (A preexisting

health condition is one diagnosed or treated in a certain period of time before entering the facility.) When can you become too sick or impaired to be cared for by the facility?

14. Can you receive Medicare and Medicaid coverage in the facility?

15. Does the facility require residents to buy private insurance or participate in a special group insurance program for residents?

16. What are the criteria and procedures for determining when a resident needs to be transferred from independent living to assisted living, or to a nursing care unit, or to an entirely different facility? Who is involved in these decisions?

### Residents' Rights

17. What rights do residents have to participate in facility management and decision-making? How are complaints handled?

18. On what grounds can residents' contracts or leases be terminated against their wishes?

19. What other rules and policies cover day-to-day operation of the facility?

20. Does the contract release the facility from any liability for injury to a resident resulting from negligence by the facility or third parties? Such waivers should be avoided.

## Nursing Home Care

### Q. What is a nursing home?

**A.** A nursing home is a facility that provides: skilled nursing care and related services for residents who require medical or nursing care; rehabilitation services for injured, disabled, or sick persons; and health-related care and services, above the level of room and board, that can be made available only through institutional facilities.

Often, nursing facilities make distinctions between three levels of care—skilled, intermediate, and custodial—for purposes of Medicare, Medicaid, or private insurance coverage. The distinction between "skilled" and "custodial" care affects Medicare and is discussed on page 595 under "Medicare" above. "Intermediate" care is a term that was previously important under Medicaid law but is no longer used. However, some state licensing laws, long-term care insurance companies, and nursing homes themselves still use the term to describe health and supportive services that are less than skilled nursing care but more than custodial.

Only about 5 percent of people age sixty-five and older live in nursing homes at any given time, but researchers estimate that older persons overall have about a 40 percent chance of spending at least some time in nursing homes. While some older nursing home residents stay for extended periods, the majority stay in a facility less than six months.

### Q. How does living in a nursing home affect my personal rights and privileges?

**A.** You do not check your rights and privileges at the door when you enter a nursing home. Although institutional care, by its very nature, substantially limits one's lifestyle and scope of privacy, one should nevertheless expect high quality, compassionate, and dignified care from nursing facilities.

The federal Nursing Home Reform Amendments of 1987, and corresponding state laws, protect residents in nearly all nursing facilities. For residents who lack decision-making capacity, the resident's agent under a power of attorney for health care or another legal surrogate recognized by state law (typically a family member) may exercise the resident's rights.

## FINDING A RETIREMENT FACILITY

- *The American Association of Homes for the Aging publishes The Consumer's Directory of Continuing Care Retirement Communities, profiling not-for-profit retirement communities around the country and providing an overview of CCRC types, terminology, and features that consumers might want to consider. For ordering information, contact AAHA Publications, 901 E Street, NW, Suite 500, Washington, DC 20004, telephone (202) 783-2242.*

- *The American Association of Retired Persons has three brochures that can help you make housing decisions. These are Selecting Retirement Housing (Stock No. D13680), Staying at Home (Stock No. D14986), and Retirement Housing: Bibliography of Housing from AARP (no stock number), AARP, 601 E. St., NW, Washington, DC 20049, telephone (202) 434-2277 or toll-free 1-800-424-3410.*

- *State or local agencies on aging frequently prepare directories or guides on housing options for older persons and persons with disabilities. Find the agency's number in your local telephone book.*

Federal law requires that nursing homes meet strong basic standards for the quality of life of each resident and for the provision of services and activities. Specific rights guaranteed by federal and state law include the following:

*Information Rights*    Nursing homes must provide:

- written information about residents' rights;
- written information about the services available under the basic rate and any extra charges for extra services;
- advance notice of changes in room assignment or roommate;
- upon request, latest facility inspection results and any plan of correction submitted to state officials;
- explanation of the resident's right to make a health care advance directive—that is, power of attorney for health care or living will—and facility policies on complying with advance directives; (See discussion of advance directives on pages 617–620 and 627–635 under "Right To Control Your Own Affairs" below.)
- information about eligibility for Medicare and Medicaid and the services covered by those programs.

*Self-Determination Rights*    Each resident has the right to:

- participate in an individualized assessment and care planning process that accommodates the resident's personal needs and preferences;
- choose one's personal physician;
- voice complaints without fear of reprisal, and to receive a prompt response;
- organize and participate in resident groups (such as a resident council) and family groups.

*Personal and Privacy Rights*    Residents have the right to:

- participate in social, religious, and community activities as they choose;
- privacy in medical treatment, accommodations, personal visits, written and tele-

phone communications and meetings of resident and family groups;

- confidentiality of personal and clinical records;
- access to the long-term care ombudsman, one's physician, family members, and reasonable access to other visitors subject to the resident's consent;
- freedom from physical or mental abuse, corporal punishment, and involuntary seclusion;
- freedom from any physical restraint or psychoactive drugs used for purposes of discipline or convenience, and not required to treat the resident's medical symptoms;
- protection of resident's funds held by the facility with a quarterly accounting.

**Transfer and Discharge Rights**    Residents may be transferred or discharged only for the following reasons:

- the health, safety, or welfare of the resident or other residents requires it;
- the nonpayment of fees;
- the resident's health improves so that he or she no longer needs nursing home care;
- the facility closes.

Normally residents must receive at least thirty days advance notice, with information about appealing the transfer and how to contact the state long-term care ombudsman program.

The facility must prepare and orient residents to ensure safe and orderly transfer from the facility.

**Protection Against Medicaid Discrimination**
Nursing homes must:

- have identical policies and practices regarding services to residents regardless of the source of payment. (However, be aware that not all facilities participate in Medicaid.);
- provide information on how to apply for Medicaid;

- explain the Medicaid "bed-hold" policy—that is, how many days Medicaid will hold the resident's bed, or ensure priority readmission, after temporary absences;
- not request, require, or encourage residents to waive their rights to Medicaid;
- not require a family member to guarantee payment as a condition of a resident's admission or continued stay;
- not "charge, solicit, accept or receive gifts, money, donations or other considerations" as a precondition for admission or continued stay for persons eligible for Medicaid.

**Q. What can I do if I think a nursing home is not providing adequate care or respecting my rights?**

**A.** Different problems require different responses. The following steps should help resolve most problems. The order may vary depending on the problem.

1. Keep a log of the relevant details, including dates and personnel involved.
2. Try to resolve the problem informally by talking to supervising staff.
3. Many facilities have active resident councils or family councils. Bring the problem before these groups.

---

**BASIC QUALITY OF LIFE STANDARD FOR NURSING HOMES**
*Federal law requires each nursing facility to "care for its residents in such a manner and in such an environment as will promote maintenance of enhancement of the quality of life of each resident."*

4. Contact your long-term care ombudsman. (See below.)

5. Contact the state regulatory agencies that license, certify, and survey nursing homes. Usually, the state department of health has this responsibility.

6. Contact a community legal assistance program, other advocacy organization, or private attorney experienced in long-term care issues.

### Q. What is the long-term care ombudsman program?

**A.** The federal Older Americans Act requires every state to operate a long-term care ombudsman program. The ombudsman is responsible for advocating on behalf of nursing home residents and residents of other long-term care facilities, such as "assisted living" or board and care facilities. The ombudsman provides education on long-term care options and residents' rights, and investigates and resolves complaints made by or on behalf of residents.

### BASIC SERVICE AND ACTIVITIES STANDARD

*Federal law requires each nursing facility to "provide services and activities to attain or maintain the highest practicable physical, mental, and psychosocial well-being of each resident in accordance with a written plan of care which . . . is initially prepared, with participation to the extent practicable of the resident or the resident's family or legal representative."*

Most states operate local or regional programs with paid or volunteer ombudsmen. Residents and family members often find ombudsman staff to be essential partners in resolving problems. Federal law requires nursing homes to allow the ombudsman access to residents and access to resident records. In addition, the ombudsman usually has special authority under state law to inspect records and take other steps necessary to respond to complaints.

## RIGHTS OF PERSONS WITH DISABILITIES

Many older people are unable to manage their daily activities as well as they once did. Others have disabilities which have worsened with age. Two major federal laws, the Americans with Disabilities Act and the Fair Housing Amendments Act, protect people with physical or mental disabilities from discrimination in virtually every aspect of their lives. In addition, these laws require employers and the providers of services to modify their rules and policies, and physical environment, to meet the needs of persons with disabilities.

### Q. Who is protected by these laws?

**A.** Both the Americans with Disabilities Act (ADA) and the Fair Housing Amendments Act (FHAA) protect people with mental or physical impairments that limit their ability to perform one or more major life activities. These activities include walking, seeing, hearing, taking care of personal or health needs, or doing everyday chores. The laws also protect people who are perceived to have a disability, or whose family members or friends are disabled.

Neither law protects people who threaten the safety or health of others, or whose behavior would result in substantial damage to the property of others. Nor do the laws protect current users of illegal drugs.

**Q. What situations does the Americans with Disabilities Act cover?**

A. The ADA protects people with disabilities against discrimination in employment, public transit and public accommodations (such as hotels, restaurants, banks, schools, and senior centers). It generally does not cover housing, although it does cover some nonhousing activities that are based in a housing facility, such as meal or activity programs to which the public is invited.

**Q. What situations are covered by the Fair Housing Amendments Act?**

A. The FHAA applies to almost all housing transactions. Most importantly for the purposes of this chapter, the law prohibits landlords from refusing to rent to older people, or asking them to move, simply because they need assistance with certain activities. The law does not apply to rental buildings that contain fewer than four units, and where the owner also lives in the building. Examples of prohibited discrimination include:

- refusing to rent to a family whose member has a mental illness;
- requiring applicants for senior housing to provide a doctor's letter stating that they are in good health and can live on their own;
- denying a resident who uses a wheelchair or a walker access to a communal dining room;
- evicting a tenant because he or she is receiving homemaking help or other services.

**Q. What does "reasonable accommodation" mean?**

A. Reasonable accommodations are changes in rules or procedures that are reasonable under the circumstances, and give a disabled person equal opportunity to participate in a specific activity, program, job, or housing situation. They are very individualized, and can often be worked out informally by the people involved. Examples include:

- providing large-print notices, leases, or other written materials;
- giving a job or housing applicant more time to fill out an application;
- waiving a no-pets rule for a tenant with a mental disability who is emotionally dependent on his or her pet, or waiving a no-guest rule for a tenant who needs a live-in aide;
- assisting a customer who needs help with packages, or with opening and closing doors, or even with dialing a telephone.

**Q. What are reasonable modifications?**

A. Reasonable modifications are changes to the physical structure of a building or property which are reasonable under the circumstances, and which give a person with disabilities equal access to the premises. Examples include:

- widening doorways and installing ramps;
- replacing doorknobs with lever handles;
- installing grab bars in bathrooms.

**Q. Who pays for these alterations?**

A. In an apartment or other housing program, the landlord pays for alterations to the common areas, such as hallways, entrances, and meeting rooms. The tenant is responsible for the costs of modifications inside the apartment. Alterations to public facilities, hotels, and other programs covered by the ADA are paid for by the owner of the facility.

**Q. How do I go about getting some changes made in my apartment?**

A. Although many housing providers are familiar with the FHAA, and are working to make sure that their buildings are accessible, they may not be aware of accommodations that would make life easier for individual tenants. All you need to do is request the changes; if they are reasonable, they should be honored. Remember that you are responsible for the costs of physical alterations inside your own apartment. Also, you may be required to return the premises to their original condition when you move.

### Q. What do I do if I believe I am being discriminated against?

**A.** These laws can be enforced through court action or by filing a complaint with an administrative agency.

If the discrimination involves housing, call the U.S. Department of Housing and Urban Development's Fair Housing Complaint Hotline at 1-800-424-8590 (voice), or 1-800-543-8294 (TDD—telecommunications device for the deaf).

If the discrimination involves employment, public accommodations, telecommunications, or public transit, contact the U.S. Department of Justice, Office on the Americans with Disabilities Act, Civil Rights Division, P.O. Box 66118, Washington, DC 20035-6116; or call (202) 514-0301 (voice), or (202) 514-0383 (TDD).

---

## RIGHT TO CONTROL YOUR OWN AFFAIRS

As we grow older, all of us face the possibility that one day we may become incapacitated mentally. The time may come when we are no longer able to make our own health care decisions, manage our own financial affairs, or act on our own behalf.

When that happens, you and your property must be protected, and people should honor your wishes wherever possible. How and where do you want to live? What decisions can you make? What decisions should you leave to someone else? Whom do you want to make decisions for you? Several alternatives will ensure that people respect your wishes whenever possible. Through planning, the decisions made on your behalf can be those you would have made yourself.

### Financial Management Issues

### Q. What may I do to make sure that people consider my wishes if I become incapacitated?

**A.** You should make plans now, while you have capacity, to be sure your wishes are met. Several planning tools guarantee you a voice in your future. If incapacity strikes, these tools will name the person you want to act on your behalf and/or tell other people how to care for you and your property.

There are different types of planning tools. Some—such as the durable power of attorney, joint property arrangements, and living trusts—cover your property and financial affairs. Others, known as the advance directives for health care, address your health care concerns, including decisions near the end of life.

The details of creating these documents vary from one state to another. However, some general principles apply.

### Durable Power of Attorney

### Q. What is a power of attorney?

**A.** It is a written document in which you (the "principal") grant certain authority to another person (the agent or "attorney in fact") to act on your behalf. A power of attorney may be very specific, authorizing a person only to sell a car for you, for example. Or it can be very broad, allowing the agent to do almost anything on your behalf.

## A LEGAL TEST OF CAPACITY

*There is no universal legal test of mental capacity or incapacity. Laws vary from state to state, but some general principles apply everywhere. First, incapacity is always evaluated in connection with specific tasks. The question is always, "Incapacity to do what?" Different legal standards of capacity may apply to different tasks, such as capacity to do a will, to drive, to enter contracts, to manage money, or to make medical decisions. In a typical guardianship proceeding, most but not all states use a two-part test to determine incapacity (sometimes called incompetency). First, some type of disability must be verified, for example, mental illness, mental retardation, and/or Alzheimer's disease. Second, there must be a finding that the disability prevents the person from performing activities essential to take care of his or her personal needs or property. Most courts will also insist that all feasible alternatives to guardianship have been explored before appointing a guardian.*

Traditionally, powers of attorney were used to authorize a trusted family member, friend, or attorney-at-law to act in your behalf in financial matters—the sale of real estate, the making of investments, and so on. When drafted to cover all financial matters, this authorization is called a "general power of attorney."

**Q. Will a power of attorney be valid when I become mentally incapacitated or incompetent?**

**A.** A power of attorney normally is not valid if you become incapacitated, unless you use a "durable" power of attorney. A durable power of attorney clearly states that you intend the power to continue if you become disabled or incapacitated. It generally remains in effect until you deliberately revoke it or until you die. However, in some states, your durable power of attorney is terminated if a guardian is appointed for you (although appointment of a guardian is usually unnecessary because the durable power of attorney takes care of the management of your affairs).

**Q. Whom should I name as my agent under a durable power of attorney? Does the person have to be an attorney-at-law?**

**A.** Your agent does not have to be a lawyer. In most states, it can be any adult or an institution. However, it should be someone who knows you well and whom you trust completely to manage your affairs. After all, decisions made by your agent can have tremendous consequences for you. Your agent has to carry out your wishes and always act as you would choose or with your best interests in mind. If there is no one whom you trust with this power, it may be best not to draw up a power of attorney. Other planning tools may suit you better.

You may name multiple agents who exercise all or some of the powers jointly (that is, all must agree) or separately (that is, any one may act). With multiple agents, some process for handling disagreements among agents should be considered, so that disagreements do not undermine the usefulness of the power. In all cases, it is a good idea to name an alternate to serve as your agent in case your first choice becomes unavailable.

**Q. What if I do not want a power of attorney to take effect now, but only if I become disabled or incapacitated?**

**A.** In general, a durable power of attorney becomes effective when you sign it. However, you may tell your agent not to act until you become incapacitated or disabled. If your agent acts prematurely, you still have the right to act on your own behalf and you may revoke the durable power of attorney at any time if you still have capacity. It may be possible to write your durable power of attorney so that it becomes effective only if you become incapacitated. This is called a "springing power of attorney." Many states allow you to write this type of durable power of attorney. Others do not. Consult a knowledgeable lawyer to find out what is possible in your state.

**Q. Do I need a lawyer to write a durable power of attorney?**

**A.** While not required, a lawyer is advisable for drafting your durable power of attorney. A lawyer should make sure that your document meets your state's requirements and that the powers you wish to give your agent are actually spelled out in language that will be legally effective. Some powers may not be presumed to be within the scope of the power of attorney unless they are specifically spelled out—for example, the power to make gifts or loans or file tax returns.

Some states require a specific format or specific wording in the document. Certain states provide a "short form durable power of attorney" that allows you to check off the powers to be granted to the agent, with state law providing an interpretation of what each power means.

**Q. My father has Alzheimer's disease. I would like him to appoint me to act for him under a durable power of attorney, since he can no longer manage on his own. May he do this now or is it too late?**

**A.** It is up to your father to decide if he wants to give you his power of attorney. And it may be too late. Durable powers of attorney and other planning tools must be made while a person is still capable. This is why advance planning is so important.

However, just because doctors diagnose someone as having a specific disease does not mean that the patient is necessarily incapacitated. Also, incapacity does not affect all functions in the same way. Thus, even people in the early stages of a disease such as Alzheimer's may have the capacity to make some decisions. They also may have more capacity at certain times of the day than at others, or their capacity may be affected by medications.

## REVOKING A POWER OF ATTORNEY

*If you change your mind about whom you want as your agent under a power of attorney (durable or not), you may revoke the document. In fact, while you are capable, you may revoke a power of attorney at any time for any reason. Simply notify the person you have named to act as your agent. For your protection, it is best to do this in writing. You also should destroy all copies of the power of attorney and notify in writing any third parties with whom this person might have done business. Where substantial assets are at stake, you may also want to file a document called a "Revocation of Power of Attorney" in the public records where you live or own real estate, and maybe even in the local newspaper(s).*

Capacity must be assessed on a case by case basis. If your father is willing to see a lawyer about writing a durable power of attorney, the lawyer can help assess whether your father understands the purpose and consequences of the durable power.

### Q. Who decides whether I'm incapacitated?

**A.** You can specify how you wish to have your incapacity and mental status determined if the need should arise. For example, in your durable power of attorney you can name a doctor to make this determination, or you can say that two doctors must decide whether you have capacity. Any doctor or clinical psychologist who makes evaluations of capacity should have experience in this area. If you provide no instructions, then a court might ultimately decide the issue, guided by generally accepted standards used by other courts in making these determinations.

## Living Trusts

### Q. What is a "living trust"?

**A.** A living trust (also called "inter vivos" trust) is an arrangement under which you transfer ownership of all or part of your property to the trust during your lifetime. As the person establishing the trust, you are called the "grantor" or "settlor." You name a "trustee," who manages the property according to the terms of your written trust document. The trustee may be an individual or an institution or yourself. The trust is for the benefit of one or more persons, including yourself, called the "beneficiaries."

Frequently, a will is used to set up a trust (called a testamentary trust) that becomes effective after the death of the person establishing the trust. A living trust, however, is effective during the lifetime of the settlor. In a living trust, the settlor and/or members of his or her family usually are the beneficiaries of the trust. A living trust may be revocable or irrevocable.

### Q. What is a living trust useful for?

**A.** Living trusts are one way of ensuring that someone (a trustee) has the legal authority to manage your estate properly if you become incapacitated or simply do not wish to manage your own estate anymore. They are especially useful where there is a substantial amount of property and professional management is desired. Like the durable power of attorney, a living trust may make it unnecessary to have a guardian or conservator appointed to manage your financial affairs. However, a trust is generally more expensive to create and to manage than a durable power of attorney.

### Q. How may I use a living trust to plan for possible incapacity?

**A.** You may design a living trust so it takes effect only if you become incapacitated. In this way, you keep control over your affairs until the proper person determines that you are incapacitated. As with a durable power of attorney, the process for such a determination should be spelled out in the document.

You may also write your living trust so that it is effective before you become incapacitated and continues even after you lose capacity. For example, you might name yourself as trustee and manage the trust's assets while you have capacity, but name a successor trustee who will take over for you if you become incapacitated. Again, you should designate in the trust document how that determination of incapacity should be made.

### Q. I thought a trust simply paid an allowance to someone. If I need a trust because I cannot manage my own finances, how would this help me?

**A.** Some trust arrangements do just pay a sum to the beneficiary periodically. However, you may design a living trust in which the trustee handles many of the daily tasks of managing the estate, including paying bills and taxes. You may state in the trust agreement exactly what you want the trustee to do and how you want your assets managed.

### Q. Is a living trust just for someone who is incapacitated?

**A.** No. While it's an excellent way for someone to plan and avoid the need for a guardian or conservator of the estate, a living trust also is useful for someone who wishes to turn over financial management of his or her affairs to another person.

Living trusts may have significant tax consequences, and may or may not reduce the amount of your estate that is subject to the probate process after your death. In addition, trusts may have an affect on your eligibility for Medicaid payment of your nursing home care. Trusts are very complicated; considerable caution is required in making them and the assistance of a lawyer is highly recommended.

To find out more about living trusts, contact a lawyer in your state. He or she will be able to give you particulars about how your state's laws affect such trusts and about the consequences of making a trust.

### Q. My father has a lot of money in his estate, but he is becoming increasingly forgetful every week. May he still write a living trust?

**A.** Like the durable power of attorney, people must prepare living trusts while they still have the capacity to do so. First of all, your father must want to make a trust. If he does, his lawyer may determine his ability to make a trust agreement. Sometimes this is done by having him examined by a family physician or perhaps a gerontologist. His lawyer will know what standard of capacity must be proven. If your father does not have that capacity, he cannot make and sign a living trust.

### Q. May I decide that I want to change, or revoke, a living trust arrangement?

**A.** It depends on whether the trust is revocable or irrevocable. If your trust is revocable and you still have capacity, then you always may change or even revoke it completely. An irrevocable trust cannot be changed or revoked.

### Q. How may I ensure that my trustee will manage my affairs properly after I become incapacitated?

**A.** Your trust instrument should contain specific instructions. You should include a precise statement of what the trustee should do on your behalf, and specify the trustee's particular duties, responsibilities, and limitations.

### Q. My wife and I hold most of our assets in common. May I still draft a living trust to protect my share of the estate?

**A.** Yes, but take care to ensure that the trust does not violate the rights or interests of your wife in her portion of the estate. You may do this through careful drafting of the document and sound financial planning before incapacity. You and your wife may need separate counseling and planning advice, as your interests may conflict with each other.

### Q. It sounds as though a living trust is a very complex type of financial planning tool. Who can help me decide if one is right for me?

**A.** It is best to consult with a lawyer or a trust officer familiar with living trusts to determine if one is right for you. Do not rely solely on mail-order or do-it-yourself trust kits, as they may contain information that is misleading or inappropriate for your circumstances or your state's law. There is more information in the chapter, "Estate Planning," beginning on page 651.

## Joint Ownership

**Q. I have most of my property and bank accounts held jointly with my spouse and an adult child. Isn't this good enough to ensure management of my property if I become incapacitated?**

**A.** No. Joint ownership, or joint tenancy with right of survivorship, is a common and simple form of ownership for property such as one's home, cars, securities, and bank accounts. It is a convenient way to allow another person access to property or money you have in a bank account or to deposit or write checks on your behalf. However, joint ownership is not a substitute for other planning tools because it has serious disadvantages. For example, an untrustworthy joint owner may withdraw all the money in a bank account and leave you with nothing. It is possible to challenge a co-owner's improper use of your money, but it may be difficult. In some states, creditors of a co-owner may be able to reach your account, even though that person is only listed on your account to help you manage your money. In addition, being listed as a co-owner of a bank account could affect the co-owner's eligibility for public benefit programs such as Medicaid. Finally, transfers of a home, a car, or securities, normally requires the signature of all owners. The loss of capacity of one owner may prevent a needed sale or transfer of the property. See discussion beginning on page 673 of the chapter on estate planning for more information on joint ownership.

**Q. I'm concerned about the disadvantages of joint bank accounts. Is there another way that I can give someone access to my bank account without giving that person ownership of my money?**

**A.** Some states have laws allowing persons to create what is referred to as an "agency bank account" or "convenience account." This works very much like a durable power of attorney. You name an agent on your bank account who then has the authority to make deposits or withdrawals and manage your account. The authority remains effective if you become incapacitated or disabled, unless you indicate otherwise. The agent has no right of ownership in the money in the account before or after your death, unless you indicate that the agent is to receive the money when you die. This may be a useful tool for you if you do not want to give someone authority over other aspects of your financial affairs through a durable power of attorney. It also may be useful as a supplement to your durable power of attorney, because some banks are reluctant to accept a durable power of attorney and prefer their own forms and procedures. Your banker or lawyer should be able to tell you whether your state's law allows agency bank accounts and how one might benefit you.

## Representative Payees

**Q. I have no income other than my social security check. Would a living trust or power of attorney help me manage my money?**

**A.** A living trust is far too costly and complicated for this kind of situation. A durable power of attorney definitely would be helpful. However, if the primary need is to take care of the social security check, a representative payee may be the simplest way to help you take care of your daily expenses and manage your small income.

**Q. What is a representative payee?**

**A.** A representative payee is a person or organization appointed by a government agency, such as the Social Security Administration (SSA) or the Veterans Administration (VA), to receive and manage public benefits on behalf of someone who is incapable of doing so. The payee actually receives your government benefits on your behalf and is responsible for managing those benefits and making sure that they are spent for your welfare.

**Q. What types of income may a representative payee manage?**

**A.** He or she may only manage the income paid by government programs (usually federal programs such as social security, veterans benefits, black-lung benefits, and supplemental security income programs). The representative payee has *no* authority over any other income or property that you might receive. If you have additional income from other sources, you may need other assistance (such as help from an agent under your durable power of attorney or from a money management program, discussed below) in addition to the help of a representative payee.

**Q. How is a representative payee set up?**

**A.** You, or someone on your behalf, must ask the Social Security Administration (or other program) to appoint a representative payee. Generally, you must have some sort of disability that prevents you from managing your own financial affairs, and you probably will need medical records of your disability. The government agency that provides the benefits must decide that you need help managing them. Your disability may be physical or mental. Although the decision is made by the agency and not by a court of law, you have the right to contest the appointment of a representative payee if you disagree, including the right to a hearing and all the appeals rights that apply to any claim before the agency.

**Q. How can I be sure a representative will manage my money properly?**

**A.** Supervising representative payees can be a problem. In principle, the payee must provide

a detailed accounting to the agency paying the benefits. However, many exceptions exist. For example, spouses and institutions (such as nursing homes) that are acting as payees do not have to make such reports. Under some benefits programs, such as the VA, reporting requirements vary with the size of the benefit. There is not much you may do to protect yourself ahead of time in such circumstances, except to plan for incapacity through other methods that allow someone else of your choice to manage your income for you.

**Q. If I regain my ability to control my own finances, may I dismiss a representative payee?**

**A.** Yes. First you need a doctor's certification that you are now able to manage your own financial affairs. You must then notify the government agency of your wish to dismiss the representative payee, and the agency must determine that you have regained the capacity to manage your own benefits.

## Money Management Services

**Q. I do not have a durable power of attorney or other legal tool for managing my property, but I have heard of some organizations offering "money management" services. What are these?**

**A.** Money management programs, also known as "daily money management" or "voluntary money management," represent a broad group of services designed to help older persons or persons with disabilities who need assistance managing their financial affairs. These services might include check depositing, check writing, checkbook balancing, bill paying, insurance claim preparation and filing, tax preparation and counseling, investment counseling, and public benefit applications and counseling.

### Q. Who provides money management services?

**A.** This assistance may be provided by an individual or an organization. An organization may provide services on a for-profit or not-for-profit basis. Services may be provided for free, on a sliding fee scale basis (where you pay according to your income), or for a flat rate.

If you receive or are considering money management services, you should make sure that your service provider has a system of cash controls to prevent or at least lessen the risk of embezzlement of client funds. The service provider should also be bonded and insured to protect clients from theft or loss of funds.

### Q. How do money management programs help me keep control of my life?

**A.** A money management program may be able to help by providing the financial management assistance you need in the way you want it. It may also help avoid the need for a guardianship. Money management services work on a voluntary basis, so you must be able to ask for help or accept an offer of help. Money management services may be particularly useful if you have no family or friends who are able or whom you trust to act as your agent or trustee.

## Guardianship

### Q. What exactly is a guardian?

**A.** A guardian is someone who is appointed by a court to make personal and/or financial decisions on behalf of another person. "Guardian" is a general term for a court-appointed surrogate (substitute) decision maker. Your state may use other terms, such as "conservator," "committee," "curator," or "fiduciary." Some terms may only apply if the decision maker has authority over financial and property matters; other terms may apply if the decision maker has authority over personal decisions such as living arrangements and health care. A person who has a guardian may be called a "ward," an "incapacitated person," or some other term.

### Q. When is the appointment of a guardian appropriate?

**A.** People need a guardian:

- when they can no longer manage their affairs because of serious incapacity;
- no other voluntary arrangements for decision making and management have been set up ahead of time, or if they have been set up, they are not working well; and
- serious harm will come to the individual if no legally authorized decision maker is appointed.

A guardianship is a serious step and should relate to a serious inability to make or understand the consequences of decisions. It should not depend on stereotypical notions of old age, mental illness, or handicaps. A person has a right to make foolish or risky decisions. These decisions by themselves do not mean that the person has a decision making incapacity.

### Q. Are there any disadvantages to the appointment of a guardian?

**A.** Yes. Although a guardianship may be necessary to protect the welfare of an incapacitated person, it also results in the loss of individual rights. The person under a guardianship may lose the right to marry, the right to vote, the right to hold a driver's license, the right to make a will, the right to enter into a contract, and other rights. Because of its serious consequences, guardianship should be considered the last resort for helping someone who is experiencing incapacity.

In addition, the court proceedings themselves can be costly, time-consuming, and emotionally trying for a family. Once in place, a guardian's ability to manage the estate is far less flexible than it would be under advance planning legal tools such as durable powers of attorney or living trusts. Guardians must operate within strict fiduciary limitations and normally must file annual accountings with the court. On the positive side, the fiduciary rules and court accountings ensure at least some oversight and accountability of the guardian.

### Q. Who appoints a guardian?

**A.** Procedures vary among the states, but generally a court of law appoints a guardian after hearing evidence that a person is incapable of making decisions and deciding that the person needs a surrogate decision maker.

In most states, the law requires some form of due process rights. These rights are intended to protect a person from being inappropriately declared incapacitated. The rights often include the right to be notified of the date and place of the hearing, the right to be present at the hearing, and the right to be represented by a lawyer.

### Q. My elderly mother is often confused. I think she ought to have a guardian to look after her interests. What do I do?

**A.** First, you may want to contact your local area agency on aging to see if there are any programs or services that might help your mother manage and make it unnecessary to obtain a guardian for her. It will also help to have her examined by a doctor or psychologist experienced in geriatric evaluation. A geriatric evaluation will typically involve evaluation by more than one specialist from different disciplines, such as medicine, nursing, and social work. Often, a person's decision making may be impaired because of physical or other causes that can be corrected.

If the evaluation supports the need for guardianship, check with a lawyer to learn the specifics of your state's guardianship law and procedures, as they vary substantially from state to state. The appointment of a guardian normally requires the filing of a petition with the court, notice to your mother and other interested parties, and a court hearing. You will probably need a lawyer to help you through it.

The court may also appoint an investigator to interview your mother and make a report to the court or an attorney to represent your mother. At the hearing, a judge will review the petition, the investigator's or attorney's report, and medical reports.

The judge may ask the person filing the petition why the other person needs a guardian. The judge may also ask the allegedly incapacitated person some questions. The hearings are usually fairly informal. If there is disagreement, the judge may set the case for a formal hearing with witness testimony, cross examination, and argument by counsel.

### Q. What if someone thinks I need a guardian, and I do not want one?

**A.** Every state gives the allegedly incapacitated person a chance to fight the petition for guardianship. If you do not think you need a guardian, you must let the court know that. Usually you do this by appearing in court on the day of the hearing or asking someone to represent you at the hearing.

It is best to get your own lawyer to represent you at the hearing. If you cannot afford one, many states require that the court appoint one at the state's expense. Some free legal services programs for older persons will help you fight a guardianship. If you cannot get to court or hire a lawyer, you may write the court about your objection to the guardianship.

### Q. This sounds very expensive. Who pays for a guardianship?

**A.** It can be expensive. There are court charges and attorney's fees and fees for the

## WHO MAY BE A GUARDIAN?

*Laws vary from one state to another. In most states, the courts may appoint almost anyone as your guardian if the person meets legal requirements. Often the court appoints the person filing the petition. Most courts like to appoint a relative who knows the person and is most likely to act in his or her best interests. However, the courts may appoint a friend or attorney, especially if no family members are available. The courts also may appoint multiple guardians, either with shared responsibilities or with responsibilities split between them. If there are no friends or family willing or able to serve as guardian, many states permit public or private agencies to act as the guardian and to charge fees for that service.*

doctor or other persons who examine the alleged incapacitated person to assess his or her capacity. If the court appoints a guardian of the estate, the estate often pays the guardian's fees. Older persons who are either seeking guardianship over a family member or who are challenging a guardianship may be able to get free legal help through legal services programs or through lawyers who volunteer their services *pro bono* (free of charge). Contact your local area agency on aging or local bar association to find these resources in your community.

**Q. If I need a guardian, may I specify whom I want and do not want to play this role?**

**A.** Yes, but the court does not have an obligation to appoint the person you choose. You should do this as part of your general planning for incapacity. Sometimes even the best plans for incapacity fail (for example, if your agent under your durable power of attorney passes away after you become incapacitated), so it is a good idea to name in your planning documents one or two people whom you want as your guardian if that becomes necessary.

**Q. May the court remove a guardian?**

**A.** Yes, a guardian may be removed if the incapacitated person can prove that he or she has regained the capacity to make decisions. It can be hard to have a guardian removed. Therefore, if someone's incapacity may be temporary, consider whether some other legal tool (such as money management or a representative payee) will meet the person's need for help and make it unnecessary to get a guardianship.

A court also may remove a guardian who is not properly carrying out his or her responsibilities. Usually a new guardian will replace the person who is removed.

**Q. My elderly aunt needs some help with her affairs. She is not totally incapable. May a guardianship meet her needs?**

**A.** In most states, if a person has partial capacity his or her guardian may be given only partial power over his or her affairs. This is generally called a "limited guardianship." In your aunt's case, the court's guardianship order would identify the specific matters over which the guardian has authority. Your aunt would retain legal authority over all other areas of her life.

In all states, the courts try to ensure that a guardianship is the "least restrictive" alternative. This means that a guardianship restricts the ward as little as possible, letting the ward do whatever the disability allows.

Suppose your aunt can no longer manage her large estate, but she can handle her daily finances. A guardianship should let her keep control over everyday expenses. Or, let us say your aunt needs placement in a nursing home by the guardian. If she can say what type of nursing home she wants to live in, the guardian should honor those wishes.

Even when a limited guardianship is not feasible, the guardian should try to involve the ward in making decisions whenever possible.

### Health Care Decision-Making Issues

**Q. What is my right to control decisions about my health care?**

**A.** With few exceptions, our system of law has historically recognized the right of capable individuals to control decisions about what happens to their bodies. This includes the right to refuse any suggested medical treatment. We normally exercise this right by talking to our doctor and other health care providers. You have a right to:

- know all the relevant facts about your medical condition;
- know the pros and cons of different treatment options;
- talk to other doctors and get their opinions, too;
- say "yes" to treatment or care that you want, and "no" to treatment or care that you do not want.

Your doctor is the expert in medicine, but you are the expert in defining and applying your personal values and preferences.

**Q. What happens to my right to make medical decisions if I am too sick to decide?**

**A.** In an emergency, the law presumes consent. In all other instances, someone else must make decisions for you. The best way to ensure that decisions are made the way you would want and by the person you want, is to do an advance directive for health care *before* you become incapacitated.

**Q. What is an advance directive?**

**A.** An advance directive is generally a written statement, which you complete in advance of serious illness, about how you want medical decisions made. The two most common forms of advance directive are a "living will" and a "durable power of attorney for health care," although in many states you may combine these into a single advance directive document.

An advance directive allows you to state your choices for health care or to name someone to make those choices for you, if you become unable to make decisions about your medical treatment. In short, an advance directive enables you to have some control over your future medical care. You can say "yes" to treatment you want, or say "no" to treatment you don't want.

**Q. What is a living will?**

**A.** A living will is simply a written *instruction* spelling out any treatments you want or don't want in the event you are unable to speak for yourself and you are terminally ill or permanently unconscious. A living will simply says, "Whoever is deciding, please follow these instructions." It is called a "living will" because it takes effect while you are still alive. It is also called a "medical directive" or "declaration."

**Q. What is a durable power of attorney for health care?**

**A.** A durable power of attorney for health care (sometimes called "health care proxy") is a document that appoints someone of your choice to be your authorized agent (or "attorney-in-fact" or "proxy") for purposes of health

# DURABLE POWER OF ATTORNEY FOR HEALTH CARE

SAMPLE*

I, _____ hereby appoint: _____

name _____

home address _____

home telephone number _____

work telephone number _____

as my agent to make health care decisions for me if and when I am unable to make my own health care decisions. This gives my agent the power to consent to giving, withholding, or stopping any health care, treatment, service, or diagnostic procedure. My agent also has the authority to talk with health care personnel, get information, and sign forms necessary to carry out those decisions.

(1) If the person named as my agent is not available or is unable to act to act as my agent, then I appoint the following person(s) to serve in the order listed below:

1.  name _____

    home address _____

    home telephone number _____

    work telephone number _____

2.  name _____

    home address _____

    home telephone number _____

    work telephone number _____

By this document I intend to create a power of attorney for health care which shall take effect upon my incapacity to make my own health care decisions and shall continue during that incapacity.

*Check requirements of individual state statute.

## Durable Power of Attorney
## for Health Care (continued)

My agent shall make health care decisions as I direct below or as I make known to him or her in some other way.

    (a) Statement of desires concerning life-prolonging care, treatment, services, and procedures:

_____

_____

_____

_____

      BY SIGNING HERE I INDICATE THAT I UNDERSTAND THE PURPOSE AND EFFECT OF THIS DOCUMENT.

             I sign my name to this form on     _____

                                              (date)

My current home address:

_____

_____

_____

                        (You sign here)

## WITNESSES

    I declare that the person who signed or acknowledged this document is personally known to me, that he/she signed or acknowledged this durable power of attorney in my presence, and that he/she appears to be of sound mind and under no duress, fraud, or undue influence. I am not the person appointed as agent by this document, nor am I the patient's health care provider, or an employee of the patient's health care provider.

# Durable Power of Attorney
## for Health Care (continued)

First Witness

Signature: _____

Home Address: _____

Print Name: _____

Date: _____


Second Witness

Signature: _____

Home Address: _____

Print Name: _____

Date: _____

(At least one of the above witnesses must also sign the following declaration.)

I further declare that I am not related to the patient by blood, marriage, or adoption, and, to the best of my knowledge, I am not entitled to any part of his/her estate under a will now existing or by operation of law.

Signature: _____

Signature: _____


I further declare that I am not related to the patient by blood, marriage, or adoption, and, to the best of my knowledge, I am not entitled to any part of his/her estate under a will now existing or by operation of law.

Signature: _____

Signature: _____


Sample form is from *A Matter of Choice*, prepared for the U.S. Senate Special Committee on Aging.

# LIVING WILL

SAMPLE*

## LIVING WILL
### Declaration

Declaration made this _____ day of _____ 199__

I, _____ , being of sound mind, willfully and voluntarily make known my desires that my dying shall not be artificially prolonged under the circumstances set forth below.

(1) If at any time I should have an incurable injury, disease, or illness certified to be a terminal condition by two (2) physicians who have personally examined me, one of whom shall be my attending physician, and (2a) the physicians have determined that my death will occur whether or not life-sustaining procedures are utilized and, (3) where the application of life-sustaining procedures would serve only to artificially prolong the dying process, including provision of food and water, I direct that such procedures be withheld or withdrawn, and that I be permitted to die naturally with only the administration of medication or the performance of any medical procedure deemed necessary to provide me with comfort, care or to alleviate pain.

If I am unable to give directions regarding the use of such life-sustaining procedures, it is my intention that this declaration shall be honored by my family and physician(s) as the final expression of my legal right to refuse medical or surgical treatment and accept the consequences from such refusal.

I understand the full import of this declaration and I am emotionally and mentally competent to make this declaration.

Signed _____

Address _____

I believe the declarant to be of sound mind and I did not sign the declarant's signature above for or at the direction of the declarant. I am at least eighteen years of age and am not related to the declarant by blood or marriage, entitled to any portion of the estate of the declarant according to the laws of intestate succession of the _____ or under any will of the declarant or directly financially responsible for declarant's medical care. I am not the declarant's attending physician, an employee of the attending physician, or an employee of the health facility in which the declarant is a patient.

* Check requirements of individual state statutes.

Living Will
Declaration (continued)

Witness _____

Address _____

Witness _____

Address _____

Before me, the undersigned authority, on this _____ day of _____ , 199__ , personally appeared _____ , _____ , and _____ , known to me to be the Declarant and the witnesses, respectively, whose names are signed to the foregoing instrument, and who, in the presence of each other, did subscribe their names to the attached Declaration (Living Will) on this date, and that said Declarant at the time of execution of said Declaration was over the age of eighteen (18) years and of sound mind.

[Seal]
My commission expires:

_____
Notary Public

Sample form is from *A Matter of Choice*, prepared for the U.S. Senate Special Committee on Aging.

care decisions. You can give your agent as much or as little authority as you wish to make some or all health care decisions for you. And in most states, you can include the same kind of instructions that you would put in a living will.

### Q. Which is better: a living will or a durable power of attorney for health care?

**A.** The most efficient approach is to combine the living will and durable power of attorney for health care in one document. In most states you can do this. However, some states have two separate statutes with inflexible rules for these advance directives. In these states, having both may be the preferred approach.

On its own, a living will is a very limited document because under most state statutes living wills apply only to terminal illness or permanent coma. They address only life-sustaining medical treatments and not other treatment decisions, and they generally provide only general instructions that may be difficult to apply in complicated medical situations.

The durable power of attorney for health care is a more comprehensive and flexible document. It may cover any health care decision and is not limited to terminal illness or permanent coma. More importantly, it authorizes someone of your choice to weigh all the facts at the time a decision needs to be made and to legally speak for you according to any guidelines you provide.

### Q. Why can't I just tell my doctor what I want?

**A.** Telling your doctor and others what you want does provide evidence of your wishes to help guide decisions if you later become incapacitated, especially if your doctor writes your wishes down in your medical record. However, written advance directives are likely to carry more weight and to be followed.

### Q. What happens if I do not have an advance directive?

**A.** If you have not planned ahead by executing an advance directive, many states have family consent (or health surrogate) statutes that authorize someone else, typically family members in the order of kinship, to make some or all health care decisions. Even in the absence of such statutes, most doctors and health facilities routinely rely on family consent, as long as there are close family members present and *no* controversial decisions to be made.

However, without an advance directive, decisions may not be made the way you would want them, or by the person you would want to make them. Making an advance directive also benefits your family members, because it spares them the agony of having to guess what you would really want.

If no close family or other surrogate is available to make decisions for you, a court-appointed guardian may be necessary. This is an option of last resort.

### Q. How do I make an advance directive?

**A.** Requirements differ from state to state. Many states provide suggested forms, and in some cases, required language for advance directives. Most states have specific witnessing or notary requirements. Follow these requirements closely. Commonly, two witnesses are required; and often, several categories of persons are disqualified from serving as a witness, such as relatives, heirs, or health care providers.

In addition to the forms included in state statutes, a variety of other advance directive forms are available—some prepared by state bars or medical associations, some published by national organizations, others published in journals or local publications or do-it-yourself books. The most important point to remember about forms is that they are supposed to *aid*, and not take the place of, communication. Therefore, a form ought to be a *starting* point, not an *end* point, for making your wishes known. There is no ideal form. Any form you use should be personalized to reflect your values and preferences. Before doing an advance directive, talk with your doctor, family members, and advisors. This will help you to understand the medical possibilities you may face and clarify your values and choices.

**Q. What should my advance directive say?**

**A.** No one can tell you exactly what to say in your advance directive. However, the most important task to accomplish is to name someone you trust to act as your agent for health care decisions. If there is no one whom you fully trust to act as your agent, then it is best not to name an agent and, instead, only include instructions about the kinds of treatment you would want or not want if you became seriously ill.

Also consider addressing:

- *Alternate proxies.* Whenever possible, name one or more alternate or successor agents in case your primary agent is unavailable.

- *Life-sustaining treatments.* Are there any specific types of treatment you want or don't want in any circumstances? Your personal or family medical history may make certain conditions or treatments more likely.

- *Artificial Nutrition and Hydration.* Some states will presume that you want nutrition and hydration in all circumstances unless you instruct otherwise.

- *Organ donation.* In many states, you can include instructions about donating organs in your advance directive.

**Q. Can I change or terminate my advance directive?**

**A.** Yes, you always have the right to change or revoke your advance directive while you have the mental capacity to do so. Normally, you can revoke it orally or in writing in any way that indicates your intent to revoke. Your intent should be communicated to your agent, your family, and doctor.

If you want to change the document, it is best to execute a new document. The same formalities of signing and witnessing are required for changes.

**Q. Whom should I select as my agent or proxy for health decisions?**

**A.** The choice of agent is the most important decision you may make in doing an advance directive. Your agent will have great power over your health and personal care if you become incapacitated. Name a person whom you trust fully. If no such person is available, it may be best not to name a health care agent.

Find out who can and cannot be your agent under state law. Some states prohibit health care providers or health care facility employees from acting as your agent. Speak to the person you wish to appoint beforehand to explain your intentions and to obtain his or her agreement. Preferably, do not name co-agents, because it opens up the possibility of disagreement among agents. Instead, name alternate or successor agents, in case the primary agent is unavailable. If there is anyone whom you absolutely want to keep out of playing any role in your health care decisions, you may be able to expressly disqualify that person in your advance directive.

**Q. What do I do with my advance directive after completing one?**

**A.** Make sure someone close to you knows where it is located. If you have named an agent, give your agent a copy or the original. Also give your physician a copy and ask that it be made part of your permanent medical record. You may also want to make a small card for your purse or wallet which states that you have an advance directive and provides the name, phone number, and address of your agent or person who can provide a copy of it.

### Q. What if my doctor or hospital refuses to follow my advance directive?

**A.** First, find out ahead of time your doctor's views about advance directives and your specific wishes. If you disagree, you may wish to find a new doctor ahead of time.

Under federal law, most hospitals, nursing homes, and home health agencies must inform you of their policies about advance directives at the time of admission. Most will respect advance directives, but some may have restrictive policies. However, no facility can require you to have, or not have, an advance directive as a requirement of admission.

If you are in a condition to which your advance directive applies and your providers will not honor your directive, state law spells out their obligations. Usually, the provider must make a reasonable effort to transfer the patient to another provider who will respect the advance directive.

### Q. If I make an advance directive in one state, will it be recognized in others?

**A.** In many states, the law is unclear about honoring out-of-state directives. Realistically, providers will normally try to follow your stated wishes, regardless of the form you use or where you executed it. However, if you spend a great deal of time in more than one state (for example, summers in Wisconsin, winters in Arizona), you may want to consider executing an advance directive for each state. Or, find out whether one document meets the formal requirements of

> ### GETTING MORE INFORMATION ABOUT ADVANCE DIRECTIVES
>
> *Most state or area agencies on aging have information on advance directives, as do many state bar associations and medical societies. State-specific information and forms are also available from these two organizations:*
>
> *Choice in Dying*
> *200 Varick Street*
> *New York, NY 10014*
> *(212) 366-5540*
> *1-800-989-WILL*
>
> *American Association of Retired Persons*
> *Legal Counsel for the Elderly*
> *P.O. Box 96474*
> *Washington, DC 20090-6474*
> *(202) 434-2277 or (202) 434-2120*
> *or 2170*

both states. As a practical matter, you may want different health care agents if the same agent is not easily available in both locations.

### Q. Is a lawyer needed to do an advance directive?

**A.** No, a lawyer is not necessary, but a lawyer experienced in doing advance directives is very helpful. A lawyer can draft a personalized document that reflects your particular wishes and ensure that all legal formalities are followed. A lawyer is especially helpful if potential family conflicts or special legal or medical concerns are present.

## Abuse and Exploitation

### Q. What is elder abuse?

**A.** Elder abuse occurs when somebody neglects or abuses older people. The abuse can be physical or mental. Definitions of elder abuse vary from state to state, but generally include:

- physical abuse, such as hitting or shoving;
- sexual abuse, including fondling, sexual intercourse, and forced intimate contact of almost any sort;
- verbal and psychological abuse, such as screaming at the older person, name calling, and threatening the person;
- neglect, such as withholding food, shelter, medical care, medication, and other necessities from the older person; and
- restraint, such as keeping the person locked up.

Also included in most states is financial exploitation. This can range from outright theft to misuse of the older person's money. Cashing an older person's social security check and not using the money for the person's care is one example. Many states also would consider misusing credit cards and funds held in joint bank accounts as financial exploitation.

Every state has specific elder abuse laws. You can get details on laws and programs from your area or state agency on aging.

## SPOUSAL ABUSE

*Suppose your spouse often hits you and pushes you around. You are both over sixty-five, and it is harder for you to run away from him or her. Is there anything you may do after all these years?*

*You do not have to live with abuse, no matter what your age. Physical abuse is against the law. It is no more legal for your spouse to hit you than for a stranger to hit you.*

*Fortunately, more and more police departments and courts are sensitive to domestic violence and are willing to help victims. If your spouse strikes you, call the police and file a complaint. You also may ask the police to help you find a domestic violence shelter. You may stay there if you wish to leave your abusive home. If you do not want to leave your home, you may seek an order of protection through the courts. With such an order, you might have your spouse removed from the home, even though he or she may be the owner. Call the National Domestic Violence number at its Denver, Colorado, office at 303/839-1852 for information. See discussion beginning on page 64 for more helpful information.*

**Q. Is elder abuse just a problem for very frail old people who live in nursing homes?**

**A.** No, elder abuse is a real problem for many older people. Some victims are very frail and are unable to seek help on their own. However, many elder abuse victims are active older adults who cannot find a solution to this difficult problem.

Elder abuse can be a problem for both the rich and the poor. It does not strike only one race, social class, or economic level.

**Q. My son shares my apartment with me. Sometimes, when I forget things or get confused, he loses his temper, pushes me, and threatens to put me in a nursing home. Is this abuse?**

**A.** Yes. Many types of elder abuse occur within the home. Even if it only happens from time to time, it is still abuse. Seek help from your local social service agency on aging.

**Q. My neighbor is very old and sick. She depends on her daughter for shopping, cooking, and cleaning. However, her daughter often leaves the older woman without food and clean clothes. Is there anything I can do to help?**

**A.** Yes, you may report this neglect to your local elder abuse reporting agency. This may be your state or local agency on aging or human services department. You may even report abuse and neglect to the police.

You should not worry about being sued for making the report. Most states protect people who make such reports acting in good faith. You may even make an anonymous report.

**Q. My son is using all my money to buy illegal drugs. He is also running up large charges on my credit cards. (His name is on my credit-card accounts and my bank accounts.)**

**Since he is a co-owner of my home, I am afraid he will mortgage it or possibly even sell it to get more money. What can I do?**

**A.** Even if he has the legal right to reach your funds, you may protect yourself from this type of financial exploitation. Ask your bank to help you transfer funds to new accounts that your son may not access. Write all your credit card companies and ask them to remove your son's name from your accounts. Have them issue new credit cards to you.

Contact a lawyer to see what you must do to protect your home. A free legal services program for older or poor persons may be able to help you. Your local area agency on aging can help you find those resources.

Finally, seek help for yourself and for your son from a local social service agency. Many of them have experience in dealing with family difficulties of this sort. You do not have to allow your son's problems to overtake your own well-being and financial security.

**Q. My son and daughter-in-law live with me in my home. They are living rent-free and give me no money for household bills or food. I feel like they are taking advantage of me. Can someone help me?**

**A.** Yes. The situation you describe is surprisingly common. If the help you provide them is not what you wish, you are being exploited. Over 75 percent of all abusers are family members. You can seek help from an elder abuse program operating in your area. It can provide counseling and other assistance.

## LEGAL SERVICES

Most of the time people prefer to resolve disputes and manage affairs on their own. Sometimes, however, they will need expert help to protect their interests. Many older people already have lawyers who have helped them with legal issues in the past. Others will need to work with a lawyer for the first time. Help from a lawyer who is an expert about social security or estate planning may be necessary.

**Q. My 45-year-old son and I are co-owners of a condominium. We have had a falling-out over some lifestyle issues. Do I need a lawyer to get me out of the joint ownership? How can my son and I resolve our differences?**

**A.** You could hire a lawyer and go to court, but some other solutions may be faster, less expensive, and produce better and more lasting solutions.

Sometimes, problems that seem to be "legal" may be solved through other means. A social worker or psychotherapist can help with family problems. Some specialize in counseling for the elderly. You also can request help from a social service agency. Your local agency on aging can provide information on counseling. Mediation is another possible means of resolving your dispute. It may be available through your local court or through a private mediator. Your local bar association also may be able to make a referral. Another option is small claims court. Small claims court gives you the opportunity to get a legal judgment without hiring a lawyer and putting up with delays, if the dollar amount is under a certain amount, for example, $2,000. There is more information about small claims court on pages 27–29 of the chapter, "How the Legal System Works."

**Q. I am having a problem with a local department store over some invalid credit card charges. Do I really need a lawyer to resolve this issue?**

**A.** Before hiring a lawyer, consider other sources of help. You may be able to get help from a consumer protection agency run by your state or county. Many law schools offer legal clinics that can provide free or low-cost help. Some stores and utility companies have their own consumer complaint departments. Mediation and conciliation programs may be able to resolve your problem without requiring you to go to court or hire a lawyer. Check with the district attorney's office, city hall or the area agency on aging.

**Q. My insurance company won't pay a claim. Is there anything I can do short of suing?**

**A.** Many insurance programs provide an opportunity to provide additional information about the claim and may provide for impartial hearings. These may be done in writing or in person. Check with the Insurance Commissioner's Office in your state about how such disagreements might be resolved. Make sure your personal insurance agent is aware of the problem. He or she wants to retain your business and may provide extra help.

For problems in specific fields, bankers, accountants, real estate brokers, and stockbrokers may be able to help. But don't rely entirely on these individuals. If they can't resolve your problems, see a lawyer. A lawyer can discuss possible actions other than lawsuits.

### Finding a Lawyer

**Q. I want to hire a lawyer to represent me who understands my problems. Are there any legal services that serve just older people?**

**A.** Yes, older adults benefit from a wide variety of legal services. One small but growing area of specialization among private attorneys has become known as "elder law." Elder law attorneys focus on the legal needs of the elderly and work with a variety of legal tools and techniques to meet these needs. An elder law practitioner typically handles general estate planning matters and counsels clients about planning for

## BEFORE YOU HIRE A LAWYER

*If you need a lawyer, you should ask some questions before hiring one.*

- *Ask about the lawyer's experience and the kinds of law he or she specializes in.*
- *Ask who will be working on your case.*
- *Ask how fees are computed and what the lawyer's estimate is for the total time and cost of handling your case.*
- *Ask about what the attorney thinks is necessary to complete what you need and whether there are alternatives.*
- *Ask how you can participate (you can save money by doing some legwork yourself, such as providing complete documents and other information).*

## LEGAL HELP FOR THE HOMEBOUND

*If you are homebound and want to speak to a lawyer, call your local agency on aging. Request its help in contacting a lawyer who may be able to come to your home. If you live in a nursing home, you should speak with the nursing home ombudsman.*

incapacity with alternative decision-making documents. The attorney might assist the client in planning for possible long-term care needs, including nursing home care, locating appropriate types of care, coordinating public benefits and private resources to finance the cost of care, and working to ensure the client's right to quality care. The National Academy of Elder Law Attorneys (NAELA) can provide more information about attorneys who specialize in elder law. In addition, NAELA can provide consumer information about what questions to ask an attorney to make sure he/she can meet your legal needs. NAELA is located at 1604 N. Country Club, Tucson, AZ 85716; (602) 881-4005.

Publicly funded legal services are also available through programs funded under the Older Americans Act. These programs have attorneys, paralegals, and advocates who specialize in the rights of older persons. Your state or local agency on aging can refer you to these programs. State and local bar associations may also have information about programs for older persons that provide referrals or legal services on a *pro bono* basis. (*Pro bono* programs operate for the good of the public and do not charge lawyer's fees.)

**Q. Do I need to be poor to get any of these legal services?**

**A.** Some bar-sponsored programs may be limited to people with low incomes. Services offered through the Older Americans Act do not have income requirements, but must give priority to those in greatest social or economic need.

You can find out more by contacting your local agency on aging or bar association.

## SPECIAL SERVICES

Many special programs and services are designed to meet the needs and enrich the lives of older adults. Some are funded with tax dollars, especially under the Older Americans Act. Others have been developed through agencies or private enterprise.

## The Older Americans Act

**Q. What kinds of services does the Older Americans Act provide?**

**A.** The Act provides funding for a wide variety of services. These include education, social services, recreation, personal assistance, and counseling. It also makes available transportation, legal and financial assistance, career and retirement counseling, advocacy, long-term-care ombudsman services, services for the disabled, crime prevention, and volunteer services. In addition, your local area agency on aging can provide information and guide you to services in your community. These might include home helpers, money management agencies, or special discounts available to seniors. The specific services offered in each category vary with locale.

**Q. How can I find out about programs that might help me?**

**A.** Start at your local or state agency on aging, or call the "Eldercare Locator" at 1-800-677-1116. The toll-free assistance helps to identify community resources nationwide. Your local area agency on aging (AAA) can tell you

### YOUR AREA AGENCY ON AGING (AAA)

*One important product of the Older Americans Act is the nationwide network of area agencies on aging (AAA). Today, every area of the country is served by either an AAA or a state unit on aging. These agencies help local communities develop services specifically for older residents. The AAAs channel funds from the Older Americans Act to local communities.*

*Each AAA operates autonomously. All of them offer information and referral services to older adults. A few provide services directly, but most only coordinate services and provide assistance to designated service agencies in the local communities.*

*AAAs provide some funding and programming for local senior citizen centers, too. Programs include recreation, social activities, meals, and educational programs. Many service organizations offer programs at the senior centers as well as at other sites in the community. Additional funds are generally provided by local and state governments, as well as by such organizations as the United Way, private foundations, corporations, and individual donors.*

*You can feel confident in calling your AAA with almost any question about services in your neighborhood for older people. You can also go directly to a senior citizen center near you and ask for help. If staff there cannot provide it, ask them to put you in touch with someone in the AAA who can help.*

about the programs in your community that provide services to seniors. Most AAAs have written materials that describe resources in the community. Some have brochures that identify common problems that the elderly might face with resources and ways to solve the particular problem. The AAA may have additional resource materials published by community, state, and national organizations. The AAA in your community is a beginning resource for many questions by the elderly.

**Q. My Aunt Minnie is in a nursing home. I fear they do not treat her well. They may even tie her in a chair part of the day. Her husband is in a board care home, and they won't let him visit Aunt Minnie. Her younger sister lives in her own home. She had an aide and nurse to help her when she left the hospital, but they just stopped visiting her. How can I be certain that all three receive quality care?**

**A.** You should call the local long-term care ombudsman, an advocate who works to ensure that older Americans receive appropriate quality care.

**Q. I have an elderly neighbor who is finding it hard to manage on her own, especially with shopping and preparing meals. Are there services that could help her?**

**A.** Yes. Under the Older Americans Act, several types of nutrition programs and chore services are available to aid older adults. These include home-delivered hot meals, as well as meals served at a "congregate" dining site. There may be limitations placed on home-delivered services because of the great need and the limited amount of funding. The AAA or someone designated will do an assessment of need. The result of such an assessment may lead to the identification of more services that may be arranged for your neighbor.

**Q. I would like to use some of the services described here, but I really can't afford to pay for helpers or home-delivered meals. How can I use these programs?**

**A.** The Older Americans Act targets services to low-income and minority elderly, as well as to those who are frail or disabled. Many of the programs funded by the Act are provided without charge, although donations may be requested. Other programs offered by, arranged for, or provided through area agencies on aging may have a small fee or use a "sliding scale," where the fee is assessed on the basis of your ability to pay. Some programs are reimbursed by other governmental programs such as Medicaid. Do not let financial concerns keep you from benefiting from the variety of programs available.

**Q. My elderly mother has been diagnosed as having Alzheimer's disease. I would like to have her live with me. Are there services available to help me provide for her needs in my own home?**

**A.** Maybe. Although the Older Americans Act authorizes grants to be made to provide such services, they may or may not be available in your community. These may include in-home supportive services for victims of Alzheimer's disease or related conditions, and for the families of these victims. The services and the extent of services vary from place to place. They might include counseling and training for family care-givers, a needs assessment and assistance in locating and securing services, and case management. A case manager acts as an advisor, broker, and coordinator of services to help pull together an appropriate plan of care.

Services might also include homemaker and home health aides, in-home respite service so family care-givers can get away for short periods, assistance in adapting a home to meet the needs of an impaired older person, and chore maintenance.

A second very important resource is the state or local Alzheimer's Association. Local chapters can be found through the National Headquarters of the Alzheimer's Association at 919 North Michigan Ave., Ste. 1000, Chicago, IL 60611, 1-800-272-3900. The Alzheimer's Association's local chapters provide extensive knowledge of resources for families of Alzheimer's victims in your specific community. Chapters also offer support from others whose loved ones are victims.

### Education and Job Training

**Q. I would like help in getting a job, since I feel able to continue working even though I have retired. Can I get help under the Older Americans Act?**

**A.** Yes. Through the Community Service Employment for Older Americans program you may be able to get help in finding a job or training opportunity. These may be part-time positions, at minimum wage. In general, this program is designed for lower-income seniors, so income and resource eligibility requirements may apply.

**Q. I'm retired and I'm looking for new experiences, but I don't really want to enroll in a school. Is there anything for me?**

**A.** Many universities, local junior colleges, and museum education programs provide special programs, reduced fees, and auditing of classes. A call to the one closest to you can provide information about such programs. The Elderhostel program meets the needs of people like you. Elderhostel is a not-for-profit agency offering educational programs for adults aged sixty years and older. Through an international network of colleges and universities, Elderhostel is able to offer low-cost residential academic programs both in America and abroad. Courses offered have included "The Literary Heritage of Oxford," offered in Oxford, England; "Political Controversies, Judicial Politics and You"; and lectures on Greek Island society, in conjunction with a cruise of the Greek Isles. The courses are usually taught by university faculty, and run from one to three weeks. Most of the time, participants are housed in dormitories. On special trips, other arrangements may be made. Students may expect to spend approximately three hours a day in class, with many field trips and opportunities for sightseeing. For more information, you can write to Elderhostel at 75 Federal St., Boston, MA 02110-1941, or call (617) 426-8056.

Elderhostel, in cooperation with the Experiment in International Living, also offers a "host family" program, where older adults from the U.S. have a chance to live with a host family in a foreign country. The only requirement is that the participant be over sixty years old, or be accompanied by someone over sixty.

# WHERE TO GET MORE INFORMATION

## General Resources

**Local:**

For most older people, their main resource is their area agency on aging (AAA). It can supply details and referrals on many topics. To find your local area agency on aging or the one serving someone you are trying to help, call the toll-free **Eldercare Locator, 1-800-677-1116,** or write to:

National Association of Area Agencies on Aging
1112 16th St., NW, Suite 100
Washington, DC 20036
(202) 296-8130

Some municipalities and townships also have their own departments or commissions on aging. Look in the telephone book or call your city or municipal general information number.

### State:

State agencies on aging oversee the activities of local area agencies on aging. These state agencies often have valuable resource materials and other statewide information about your rights or services available. To find your state agency on aging, ask your local agency, or contact:

National Association of State Units on Aging
1225 I Street, NW, Suite 725
Washington, DC 20005
(202) 898-2578

### National:

Many associations promote the interests of older adults. The best known—and the largest—is the American Association of Retired Persons (AARP). You can join if you are over age 50. AARP has regional and local groups nationwide, and it provides booklets and other resources on virtually any topic of interest to older persons. Look in the telephone directory for the nearest group. Or contact:

American Association of Retired Persons
601 E Street, NW
Washington, DC 20049
(202) 434-2277

Other associations also promote the interests of older persons. They also provide information and education to senior citizens. These include:

National Council on the Aging
409 Third Street, SW, Suite 200
Washington, DC 20024
(202) 479-1200

Older Women's League
666 11th Street, NW, Suite 700
Washington, DC 20001
(202) 783-6686

National Council of Senior Citizens
1331 F Street, NW
Washington, DC 20004
(202) 347-8800

## Consumer Issues

The Consumer's Resource Handbook can help you locate the proper source of help for many different consumer problems. It includes a directory of federal agencies. The handbook is available free of charge from the Consumer Information Center, Pueblo, CO 81002, telephone (719) 948-3334.

The Federal Trade Commission (FTC) has a variety of consumer protection programs and publications. To request reports, brochures, or a list of publications, contact:

Public Reference Branch, Room 130
Federal Trade Commission
Washington, DC 20580
(202) 326-2222

Consumer problems involving the U.S. mail in any way can be brought to the attention of:

U.S. Postal Service
Consumer Complaints
900 Brentwood Road, NE
Washington, DC 20066-7203
(202) 636-1400

The National Consumers League (NCL) publishes a variety of booklets and guides on several topics of importance to consumers. NCL is a not-for-profit membership group, conducting research, education, and advocacy on consumer issues. Call or write them at:

National Consumers League
815 Fifteenth Street, NW, Suite 928-N
Washington, DC 20005
(202) 639-8140

## Credit

Many federal agencies enforce the Equal Credit Opportunity Act. However, you generally can direct questions to the Federal Trade Commission (FTC). To find out how to contact the FTC, see "Where to Get More Information" at the end of the "Consumer Credit" chapter.

## Discrimination Based on Age or Disability

You should direct questions regarding age discrimination in the workplace to a local office of the Equal Employment Opportunity Commission (EEOC). Look in the "U.S. Government" section of the telephone directory for a listing or call its nationwide toll-free number: 1-800-669-4000. You may also write to:

Equal Employment Opportunity Commission
1801 L St., NW
Washington, DC 20507

Housing discrimination questions can be answered by your local office of the U.S. Department of Housing and Urban Development (HUD). The national office of HUD offers information on problems unique to the elderly. For assistance with housing discrimination, call:

HUD's Fair Housing Complaint Hot Line
1-800-424-8590

For problems involving discrimination based on disability in areas of employment, public accommodations, telecommunications, or public transit, contact:

Office on the Americans with Disabilities Act
U.S. Department of Justice
Civil Rights Division
P.O. Box 66118
Washington, DC 20035-6116
(202) 514-0301 (voice)
(202) 514-0381 (TDD)

## Education and Training

A wide variety of local and state agencies might be able to provide details on educational and training programs for the elderly. For information about federal programs, you can direct questions to the U.S. Department of Education. Or you also can contact the specific government agency, such as the U.S. Department of Labor, that provides funding for the particular program in which you are interested.

For information on Elderhostel, call or write:

Elderhostel
75 Federal Street
Boston, MA 02110-1941
(617) 426-8056

## Elder Abuse

Elder abuse programs exist in many areas. For details, contact your local area agency on aging or your state unit on aging. If you need immediate help, call the police. They have the power to step in and investigate immediately. They may also have a special senior citizen's unit.

## Health and Long-Term Care

For brochures and other information about Medicare, contact your local Social Security Administration office. It also publishes a free booklet on

Medicare supplemental (or "medigap") insurance, *Guide to Health Insurance for People with Medicare*. This is available from local Social Security Administration offices or from:

The Consumer Information Center
Department 70
Pueblo, CO 81009
(719) 948-3334

A variety of publications on health insurance, long-term care, and related financial issues is available from AARP, listed earlier, and from the United Seniors Health Cooperative, a not-for-profit consumer organization. For information, call or write:

United Seniors Health Cooperative
1331 H Street, NW, Suite 500
Washington, DC 20005-4706
(202) 393-6222

Information about the Medicaid program is usually available from local offices on aging, publicly funded legal services programs, and your local government's health or social services department.

For information about resources relating to Alzheimer's disease and related disorders, contact:

The Alzheimer's Association
919 N. Michigan Avenue, Suite 1000
Chicago, IL 60611
1-800-272-3900

If you have questions or problems concerning nursing homes, contact your state or local long-term care ombudsman program. Every state operates an ombudsman program through its state office on aging.

If your interest is in health policy and advocacy, you can obtain a variety of resource materials and information from:

Families USA
1334 G Street, NW
Washington, DC 20005
(202) 628-3030

## Health-Care Advance Directives

Health care advance directive information and forms may be available from your state or local area agency on aging, bar association, or hospital. Health care advance directives include living wills, durable powers of attorney for health care, and other instructions for health care decision making. Nationally, Choice in Dying offers free health care advance directives complying with the legal requirements of each state (and the District of Columbia). Contact its office at:

> Choice in Dying
> 200 Varick Street
> New York, NY 10014
> (212) 366-5540 or 1-800-989-WILL.

AARP and the American Bar Association Commission on Legal Problems of the Elderly offer a booklet on health-care powers of attorney. Single copies are free. To order, write to:

> AARP Fulfillment
> (Stock Number D13895)
> 601 E Street, NW
> Washington, DC 20049

AARP's Legal Counsel for the Elderly program also publishes *Planning for Incapacity: A Self-Help Guide.* An individual guide is written for each state and contains legal forms for health care advance directives and instructions. For information on costs and ordering, contact:

> Legal Counsel for the Elderly/AARP
> P.O. Box 96474
> Washington, DC 20090-6474
> (202) 434-2120, 2170, or 2277

### Housing

The American Association of Homes for the Aging (AAHA) offers information on retirement housing. It publishes *The Consumer's Directory of Continuing Care Retirement Communities.* You can call (202) 783-2242, or write to:

> American Association of Homes for the Aging
> AAHA Publications
> 901 E Street, NW, Suite 500
> Washington, DC 20004

The American Association of Retired Persons (AARP) maintains a computer database of retirement housing and will provide members a free printout for your geographic area. Request a printout (specify your geographic area) from:

> Membership Communications
> AARP
> 601 E Street, NW
> Washington, DC 20049
> (202) 434-2277

AARP offers other excellent materials on housing options, including:

- "Home-Made Money: A Consumer's Guide to Home-Equity Conversions" (stock number D12894). This guide discusses how to benefit from the equity you have built up in your home while you remain in your home.

## Insurance

Your basic resources on insurance are your state's insurance office and, in many states, your state office on aging. Health insurance is discussed below.

## Legal Assistance

You can get details on legal assistance from various sources. Your area agency on aging should be able to tell you about legal services funded by the Older Americans Act. Local or state bar associations can direct you to legal aid and *pro bono* services. Some bar associations also operate lawyer referral services. Many bar associations also publish handbooks on the legal rights of the elderly. In addition, you can obtain other information from:

American Bar Association
Commission on Legal Problems of the Elderly
1800 M Street, NW, Suite 200
Washington, DC 20036
(202) 331-2297

National Academy of Elder Law Attorneys
1604 N. Country Club
Tucson, AZ 85716
(606) 881-4005
(602) 325-7925 (Fax)

Legal Counsel for the Elderly/AARP
601 E Street, NW
Washington, DC 20049
(202) 434-2120, 2170, or 2277

## Medigap

For an annual Medicare and Medigap Update, write to United Seniors Health Cooperative, 1331 H St., NW, Suite 500, Washington, DC 20005.

## Retirement Benefits and Pensions

A source of facts about pensions, particularly as the Employee Retirement Income Security Act (ERISA) affects them, is the Department of Labor (DOL). The DOL can provide a wide variety of literature and information on ERISA. For assistance, call (202) 219-6666, or write to:

Pension and Welfare Benefits Administration
U.S. Department of Labor
Division of Technical Assistance and Inquiries
200 Constitution Avenue, NW
Washington, DC 20210

Another resource is the Pension Rights Center. It is a public interest group that works to protect the pension rights of workers, retirees, and their families. Several publications are available. To contact the center, call (202) 296-3776, or write to:

Pension Rights Center
918 16th St., NW, Suite 704
Washington, DC 20006

Brochures and other information on social security retirement benefits or benefits for disabled persons, dependents, and survivors are available from your local Social Security Administration office. Again, AARP has useful material on all these topics.

## Reverse Mortgages

Write to AARP Fulfillment (EE0597) for "Home-Made Money: A Consumer's Guide to Home Equity Conversions," stock no. D12894, and "Reverse Mortgage Lenders List," stock no. D13253. The address is P.O. Box 22796, Long Beach, CA 90801-5796.

Write to the National Center for Home Equity Conversion, Suite 115, 7373 147th St. West, Apple Valley, MN 55124 for a copy of "Reverse Mortgage Locator," with information on lenders. It also offers a book on reverse mortgages, *Retirement Income on the House.*

## Tax Benefits

The IRS is a useful source of information on tax questions. The IRS's tele-tax service has recorded tax information on 140 topics. You can find the toll-free 800 number for your state by calling the IRS office in your area. Topics of interest to older persons include pensions and annuities, power-of-attorney information, lump-sum distributions, and social security and equivalent railroad retirement benefits.

In addition, IRS representatives are available to help you with your tax questions. Consult your local IRS office to find out about assistance by phone, by mail, or in person.

The IRS also publishes a number of free pamphlets dealing with common tax questions. They are available from your local IRS office. The basic Internal Revenue Service (IRS) publication for older Americans is Publication 554, *Tax Information for Older Americans.*

# Estate Planning

# INTRODUCTION

ESTATE PLANNING IS PLANNING FOR DEATH. We're all a little squeamish about death, especially when we're the ones involved. This discomfort can lead to procrastination that might account for the fact that only about two out of every five Americans have a will.

The fact that so few Americans have a will is ironic. We spend our lives working hard to earn enough money and property to make the lives of our children and spouses, friends and business associates happier, wealthier, and more secure than our own. And, yet, most of us fail to do the one thing that's essential to make sure those we care about receive the fruits of our labor—we fail to plan for them because we fail to plan our estates.

Estate planning pays real dividends—in results achieved, in dollars saved, and, most importantly, in security and peace of mind. Moreover, estate planning doesn't have to be expensive, traumatic, or, even, especially time-consuming. Estate planning often saves money by reducing taxes and the expenses of death. It saves time by speeding the process by which property passes from you, at your death, to your family, friends, or anyone else you want to have it. Finally, estate planning allows you to make the crucial decisions about the disposition of your property and the care of your family. In a very real sense, estate planning makes you the boss.

This chapter answers, in nonlegal terms, commonly asked questions about estate planning. Keep in mind that the rules governing estate planning, wills, probate, and trusts are determined by state law, which means that the principles discussed in this chapter may not apply in your state. Similarly, the costs of estate planning vary depending on such factors as where you live, the nature of your estate, and your particular needs. As you begin the process of estate planning, consult one or more attorneys with experience in this area of the law. After a consultation, they can give you a good idea of the cost of ensuring that your estate is in order for today and tomorrow.

## Q. *What is an "estate"?*

**A.** Almost everyone, single or married, has an estate. It consists of all your property, including for example:

- real estate, for example, a home;
- personal property such as cars and furniture;
- intangible property such as bank accounts, stocks and bonds, and pension and social security benefits, and the face value of your life insurance policies.

An estate plan is your direction for the distribution of all your property after you die.

## Q. *Isn't a will all I need?*

**A.** Not necessarily. While a will often is the most important piece of an estate plan, it's not the only part. These days, it's common for a person to have a number of options, in addition to or in place of a will, for distributing property. Pensions, life insurance, joint ownership, and trusts can be used in lieu of a will to transfer property upon your death. As you plan your estate, you might want to consider these, or similar alternatives, to the traditional will.

### Q. How can an estate plan distribute my property quickly?

**A.** You want your beneficiaries to receive promptly the property you've left them as part of your estate plan. Options include: gifts made before you die; insurance or pension benefits paid directly to them as the named beneficiaries; a living trust; using expedited will probate available in many states for smaller estates; and taking advantage of laws in certain states that provide partial payments to beneficiaries while the estate is in probate.

Estate planning can also minimize expenses by keeping the cost of transferring property to beneficiaries as low as possible. For example, choosing a competent executor for your estate and giving the executor the necessary authority to carry out your directives can save money and simplify the administration of your estate.

### Q. Would an estate plan help if I become mentally or physically incapacitated?

**A.** Yes. During estate planning, many people also plan for possible mental or physical incapacity. This planning is especially important for a single person who may want to designate someone other than a relative to manage his or her property and affairs in the event of incapacity. A living will or a durable health-care power of attorney can enable you to pick someone to make decisions for you about medical treatment, including decisions about using or terminating life support systems.

You can select someone to direct your financial affairs in the event of your incapacity by executing a durable power of attorney for financial matters. This type of power of attorney gives a specific named individual access to your assets and the authority to manage those assets, to pay bills, and to take any other action needed to keep your financial house in order during your incapacity. See the chapter titled "Rights of Older Americans" beginning on page 571 for more information on living wills and similar legal documents designed for the purpose of providing health care in the event of incapacity.

### Q. I have a business. Should I account for it in my estate plan?

**A.** Yes. An estate plan can make sure your business is not thrown into chaos upon your death or incapacity. You can provide for an orderly succession and continuation of its affairs by spelling out in your plan what will happen to your interest.

### Q. Can I help a favorite cause through my estate planning?

**A.** Yes. Your estate plan can help support religious, educational, and other charitable causes, either during your lifetime or upon your death, while at the same time take advantage of tax laws designed to encourage private philanthropy.

### Q. Can an estate plan help reduce taxes on my estate?

**A.** Yes. Every dollar your estate has to pay in estate taxes is a dollar that your beneficiaries won't receive. A good estate plan gives the maximum allowed by law to your beneficiaries and the minimum to the tax collector. This becomes especially important as your estate approaches the magic number of $600,000, the current level at which the federal estate tax becomes payable.

### Q. Isn't an estate plan just for old people?

**A.** Emphatically not. One glance at the news demonstrates that far too many young and middle age people die suddenly or, what is even more likely, become mentally or physically incapacitated. An estate plan can be tailored to anticipate both of these contingencies.

### Q. When should I plan my estate?

**A.** The time to plan for death or disability is when you're healthy. As a general rule, people make better decisions when they feel good and tend to make worse decisions when coping with mental or physical stress, strain, or illness. Moreover, a so-called deathbed will, or one made by someone whose mental competence is questionable, may invite a legal challenge.

It's also important not to procrastinate. Don't put off making your estate plan until your estate reaches a certain level or value. Even if you don't have as many assets now as you expect to have someday, it's easy to update the plan every few years as your assets increase and your life circumstances change. If you put in a few hours now learning the basics and setting up your plan, you'll know you're covered in case of an unexpected event.

### Q. My spouse doesn't like to talk about finances or estate planning. What should I do?

**A.** You can't plan your estate if you don't know all the facts about your family's assets. Yet many people don't have basic information about their spouse's income—how much is earned, what benefits he or she is entitled to, what his or her assets and debts are, and where assets are invested.

You need to know this information when planning your estate. It's especially important to know who holds title to real estate and what is known as titled personal property, for example, automobiles, boats, and recreational vehicles. It is also important for you to know the beneficiaries of your spouse's insurance policies, pension plans, retirement accounts, and other similar assets.

### Q. What can I do to minimize the costs of estate planning?

**A.** A lawyer or other professional often charges by the hour for the amount of work put into the estate plan. Ask about fees at your first consultation and inquire about how much your total estate plan might cost. If your legal advisor charges by the hour, the more time you invest in locating relevant documents and putting your wishes in writing, the less preparatory work your advisor will have to do. This should go a long way toward reducing the final cost of your estate plan.

## WORKING WITH A LAWYER

### Q. Should I consult an attorney as I plan my estate?

**A.** If your estate is relatively small and your objectives straightforward, you might plan your estate mostly on your own, with the help of the ABA's forthcoming *Guide to Estate Planning* and other resource materials, using professional help largely for tasks like writing a will or trust. However, a caveat is in order. "How-to" guides can assist you as you start the estate-planning process. But in these matters, certainty, above all, is golden. So, before finalizing anything, consult with an experienced estate lawyer to make sure that your property goes exactly where you want it to; that your family is protected fully; and that you are assured of proper care in the case of incapacity. As a general rule, the larger your estate, the more important it is to consult an attorney.

### Q. How do I find a lawyer to help me plan my estate?

**A.** The trust department of your local bank can give you the names of one or more attorneys experienced in estate planning. If you have a friend or relative who has executed a will

## INFORMATION YOU NEED TO PLAN YOUR ESTATE

*For an individual with a sizable estate or for the person who wants to divide his or her estate among many people, it's helpful to know as much of the following information as possible. If you use a lawyer, you can save the lawyer's time and your money by having this information readily available.*

- *the names, addresses, and birth dates of all persons, whether or not related to you, you expect to name in your will;*
- *the name, address, and telephone number of the person(s) you expect to name as the executor of your will;*
- *if you have minor children, the names, addresses, and telephone numbers of possible guardians;*
- *amount and source of your principal income and other income such as interest and dividends;*
- *amount, source, and beneficiaries, if any, of your retirement benefits, including IRAs, pensions, Keogh accounts, government benefits, and profit-sharing plans;*
- *amount, source, and beneficiaries, if any, of other financial assets such as bank accounts, annuities, and loans due you;*
- *amount of your debts, including mortgages, installment loans, and business debts, if any;*
- *a list (with approximate values) of valuable property you own, including real estate, jewelry, furniture, collections, heirlooms and other assets;*
- *a list and description of jointly owned property and the names of co-owners;*
- *any documents that might affect your estate plan, including prenuptial agreements, marriage certificates, divorce decrees, recent tax returns, existing wills and trust documents, property deeds, and so on;*
- *location of any safe deposit boxes and an inventory of the contents of each.*

recently, ask for the name of the attorney. Another source is your local bar association's referral program, which lists attorneys knowledgeable in estate practice.

Attorneys often offer an initial consultation without charge. At this get-acquainted session, you can ask about the attorney's experience in estate planning and get a firm idea of fees.

Be comfortable with the attorney you choose! A good estate attorney will have to ask questions about many private matters; it's important for you to be comfortable discussing these personal considerations. Frank and open communication with your attorney is important in ensuring that you get an estate plan that fits *your* needs.

### Q. How does the process of estate planning work?

**A.** Don't just expect to pile some papers on your lawyer's desk and have a will or trust magically appear in a few weeks. Preparing these documents is seldom as simple as filling in blanks on a form. Most people will meet with their attorney several times, with more extensive estates requiring more consultations.

At the first meeting, be prepared to tell your lawyer about some rather intimate details of your life—how much money you have; how many more children you plan to have; which relatives, friends, or other associates you want to get more or less of your estate. Bring as many of the documents listed in the accompanying sidebar (page 655) as possible.

After talking with you, your attorney will explain the options the law provides for accomplishing your estate-planning goals. Based on your direction, your attorney can draft a will or trust or both, depending on your circumstances.

It's a good idea to ask your attorney to send you a draft of the will or trust document for your review. After examining the draft, ask for any clarification you might need and provide any necessary changes to effectuate your wishes. This information will assist your attorney in preparing the finalized will or trust document which, upon signing, will become legally effective to distribute your estate.

---

## WILLS

### Q. Do I have to have a lawyer to write my will?

**A.** No. If your will meets the legal requirements established by the law of your state, it is valid, whether or not you wrote it with a lawyer's help. However, a lawyer can help ensure that your will is more than just valid. Your lawyer can make sure that the will does what you really want it to do. It is for this reason that more than 85 percent of Americans who have wills worked with a lawyer.

### Q. Can't I just use one of the books or computer programs I've seen to write my will without a lawyer involved?

**A.** For small estates involving little money and other assets and in which everything is to go to few people, a well-done book or software program might enable you to make your will without hiring a lawyer. However, keep in mind that it's not always easy to determine whether a given book or kit is up-to-date and thorough, especially since the laws governing estates vary from state to state. Do-it-yourself books, some lawyers say, have caused more work for them, and bills for estates, than they have avoided. In addition, filling in the blanks often takes a lot more thought and knowledge than it seems.

The consequences of a mistake—an invalid will or a contested will—make do-it-yourself will writing too risky for most estates. The complexities of many wills and the many tax considerations involved makes a lawyer's expertise important if not invaluable.

You most certainly should use a lawyer if you own a business, if you have a complicated family situation (for example, children from more than one marriage), or if you anticipate a challenge to the will. And, before deciding to write your own will, you might want to at least consult a lawyer. You might conclude that you can get the plan you want and the accompanying peace of mind at a price you can more than afford.

### Q. If I use a lawyer, how much should I expect to pay?

**A.** Among other factors, it depends on the size and complexity of your estate, the average legal fees for estate planning in your area, and your lawyer's experience. You'll pay more if your estate exceeds $600,000 and you are interested in minimizing federal estate taxes and state inheritance taxes.

Many lawyers will see you for an initial consultation at no charge. By taking advantage of this opportunity, you'll be able to discuss fees based on the specifics of your financial situation and exactly how you wish to distribute your estate.

If you are among the 74 million Americans belonging to group legal service plans, usually through employers, unions, or membership groups such as the American Association of Retired Persons, you might be able to consult a lawyer for a smaller-than-normal fee. Group plans enable members to obtain a variety of legal services, including will preparation, at reduced cost.

### Q. Why should I go to the trouble of writing a will?

**A.** A will lets you control what happens to your property.

If you have minor children, a will enables you to designate the best available person to care for them after your death. Through a will you can nominate a legal guardian for your children and name an executor to handle the distribution of your estate to your designated beneficiaries.

### Q. What happens if I die without a will?

**A.** If you die without a will, your property still must be distributed. The probate court in your area will appoint someone (who may or may not be the person you would have wanted to comb through all your affairs) as the administrator of your estate who will be responsible for distributing your property in accordance with the law of your state.

The probate court will closely supervise the administrator's work and may require the administrator to post bond to ensure that your estate will not be charged with the costs of any errors made by the administrator. Of course, all this involvement may be much more expensive

## THE VIDEO WILL

*More and more people are preparing a "video will," which is a videocassette showing them reading the will aloud and, perhaps, explaining why certain gifts were made and others not made. The video recording might also show the execution of a will. Should a disgruntled relative decide to challenge the will, the video can provide compelling proof that the testator, that is, the person making the will, really intended to make a will, was mentally competent to do so, and observed the formalities of execution. You should consult a lawyer before making such a video and find out whether your state's law permits a video will to substitute for, rather than supplement, a properly prepared written will.*

than administering an estate under a will—and these costs come out of your estate before it is distributed. Some of your property may have to be sold to pay these costs, instead of going to family or friends.

### Q. Who gets my property if I die without a will?

**A.** By not leaving a valid will or trust, or by not transferring your property in some other way before death, you've left it to the law of your state to write your "will" for you. In the absence of a will, the law of your state has made certain judgments about who should receive a

# Property Distribution After Dying Without a Will

The laws governing the distribution of property belonging to a person who dies intestate (that is, without a will) can be very complicated, reaching out to the descendants of the deceased's great-grandparents and even beyond.

The example below is based on the rules of descent and distribution in Illinois. It is offered only as a simplified version of the law. It is not intended to be representative of other states. This example merely demonstrates that the failure to leave a properly drawn will can lead to a distribution of property that is unintended by the deceased.

| *Survivors* | *Shares to Survivors of Illinois Intestate Deceased* |
| --- | --- |
| Spouse and child or descendant | 50 percent to spouse and 50 percent to child or descendant. |
| Child or descendant; no spouse | 100 percent to child or descendant. |
| Spouse, no descendant | 100 percent to spouse. |
| Parent; brother or sister; no spouse; no child or descendant | 100 percent in equal shares among parents, brothers, and sisters. If only one parent survived the deceased, that parent receives a double share. Descendants of a deceased brother or sister take their ancestor's share, *per stirpes.*[1] |
| Grandparent or descendant of grandparent; no spouse; no child or descendant; no parent; no brother, sister, or descendant of brother or sister | 50 percent to maternal grandparent, or if none, to descendant of maternal grandparent, and 50% to paternal grandparent, or if none, to descendant of paternal grandparent. If there is no grandparent and no descendant of a grandparent of one category, 100 percent to grandparent or descendant of grandparent of the other category. |
| Great-grandparent or descendant of great-grandparent; no grandparent or descendant of grandparent; no spouse; no child or descendant; no parent; no brother, sister, or descendant of brother or sister | Distribution to great-grandparent and descendant of great-grandparent is similar to example immediately above. |
| None of the above | 100 percent to nearest kindred by rules of civil law. |
| No known kindred | 100 percent to county. |

[1] Descendants of a deceased child, brother, sister, grandparent, or great-grandparent take *per stirpes* the share that their ancestor would have taken. Suppose, for example, that the deceased (Grandparent A) had two children (Parents A and B), both of whom died before the deceased. In addition, one of the deceased's children (Parent A) left two children and the other child of the deceased (Parent B) left three children. In that case, the two children of Parent A would each take one half of their parent's share and the three children of Parent B would each take one third of their parent's share.

SOURCE: Morton John Barnard, attorney, Miller, Shakman, Hamilton, Kurtzon, and Schlifke, Chicago, Illinois.

## ALTERNATIVES TO WRITTEN WILLS

*The best rule to follow in creating a will is "put it in writing." By executing a written will, you are ensuring that your intentions are clear and that you have a degree of certainty about the exact distribution of your estate upon your death.*

*As with all general rules, there are exceptions. Some states recognize oral wills or holographic wills—handwritten, unwitnessed wills—only under extremely limited circumstances.*

*A few states have statutory wills that are created by state law and allow people to fill in the blanks on a standard form. However, these form wills are designed for simple estates and provide little flexibility. They will not be useful if you have a large estate or if your wishes are complicated.*

*Also keep this caveat in mind—make sure your state treats as valid these alternatives to the traditional, time-tested written will and then make certain that you follow all the steps the law requires.*

decedent's property. Those judgments may or may not bear any relationship to the judgments you would have made if you had prepared a will or executed a trust.

As a general rule, state law gives your property to the persons most closely related to you by blood, marriage, or adoption. As a result, your hard-earned money might end up with relatives who don't need it, while others, whether or not related to you, who might be in greater need or who are more deserving, are passed over. In the unlikely event that you have no relatives or in the event that your relatives cannot be located after diligent efforts, your property will go to the state—a big reason to have a will or trust.

### Q. Does a will cover all my property?

**A.** Probably not. It is easy to think that a will covers all of your property. But because property can be passed to others by gift, contract, joint tenancy, life insurance, or other methods, a will might best be viewed as just one of many ways of determining how and to whom your estate will be distributed at your death.

The various methods of distributing your estate are discussed in this chapter. In the meantime, keep in mind the kinds of property that a will may not cover and include them in your estate planning.

### Q. Are there any special legal formalities required to make my will legally valid?

**A.** After you've drawn up your will, there remains one step: the formal legal procedure called "executing the will." This requires witnesses to your signing the will. In almost all states, the signature of at least two witnesses is required. In some states, a will is not deemed legally valid unless the witnesses appear in

## THE ESSENTIALS OF A VALID WILL

*To be valid, your will doesn't have to conform to a specific formula. However, certain elements must be present and are set forth below:*

1. *You must be of legal age—18 in almost all states.*

2. *You must be mentally competent, which means that you know you are executing a will, know the general nature and extent of your property, and know your descendants and other relatives who would ordinarily be expected to share in your estate.*

3. *The will must have a substantive provision that disposes of property and it must indicate your intent to make the document your final word on what happens to your property.*

4. *With rare exceptions as, for example, when death is imminent, a will must be written.*

5. *You must sign the will unless illness, accident, or illiteracy prevents it. In these circumstances, you can designate someone to sign for you at your direction and in your presence.*

6. *In almost all states, your signature must be witnessed by at least two adults who understand that they are witnessing a will and are competent to testify in court. In most states, the witnesses should be disinterested, that is, not named in your will as receiving any part of your estate. As a general rule, the witnesses watch you sign the will. Each witness then signs the will in the presence of the other.*

   *If your will doesn't meet these conditions, it might be disallowed by a court and your estate would then be distributed according to any prior will or, if there is no will, in accordance with state law.*

court and testify about witnessing the will. However, in a growing number of states, a will can be "self-proved"—that is, the will is accepted as valid and the witnesses will not be required to appear and testify if, at the time the will was executed, the witnesses' signatures were notarized and each witness submits an affidavit attesting to the fact that he or she witnessed the signing of the will.

### Q. Who shouldn't be witnesses?

**A.** The witnesses should have no potential conflict of interest, that is, they should not be people who receive gifts under the will or who might benefit from your death. Thus, in some states, a will is invalid if witnessed by a beneficiary. In other states, a beneficiary can serve as a witness but, in doing so, might lose whatever property or interest you left to that person in your will.

## Q. In my will, can I leave my property to anyone I wish?

**A.** In general, you can pick the people you want your property to go to and leave it to them in whatever proportions you want, but there are a few exceptions. For example, a surviving husband or wife may have the right to take a fixed share of the estate regardless of the will. Some states limit how much you can leave to a charity if you have a surviving spouse or children, or if you die soon after making the provision.

Some people try to make their influence felt beyond the grave by attaching bizarre or excessive conditions to a gift made in the will. Most lawyers will advise you not to try this. Courts don't like such conditions, and you're inviting a will contest if you try to tie multiple, unreasonable conditions to a gift. For the most part, though, it's your call.

## Q. Can I disinherit my spouse and children?

**A.** You usually can't disinherit your spouse. State laws generally entitle a spouse to take a portion of the other spouse's estate (except in community property states)—regardless of the other spouse's will or estate plan.

The situation with children is dramatically the opposite. Except for Louisiana, every state permits you to disinherit your children. However, to be effective, your intent to disinherit must be express, which usually means it has to be stated in writing.

## Q. What share will my spouse receive under state law?

**A.** If a husband or wife dies with a will that makes no provision for the surviving spouse, or conveys to that person less than a certain percentage of the deceased spouse's assets, the sur-

viving spouse can take a statutorily defined elective share of the estate. This means he or she can choose to accept the amount allowed by law, usually one third or one half of the estate.

The surviving spouse doesn't have to take an elective share of the estate—it's his or her choice. If he or she doesn't exercise the choice, the will stands and the property is distributed as stated in the will.

Elective share provisions are troubling to many people entering into second marriages, particularly late in life. There may be substantial concern that the surviving spouse of only a few years would be eligible to take up to one half of the deceased spouse's property, even though the latter wanted it to go to his or her own children. Recent revisions to the Uniform Probate Code provide a "sliding scale" for surviving spouses who take action against the will. Under this approach, which a few states have adopted, the longer the marriage, the higher the elective share. If the marriage lasted only a few years, the percentage could be quite low, minimizing one source of worry for older couples.

## Q. Is a surviving spouse protected by other laws?

**A.** Yes. Depending on the state, a surviving spouse may have the protection of homestead laws, exempt property laws, and family allowance laws. Typically, these protections are in addition to whatever the spouse receives under the will, the elective share that the spouse can choose to take under the will, or the statutory share that he or she receives if there is no will.

*Homestead laws* protect certain property from the deceased spouse's creditors. Typically, they permit the surviving spouse to shelter a certain value of the family home and some personal property from creditors. In some states, the homestead exemption protects a statutorily

## KINDS OF WILLS

*Here's a brief glossary of terms used in the law for various kinds of wills:*

**Simple will.** *A will that provides for the distribution of the entire estate to one or more persons or entities, known as beneficiaries, so that no part of the estate remains undistributed.*

**Testamentary-trust will.** *A will that sets up one or more trusts into which designated portions of your estate are placed after you die.*

**Pour-over will.** *A will that leaves your estate to a trust established before your death.*

**Holographic will.** *A will that is unwitnessed and in the handwriting of the will maker. About twenty states recognize the validity of such wills.*

**Oral will (also called "noncupative will").** *A will that is spoken, not written down. A few states permit these.*

**Joint will.** *Two wills—the wife's and the husband's—contained in one document.*

**Living will.** *Not really a will at all—since it has force while you are still alive and doesn't dispose of property. A living will is often executed at the same time you make your true will. It tells doctors and hospitals whether you wish life support in the event you are terminally ill or, as a result of accident or illness, cannot be restored to consciousness. (A power-of-appointment for health or a durable health care power of attorney can be used to address this concern.)*

specified sum of money from creditors, rather than the deceased's real or personal property. As a general rule, the protection is temporary, extending to the lifetime of the surviving spouse or until any minor children reach legal adulthood. However, in a few states, homestead laws permanently shelter specified property from creditors of the deceased.

*Exempt property laws* give the surviving spouse certain specified property; provide protection from creditors; and protect against disinheritance.

*Family allowance laws* make probate less of a burden on family members. Under these laws, the family is entitled to a certain amount of money from the estate while the estate is being probated, regardless of the claims of creditors.

### Q. What is an "independent executor"?

**A.** About a dozen states permit the appointment of an independent executor, who, after appraising the estate's assets and filing an inventory of assets with the probate court, is free to administer the estate without intervention from the court. This saves time and money. However, a court could become involved in the event someone challenges the independent executor's administration of the estate.

The independent executor has the power to do just about anything necessary to administer the estate. He or she can sue and be sued, settle claims made by others against your estate, deny or pay claims made by others against your estate, pay debts, taxes and administration expenses, run a business if part of the estate, and distribute the assets of your estate to your beneficiaries as spelled out in your will. In some states, the independent executor can sell your property without first securing a court order to do so.

### Q. Whom should I make the executor of my will?

**A.** There's no consensus about who makes the best executor. It all depends on your individual circumstances.

One approach is to appoint someone with no potential conflict of interest—that is, someone who doesn't stand to gain from the will. Under this approach, you can minimize the likelihood of a will contest from a disgruntled beneficiary who might be tempted to accuse the executor of taking undue advantage of his or her role to the detriment of others named in the will. On the other hand, if you believe that there is little possibility of a will contest, you could choose a beneficiary as executor. Since an executor who is a beneficiary usually waives the executor's fee to which he or she is entitled, your estate will save money.

For most people whose assets amount to less than half a million dollars, a good choice is your spouse or the person who will be the main beneficiary of your will. This person will naturally be interested in making sure the probate process goes efficiently and with minimal expense. For larger estates and those that involve running a business, it may be advisable to use the estate-planning department of your bank, your accountant, or your attorney.

Whomever you choose as executor, be sure to provide in your will for a successor executor

in case the first named executor dies or is unable or unwilling to perform. Without a back-up executor, the probate court will have to appoint someone, and that person may not be to your liking.

One final caution—don't name someone as your executor unless you have spoken to the person and he or she agrees. This will ensure that your estate will be administered by the person of your choice, not the court's.

### Q. Can I appoint more than one executor?

**A.** Yes, naming coexecutors is popular with small business owners who name a spouse or relative to oversee the personal side of matters and a second person with business expertise to oversee the management of the business.

Naming coexecutors may be a good idea if one of the executors lives in a different state and is unable to make the often frequent trips necessary to handle the many details involved in administering an estate. While this person could be a coexecutor, another coexecutor living in the same state could be named to handle the day-to-day administration. Finally, don't forget to name one or more successor executors so that, if one coexecutor dies or declines the position, someone else of your choice will be available.

### Q. Is there anyone whom I shouldn't appoint as executor?

**A.** As a general rule, the executor can't be a minor, a convicted felon, or a non-U.S. citizen. In addition, while all states allow an out-of-state resident to act as executor, some require that the nonresident executor be a primary beneficiary or close relative. Some states require that a nonresident executor obtain a bond or engage a resident to act as the nonresident executor's representative. For these reasons and because handling an estate can take months and require a lot of travel to your state of residence, it's a good idea to pick at least one executor who is a legal resident of the state in which your estate will be administered.

### Q. How much does an executor charge for his services?

**A.** If the executor is a beneficiary, for example, a family member, he or she may choose to forgo the statutory executor's fee, but you can expect any executor who is not a beneficiary, such as a bank or lawyer, to charge a fee. Fees vary by state and are usually set as a percentage of the estate's value. For small and mid-sized estates—estates under $200,000 for example—expect a fee of one to four percent of the total estate. Although these fees usually are regulated by probate courts and state law, non-beneficiary executors generally charge the maximum fee even if the estate requires less work than the complicated estates the statutory fee structure contemplates.

### Q. Where should I keep my will?

**A.** Keep it in a safe place, such as your lawyer's office, a fireproof safe at home, or a safe deposit box. If you do keep your will in a safe deposit box, make sure to provide that the executor can take possession of the will when you die. Also, keep in mind that some jurisdictions require a decedent's safe deposit box to be sealed immediately after death until certain legal requirements have been satisfied.

### Q. What other estate documents should I keep with the will?

**A.** You should also keep a record of other estate planning documents with your will, such as trust documents, IRA's, insurance policies, income savings plans such as 401(k) plans, stocks and bonds, and retirement plans.

## TRUSTS

### Q. What is a trust?

**A.** A trust is a legal instrument used to hold and manage real property and tangible or intangible personal property, for example, antiques (tangible personal property) or the right to royalty payments (intangible personal property). Putting property in trust transfers it from your personal ownership to the ownership of a legal entity called a "trust" which holds the property for your benefit or the benefit of anyone else you might name. Upon transfer, the law looks at these assets as if they were owned by the trust. Many trusts are set up in wills, and take effect upon death. Others can be established while you are still alive (see below and next section).

### Q. What is a living trust?

**A.** A living trust is simply a trust established while you are still alive. It can serve as a partial substitute for a will. Therefore, upon the death of the person creating the trust, his or her property is distributed as specified in the trust document to beneficiaries also specified in the document.

There are three parties to a living trust:

- the creator of the trust (also referred as the grantor, settlor, or donor);
- the trustee (the person who holds and manages the property for the benefit of the creator or other beneficiaries); and
- one or more beneficiaries (the person or persons named to receive the benefits of the trust).

### Q. Why do people use trusts?

**A.** The reasons vary. Parents, for example, might use a trust to manage their assets for the benefit of their minor children in the event the parents die before the children reach the age of legal adulthood. The trustee can decide how best to carry out the parents' wishes that the money be used for education, support, and health care.

A trust is a good idea for anyone whose intended beneficiary is unable to manage money and other assets prudently. A trust established for such a beneficiary is sometimes known as a "spendthrift trust."

For someone who is unable to manage his or her estate because of mental or physical incapacity, a trust is an effective way to avoid the expense and undesirable aspects of a court-appointed guardian.

## THINGS A TRUST CAN DO FOR YOU

*A trust is an important estate-planning tool. The flexibility of trusts makes them useful for many different people with all kinds of needs. In addition, trusts can do a number of things wills can't do such as:*

- *manage assets efficiently if you should die while your beneficiaries are minors;*

- *protect your privacy (unlike a will, trusts are confidential);*

- *depending on how they're written and on state law, protect your assets by avoiding creditors and reducing taxes;*

- *manage property for you while you're alive; provide a way to care for you if you should become disabled; avoid probate; and speed transfer of your assets to beneficiaries after your death.*

**Q. Can you change a trust after you set one up?**

**A.** It depends. A trust can be revocable—that is, subject to change or termination; or irrevocable—that is, difficult to change or terminate.

A revocable trust gives the creator great flexibility but no tax advantages. An irrevocable trust is the other side of the coin—less flexibility but considerable tax benefits. For example, an irrevocable trust can minimize federal and state taxes. In addition, an irrevocable trust may protect trust property from the creditors of the trust creator. However, an irrevocable trust often doesn't avoid taxes entirely. Because it can be difficult to balance the costs and benefits of an irrevocable trust, it's wise to consult with an estate-planning attorney before you proceed.

**Q. Should I consider setting up a trust?**

**A.** It depends on the size of your estate and what you want to do with it. For example, if you are primarily interested in protecting yourself in the event you become unable to manage your estate, a revocable living trust is a good option. It can avoid the expense and delay of a court hearing on your mental or physical condition and the appointment of a legal guardian to oversee you and your estate in the event you are declared legally incompetent. If you want to provide for minor children, grandchildren, or a disabled relative, a trust might be appropriate. Before making a decision, consult an estate-planning lawyer.

**Q. I can see the advantages of a trust, particularly a revocable living trust. What are some disadvantages?**

**A.** Besides preparing the trust document itself, you will have to transfer all of the assets specified in the trust document into the trust. This can require executing deeds or bills of sale,

## KINDS OF TRUSTS

**Self-declaration of trust** *provides support for the owner during his or her lifetime. Like a will, it also contains provisions for disposing of the trust property at the owner's death.*

**Support trust** *directs the trustee to spend only as much income and principal as may be needed for the education, health care, and general support of the beneficiary.*

**Discretionary trust** *permits the trustee to distribute income and principal among various beneficiaries as he or she sees fit.*

**Charitable trust** *supports a charitable purpose. Often these trusts will make an annual gift to a worthy cause of your choosing.*

**Spendthrift trust** *benefits individuals who the grantor believes can't or won't be able to manage their own affairs—like an extravagant relative. It may also be useful for beneficiaries who need protection from creditors.*

**Insurance trust** *is a device used to avoid or, at least, minimize federal and state estate taxes. Here, trust assets are used to buy a life insurance policy whose proceeds benefit the creator's beneficiaries.*

**Totten trust** *is not really a trust at all. It is one or more joint bank accounts that pass to a named beneficiary immediately upon the owner's death.*

**Medicaid trust** *is a trust that helps you qualify for federal Medicaid benefits. This device is mostly used when family members are concerned with paying the costs of nursing home care.*

submitting tax forms, retitling assets, and other registration procedures.

You have to be sure to keep transactions involving your trust separate from those involving property owned in your name. After creating the trust, each time you buy, inherit or otherwise acquire an asset that you don't want subject to probate, you have to remember to buy it in the name of the trust or transfer it into the trust after receipt.

Cost is also a factor. While a lawyer isn't required for setting up a revocable living trust, it's usually a good idea to work with one. Also, a trust generally costs more than a will to prepare. In addition, there may be an annual management fee, particularly if the trustee is a bank or trust company. (However, if all of your property is in trust so that there is no estate to probate at your death, these higher initial costs may be offset by costs that would have gone to probate.)

There are other problems too. Depending on the state the property is located in, putting your home in a revocable trust might jeopardize a homestead exemption, might require a trans-

## SOME RESPONSIBILITIES OF THE SUCCESSOR TRUSTEE

*If you become the successor trustee because of the death of the original trustee:*

- *obtain a copy of the deceased trustee's death certificate as well a copy of the trust creator's death certificate if the creator has died;*
- *tell the trust creator's family that you are the successor trustee;*
- *make sure each trust beneficiary has a copy of the trust document;*
- *inform all financial institutions holding trust assets that you are the new trustee;*
- *collect and pay all taxes and other debts;*
- *monitor all income;*
- *make sure there is an accurate inventory of all trust property;*
- *ensure that the trust property has been or will be distributed to beneficiaries;*
- *prepare and file all appropriate tax returns;*
- *When the trust terminates, prepare a final accounting and distribute the trust property to the named beneficiaries.*

*If you become a successor trustee because the creator of the trust, who was also the trustee, has become incapacitated:*

- *obtain a medical opinion confirming the creator/trustee's incapacity;*
- *inform the family of the trust creator that you are his or her successor trustee;*
- *provide each beneficiary with a copy of the trust document;*
- *inform all financial institutions holding trust property that you are the successor trustee;*
- *pay all taxes and debts;*
- *monitor all income.*

fer fee, or might cause your property to be reassessed for property tax purposes. Moreover, this type of trust will not reduce estate taxes.

In some states, a revocable living trust, unlike a will, is not automatically revoked or amended on divorce. If you don't amend the trust, your ex-spouse could end up being the beneficiary.

Conflicts can arise between trustees and beneficiaries. For example, beneficiaries often prefer riskier, higher-income investments than trustees, who have a duty to preserve the original assets of the trust as well as the duty to invest the assets prudently. Conflict of this sort is especially likely to occur if the trust is designed for the benefit of more than one generation.

Conflicts also might arise among different classes of beneficiaries. For example, your child may be the current beneficiary, with your grandchildren becoming beneficiaries after your child dies. In this situation, your child and grandchildren may have conflicting interests in the trust. As the creator of the trust, you can minimize any conflict by clearly stating in the trust document whose interests are paramount.

### Q. Whom should I pick as trustee?

**A.** A trustee's duties can continue for generations and, in many cases, require expertise in collecting estate assets, investing money, paying bills, filing periodic accountings, and managing money for beneficiaries.

The biggest decision to make in designating a trustee is whether to use a family member, a professional trustee, or both. Many trust creators choose a family member as a trustee. A family member usually won't charge a fee and, generally, has a personal stake in the trust's success. If the family member is competent to handle the financial matters involved, has the time and interest to do so, and if you're not afraid of family conflicts, naming a family member as trustee may be a good move, particularly for a small- or medium-sized estate.

A professional trustee such as a bank will charge a management fee which, in some cases, can be substantial. Professional trustees also have been criticized for being impersonal in their dealings with beneficiaries who require, or at least desire, more personal attention. On the other hand, a professional trustee is immortal, unlikely to take sides in family conflicts, and commands the kind of investment and money-management expertise that a lay trustee may not possess. Particularly if you have a large estate, give serious consideration to a professional trustee.

### Q. Can I name more than one trustee?

**A.** Yes. Many trust creators name co-trustees. For example, when a married couple decides to establish a trust, the spouse creating the trust often names himself or herself as one cotrustee and the spouse as the second cotrustee. As a further protection, the creator will name a successor trustee who would manage the trust in the event that one or both of the cotrustees die or resign their trustee duties.

### Q. How do I choose a lawyer to help me set up a trust?

**A.** First, make sure the lawyer you select has expertise in trust and estate law in your state and is willing to work with you to tailor the trust to your particular needs; otherwise the primary benefit of a trust—its flexibility—might be lost. A knowledgeable lawyer will provide you with the financial expertise necessary to ensure that the trust property is preserved and, where possible, is invested wisely to ensure that the assets placed in trust actually grow in value.

Second, because trusts have tax consequences and are scrutinized closely by the IRS, choose a lawyer who understands the interplay between various types of trusts and their tax obligations.

### Q. When does a trust come to an end?

**A.** Except for charitable trusts, a trust ends upon a date specified in the trust document or upon the occurrence of a particular event stated in the document. For example, in a trust to benefit children, the date of termination usually is the date the youngest child reaches a stated age.

### Q. What if I set up a trust and then move to another state? Which law applies?

**A.** The trust document usually contains a clause specifying which state's law applies. As a general law, the law of the state of your residence at the time you created the trust is the applicable law and remains so if even if you later move to another state. However, it's probably a wise idea to check with a lawyer familiar with the statutes of your new state of residence to see if the trust should be revised to account for differences in the law between the two states.

## LIVING TRUSTS

**Q. Who can advise me about setting up a revocable living trust?**

**A.** Your attorney is the obvious choice, but not the only one. Most banks provide trust services, for example, establishing the trust and managing the trust assets. Of course, the bank's management charges can add up and could exceed the cost of probating your estate. In addition, the bank may insist on managing the trust, which means that you won't be in control. Be sure to weigh these factors before deciding to use a bank as your trustee.

For people with more assets or people who don't want the uncertainty and work of writing and funding their own trust, it's definitely wise to work with an attorney. It's especially good to have an attorney's assistance in determining which assets to put into the trust and which to dispose of through a will.

**Q. I just received a call from someone purporting to sell living trusts. Should I buy one?**

**A.** No. A number of dubious companies, playing on people's fears of probate and suspicions about lawyers, have taken to selling living-trust kits door to door, by mail, or through seminars. Often, they deliberately exaggerate the costs and difficulties of the probate process, even though probate procedures and fees in many states, especially for simple estates, are increasingly more manageable and less costly. Authorities in several states have filed consumer fraud suits against these promoters for

### YOU MIGHT BENEFIT FROM A LIVING TRUST IF...

1. *Your estate has substantial property or assets that are difficult or costly to dispose by a will.*

2. *You don't want the task of managing your property (say you rent out a number of condos). A revocable living trust allows you to give those duties to your trustee while you receive the income, minus the trustee's fee, if any.*

3. *You want your estate administered by a someone who doesn't live in your state. A living trust might be better than a will because the trustee probably won't have to meet the residency requirements some state laws impose upon executors.*

4. *You have property in another state. Many lawyers recommend setting up a revocable living trust to hold the title to that property. This helps you avoid time-consuming, complicated, "ancillary probate" procedures.*

misrepresenting themselves and deceiving consumers.

Most lawyers and financial advisers urge you to avoid such pitches, whether they're made in unsolicited telephone calls, through the mail, or in seminars. The products seldom

## YOU MAY NOT BENEFIT FROM A REVOCABLE LIVING TRUST IF...

1. *Your probate system has simple and easy procedures for administering estates of your size.*

2. *You're young and healthy and don't have a lot of money. A will can usually take care of the immediate needs of a young family. You can think about a trust when you have children and your assets have grown.*

3. *You are not rich but you have enough assets that reregistering them all would cost more than it's worth. For example, you might own a number of parcels of property, none particularly valuable, but all of the property would require retitling if placed into a trust.*

live up to their touts and often cost $2,500 or more—far above what you'd typically pay to get a good personalized trust prepared by a lawyer. Because revocable living trusts should be crafted to fit your particular situation, it's next to impossible to find a prepackaged one that will suit your needs as well as one prepared by your lawyer.

### Q. How do I set up a revocable living trust?

**A.** Requirements for setting up a revocable living trust vary with each state. In general, you execute a document saying that you're creating a trust to hold property for your benefit and that

of any other designated beneficiary. Some trust declarations list the major assets (home, investments) that you're putting into trust; others refer to another document (a "schedule") in which you list the exact property that will be in the trust. In either case, you can add and subtract property whenever you want. You will have to change the ownership registration on all property put into the trust—deeds, brokerage accounts, stocks or bonds, bank accounts, etc.—from your own name to the name of the trust (for example, The John A. Smith Trust). If you make yourself the trustee, you will have to remember to sign yourself in trust transactions as "John A. Smith, Trustee," instead of using only your name.

### Q. How can I reduce the costs of a revocable living trust?

**A.** By doing some preparation, you can minimize the time the lawyer spends on setting up the trust and reduce your legal costs. As in making a will, ask your lawyer what documents are important. After collecting the necessary records, deeds, bank statements etc., make a list of your assets and where you want them to go when you die.

### Q. Once I put my property in a revocable living trust, can I still manage it or sell it?

**A.** Yes. In a revocable living trust, you can retain the right to manage the trust property. This right includes the right to sell any of the property you placed into the trust.

### Q. Does a revocable living trust save taxes?

**A.** No. When you put property in a revocable living trust, the trust becomes its owner, which is why you must transfer title to the property from your own name to that of the trust. But you retain the right to use and enjoy the property and, because you do, under the tax

## WHAT A REVOCABLE LIVING TRUST WON'T DO

*A revocable living trust is a very important estate-planning tool. But it can't do everything. Here's a summary of what it can't do.*

1. *Won't help you avoid taxes. A revocable living trust doesn't save any income or estate taxes that couldn't also be saved by a properly prepared will. Trust property is still counted as part of your estate for the purposes of federal and state income and estate taxes. Your trustee or successor trustee still has to pay income taxes generated by trust property and owed at your death. (Your executor would have to pay such taxes out of your estate if the property was controlled by a will instead of a trust.) And if the estate is large enough to trigger federal or state estate or inheritance taxes, your trustee will be required to file the appropriate tax returns. These and other duties can make the cost of administering an estate distributed by a revocable living trust almost as high as traditional estate administration, at least in some states.*

2. *Won't make a will unnecessary. You still need a will to take care of assets not included in the trust. If you have minor children, you probably need a will to suggest or nominate a guardian for them. While only a court can appoint a guardian, courts strive to implement your wishes in this regard if you have stated them.*

3. *Won't affect nonprobate assets. Like a will, a revocable living trust won't control the disposition of jointly owned property, life insurance, pension benefits or retirement plans payable to a beneficiary, and other nonprobate property.*

4. *Won't protect your assets from creditors. Creditors can attach the assets of a revocable living trust. In fact, since the assets you put in a living trust don't have to be probated, they could lose the protection of the statute of limitations, which means that your creditors have longer to get at them.*

5. *Won't necessarily protect your assets from disgruntled relatives. While it is harder to challenge a living trust than a will, a relative can still bring suit to challenge the trust on grounds of fraud, undue influence, or duress.*

6. *Won't entirely eliminate delays. A living trust might well lessen the time it takes to distribute your assets after you die, but it won't completely eliminate delays. Many state laws impose a waiting period for creditors to file claims against estates of people with living trusts. The trustee still has to collect any debts owed to your trust after you die, prepare tax returns, pay bills, and distribute assets, just as would the executor of a will. All this takes time.*

law, the property in the trust belongs to you for tax purposes. Thus, if the trust receives income from the assets, you must report the income from the trust on your individual income tax return.

### Q. What happens to the property in the trust when I die?

**A.** When you die, your trustee distributes the property according to the terms of the trust.

### Q. How can a revocable living trust help if I become disabled?

**A.** You would set up a revocable living trust, fund it adequately (or give someone in whom you have confidence power of attorney to fund it in the event of your incapacity), and name one or more reliable trustees to manage your property contained in the trust should you become ill. This avoids the delay and red tape of expensive, court-ordered guardianship. And, at the same time, the trustee can take over any duties you had of providing for other family members. For more, see page 620 of the chapter, "The Rights of Older Americans."

### Q. Once the trust is set up, do I have to do anything else?

**A.** Setting up the trust is actually the easy part. The harder part is putting something in it—what's called funding the trust. This includes not just depositing money in the trust account, but also transferring title of assets to the name of the trust.

### Q. How do I transfer titles to the trust?

**A.** Take a copy of the trust agreement to your bank, stockbroker, mortgage and title insurance companies, and anyone else who controls title to your assets and then request a transfer of ownership from your name to that of the trust. Make sure to keep a record of these transfers; it will make your trustee's job much easier.

### Q. What should I leave out?

**A.** The special tax treatment given Individual Retirement Accounts (IRAs) might encourage you to leave them in your name. The fees your state charges to transfer title of a mortgage or other property could make the cost of transfer prohibitive. You might want to hold off on transferring your home to the trust until the mortgage is paid off or one spouse dies. Some people worry about taking the family home out of the husband and wife's names in joint tenancy and putting it into a living trust in the name of one of the spouses. In such cases, a lawyer may suggest putting the living trust in both your names, for example, "The James and Ima Hogg Trust," with both spouses as cotrustees, instead of just one name.

If the trust is in one name only and the other spouse is not a cotrustee or successor trustee, many lawyers recommend leaving some property, for example, a sizable bank account, outside the trust. If you use a bank account, it should be in the names of both spouses so that, if one should die, the other will have access to the funds. A word of caution is in order, however. The law in some states will freeze such accounts for a specified period of time after the death of the cosignator. Consult your attorney to get the specifics.

Finally, keeping a few assets out of the living trust can help protect against creditors' claims down the line. When your estate contains some property and goes through probate, it triggers the running of the statute of limitations on claims against your entire estate. Creditors are put on notice that you have died and, once the statutory period expires, the estate is safe from most creditor's claims.

The important point: be sure to go through each of your assets with your lawyer to determine whether it's wise to transfer that asset to the trust.

### Q. If I set up a revocable living trust, do I still need a will?

**A.** In order to avoid probate, some people use a revocable living trust instead of a will to transfer property upon their death. However, a trust alone can't accomplish many of the most important goals of estate planning. For example, you may require a will to name a personal guardian for your children, even if you have a trust. And, even with a revocable living trust, you'll need a will to dispose of property that you didn't put into the trust.

Probate is also no longer the costly, time-consuming demon it used to be. So preparing at least an auxiliary will is recommended for just about everyone.

## OTHER ESTATE PLANNING ASSETS AND TOOLS

### Q. My wife and I own our house in joint tenancy. Can't I use joint tenancy to pass property without having to draw up a will?

**A.** Yes. Joint tenancy is a form of co-ownership. If you and your wife buy a house or car in both your names and as joint tenants, each of you is considered a joint tenant and has co-ownership. When one of the co-owners dies, joint ownership usually gives the other co-owner instant access to the jointly held property.

### Q. What's the difference between joint tenancy and tenancy in common?

**A.** In joint tenancy, you and your spouse, or other co-owner, own the property, for example, a home. Joint tenancy means, among other things, that each owner must agree on such issues as whether to sell the home.

In tenancy in common, on the other hand, each owner owns an equal share of the property. In some states a tenant in common may sell his or her share of the property without the consent of the other owners. Keep in mind, however, that few buyers are interested in purchasing what amounts to part of a home. In tenancy in common, different partners can own unequal shares of the property.

If you own an asset in joint tenancy with anyone and you die, ownership of that asset passes to the other joint tenant automatically. In a tenancy in common, your share passes as provided in your will or trust, with possible consequences of probate, estate taxes, and so on.

### Q. Is there another way to give money to minor children besides a will or trust?

**A.** Yes. The most common way is through the Uniform Gift to Minors Act or Uniform Transfers to Minors Act, which are straightforward enough that you may be able to make a gift without consulting a lawyer. These statutes allow you to open an account in a child's name and deposit money or property in it. If the child is over age 13, the income is taxed at his or her tax rate, which, almost certainly, will be lower than yours. For younger children, the government taxes income from the account at your tax rate. However, if you name yourself as custodian and die while the child is a minor, the property will be included in your estate for tax purposes.

### Q. How can I use life insurance in my estate plan?

**A.** Life insurance is often a very good estate planning tool, because you pay relatively little up front, and your beneficiaries get much more when you die. When you name beneficiaries other than your estate, the money passes to them directly, without probate.

# TEN TIMES YOU DON'T WANT TO USE A JOINT TENANCY

1. *When you don't want to lose control. By giving someone co-ownership, you give him or her co-control. If you made your son co-owner of the house, you couldn't sell or mortgage it unless he agrees.*

2. *When the co-owner's creditors might come after the money. If creditors come after your co-owner, they may be able to get part of the house or bank account held in joint tenancy.*

3. *When you can't be sure of your co-owner. You and your co-owner could have a falling out and he or she could take all the money out of the bank account.*

4. *When you're using co-ownership to substitute for a will. Often, parents with several children will put one child's name on an account, assuming he or she will divide the money equally among the other children. But this method provides no control over the money. The surviving joint tenant can do with it what he or she pleases.*

5. *When it might cause confusion after your death. Unplanned ownership of property often leads to unwanted results—especially for people unable to manage assets.*

6. *When it won't speed the transfer of assets. Some states automatically freeze jointly owned accounts upon the death of one of the owners until the tax authorities can examine it. As a result, the survivor can't count on getting to the money immediately.*

7. *When it compromises tax planning. Careful planning to minimize the taxes on an estate can be completely thwarted by an inadvertently created joint tenancy that passes property outright to the surviving tenant.*

8. *When you're in a shaky marriage. Your individual property may become marital property once it's transferred into joint tenancy.*

9. *When one of the joint tenants could become incompetent. If this happens, part of the property may go into a conservatorship, making it cumbersome at best if the other joint tenant wants to sell some or all of the jointly held property.*

10. *When you don't want to transfer assets all at once. Joint tenancies deprive you of the flexibility of a will or trust in which you can use gifts and asset shifts to minimize taxes or pay out money over time to beneficiaries, instead of giving it to them all at once.*

*If you have an estate below the federal estate tax level—currently $600,000—it might be all right to use joint tenancy—but you should check with a lawyer. Most of the advantages of joint tenancy can be achieved using a revocable living trust.*

## Uniform Acts Concerning Gifts and Transfers to Minors

| State | UGMA* | Rev. UGMA | UTMA** | Other | Provides for Testamentary Gifts |
|-------|-------|-----------|--------|-------|--------------------------------|
| AL | | | X | | X |
| AK | | | X | | |
| AZ | X | | | | |
| AR | | | X | | X |
| CA | | X | | | X |
| CO | | X | | | X |
| CT | | X | | | X |
| DE | X | | | | |
| DC | | X | | | |
| FL | | | X | | X |
| GA | | X | | | |
| GUAM | | | X | | |
| HI | | | | | |
| ID | | | X | | X |
| IL | | X | | | |
| IN | | X | | | X |
| IO | | | X | | |
| KS | | | X | | X |
| KY | | X | X | | |
| LA | | | | X | X |
| ME | | | X | | |
| MD | | X | | | X |
| MA | X | | | | |
| MI | X | | | | |
| MN | | X | | | X |
| MS | | X | | | |
| MO | X | | | | |
| MT | | | X | | X |
| NE | X | | | | |
| NV | | | X | | X |
| NH | | | X | | X |
| NJ | | | | X | X |
| NM | X | | | | X |
| NY | | X | | | X |
| NC | X | | | | X |
| ND | | | X | | X |
| OH | | | X | | |
| OK | | | X | | |
| OR | | | X | | X |
| PA | | X | | | |
| PR | | | | | |
| RI | | X | | | X |
| SC | X | | | | |
| SD | | X | | | X |
| TN | | X | | | |
| TX | | X | | | X |
| UT | X | | | | |
| VT | X | | | | |
| VI | X | | | | |
| VA | X | | | | |
| WA | | X | | | X |
| WV | | | X | | |
| WS | | | X | | |
| WY | | X | | | |
| **54** | **12** | **20** | **18** | **2** | **26** |

*Uniform Gifts to Minors Act.
**Uniform Transfers to Minors Act.

Life insurance is often used to pay the immediate costs of death (funeral or hospital expenses), set up a fund to support your family so they won't have to return to work while still under stress from your death, replace your lost income, pay for children's education, and so on.

You can use life insurance to distribute assets among children from different marriages. And, if your estate is large enough, you can set up an irrevocable trust for your children that's funded with the life insurance policy. You pay the premiums but the trust actually owns the policy. When you die, your children receive the benefits from the trust, while your spouse gets the rest of your estate.

### Q. How do retirement benefits affect my estate plan?

**A.** Many of us are entitled to retirement benefits from an employer. Typically, a retirement plan will pay benefits to beneficiaries if you die before reaching retirement age. After retirement, you can usually pick an option that will continue payments to a beneficiary after your death. In most cases, the law requires that some portion of these retirement benefits be paid to your spouse.

IRAs (Individual Retirement Accounts) provide a ready means of cash when one spouse dies. If your spouse is named as the beneficiary, the proceeds will immediately become his or her property when you die. Like retirement benefits (and unlike assets inherited via a will), they will pass to the named beneficiary without having to go through probate. Check with a lawyer to see how such plans can best be coordinated with your estate plan.

### Q. Do prenuptial agreements play a role in estate planning?

**A.** Any couple in a situation where one partner has a lot more money or property than the other or where one partner is substantially older than the other, should consider entering

into a prenuptial agreement as part of their estate planning.

Older people with grown children from another marriage may want their property to go to their own children after they die, rather than to the new spouse and his or her children. A prenuptial agreement can accomplish this purpose. See page 56 of the "Family Law" chapter for more information about premarital agreements.

### Q. I live in a community property state. How does this affect my estate plan?

**A.** The laws of Puerto Rico and nine states—Arizona, California, Idaho, Louisiana, Nevada, New Mexico, Texas, Washington, and Wisconsin—provide that most property earned during the marriage by either spouse is held equally by husband and wife as community property—that is, as property belonging to both spouses. (The major exceptions are property acquired during the marriage by inheritance or gift.) In a community property state, when one spouse dies, his or her half of the property passes either by will or operation of law; the other half of the property belongs to the surviving spouse.

If you live in a community property state, you can only dispose of your half of the community property via a will or trust. If you and your spouse have the same estate planning objectives, it's no problem. But if you don't, living in a community property state could make it more difficult to meet your estate-planning goals.

### Q. I live in a separate property state but own property in a community property state. Which law applies?

**A.** If the property is real estate, state laws may treat it as community property for estate-planning purposes. Thus, if you live in Arkansas (a separate property state) but own land in Texas (a community property state), an Arkansas court probating your will would treat the Texas property just as Texas would—as community property. But not every state would extend the same courtesy.

This separate/community property division can get pretty complicated—and this is only one example of how state laws differ. If you own property in more than one state, consult an estate-planning lawyer who is conversant with the estate laws of each different state.

### Q. Should I give some of my property away before I die?

**A.** Making gifts during your lifetime can be a good idea, especially if you have a large estate. They can help you avoid high estate and inheritance taxes. In some states, they might enable you to reduce a relatively small estate to one that is small enough to avoid formal probate procedures. Another advantage of giving property away before you die is that you get to see the recipient's appreciation for your generosity.

But watch out for a few pitfalls. These gifts will be subject to gift taxes if they're larger than the amount provided by law. Current law allows you to give up to $10,000 per person per year ($20,000, if a couple makes the gift) before the gift tax applies. You can make gifts to any number of people, whether or not related to you. You can also make gifts to trusts but keep in mind that not all trust gifts qualify for this exclusion.

You need to put in your will a statement that any gifts you have given before you died are not to be considered advances. Without such a clear statement of intent, the probate courts in some states may subtract the amount of the gift from the amount you left in the will.

## CHANGING YOUR MIND

### Q. Once I've planned my estate, do I have to worry about it again?

**A.** Yes. Life doesn't stand still. After you've crafted your initial estate plan, your circum-

stances are likely to change—you may have more children, acquire more assets, have a falling out with your spouse, other relatives, or friends you've named as beneficiaries. These and other life changes will occasion a change in your estate plan.

It's a good idea to review your will or trust document along with your inventory of assets and list of beneficiaries every three or four years to make sure your past decisions continue to meet your current needs. Think of estate planning not as a one-time transaction, but as a process that works best if periodically reviewed.

### Q. How do I change my will after it has been executed?

**A.** You can change, add to or even revoke your will any time before your death as long as you are physically and mentally competent to make the change. An amendment to a will is called a codicil.

You can't simply cross out old provisions in your will and scribble in new ones if you want the changes to be effective. You have to formally execute a codicil, using the same procedures as were used when you executed the will itself. The codicil should be dated and kept with the will. It's a good idea to check with your lawyer before signing a codicil or revoking your will.

### Q. When should I update my will?

**A.** You may need to modify your present will by executing a codicil or preparing an entirely new will to account for major changes in your life or in your financial situation—for example, the purchase of a new house, divorce or remarriage, moving to another state, big jump (or decline) in income, birth of children, death of relatives, etc. In fact, it's a good idea to periodically review your will and update it as necessary.

## DO I NEED TO UPDATE MY ESTATE PLAN? A CHECKLIST.

*Ask yourself if any of these changes have occurred in your life since you last read over your will or trust document.*

*Have you married or been divorced?*

*Have beneficiaries died or has your relationship with any of them changed substantially?*

*Has the executor of your will or trustee of your trust died?*

*Has the mental or physical condition of any beneficiaries, executor, or trustee changed substantially?*

*Have you had children or have children gone to college or moved out of, or into, your home?*

*Have you moved to another state?*

*Have you bought, sold, or mortgaged a business or real estate?*

*Have you acquired major assets (car, home, bank account)?*

*Have your business or financial circumstances changed significantly (estate size, pension, salary, ownership)?*

*Has the law changed in your state (or has the federal tax law changed) in a way that might affect your tax and estate planning?*

**Q. When and how should I revoke my will entirely?**

**A.** Sometimes, when you have a major life change, such as a divorce, remarriage, winning the lottery, having more children, getting the last child out of the house, it's a good idea to rewrite your will from scratch rather than making a lot of small changes through codicils. You can do this by executing a formal statement of revocation and executing a new will that revokes the old one.

If you write a new will, be sure to include the date it's signed and executed and put in a sentence that states that the new will revokes all previous wills. Otherwise, a court might rule that the new will only revokes the old one where the two conflict.

**Q. What happens if I fail to keep my will up-to-date?**

**A.** Some life changes may be accommodated by the law, regardless of what your will says. For example, if you have a new child, and don't explicitly say you don't want him or her to inherit anything, the law will give the child his or her legal share of your estate. Likewise a new spouse.

If you come into property that is not accounted for by the will, it becomes part of your "residuary estate"—that is, it will pass to the person or institution who gets everything not specifically identified in the will.

It's best to modify your will periodically to account for such life changes or "after-acquired assets." If you don't, you run the risk of paying higher taxes, giving property to people you don't want to have it, or creating confusion (and possibly probate delays or even litigation) among your grieving relatives after you're gone.

Other estate-planning documents you should take care to keep up-to-date include IRAs, insurance policies, income savings plans such as 401(k) plans, government savings bonds (if payable to another person), and retirement plans. You should keep a record of these documents with your will and update them as needed when you update your will.

**Q. What if I set up a revocable living trust, then change my mind about it?**

**A.** You modify a trust through a procedure called an amendment. You should amend your trust when you want to change or add beneficiaries, take assets from the trust, or change trustees. You amend a trust by adding a new page for every change, specifying the new additions. To avoid a legal challenge from a disgruntled nonbeneficiary, you should not detach a page from the trust document, retype it to include the new information, and put it back in its original place.

You don't have to write a formal amendment to the trust to add property to it, because a properly drafted trust will contain language giving you the right to include property acquired after the trust is drafted. Just make sure the new property is titled as being owned by the trust and list it on the schedule of assets in the trust. You do have to amend the trust if the newly acquired property is going to a different beneficiary than the one already named in the trust or if the trust has more than one beneficiary listed.

You should revoke, not amend, your trust when making major changes. You revoke a trust by destroying all copies of it or writing "revoked" on each page and signing them. When you create a new trust to replace a revoked one, give the new trust a different name, usually one containing the date the new document was executed.

## SPECIAL CONSIDERATIONS

**Q. I own a vacation house in a state other than the one where I have my primary res-**

**idence. Which law applies to property in different states?**

**A.** The laws of the state where your primary home is located determines what happens to your personal property—car, stocks, cash.

Distribution of any other real property is governed by the laws of the state in which the property is located. If you do own homes or real property in different states, it's a good idea to make sure that the provisions of your estate planning documents comply with the laws of the appropriate states.

**Q. My life partner and I aren't married. Are there any special estate-planning strategies about which we should be aware?**

**A.** It's especially important to write a will or trust if you're involved in an unmarried relationship, because a will or trust lets you leave your property to anyone or any organization you wish. A will or trust also lets you name an executor or trustee for your estate to supervise distribution of your assets. If you want your partner to inherit a good share of your property, naming your partner or someone sympathetic to the relationship as executor or trustee can help to ensure that your wishes are carried out.

Furthermore, if you want your partner to receive the proceeds from a life insurance policy, IRA, bank accounts, and so on, you need to name your partner as the beneficiary in each of those documents separately. The advantage of using beneficiary designations and other non-probate arrangements (such as holding property in joint tenancy with your partner) is that the transfers will take place automatically on your death; no disgruntled relatives can hold up your desires as they can in a will contest.

**Q. How do gay or unmarried couples keep control over funeral arrangements?**

**A.** Funeral arrangements can be an especially sensitive subject for an unmarried couple. Since tradition and the law often gives the deceased's blood or legal relatives—not an unmarried partner—the right to control funeral arrangements, many nonmarital partners have been infuriated to find out at the funeral that no mention was made of the relationship or of the fact that the deceased had a life partner.

To prevent this, put into writing your funeral instructions and name your partner as the person responsible for carrying out those instructions. You might mention these instructions in your will as well, although you should remember that sometimes a funeral is over before the will is read. Still, the mention of your wishes in a will and a signed statement of funeral instructions should go a long way toward convincing funeral directors of your partner's authority in the event of a dispute between the partner and other family members.

Sometimes unmarried people create cohabitation agreements to cover the rights and responsibilities of each partner. These agreements cover such contingencies as each partner's disability and division of property in case the relationship ends. They are often coordinated with wills and trusts. You'll want a lawyer who's experienced in nonspousal domestic partnerships to help you write yours.

A word of caution is in order, however. In many states, cohabitation, regardless of the sex of the parties, is thought to be against sound public policy. In these states, the courts will not enforce cohabitation agreements.

### Q. My marriage is on the rocks. How does divorce affect my estate plan?

**A.** Depending on your state's law, a divorce may revoke your will in its entirety or those provisions of your will that favored your former spouse. Either way, be sure to revise your will or write a new one when you get divorced, changing the provisions that relate to your former spouse and his or her family. Be sure to modify other related documents such as living wills, survivorships, and insurance policies.

Trusts may need to be specifically amended, and names of trustees changed if they were members of your ex-spouse's family. Settlement negotiations at the time of the divorce should include all these issues. Retirement benefits subject to ERISA (see page 460 of the chapter "Law in the Workplace" and page 578 of the chapter "The Rights of Older Americans") especially need to be looked into. Since ERISA rules preempt state law, the designation of your now ex-spouse as beneficiary will have to be changed.

**Q. I'm divorced and considering remarrying. How will this affect my estate plan?**

**A.** If you're one member of an older couple in which both you and your spouse have children from a previous marriage, you might want to arrange things so your own money goes to your own children and your spouse's money goes to his or her children.

The versatility of a revocable living trust makes it a useful instrument for allocating assets among different families. You can set up a separate trust for the children of different marriages, or even for each family member.

Some families are using Qualified Terminable Interest Property Trusts to address the special concerns of stepfamilies. This type of trust allows you to do several things: 1) leave your property in trust for your spouse during your spouse's lifetime; 2) give the trust property to someone else after your spouse's death; and 3) reduce estate inheritance taxes. Talk to your lawyer about the details of such a trust.

## DEATH AND TAXES

**Q. I'm not rich. Do I have to worry about federal estate taxes?**

**A.** Under current law, your estate isn't liable for federal estate taxation unless it exceeds $600,000. For married couples the threshold is $1.2 million.

In deciding what your estate is worth, the IRS generally uses the fair market value of property you own at your death, not what you originally paid for it. In many cases especially if you've owned your home, stocks, or other assets for many years, the appreciation in value of large assets could put you over the limit. For appraisal purposes, the government uses the face value of all insurance policies in your name, including most group policies from work or professional organizations.

Assets subject to tax at death may include the family home, the family farm, life insurance, household furnishings, benefits under employee benefit plans, and other items that produce no lifetime income. In short, you may be richer than you think. If your estate is likely to exceed the $600,000 threshold, however, good estate planning can sharply reduce the amount of money that goes to the government instead of to your beneficiaries.

**Q. What should I do if I may be liable for the estate tax?**

**A.** Although the federal estate tax misses most people, those it hits, it hits hard. At the moment, the rate begins at 37 percent and goes up to 50 percent. So if you are in jeopardy of exceeding the threshold, see your lawyer for some tax-planning advice.

Warning: Tax laws change frequently. Be sure to review your estate plan periodically. Provisions that may be changed in coming years include the threshold amount subject to taxation, the number of tax-free $10,000 gifts allowed (presently, there is no limit), the tax rate in upper brackets of estate income (it might go higher than the current 50 percent), and a capital gains tax at death.

**Q. What about state death taxes?**

**A.** Five states charge an additional estate tax similar to tax imposed by the federal gov-

## YOUR FINAL INSTRUCTIONS

*Your final instructions should list:*

- *disposition of your body—buried, cremated, donated to science;*

- *provision for donating certain specified organs for transplants;*

- *funeral arrangements—information about any funeral plan you've bought or account you've set up to pay burial expenses; location of cemetery and burial plot; choice of funeral director and services, etc.;*

- *name of any charity or cause to which you wish contributions sent in your name;*

- *location of your will and the identity and telephone number of the executor and your lawyer;*

- *location of any trust document and the identity of any trustee, co-trustee or successor trustee;*

- *location of your safe deposit box, the key to it, and any important records not located in it, such as birth certificates; marriage, divorce, and prenuptial documents; military discharge records and your service number; important business, insurance and financial records; and pension and benefit agreements;*

- *inventory of assets including documents of debts owed and loans outstanding, credit card information, post office box and key, information on any investments, household contents, bank accounts, list of expected death benefits, etc.;*

- *important information: names, addresses, dates and places of birth for you and your spouse, family members and other heirs, and ex-spouses, if any; social security numbers for you and your spouse and dependent children along with the location of social security cards; policy numbers and telephone numbers and addresses of insurance companies and agencies that control your death benefits (employer, union, Veterans Affairs office, etc.);*

- *information you want in your obituary.*

ernment; seventeen states impose an inheritance tax. (Inheritance taxes are charged to beneficiaries; estate taxes are charged to the deceased person's estate.)

What is taxed and at what rate depends on state law, not only of the state in which you live but also the state where the property is located. Unless your state has an inheritance tax, your beneficiaries don't pay tax when they receive money or other property from your estate. But they will have to pay income tax on any earnings after they invest the bequest. In addition,

death itself may produce numerous tax consequences, including taxes on insurance (if paid to the estate) and employee benefits.

### Q. *What if I receive a bequest and don't want it?*

**A.** Because of taxes or other reasons, those named as beneficiaries in a will or trust document may not want the property left to them. For example, if you go bankrupt and then your father dies, your creditors may be entitled to the first shot at the property he left to you. You might want to give up this property so that it will go, for example, to your sister instead of to your creditors. Or you may receive property that is subject to liens and mortgages greater than its market value, so it is a burden you would rather not have.

Most states permit beneficiaries to disclaim (that is, refuse) an inheritance or benefit. The Internal Revenue Code describes how a beneficiary may disclaim an interest in an estate for estate-tax purposes. See a knowledgeable tax lawyer if you intend to disclaim any gift.

## PROBATE

### Q. What is probate?

**A.** Probate is the court-supervised legal procedure that determines the validity of your will. Probate affects some, but not all of your assets. Nonprobate assets include things like a life insurance policy paid directly to a beneficiary.

The term probate is also used in the larger sense of administering your estate. In this sense, probate means the process by which assets are gathered, applied to pay debts, taxes, and expenses of administration, and distributed to those designated as beneficiaries in the will.

### Q. I've heard that probate is expensive, time-consuming, and bureaucratic. True?

**A.** Probate used to be all that and more. But times have changed and so has the probate process in most states. Today, it is seldom as costly and time-consuming as in the past.

### Q. How much does probate cost?

**A.** The expenses of probate (which can include court and appraiser fees) depend on the state where you live and the size of your estate.

According to the American Association of Retired Persons (AARP), the typical cost of probate runs $1,500. But this is a very rough estimate. If there are complications—for example, an invalid will or a will contest—all bets are off.

Good estate planning can minimize expenses by passing most of your property through a living trust or by joint tenancy or some other means that avoids probate, so that very little property is left to be distributed through your will. The smaller the size of the probate estate, the lower the costs, especially if it is small enough to qualify for expedited processing.

Most states have adopted alternatives to the probate procedures for families with no real property or with assets of, say, $50,000 or less. These procedures can help save the court fees, attorney's fees, and executor fees that have given probate its nasty reputation.

### Q. What if my estate doesn't qualify for such simplified probate?

**A.** If your estate is relatively small or uncomplicated and your will is well-drafted, your spouse or other executor may not need a lawyer to help with the probate process. If

## WHAT HAPPENS IN PROBATE?

- *Your will is filed with the probate court and its validity determined.*
- *All property, debts and claims of the estate are inventoried and appraised.*
- *All valid claims of the estate are collected.*
- *The remainder of the estate is distributed to beneficiaries according to the will.*

things get more complex, the need for a lawyer becomes greater. The more complex the probate process, the more hours the lawyer will have to put in—and the more it will cost.

### Q. How long does probate take? How does my family survive before my estate is freed up?

**A.** The average estate completes the probate process in six to nine months, depending on the state's probate laws. The reformed probate procedures in many states now make it possible for your survivors to obtain funds to live on while your estate is being probated.

### Q. Should I plan my estate to try to avoid probate?

**A.** For people with substantial assets, probate can be expensive and time-consuming, tying up money and property that could go directly to your beneficiaries. Probate is also a public process. For these reasons, probate avoidance may be an element of an estate plan. But for families of moderate means, it may be more trouble to avoid probate than to go through it.

Even more than other aspects of estate planning, the details of probate vary by state. So you'll have to ask a lawyer if probate avoidance should be your principal estate-planning goal.

### Q. Who is involved in the probate process?

**A.** The main players are the probate court and your personal representative. The probate court's involvement varies depending on what kind of probate procedure exists in your jurisdiction. There are various degrees of court supervision required in different areas.

If you have a will, the personal representative is called your executor—the person you appointed in your will to administer your estate. The executor named in the will is in charge of this process, and probate provides an

> ## PROPERTY THAT AVOIDS PROBATE
> - *Property in a trust*
> - *Property that is jointly held (but NOT community property)*
> - *Death benefits from insurance policies, the government, and employers and other benefits controlled by a designation of beneficiary*
> - *Gifts made before your death*
> - *Individual Retirement Accounts*
> - *Money in a pay-on-death accounts*

orderly method for administration of the estate. If you don't have a will, the court will appoint someone to handle these tasks, usually at more expense to your estate than if you had appointed an executor and given him or her the necessary powers to settle the estate.

### Q. Is a lawyer necessary for probate?

**A.** It depends largely on what state you live in and the size of your estate. Even though probate laws have become simpler in most states, the process can be complex and time-consuming. As a result, it may be more expensive for a nonlawyer to negotiate than it is for an experienced estate lawyer.

Some states even prohibit executors from handling probate without a lawyer's assistance. On the other hand, a few states (California, Wisconsin, and Maryland) have simplified probate procedures so much that it is often possible for a nonlawyer to probate a small estate.

There is good news if you're in one of the categories of people who can profit from probate avoidance techniques like a revocable living trust or other nonprobate transfers of property, such as joint tenancy or life insurance.

Even though in these cases you still need a will to dispose of residual property (most of your assets will be distributed in other ways), the cost and time to probate such a simple will is minimal, even with a lawyer's assistance.

### Q. What can my family do to reduce the costs of probating my estate?

**A.** For most estates, you can appoint a non-lawyer as executor (usually a family member) to do most of the work such as gathering information and records. The executor files the required forms, figures and pays the taxes, and distributes the estate assets. If the executor has any questions, he or she can consult an experienced estate lawyer.

### Q. What does it mean when a will is contested?

**A.** Human nature being what it is, some people who don't receive what they consider a fair share from a dead relative's will may want to challenge, that is, contest, the will.

Chief among the grounds for a will contest is that the will was not properly executed; the testator lacked "testamentary capacity" (the ability to make a will—for example, he was senile when he left his estate to the named beneficiary); undue influence (the evil sister hypnotized her dying brother into leaving her the whole estate); fraud (the evil brother retyped a page of the will to give himself the Porsche collection); or mistake (you will your million dollar summer home to "my cousin John" and it turns out you have three cousins named John).

### Q. How can I plan to avoid a will contest?

**A.** There's an old saying that you never really know someone until a will is read. However, if your will conforms to legal requirements, a challenge is unlikely to be successful. It's also another reason to consult with an experienced estate-planning lawyer and to update your will periodically.

There are other concrete steps you can take to reduce the chances of a will contest. One is called a "no-contest" clause, which in some states allows you to disinherit a beneficiary who unsucessfully contests the will. Of course, be aware that any heir can always challenge a trust or will by claiming that the person who executed the document did not have the legal capacity or did so as a result of fraud or undue influence. But if you exercise care and obtain good legal advice, these challenges will be defeated and your intentions will be carried out.

## WHERE TO GET MORE INFORMATION

Your banker, lawyer, financial planner, and even some accounting firms offer advice on estate planning. Many self-help books, tapes, kits, and software also attempt to help you understand estate planning or even do it yourself. These are available at many law libraries and at most general libraries and bookstores.

Several public interest organizations will provide help or referrals for people who want to plan their estate. Your local or state bar association is a good place to start. The American Association of Retired Persons is another.

### Concerns of the Elderly

For information on matters of concern to the elderly, contact:

American Bar Association
Commission on Legal Problems of the Elderly
1800 M St. NW
Washington, DC 20036
(202) 331-2200

Do Yourself Justice
AARP
601 E Street, NW
Washington, DC 20049
(202) 434-2277

Legal Counsel for the Elderly, Inc.
P.O. Box 96474
Washington, DC 20090-6474
(202) 434-2120, 2170, or 2277

For a living will chart giving information on state laws, contact:

Choice in Dying
200 Varick Street
New York, NY 10014
(212) 366-5540
1-800-989-WILL

Hemlock Society, U.S.A.
P.O. Box 11830
Eugene, OR 97440
1-800-246-6406

## Estate Planning

*Plan Your Estate*, Dennis Clifford. (Berkeley, Nolo Press, 1990.) ISBN-0-87-337-239-5. Call (510) 549-1976 to order.
*Federal and Estate Gift Taxes*, U.S. Government Printing Office, IRS publication No. 448, Washington, DC 20402. Order by calling (202) 512-2457 or faxing (202) 512-2164.

## AARP Publications

*Final Details: A Guide for Survivors When Death Occurs*
*Prepaying Your Funeral*
*Product Report: Funeral Goods and Services*

AARP, 601 E Street NW, Washington, DC 20049. Order by calling (202) 434-2277, or 1-800-424-3410 or 3525.

## Gay and Unmarried Partners

*A Legal Guide for Lesbian and Gay Couples*, Hayden Curry and Dennis Clifford. (Berkeley, Nolo Press) ISBN-0-87-337-199-2. Call (510) 549-1976 to order.

# GLOSSARY

## A

**abstract of record** - A complete history of the case in a concise, abbreviated form.

**acquittal** - A trial verdict that indicates that the defendant in a criminal case has not been found guilty of the crime charged, beyond a reasonable doubt.

**action** - A legal dispute brought to court for trial and settlement (see also case, lawsuit).

**actus reus** - A criminal act.

**ademption** - Failure of a gift because the will-maker, by the time of death, no longer owns the property that the will-maker attempted to bequeath in the will.

**adjudication** - Giving or pronouncing a judgment or decree; also the judgment given.

**administration** - The process of collecting the estate's assets; paying its debts, taxes, expenses, and other obligations; and distributing the remainder as directed by the will.

**administrator** - A personal representative, appointed by a probate court, who administers the estate of someone who dies without a will or leaves a will naming an executor who dies before the will-maker or who refuses to serve.

**admissible** - Evidence that can be legally introduced in court.

**adversary system** - The system of trial practice in the U.S. and some other countries in which each of the opposing or adversarial parties has full opportunity to present and establish its contentions before the court.

**affidavit** - A written statement of fact given voluntarily and under oath. For example, in criminal cases, affidavits are often used by police officers seeking to convince courts to grant a warrant to make an arrest or a search. In civil cases, affidavits of witnesses are often used to support motions for summary judgment.

**affirmative defense** - Without denying the charge, the defendant raises extenuating or mitigating circumstances such as insanity, self-defense, or entrapment to avoid civil or criminal responsibility. The defendant must prove any affirmative defense he or she raises.

**allegation** - The assertion, declaration, or statement of a party to an action, made in a pleading, setting out what he or she expects to prove.

**alimony** - A court-ordered payment for the support of one's estranged spouse in the case of divorce or separation.

**alternative dispute resolution** (ADR) - Means of settling a dispute without a formal trial.

**amicus brief** - A document filed by an amicus curiae in support of a party in a lawsuit.

**amicus curiae** - Friend of the court. A party who volunteers information on some aspect of a case or law to assist the court in its deliberation.

**ancillary bill or suit** - A cause of action growing out of and supported by another action or suit, such as a proceeding for the enforcement of a judgment.

**answer** - A pleading by which a defendant resists or otherwise responds to the plaintiff's allegation of facts.

**anti-lapse statute** - A state law that provides for a gift to go to the descendants of certain will beneficiaries who die before the will-maker dies.

**appeal** - A request by the losing party in a lawsuit for higher court review of a lower court decision.

**appearance** - The formal proceeding by which a defendant submits himself or herself to the jurisdiction of the court.

**appellant** - The party appealing a decision or judgment to a higher court.

**appellate court** - A court having jurisdiction to review the judgments of a "trial court."

**appellee** - The party against whom an appeal is filed.

**arbitration** - Dispute settlement conducted outside the courts by a neutral third party. May or may not be binding.

**arraignment** - The proceeding in criminal cases where an accused individual is brought before a judge to hear the charges filed against him or her, and to file a plea of guilty, not guilty, or no contest. Also called a preliminary hearing, or an initial appearance.

**arrest** - To take into custody by legal authority.

**assignment** - The transfer of one's interest in a right or property to another person or entity.

**attorney-at-law** - A lawyer licensed to provide legal advice and to prepare, manage, and try cases.

## B

**bail** - Security given for the release of a criminal defendant or witness from legal custody (usually in the form of money) to secure his or her appearance on the day and time appointed (also called bail bond).

**bailiff** - A court attendant whose duties are to keep order in the courtroom and to have custody of the jury.

**bankruptcy** - Refers to statutes and judicial proceedings involving persons or businesses that cannot pay their debts and seek the assistance of the court in getting a fresh start. Under the protection of the bankruptcy court, debtors may discharge their debts, perhaps by paying a portion of each debt.

**bench trial** - A trial heard by a judge without a jury.

**bench warrant** - Order issued by a judge for the arrest of an individual.

**beneficiary** - Someone named to receive property or benefits in a will. In a trust, a person who is to receive benefits from the trust.

**bequeath** - To give a gift to someone through a will.

**bequests** - Gifts made in a will.

**binding instruction** - An instruction in which a jury is told that if it finds certain conditions to be true, it must decide in favor of the plaintiff, or defendant, as the case might be.

**breach of contract** - A legally inexcusable failure to perform a contractual obligation.

**brief** - A written statement prepared by each side in a lawsuit to explain to the court its view of the facts in a case and the applicable law.

**burden of proof** - The standard by which a case is decided. In criminal cases, the prosecutor must prove his/her case "beyond a reasonable doubt." In civil cases, the plaintiff must prove his/her case by a "preponderance of evidence," or, in some cases, by "clear and convincing" evidence.

## C

**calendar** - The clerk of the court's list of cases with dates and times set for hearings, trials, or arguments.

**calling the docket** - The public calling of the docket or list of cases, for the purpose of setting a time for trial or entering orders.

**caption** - The heading or introductory clause on documents filed that shows the names of the parties, name of the court, number of the case, etc.

**case** - A legal dispute.

**case law** - Law based on published judicial decisions.

**cause** - A lawsuit, litigation, or legal action.

**cause of action** - Facts giving rise to a lawsuit.

**caveat emptor** - Let the buyer beware. This phrase expresses the 19th-century rule of law that the purchaser buys at his own risk.

**certiorari** - Order to a lower court to deliver the record of a case to an appellate court.

**challenge for cause** - The objection to the inclusion of a person on a jury for a stated reason. Attorneys can make this challenge as necessary during voir dire.

**change of venue** - Moving a trial to a new location, generally because pretrial publicity has made it difficult to select an impartial jury.

**charge to the jury** - The judge's instructions to the jury concerning the law applicable to the case.

**charitable trust** - A trust set up to benefit a charity.

**circuit courts** - In several states, the name given to a tribunal, the territorial jurisdiction of which may comprise several counties or districts. In the federal system, the courts of appeal beneath the U.S. Supreme Court.

**citation** - A reference to a source of legal authority. Also, a direction to appear in court, as when a defendant is cited into court, rather than arrested.

**civil actions** - Noncriminal cases in which one private individual or business sues another to protect, enforce, or redress private or civil rights.

**claim** - An assertion of a right to money or property made by the injured party that is suing.

**clear and convincing evidence** - A level of proof requiring the truth of the facts asserted to be highly probable.

**clerk of the court** - A court employee who is responsible for maintaining permanent records of all court proceedings and exhibits, and administering the oath to jurors and witnesses.

**codicil** - An amendment to a will.

**common law** - Law arising from tradition and judicial decisions rather than laws passed by the legislature.

**common law action** - A case in which the issues are determined by common law legal principles established by courts and tradition, as opposed to statutes.

**comparative negligence** - A legal doctrine where the actions of both parties to a civil suit are compared to determine the liability of each to the other.

**complainant** - The individual who initiates a lawsuit; synonymous with "plaintiff."

**complaint (civil)** - Initial document filed by the plaintiff in a civil case stating the claims against the defendant.

**complaint (criminal)** - A formal accusation charging that a person has committed an offense.

**conditional release** - A release from custody, without the payment of bail, which imposes regulations on the activities and associations of the defendant.

**conservatorship** - Legal right given to a person to manage the property and financial affairs of a person deemed incapable of doing that for himself or herself.

**consideration** - Something of value given in return for another's performance or promise of performance; generally required to make a promise binding and to make agreement of parties enforceable as a contract. Consideration may be either executed or executory, express or implied.

**contempt of court** - Any act calculated to embarrass, hinder, or obstruct a court. Contempts are of two kinds: direct and indirect. Direct contempts are those committed in the immediate presence of the court; indirect is the term mostly used with reference to the failure or refusal to obey a court order. Any party found in contempt of court normally receives sanctions.

**continuance** - The postponement of a proceeding to a later date.

**contract** - A legally enforceable agreement between two or more competent parties made either orally or in writing.

**contributory negligence** - Legal doctrine which says that a plaintiff cannot recover damages in a civil action for negligence if the plaintiff was also negligent.

**conviction** - A trial verdict or judgment that a criminal defendant is guilty of a crime.

**copyright** - The right to literary property, giving authors, composers, and other creators the sole right to reproduce and distribute their work for a limited period of time.

**corpus delecti** - Body of the crime. The objective proof that a crime has been committed.

**corroborating evidence** - Supplementary evidence that supports the initial evidence.

**counsel** - Legal advice; also a term used to refer to lawyers in a case.

**counterclaim** - A claim by a defendant in a civil case that he or she has been injured by the plaintiff.

**court costs** - The expenses in addition to legal fees of prosecuting or defending a lawsuit.

**court of last resort** - The final court that decides a case on appeal (for example, the Supreme Court of the United States or the supreme court of any state ).

**courts of record** - Courts whose proceedings are permanently recorded, and which have the power to fine or imprison for contempt.

**court reporter** - A person who records, transcribes, or stenographically takes down testimony, motions, orders, and other proceedings during trials, hearings, and other court proceedings.

**criminal case** - Case brought by the government against an individual accused of committing a crime.

**cross-examination** - Questioning of a witness by an attorney for the side against which the witness testified.

## D

**damages** - Monetary compensation that may be recovered in the courts by any person who has suffered loss, detriment, or injury to his or her person, property or rights, through the unlawful act or negligence of another.

**decision** - The judgment reached or given by a court of law.

**declaratory judgment** - A judgment that declares the rights of the parties or expresses the opinion of the court on a question of law, without ordering anything to be done.

**decree** - A decision or order of the court. A final decree is one that finally disposes of the litigation; an interlocutory decree is a provisional or preliminary decree that is not final.

**defamation** - That which tends to injure a person's reputation. **Libel** is published defamation, whereas **slander** is spoken.

**default** - Occurs when a defendant does not file the proper response within the time allowed or fails to appear at the trial.

**defendant** - In a civil case, the defendant is the person against whom the lawsuit is brought. In a criminal case, the defendant is the person accused of committing the crime.

**deliberation** - The process by which a jury reaches a verdict at the close of a trial.

**demur** - In some state courts, to file a pleading (called a demurrer) admitting the truth of the facts in the complaint, or answer, but contending they do not make out a cause of action.

**de novo** - Latin for anew or afresh. A "trial de novo" is the retrial of a case. A "de novo" standard of review permits an appellate court to substitute its judgment for that of a trial judge.

**deposition** - An oral statement made before an officer authorized by law to administer oaths. Before trial, such statements are often taken to examine potential witnesses and to obtain information.

**descent and distribution statutes** - State laws that provide for the distribution of estate property of a person who dies without a will. Same as **intestacy laws**.

**direct examination** - The first interrogation of a witness by the party on whose behalf he or she is called.

**directed verdict** - An instruction by the judge to the jury to return a specific verdict because one of the parties failed to meet its burden of proof.

**discovery** - The pretrial process by which each party ascertains evidence the other party will rely upon at trial.

**dismissal** - A court order terminating a case. May be voluntary (at the request of the parties) or involuntary.

**dissent** - A term commonly used to denote the disagreement of one or more judges of a court with the decision of the majority.

**district attorney** - A state government lawyer who prosecutes criminal cases. Also referred to as a prosecutor.

**district courts** - U.S. district courts are trial courts. State district courts are also often trial courts of general jurisdiction.

**diversion** - The process of removing some minor criminal, traffic, or juvenile cases from the full judicial process, on the condition that the accused undergo some sort of rehabilitation or make restitution for damages. Diversion may take place before the trial or its equivalent, as when a juvenile accused of a crime may consent to probation without an admission of guilt. If the juvenile completes probation successfully (takes a course or makes amends for the crime), then the entire matter may be expunged (erased) from the record.

**docket** - A log containing brief entries of court proceedings and filings of legal documents in a case.

**domicile** - The place where a person has his or her true and permanent home. A person may have several residences, but only one domicile.

**donor** - The person who sets up a trust. Also known as its **grantor** or **settlor**.

**double jeopardy** - The common-law and constitutional prohibition against more than one prosecution for the same crime, transaction, or omission.

**due process** - United States law in its regular course of administration through the courts. The constitutional guarantee of due process requires that everyone receive such constitutional protections as a fair trial, assistance of counsel, and the rights to remain silent, to a speedy and public trial, to an impartial jury, and to confront and secure witnesses.

**duress** - Refers to conduct that has the effect of compelling another person to do what he or she would not otherwise do. It is a recognized defense to any act, such as a crime, contractual breach or tort, all of which must be voluntary to create liability or responsibility.

## E

**en banc** - All the judges of an appellate court sitting together to hear oral arguments in a case of unusual significance and to decide the case.

**enjoin** - To require a person, through the issuance of an injunction, to perform or to abstain from some specific act.

**equal protection of the law** - Guarantee of the Fourteenth Amendment of the U.S. Constitution that all persons receive equal treatment under law.

**equitable action** - An action that may be brought for the purpose of restraining the threatened infliction of wrongs or injuries, and the prevention of threatened illegal action. An action seeking an injunction is an equitable action.

**escheat** - The process by which a deceased person's property goes to the state if no heir can be found.

**escrow** - Money or a written instrument such as a deed that, by agreement between two parties, is held by a neutral third party (held in escrow) until all conditions of the agreement are met.

**estate** - Applies to all that a person owns. An estate consists of personal property (car, household items, and other tangible items), real property, and intangible property, such as stock certificates and bank accounts, owned in the individual name of a person.

**et al.** - And others.

**evidence** - Any form of proof presented by a party for the purpose of supporting its factual allegations or arguments before the court.

**exclusionary rule** - A judge-made rule that prevents unconstitutionally obtained evidence from being used in court to build a case against a criminal defendant.

**execute** - To complete the legal requirements (such as signing before witnesses) that make a will valid. Also, to execute a judgment or decree means to put the final judgment of the court into effect.

**executor** - A personal representative, named in a will, who administers an estate.

**exemplary damages** - An order to pay money as a form of punishment or deterrence from future error that has caused legal injury; also known as punitive damages.

**exhibit** - A paper, document, or other article produced and exhibited to a judge or jury during a trial or hearing.

**ex parte** - By or for one party; done for, on behalf of, or on the application of, one party only.

**ex post facto** - After the fact. The Constitution prohibits the enactment of ex post facto laws—laws that make punishable as a crime an act done before the passing of the law.

**expungement** - The official and formal elimination of part of a record.

**extradition** - The process by which one jurisdiction (state or nation) surrenders to another jurisdiction a person accused or convicted of a crime in the other state.

## F

**family allowance** - Money set aside from the estate of the deceased. Its purpose is to provide for the surviving family members during the administration of the estate.

**felony** - A serious criminal offense generally punishable by imprisonment of one year or more.

**fiduciary** - A person having a legal relationship of trust and confidence to another and having a duty to act primarily for the other's benefit, for example, a guardian, trustee, or executor.

**finding** - A formal conclusion by a trial judge or jury regarding the facts of a case.

**first appearance** - The initial appearance of an arrested person before a judge to determine whether or not there is probable cause for his or her arrest. Generally the person comes before a judge within hours of the arrest. Also called initial appearance.

**fraud** - Intentional deception designed to deprive another person of property or to injure him or her in some other way.

### G

**garnishment** - A legal proceeding in which a debtor's money, in the possession of another (called the garnishee), is applied to the debts of the debtor, such as when a creditor garnishes a debtor's wages.

**good time** - A reduction in sentenced time in prison as a reward for good behavior. It usually is one-third to one-half off the maximum sentence.

**grand jury** - A group of citizens assembled in secret to hear or investigate allegations of criminal behavior. A grand jury has authority to conduct criminal investigations and to charge a crime through an indictment.

**grantor or settlor** - The person who sets up a trust.

**guardian** - A person appointed by will or by law to assume responsibility for incompetent adults or minor children. If a parent dies, this will usually be the other parent. If both die, it probably will be a close relative.

**guardianship** - Legal right given to a person to be responsible for the food, housing, health care, and other necessities of a person deemed incapable or providing these necessities for himself or herself. Can also include financial affairs, and thus perform additionally as a conservator.

### H

**habeas corpus petition** - In federal court, a means by which a state prisoner may challenge the constitutionality of his or her conviction and imprisonment.

**harmless error** - In appellate practice, an error committed by a trial court during a trial, but not harmful to the rights of the party and for which the court will not reverse the judgment.

**hearing** - Any form of judicial, quasi-judicial or legislative proceeding at which issues are heard, or testimony taken.

**hearing on the merits** - A hearing before a court on the legal questions at issue, as opposed to procedural questions.

**hearsay** - Statements by a witness who did not see or hear the incident in question but heard about it from someone else. Hearsay is usually not admissible as evidence in court.

**holding** - The legal conclusion or principle that provides the basis for a court's judgment.

**holographic will** - A handwritten will.

**hostile witness** - A witness who is subject to cross-examination by the party who called him or her to testify, because of his or her evident antagonism toward that party as exhibited in his or her direct examination.

**hung jury** - A jury that is unable to reach a unanimous verdict.

### I

**immunity** - A grant by the court against prosecution in return for providing criminal evidence against another person or party.

**impeachment of witness** - An attack on the credibility of a witness by the testimony of other witnesses or other evidence.

**implied contract** - Not explicitly written or stated; determined by deduction from known facts or from the circumstances or conduct of the parties.

**inadmissible** - Evidence that cannot under the rules of evidence be admitted in court.

**in camera** - In chambers or in private. A hearing or inspection of documents that takes place outside the presence of the jury and public.

**independent executor** - A special kind of executor, permitted by the laws of certain states, who performs the duties of an executor without intervention by the court.

**indeterminate sentence** - A sentence of imprisonment to a specified minimum and maximum period of time, specifically authorized by statute, subject to termination by a parole board or other authorized agency after the prisoner has served the minimum term.

**indictment** - The formal charge issued by a grand jury stating that there is enough evidence that the defendant committed the crime to justify having a trial; it is used primarily for felonies.

**indigent** - Meeting certain standards of poverty, thereby qualifying a criminal defendant for representation by a public defender.

**inferior court** - Courts of limited jurisdiction.

**in forma pauperis** - In the manner of a pauper. Permission given to a person to sue without payment of court fees on claim of indigence or poverty.

**information** - A formal accusation by a prosecutor that the defendant committed a crime. An information is an alternative to an indictment as a means of charging a criminal.

**infraction** - A violation of law not punishable by imprisonment. Minor traffic offenses generally are considered infractions.

**inheritance tax** - A state tax on property that an heir or beneficiary under a will receives from a deceased person's estate. The heir or beneficiary pays this tax.

**injunction** - An order of the court prohibiting (or compelling) the performance of a specific act to prevent irreparable damage or injury.

**instructions** - Judge's explanation to the jury before it begins deliberations of the questions it must answer. Judge's instructions include information about law governing the case.

**intangible assets** - Nonphysical items such as stock certificates, bonds, bank accounts, and pension benefits that have value and must be taken into account in estate planning.

**integrated bar** - The organized state bar association to which every lawyer in a state must belong in order to be permitted to practice in that state.

**interlocutory** - Provisional; temporary; not final. Refers to orders and decrees of a court.

**interrogatories** - Written questions asked by one party of an opposing party, who must answer them in writing under oath; a discovery device in a lawsuit.

**intervention** - A proceeding in a lawsuit in which a third person is permitted by the court to make him or herself a party.

**inter vivos gift** - A gift made during the giver's life.

**inter vivos trust** - Another name for a living trust.

**intestate** - Dying without a will.

**intestate succession** - The process by which the property of a person who has died without a

will passes on to others according to the state's descent and distribution statutes.

**irrevocable trust** - A trust that, once set up, the grantor may not revoke.

**issue** - The disputed point in a disagreement between parties in a lawsuit.

## J

**joint tenancy** - A form of legal co-ownership of property (also known as survivorship). At the death of one co-owner, the surviving co-owner becomes sole owner of the property.

**judgment** - The final disposition of a lawsuit.

**judgment notwithstanding the verdict** - A judge's decision to rule in a case contrary to the jury's verdict.

**judicial review** - The authority of a court to review the official actions of other branches of government. Also, the authority to declare unconstitutional the actions of other branches.

**jurisdiction** - The power, right, or authority to apply the law. A court's authority to hear cases.

**jury** - A certain number of persons, usually selected from lists of registered voters or licensed drivers, and sworn to inquire of certain matters of fact, and declare the truth upon evidence laid before them during a trial.

**jury panel** - A list of prospective jurors to serve in a particular court, or for the trial of a particular action; denotes either the whole body of persons summoned as jurors for a particular term of court or those the clerk selects by lot.

**justiciable claim** - A claim that is capable of being resolved in the courts.

**juvenile court** - Court specifically established to hear cases concerning minors.

## L

**lawsuit** - A legal action started by a plaintiff against a defendant based on a complaint that the defendant failed to perform a legal duty, resulting in harm to the plaintiff.

**leading question** - A question that instructs a witness how to answer or suggests which answer is desired. These questions are usually prohibited on direct examination.

**liable** - Legally responsible.

**libel** - Published words or pictures that falsely and maliciously defame a person, that is, injure his or her reputation. Libel is published defamation; slander is spoken.

**lien** - A legal claim against another person's property as security for a debt. A lien does not convey ownership of the property, but gives the lienholder a right to have his or her debt satisfied out of the proceeds of the property if the debt is not otherwise paid.

**limitation (statute of)** - A certain time allowed by statute in which litigation must be brought.

**liquidated damages** - A form of money payment in an amount specified in advance by a contract or agreement as the sum to be paid if terms were violated.

**litigant** - Individual bringing a lawsuit. Participants (plaintiffs and defendants) in lawsuits are called litigants.

**litigation** - A case, controversy, or lawsuit.

**living trust** - A trust set up and in effect during the lifetime of the grantor. Also called inter vivos trust.

**long-arm statute** - State laws that give a court jurisdiction to try civil cases in which persons from other states have been sued. Long-arm statutes are commonly employed to allow a local court to exercise jurisdiction over out-of-state motorists who cause automobile accidents within the state.

## M

**magistrate judges** - Judicial officers who assist U.S. district judges in getting cases ready for trial, who may decide some criminal and civil trials when both parties agree to have the case heard by a magistrate judge instead of a judge.

**mala in se** - Evil in itself—behavior that is universally regarded as criminal, such as murder.

**mala prohibita** - Wrong because prohibited—behavior that is criminal only because a society defines it as such. An example is the manufacture of alcoholic beverages during Prohibition.

**mandate** - A judicial command directing the proper officer to enforce a judgment, sentence, or decree.

**manslaughter** - The unlawful killing of another without premeditation, either voluntary—upon a sudden impulse, for example, a quarrel erupts into a fistfight in which one of the participants is killed; or involuntary—during the commission of an unlawful act not ordinarily expected to result in great bodily harm, or during the commission of a lawful act without proper caution, for example, driving an automobile at excessive speed resulting in a fatal collision.

**mediation** - A form of alternative dispute resolution in which the parties bring their dispute to a neutral third party, who helps them agree on a settlement.

**memoranda of law** - Formal written arguments in support of a motion filed in a case.

**mens rea** - The "guilty mind" necessary to establish criminal responsibility.

**merits** - Issues of legal substance at stake in a case, as opposed to procedural considerations.

**Miranda warning** - The warning police must give suspects regarding their constitutional right to remain silent and their right to an attorney.

**misdemeanor** - Less serious criminal offense usually punishable by a sentence of one year or less.

**mistrial** - An erroneous or invalid trial; a trial that cannot stand in law because of lack of jurisdiction, incorrect procedure with respect to jury selection, or disregard of some other fundamental requisite; an invalid trial because of the inability of a jury to reach a verdict.

**motion to dismiss** - A formal request for the court to dismiss a complaint because of insufficiency of evidence or because the law does not recognize the injury or harm claimed.

**multiplicity of actions** - Numerous and unnecessary attempts to litigate the same right.

**municipal courts** - In the judicial organization of some states, courts whose territorial authority is confined to a city or community.

**murder** - The unlawful killing of a human being with malice aforethought (deliberate intent to kill). Murder in the first degree is characterized by premeditation; murder in the second degree is characterized by a sudden and instantaneous intent to kill or to cause injury without caring whether the injury kills or not.

## N

**negligence** - Failure to exercise ordinary care.

**nolo contendere** - No contest. Has the same effect as a plea of guilty, as far as the criminal sentence is concerned, but may not be considered as an admission of guilt for any other purpose.

**nominal party** - One who is joined as a party or defendant merely because the technical rules of pleading require his or her presence in the record.

**notice** - A formal notification to a party that a lawsuit has been initiated.

**notice to produce** - A notice in writing requiring the opposite party to yield a certain described paper or document in advance or at the trial.

**nuncupative will** - An oral (unwritten) will.

## O

**objection** - The act of taking exception to some statement or procedure in trial. Used to call the court's attention to improper evidence or procedure.

**objection overruled** - A judge's rejection of an objection as invalid.

**objection sustained** - Support or agree with an objection. Used by the judge to indicate agreement with a motion or request.

**of counsel** - A phrase commonly applied to counsel employed to assist in the preparation or management of the case, but who is not the principal attorney of record.

**offer** - An act of willingness to enter into a purchase agreement that justifies to another person an understanding that his assent to that purchase agreement is invited and will establish a contract.

**one day–one trial jury service** - System used in many jurisdictions where potential jurors serve either for the length of a trial if assigned to a jury or, if not, complete their service in one day.

**opinion** - A written explanation of a decision of a trial court or of the decision of a majority of judges of an appellate court. At the appellate level, a dissenting opinion disagrees with the majority opinion because of the reasoning and/or principles of law on which the decision is based. A concurring opinion agrees with the decision of the court but offers further comment.

**option** - A contract that gives the holder a right or option to buy or sell specified property, such as stock or real estate, at a fixed price for a limited period of time.

**oral argument** - An opportunity for lawyers to summarize their position before the court and also to answer the judges' questions.

**order** - A command from the court directing or forbidding an action.

**original jurisdiction** - A court's authority to hear a case in the first instance.

## P

**parole** - The supervised, conditional release of a prisoner.

**parties** - The persons who are actively involved with the prosecution or defense of a legal proceeding. Plaintiffs and defendants are parties to lawsuits, appellants and appellees are parties in appeals. (They may also be known as petitioners and respondents.)

**patent** - A government grant giving an inventor the exclusive right to make or sell his or her invention for a term of years.

**peremptory challenge** - A motion to reject a juror for an unspecified race-neutral reason. May only be used a limited number of times.

**perjury** - The criminal offense of making a false statement under oath.

**personal property** - Tangible physical property (such as cars, clothing, furniture, and jewelry) and intangible personal property, but not real property—that is, not land or rights in land.

**personal recognizance** - When a person is released from custody before trial on his or her promise to return for further proceedings.

**petit jury** - The twelve (or fewer) jurors selected to sit in the trial of a civil or criminal case.

**petitioner** - Person filing an action or appealing from a lower court's judgment.

**plaintiff** - A person who brings an action; the party who complains or sues in a personal action and is so named on the record. The person who files the complaint in a civil lawsuit.

**plea** - The defendant's declaration of guilty or not guilty, in response to the criminal charges contained in the information or indictment.

**plea bargain** - The process by which an accused person agrees to plead guilty to some of the charges in return for the government's promise to drop some of the charges.

**pleadings** - Written statements of fact and law filed by the parties to a lawsuit; consists of complaints, answers, and replies.

**polling the jury** - A practice whereby the jurors are asked individually whether they agreed, and still agree, to the verdict.

**pour-over will** - A will that leaves some or all estate assets to a trust established before the will-maker's death.

**precedent** - Previously decided case that guides future decisions.

**prejudicial error** - Synonymous with "reversible error"; an error that warrants the appellate court in reversing the judgment before it.

**preliminary hearing** - Criminal hearing at which a judge determines whether sufficient evidence exists to warrant trying an individual charged with a crime.

**preponderance of evidence** - The greater weight of evidence, or evidence that is more credible and convincing to the mind, but not necessarily the greater number of witnesses.

**pre-sentence investigation** - An inquiry conducted at the request of the court after a person has been found guilty of a criminal offense. Provides the court with extensive background information to determine an appropriate sentence.

**presumption** - A rule of law that courts and judges will draw a particular inference from a particular fact, or from particular evidence.

**pretermitted child** - A child born after a will is executed, who is not provided for by the will. Most states have laws that provide for a share of estate property to go to such children.

**pretrial conference** - A meeting in which attorneys for both sides meet the judge in advance of the trial to seek to clarify or narrow the issues.

**prima facie case** - The minimum amount of evidence a plaintiff must produce to overcome a motion to dismiss.

**principal** - In criminal law, one who commits an offense, or an accomplice who is present during the commission of the crime. In commercial law, the amount received in loan, or the amount upon which interest is charged. In the law of agency, one who has permitted or engaged another to act for his or her benefit, in accordance with his or her direction and subject to his or her control.

**probable cause** - Reasonable belief that an individual has committed a crime.

**probate court** - The court with authority to supervise estate administration.

**probate estate** - Estate property that may be disposed of by a will.

**probation** - A sentencing alternative to imprisonment in which the court releases convicted defendants under supervision as long as certain conditions are observed.

**pro se** - A Latin term meaning "on one's own behalf"; in courts, it refers to persons who present their own cases without lawyers.

**prosecutor** - Government lawyer who tries criminal cases.

**public defender** - Lawyer employed by the government to represent individuals accused of crimes who cannot afford to hire their own attorney privately.

**puffing** - A statement of belief not meant as fact; a seller's extravagant statements to enhance his wares and induce others to buy the product. Salesmanship talk, characterized as puffing, cannot be the basis of a charge of fraud or express warranty, since the buyer is said to have no right to rely on sales talk.

### Q

**quash** - To overthrow; vacate; to annul or void a summons or indictment.

### R

**real property** - Land, buildings, and other improvements affixed to land.

**reasonable doubt** - Uncertainty that might exist in the mind of a reasonable person applying reason to the evidence introduced.

**rebuttal** - The introduction of contrary evidence; the showing that statements of witnesses as to what occurred are not true; the stage of a trial at which such evidence may be introduced.

**record** - A written account of all the acts, proceedings and testimony in a lawsuit.

**redirect examination** - Follows cross-examination and is exercised by the party who called first and questioned the witness.

**reliance** - Confidence or dependence upon what is deemed sufficient authority such as a warranty that provides a written guarantee of the integrity of a product.

**remand** - When an appellate court sends a case back to a lower court for further proceedings.

**removal, order of** - An order by a court directing the transfer of a case to another court.

**reply** - A pleading in response to an answer.

**repossession** - To take back—as in a seizure or foreclosure—to satisfy the obligation to the seller, bank, or finance company after the debtor defaults on his or her payments.

**rest** - A party is said to "rest" or "rest its case" when it has presented all the evidence it intends to offer.

**reverse** - When an appellate court sets aside the decision of a lower court because of an error. A reversal is often accompanied by a remand.

**revocable trust** - A trust that the grantor may change or revoke.

**revoke** - To cancel or nullify a legal document.

**rule of court** - An order made by a court having jurisdiction. Rules of court are either general or special: the former are the regulations by which the practice of the court is governed; the latter are special orders made in particular cases.

**rule to show cause** - A court order obtained on motion by either party to demonstrate why the particular relief sought should not be granted. Generally, used in connection with contempt proceedings.

## S

**search warrant** - A written order issued by a judge that directs a law enforcement officer to search a specific area for a particular piece of evidence.

**self-proving will** - A will whose validity does not have to be testified to in court by the witnesses to it, since the witnesses executed an affidavit reflecting proper execution of the will prior to the maker's death.

**sentence** - The punishment ordered by a court for a defendant convicted of a crime.

**separation of witnesses** - An order of the court requiring all witnesses to remain outside the courtroom until each is called to testify, except the plaintiff or defendant.

**sequester** - To separate. Sometimes juries are sequestered from outside influences during their deliberations.

**serve** - To deliver a legal document, such as a complaint, summons, or subpoena. Service constitutes formal legal notice.

**settlement** - Agreement resolving a dispute between parties in a lawsuit without trial. Settlements often involve the payment of compensation by one party in satisfaction of the other party's claims.

**settlor** - The person who sets up a trust. Also called the **grantor** or **donor**.

**sheriff** - An officer of a county, often chosen by popular election, whose principal duties are to aid the courts. The sheriff serves processes, summons juries, executes judgments, and holds judicial sales.

**sidebar conference** - Confidential discussion between judge and attorneys to resolve legal matters, which could be prejudicial if aired before the jury.

**slander** - False and defamatory spoken words tending to harm another's reputation, business, or means of livelihood. Slander is spoken defamation; libel is published.

**small claims court** - A court that handles civil claims for small amounts of money. People often represent themselves rather than hire an attorney.

**special appearance** - Notice of the party that has been sued that he or she is aware of the lawsuit, but contests the court's authority over himself or herself. This prevents a defendant from losing a case by default.

**special damages** - A form of compensatory damages ordered paid when the injury done resulted from the other side's wrong but was not a natural or necessary consequence.

**specific performance** - Where damages would be inadequate compensation for the breach of a contract, the party who breached the contract will be compelled to perform specifically what he or she originally agreed to do.

**spendthrift trust** - A trust set up for the benefit of someone who the grantor believes would be incapable of managing his or her own financial affairs.

**standing** - The legal right to sue or enter a lawsuit on a particular matter.

**stare decisis** - The doctrine that, when a court has once laid down a principle of law as applicable to a certain set of facts, it will adhere to that principle and apply it to future cases where the facts are substantially the same.

**statute** - Law enacted by legislatures or executive officers, such as codes.

**statute of limitations** - A law that sets the time within which parties must take action to enforce their rights.

**stay** - A suspending of a judicial proceeding by order of the court.

**stipulation** - An agreement by attorneys on opposite sides of a case as to any matter pertaining to the proceedings or trial. It is not binding unless agreed to by the parties.

**strike** - To remove improperly offered evidence from the court record.

**style** - The title of a lawsuit.

**subpoena** - A document issued by the court to compel a witness to appear and give testimony or to procure documentary evidence in a proceeding.

**subpoena duces tecum** - A process by which the court commands a witness to produce certain documents or records in a trial.

**substantive law** - Law dealing with rights, duties, and liabilities, as distinguished from law that regulates procedure.

**suit in equity** - A civil case in which a court forbids or allows another person to take an action.

**summary judgment** - A court order that decides a case in favor of one side on the basis of affidavits or other evidence, before the trial commences. It is used when there is no dispute as to the facts of the case, and one party is entitled to judgment as a matter of law.

**summons** - Legal notice informing an individual of a lawsuit and the date and location of the court where the case will be heard.

**support trust** - A trust that instructs the trustee to spend only as much income and principal (the assets held in the trust) as needed for the beneficiary's support.

**surety bond** - A bond purchased at the expense of the estate to insure the executor's proper performance. Often called a fidelity bond.

**survivorship** - Another name for joint tenancy.

## T

**talesman** - A person called to act as a juror from among the bystanders in a court.

**tangible personal property memorandum (TPPM)** - A legal document that is referred to in a will and used to guide the distribution of tangible personal property.

**temporary restraining order (TRO)** - Prohibits a person from an action that is likely to cause irreparable harm. This differs from an injunction in that it may be granted immediately, without notice to the opposing party, and without a hearing. It is intended to last only until a hearing can be held.

**testamentary capacity** - The legal ability to make a will.

**testamentary trust** - A trust set up by a will.

**testimony** - Evidence given by a competent witness, under oath, as distinguished from evidence derived from writings and other sources.

**third-party claim** - An action by the defendant that brings a third party into a lawsuit.

**title** - Legal ownership of property, usually real property or automobiles.

**tort** - A civil wrong or breach of a duty to another person, as outlined by law. A very common tort is negligent operation of a motor vehicle that results in property damage and personal injury in an automobile accident.

**transcript** - The official record of proceedings in a trial or hearing.

**transitory** - Actions are "transitory" when they might have taken place anywhere, and are "local" when they could occur only in some particular place.

**traverse** - In pleading, to traverse signifies to deny. When a defendant denies any material allegation of fact in the plaintiff's declaration, he or she is said to traverse it.

**trust** - A legal device used to manage property—real or personal—established by one person (the donor, grantor, or settlor) for the benefit of another (the beneficiary). A third person or the grantor manages the trust. This person is known as the trustee.

**trust agreement or declaration** - The legal document that sets up a living trust. Testamentary trusts are set up in a will.

**trustee** - The person or institution that manages the property put in trust.

## U

**undue influence** - Influence of another that destroys the freedom of a testator or donor and creates a ground for nullifying a will or invalidating a future gift. The exercise of undue influence is suggested by excessive insistence, superiority of will or mind, the relationship of the parties or pressure on the donor or testator by any other means to do what he is unable, practically, to refuse.

**unilateral mistake** - An act or omission arising from ignorance or misconception of a party to a contract, which may, depending upon its character or the circumstances surrounding it, justify repealing a contract.

## V

**venire** - The panel of citizens called for jury service from which a jury will be selected.

**venue** - The particular county, city, or geographical area in which a court with jurisdiction may hear and determine a case.

**verdict** - Formal decision made by a jury, read before a court, and accepted by the judge.

**voir dire** - To speak the truth. Process in which prospective jurors are questioned to determine whether they can perform their duties in an impartial manner.

## W

**waive** - To voluntarily give up a right or a claim.

**warranty** - A written or oral statement by one party to a contract that a fact is or will be as it is expressly declared or promised to be.

**weight of evidence** - The balance or preponderance of evidence; the inclination of the greater amount of credible evidence, offered in a trial, to support one side of the issue rather than the other.

**will** - A legal declaration that disposes of a person's property when that person dies.

**with prejudice** - As applied to a judgment of dismissal, the term refers to the adjudication of a case on its merits, barring the right to bring or maintain another action on the same claim.

**without prejudice** - A dismissal "without prejudice" allows a new suit to be brought on the same cause of action.

**witness** - One who testifies under oath as to what she or he has seen, heard, or otherwise observed.

**writ** - An order issued from a court requiring the performance of a specified act, or giving authority and commission to have it done.

# ACKNOWLEDGMENTS

*The American Bar Association Family Legal Guide* was written by a wide range of legal experts, including lawyers, law professors, professors from other university disciplines, and legal journalists. The authors and their professional titles and affiliations are listed below by chapter.

The material in each chapter has also been reviewed by various experts. They include the chairpersons and members of American Bar Association (ABA) committees specializing in important legal areas, as well as law professors, university professors, ABA staff, and others with appropriate expertise. These people volunteered their time to review chapters. You will find each of them listed below by chapter.

At the ABA, assigning and reviewing copy was the responsibility of Charles White, Publications Director of the Public Education Division. Providing considerable assistance were Jane Moisant, Charles F. Williams, L. Anita Richardson, and May Nash of the division staff.

The "When and How to Use a Lawyer" chapter: Written by Barbara Kate Repa, legal journalist, San Francisco, California. Reviewed by Sherwin M. Birnkrant, Attorney, Sommers, Schwartz, Silver & Schwartz, Southfield, Michigan; Louis M. Brown, Attorney, Sanders, Barnet, Goldman, Simons & Mosk, Los Angeles, California; John R. DeBarr, Chair, ABA Commission on Legal Assistance for Military Personnel, Coronado, California; Adrian Hochstadt and William Hornsby, Attorneys, ABA Legal Services Department; Christel E. Marquardt, Attorney, Levy and Craig, P.C., Overland Park, Kansas; and Larry Ray, Staff Director, ABA Standing Committee on Dispute Resolution, Washington, D.C.

The "How the Legal System Works" chapter: Written by Charles F. Williams, Assistant Publications Director, ABA Public Education Division. Reviewed by the Honorable Shirley S. Abrahamson, Justice, Supreme Court of Wisconsin, Madison, Wisconsin; Luther J. Avery, Attorney, Avery & Associates, San Francisco, California; Sherwin M. Birnkrant; Steve Goldspiel, Assistant Director, ABA Judicial Services Division; the Honorable David Ramirez, Judge, District Court, Denver, Colorado; and the Honorable Ricardo M. Urbina, Associate Judge, Superior Court of District of Columbia, Washington, D. C.

The "Family Law" chapter: Written by Jeff Atkinson, Professor of Law, DePaul University School of Law, Chicago, Illinois; Marcia O'Kelly, Associate Professor of Law, University of North Dakota School of Law, Grand Forks, North Dakota; Jesse Trentadue, Attorney, Suitter, Axland, Armstrong & Hanson, Salt Lake City, Utah; and Diane Geraghty, Associate Professor of Law, Loyola University School of Law, Chicago, Illinois. Reviewed by Jeff Atkinson; Linda Elrod, Professor of Law, Washburn University School of Law, Topeka, Kansas; Marcia O'Kelly; Arnold H. Rutkin, Attorney, Rutkin & Effron, P.C., Westport, Connecticut; Peggy L. Podell, Attorney, Podell & Podell, Milwaukee, Wisconsin; and Philip Schwartz, Attorney, Schwartz, Ellis and Moore, Arlington, Virginia.

The "Buying and Selling a Home" chapter: Written by Lynn Orr Miller, legal and financial journalist, Boston, Massachusetts. Reviewed by Stanley B. Balbach, Attorney, Balbach, Fehr & Hodson, Urbana, Illinois; Gurden Buck, Attorney, Robinson & Cole, Hartford, Connecticut; Bernice

Cilley, Attorney, Mays & Valentine, Richmond, Virginia; Edward T. Flynn, Attorney, Attorneys' Title Guaranty Fund, Inc., Chicago, Illinois; Richard M. Frome, Attorney, New York, New York; Jerry T. Gorman, Vice President and Corporate Counsel, Attorneys' Title Guaranty Fund, Inc., Champaign, Illinois; David L. Haron, Attorney, Frank & Stefani, Troy, Michigan; Jonathan Hoyt, Attorney, Clinton, Connecticut; Ronald J. Maas, Secretary and General Counsel, Weichert Realtors, Morris Plains, New Jersey; Frank A. Melchior, Vice President and Associate Regional Counsel, 1st American Title Ins. Co., Iselin, New Jersey; and Julius J. Zschau, Attorney, Baynard, Harrell, Ostow & Ulrich, P.A., Clearwater, Florida.

The "Home Ownership" chapter: Written by Jane Easter Bahls, legal journalist, Missoula, Montana. Reviewed by Stanley B. Balbach; David L. Haron; Ronald J. Maas; Amy Meland, Law Clerk, Attorney's Title Guaranty Fund, Inc., Chicago, Illinois; and Frank A. Melchior.

The "Renting Residential Property" chapter: Written by Michael Pensack, Director, Tenants Union of Illinois, Chicago, Illinois, and Celeste Hammond, Professor of Law, John Marshall Law School, Chicago, Illinois. Reviewed by Richard E. Blumberg, Attorney, Blumberg, Farber & Smith, Berkeley, California; Christopher Hanback, Attorney, Jackson and Campbell, Washington, D.C.; Sharon Johnson, Director, Resident Relations Foundation, San Diego, California; Myron Moskovitz, Professor of Law, Golden Gate University School of Law, San Francisco, California; Jean K. Tullius, Assistant Professor, University of Baltimore Clinical Law Program, Baltimore, Maryland; and Frederic White, Professor of Law, Cleveland State University, Cleveland-Marshall College of Law, Cleveland, Ohio.

The "Consumer Credit" chapter: Written by Robert W. Johnson, Director, Credit Research Center, Krannert Graduate School of Management, Purdue University, West Lafayette, Indiana. Reviewed by John L. Culhane, Jr., Attorney, Wolf, Block, Schorr and Solis-Cohen, Philadelphia, Pennsylvania; Michael M. Greenfield, Professor of Law, Washington University School of Law, St. Louis, Missouri; Hugh M. Hayden, Attorney, Dean Witter Financial Services Group, River-

woods, Illinois; Frederick H. Miller, Kenneth McAfee Centennial Professor of Law and George Lynn Cross Research Professor, University of Oklahoma College of Law, Norman, Oklahoma; and Irene Vawter, Federal Trade Commission, Washington, D.C.

The "Consumer Bankruptcy" chapter: Written by Robert W. Johnson. Reviewed by the Honorable Bernice Bouie Donald, Judge, United States Bankruptcy Court, Western District of Tennessee, Memphis, Tennessee; John P. Hennigan, Jr., Professor of Law, St. John's University School of Law, Jamaica, New York; Scott H. McNutt, Attorney, Severson & Werson, San Francisco, California; Vicki S. Porter, Attorney, Denver, Colorado; and Lawrence Avery Young, Attorney, Baker & Hostetler, Houston, Texas.

The "Contracts and Consumer Law" chapter: Written by Ron Coleman, Attorney, Lowenstein, Sandler, Kohl, Fisher & Boylan, Roseland, New Jersey. Reviewed by Bernard Diederich, Office of the General Counsel, Department of Transportation, Washington, D.C.; Harry J. Haynsworth, Dean, Southern Illinois University School of Law, Carbondale, Illinois; Mark R. Lee, Professor of Law, Southern Illinois University School of Law, Carbondale, Illinois; Frederick H. Miller; and A. A. Sommer, Jr., Attorney, Morgan, Lewis & Bockius, Washington, D.C..

The "Automobiles" chapter: Written by Jill Tapper, Attorney, Belmont, Massachusetts, and Shel Toplitt, Attorney, Jager, Smith, Stetler and Arata, Boston, Massachusetts. Reviewed by James J. Ahern, Attorney, Ahern & Maloney, Skokie, Illinois; Larry A. Davis, Attorney, Davis & Riebman, Des Plaines, Illinois; Daniel W. Kummer, Senior Personal Lines Specialist, National Association of Independent Insurers, Des Plaines, Illinois; Henry L. Sarpy, Attorney, Jones, Walker, Waechter, Poitevent, Carrere & Denegre, New Orleans, Louisiana; and Kelly Carbetta Scandy, Attorney, Montgomery, Rennie & Jonson, Cincinnati, Ohio.

The "Law and the Workplace" chapter: Written by Barbara J. Fick, Associate Professor of Law, Notre Dame Law School, Notre Dame, Indiana. Reviewed by Linda H. Lamel, Attorney, Teachers Insurance and Annuity Association, New York,

New York; James B. Lewis, Attorney, Paul, Weiss, Rifkind, Wharton & Garrison, New York, New York; Adrianne Mazura, Attorney, Rudnick & Wolfe, Chicago, Illinois; and Theodore St. Antoine, James E. and Sarah A. Degan Professor of Law, University of Michigan Law School, Ann Arbor, Michigan.

**The "Small Business" chapter: Written by Harry Haynsworth, Dean, University of Southern Illinois School of Law, Carbondale, Illinois.** Portions of this chapter are based on material in the following books by Harry Haynsworth, published by the American Law Institute-American Bar Association Committee on Continuing Professional Education: *Organizational Forms for the Closely Held Corporation; Selecting the Form of a Small Business Entity; Organizing a Small Business Entity.* These materials are adapted by permission of ALI-ABA. Chapter reviewed by Pamela Baker, Attorney, Sonnenschein, Nath & Rosenthal, Chicago, Illinois; Allan G. Donn, Attorney, Wilcox & Savage, P.C., Norfolk, Virginia; Sidney S. Goldstein, Attorney, Kreindler & Relkin, New York, New York; Robert R. Keatinge, Attorney, Holland & Hart, Denver, Colorado, and Senior Editor, *Taxation,* Shepard's McGraw-Hill, Colorado Springs, Colorado; Karl Brian Kuppler, Attorney, Sutkowski & Washkuhn, Ltd., Peoria, Illinois; H. F. Riebesell, Jr., Attorney, Englewood, Colorado; Fredric A. Rubenstein, Attorney, Kelley, Drye, et al., New York, New York; and William H. Schorling, Attorney, Klett, Lieber, Rooney & Schorling, Pittsburgh, Pennsylvania.

**The "Personal Injury" chapter: Written by Martha Middleton, legal journalist, Oak Park, Illinois.** Reviewed by Phillip D. Blomberg, Attorney, Leonard M. Ring & Associates, P.C., Chicago, Illinois; Philip H. Corboy, Attorney, Corboy & Demetrio, Chicago, Illinois; Marvin E. Duckworth, Attorney, Hopkins & Huebner, P.C., Des Moines, Iowa; William R. Levasseur, Attorney, Semmes, Bowen & Semmes, Baltimore, Maryland; Stephen I. Richman, Attorney, Ceisler, Richman & Smith, Washington, Pennsylvania; Mark L. Sklan, Attorney, Smith, Smith & Kring, Irving, California; and Mark Solomons, Attorney, Arter & Hadden, Washington, D.C.

**The "Criminal Justice" chapter: Written by Darlene Ricker, legal journalist, Fountain Valley, California.** Reviewed by Rita Fry, Public Defender, Office of the Cook County Public Defender, Chicago, Illinois; B. J. George, Professor of Law, New York Law School, New York, New York; and John R. Nussbaumer, Professor of Law, Thomas M. Cooley Law School, Lansing, Michigan.

**"The Rights of Older Americans" chapter: Written by the staff of the ABA Commission on Legal Problems of the Elderly, Washington, D.C.** Reviewed by Gary French, Executive Director, ProSeniors, Inc., Cincinnati, Ohio; Sally Herme, Attorney, Legal Counsel for the Elderly, Washington, D.C.; Marilyn Park, Attorney, Pension Rights Center, Washington, D.C.; John J. Regan, Jack & Freda Dicker Distinguished Professor of Health Care Law, Hofstra University School of Law, Hempstead, New York; and William A. Schneeberg, Attorney, Garland, Texas.

**The "Estate Planning" chapter: Written by Brett Campbell, legal journalist, San Antonio, Texas.** Reviewed by Morton John Barnard, Attorney, Miller, Shakman, Hamilton, Kurtzon, and Schlifke, Chicago, Illinois; Alexander J. Bott, Associate Professor, University of North Dakota School of Law, Grand Forks, North Dakota; Edgar T. Farmer, Attorney, Ziercher & Hocker, St. Louis, Missouri; William D. Haught, Attorney, Little Rock, Arkansas; J. Rodney Johnson, Professor of Law, University of Richmond, Richmond, Virginia; Mildred Kalik, Attorney, Simpson, Thacher & Bartlett, New York, New York; and Susan S. Westerman, Attorney, Ann Arbor, Michigan.

# STATE BAR ASSOCIATIONS

THE FOLLOWING LIST of state bars provides phone numbers and addresses. Where two addresses are given for a bar, the Post Office Box address is preferred, but the street address is included for deliveries. A zip code is provided for each.

**Alabama State Bar**
P.O. Box 671 (36101)
415 Dexter St.
Montgomery, AL 36104
205/269-1515

**Alaska Bar Association**
P.O. Box 100279 (99510)
510 L St. #602
Anchorage, AK 99501
907/272-7469

**State Bar of Arizona**
111 W. Monroe St.
Phoenix, AZ 85003-1742
602/252-4804

**Arkansas Bar Association**
400 W. Markham
Little Rock, AR 72201
501/375-4605

**State Bar of California**
555 Franklin St.
San Francisco, CA 94102
415/561-8200

**The Colorado Bar Association**
1900 Grant St. #950
Denver, CO 80203
303/860-1115

**Connecticut State Bar Association**
101 Corporate Place
Rocky Hill, CT 06067
203/721-0025

**Delaware State Bar Association**
1225 King Street
Wilmington, DE 19801
302/658-5279

**Bar Association of the District of Columbia**
12th Floor
1819 H Street, NW
Washington, DC 20006-3690
202/223-6600

**The District of Columbia Bar**
6th Floor
1250 H Street, NW
Washington, DC 20005-3908
202/737-4700

**The Florida Bar**
650 Apalachee Parkway
Tallahassee, FL 32399-2300
904/561-5600

**State Bar of Georgia**
800 The Hurt Bldg.
50 Hurt Plaza
Atlanta, GA 30303
404/527-8700

**Hawaii State Bar Association**
Penthouse 1, 9th Floor
1136 Union Mall
Honolulu, HI 96813
808/537-1868

**Idaho State Bar**
P.O. Box 895 (83701)
525 W. Jefferson
Boise, ID 83701
208/334-4500

**Illinois State Bar Association**
424 S. Second St.
Springfield, IL 62701
217/525-1760

**Indiana State Bar Association**
230 E. Ohio Street, 4th Flr.
Indianapolis, IN 46204
317/639-5465

**The Iowa State Bar Association**
521 E. Locust
Des Moines, IA 50309
515/243-3179

**Kansas Bar Association**
P.O. Box 1037 (66601-1037)
1200 Harrison Street
Topeka, KS 66612
913/234-5696

**Kentucky Bar Association**
514 West Main
Frankfort, KY 40601-1883
502/564-3795

**Louisiana State Bar Association**
601 St. Charles Ave.
New Orleans, LA 70130
504/566-1600

**Maine State Bar Association**
P.O. Box 788 (04332-0788)
124 State St.
Augusta, ME 04330
207/622-7523

**Maryland State Bar Association**
520 W. Fayette St.
Baltimore, MD 21201
410/685-7878

**Massachusetts Bar Association**
20 West St.
Boston, MA 02111-1218
617/542-3602

**State Bar of Michigan**
306 Townsend St.
Lansing, MI 48933-2083
517/372-9030

**Minnesota State Bar Association**
514 Nicollet Mall
Suite 300
Minneapolis, MN 55402
612/333-1183

**Mississippi State Bar**
P.O. Box 2168 (39225-2168)
643 N State Street
Jackson, MS 39202
601/948-4471

**The Missouri Bar**
P.O. Box 119 (65102)
326 Monroe
Jefferson City, MO 65102
314/635-4128

**State Bar of Montana**
P.O. Box 577 (59624)
46 North Last Chance Gulch
Helena, MT 59624
406/442-7660

**Nebraska State Bar Association**
P.O. Box 81809 (68501)
635 S. 14th Street, 2nd Floor
Lincoln, NE 68508
402/475-7091

**State Bar of Nevada**
201 Las Vegas Blvd.
Suite 200
Las Vegas, NV 89101
702/382-2200

**New Hampshire Bar Association**
112 Pleasant St.
Concord, NH 03301
603/224-6942

**New Jersey State Bar Association**
One Constitution Sqr.
New Brunswick, NJ 08901-1500
908/249-5000

**State Bar of New Mexico**
P.O. Box 25883
Albuquerque, NM 87125
505/842-6132

**New York State Bar Association**
One Elk St.
Albany, NY 12207
518/463-3200

**North Carolina State Bar**
P.O. Box 25908 (27611)
208 Fayetteville Street Mall
Raleigh, NC 27611
919/828-4620

**North Carolina Bar Association**
P.O. Box 12806 (27605)
1312 Annapolis Drive
Raleigh, NC 27608
919/828-0561

**State Bar Association of
North Dakota**
515-1/2 E. Broadway
Suite 101
Bismarck, ND 58502
701/255-1404

**Ohio State Bar Association**
P.O. Box 6562 (43216-6562)
1700 Lake Shore Drive
Columbus, OH 43216-6562
614/487-2050

**Oklahoma Bar Association**
P.O. Box 53036 (73152)
1901 N. Lincoln
Oklahoma City, OK 73105
405/524-2365

**Oregon State Bar**
P.O. Box 1689
Lake Oswego, OR 97035
503/620-0222

**Pennsylvania Bar Association**
P.O. Box 186 (17108)
100 South Street
Harrisburg, PA 17108
717/238-6715

**Puerto Rico Bar Association**
P.O. Box 1900 (00903)
Ponce de Leon Avenue
808 Stop II
San Juan, PR 00903
809/721-3358

**Rhode Island Bar Association**
115 Cedar Street
Providence, RI 02903
401/421-5740

**South Carolina Bar Association**
P.O. Box 608 (29202)
950 Taylor Street
Columbia, SC 29202
803/799-6653

**State Bar of South Dakota**
222 E. Capitol
Pierre, SD 57501
605/224-7554

**Tennessee Bar Association**
3622 West End Avenue
Nashville, TN 37205
615/383-7421

**State Bar of Texas**
P.O. Box 12487 (78711)
1414 Colorado
Austin, TX 78701
512/463-1463
800/204-2222

**Utah State Bar**
645 S. 200 East, #310
Salt Lake City, UT 84111
801/531-9077

**Vermont Bar Association**
P.O. Box 100 (05601)
35-37 Court Street
Montpelier, VT 05602
802/223-2020

**Virginia State Bar**
707 E. Main Street
Suite 1500
Richmond, VA 23219-2803
804/775-0500

**Virginia Bar Association**
7th & Franklin Bldg.
701 E. Franklin St., #1515
Richmond, VA 23219
804/644-0041

**Virgin Islands Bar Association**
P.O. Box 4108 (00822)
Pithany Bldg. (Ground Flr.)
Christiansted, VI 00820
809/778-7497

**Washington State Bar Association**
500 Westin Bldg.
2001 6th Ave.

Seattle, WA 98121-2599
206/727-8200

**West Virginia Bar Association**
P.O. Box 346 (25322)
904 Security Bldg.
100 Capitol Street
Charleston, WV 25301
304/342-1474

**West Virginia State Bar**
2006 Kanawha Blvd. E
Charleston, WV 25311
304/558-2456

**State Bar of Wisconsin**
402 W. Wilson
Madison, WI 53703
608/257-3838

**Wyoming State Bar**
P.O. Box 109 (82003-0109)
500 Randall Avenue
Cheyenne, WY 82001
307/632-9061

# INDEX

# NOTES

# NOTES

# NOTES

# NOTES

# NOTES

# NOTES